The Complete Guide to
UNDERSTANDING AND USING THE INTERNET

LINDA BIRD
Software Solutions

Upper Saddle River, New Jersey, 07458

Library of Congress Cataloging-in-Publication Data
Bird, Linda.
  The complete guide to understanding and using the Internet / Linda Bird.
    p. cm.
  ISBN 0-13-140289-7
  1. Internet. I. Title.
  TK5105.875.I57 B545 2003
  004.67'8—dc21

2003006656

VICE PRESIDENT/PUBLISHER: Natalie E. Anderson
EXECUTIVE ACQUISITIONS EDITOR: Jodi McPherson
ASSOCIATE DIRECTOR, IT PRODUCT DEVELOPMENT: Melonie Salvati
SENIOR PROJECT MANAGER, EDITORIAL: Eileen Clark
EDITORIAL ASSISTANT: Jodi Bolognese
MARKETING MANAGER: Emily Williams Knight
MARKETING ASSISTANT: Nicole Beaudry
MEDIA PROJECT MANAGER: Cathleen Profitko
PROJECT MANAGER: Melissa Edwards
PRODUCTION MANAGER: Gail Steier de Acevedo
PROJECT MANAGER: Audri Anna Bazlen
MANUFACTURING BUYER: Natacha St. Hill Moore
MANAGER PRINT PRODUCTION: Christy Mahon
PERMISSIONS COORDINATOR: Suzanne Grappi
ASSOCIATE DIRECTOR, MANUFACTURING: Vincent Scelta
DESIGN MANAGER: Maria Lange
ART DIRECTOR: Patricia Smythe
INTERIOR DESIGN: Lee Goldstein
COVER DESIGN: Majory Dressler
ILLUSTRATOR (INTERIOR): Precision Graphics
FULL-SERVICE COMPOSITION: Impressions Book and Journal Services, Inc.
COVER PRINTER: Coral Graphics Services, Inc.
PRINTER/BINDER: Quebecor World Color-Dubuque

Credits and acknowledgments borrowed from other sources and reproduced, with permission, in this textbook appear on appropriate page within text.
Copyright © 2004 by Pearson Education, Inc., Upper Saddle River, New Jersey, 07458.

All rights reserved. Printed in the United States of America. This publication is protected by Copyright and permission should be obtained from the publisher prior to any prohibited reproduction, storage in a retrieval system, or transmission in any form or by any means, electronic, mechanical, photocopying, recording, or likewise. For information regarding permission(s), write to: Rights and Permissions Department.

Pearson Education LTD.

Pearson Education Australia PTY, Limited

Pearson Education Singapore, Pte. Ltd

Pearson Education North Asia Ltd

Pearson Education, Canada, Ltd

Pearson Educación de Mexico, S.A. de C.V.

Pearson Education–Japan

Pearson Education Malaysia, Pte. Ltd

10 9 8 7 6 5 4

ISBN 0-13-140289-7

*I would like to dedicate this book to my family:
Lonnie, my best friend and supporter
(as well as a published author),
and Rebecca and Sarah—our awesome and
articulate communicators.*

BRIEF CONTENTS

Part 1 UNDERSTANDING THE INTERNET 1
1 How the Internet is Changing the World 1
2 The Good, the Bad, the Ugly: Uses and Misuses of the Internet 22

Part 2 GETTING UP AND RUNNING WITH THE INTERNET 46
3 Necessary Equipment and Internet Connections 46
4 Internet Service Providers 62

Part 3 USING MAIL AND MESSAGING TOOLS 73
5 Mail and Messaging Software Overview 73
6 E-Mail Basics 88
7 Beyond the Basics: Using E-Mail Safely and Effectively 104

Part 4 GETTING AROUND THE WORLD WIDE WEB 118
8 Getting to Know the World Wide Web 118
9 Surfing Basics 130
10 Beyond the Basics: Advanced Surfing 150

Part 5 RUNNING EFFECTIVE INTERNET SEARCHES 166
11 Search Basics 166
12 Beyond the Basics: Searching Seamlessly 181

Part 6 TAKING CONTROL OF THE INTERNET 195
13 Communicating via the Internet 195
14 Pulling Information from the Internet 210
15 Working with Various File Types and Plug-Ins 227
16 Beyond the Basics: Taking Advantage of the Internet's Multimedia Capabilities 244

Part 7 PRIVACY AND SECURITY ISSUES 259
17 Beyond the Basics: A Closer Look at Privacy Issues 259
18 Beyond the Basics: A Closer Look at Security Issues 281

Part 8 CREATING A WEB SITE 306
19 Designing a Great Web Site 306
20 Tools You Can Use to Create a Web Site 318
21 Using FrontPage to Develop a Web Site 330
22 Adding Graphics to Your Web Site 356
23 Publishing to the World Wide Web 376

Appendix A
   Interfacing the Internet with Cell Phones and PDAs 393

Appendix B
   Useful Web Sites 399

INDEX 409

GLOSSARY 417

CONTENTS

Preface xvii

Acknowledgments xxi

Part 1 UNDERSTANDING THE INTERNET — 1

1 How the Internet is Changing the World — 1
Understand What the Internet Is   4
Understand the Origins of the Internet   6
Know How the Internet is Structured   8
Understand the Internet's Impact on the World   10
   Electronic Commerce and Online Shopping   10
   Stock Trading and Finances   12
   Communications   13
   Information Sharing   14
   Telecommuting and Home-Based Businesses   15
   The Internet's Effect on Jobs   15
   The Internet's Effect on Education   16
   The Internet's Effect on Entertainment and Travel   17
Identify Controversial Issues Related to the Internet   18
   Privacy   18
   Security   18
   Free Speech   18
   Government Control and Surveillance   18
Be Aware of Emerging Internet Technologies and Trends   19

2 The Good, the Bad, the Ugly: Uses and Misuses of the Internet — 22
Know How the Internet is Misused   25
   Malicious Code: Viruses, Worms, and Trojan Horses   26
   Methods of Spread   26
   Invasion of Privacy   29
   Harmful Web Sites   37
   Copyright and Intellectual Property Infringements   38
   Some of the Bad Guys   39

Understand the Legitimate and Ethical Uses of the Internet   41
  Listserv and Distributed Mailing Lists   41
  Usenet Newsgroups   42
  FTP Sites   42

Part 2 GETTING UP AND RUNNING WITH THE INTERNET   46

3 Necessary Equipment and Internet Connections   46

Know the Hardware Necessary to Access the Internet   49
  Computer Systems   49
  Internet Appliances and Special-Purpose Computers   50
  Wireless Devices   51
Know the Software Necessary to Access the Internet   52
  Web Browsers   52
  ISP Proprietary Software   53
  Mail-Messaging Software   53
Understand the Various Types of Internet Connections   53
  The Need for Speed: Data Transfer Rates   53
  Dial-Up   55
  Integrated Services Digital Network (ISDN)   56
  Cable Modem   57
  ADSL and DSL   57
  Satellite   58
  Fixed Wireless   59
  Summary   59

4 Internet Service Providers   62

Be Able to Evaluate and Compare Internet Service Providers   64
  Checklist for Evaluating ISPs: 64
  Asking ISPs about Connection Type, Speed, Reliability . . .   64
  Asking ISPs about Privacy and Security . . .   65
  Asking ISPs about Customer and Technical Service . . .   66
  Asking ISPs about Rates . . .   66
Recognize the Major Internet Service Providers   67
  America Online (AOL)   68
  Microsoft Network (MSN)   68
  EarthLink   68
  AT&T WorldNet Service   68
  SBC/Prodigy   69
  Regional and Local ISPs   69
Evaluate Whether or Not Free ISPs are Really Free   69
Know About Accessing the Internet via College and Business Networks   70

Part 3 USING MAIL AND MESSAGING TOOLS   73

5 Mail and Messaging Software Overview   73

Understand Why E-Mail is Popular ... and Why It's Not   76
Know How E-Mail Works   78
  Addressing, Sending, and Receiving   78

Setting the Standards 79
Be Familiar with Common Mail Client Software 80
   Outlook 81
   Pegasus Mail 82
   Eudora 82
   Outlook Express 82
   Software to Make E-Mail Secure 83
Understand the Basics of Web-Based Mail Services 83
   Microsoft MSN Hotmail 83
   Yahoo! Mail 84
   Mail.com 84
   Mail2Web 84

6 E-Mail Basics   88

Explore the Outlook Express Application Window 90
Know How to Create an E-Mail Message 92
Be Able to Format a Message 95
Know How to Use Attachments 97
Understand How to Receive a Message 99
Know How to Reply to a Message and Forward a Message 100

7 Beyond the Basics: Using E-Mail Safely and Effectively   104

Explore the Advanced Options in Outlook Express 106
Know How to Use the Address Book 108
Know How to Find E-Mail Addresses and Contact Information 109
Know How to Avoid Viruses and Virus Hoaxes 110
   Recognizing Virus Tricks 110
   Recognizing Virus Hoaxes 111
   Using the Outlook Express Anti-Virus Features 112
Know How to Avoid Spam 113
Understand About E-Mail Privacy in the Workplace 114

Part 4 GETTING AROUND THE WORLD WIDE WEB   118

8 Getting to Know the World Wide Web   118

Understand Why the Web and the Internet are Not the Same 120
Know About the Origins of the World Wide Web 121
Understand How the Web is Administered by Web Servers 122
   Serving Up the Data: Clients and Servers 123
   What's in a (Web) Name? 123
Understand the Process of Getting Information from a Web Server to Your System 125
Know the Basics of How Proxy Servers and Mirror Sites Work 126
Know the Major Browsers in Use 126

9 Surfing Basics   130

Know How to Navigate the Web 132
   Using URLs 132

Troubleshooting Error Messages 133
Refreshing Your Data 134
Tips and Tricks for Entering URLs 134
Scrolling Through Visited Web Sites 135
Using Hyperlinks and Shortcuts 136
Keep Track of Web Sites 136
Bringing Up the Past 137
Finding Your Favorites 137
Creating Web Shortcuts on the Desktop and the Links Bar 139
Know How to Use Search Tools 140
Using Search Engines and Search Directories: The Basics 141
Conducting More Effective Searches 142
Searching from within Internet Explorer 144
Understand How to Get Around a Web Page 145
Find Information on a Web Page 146
Know How to Use Information Offline 146
Saving Web Data 146
Printing and E-Mailing Web Pages 147

10 Beyond the Basics: Advanced Surfing — 150

Know How to Speed Up Surfing 153
Using Multiple Browser Sessions 153
Using Multiple Browsers 154
Disabling Graphics and Multimedia 155
Blocking Advertisements 156
Surfing During Off-Times 157
Be Able to Use Browser Settings 158
Using the Standard Buttons Toolbar 158
Setting the Home Page 159
Managing ActiveX Controls and Java 160
Understand the Basics of Managing the Cache 161

Part 5 RUNNING EFFECTIVE INTERNET SEARCHES — 166

11 Search Basics — 166

Know How to Generate Search Engine Results 168
Understand How to Use Keywords to Query Search Engines 169
Know How to Use a Web Directory 172
Know How to Use a Combination Search Engine/Web Directory 174
Be Able to Use a Natural Language Search Engine 175
Know How to Use a Metasearch Engine 178

12 Beyond the Basics: Searching Seamlessly — 181

Know How to Use Operators in a Search 183
Using the AND, OR, and NOT Operators 184
Limit Results by Using Multiple Keywords and Boolean Operators 185
Limit Searches by Using Quotation Marks 186
Know Some of the Advanced Search Engine Options 188
Use Some of the Specialized Search Sites 190

Part 6 TAKING CONTROL OF THE INTERNET 195

13 Communicating via the Internet 195

Know About Instant Messaging 197
    How Instant Messaging Works 197
    Messaging Clients 198
    The Rise of Instant Messaging's Popularity 199
    Security and Privacy Concerns 200

Understand the Basics of Using Chat 201

Know About Newsgroups and Bulletin Board Systems 202
    How a Newsgroup Works 202
    Finding a Newsgroup 203
    Keeping Control: Moderated and Unmoderated Groups 204
    Bulletin Board Systems 205

Know About LISTSERV and Mailing Lists 205

Understand the Trends Associated with Real-Time Conferencing 206
    Video Conferencing 207

14 Pulling Information from the Internet 210

Understand the Types of Information You Can Download 213
    Text Documents 214
    Audio and Music Files 214
    Images, Photographs, and Clip Art 214
    Commercial Software Programs, Patches, and Updates 215
    Trialware 215
    Shareware and Freeware 215

Copy Information from a Web Site 216
    Copying Text from a Web Site 217
    Copying Graphics and Other Objects from a Web Site 217

Save an Entire Web Page 218

Download Files from a Web Page 219

Understand the Basics of FTP 220

Download an FTP Client 221

15 Working with Various File Types and Plug-Ins 227

Be Familiar with Common File Types 230

Examine the Main File Types 232
    Text Formats 232
    Web Page Formats 233
    Graphic File Formats 233
    Media File Formats 234
    Portable Document Format 237
    Compression File Format 237

Know About Common Plug-Ins 238
    Adobe Acrobat Reader 238
    Macromedia Flash Player and Macromedia Shockwave Player 239
    QuickTime 240

16 Beyond the Basics: Taking Advantage of the Internet's Multimedia Capabilities — 244

Understand Streaming Media   248

Know About Some of the Technologies Used for Streaming Media   249
- Compression Schemes (COder/DECoders)   249
- Media Players   251
- Media Encoders   252
- Standardizing the Digital Media Platform   252

Know About Webcasting and Web Cams   253
- Webcasting   254
- Web Cameras   254

Part 7 PRIVACY AND SECURITY ISSUES — 259

17 Beyond the Basics: A Closer Look at Privacy Issues — 259

Understand How Lack of Privacy Can Lead to More Control by Others   262

Understand Data Snooping and How Others Can Track Your Activities   262
- The Technology and Methods Used for Data Snooping   262
- The Data Snoops   264

Know About Government Surveillance and Control Issues   264
- Carnivore   264
- Magic Lantern   266
- Other Government Data Snooping Techniques   266

Understand Privacy Issues in the Workplace   267
- Reasons Why Organizations Track Employees   267
- How Organizations Monitor Internet Usage   269

Understand Children's Online Privacy Rights   271

Understand Privacy Issues Related to Biometrics   272
- Fingerprint Scanning   273
- Hand and Palm Recognition Technologies   273
- Eye Scanning Technologies   274
- Facial Recognition Technologies   274
- Concerns About Biometrics   275

Implement the Best Practices for Protecting Your Privacy   275
- Checklist for Evaluating ISPs   276
- Best Practices for E-Mail Privacy   276
- Best Practices for Surfing   276

18 Beyond the Basics: A Closer Look at Security Issues — 281

Understand the Importance of Internet Security   285
- Financial Losses Due to Internet Security Breaches   285
- Know About Recent Developments in Internet Security Threats   286

Understand the Main Types of Internet-Based Attacks   287
- Denial of Service Attacks   288
- Potential Attacks Against Critical Infrastructures   289
- Common Attacks on Home Systems   289

Understand the Potential for Damage from Mobile Code: Java, JavaScript, VBScript, and ActiveX   291
- Types of Mobile Code   291

Controlling Mobile Code   292
Know Ways to Prevent Malicious Code from Executing   293
  Malicious Code and How It Spreads   293
  How Antivirus Companies Help You Ward Off Malicious Code   295
  Assessing the Threat: Rating Systems for Malicious Code   295
  Best Practices for Protecting Yourself from Malicious Code   296
Understand the Importance of Using a Firewall   297
Know How to Create Strong Passwords   298
  Password Trickery   299
  Guessing and Cracking   299
  Creating Secure Passwords   299
Know the Best Practices for Conducting Safe E-Commerce   300
Implement the Best Practices for Security   301

Part 8 CREATING A WEB SITE   306

19 Designing a Great Web Site   306
Understand Some of the Reasons for Creating Web Pages   309
Understand the Main Types of Web Sites   309
Know the Basics of How Web Sites are Developed   310
Understand Design Considerations   310
  Think Goals and Market   310
  Think Usability   311
  Think Structure   312
  Think Carefully about the Home Page's Design   313

20 Tools You can Use to Create a Web Site   318
Know About Using Web Page Editors   321
Know About Using Free Web Creation Tools   322
Understand the Basics of Using HTML Markup Tags   324

21 Using FrontPage to Develop a Web Site   330
Start FrontPage and Create a Simple Web Site   333
Enter and Edit Text on a Web Page   337
Switch Between the Normal, HTML, and Preview Panes   340
Develop a List and a Table   343
Apply a Theme   346
Revise and Create Hyperlinks   347
Create an E-Mail Hyperlink   349
Examine a Link Bar's Properties   349
Change a Web's Structure   351
Test Your Web   352

22 Adding Graphics to Your Web Site   356
Use Clip Art   359
Save Your Web Files   362
Insert Picture Files   364
Create and Test Thumbnails   366

Create a Photo Gallery 368
Modify a Photo Gallery 371

23 Publishing to the World Wide Web 376

Know How to Evaluate and Choose a Web Host 379
Know the Options for Getting Free Web Space 381
Understand the Essentials of Web Site Positioning 382
    Carefully Construct the HTML Title for Your Home Page 383
    Sprinkle Keywords Appropriately Throughout Your Home Page 384
    Develop High-Quality Links 386
    Realize the Importance of Submitting Your Site to Search Engines 386
Understand the Basics of Publishing to the Web 388

Appendix A: Interfacing the Internet with Cell Phones and PDAs 393

PDA Overview 393
Entering Data 394
E-Mail and Internet Access 395
Popular PDA Companies and Operating Systems 397
Security and Privacy Issues 398

Appendix B: Useful Web Sites 399

Biometrics 399
Children's Sites 399
Domain Name Registration 399
E-Mail Abuse and Spam 399
Hardware and Software Vendors 400
Instant Messaging and Communication 401
Internet Background Information, Surveys, and Statistics 401
Internet Service Providers 402
Job Search Sites 402
Multimedia Sites 403
News and Weather Sites 403
Online Manners 403
Online Shopping and Auctions 403
People Search Sites 403
Privacy and Security Sites 404
Scholarship and Financial Aid Sites 405
Search Engines and Directories 405
Sites Related to Downloading Files 406
Specialized Search Engines and Sites 406
Travel Sites 407
Usability and Web Site Development 407
Web Site Optimization and Hosting 407

Index 409

Glossary 417

PREFACE

THE COMPLETE GUIDE TO UNDERSTANDING AND USING THE INTERNET is designed as a course of study in Internet literacy. This book includes concepts and hands-on activities to equip students with the tools they need to become skilled and knowledgeable Internet users. Because of the scope and sequence of the book, it can be effectively used by college students, adult learners, or advanced and motivated high school students.

The book includes extensive research and cutting-edge information on topics and issues related to using and understanding the Internet, making this comprehensive and easy-to-understand presentation the ultimate Internet guide. The text provides a strong emphasis on Internet security and privacy issues as well as hands-on tips and tools for working online. It also shows students how to apply Internet skills in real-life situations, and clearly presents both the positive and negative aspects of the Internet.

KEY FEATURES

COMPREHENSIVE INFORMATION IN AN EASY-TO-UNDERSTAND PRESENTATION.

- Enables students to readily understand concepts related to using the Internet.
- The scope and sequence of the topics provides a logical presentation of Internet literacy concepts.
- Analogies and explanations provide the instructor with numerous ways to explain Internet concepts.

SECURITY AND PRIVACY ISSUES ARE EXTENSIVELY COVERED in the narrative, *Alert!* note boxes, and the security and privacy questions that conclude each chapter.

- Provides students with comprehensive coverage of the most important Internet issues today with references to related Web sites.
- Provides instructors with a springboard for discussion.

MODULAR DESIGN.

- Provides instructors with the flexibility to customize and organize the course to their specifications.
- Helps students better retain information.

OBJECTIVES AND KEY TERMS precede and define the contents of each chapter; the **summary, matching, multiple choice, discussion questions**, and **hands-on exercises** round off the chapter.

- Focuses students' attention on the chapter goals, key concepts and terms; reinforces and emphasizes the most important material.
- Gives the instructor a clear roadmap of which concepts will be covered in a chapter.
- Key term definitions appear in bold when they are introduced in the text.
- A glossary includes clear definitions for the key terms to provide a quick reference.

"THE BIG PICTURE" FEATURE INTRODUCES EACH CHAPTER.

- Provides students with an interesting overview of the concepts that will be covered in the chapter.
- Sets up the framework for the instructor to present the concepts in the chapter.

"A WINDOW ON THE WEB" feature provides a visual summary of the information that will be covered in the chapter.

- Provides students who learn visually with a quick overview of the chapter's contents.
- Helps the instructor prepare students for the concepts that will be covered.

NUMEROUS AND HELPFUL BOXED FEATURES. *What If? Notes* raise questions about ethical use of the Internet; *Inside Track Notes* give readers tips that will help them become more productive; *Heads Up Notes* warn students of potential problems; *Alert! Notes* raise privacy and security issues; *On the Horizon Notes* describe new technology.

- Provides students with easy-to-find information and multiple opportunities to think analytically; raises their awareness of potential problems or issues associated with using the Internet.
- The boxed notes reinforce or expand on the concepts presented, making it easy for instructors to stimulate classroom discussion.

REFERENCES TO WEB SITES.

- Provides students with resources so they can readily access more information about a topic or reinforce concepts presented in the text.
- Gives instructors easy-to-find Web sites that can be used for additional assignments or to reinforce learning.

HANDS-ON ACTIVITIES.

- Provides students with easy-to-follow activities to work hands-on with the Internet and related technologies.
- Instructors have flexibility in presenting the activities; the exercises can be given as independent assignments or worked through as a class.

DON'T FORGET ELEMENT summarizes the main points of the chapter.

- Provides a checklist of the most important information presented in the chapter.
- Helps students to review the main concepts.
- Provides instructors with a list of discussion items.

CHECK THIS OUT ELEMENT. Multiple choice, matching, and discussion questions.

- Provides reinforcement of concepts presented or a quick check to see whether students understand the chapter's main points.
- Provides the instructor with a method of quickly checking a student's basic knowledge of the chapter.

"REAL LIFE" QUESTIONS AND EXERCISES provide "real life" applications and practice using the Internet and related technologies.

- Helps students reinforce concepts and apply them in new ways.
- Provides instructors with material that can be used for assignments and projects.

I SPY: SECURITY AND PRIVACY ISSUES. Questions and exercises to stimulate discussion and raise current issues.

- Helps students synthesize their knowledge and conduct online research.
- Causes students to evaluate and analyze security and privacy issues surrounding the proper and improper use of the Internet.

FOR THE INSTRUCTOR

INSTRUCTOR'S RESOURCE CD-ROM

The **Instructor's Resource CD-ROM** that is available with *The Complete Guide to Understanding and Using the Internet* contains:

- Instructor's Manual in Word and PDF.
- Solutions to all questions and exercises from the book.
- PowerPoint lectures.
- A Windows-based Test Generator and the associated test bank in Word format.

TOOLS FOR ONLINE LEARNING
www.prenhall.com/bird

This text is accompanied by a companion Web site at *www.prenhall.com/bird*. This Web Site is designed to bring you and your students a richer, more interactive Web experience. Features include: online End-of-Chapter materials, interactive study guide, internet exercises, and much, much more!

ACKNOWLEDGMENTS

To Jodi McPherson for providing the vision and leadership for this book and for giving me the opportunity to write it.

To Jan Snyder, Thomas Park, Christy Parrish, Nancy Sixsmith, the team at Impressions, Audri Anna Bazlen, and the small army of other people who were involved in the editing and production of this book.

To the college professors who reviewed this book and offered their valuable insights and feedback.

Most of all, to my family who strongly supported me during the long days I spent writing: Lonnie, who helped out in countless ways, and Rebecca and Sarah who always cheered me on.

ABOUT THE AUTHOR

Linda Bird specializes in corporate training and support through Software Solutions, her own company. She has successfully trained users from more than 75 businesses, including numerous Fortune 500 companies. Her clients have included Appalachian Electric Power Co., Goodyear, Pillsbury, Rockwell, and Shell Chemical. Her background also includes teaching at Averett College and the University of Rio Grande.

Using her training experience as a springboard, Linda has authored more than 15 books on a variety of computer topics, including the Internet, PowerPoint, Word, Excel, Access, and Windows. Additionally, she has written more than 20 instructor's manuals and contributed to books on HTML, desktop applications, and the Internet. She has also penned more than 200 magazine articles for *Smart Computing* and *Computer Power User* magazines on wide-ranging computer topics—from using the Internet to troubleshooting hardware and software problems. She also writes monthly how-to columns on PowerPoint and Excel.

Linda, a graduate of the University of Wisconsin, lives on a small farm near the Great Smoky Mountains with her husband, Lonnie, and her daughters, Rebecca and Sarah. Besides authoring books, Linda home-educates her daughters. When she's not writing, you can probably find her with her family—trekking around the mountains or horseback riding.

SECTION CHAPTER

One
UNDERSTANDING THE INTERNET

1

HOW THE INTERNET IS CHANGING THE WORLD

Key Terms

When you finish this chapter, you'll understand the following terms:

ARPANET
backbone
banner ads
client
client-server architecture
computer network
download
e-commerce
e-mail
Extensible Markup Language (XML)
fiber optics
gigaPoP
hub
hypertext link
Hypertext Markup Language (HTML)
Internet
Internet Service Provider (ISP)
intranet
Metropolitan Area Exchange (MAE)
Military Network (MILNET)
Network Access Point (NAP)
NSFnet
online shopping
packet
platform
Point of Presence (PoP)
protocol
router
Secure Sockets Layer (SSL)
server
spam
switches
telecommuting
Transmission Control Protocol/Internet Protocol (TCP/IP)
Web browser
World Wide Web (Web or WWW)

Chapter Objectives

After you complete this chapter, you'll

- Understand What the Internet Is
- Understand the Origins of the Internet
- Know How the Internet is Structured
- Understand the Internet's Impact on the World
- Identify Controversial Issues Related to the Internet
- Be Aware of Emerging Internet Technologies and Trends

The Big Picture

The Internet. All you have to do is mention it and most people have at least some idea of what it is and how it's used. But what exactly is it?

The simplest explanation is that the **Internet** is a huge collection of computers all over the world that are connected to one another in various ways. Through these connections, you can perform a variety of tasks. Here are some of the most common services people use the Internet for:

- *Electronic mail (e-mail).* In its simplest form, **e-mail** is sending and receiving messages electronically and inexpensively through the Internet. E-mail has several advantages over conventional postal services. Not only is sending e-mail practically free, it's also instantaneous. An e-mail message you send to your friend in Kenya, for example, will be received in a matter of seconds—not days or weeks.

- *Information sharing and resources.* If there's a topic in which you're interested, it's a sure bet that there's information about it online. From online news, weather, and sports to research papers, medical information, and buying cars . . . you name it; the Internet has vast resources about it. After all, it's called the Information Superhighway for good reason.

- *Business Communications.* Many business and commercial organizations, and schools and universities use the Internet as their main way to communicate and share information. As you'll soon find out, the forerunner to the Internet was a *computer network* designed for the university and scientific community to communicate. The business community now uses it for many of the same things.

- *Advertising.* No longer confined to print media and television, advertising is big business on the Internet. Most companies maintain a Web site for their products or services; many advertise on related sites as well.

- *Online Shopping.* Want to order a book, subscribe to a magazine, buy concert tickets, or reserve a beach house online? You probably can. In fact, more and more businesses sell services and products online, making this a viable alternative to going to a traditional "brick-and-mortar" store.

- *Stock Trading.* You can track, buy, and sell stocks online. You also can use the Internet to complete financial and business transactions.

- *Discussions and Chat.* If you're interested in a topic, most likely a number of other people are, too. The Internet allows you to talk about the topic via discussion groups, forums, and chat rooms. You can discuss a subject with hundreds or thousands of people worldwide—not just those who are located in the same town or geographical region.

- *Entertainment.* You can use the Internet to find out about upcoming concerts and activities. You also can use the Internet to play interactive games with others from around the world, listen to music and radio stations, and even view videos—all in real-time.

- ***Program Downloads.*** You'll find a wealth of programs and files you can download from the Internet, such as utilities, graphics, games, music, and videos. **Downloading** is copying a file or program from the Web directly onto your computer.

In this chapter, we'll take you on a brief tour of the Internet: What it is, how it's set up, and how the entire thing got started in the first place. After that, we'll look at how the Internet has changed the face of the world. Next, we'll turn our attention to some of the issues swirling around the Internet—such as privacy and security concerns, illegal or improper uses of the Internet, and government control. We'll wrap up this chapter by checking into cutting-edge technologies and trends related to the Internet. In later chapters, we'll expand and build on this information so that you can gain the knowledge and skills necessary to operate effectively on the Internet.

Window on the Web

If the Internet is a series of linked computers, you need a way to connect them, right? The Internet's **backbone** is just what it sounds like—the internal infrastructure that supports the entire system, including the cabling and routers. In our bodies, a skeleton provides the structure; in the online world, high speed cables and **routers** provide the structure on which information travels.

There are a number of commercial backbones that comprise the Internet. Although the organizations that maintain each backbone typically work out agreements to connect with other backbones, no one group "runs" the Internet. This prevents control by any particular government or organization. Take a look at AT&T's backbone in the United States, keeping in mind that this backbone is connected to many others (see Figure 1.1).

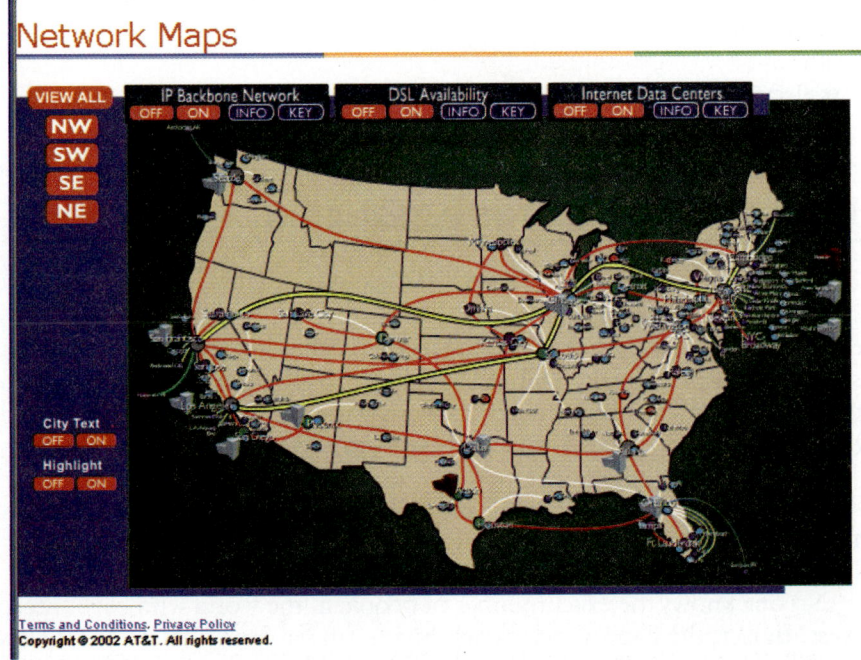

Figure 1.1.
A graphical example of how the Internet provides a backbone, or electronic roadway, on which to send information.

So, what can you do with the information that travels via the Internet's infrastructure? Figure 1.2 shows just a few of the possibilities.

Figure 1.2.
The Internet connects the world in many ways.

It's clear that the Internet is a vast electronic empire—and that it will take a while to explore. Let's get started!

UNDERSTAND WHAT THE INTERNET IS

You already have a general idea that the Internet is a loose-knit collection of computers that are connected so that you can share information and resources. Computers that are linked to each other in this way are referred to as a **computer network**. You can think of the Internet as a huge network comprised of millions of computers worldwide. The network is set up with clients and servers (logically called **client-server architecture**).

A **server** is a machine that provides services, such as distributing e-mail or Web pages; a **client** is a user machine that connects to the server and receives information from it. (You'll learn more about clients and servers in Chapter 8, Getting to Know the World Wide Web.)

No one knows the exact number of people in the world who have Internet access. In fact, the figures vary wildly, as you can see from Table 1.1. However, we can safely assume that the actual number is somewhere around 500 million, and growing each year.

4 Chapter 1 How the Internet is Changing the World

TABLE 1.1	Who in the World Has Internet Access?
Worldwide Internet Population— Unique Users (2001 Estimates)	**Projection for 2004:**
498 million (Nielsen//NetRatings)	709.1 million (Nielsen//NetRatings)
533 million (Computer Industry Almanac)	945 million (Computer Industry Almanac)

Even though the Internet is technically only the infrastructure, most people think of the Internet as including both the network and the data it comprises. Furthermore, the most well-known part of the Internet (with the possible exception of e-mail) is the World Wide Web. The **World Wide Web** (usually just called the Web, or WWW) is the graphical, user-friendly side of the Internet.

But keep in mind that the Web is not synonymous with the Internet. Instead, the **Web** is a service that enables users to view and share graphic and multimedia documents electronically and remotely over the Internet. What does that mean? Simply that people can view documents that have been saved using a specific file format, called **Hypertext Markup Language (HTML)**. This programming language has critical features that are important for distributing information remotely.

First, documents saved using HTML can be viewed on computers at faraway locations—and those that use a variety of operating systems and software applications. Just as important is the fact that HTML lets Web page developers link documents together. They can link to their own documents or to other locations on the Web. The documents are interconnected through a series of **hypertext links** (usually just called **links**). Despite their name, hypertext links can be text or objects; clicking a link causes the associated page to display (see Figure 1.3).

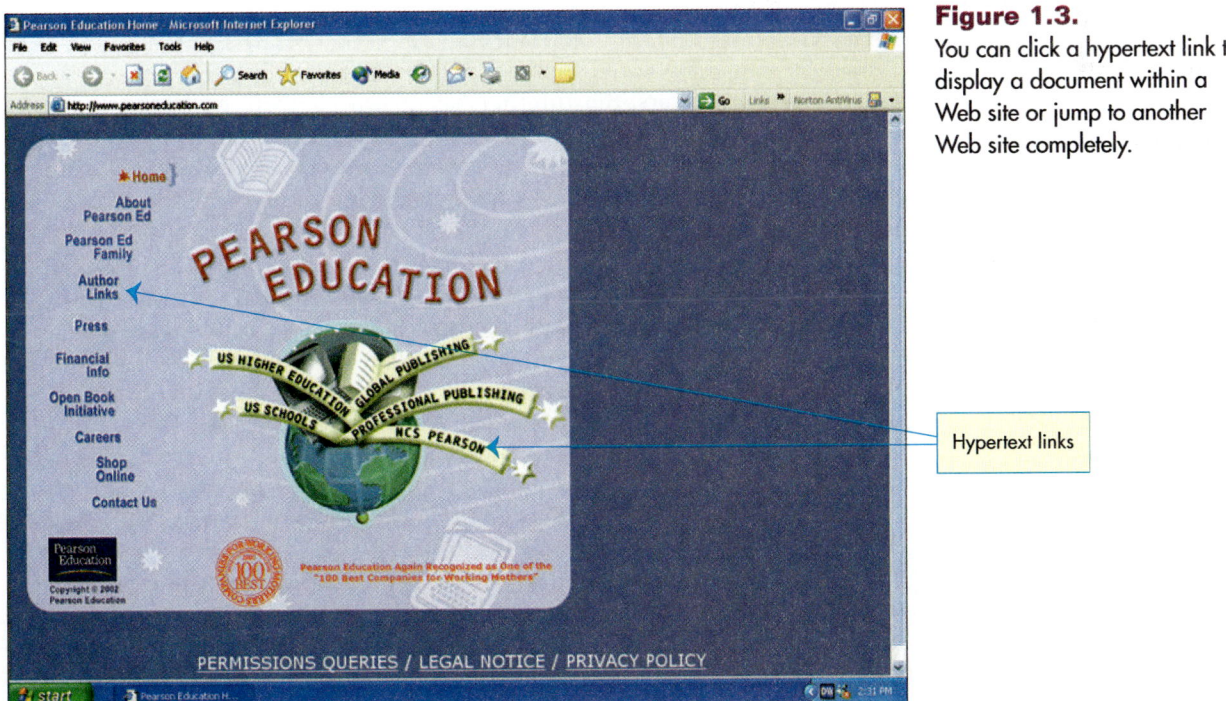

Figure 1.3.
You can click a hypertext link to display a document within a Web site or jump to another Web site completely.

> ### ON THE HORIZON
>
> HTML isn't the only player in the markup language game. **Extensible Markup Language (XML)** is the up-and-coming standard that will be used to develop Web pages in the future. This language is more portable and flexible than HTML. However, after you learn how to work with HTML, you shouldn't have any problem learning to work with XML-based programs.

To view information on the Web, you need a few things. The most obvious of these is a computer (or TV) and a way to connect it to the Internet, such as a phone line or cable modem. But to view Web content, you also need a program that's designed to display Web sites, which is called a **Web browser**. The two most popular Web browsers are Microsoft Internet Explorer and Netscape. Because Internet Explorer is by far the most widely used, in this book we'll focus on it.

How does it work? In brief, your browser software locates information that you request by looking for the Web site's address, also called a Uniform Resource Locator (URL) or a domain name. The domain name is set up using certain rules so the browser knows how to find the Web page. In fact, if you've spent much time on the Web, you probably already recognize the basic setup for a Web address: *http://www.domainname.com*. The *http:* portion of the address indicates the method your browser will use to retrieve the page (in this case, hypertext transport protocol); the remainder of the address indicates the Web site location. (You'll learn much more about domain names in Chapter 8, Getting to Know the World Wide Web.)

Of course, there are many information sites and services on the Internet that are not Web-dependent, such as e-mail and ftp sites. In future chapters, we'll cover all the great things you can do with the Internet in detail. We'll also let you know exactly what equipment, software, and services you need to access the Internet. For now, let's take a tour through the brief, but explosive history of the Internet.

UNDERSTAND THE ORIGINS OF THE INTERNET

Over the past 40 years, the Internet has grown—sometimes haphazardly and without any apparent control or direction. Although this lack of central control by any one organization or government seems confusing at times, most people agree that it's a positive thing. Just think of the consequences if one group *could* control the Internet! Let's take a look at how it began.

Back in the early 1960s, the United States Department of Defense (DoD) wanted to develop a computer network system that would work in spite of natural or man-made disasters, such as a nuclear attack or a flood. If part of the computer system was destroyed (by a bomb, for example), the information would automatically be rerouted and still reach its destination. In 1969, the Advanced Research Projects Agency (ARPA) branch of the Department of Defense created a network called **ARPANET**. Originally, this network was relatively small-scale: only three universities and one government agency were connected. On October 1, 1969, the first message was sent over the network . . . promptly causing a system crash!

As additional university and government agencies were added to the network, it became apparent that certain rules, or **protocols**, for sending and receiving information needed to be in place. Following the rules allowed a smooth transfer of data, even when individual organizations used various hardware and software for their computer systems (collectively referred to as the **platform**). Because of the wide variety of platforms represented by organizations, following the protocols was critical.

The Network Control Protocol (NCP) was the first protocol used, followed by the **Transmission Control Protocol (TCP)** and the **Internet Protocol (IP)**. The latter two (TCP and IP), which were developed by Vinton Cerf and Robert Kahn, became known as TCP/IP. **TCP/IP** includes rules for establishing connections and for transmitting information. These standards are still in use today.

By the early 1980s, more and more university computers were connected to the ARPANET. When the DoD determined that the increased usage might pose a security risk, they broke off from ARPANET and formed their own **Military Network (MILNET)** in 1983.

INSIDE TRACK

Cerf and Kahn were noted for another contribution to the modern Internet in addition to the development of TCP/IP. In an article they penned in 1974, the term "Internet" was first used.

Meanwhile, the National Science Foundation (NSF) developed **NSFnet** in 1985, based on ARPANET. Following the same protocols as ARPANET, NSFnet's main infrastructure enabled research and educational institutions to continue to share information. Additionally, regional networks were linked to the national backbone—and the network continued to grow.

At the same time, another, parallel development in business was occurring. Until the advent of the national-wide network, most companies had their own internal networks, called **intranets**, which they used to communicate with those within their organization. But as NSFnet expanded, corporations became increasingly interested in the potential for using the NSF's network for their own purposes, such as communication and publicity. Naturally, the idea of a nation-wide network appealed to many of these companies, as they realized the potential to market their products to a huge audience and communicate more effectively with those outside their companies. Although the NSF originally set up the network for non-commercial uses, the organization gradually began to respond to pressure to also allow commercial uses.

In 1989, the NSF allowed two commercial e-mail services (MCI Mail and CompuServe) to set up limited connections to the Internet. They reasoned that non-commercial users, such as those in the academic and scientific communities, would benefit the most from this deviation from the network's original purpose. Of course, this simply whetted the private sector's appetite for more. Beginning in 1991, the NSF began plans to privatize the Internet. In increasing numbers, telecommunication companies, such as MCI and Sprint, built their own networks, which they then linked to NSFnet. As time passed, the huge network was increasingly referred to as "The Internet." Finally, in 1995, the NSF stopped funding the public part of the Internet completely and commercial firms and regional network providers took over the major Internet arteries. Most of the infrastructure (such as the communication lines and *routers*) was sold to telecommunication conglomerates, such as Sprint and WorldCom. GTE, BBN Planet, and UUNet also bought pieces of the infrastructure as well.

To make sure that data would still flow smoothly through the system, the TCP/IP protocol continues to be used with the now commercially run Internet. Additionally, so that commercial enterprises could continue to communicate with universities and the private sector, main connection *hubs* in the United States were established. These connection points became known as **Metropolitan Area Exchanges (MAEs)** and included extremely fast *routers* that could speedily send data to the correct location. The West coast MAE was located in San Jose (MAE West); the East coast MAE (MAE East) was set up near Washington D.C. Since that time, other MAEs have been added in Chicago, Dallas, Atlanta, and New York. (If you're particularly interested in MAEs, you can check out the current information about them at *www.mae.net*.)

Figure 1.4.
The rapid increase in online commerce is just one sign of the Internet's explosive growth.

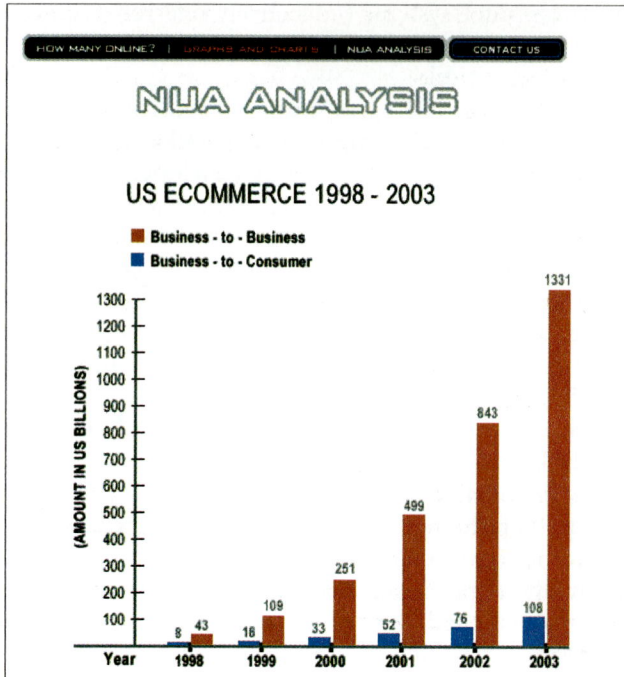

Of course, many smaller *hubs* have also been created to help route electronic information around the country. These exchange *hubs* are referred to as **Network Access Points (NAPs)** and are found in most major cities, such as New York.

Today the Internet continues to grow at a rapid rate. The latest statistics estimate that more than 166 million in the United States/Canada and 500 million people worldwide have access to the Internet. Figure 1.4 shows one sign of the Internet's growth: actual and projected online commerce in the United States from 1998–2003.

KNOW HOW THE INTERNET IS STRUCTURED

By now you're probably wondering how all of this works. After all, something's got to be responsible for moving all that data around, right? In this section we'll get you up to speed on how everything's connected. In doing so, you'll become more familiar with terms like backbone, hubs, routers, and switches.

A backbone is simply a high-speed data connection (or series of connections) between major telecommunication centers and cities. These connections form the major pathways within the Internet and are able to transport large volumes of data between central points, called nodes. To facilitate the transfer of huge amounts of information, backbones are usually made up of fiber optic cable bundles.

Of course, it wouldn't make sense to give each user on the Internet direct access to the nation's major backbones. Instead, connections are made through progressively larger networks, beginning at an individual computer and traveling through bigger and bigger networks until the information is routed to a major backbone.

Think of the system as a small spring that flows into a stream . . . which in turn pours into a river (such as the Ohio River) . . . which surges into the mighty Mississippi. Logically, the Mississippi River can carry a much larger volume than can the stream. In the same way, the Internet's major backbones can carry more data traffic than can your local network.

The major backbones include key points, called **hubs**, so that data can be rerouted to its destination. MAEs and NAPs are examples of hubs. A hub typically includes **switches** to provide a physical place to plug in the connections and a router. A **router** is a device that takes a look at the data and decides where to send it. Think of a router as a sorter or interpreter that finds out the addresses where data is stored and then passes it along to its intended destination, kind of like an Internet traffic cop that directs information to the right place.

If you send data over the Internet, however, it doesn't travel as a complete chunk. Instead, it's broken up into small blocks of data, more-or-less uniform in size, called **packets**. Each packet is given a unique number so that the packets can be reassembled at the destination point (Of course, you don't actually see this happening). The TCP/IP protocols make sure that everything's done for you. So when you send that great digital photo to your parents across the country, they don't have to reassemble the packets into something recognizable. Instead, they can just pull up the reassembled picture—without ever realizing that it was broken into pieces in the first place.

Let's take a look at how the data actually travels. Imagine that you live in New York City and want to find out information about traveling to Pismo Beach, California. The trouble is, the Web pages for Pismo Beach are located in California (although, of course, they could actually be stored anywhere . . . but that's another story). You connect to the Internet by using a local Internet Service Provider (ISP) and a PoP to do so. An **Internet Service Provider (ISP)** is the company that provides the computer system, software and other support so that you can access the Internet. A **Point of Presence (PoP)** is an ISP's connection point.

After you're connected, you can use your Web browser software to request information about Pismo Beach. Your request travels from the local Internet Service Provider's PoP to the regional ISPs and then through a central hub in Washington D.C. The hub routes the request via the most efficient set of connections to the West coast. After the data reaches the central hub in San Francisco, it's routed through the regional and local networks to the Web server in which the Pismo Beach Web pages are stored. Of course, the process is more-or-less reversed to send the information.

We say more-or-less because the information you receive may actually take a wide variety of electronic pathways to reach you, depending on what else is happening on the Internet. For example, if a regional network is not working, the information is automatically rerouted so that it can still reach its destination. Remember, this capability to quickly reroute data as needed has its roots in the military's original purpose for ARPANET. So although your request for beach accommodations may have been sent via Chicago, the information from Pismo Beach may be returned to you via Dallas.

The speed at which Internet data travels to and from your computer depends on many factors, one of which is the bandwidth of your connection. (We'll talk more about bandwidth in Chapter 3, Necessary Equipment and Internet Connections. For now, just realize that Internet connections with more bandwidth can carry data more rapidly than those with less.)

Think of the Internet as a superhighway and network backbones as major Interstate highways. Regional networks are similar to state highways, and your local ISP is like the road outside your house. Your data is like a car.

You begin your travels locally by connecting to your local ISP and making your request. Your ISP sends the request to the state highway (the regional network); it then takes a ramp (a router) to get on the Interstate (a major backbone). In major cities (MAE or NAP), there is usually an intersection of the major interstates (a router). This intersection is used to help traffic flow and to reroute cars (data) to other destinations. If there are enough lanes (bandwidth) to accommodate the traffic, everything flows smoothly.

But imagine that a NAP is not working, which is similar to a traffic accident on a major Interstate highway. In the physical world, you might be stuck in traffic for hours. On the Internet, your data is automatically (and speedily) rerouted.

Of course, to perform this miracle of cooperation, all the organizations that own part of the Internet's structure have to abide by some rules. The first is that Internet traffic changes networks only at a NAP or MAE. Second, data is supposed to travel as far along a network's own backbone as possible before jumping to another network's infrastructure. Third, the data has to be transferred using standard protocols.

What does the future hold for the Internet's structure? Telecommunication companies are already scrambling to keep up with the explosive demand for increased Internet access by adding fiber optic lines. **Fiber optics** involves converting data into light so that incredibly huge volumes of data can be transported extremely fast over specialized fiber optic lines. As you can imagine, the major backbones on the Internet transport data in this manner.

Another recent development in Internet design is the use of gigaPoPs. A **gigaPoP** is like a little NAP; it is usually located in a smaller city and connects the networks from two or more ISPs to the regional backbone. Furthermore, several gigaPoPs can be connected to form a "mini" backbone that can take some of the pressure off of the regional networks and major backbones.

By now, you should have a pretty good idea of how the Internet is structured and about some of the changes in store. In the future, the Internet will both take advantage of and drive some of the changes in technology. Fasten your seatbelt. It promises to be a fast ride.

UNDERSTAND THE INTERNET'S IMPACT ON THE WORLD

The Internet has changed millions of lives. From the way we conduct business and attend school to how we communicate . . . just about everything is affected by the Internet. A study published by the National Telecommunications and Information Administration, "A Nation Online: How Americans are Expanding Their Use of the Internet," showed that there are two million new Internet users each month. From August 2000 to September 2001, there was a 22 percent increase in the number of Americans who used the Internet. In April 2002, the Nielsen//NetRatings showed that 166 million Americans (approximately 55 percent of the total population) used the Internet. Although we'll go over the Internet's impact in more depth throughout this book, here are some main ways that it is influencing lives.

ELECTRONIC COMMERCE AND ONLINE SHOPPING

One of the main ways that the Internet has been used is for electronic commerce (e-commerce) and online shopping. **E-commerce** involves any business or financial transaction that takes place over a network. **Online shopping** typically involves a specialized Web site in which a catalog of a company's products is stored. Internet users can locate an item to purchase and then complete the transaction electronically by entering their credit card, address, and shipping information on an online form. The most popular commerce sites listed by the Nielsen//NetRatings in April 2002 are shown in Table 1.2.

TABLE 1.2	
Web site	Number of unique visitors/month
Amazon	30,337
Yahoo! Shopping	25,701
Ebay	23,736
MSN Eshop	9,341
DealTime	5,686

The biggest hurdle that companies have had to overcome to market their goods online has been to convince shoppers that the confidential information they enter in the online form is safe. To do so, most legitimate shopping sites use a Web site that encrypts (scrambles) your credit card information. You can also check out the firm's reputation by contacting the Better Business Bureau (*www.bbb.org*—see Figure 1.5) or the National Fraud Information Center.

Businesses also use the Internet as an advertising medium that can potentially reach millions of customers. Organizations maintain Web sites mainly to share information about the products and services they offer. They also can place electronic advertisements on non-competitive related sites. For example, a general travel site might contain advertisements for phones or other items. These advertisements are often displayed across the width of the Web page, which gives them the name **banner ads** (see Figure 1.6).

Of course, people don't like banner ads much more than they do television ads. If Internet advertising annoys you, you can turn it off . . . and in a later chapter, we'll show you how.

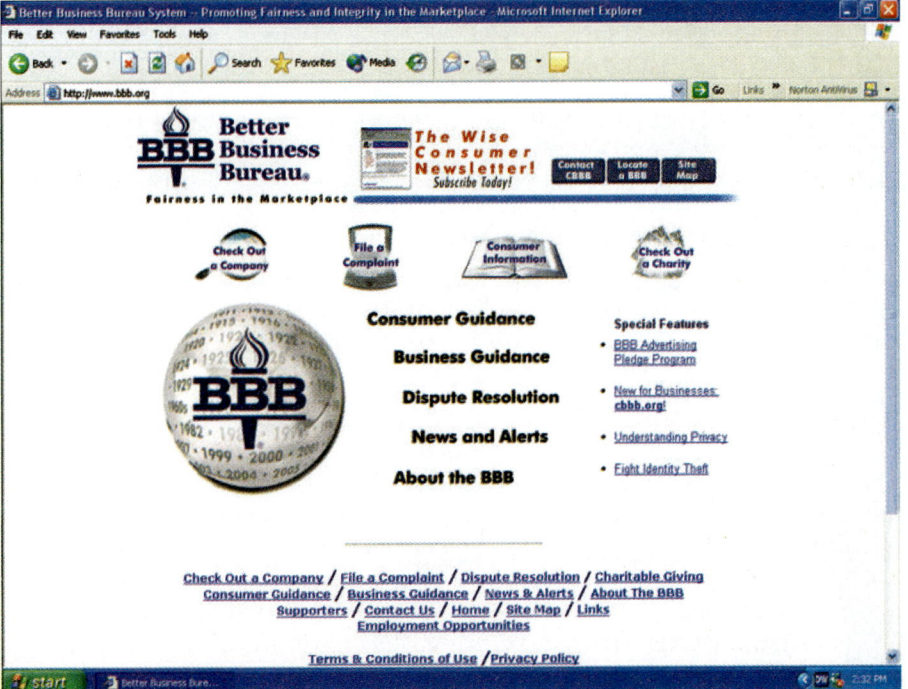

Figure 1.5.
The Better Business Bureau tries to help curb Internet fraud.

Understand the Internet's Impact on the World

Figure 1.6.
When you work on the Internet, you'll see plenty of ads.

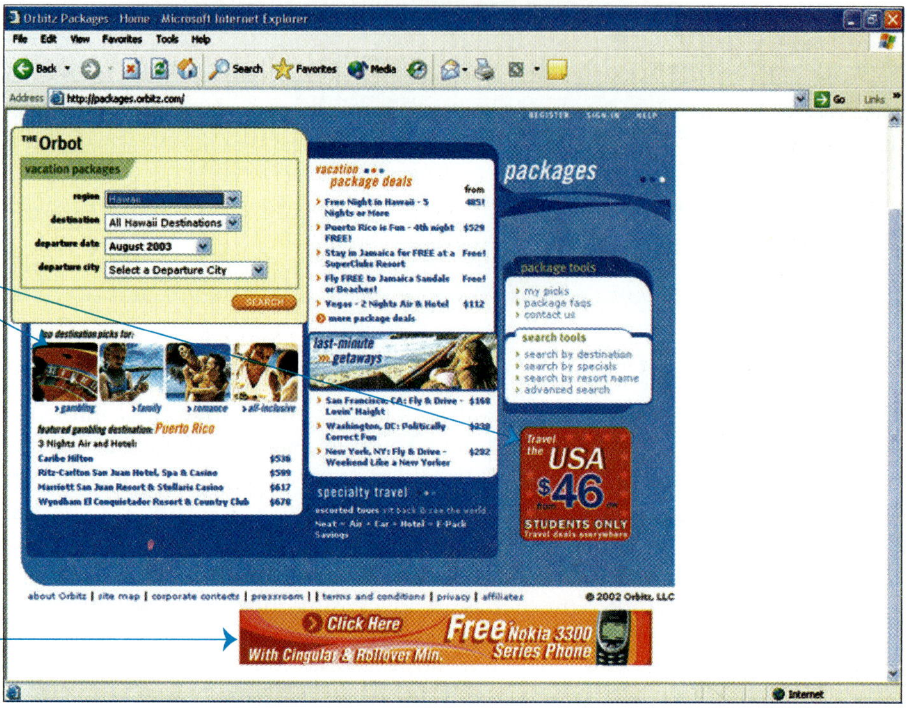

STOCK TRADING AND FINANCES

You can quickly lay your hands on financial and investment tools and information via the Internet. Some of the most well-known brokerage firms in the country, such as Merrill Lynch and Charles Schwab, maintain Web sites (see Figure 1.7).

Financial planning sites include a variety of helpful investment tools, such as online interactive tools that help you plan for college, retirement, invest-

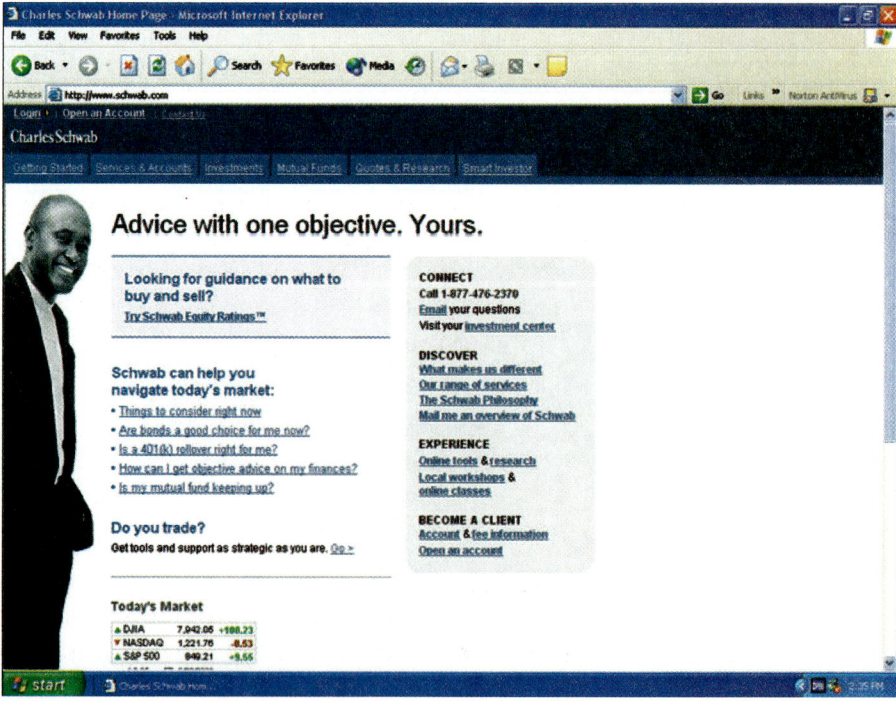

Figure 1.7.
Investment companies include a number of financial tools on their Web sites.

ments, and stock trading. Additionally, you can check out the current price of stocks and mutual funds online.

But investment firms aren't the only financial institutions who maintain Web sites. Banks are also encouraging customers to conduct business online, such as view their balances or pay their mortgages. The concept of online banking e-commerce has been relatively slow to catch on, however, because people are reluctant to send confidential information over the Internet. Web designers for commercial sites have to add security to their sites—both to protect data and to build customer confidence. For example, many e-commerce sites use **Secure Sockets Layer (SSL)** technology, which encrypts data sent over the Internet. SSL and other technologies are critical for conducting online financial transactions. We'll look more closely at these issues in future chapters.

 Hackers could get through the Secure Sockets Layer (SSL) of major banks or e-commerce sites?

COMMUNICATIONS

One of the most important ways that the Internet has impacted lives has been to revolutionize the way we communicate with each other. In this section, we'll show you a few of the most important ways that the Internet has done this.

ELECTRONIC MAIL. One of the most popular ways to use the Internet is to send and receive e-mail. How does it work? You use a specialized mail program (an e-mail client) in conjunction with the Internet to communicate with people all over the world by sending and receiving electronic messages.

Not only is e-mail fast and convenient, it's practically free. In fact, if you access a free Web-based e-mail service at the library, it doesn't cost you anything; otherwise, you might have the initial costs of buying a computer system and ordering an ISP.

The growth in electronic mail has been explosive. Some surveys indicate that as many as 96% of the online users regularly use e-mail (Jupiter Media Metrix, July 1999). In fact, the typical American Internet user sends or receives 75 legitimate e-mail messages each month.

We emphasize *legitimate* because the use of commercial e-mail pitches (commonly called junk e-mail or **spam**) is also on the increase. It's projected that by 2004 Americans will receive 200 billion pieces of spam, compared with 88 billion pieces of U.S. Postal Service junk mail (Forrester Research). Sending advertising via e-mail is attractive to businesses, since they can save approximately 60% of the cost of a direct mailing by using e-mail instead of the United States Post Office. Some technical gurus, such as Eric Allman who invented the first commercial e-mail program, are concerned that spam may eventually become so out-of-control that users will completely abandon e-mail. At this point, however, e-mail still provides a fast, viable link between computer users. (We'll give you some hints on how to better control spam in Chapter 7, Beyond the Basics: Using E-Mail Safely and Effectively.)

REAL-TIME COMMUNICATIONS. There are ways to communicate in real-time on the Internet. In contrast to e-mail, real-time communication means that you interact with others at the moment you type or speak your message. Instant messaging and chat are two examples of real-time communication tools that are available. In Chapter 13, Communicating via the Internet, we'll go over how to use these tools in more depth.

BUSINESS COMMUNICATIONS. Businesses have heavily used the Internet to communicate—both with those within their company and those who are not. They use the Internet to send e-mail as well as to communicate information about their products and services to prospective customers. Savvy companies quickly realized the power inherent in the Internet and leverage it to their advantage: Small businesses that use the Internet grow 46% more rapidly than those that don't (Source: *American City Business Journals*). It's expected that businesses will continue to use the Internet for advertising and communication.

INFORMATION SHARING

With the advent of the World Wide Web, users were able to easily view graphical and multimedia content online. This opened the doors to finding out information on almost any imaginable topic. According to the U.S. Department of Commerce, there were 26,000 registered domain names in 1993; by 1999, just six short years later, there were five million Web sites. What are the most popular types of sites? Those having to do with travel, job searches, finances, and medical information tend to attract the most users. (See Appendix B, Useful Web Sites, for a listing of popular Web sites.)

Another way that the Internet greases the wheels of information sharing is by allowing you to download software. For years, people have downloaded software for free (freeware) or by paying a small fee (shareware). However, it's becoming increasingly common to purchase complete programs via the Internet. For example, you can buy Microsoft Office or Norton AntiVirus directly from the vendor's Web sites in much the same way as you do other online purchases. The advantage of downloading a program instead of buying the boxed version is twofold: You can immediately begin using the program and it's easier to get updates for the software (see Figure 1.8).

Figure 1.8.
You can download software from the Internet.

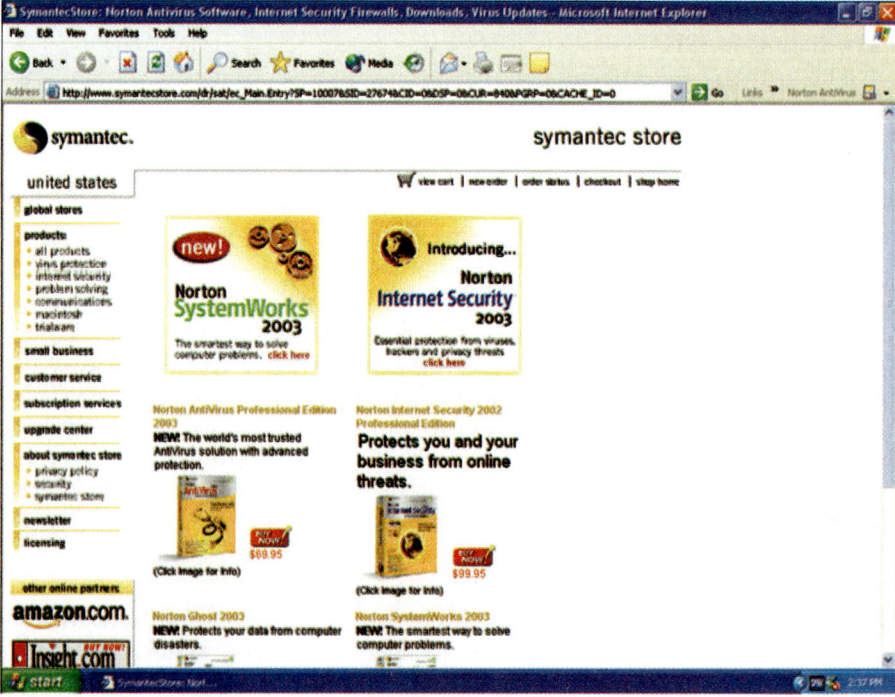

Chapter 1 How the Internet is Changing the World

TELECOMMUTING AND HOME-BASED BUSINESSES

Advanced technologies, such as the Internet (and e-mail), were pivotal in opening the doors for some people to work from home. **Telecommuting** involves working as an employee for a company, but from a remote location. Telecommuting has grown rapidly since 1995 (the same time the Internet was commercialized). By 2000, the United States Government's Bureau of Transportation Statistics estimated that there were 14 million home-based workers in the United States.

The trend for telecommuting and home-based workers has been strengthened by an increased acceptance of the workstyle by corporate America. Part of this is due to the fact that employers began to see the benefits of the arrangement: Telecommuting was used to keep self-starting workers happy, improve productivity, and reduce office costs. Employees liked the workstyle as well because it gave them lower commuting costs, flexible hours, and more family time.

A related trend is the increase of home-based businesses. Many jobs that formerly required an on-site presence by an employee can be performed remotely via the Internet. Additionally, as companies downsize, they unwittingly contribute to the startup of small, home-based businesses in two ways: skilled or professional employees that are laid off will frequently decide to run their own businesses, and companies outsource more and more work to these types of people.

THE INTERNET'S EFFECT ON JOBS

The presence of the Internet has had numerous effects on the job market. As the technology changed rapidly, so did jobs. Workers needed to be retrained to perform the new jobs, spawning an entire training industry. For example, many workers needed to attend computer classes to learn how to operate the newly available software and how to get around the Internet. Administrative assistants and office personnel needed different (or additional) skills than for which they had been originally trained. For example, although keyboarding remained a critical skill, knowing how to actually operate a typewriter was no longer necessary.

Middle managers were also affected by the introduction of the Internet into the workplace. They were required to learn new skills and use computers for a greater percentage of their workday. In some cases, jobs were combined or eliminated because the computer enabled workers to operate more efficiently.

But not all of the changes were negative. The Internet, although it displaced some workers, has simultaneously opened doors of opportunity for them. The Internet facilitates outsourcing and working from home. Additionally, many workers can work remotely as consultants or freelancers, using the Internet to stay connected with others. Entire new industries and jobs (such as Web designers) have been born. Finally, a host of job search sites, such as CareerBuilder (*www.careerbuilder.com*) and Monster.com (*www.monster.com*), aid people in their search for new careers (see Figure 1.9).

Figure 1.9.
You can use the Internet to find a new job.

THE INTERNET'S EFFECT ON EDUCATION

Like most other aspects of life, the Internet has also changed education. Students are computer-literate at younger and younger ages—in some cases, they are more adept at getting around a computer (and the Internet) than are their teachers! The Internet has also become a learning tool that students can use to learn interactively. For example, kids can learn about science and nature by using hands-on games and computer-based activities (see Figure 1.10).

Students can also conduct online research, tapping into online libraries, government Web sites, and professional journals. Additionally, online courses

Figure 1.10.
The Internet includes a number of interactive learning tools.

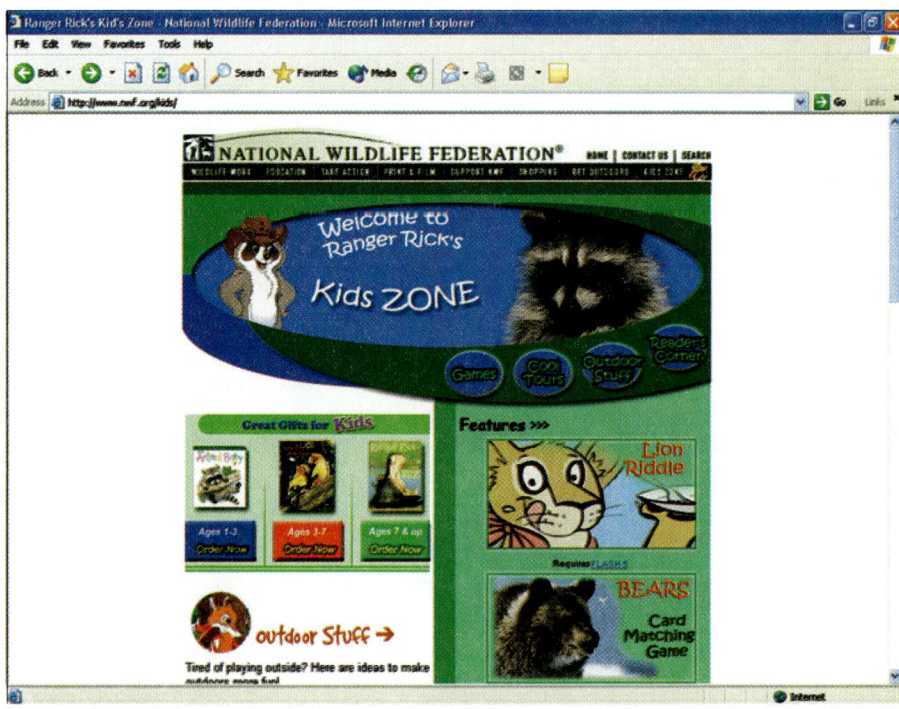

16   Chapter 1   How the Internet is Changing the World

on a wide variety of topics are available for high school and college students. In fact, it's possible to earn a college degree without ever stepping into a traditional college classroom. Online classes have enabled many people to fit a college course into a schedule that might otherwise be cram-packed with family and job responsibilities.

Although the Internet *can* be employed as an educational tool, there are some dangers related to using it. Some people's learning styles make it difficult for them to learn remotely over a computer network. Furthermore, online courses can contribute to an over-reliance on technology if the learning isn't paired with hands-on, practical life application of the knowledge. Additionally, some educators feel that the quality of online learning isn't as good as the traditional classroom or other life experiences.

Finally, the Internet has not only made it easier for students to conduct research, but also to easily copy the information they find from the Web directly into a paper or report. Although the Internet doesn't cause plagiarism, it does make it significantly easier for students to copy others' work. (We'll go over copyright considerations related to using online information in Chapter 14, Pulling Information from the Internet.)

THE INTERNET'S EFFECT ON ENTERTAINMENT AND TRAVEL

The Internet has enabled users to listen to online radio stations, share digital music files, and research travel online. For example, the music industry has been revolutionized by the development of software (such as Napster) that allowed users to download MP3 files.

Although the recording industry was able to effectively shut down Napster, there are now a number of music file sharing software programs available on the Internet. In response, the recording industry is beginning to sell music on a subscription basis.

The travel industry has also been given a boost by its presence on the Internet. Not only can you research travel destinations, but you can also make online reservations. Expedia was the most popular travel site according to the Nielsen//Net Ratings in April 2002 (see Figure 1.11).

Figure 1.11.
Travel sites remain a popular destination on the Internet.

IDENTIFY CONTROVERSIAL ISSUES RELATED TO THE INTERNET

Although the Internet has been used in many legitimate and helpful ways, it has also raised some troubling and controversial issues. In later chapters, we'll discuss these issues in more detail, but here are some things to think about until then:

PRIVACY

The beauty of the Internet is that information is freely available. It's also a drawback if there is information about you (such as your personal e-mail address or maybe even that terrible senior picture from high school) that you don't want shared. Even worse is the problem of identity theft and fraud—when someone uses your personal information to masquerade as you or make purchases in your name. (You'll learn more about privacy issues in Chapter 2, The Good, the Bad, the Ugly: Uses and Misuses of the Internet, and in Chapter 17, Beyond the Basics, A Closer Look at Privacy Issues.)

SECURITY

You'd like to think that your personal computer system is secure from invasion by cybercriminals. But the reality is that hackers and other bad guys are eager to crack into your system for a variety of reasons—to find out information or to send you a virus just for spite. There are ways to fight back, though, through the use of anti-virus software, filters, and passwords. (You'll learn more about security issues in Chapter 2 and in Chapter 18, Beyond the Basics, A Closer Look at Security Issues.)

FREE SPEECH

The Internet is a completely free forum and exchange of information. Although this has a good side to it, it also has some serious negatives as well. Take, for example, the presence on the Internet of pornographic and other harmful sites, and the way that terrorists have used the Internet to communicate. In light of this, throughout the book we'll look at the role (if any) of government in regulating or monitoring these types of communications.

GOVERNMENT CONTROL AND SURVEILLANCE

Since the terrorist attack on September 11, 2001, the United States government has become increasingly proactive in its desire to monitor the Internet for possible criminal activity. In October, 2001, congress passed the USA PATRIOT Act, which included changes to the electronic surveillance laws already in place.

But even before the attack, the Federal Bureau of Investigation (FBI) announced that the agency was using an Internet monitoring system called "Carnivore." Although the details are not public knowledge, it's believed that the Carnivore diagnostic tool examines packets and determines whether the FBI has a legal right to the information. As of this writing, the Electronic Privacy Information Center (EPIC) had filed under the Freedom of Information Act (FOIA) to gain public release of records regarding Carnivore. If you want to know more, take a look at EPIC's Web site at *www.epic.org*, the FBI site at *www.fbi.gov/hq/lab/carnivore/carnivore.htm*, or the Center for Democracy and Technology at *www.cdt.org* (see Figure 1.12).

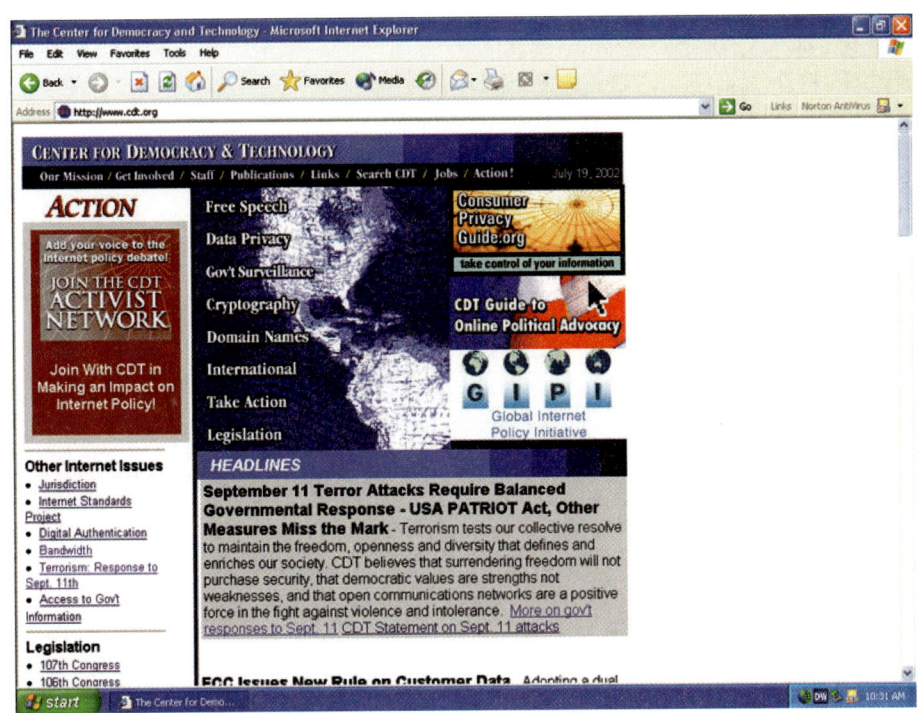

Figure 1.12.
The Center for Democracy and Technology is just one of many sites set up to educate people about privacy and security issues.

BE AWARE OF EMERGING INTERNET TECHNOLOGIES AND TRENDS

The Internet will continue to grow and change in response to the new technology and to user demands. Watch for many of the following trends and technologies in the future:

- Greater concerns over securing data, maintaining privacy, and fighting cybercriminals
- More universal access to the Internet
- An increasing number of people using high-speed (broadband) Internet access
- More fiber-optic cable and other cutting-edge technologies
- Increased use of wireless devices and personal digital assistants (PDAs)
- Greater government control over Internet content
- Increased electronic surveillance by the government
- The use of biometrics (the process of authenticating a person's identity based on their biology; for example, using retina scanning to verify a person's identity before letting them access a computer system)

Throughout the book, we'll look at these technologies and discuss privacy and security issues related to them.

Don't Forget...

- The Internet has a colorful and interesting background. Beginning as a means for the Department of Defense to communicate remotely, the Internet has mushroomed into a gigantic conglomeration of networks that span the world.

- The supporting structure for the Internet isn't controlled by any one organization. This de-centralization is intentional so that communications can continue even if part of the Internet is destroyed by a natural or man-made disaster.

- The Internet is used for a wide variety of tasks, including the ever-popular e-mail, online shopping, stock trading, sharing information, real-time communications, and job-related tasks.

- The Internet, by its very nature and strategic position, raises issues regarding privacy, security, freedom of speech, and government control and monitoring. As new technologies emerge and more people begin to use the Internet, these issues will likely become even more prominent.

Check This Out

MULTIPLE CHOICE

1. What was the forerunner to the Internet that was originally set up by the United States Department of Defense?
   a. The World Wide Web
   b. ARPANET
   c. NSFnet
   d. TCP/IP

2. What is a protocol?
   a. A set of guidelines used to ensure uniform transfer of data across the Internet
   b. A router that directs Internet traffic
   c. A hub location, such as MAE West
   d. None of the above

3. Which of the following is not directly responsible for transferring data on the Internet?
   a. Router
   b. Switch
   c. Hypertext
   d. Backbone

4. Which of the following groups controls and runs the Internet?
   a. A group of investors from New York
   b. The science and academic community
   c. Businesses
   d. No one single group—it's decentralized

5. In which of the following ways has the Internet impacted life?
   a. Communications (e-mail)
   b. Job structure and tasks
   c. E-commerce
   d. All of the above

MATCHING

a. ISP
b. PoP
c. fiber optics
d. HTML
e. router
f. backbone
g. NAP
h. packet
i. telecommuting
j. intranet

1. The vendor who provides access to the Internet, usually by charging a monthly fee
2. The programming language used to develop pages for the World Wide Web
3. A way to convert data into light so that it can be transported quickly
4. The major communication pathway for the Internet
5. The hardware device or software responsible for sending data to the correct destination
6. A major hub on the Internet
7. A workstyle in which the employee uses the Internet to work from home
8. A company's internal computer network
9. Data that is broken into chunks so that it can be transported across a network
10. The connection used by the vendor to provide access to the Internet; a jumping-on place

Real Life

1. The Internet has impacted many aspects of everyday life. Spend a few minutes listing the ways that the Internet has affected your life and the lives of people you know. Discuss with other students which changes you feel are positive and which ones appear to be detrimental.
2. If you have access to the Internet, find out which courses at your school (or schools in your area) are taught online. List the pros and cons of online courses.
3. Interview several professors at your school to find out if they feel online courses are instructionally sound. If there is a difference in opinions between the teachers, analyze where the variance lies. For example, is it rooted in the instructor's background and experience with the computers or due to the subject matter?
4. Analyze your major (or career) to determine if you could perform the job tasks via telecommuting. Additionally, use the Internet to research which professions are most conducive to telecommuting. What qualities or characteristics would a person need to work independently from home?
5. List the pros and cons of online shopping. If you have access to the Web, look at some of the major shopping sites, such as Amazon.com. In what ways has online shopping transformed the way people research and make purchases? What hurdles do online shopping companies need to overcome to be profitable?

I Spy: Privacy and Security Concerns

1. The Internet has enabled people to be connected in ways that they could never have imagined just a few years ago. What impact does being connected electronically with others have on our personal privacy?
2. List and describe some of the ways that you think people might use the Internet to infringe on others' privacy (see the Center for Democracy and Technology at *www.cdt.org* for ideas and discussion).
3. Find several Web sites that include information on Carnivore and the US PATRIOT Act of 2001. Start by looking at EPIC's Web site at *www.epic.org* and the FBI site at *www.fbi.gov/hq/lab/carnivore/carnivore.htm*. Is the United States government overstepping its power by monitoring Internet communications? In relation to the Carnivore diagnostic tool, what is the balance between privacy, freedom, and security?
4. For the government to monitor e-mail and instant messaging communications, it will have to use surveillance tools and technologies that seriously concern privacy groups and may step on constitutional rights. Which is more important: protecting the American public or safeguarding an individual's right to privacy on the Internet?

CHAPTER 2

THE GOOD, THE BAD, THE UGLY: USES AND MISUSES OF THE INTERNET

Chapter Objectives

After you complete this chapter, you'll

- Know How the Internet Is Misused
- Understand the Legitimate and Ethical Uses of the Internet

Key Terms

When you finish this chapter, you'll understand the following terms:

adware
click stream data
cookie
cracker
cybercrime
File Transfer Protocol (FTP)
firewall
hacker
identity theft
Internet fraud
Listserv
log files
macro virus
malicious code
malware
online profiling
payload
payload trigger
privacy policy
social engineering
spyware
Trojan horse
Usenet
virus
virus hoax
Visual Basic for Applications (VBA)
Web bug
worm

The Big Picture

At times, it's like the Wild, Wild West. The Internet definitely has its share of bad guys, traps, harmful Web sites, illegal acts, and other dangers. This type of bad-news activity on the Internet ranges from merely annoying (receiving junk e-mail, for example) to downright illegal or dangerous.

Why is this? Human nature being what it is, traditional crime has been electronically mirrored in the murky portions of the Internet. In this chapter, we'll take a look at some of the ways people can potentially use the Internet to negatively impact your life, cause damage to your system, invade your privacy, steal your money, and cause general havoc. We'll also give you some practical ideas about how you can protect your privacy, the security of your computer, and even your personal safety.

We'll wrap up the chapter by recapping some of the legitimate uses of the Internet covered in Chapter 1, How the Internet is Changing the World, and then expand on your knowledge by discussing some additional ways in which the Internet can be used in a positive way. For example, we'll briefly discuss Usenet, Listserv, and FTP sites. After all, there are still a lot of good guys out there, too!

In an ideal world, no nasty computer virus or hacker would attempt to take over your computer (see Figure 2.1).

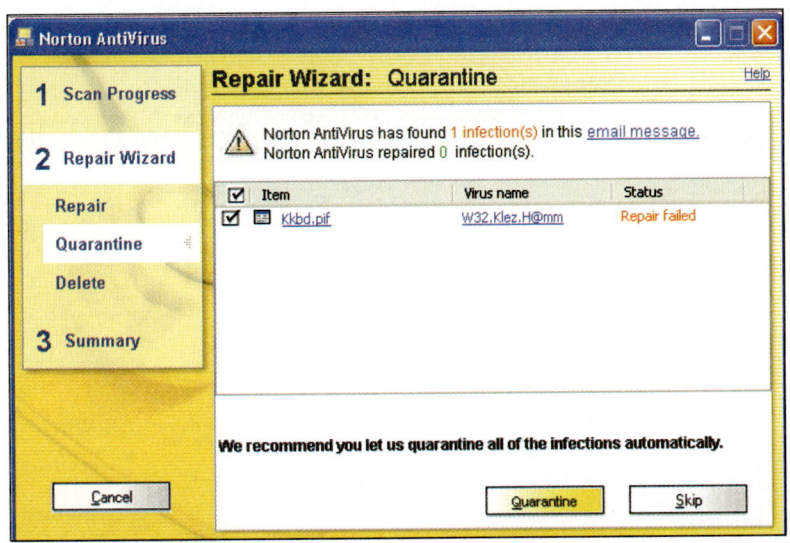

Figure 2.1.
Personal firewall and anti-virus software can help you ward off hackers and viruses.

Fortunately, access to the computer was blocked by a personal firewall in this case. What would be the worst-case scenario? A malicious computer virus has actually been unleashed on your system and is now causing you major headaches—like erasing your entire hard drive. Unfortunately, if you work on the Internet for any length of time, chances are good that you'll run into one of these Web-based bandits. In fact, according to the Community Emergency Response Team (CERT, with a Web site at *www.cert.org*), the number of security-related incidents has increased drastically from 1988 through 2002 (see Figure 2.2).

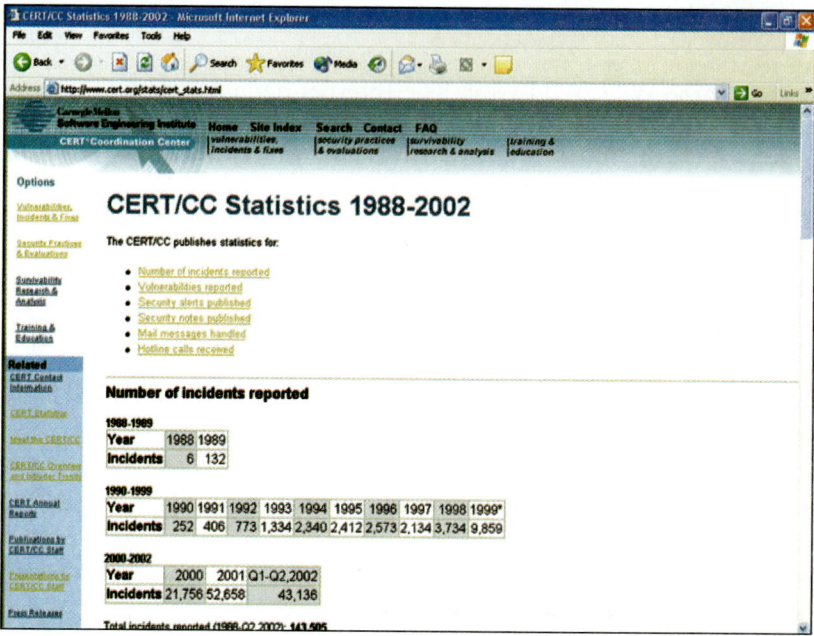

Figure 2.2.
Unfortunately, attacks on computer systems are on the rise.

Another type of attack is on your privacy. For example, one common practice of marketing companies is to collect demographic and marketing information about you and then bombard you with electronic ads or links to related products. Many Internet-based companies keep track of the Web pages you've viewed and then show links to related products or services. For example, Amazon.com, which sells a number of products online (including books, videos, tools and toys) personalizes pages you view, based on your browsing habits. It does this by tracking your online movements, such as how long you view a page, which links you click, and so on (see Figure 2.3). Some people like the fact that the site is customized for their interests; others feel that it's an invasion of privacy.

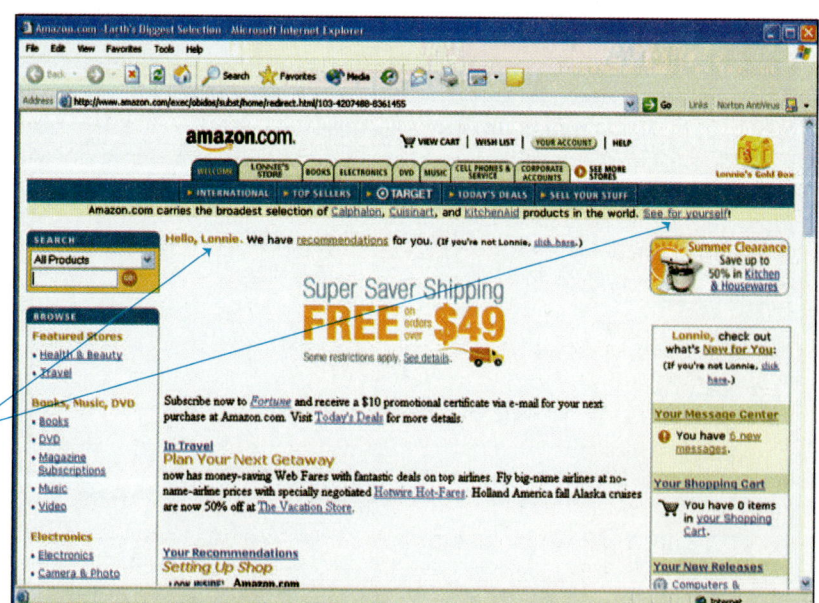

Figure 2.3.
Many Web sites track the pages you view and then use the demographic information to display ads or personalized information.

But don't despair. If you're aware of Internet-based problems and snares, you can avoid them—or at least minimize their impact. For example, to help secure your computer system, you can install a **firewall**, which is a type of software that specifically prevents others from accessing your system via the Internet. To protect your online privacy, you can turn off or delete the programs used to track your movements.

Finally, it's important to remember that even with its problems, the Internet also has a useful, friendly side. We'll expand on some of the positive ways you can use the Internet, such as joining a newsgroup, sharing files and information, utilizing a distributed mailing list, or just having fun (see Figure 2.4).

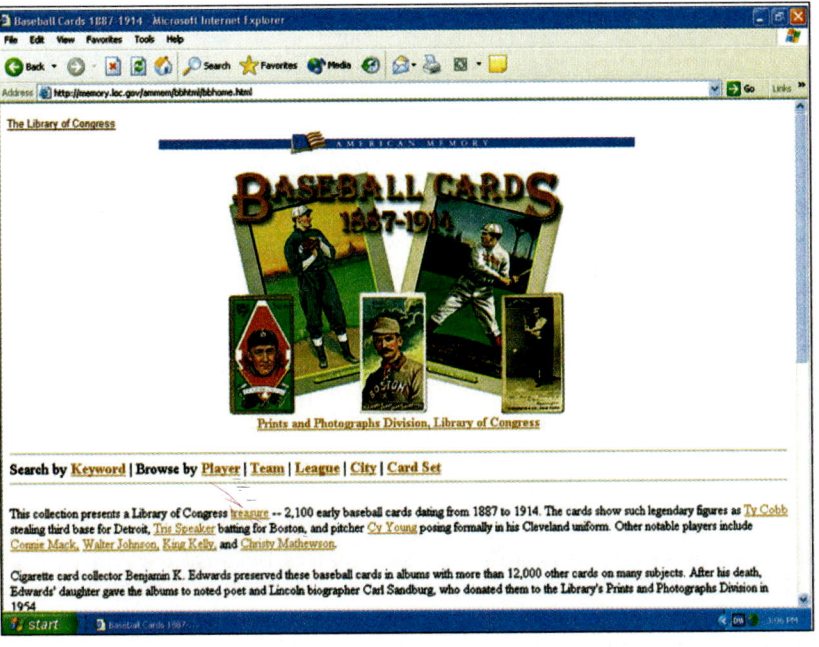

Figure 2.4.
The Internet has a good side: You can find out information, play games, or participate in online activities.

KNOW HOW THE INTERNET IS MISUSED

Almost anything in life can be misused in the hands of the wrong people—and the Internet is no exception. In fact, the apparent anonymity that most people enjoy as they surf the Web and use other Internet services lends itself to improper, immoral, or illegal uses. In this section, we'll take a look at some of the major issues surrounding these negative uses.

The Internet is a strong powerful tool when it's used ethically and legally, but dangerous and destructive when it's not. Problems can range from damage to your system caused by viruses to serious infringements on your privacy. The negative impacts of cybercrime are even worse. **Cybercrime** is criminal activity that is facilitated through use of the Internet and can involve terrorist activities, fraud schemes, copyright infringements, exploitation of children, or online stalking. Cybercrime can take many forms: spreading viruses and other malicious programming code, hacking into computer systems, stealing identities, copyright infringements, and exploitation of children are just to name a few. As we discuss each, we'll warn you about the traps and give you ideas of how to protect yourself.

Like the technology it uses to cause its damage, cybercrime is constantly changing, making it difficult to completely avoid when you're online. To compound the problems, enforcement against cybercriminals is often difficult. However, filtering, anti-virus software, personal firewalls, and a healthy dose of common sense can help to keep you from becoming a cybervictim.

MALICIOUS CODE: VIRUSES, WORMS, AND TROJAN HORSES

Malicious code—also known as **malware** (a shortened version of *mal*icious soft*ware*)—can be any computer program or code that's purposely developed to invade systems and cause problems. Viruses, worms, and Trojan horses are all common types of malware. What's the difference between each of these types of malicious code? Simply that they use different means to spread from one computer system to another.

A **virus** is a renegade program that's designed to modify the way a computer works without the permission or knowledge of the end user. Computer viruses got their name from a well-known analogy: Much like a biological virus takes over a person's cells and replicates itself to bring about infection, a computer virus takes over control of your system, reproduces itself, and then causes infection or damage.

INSIDE TRACK

Keep in mind that most people use the term virus to refer to any malicious code that causes damage to a computer system—although technically a virus is a specific type of nasty code that is spread in a specific manner.

The damage caused by a virus is called the virus **payload**. The payload of a virus can range from minor annoyances (such as a screen saver that suddenly begins to flash wildly) to major economic losses (such as erasing hard drives or crashing a company's computer network or Web site). Even the tamest viruses—those that merely play visual or audio messages—take up system resources and can eventually lead to a crash.

Like many biological viruses that can remain dormant for a length of time, computer viruses can also lurk undetected in your computer system until activated. The **payload trigger** is the condition or event that activates the virus, such as a date, the execution of a particular program, or even connecting to the Internet.

ALERT!

It's risky to open a file attached to an e-mail message unless you first scan it with anti-virus software. It may include malicious code that could damage your computer. We'll talk more about this issue in Chapter 7, Beyond the Basics: Using E-Mail Safely and Effectively. For now, just take our advice and make sure to scan these files before opening them.

Like a virus, a **worm** makes a copy of itself and causes damage to computer systems; however, worms differ from viruses because they do not attach to other programs. Worms typically spread via an e-mail program, but they can also spread across network connections or through security holes in a browser. In many cases, worms have the capability to be self-activating and spread without *any* human intervention. Because of this, they can spread quickly and be hard to control.

Another type of malware is a Trojan horse. Like its namesake in Greek mythology, a **Trojan horse** is a malicious program that enters your computer hidden within a legitimate program. In contrast to viruses and worms, a Trojan horse isn't able to replicate itself. For example, you might download a music file, a utility program, or a game from a Web site. You're expecting, of course, that the file or program is useful. However, when you open it, a nasty Trojan horse program instead unleashes itself.

ALERT!

One infamous piece of malware, Badtrans (W32.Badtrans) spreads via e-mail and then installs a Trojan horse program on your system that can track keystrokes. This can be a severe compromise of your system's security, because Badtrans can potentially find out passwords, credit card numbers, and other confidential information.

Although a Trojan horse can cause the same types of damage to an individual system as do viruses and worms, it doesn't spread as quickly or by itself as does a worm or virus, and the damage is typically more limited in scope.

METHODS OF SPREAD

Before the mid-1990s, the main way viruses spread was from sharing floppy disks. Nowadays, malicious programming code can be spread by using a variety of methods. For example, a virus or worm can enter your computer as an e-mail attachment or embedded in a program or file. In this section, we'll give a few examples of some of the most infamous malware and briefly describe the method each used to spread. If you understand how malware spreads, you'll be in a much better position to protect your system's security.

The most common method of spreading malware is via e-mail attachments: files that are sent along with a message. One of the most infamous worms that spread using this method was the Love Bug, also known as LoveLetter or VBS.LoveLetter. It spread rapidly in May 2000, and caused up to $15 billion dollars in damage due to lost productivity and destroyed files.

Chapter 2 The Good, the Bad, the Ugly: Uses and Misuses of the Internet

This worm mailed itself to everyone in the victim's Outlook address book, with "I LOVE YOU" in the subject line. It was particularly effective because it used a known name as the sender so the recipients felt comfortable opening the attached message (especially if they felt it was true!).

Using deception to trick a user into opening a message is called **social engineering**. More recently, the W32.Klez worm (and variations of it, such as W32.Klez.H) used mass-mailing techniques and social engineering—in the form of alluring subject lines that encouraged victims to open the attachment—to spread rapidly throughout the Internet community.

W32.Nimda and W32.Gomer, two other infamous malware programs, use multiple methods of spread, including e-mail attachments. These viruses can also be spread if you download messaging files from the Internet without first scanning them.

Finally, viruses can spread via macros in Excel or Word, programs included in Microsoft's Office Suite. **Macro viruses** spread by using the programming portion of these programs, called **Visual Basic for Applications (VBA)**. Although macros can perform useful tasks, people can develop destructive macros and then include them in an Office file. To protect yourself against macro viruses, don't use Office files from others unless you're sure they don't include malicious code. As an added security measure, you can also change your security settings within the Office programs. To see how to do this, consult Help in the Office program with which you're working.

INSIDE TRACK

Symantec (makers of Norton AntiVirus software) maintains a comprehensive database that includes more than 50,000 Internet security-related threats, categorized by the risk that the threat poses. You can view this helpful information at Symantec's Web site (*www.symantec.com*).

For a non-commercial source of information on viruses and security issues, take a look at the CERT Coordination Center (*www.cert.org*), which is a federally funded research center.

PROTECTING YOUR SYSTEM FROM MALICIOUS CODE. The old saying, "an ounce of protection is worth a pound of cure" is certainly true when you're referring to keeping your system virus-free. First, it's *strongly* recommended that you install anti-virus software on your system and run the software on a regular basis. Because new malicious code is always being developed, you should download the current virus definitions on a weekly basis to keep your anti-virus software up-to-date. Both McAfee (*www.mcafee.com*) and Symantec/Norton (*www.symantec.com*) produce highly rated anti-virus software that you can use to protect your system (see Figure 2.5). A lesser-known, but very effective anti-virus program is produced by Kaspersky Labs (*www.kaspersky.com*).

Figure 2.5.
It's strongly advisable to install and run anti-virus software.

Second, you should carefully consider whether it's safe to download programs from the Web—especially if you don't know the source. Unfortunately, Trojan horses and viruses that are attached to executable programs are well-hidden. (Executable files are those that include a program the computer can directly run.) Often, the reputation of the file's source is your only indication of potential trouble. For example, downloading an executable file from Microsoft's site is probably safe, whereas "free" software from a suspicious-looking site such as *www.imgoingtoinfectyoursystem.com* is probably not.

Additionally, the following practices will help minimize the chances of infection:

INSIDE TRACK

Fortunately for us, most viruses aren't successful at spreading rapidly throughout the online community on a regular, day-to-day basis. However, when they do, they're referred to as "in the wild." The W32.Klez worm was "in the wild" and accounted for more than 67% of the malware damage done to systems in the first half of 2002.

- Don't leave a floppy disk in your computer's disk drive when you start the computer. This is one way that a certain type of virus, called boot sector viruses, spreads.
- Be wary of e-mail attachments. Don't open attachments from people you don't know or if the attachment has been forwarded to you.
- Verify that e-mail attachments have actually been sent from the person indicated. Some worms spread by sending messages to everyone in an address book.
- Perform a virus scan on all e-mail attachments and software downloads before opening them.
- Prevent macro viruses from executing by changing Office's security settings to High. To do this, choose Tools, Options in Word or Excel. On the Security page, click the Macro Security button. Click the High option button and then close all open dialog boxes.
- Finally, be sure to back up your data on a regular basis. If your system is attacked, a recent backup of your data can save you considerable time and effort in restoring your work.

RECOGNIZING MALICIOUS CODE. Hopefully, the measures you take to protect your system from malicious code are successful. If not, some of the following symptoms *might* indicate that your computer system is infected with malicious code:

- New files mysteriously appear on your system
- The Windows registry (the master file that dictates how Windows operates) is changed
- Program file size changes
- Your computer sends out e-mail messages on its own and/or your friends tell you that they received a virus sent from your e-mail account
- You run out of disk space
- Your computer suddenly takes longer to boot up (or won't start up at all)
- Software acts in unusual ways
- The system slows down drastically
- A screen saver you didn't download or choose is activated

But don't panic the first time your computer acts erratically. Remember that unpredictable behavior can also be due to hardware problems or software conflicts—or even operator error. However, if you suspect that your computer has been infected, you should immediately scan your system with anti-virus software. If you haven't installed an anti-virus program, you can sometimes perform a trial scan of your system from some of the major anti-virus software's Web sites.

ON THE HORIZON

For several years, computer experts have been warning users against opening e-mail attachments that can contain dangerous code, although it was believed that simply viewing an e-mail message was safe. However, the recent development of the BubbleBoy virus changed all of that. Although the first variant of BubbleBoy didn't deliver a destructive payload, it was activated without opening any attachment. It could also e-mail itself to contacts in your address book. Unfortunately, this is probably only the beginning of a new way to spread malicious code.

VIRUS HOAXES. Finally, not all virus damage is due to malicious programming code. **Virus hoaxes** are false reports about non-existent viruses. They usually involve sending an electronic chain letter that warns of a highly devastating virus and directs you to send the warning to everyone in your address book. These hoaxes tie up e-mail servers, which leads to decreased productivity. Some hoax messages even direct the recipient to delete legitimate files on his system to clean a fictitious virus from his system, causing system integrity problems. You can usually spot these hoaxes because of their extreme claims and the fact that they're not validated by any reputable organization. If you have any questions about the validity of an e-mail message, take a look at the virus hoax information on the major anti-virus program's Web sites (such as *www.symantec.com* or *www.mcafee.com*).

INVASION OF PRIVACY

Another way the Internet can be misused is to use it to gather information about you—usually without your knowledge. A Lou Harris poll determined that almost 90% of people are concerned about their privacy—an increase from 34% in 1970.

In most cases, personal information isn't collected for malicious reasons. For example, marketing companies collect data to develop a profile of you based on your surfing habits, which allows advertisers to market their products or services to you electronically. This process is known as **online profiling**.

Online profiling is considered an invasion of privacy and is annoying to most people. But there are worse problems that can result when your online movements are tracked. Cybercriminals view the Internet as a good tool to steal your personal information. After they have identifying information, they can then use it to impersonate you and/or access your finances, a crime referred to as **identity theft**. Another major privacy-related problem is **Internet fraud**, in which Internet resources (such as Web pages or e-mail) are used to deceive others into giving the perpetrator money. Let's look at each of these problems.

ONLINE PROFILING. Marketing companies use online profiling to collect information to determine your interests and to target advertising accordingly. For example, if you visit several snorkeling and travel Web sites, the data can be combined to determine that you might be taking a vacation soon. Consequently, chances are good that the banner and pop-up ads displayed as you move through the Internet will be related to purchasing snorkeling equipment or vacation packages.

This gathering of information takes place with the permission of the Web sites you visit—but not necessarily with your permission. An identifier is placed on your computer so that the marketing company can follow your online movements. The factual data (such as the actual sites visited) is sometimes

INSIDE TRACK

If you're on mailing lists or receive telemarketing calls, you can let companies know that you don't want to be included on their marketing lists or have your identifying information sold. You do this by using the organization's opt-out option. Most companies that ask you to provide information about yourself should have an opt-out policy in place. You can usually locate opt-out information by clicking the company's Privacy Policy link on their Web site or by calling the company. You can also go to Junkbuster's Web site (*www.junkbusters.com/optout.html*) to find a list of opt-out forms you can use to tell companies that you don't want to receive advertising.

called **click stream data**. In addition to your click stream data, the marketing company may also develop a profile based on inferences about your interests, associations, habits, and so on. If the marketing company is successful in tying this information to personally identifying information (such as an e-mail address), they have access to many things about you—all without your permission.

Much of the Web tracking that occurs does so by using log files and cookies. **Log files** track the activity that occurs on a Web site. Webmasters (people who administer the Web site) like to use the log files to evaluate how effective their sites are. However, log files can also be used to gather marketing information—including your interests, the type of computer and operating system you have, and so on—typically provided by the user via an online form.

Another way that your activity on the Internet can be traced is through use of cookies. A **cookie** is a text file that a server places on the visitor's hard drive. This file is a unique identifier, such as a serial number that the server can use to retrieve your records from their database. When the user accesses the site again, the server will read the cookie's contents to gather information about the person. For example, if you buy a woodworking tool from Amazon, you'll most likely be shown a number of advertisements for woodworking books or magazines the next time you visit the site. Although cookies were originally developed so that Web sites could recognize and respond appropriately to repeat visitors (or facilitate online shopping), cookies have been embraced by marketing companies as a way to track individuals' activities so that they can customize advertisements and content.

ALERT!
DoubleClick's methods of collecting data on Web surfers led to lawsuits by privacy advocates. After a 30-month investigation into their privacy practices, DoubleClick struck an agreement with 10 states. The agreement stipulates that DoubleClick needs to disclose to Web surfers that it is tracking usage. However, it doesn't stop DoubleClick from continuing to gather data.

Although letting servers place cookies on your hard drive may make subsequent visits to a Web site easier, doing so may simultaneously compromise your privacy. In some cases, the information stored in cookies is collected, cross-referenced, and shared with other advertisers. Every time you click on a banner or pop-up ad, a marketing collection agency, such as DoubleClick, can potentially collect and sell information about your interests.

Another way your online movements can be traced is through the use of **adware** or **spyware** programs. These programs are installed on your computer and can track your online movements. This information can then be used to show you targeted pop-up ads or sold to other marketing companies.

ALERT!
Adware and spyware can be attached to file-sharing programs. If you download free file-sharing software programs, keep this possibility in mind.

How do these programs get on your computer in the first place? Unknown to many users, some file-swapping and utility programs include adware or spyware code. When the desired program is installed on your computer, the "parasite" program is simultaneously loaded. After they're placed on your system, adware and spyware programs can display pop-up advertisements and/or track your browsing habits, such as how long you view certain Web pages, what you buy online, or which ads you click.

Here's an example: You download and install a utility called Gator, which helps you manage passwords and addresses. Simultaneously, embedded adware called OfferCompanion is also installed. OfferCompanion can then track your online movements, profile your surfing habits, and shower you with pop-up advertisements (see Figure 2.6).

You can take a few practical precautions to control adware and spyware. First, educate yourself about these types of programs. The CERT Web site (*www.cert.org*) includes extensive information about this class of software. Second, if you plan to download programs, make sure to carefully read the associated license agreement. You may be surprised at what it contains. For example, one company includes a clause that you agree to let them use (for free) any unused portion of your computer's hard drive! Third, delete the adware already on your system. If you're not sure whether you unknowingly installed this software on your system, you can use Lavasoft's Ad-Aware utility (*www.lavasoftusa.com*) to locate and delete adware (see Figure 2.7). Keep in

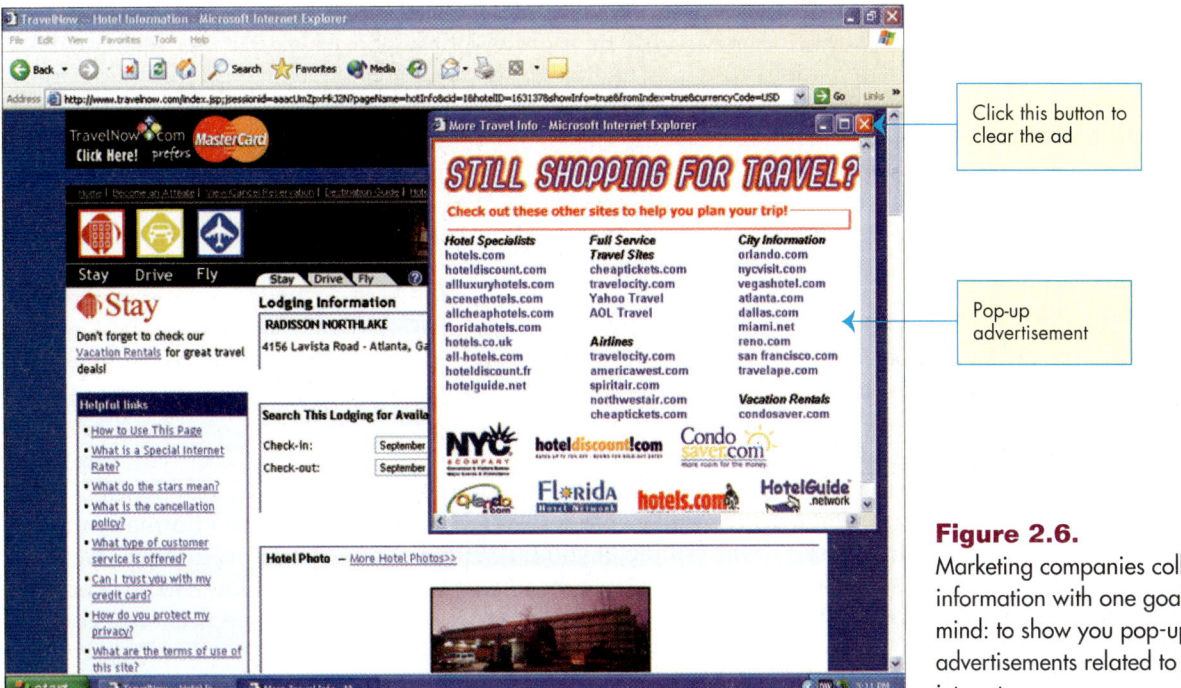

Figure 2.6.
Marketing companies collect information with one goal in mind: to show you pop-up advertisements related to your interests.

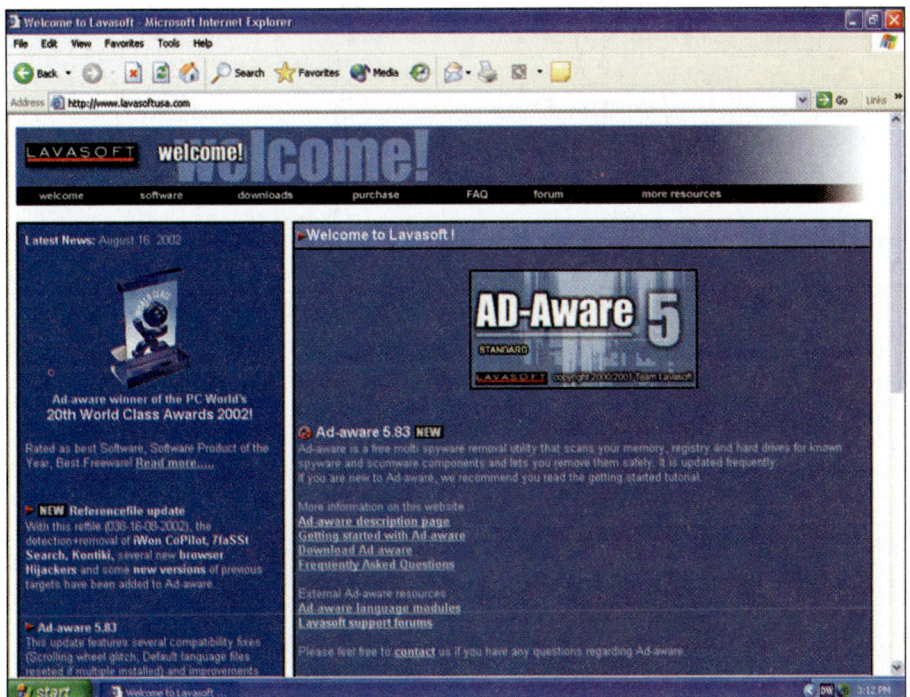

Figure 2.7.
You can ferret out adware by using Lavasoft's Ad-Aware utility.

 ALERT!
Another way your online surfing habits can be tracked is through use of Web bugs. A **Web bug** is a graphic on a Web page or in an e-mail message that is capable of monitoring who is viewing the Web page or message. This information is usually sent to a marketing company. Web bugs are typically very small (such as one-by-one pixel in size) and appear invisible—so you don't know you're being tracked. If you want to find out more about Web bugs, take a look at the Privacy Foundation's Web site (www.privacyfoundation.org).

mind, however, that uninstalling adware also probably uninstalls the program to which it is linked.

Although adware and spyware certainly constitute an invasion of privacy, they haven't been used to introduce malicious code on your system—at least not so far. You'll learn more about adware, spyware, and the potential they have for causing trouble in Chapter 17, Beyond the Basics: A Closer Look at Privacy Issues.

PROTECTING YOURSELF FROM ONLINE PROFILING. Because the U.S. Constitution guarantees the right to privacy, many people are uncomfortable with the idea that information about them is being collected and shared without their consent or knowledge. Some commercial sites are self-regulated, which involves divulging the kind of information that they collect and how it's being shared with others. TRUSTe is a watchdog program that certifies companies that follow tight guidelines about sharing their privacy and collection policies. Web sites that show the TRUSTe logo still probably collect information about you—they're just more upfront about it.

Besides using online profiling to display banner ads, advertisers like to gather marketing and identifying information about you so that they can send unsolicited advertisements, called spam, to your electronic mailbox. However, the ease with which people can pass around your e-mail address (and the fact that it's practically free to send spam) can potentially make electronic e-mail junk more prevalent and annoying than the postal junk mail you receive in your mailbox.

There are a number of measures you can take to prevent online profiling by the marketing giants. First, you can use cookie-management software, such as Cookie Crusher, which prevents or limits your computer from accepting cookies. You can also limit (or turn off) your browser's acceptance of cookies. The process for disabling cookies varies depending on your browser, but the following works if you use Internet Explorer:

> **ALERT!**
> If you receive spam in your mailbox, don't respond directly to the sender! By doing so, you just validate the fact that the spammer has sent mail to a valid e-mail address. At the very least, asking the spammer to "unsubscribe" you from the list won't be effective; at worst, you may end up with more e-mail. We'll give you some strategies for dealing with unwanted electronic junk mail in Chapter 7.

ACTIVITY 2.1
Disabling Cookies in Internet Explorer

1. Choose Tools, Internet Options.
2. Click the Privacy tab (see Figure 2.8).

Figure 2.8.
Use Internet Explorer to help control cookies.

3. Drag the slider until the Block All Cookies setting is displayed.
4. Move the slider up or down to choose other levels of privacy.
5. Choose OK.

Chapter 2 The Good, the Bad, the Ugly: Uses and Misuses of the Internet

But be forewarned. The decision to disable cookies has some consequences. Some Web sites absolutely require that you accept cookies or they won't display correctly. Additionally, electronic shopping carts are difficult or impossible to use without cookies on your computer.

Another way of protecting your privacy is to use an address that is different from your "real" one when you register or fill out a form at a Web site. If you don't, you may soon find your mailbox filling regularly with electronic junk. (You'll learn about Web-based e-mail services in Chapter 5, Mail and Messaging Software Overview.)

Finally, avoid clicking on banner and pop-up advertisements. When you do so, chances are strong that your online movements are being traced . . . and you'll start seeing more and more of the same type of ads. (We'll show you how to squash these ads in Chapter 10, Beyond the Basics: Advanced Surfing.)

To find out more about how cookies are used to track your online actions, go to the Junkbusters site (*www.junkbusters.com/ht/en/cookies.html*). Another helpful Web site is Cookie Central (*www.cookiecentral.com*). This site includes a detailed description of how cookies work, lets you view sample code, and gives suggestions for squashing cookie files on your system.

IDENTITY THEFT.   Identity thieves steal personal information, such as your social security number, driver's license number, or credit card number. They can then use the information to set up credit cards or bank accounts in your name or to charge items against existing accounts. Identity theft has been an increasing problem in recent years and the Internet has handed criminals even more ways to find personal information. In fact, the Federal Trade Commission maintained in 1999 that identity theft was the fastest growing crime in the United States. During 2001, approximately 700,000 Americans were victims of identity theft.

There are some things you can do to help prevent your personal information from being hijacked. Here's a quick checklist:

INSIDE TRACK

Most legitimate Web sites include a link to information on their privacy policy. A **privacy policy** is an organization's statement about its use of personal information that you provide. It outlines information about what type of data they collect at the site about you and what they plan to do with it.

- Find out how personal identifying information that you share will be used by those who request it. Refuse to share information if you're not comfortable with the situation.
- In the same way that you should carry as little identifying information in your purse or wallet as possible, don't share information online without considering how it may be used. For example, don't share identifying information with others in a chat room.
- Don't use your main e-mail address when you fill out forms online. If possible, avoid filling out the forms at all; when you do, include as little information as you can. Also consider setting up a second, Web-based e-mail account just for filling out these forms. (You'll learn how to do this in Chapter 5).
- Don't send personal information (such as a credit card number) in an e-mail unless you're sure the message will be encrypted.
- Install anti-virus software. Programs can (and have) been developed that record all your keystrokes—including those for credit card or social security numbers.

ALERT!

The Federal Trade Commission (FTC) received 204,000 complaints in 2001. Of these, 42 percent involved identity theft.

Unfortunately, by the time ID thieves are caught, it's usually extremely difficult to untangle the financial mess they cause. If you're a victim of identity theft, you'll most likely find it extremely difficult and time-consuming to restore your reputation and obtain credit or loans. In fact, according to the Privacy Rights Clearinghouse, identity theft victims spent an average of 175 hours and $1,000 in out-of-pocket expenses to clear their names.

If you suspect that someone has grabbed your identity, take action immediately. Here are some things you can do:

- Contact the three major credit bureaus to report the theft and request that a "fraud alert" be placed in their files. Also ask these bureaus to stop issuing any new credit in your name. The three main credit bureaus are Equifax (*www.equifax.com*, 1-800-525-6285), Experian (*www.experian.com*, 1-888-397-3742) and TransUnion (*www.tuc.com*, 1-800-680-7289).
- File a report with the police where the ID theft occurred. Make sure to obtain a copy of the report (and the report number). You may need this to prove to the bank or other lending institutions that you were a victim of the crime.
- Report the theft to the ID Theft Clearinghouse (1-877-438-4338). This is a central repository maintained by the Federal Trade Commission that is used to help combat identity theft.
- Close any accounts that have been fraudulently used. Contact the security department(s) of the bank or financial institution to alert them to the situation. When you open new accounts, make sure to password-protect them with something other than your mother's maiden name or your social security number.

The U.S. government maintains a Web site (*www.consumer.gov/idtheft*) with useful information related to fighting identity theft and forms for filing complaints (see Figure 2.9).

You can also find out information about this gross invasion of privacy on the Federal Trade Commission's Web site (*www.ftc.gov*) and the Identity Theft Resource Center's Web site (*www.idtheftcenter.org*). The Privacy Rights Clearinghouse (*www.privacyrights.org*) also includes valuable information as well as a list of related privacy links.

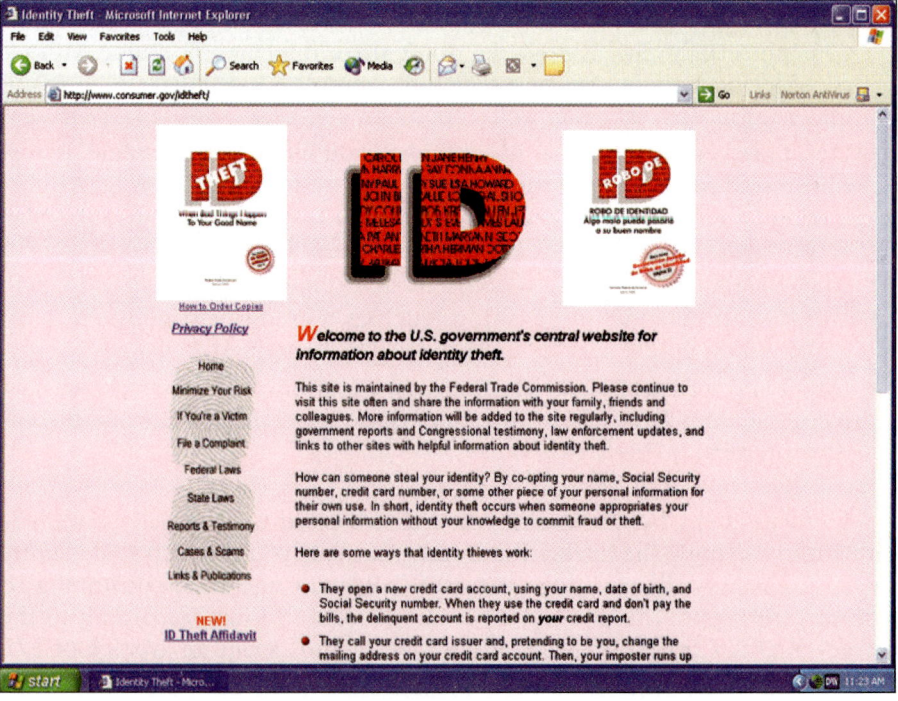

Figure 2.9.
It's important to act quickly if you suspect that your identity has been stolen.

INTERNET FRAUD. The Internet has a strong infrastructure for trade and commerce. Although it has generally helped businesses to offer their goods and services online, it has also opened the door for the electronic version of fraud. Internet fraud is where an Internet resource (such as a forum, auction, Web site, or e-mail) is used to deceive others so that the fraud victim transfers money to the perpetrator. The Internet provides an environment for cyber-criminals to thrive because they can anonymously try to snare thousands of users by sending e-mail messages, posting items on bulletin boards or auction sites, entering chat rooms, or building Web sites. E-mail and Web sites comprise the two most common Internet resources used in fraud (see Figure 2.10).

In an effort to help prevent online fraud, the U.S. government established the Internet Fraud Complaint Center (IFCC), a cooperative endeavor between the Federal Bureau of Investigation (FBI) and the National White Collar Crime Center (NW3C). You can use this center's Web site (*www.ifccfbi.gov*) to report possible fraud or to learn how to prevent becoming a victim.

According to the IFCC's 2001 report, the most common type of Internet fraud involves online auctions (42.8%); another 20.3% involves the non-delivery of merchandise (see Figure 2.11).

Here are some typical types of fraud that are easily facilitated by the Internet:

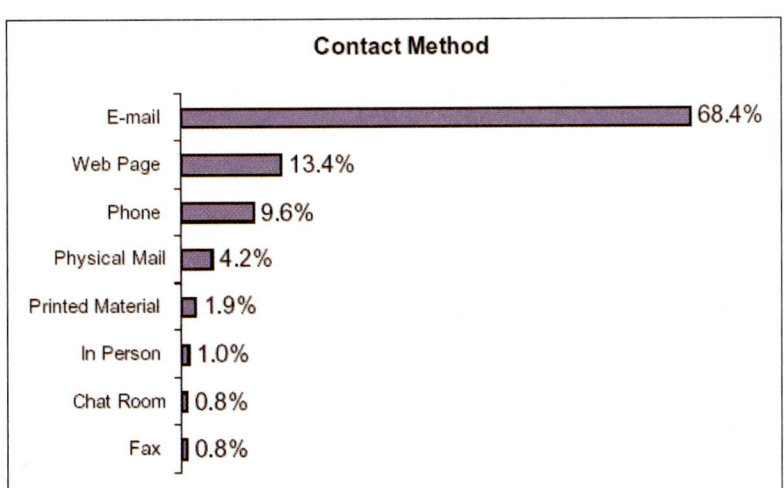

Figure 2.10.
E-mail and Web sites can be used to facilitate online fraud.

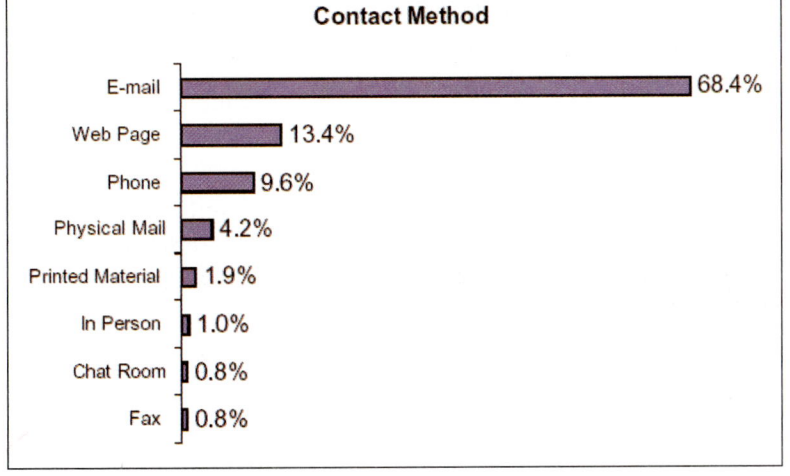

Figure 2.11.
Online auctions can be a hotbed for Internet fraud (source: IFCC).

Know How the Internet is Misused 35

- Unsolicited e-mail messages asking for donations to charitable organizations. Typically, the messages include links to fraudulent Web sites where the victim enters credit card information.
- Unsolicited e-mail messages from seemingly legitimate government agencies or banking institutions with which the victim is familiar. The message typically indicates that the organization is updating their records and needs identifying information, such as credit card information. In July 2001, for example, the IFCC received complaints that people were receiving e-mail from the "FBI" or "fbi.gov." The message simply stated that the intended victim's application was approved and then asked for identifying information, such as the person's name, address, and credit card number.
- E-mail letter scams (such as the Nigerian Letter Schemes), in which someone posing as a bank official in another country claims to have a large sum of money that they need to transfer out of the country. Even though there are many variations on this scam, most promise large sums of money to the intended victim in return for help in transferring the money to an overseas bank account. Not only is the victim required to provide bank account numbers, but is also asked to pay money upfront for "processing."
- Web sites that advertise popular items (such as electronic equipment, cameras, or software) at a substantial discount, then never deliver the item. A variation to this scam is delivering goods that are of lower quality or different than those advertised. For example, some items may have been obtained via black market (or so-called gray market) channels.
- Auction sites, in which scam artists post non-existent items. Alternatively, the item is delivered, but was misrepresented and is of substantially poorer quality than advertised. Other potential problems with Internet auction fraud involve selling black-market goods or the seller bidding under multiple, faked names to drive up the price. In their May, 2001 report, the IFCC reported that victims of Internet fraud related to online auctions lost an average of $776.

The six most common fraudulent items auctioned by cybercriminals in 2001 were Beanie Babies, cameras/camcorders, desktop computers, jewelry, laptop computers, and video consoles/games/tapes (see Figure 2.12).

INSIDE TRACK

Some Internet fraud schemes use scare tactics to get people to give up their credit card number. For example, a scheme involving eBay's auction site surfaced in January 2001. Many eBay subscribers received an e-mail, telling them that their "purchase had been made for a computer and credit card had been charged for $1460." If the subscriber wanted to cancel the order, they had to go to a special Web site and enter certain information (including social security and credit card numbers). Of course, the entire thing was a scam.

To prevent fraud, some online auctions offer to have a third party facilitate the transaction. The buyer sends payment to the third party who then notifies the seller. After the buyer receives the product and determines that it is as advertised, the third party pays the seller. If the product is not as advertised, the buyer sends it back and notifies the third party who refunds the buyer's money.

Figure 2.12.
Online auctions, while enjoyable for many, can also be used by criminals who specialize in fraud.

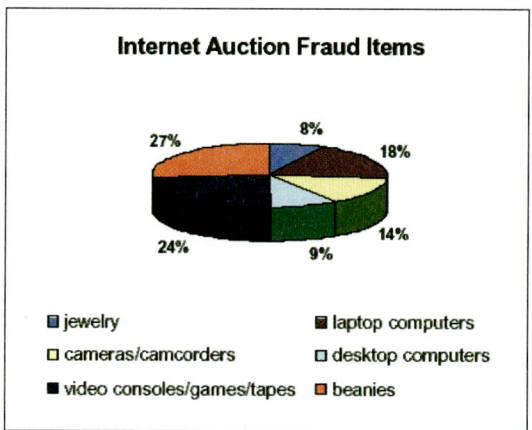

TABLE 2.1	Loss per item due to online auction fraud (Source: Internet Fraud Complaint Center)	
Items	Total Loss Amount	Average Per Item
Laptop computers	$253,361	$1,280
Video consoles/games/tapes	$116,869	$448
Cameras/camcorders	$106,898	$685
Desktop computers	$96,556	$966
Jewelry	$81,873	$952
Beanies	$28,670	$101

Although Beanie Babies are the items most often associated with online auction fraud, laptop computers are the items that cost the most per incident (see Table 2.1).

Your best defense to keep from becoming a victim of Internet fraud, keep the following items in mind:

- Use common sense. If an item's price seems too good to be true, it probably is. Although the overhead of selling items over the Internet may be less than those sold in a traditional store, you should be suspicious of drastically slashed prices or exaggerated claims.
- Make sure you understand what you're actually receiving when you buy an item online. For example, if you buy a camera online, make sure it includes all the accessories, an instruction manual, and a valid warranty.
- Don't buy or bank over the Internet unless you know and trust the company.
- If you are unfamiliar with a company, contact the Better Business Bureau (*www.bbb.org*) to make sure there are no complaints filed against the company. Also verify the company's physical address, e-mail address, and phone number.
- Check out other Web sites that include information about the company in question. Pay close attention to others' feedback about the organization.
- When using an online auction, get as much information about the seller as possible (phone number, physical address, and so on) before sending a check or money order. Be cautious if the person only provides a P.O. box for a mailing address.
- If you receive e-mail (supposedly) from a well-known organization, check directly with representatives of the company to make sure the message is legitimate. For safety, you may want to cross-check the information multiple ways. For example, you can call both the organization's regular and toll-free numbers and then send a postal letter to verify the information.
- Do not give your social security or driver's license number to the seller.
- If an online auction lists feedback about a seller, evaluate the comments before bidding.
- Keep in mind that it's much more difficult to recover costs when you're dealing with a seller in another country. Decide if the risk is worth getting the item at a lower price.

HARMFUL WEB SITES

Another unethical (and sometimes illegal) use of the Internet is to spread harmful or damaging information. For example, some Web sites include information on

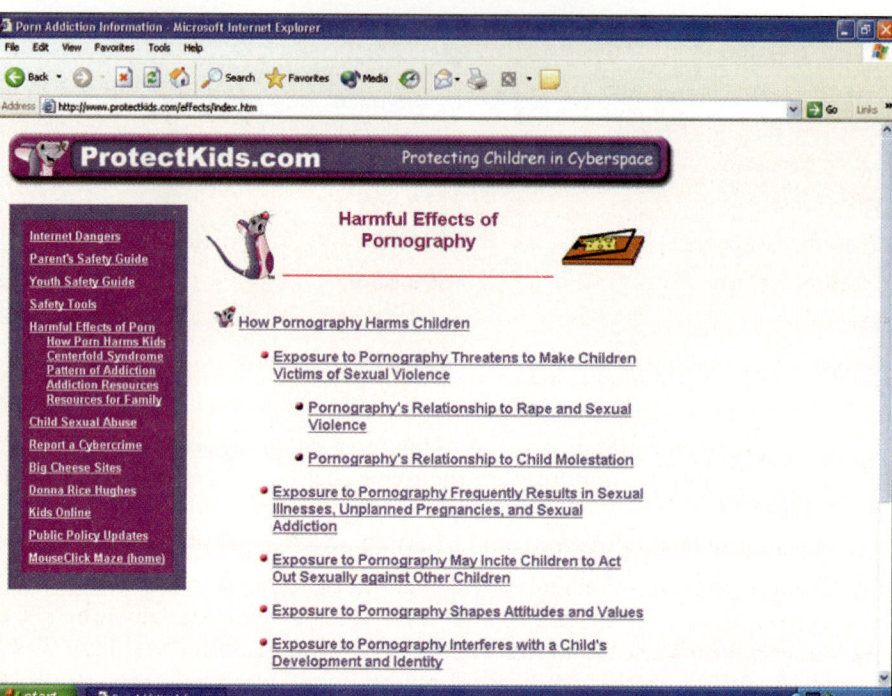

Figure 2.13.
ProtectKids is concerned with keeping children safe online.

 how to construct weapons with the intent that others would actually make and use them in destructive ways. Additionally, the Internet can be used as a means to display pornographic sites, causing untold damage to society and families, especially children. Although illegal, child pornography sites are still present on the Internet. One site that includes statistics about the harmful effects of pornography on children is ProtectKids.com (*www.protectkids.com/effects/index.htm*). This site also includes general information about protecting children online (see Figure 2.13).

Unfortunately, the potential for accidentally stumbling upon an offensive site is great. In fact, some people deliberately redirect users to their sites if a commonly used word is misspelled or mistyped. Because of the problems associated with these pornographic and offensive sites, the use of software that filters out the sites (based on keywords) is advisable. Unfortunately, because one in five potentially harmful sites still makes it through many filtering programs, many people feel the only sure solution is to force the shutdown of these illegal and unethical sites.

COPYRIGHT AND INTELLECTUAL PROPERTY INFRINGEMENTS

Another common misuse of the information that is so freely available on the Web is plagiarism. For example, students can easily copy and paste information from a Web site for a report, passing it off as their own work. If the information is protected by a copyright, using it without permission can infringe on the copyright.

A recent well-publicized case of possible copyright infringement involved Napster versus the Recording Industry Association of America (RIAA). Napster software, initially developed by Shawn Fanning, allowed one-to-one sharing of MP3 music files between computer users as they swapped the files from their personal hard drives. In a year's time, the number of people who had downloaded Napster to share music files mushroomed to approximately 20 million. This peer-to-peer sharing (for free) of copyrighted music files raised the hackles of the recording industry.

Napster believed that sharing music was legal, using the Federal "Audio Home Recording Act" (AHRA) as the basis for its argument. This statute gives consumers the right to create and share digital music for noncommercial uses. Of course, the RIAA held the opposite opinion and took Napster to court over copyright violations in December 1999. The court eventually ruled that Napster had to prevent users from obtaining access to copyrighted material. But even though Napster was crippled, the cat was out of the bag. At the time of this writing, there were dozens of Napster-style MP3 file sharing software programs, such as Napigator and Gnutella, available on the Internet.

SOME OF THE BAD GUYS

The negative uses of the Internet are propelled by crackers, hackers, and cybercriminals. In this section, we'll find out how these people operate and how you can protect yourself from them.

HACKERS AND CRACKERS. **Crackers** are cybervandals who use their programming skills to write malicious programs or to break into a system without authorization. Usually, crackers do this with the intent of damaging a system or network, or crashing an entire Web site. Alternatively, they may try to steal information, such as your username, password, or credit card number. **Hackers** are simply programming experts who share their skills and information with others without actually causing harm. However, we'll use the terms cracker and hacker interchangeably in this discussion.

Hackers are typically skilled at getting around computer systems and adept at using programming code to gain the results they want. One notable case occurred in 1998; Jason Allen Diekman hacked into computers at NASA and numerous universities. The control that he gained enabled him to modify files and alter security on the systems. Diekman also attempted to make wire transfers from Western Union in 2001. Although laws are in place to prosecute the people who commit these illegal acts, it is often hard to catch the people responsible for them.

To protect your system from unauthorized entry by crackers, it's advisable to use a firewall, which is a program that prevents others from remotely accessing your system and the information it includes. Obviously, the firewall used by a business to protect its network must be more extensive than one you would use at home. For homes or small businesses, however, you have several good options. You can download ZoneAlarm, a personal firewall (*www.zonelabs.com*) or buy a commercial firewall package, such as Norton Personal Firewall (*www.symantec.com*), as shown in Figure 2.14.

STALKERS AND OTHER NASTY PEOPLE. Internet stalkers are people who deliberately harass and pose emotional (and possibly physical) danger to others. Most often, stalkers badger women and children. They can do this through e-mail, chat rooms, and newsgroups. These dangerous strangers can hassle children; after they find out identifying information, they can even arrange for face-to-face meetings.

So, how can you protect yourself (and your children) online? Here are some ideas:

- Make sure that everyone who uses the Internet understands the inherent dangers of communicating with strangers. Help them realize that criminals wander on the Internet, just as they wander the streets, and that people who are on the Internet may not be who they say they are.

ALERT!
There are criminals online, just as there are in real life. The Family Internet Safety Pact (www.childlures.com/parents/pact.asp) lists a number of principles and safety rules that you can discuss with your children related to interacting with strangers online.

Figure 2.14.
Use a firewall to prevent intrusions into your system.

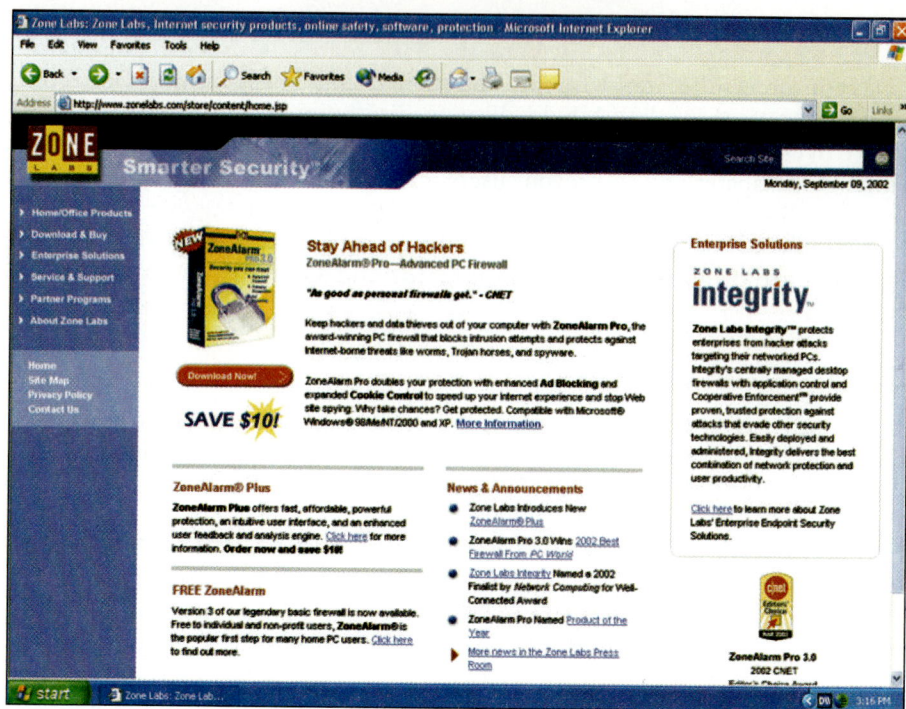

- Emphasize that children should never share any identifying information (name, e-mail address, physical address, photographs, or phone number) with others on the Internet.
- Route children's mail to a responsible adult's e-mail account.
- Tell children not to enter contests, fill out forms, or buy items online.
- Emphasize to children the danger of physically meeting a person whom they have met through the Internet, especially without adults present. Make sure that they understand that the person is a stranger, and they should act in the same way as they would for other strangers they meet.
- Use filtering software. Some ISPs provide this software as part of their service. You can also buy commercial software, such as CyberPatrol (*www.cyberpatrol.com*), SurfWatch (*www.surfwatch.com*), or CyberSitter (*www.cybersitter.com*). These software packages typically let you set different filtering levels, depending on the age or maturity of the child.

Finally, if you're already being stalked, you can get some help from Internet safety organizations. The largest one is CyberAngels (*www.cyberangels.com*), which is manned by computer-savvy and law enforcement volunteers. Its Web site includes many helpful links related to security, safety, and privacy (see Figure 2.15).

 People made a wholehearted effort to protect children online? If you're concerned about some of the negative ways in which the Internet is used to exploit children, you can help in practical ways. For example, the National Center for Missing and Exploited Children (*www.ncmec.org*) includes educational information and links for reporting exploitation of children. You can also volunteer to help in a variety of ways, such as placing a banner ad for a missing child on your Web page.

40 Chapter 2 The Good, the Bad, the Ugly: Uses and Misuses of the Internet

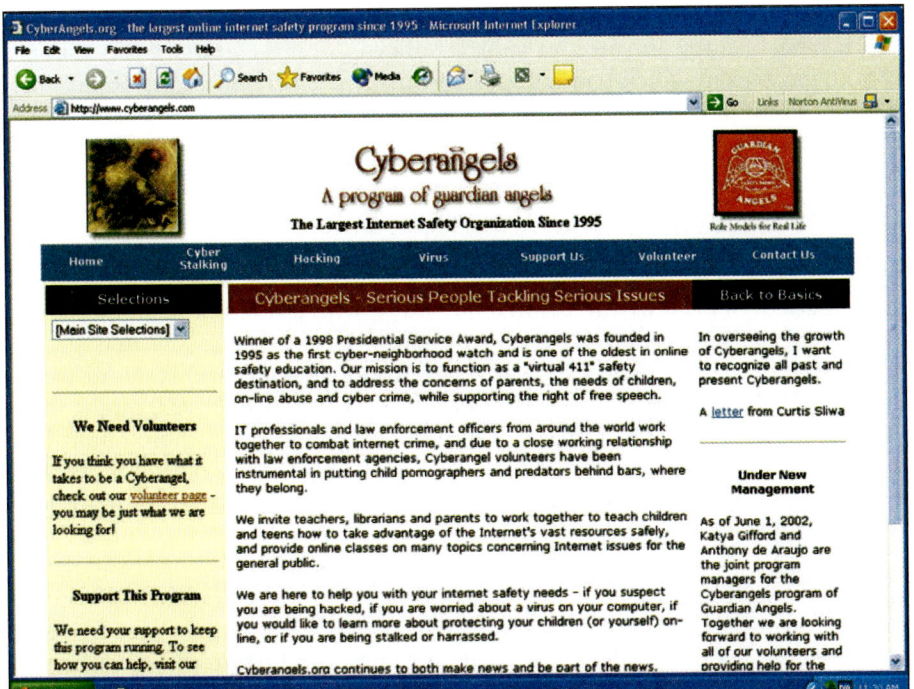

Figure 2.15.
If you're being harassed by a cybercriminal, you can get help through several legitimate Internet safety organizations.

UNDERSTAND THE LEGITIMATE AND ETHICAL USES OF THE INTERNET

In Chapter 1, we discussed some of the ways in which the Internet has been a positive and useful force in the world. Not only has it become the main way information is shared, but it has also had widespread influence on almost every aspect of life—from how jobs are performed to how you order a pizza. Here's a quick recap:

The Internet can be used for . . .

- Information sharing
- Advertising
- Company Web sites
- Online shopping
- E-commerce
- E-mail
- Real-Time communication (chat rooms)

With those ideas firmly in mind, let's take a closer look at some of the less well-known uses for the Internet: mailing lists, Usenet newsgroups, and FTP sites.

LISTSERV AND DISTRIBUTED MAILING LISTS

A **Listserv** is simply a distributed mailing list, in which the same e-mail message is sent to all the people who are on the list. For example, if you were on a listserv about golf, you could send a message about an upcoming tournament, and everyone would be e-mailed the same message. Anyone on the list could then respond to the message. Just keep in mind that your reply is sent by default to everyone on the list, so be careful what you say!

Users typically subscribe to a list, which focuses on a particular topic, such as a hobby, business, finance, or sports. Yahoo! Groups (*groups.yahoo.com*) is a central location in which you can locate, join, or even create a distributed mailing list. You'll learn more about joining a mailing list in Chapter 13, Communicating via the Internet.

USENET NEWSGROUPS

Usenet is a worldwide distributed discussion system, in which topical newsgroups are organized by subject in a hierarchy, with a series of main topics and their associated subtopics. Articles (messages) are posted to the newsgroup, and everyone who subscribes to the newsgroup can view and respond to the message. For example, one group, located at *rec.pets.dogs.breeds*, might focus on discussing the merits of different dog breeds. In contrast, there might be a newsgroup on various activities you can do with your dog, called *rec.pets.dogs.activities*. Each has a long listing of messages related (more or less) to the main topic (see Figure 2.16).

Don't be mislead by the word "news" in "newsgroups"—messages may be on any topic and the messages are not always factual. You can view newsgroup messages by going to Google (*groups.google.com*) or Usenet (*www.usenet.org*) to name a few. You can click the links to work your way through the list of available newsgroups or enter a keyword in the search box (see Figure 2.17). After you locate the newsgroup you want, you can view current articles or link to the archives (older articles). You'll learn more about newsgroups in Chapter 13.

FTP SITES

File Transfer Protocol (FTP) is the protocol used for transferring files over a TCP/IP network, such as the Internet. When you use FTP, you are using a client program to transfer files to or from a server that stores the files.

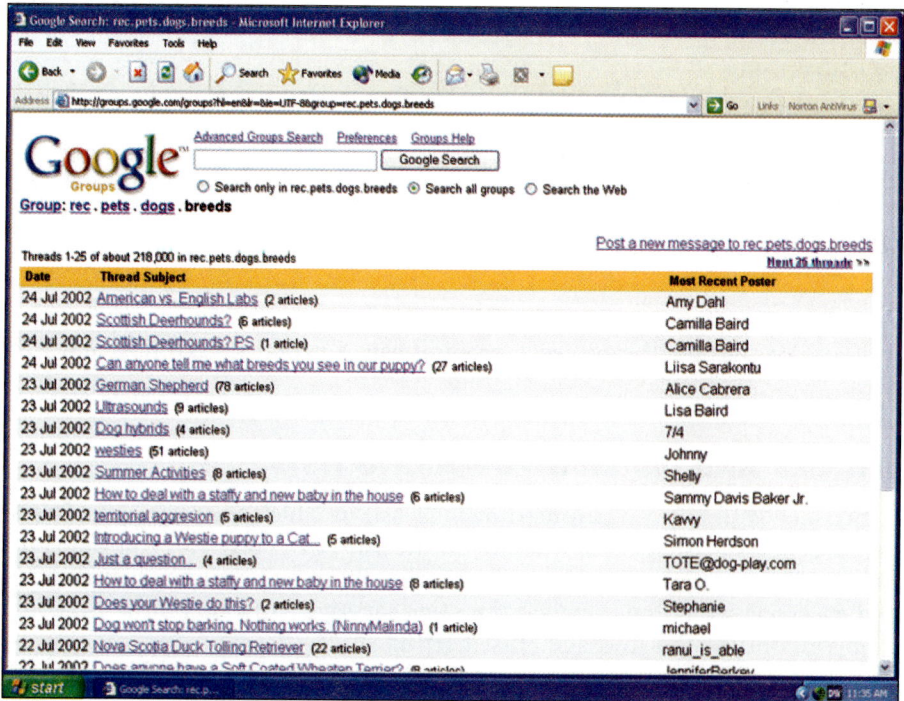

Figure 2.16.
Newsgroups are message boards that are available on just about any subject.

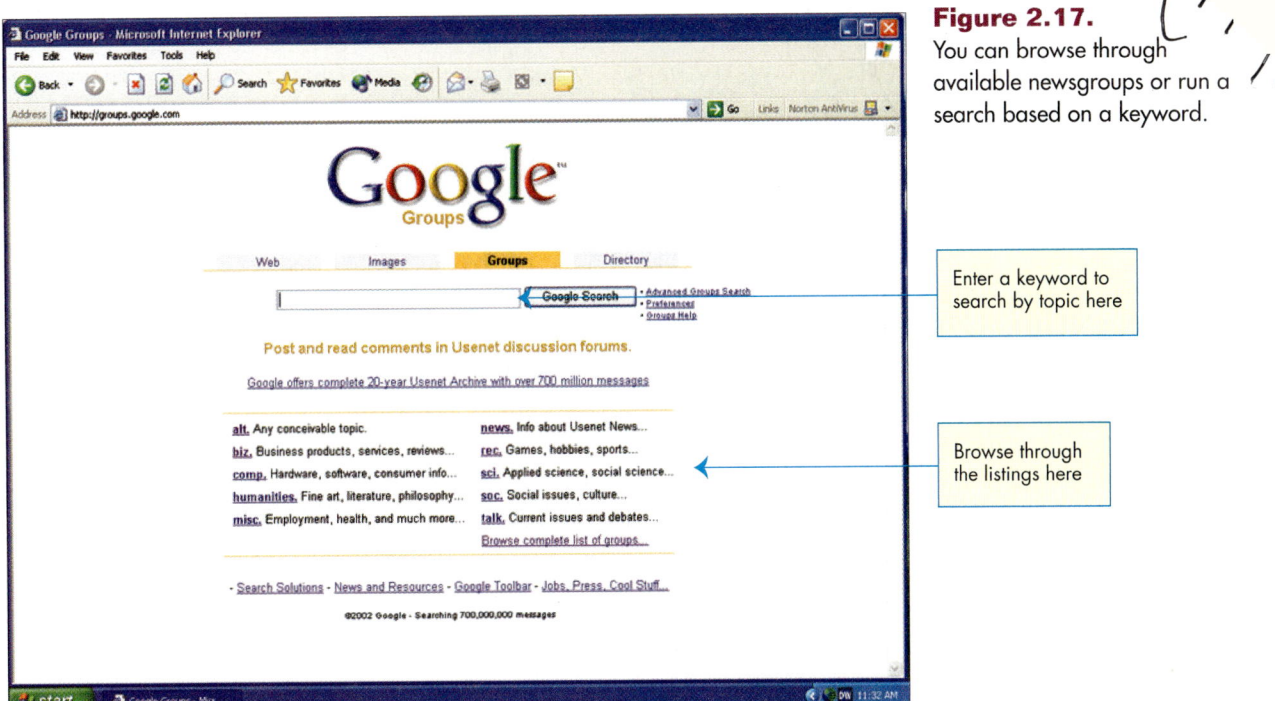

Figure 2.17.
You can browse through available newsgroups or run a search based on a keyword.

Anonymous FTP is an Internet FTP site that contains files that can be downloaded by anyone. The anonymous FTP directory is isolated from the rest of the system and will generally not accept uploads from users. You can access and transfer files to your own system without having an account on the FTP site. You'll learn more about using FTP in Chapter 14, Pulling Information from the Internet.

Don't Forget...

- The Internet can be powerful and positive. However, it's important to be aware of the major dangers and traps on the Internet.
- Some of the potential problems you can encounter if you use the Internet include viruses, fraud, invasion of privacy, security breaches, and crackers.
- Making sure appropriate security measures are in place will help considerably in warding off trouble.
- Install current anti-virus software, limit the amount of identifying information that you share, disable or limit your computer's capability to accept cookies, and be smart about opening e-mail attachments.
- Use common sense when working on the Internet.

Check This Out

MULTIPLE CHOICE

1. You open an e-mail attachment and suddenly a message is sent to all the people in your address book. Most likely you've encountered a _____.
   a. CyberChip
   b. worm
   c. lacker
   d. None of the above

2. Which of the following measures help prevent a virus from infecting your system?
   a. Installing anti-virus software, such as Norton Anti-Virus
   b. Scanning e-mail attachments before opening them
   c. Installing a personal firewall
   d. All of the above

3. The term used for someone who maliciously breaches security on a computer system is _____.
   a. lacker
   b. cracker
   c. cyberdog
   d. virus

4. A *cookie* is a _____.
   a. Web site that helps maintain your privacy
   b. data file that a server stores on your computer
   c. Trojan horse program
   d. None of the above

5. Fraud, hacking into a system, and stealing someone's identity are all examples of _____.
   a. cookies
   b. cracking into a system
   c. cybercrime
   d. online profiling

MATCHING

a. cookie
b. social engineering
c. payload
d. virus hoax
e. Trojan horse
f. worm
g. cybercrime
h. online profiling
i. fraud
j. payload trigger

1. A condition or event that causes malware to be activated
2. The damage done by a virus
3. A destructive program that is hidden within another legitimate program
4. A destructive program, such as Love Bug, that is commonly spread through e-mail attachments
5. A marketing practice whereby your actions on the Web are traced and the information compiled for the purpose of sending you targeted advertisements
6. A small data file that a Web site server stores on your computer
7. Illegal acts that are facilitated by using the Internet
8. Information spread about a non-existent virus
9. An illegal act in which a perpetrator deceives another person so that the victim transfers money to the perpetrator
10. Using deception to trick a user into opening a message that contains malicious code

Real Life

1. Using the information in Chapters 1–2 as a basis, make a comprehensive list of Internet resources, such as e-mail, Web sites, distributed mailing lists, and so on. After you've developed the list, jot down a positive and a negative way in which each resource can be used.
2. Use the Internet to find out about real-life cases involving Internet fraud, online profiling, and identity theft. (You can begin your search by using the Web sites listed in this chapter.)
3. What are the pros and cons of using online auctions to purchase items? If you've used online auctions before, share your experiences (good or bad) with others in the class. As a group, develop a list of ways in which you can protect yourself when purchasing goods in this manner.
4. Develop a checklist of questions to ask (or of ways to check the validity of) an online merchant. If you've ever purchased an item online before, also share your experiences with the class.
5. Spend time researching the Junkbusters Web site (*www.junkbusters.com*), especially the pages related to privacy. Read over the information about protect-

ing your privacy. If you wish, go through the steps they suggest for eliminating junk e-mail, telemarketing calls, and other threats to your privacy.

6. Look over a few examples of malware on the Web sites for Norton AntiVirus (*www.symantec.com*) and McAfee (*www.mcafee.com*). Develop a list of the most problematic viruses, worms, and Trojan horse programs. Also, spend time finding out about common virus hoaxes. A good Web site to use for this is *hoaxbusters.ciac.org*. What are the common traits that most hoaxes share?

I Spy: Privacy and Security Concerns

1. Explore the Privacy Rights Clearinghouse Web site (*www.privacyrights.org*) and related links. Develop a short report (or list) that outlines your personal concerns related to privacy.
2. You can use cookie-management software to prevent your computer from automatically accepting cookies. Do an Internet search to find out about several cookie-management programs and then draw up a list of pros and cons for using this type of program. Finally, determine which program currently on the market offers the best features.
3. Go to the Web site for CERT (*www.cert.org*) and research current security issues. For example, find out which malware is currently the most prevalent and problematic. Also, learn how to protect the security of different types of computer systems: home, small business, and a business network. How does the level and type of security differ between these systems? Develop a short written or oral report that outlines your findings.
4. Research information on firewalls and then write a report on them. Include information about the purpose of a firewall, how it functions, and which firewalls are on the market.
5. Find out information about victims of identity theft. Write up a report (or develop a PowerPoint presentation) that explains the growing problem of identity theft, and what can be done about it. Make sure to include some examples of identity theft victims.

SECTION Two
GETTING UP AND RUNNING WITH THE INTERNET

CHAPTER 3
NECESSARY EQUIPMENT AND INTERNET CONNECTIONS

Chapter Objectives

After you complete this chapter, you'll

- Know the Hardware Necessary to Access the Internet
- Know the Software Necessary to Access the Internet
- Understand the Various Types of Internet Connections

Key Terms

When you finish this chapter, you'll understand the following terms:

- always on connection
- asymmetric
- Asymmetric Digital Subscriber Line (ADSL)
- bandwidth
- Bluetooth
- broadband
- Broadband Service Provider (BSP)
- cable modem
- demodulate
- dial-up
- Digital Subscriber Line (DSL)
- downloading
- downstream
- Ethernet
- high speed access
- Integrated Services Digital Network (ISDN)
- Kbps
- mail client
- Mbps
- modem
- modulate
- narrowband
- network interface card (NIC)
- open source
- Personal Digital Assistant (PDA)
- plain old telephone service (POTS)
- satellite
- set-top box
- special-purpose computers
- symmetric
- Symmetric Digital Subscriber Line (SDSL)
- transport medium
- uploading
- upstream
- wireless

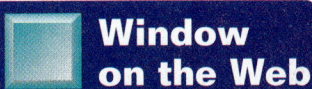

The Big Picture

In the old days (like eight or ten years ago) you had limited choices for connecting to the Internet. Most people simply used a computer, modem, and standard phone line to dial into the Internet—mainly because they didn't have many other options.

Not so anymore. Nowadays, you have a variety of access options from which to choose. The alternatives vary a great deal in transmission speed, cost, and availability. In this chapter, we'll run through the current connection technologies so that you can make a wise choice about the best one for your pocketbook and situation. We'll also talk about the hardware and software you need to connect to the Internet.

Window on the Web

Data communication technology has advanced rapidly, so the number of options for connecting to the Internet has also increased. Take a look, for example, at the speed comparisons among the different technologies currently available (see Table 3.1).

TABLE 3.1 Technologies You Can Use to Connect to the Internet

Connection Type	How It Works to Connect and Transfer Data	Speed	Advantages	Disadvantages
Dial-up access	Uses a modem and regular telephone line	28Kbps–56Kbps	Readily available Relatively inexpensive	Slow Ties up phone line; must dial in to an ISP
ISDN Integrated Services Digital Network	Uses digital phone lines	64Kbps–128 Kbps	Not as fast or cost-effective as DSL or other new technologies, but faster than dial-up modems	More expensive than dial-up access Not available in all locations
Cable modem	Uses television cable	500Kbps–2,000 Kbps	Very fast Always on	Not available in all areas; must first have cable available Users share bandwidth with others in area, which can cause fluctuating speeds Possible security problems (because it is always on)
ADSL/DSL Asymmetric Digital Subscriber Line/Digital Subscriber Line	Uses the digital portion of a regular copper telephone line	128Kbps–1,500 Kbps	Doesn't tie up phone line; can transmit voice simultaneously Very fast Always on	Bandwidth is affected by the distance from the network hubs Very limited availability Possible security problems (because it is always on)
Satellite	Uses a satellite dish	60Kbps–400 Kbps	Bandwidth is not shared Doesn't require a phone line Available in locations where DSL and ISDN are not Always on	Relatively expensive startup costs due to the necessity of buying a satellite dish Possible security problems (because always on)
Wireless	Uses radio signals	128Kbps–2Mbps	Very fast Doesn't require a phone line Available in locations where DSL and ISDN are not Always on	Must be within a few miles (usually 10 miles–20 miles) of the nearest access point Limited availability Relatively high startup costs

So how do these numbers translate into speed? Take a look at the following chart (see Figure 3.1), which compares how long it takes to transmit a 10MB movie.

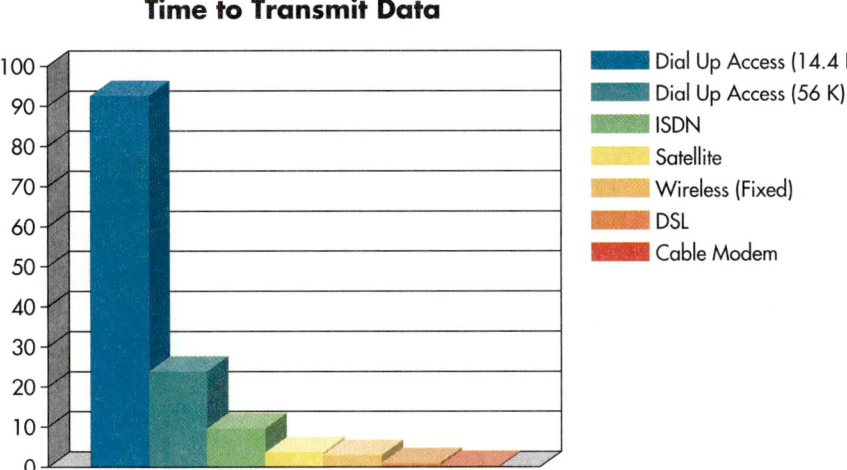

Figure 3.1.
The equipment and connection technology you choose can make a big difference in speed.

Besides the actual connection, you need three main things in place to link effectively to the Internet:

- Hardware equipment (to view and interact online)
- Software (to connect to the Internet and view Web or mail content)
- An Internet Service Provider (ISP)

In this chapter, we'll guide you through the options for the equipment, software, and connections necessary to get you up and running on the Internet; in Chapter 4, Internet Service Providers, we'll show you how to analyze ISPs and choose the best one for your needs. Let's get going.

KNOW THE HARDWARE NECESSARY TO ACCESS THE INTERNET

The hardware (physical equipment) that you need to hook up to the Internet depends on which type of connection option that you select: If you choose satellite, you'll need a satellite dish; if you choose cable modem, you'll need the coaxial cable, and so on. However, no matter which connection type you choose, you'll still need some way to *view* Internet content, such as e-mail or Web pages—and a monitor or TV screen comes in pretty handy to do so. It's also helpful to have the necessary equipment so that you can respond to the content you view. For example, to reply to an e-mail message, you'll need a keyboard or other input device. In this section, we'll go over all the hardware you need to work online.

COMPUTER SYSTEMS

The most popular hardware for viewing and interacting with Internet content is a computer system. The majority of systems sold include all the components you need to tap into dial-up Internet access, such as a dial-up modem or a Universal Serial Bus (USB) port. Most computers also include a sound card and microphone to communicate with others on the Internet and speakers to listen to your favorite online radio station. Additionally, it's helpful to have plenty of storage space on your hard drive if you plan to download graphic, movie, or music files.

Whatever memory comes with a new system should be sufficient for 'net surfing. Computers, of course, come standard with input devices (such as keyboards and mouse units) and output devices (such as monitors). And although any input and output device will work fine for basic Internet use, you will be much more comfortable if you buy an ergonomic keyboard/mouse and a high-resolution monitor, especially if you think you'll spend much time online.

If you want to tap into the new *broadband* technologies that are available (such as DSL or cable modem), make sure that you have a network card preinstalled in the computer. **Network Interface Cards (NICs)** are generally offered as an option (but are not standard) on many new computers. They're necessary when using *broadband* modems, such as DSL or cable, or when setting up a computer network. **Ethernet** is the most widely used protocol for local area networks. The bandwidth for an Ethernet network is 10Mbps (10 million bits per second); Fast Ethernet has a bandwidth of 100Mbps.

The bottom line? Make sure that any new computer you purchase includes the hardware that will let you connect to the Internet effectively—although it probably already includes almost everything you need.

INTERNET APPLIANCES AND SPECIAL-PURPOSE COMPUTERS

As an alternative to employing a traditional computer system, you can use a special purpose computer or an Internet appliance to connect to the Web. **Special-purpose computers** are stripped-down computer systems that have one basic function: to let you work on the Internet. Several companies have tried (more or less unsuccessfully) to promote the idea that buying a less-expensive, special-purpose computer was cost-effective for those who simply wanted to use the Internet, but didn't want to do much else with a computer. However, the relatively low price of high-powered, full-fledged computer systems (coupled with the fact that most people *do* use their computers as all-purpose tools) has prevented the special-use computer from catching on. For example, a limited use, Internet-only computer cost about $500 at one point; a full-fledged computer system cost only a couple hundred dollars more. Buying the complete computer system made sense to most people, even if their computing needs were simple: such as keeping their finances straight, penning a Christmas letter, or playing a game.

One Internet appliance that has enjoyed modest success is a **set-top box**, which is the generic name for the special Internet appliance popularized by WebTV—now called MSN TV (MSN is an abbreviation for Microsoft Network).

Another ISP, America Online (AOL), also has a set-top unit on the market. The service associated with its set-top box is appropriately called AOLTV. AOLTV combines the content and services traditionally associated with this ISP, such as instant messaging, buddy lists, mail, and Web browsing, with the capability to simultaneously watch TV and videotape shows. For example, you can simultaneously surf the Web, get a message that a buddy is online, and be reminded that your favorite TV show is about to begin (see Figure 3.2).

The set-top box is actually a receiver that connects to your television to provide Internet access; users communicate with the device from the comfort of their couch by using a wireless keyboard. The initial cost for using WebTV or a similar appliance and service is approximately $100. The relatively low cost has helped people to get online inexpensively and easily. Set-top boxes appeal to people who are looking for an uncomplicated way to connect to the Web and don't want to buy much new equipment or learn how to operate a computer. But keep in mind that you're required to use MSN's or AOL's Internet access service if you use their devices, which can severely limit your options for using new technology or switching services if you're unhappy.

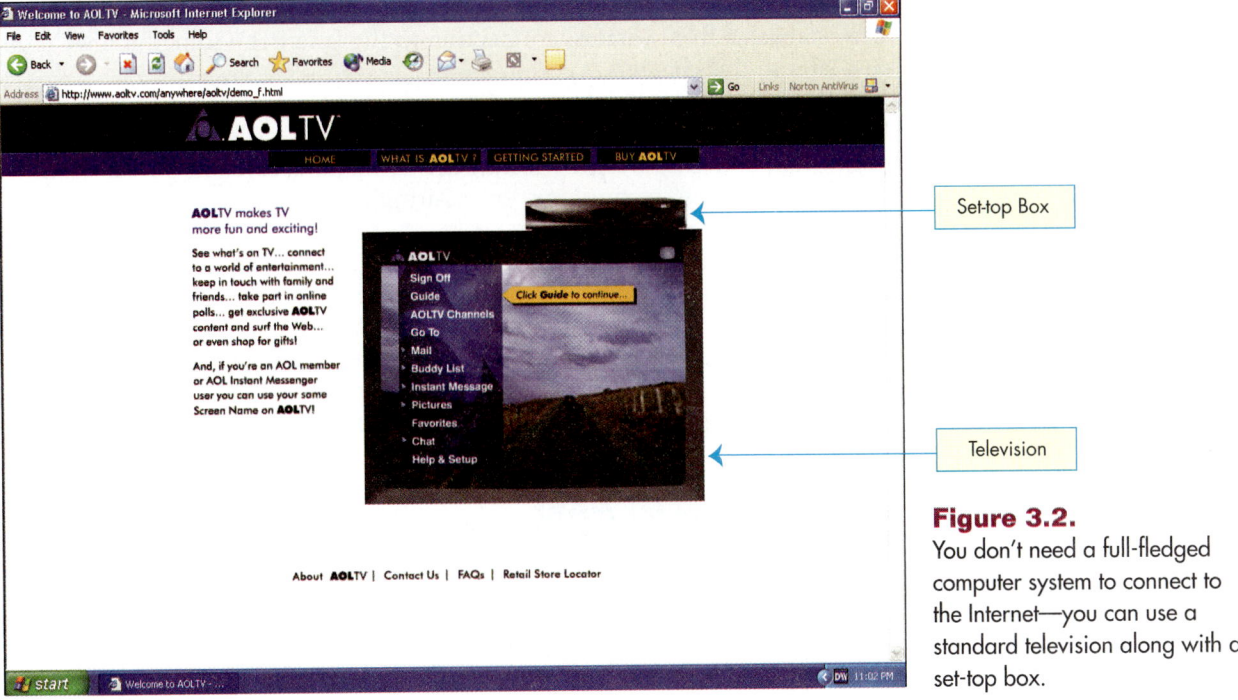

Figure 3.2.
You don't need a full-fledged computer system to connect to the Internet—you can use a standard television along with a set-top box.

WIRELESS DEVICES

People are increasingly using handheld devices to access the Internet. A **Personal Digital Assistant (PDA)** is essentially a small computer that is pocket- or handheld size, making it mobile and useful for busy business professionals. Two of the most well known companies that produce PDAs are Palm (*www.palm.com*) and Handspring (*www.handspring.com*). Microsoft's Pocket PC handheld also has a following.

Besides PDAs, some cellular phones have built-in technology that lets them use e-mail or the Web. For the most part, these devices use **wireless** connections. Wireless connections use technology that doesn't employ lines or wires, working in much the same way as radio signals do (see Figure 3.3).

Figure 3.3.
Many PDAs and cell phones include the capability to access the Web.

Know the Hardware Necessary to Access the Internet 51

Cell phones and PDAs are considered mobile devices. However, you can also establish a fixed wireless connection to the Internet—something we'll discuss later in this chapter.

Bluetooth is a technology that uses short-range radio links between PDAs, cell phones, and other wireless devices. This technology is developed, promoted, and employed by a number of manufacturers. You can find out more about this technology by visiting Bluetooth's official Web site (*www.bluetooth.com*).

Wireless communications are still somewhat in their infancy; promises of seamless mobile Web surfing haven't proven true—at least not yet. Many users still consider the technology expensive and slow, with poor compatibility. However, as new technology emerges, you can expect an increase in the use of mobile, wireless Internet access. (If you want to find out more about PDAs and other mobile devices, see Appendix A, Interfacing the Internet with Cell Phones and PDAs.)

KNOW THE SOFTWARE NECESSARY TO ACCESS THE INTERNET

The equipment you need to connect to the Internet is just the beginning: You'll also need software to connect to your ISP and to surf the Web. Additionally, if you want to use mail, it's helpful (although not totally necessary) to install mail-messaging software.

WEB BROWSERS

INSIDE TRACK

Netscape Navigator is the browser software associated with Netscape 6.2/7.0. Netscape 6.2/7.0 is a collection of programs, including Netscape Navigator, Netscape Mail, Netscape Instant Messenger, Netscape Composer, and Netscape Address Book. Because the browser (Navigator) is the most well-known component of this suite, Netscape, Netscape Navigator, and Navigator are used interchangeably when referring to this browser.

A Web browser is specialized software that lets you view Web pages. As you probably remember from Chapter 1, How the Internet is Changing the World, Web pages are developed by using a special markup language (HyperText Markup Language, or HTML). Web browsers allow you to display and view Web content on your computer. The two major browsers at the time of this writing are Microsoft Internet Explorer and Netscape.

In the beginning of modern Internet time (1995), Netscape was king of the Web browsers. Most people who wanted to use a Web browser chose Netscape. But as Microsoft gained dominance, it trotted out its own browser, Internet Explorer. By 1997, Microsoft had captured market share and Netscape was used by fewer and fewer people. Currently, Internet Explorer is strongly in front, with approximately 92% of users in its pocket (see Figure 3.4).

Figure 3.4.
Microsoft Internet Explorer dominates the market (Source: W3Schools).

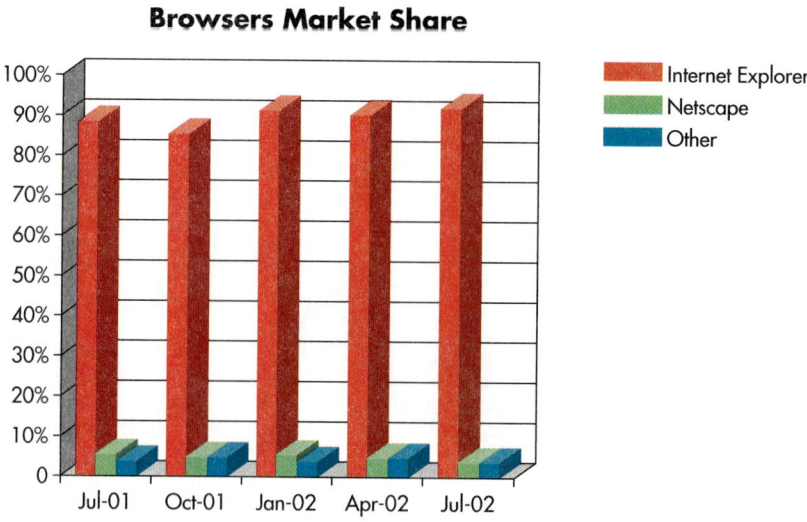

ON THE HORIZON

For years, Internet Explorer and Netscape have fought it out in the browser wars—at least until Microsoft took over market share. However, there might soon be a new player in the game: Mozilla, which is a Netscape-backed, free, open source browser. (An **open source** program is one in which the programming code is shared for free with any software developer who wants it.) For more information on the status of this free browser or to view the source code, take a look at Mozilla's Web site (*www.mozilla.org*).

ISP PROPRIETARY SOFTWARE

To access the Internet through an ISP, you usually (but not always) need that company's software. For example, to connect to AOL, you install its software as part of the setup process. ISP proprietary software sometimes includes a Web browser, merging the two types of software that you typically need to get online.

As you can imagine, ISPs provide the software at no charge and they are more than eager to give it to you. You can get your hands on the software in several ways. You can call the company and ask them to send it to you via postal mail or by downloading it from the Internet. Some ISPs place their free software in the checkout area of major office supply stores, in the hopes that you'll sign up for their service.

One final note of caution: Make sure that you have the toll-free technical support phone number available when you install the software; some of the setup procedures aren't as intuitive or seamless as you want.

MAIL-MESSAGING SOFTWARE

Although not necessary to get connected to the Internet, you need mail-messaging software (sometimes called a **mail client**) to effectively send and receive e-mail. The most popular e-mail programs include Outlook (part of the Microsoft Office suite of programs) and Outlook Express. There are also a number of alternative or free e-mail programs. For example, you can employ Web-based e-mail, in which you use a Web site to access messages instead of a mail client. You'll learn more about working efficiently with mail clients in Section III, Using Mail and Messaging Tools.

UNDERSTAND THE VARIOUS TYPES OF INTERNET CONNECTIONS

Okay, so now you have all the necessary equipment and software to get online. Only one thing is missing: how to actually connect your system to the Internet. In this section, we'll get you up to speed on the various types of connections currently available and discuss the pros and cons for each. When we're finished, you'll have a good handle on the various types of technology and be able to determine which one is best suited for your life situation.

THE NEED FOR SPEED: DATA TRANSFER RATES

Before we begin to discuss the various connections, however, we'll take a quick look at the effect that bandwidth and transport medium have on the speed at which Web pages display, files download, and e-mail is transferred. The

transport medium is the physical connection and equipment that is used to transfer information. For example, the Internet's backbone is a transport medium.

Bandwidth refers to the transmission capacity of a communications line—the data transfer rate. Bandwidth is measured in how many bits per second (bps) can travel over the line. Think of bandwidth as a highway and your data as cars. In relation to this, a six-lane Interstate can accommodate much more traffic simultaneously than can a single-lane country road.

Imagine that you need to move six cars from New York City to Chicago: If you arrange them six abreast on the Interstate, you can move them much more quickly to their destination than if you have to line them up, one behind another, on a narrow road. The same is true for data: Wider is better and translates into faster speeds.

As we said, the speed at which data is transferred in a communications system is measured as bits per second, or bps. A transfer rate of 1,000 bits per second is called kilobits per second (**Kbps**). Sending one million bits per second down the communications pipeline is known as megabits per second (**Mbps**).

Uploading is when data is transferred from your computer system to the Internet; **downloading** is when data is transferred from the Internet to your system. A related set of terms is upstream and downstream. **Downstream** refers to the transfer of data from the provider to you, such as downloading files or displaying a Web page. In contrast, when you send a request from your computer to the Internet (such as asking for a particular Web page, or checking e-mail), it's referred to as **upstream**.

Now the plot thickens. Some of the communication technologies use the same data transfer rate for both the downstream and upstream pathways. For example, if you use a dial-up connection, your request for a Web page travels at the same rate as the downloaded information does. This type of data transfer is called **symmetric**. But some technologies have different data transfer rates for the upstream and downstream, known as **asymmetric**. For example, DSL can pull data down from the Internet at a rate of 1.5Mbps; whereas the upstream side of things operates at only about 128Kbps. Because of this, DSL was originally referred to as **Asymmetric Digital Subscriber Line (ADSL)**. Figure 3.5 shows that the download and upload speeds of many of the technologies differ.

Broadband refers to a network that is capable of high-speed transmission of data. For example, the line might be able to transmit several data streams at the same time. Alternately, broadband can refer to the service used to transfer

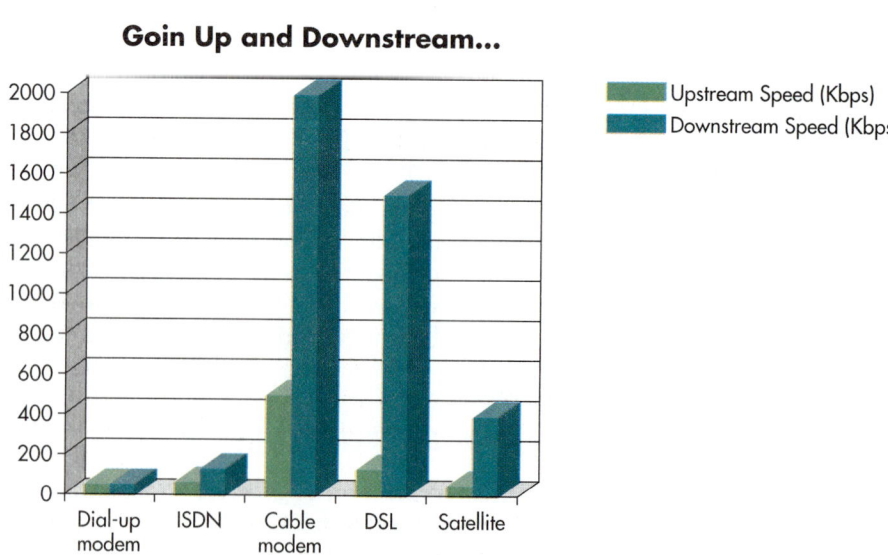

Figure 3.5.
Most broadband services have different upload and download speeds.

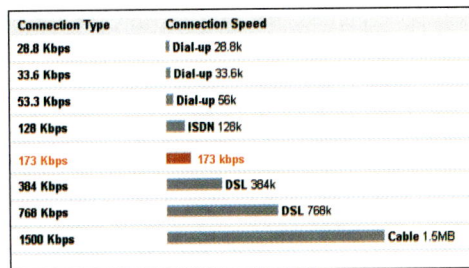

Figure 3.6.
The need for speed... broadband services are quicker on their feet.

the data, such as DSL. Another term for broadband services of this type is **high speed access**. Companies that provide Internet access via a broadband service are sometimes referred to as **Broadband Service Providers (BSPs)** instead of ISPs.

So, what constitutes broadband? Some people consider any communication lines or data transfer above 1.544Mbps (which is the transfer rate for T1 lines) to be broadband, such as services such as cable modem and DSL. In contrast, **narrowband** includes transmission rates up to 1.544Mbps. Figure 3.6 shows a comparison of the average transfer rates for some of the current connection technologies.

However, there are potential bottlenecks in the entire system, such as your computer's connection to the Internet or old phone lines that can't move data as fast as your modem can process it. The rate at which data can flow between two points on a network is limited to the narrowest bandwidth that exists on the network. When you're choosing an ISP, make sure to evaluate the bandwidth offered by the service and find out how many users share it. You also need to carefully evaluate the types of connection technologies available, try to eliminate any bottlenecks, and then enjoy the increased speed. Let's go through the currently available technologies, starting with the slowest (but least expensive): dial-up connections.

DIAL-UP

Dial-up connections (also called dial-up analog connections) are still used by the vast majority of Internet users. The concept is pretty simple: Your computer, through a modem, uses existing telephone lines in your home or office to dial into the ISP's network. To use this service, all you need is **plain old telephone service (POTS)**.

A **modem** (the term comes from combining *mo*dulate and *dem*odulate) is a device that provides an interface between the computer and communication lines, such as cable or phone lines. It converts the computer's digital transmission into an analog signal so that it can be carried via the communication lines, a process called modulation. When an analog signal arrives at the receiving computer, the modem then demodulates (converts) the signal back to digital (see Figure 3.7). This technology is symmetric because both the upstream and downstream data rates are the same.

Through the years, the speed at which modems can process data has increased: In 1995, 14,400bps (14.4Kbps) modems were common; nowadays 56Kbps (usually just referred to as *56K*) modems are the norm.

But even if you have a speedy 56K modem, you're not guaranteed that communications will flow at that rate to and from your computer. The phone lines, routers, and switches that the data passes through on the way to your computer might be using older technology that creates data bottlenecks. Consequently, your computer will probably connect to the Internet at speeds that are slower than your modem is capable of handling.

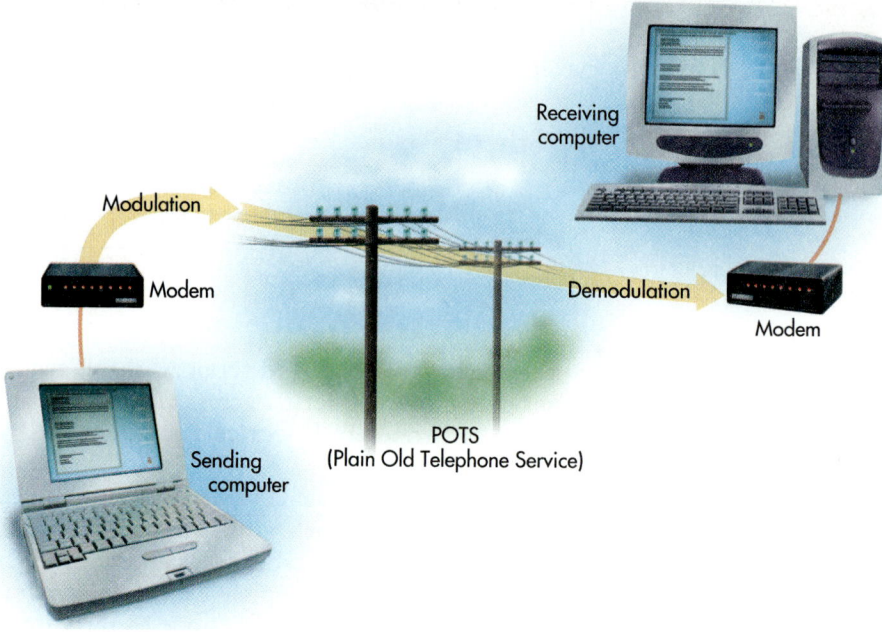

Figure 3.7.
Modems convert digital signals to analog and then back to digital.

Dial-up access is still used by the majority of Internet users for good reasons: It's readily available, a claim many of the other technologies can't match. All you really need is a phone line, modem, and computer. It's also relatively inexpensive, too. The only real cost is the monthly ISP fee, typically around $22/month. (The exception to this is if you have to use long distance to dial in to your ISP.)

However, this technology has some drawbacks, too. It ties up your phone line while you're on the Internet. To get around this, many people pay for a second telephone line, which bumps up the overall cost of dial-up access—perhaps even doubling it. It's also slow compared with the newer broadband technologies, and dropped connections (being disconnected from the Internet) are relatively common. Because of these disadvantages, there is a steady movement of users to fast access services, such as DSL, cable modem, and satellite.

According to Jupiter Media Metrix, a company that specializes in analyzing technology trends, more than 80% of all online users still use dial-up. However, according to a survey that Jupiter conducted in April, 2002, 24% of all dial-up customers were thinking about switching to broadband within the following year.

INTEGRATED SERVICES DIGITAL NETWORK (ISDN)

In the mid-1990s, when many people still had 14.4K dial-up modems, **Integrated Services Digital Network (ISDN)** promised fast Internet access. ISDN is a type of technology that can simultaneously carry digital voice and data transmissions. It works by using a portion of existing phone lines to send and receive digital communications. The data is sent using D or B channels that run simultaneously over a single phone line. Using different channels to carry the data means that you can access the Internet and talk on the phone at the same time.

To use ISDN, your local phone company must use digital phone lines. Depending on where you live, this fact alone might preclude you from using ISDN. Using digital phone lines usually costs more than standard phone service, too. Besides digital phone lines, you also need some equipment in place to use this technology: an ISDN terminal adapter that prepares your computer to use ISDN transmissions and an ISDN network terminator to ready a standard phone line for ISDN use.

ISDN is faster than dial-up, but is no longer considered competitive with the newer technologies, such as cable-modem. The upstream speed is 64Kbps; the downstream speed 128Kbps. Like many other connection types, this represents the *theoretical* top speed. The actual data transfer rate depends on several factors. For example, performance can drop if the terminal adapter connected to your computer uses a serial port instead of a USB because serial ports allow for slower data transfer. Speed can also be affected by the routers, switches, and lines used by the phone company.

CABLE MODEM

Cable modem is a technology that uses a cable TV connection rather than a phone line to connect to the Internet. The cable is attached to an Ethernet device in your computer. The service costs approximately $30–$50/month, which compares favorably with dial-up connections (if you factor in the second phone line usually needed by modem users).

The bandwidth of the coaxial cable used is significantly greater than that used for a standard phone line, which translates into lightning-fast data transfer and super-fast access. The speeds average 500Kbps upstream and as high as 2,000Kbps downstream.

Of course, these numbers are only averages and they depend on a number of factors. One of the most important is the fact that the bandwidth is a shared resource. If everyone in the neighborhood signs up for cable modem service and uses it simultaneously (let's say to download MP3 music files), the available bandwidth—and speed—drop like a rock. The other major drawback to cable modem technology is that it's not available in all locations. At the time of this writing, cable modem could be purchased by only 40% of the people in the United States.

Finally, cable modem, like DSL and satellite, provides an always on connection without having to tie up a phone line or dial into the ISP. An **always on connection** is one that you don't have to specifically dial up or specifically access. Instead, any time your computer is on, so is the connection. This hands the user great convenience, but also necessitates using virus-protection software and a firewall to ward off intrusions into your system.

ADSL AND DSL

Digital Subscriber Line (DSL) is a technology that provides a wide pipeline for data to travel. This translates into very fast Internet access and data transfer rates. DSL has several variations, with ADSL being the most well-known in the United States. Asymmetric DSL, true to its name, has different upload and download speeds. For example, data can be transmitted at top speeds of 1.5Mbps–2.0Mbps downstream; 400Kbps upstream. Despite the fact that ADSL is only one type of DSL, you'll find that the terms ADSL and DSL are used more or less interchangeably in the United States.

DSL technology works by taking advantage of the unused frequencies on copper phone lines to transmit data. DSL can transmit voice and high-speed data simultaneously over a single phone line, which enables you to carry on a conversation and surf online—all at once.

To use DSL, you'll need some basic equipment, including a network interface card (NIC) and a DSL modem that connects to your computer. DSL is an increasingly cost-effective method of getting fast access. Setup costs are usually relatively low (or waived with a year-long commitment), and the monthly fee usually ranges from $30–$50.

INSIDE TRACK
Even though ISDN is being eclipsed by DSL and cable modem technologies in the United States, it still continues to be used regularly in other countries (in parts of Europe, for example) because strict government regulation in these countries led to the early installation of ISDN-capable communication lines. Because of the international use of ISDN technology, it's important to understand a little bit about it.

INSIDE TRACK
Residential, home office, and small office personnel generally use the connection types discussed in this chapter. However, larger companies sometimes lease high-bandwidth T1 or T3 telephone connections. These connections have a capacity of 100–10,000 users at once, but are also priced accordingly: A leased T1 connection might accommodate 100 users at once, but costs about $1500 per month. A T3 connection is even pricier: It can cost $5,000–$12,000 per month, but is extremely fast (44,700Kbps) and allows for 1,000–10,000 users simultaneously.

ALERT!
When you use satellite, DSL, or cable modem technologies, your system is connected to the Internet whenever the computer is turned on. Although this provides convenience, it also creates more exposure to cyber vandals because of the fact that the system is "always on." This gives the bad guys ample opportunity to search for security holes in your system and exploit them. If you employ these technologies, make sure you also install firewall and anti-virus software. Also consider turning off your computer when you're not actively using it.

INSIDE TRACK

DSL actually comes in several variations. The most well-known (besides ADSL) is **Symmetric Digital Subscriber Line (SDSL)**. SDSL has the same upload and download speeds (hence the term symmetric). This connection technology is more expensive than ADSL, however, and is mainly used by businesses that need matching upload and download speeds to transfer data.

All of this combines to make DSL a great option—if you can get it. Unfortunately, it's not available in all locations, so before you run out and buy that DSL modem, make sure that the service is up and running in your area. You can find this out by calling your local phone companies, or by conducting an area code search on DSL Web sites.

SATELLITE

Despite the technological advantages of DSL and cable modem, many people in the United States don't have access to these services, especially those who don't live in a large city. If you're one of those who can't take advantage of these broadband services, don't despair. Even if you live in a rural area, you can still get faster access than that provided by dial-up: Use satellite.

Satellite Internet access works by sending your request from the computer system, via a satellite dish, to a satellite approximately 22,000 miles above the earth. This signal is sent to the ISP's hub, in which it routes the request through the Internet's backbone to the appropriate location. The information (such as a Web page) is routed back via the reverse route and then "beamed" down to your satellite dish, at which it is downloaded into your computer (see Figure 3.8). The good news is that this all takes place at a significantly faster speed than either dial-up or ISDN. Upstream speeds are only in the range of 60Kbps (just slightly faster than a 56K modem) but download speeds zip along at 200Kbps–400 Kbps.

Until recently, satellite broadband could transmit data only one way. This meant that you still had to send upstream data. One-way data transmission tied up a phone line and also translated into slower upstream speeds. However, most broadband satellite services now offer two-way service, in which information is both uploaded and downloaded via satellite.

Although not nearly as quick on its feet as DSL and cable modem, satellite broadband provides an option for those who can't get DSL or cable modem. The advantages of satellite include its almost universal availability, fast speed, and the cost savings of not having to install a second phone line.

But there are drawbacks. Satellite can cost several hundred dollars to set up. Not only is the dish expensive, but it usually requires professional installa-

Figure 3.8.
Fast Internet access via satellite eliminates the need for dial-up connections.

58   Chapter 3   Necessary Equipment and Internet Connections

tion. Additionally, satellite service, although generally reliable, can vary with weather and solar conditions. For example, an upcoming storm can prevent uploading or downloading information. Because of this, some satellite services include a few hours of dial-up access in their plan so that you have an alternative way to connect to the Internet when these conditions exist.

FIXED WIRELESS

A relatively new option for connecting to the Internet is fixed wireless. This technology involves sending data via radio signals. The biggest drawback to the service is availability because users need to be within a few miles of the nearest access point (the point from which the signal is transmitted).

Wireless services use a variety of frequencies and technologies to send and receive data. As a result, data transfer rates can differ significantly. Additionally, your proximity to the point where the signal originates also affects the connection speed. Because of the difference in speed, some wireless ISPs structure their pricing plans based on the transfer rate. For example, you might pay from $40/month (for a 128Kbps transfer rate) to $800/month (for a 2Mbps transfer rate). Obviously, more businesses than individuals will be paying for these higher speeds!

SUMMARY

The conclusion? You should carefully weigh the cost, speed, availability, and convenience of each connection technology before deciding the best one for you. To help you evaluate your options, Table 3.2 recaps the speed and costs associated with each technology.

> **ALERT!**
> When checking for the availability of broadband services in your area, you'll probably be prompted to enter your address and phone number in an online form. To protect your privacy (but still accurately find out about availability), consider entering information that approximates—but isn't exactly the same as—your phone number and zip code.

TABLE 3.2	Summary of costs and speeds for the various connection technologies			
Technology	Upstream Speed (Kbps)	Downstream Speed (Kbps)	Start-Up Costs	Monthly Costs
Dial-up modem	28–56	28–56	$0–$20	$20–22*
ISDN	64	128	$150–$200	$20–$100
Cable modem	500	1,000–2,000	$100	$30–$60
DSL	128	1,500	$0–$100	$30–$60
Satellite	60	400	$600–$1200	$60–$70
Wireless (fixed)	128–2,000	128–2,000	$250–$1,000	$40–$800

*You may also need a second phone line

Don't Forget...

- You need a combination of hardware, software, and connection technologies to get online.
- There are many ways to connect to the Internet. The main types used today are dial-up access, ISDN, cable modem, ADSL and DSL, satellite, and fixed wireless.
- Connection technologies vary widely in speed, price, and availability.
- Despite the number of available choices, most people who use the Internet are still employing dial-up access.
- Broadband services are steadily gaining a following, while simultaneously dropping in price.

Check This Out

MULTIPLE CHOICE

1. Which of the following is not considered a broadband service?
   a. Dial-up
   b. Satellite
   c. DSL
   d. Cable modem
2. Which of the following currently provides the slowest connection to the Internet?
   a. Cable modem
   b. ISDN
   c. Dial-up
   d. DSL
3. Which of the following services includes the highest startup cost for residential users?
   a. Dial-up
   b. Cable modem
   c. Satellite
   d. DSL
4. What is the main advantage of satellite over DSL?
   a. It is less expensive.
   b. It is available in many areas where DSL is not.
   c. Satellite is much faster than DSL, providing speeds of up to 1.5Mbps.
   d. It doesn't require professional installation.
5. What is one disadvantage of always on connections, such as cable modem?
   a. It provides more opportunities for others to breach your system's security.
   b. You don't have to dial in to the ISP.
   c. They are not as fast as dial-up.
   d. None of the above

MATCHING

a. Kbps
b. broadband
c. POTS
d. dial-up
e. asymmetric
f. DSL
g. Ethernet
h. set-top box
i. cable modem
j. satellite

1. Includes standard telephone lines
2. Digital subscriber line
3. A group of technologies that provides high-speed access to the Internet
4. Data transmission rate of 1000 bits per second
5. A standard network protocol
6. A broadband service that uses coaxial cable to transmit data
7. A device you can use with your television to access the Web
8. Upload and download speeds differ
9. Uses a modem and phone lines to access the Internet
10. A broadband service available in rural areas even when DSL, cable modem, and ISDN aren't

Real Life

1. The number of people using broadband services in the United States doubled during 2001. Use the Internet to determine whether the trend to using fast access services is continuing. Start by looking at the following Web sites: *www.nua.com/surveys* and *www.nielsen-netratings.com*. If you have the appropriate software (such as Excel or PowerPoint), develop a chart that shows your findings.
2. Explore the surveys, reports, and press releases on Jupiter Media Metrix's Web site (*www.jmm.com*) regarding the growth and trends in Internet usage. Write a short report or develop a PowerPoint presentation that documents your findings.
3. Find out which connection technologies (narrowband and broadband) are available in your area. Analyze the cost, speed, and availability of the services. If you needed to sign up for Internet access, which one would you choose? Why?
4. Using the Internet, compare and contrast the connection technologies available in the following five locations: New York, New York; Boulder Junction, Wisconsin; Knoxville, Tennessee; St. Maries, Idaho; and West Plains, Missouri. What conclusions can you draw about the relationship between population density and broadband technology?
5. Explore the Web sites for several BSPs, such as Road Runner (*www.rr.com*) and EarthLink (*www.earthlink.net*). Also spend time looking over the services offered by MSN TV (*www.msntv.com*) and AOLTV (*www.aoltv.com*). View the demonstrations on each Web page that show the difference in speed between dial-up and broadband access.

I Spy: Privacy and Security Concerns

1. What are the security issues surrounding an always on connection to the Internet? What types of measures do you need to put in place to prevent security breaches to your system if you use one of these technologies?

2. Research the three firewall programs that are currently available. For example, find out about BlackICE PC Protection, Zone Labs' ZoneAlarm, and Symantec's Norton Personal Firewall. Compare and contrast the features of each program; then determine which one would be best if you were using a broadband service.

CHAPTER 4

INTERNET SERVICE PROVIDERS

Key Terms

When you finish this chapter, you'll understand the following terms:

Acceptable Use Policy (AUP)
flat rate
metered rate
Parental controls

Chapter Objectives

After you complete this chapter, you'll

- Be Able to Evaluate and Compare Internet Service Providers
- Recognize the Major Internet Service Providers
- Evaluate Whether or Not Free ISPs Are Really Free
- Know About Accessing the Internet via College and Business Networks

The Big Picture

Unless you're able to get on the Internet through a school, business, or library, you'll soon find yourself shopping for an Internet Service Provider (ISP). After all, the ISP you choose can profoundly influence your online experience; select an unreliable or slow provider (or one that sells your personal contact information to others), and you'll soon regret your decision.

Fortunately, there are a number of well-run, reliable ISPs available. But how do you find the right one for you? In this chapter, we'll give you a checklist of things to consider when you're looking for an ISP. Although you might not be looking for an ISP right now, you probably will be at some point.

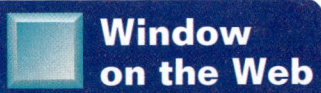

Window on the Web

To find the best ISP for your needs, you should consider several factors: availability, price, service, and fast and reliable connections. Luckily, the Web includes a number of resources to help you do this. For example, you can use the Web pages for several ISPs to compare features and pricing. Additionally, you find out other people's experience with the various ISPs through Usenet groups or in chat rooms.

One great place to start researching information about ISPs on the Web is The List, located at *www.thelist.com* (see Figure 4.1). This Web site includes information on evaluating ISPs as well as a search feature that helps you locate which providers service your area.

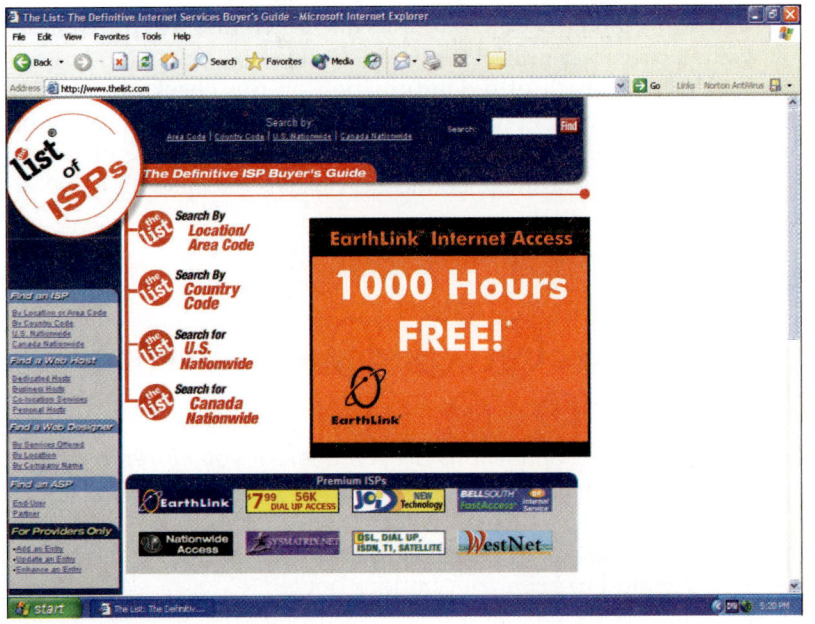

Figure 4.1.
Looking for an ISP? Start with The List.

Window on the Web 63

We'll also show you some options for finding free or discounted ISPs, such as Juno, which recently merged with NetZero to form United Online. These discounted ISPs can save you money, especially if you're online only a limited number of hours each month.

In this chapter, we'll give you some guidelines so that you can make a wise decision about choosing an ISP. Who knows? If you become analytical enough, you just might become the local expert on choosing and using ISPs!

BE ABLE TO EVALUATE AND COMPARE INTERNET SERVICE PROVIDERS

There's more to choosing an ISP than meets the eye. You know you want fast and reliable connections, pleasant service, and a fair price. But that's not all that you need for a pleasant online experience.

Begin by determining what type of connection you want to use. If you plan to get a broadband service, you'll most likely have to use the ISP associated with the service. For example, if you decide to use cable modem, the cable company will be your ISP. However, if you instead opt for dial-up (like 80% of Americans still do), you have many more choices for an ISP.

After you decide on the type of connection you want to use, think about your other requirements for Internet access: How much time do you plan to spend online? Do you need multiple mailboxes for e-mail? Are you interested in safety and privacy features, such as parental controls and firewalls? After you've laid the groundwork by asking yourself these questions, you're ready for some heavy-duty research.

First, ask others which ISP they use and whether or not they like the service. Although rather informal, this feedback can provide useful information. Next, take a look under Internet Service Providers in the yellow pages of your phone book. Finally, go to your school or library and run searches on the Web. Some Web sites include helpful information on evaluating ISPs and can help you determine which organizations are available in your area. Besides the major ISPs (such as EarthLink, MSN, and AOL), you'll probably find that there is a number of small, locally based providers as well.

Assuming that you've narrowed your choice of ISPs to three or four, you're ready to interview them to find out which one will provide the services you want. You can use the following checklist to help you determine what questions to ask. Much of the information on this checklist pertains to using dial-up ISPs. But you can use the same list, even if you plan to use broadband through a Broadband Service Provider (BSP). If you do use broadband, don't forget to find out the average connection speeds for uploading and downloading data.

CHECKLIST FOR EVALUATING ISPS:

ASKING ISPS ABOUT CONNECTION TYPE, SPEED, RELIABILITY . . .

✔ *What types of connections do you offer? If you currently offer only dial-up, do you plan to provide broadband services in the next year?*

You may decide to switch connection technology if the price drops, so it's helpful to keep your options open.

✔ *How does your service connect to the Internet?*

> A service that uses a T1 or T3 line is better than one that uses an ISDN line or modem to connect. It's also advantageous if the ISP has multiple ways to connect to the Internet; if one connection goes down, another can act as a backup.

✔ *How much bandwidth do you have? What is the ratio of bandwidth to subscribers?*

> This is important to know because ISPs buy a certain amount of bandwidth; if they add too many subscribers to the line, you may get busy signals when you try to dial in. To research this information on your own, go to ISPWorld's Web site (*www.ispworld.com*) and follow the links for the ISP Directory.

✔ *Are there multiple local numbers available to access the ISP?*

> The availability of multiple phone numbers in the local area is advantageous; if the first number is busy, you can try another without incurring long distance charges.

✔ *Are there toll-free dial in numbers available?*

> This is a helpful feature: You can still access the Internet and your e-mail when you're traveling. Unlike the smaller local ISPs, major providers will most likely have local access numbers, no matter where you travel in the United States.

✔ *Do the local dial-up numbers support the modem speed on your computer?*

> Smaller ISPs may have older modems, routers, and switches that can create bottlenecks, even if you have a 56K modem in your computer.

✔ *Is there a maximum size for file attachments?*

> Some ISPs truncate files beyond a certain length. You may not think you need to send files bigger than 2MB, for example, but as you become more Web-savvy, you might be regularly sending large graphic and music files.

ASKING ISPS ABOUT PRIVACY AND SECURITY...

✔ *Does the ISP provide firewall software for its subscribers?*

> Using firewall software is an important part of your overall security plan. Although an ISP's firewall is a nice extra, most of the time you can find other low-cost options for obtaining a firewall.

✔ *Does the ISP's software include parental controls?*

Some (though not all) ISPs have options to limit what children can view on the Internet. AOL includes a solid set of parental controls. **Parental controls** are software programs that limit which sites someone can view on the Web (or how long they can be online).

✔ *Does the ISP sell or share identifying information with anyone?*

Some ISPs sell or give your information to commercial marketing services. Make sure that yours won't do this unless you don't mind receiving lots of online offers and spam.

ASKING ISPS ABOUT CUSTOMER AND TECHNICAL SERVICE...

✔ *How helpful is their Customer Service? Is there a toll-free number you can use to contact them? What hours are they open?*

✔ *How long does it take to contact technical help? Is there a toll-free number you can use to contact them? What hours are they open?*

It's a good idea to test the ISP's technical support by calling them yourself to find out how long it takes to get through to a real person.

ASKING ISPS ABOUT RATES...

✔ *Is there a startup fee? What does this fee include?*

Some ISPs charge a $20–$35 fee to set you up with their service. Sometimes, this also includes the necessary software to access their service. (Hint: Negotiate this fee if there is one. In most cases, you can get the fee waived and even get a free month of service.)

✔ *What is your monthly access fee?*

Obviously, price is a consideration—although not the only one. You might be able to bargain a little: Ask for a student rate, a free month of service, or a domain name. You just might get it.

✔ *Do you charge a flat rate (unlimited) fee, or a metered rate?*

A **flat rate** gives you unlimited access to the Internet. A **metered rate** includes limited hours; if you exceed the allowed hours, you pay extra charges on a per-hour basis. Because of this, a flat rate is usually preferred unless you are certain that you will spend only a few hours per month online.

✔ *What does the fee include?*

ISPs routinely include space on their service for your own Web site and several mailboxes in addition to access to the Internet.

✔ *Am I committed to a particular length of contract?*

Some ISPs offer free merchandise (such as an inexpensive digital camera) or a free month of service as long as you commit to the provider for a certain length of time. BSPs are more likely to ask you to sign a contract for a specific length of time to help offset their upfront installation costs.

✔ *Do you offer a trial account?*

If the service offers a trial period, consider "trying before you buy" so that you can make sure that the ISP will fit your needs.

 **HEADS UP!** Some ISPs offer free trials. However, if you do sign up for an ISP's trial period, keep in mind that they'll probably make it much easier to sign up for the service than to cancel. If you do cancel, be prepared to receive some pressure to continue.

Now that you have an idea of how to evaluate prospective ISPs, let's take a look at some of the largest providers you can use. Even if you decide to use a smaller, local, or regional ISP, it's helpful to know a little about the main providers.

RECOGNIZE THE MAJOR INTERNET SERVICE PROVIDERS

One of your decisions involves using a large, national ISP or a smaller, locally based organization. Using a sizable ISP has certain advantages over using a lesser-known one. The infrastructure, including the ISP's connection to the Internet's backbone, is usually better. Additionally, it's likely that technical support for major ISPs will be available 24 hours per day, seven days per week. Finally, you won't have to change your e-mail address or ISP if you move.

On the other hand, the fees are generally a little lower for local companies than they are for the national ISPs. You might find more personable service with a local group, too.

You've probably already heard the names of most of the big Internet Service Providers. Which company holds the largest part of the market varies from year to year, but as of April 2002, those shown in Table 4.1 were the major players in the ISP game.

 ALERT! The biggest complaint against AOL involves this ISP's use of its customers' contact information and other infringements on their privacy. Users of AOL have complained that they have to endure endless banner advertisements and regularly receive spam in their AOL mailboxes.

TABLE 4.1	The Top ISP Providers (April, 2002)
Internet Service Provider	**Subscribers (in millions)**
America Online (Dial-up)	26.1
MSN (Dial-up)	7.7
United Online (Dial-up)	5.2
EarthLink (Dial-up)	4.9
SBC/Prodigy (SBC/Prodigy DSL and Dial-up)	3.3
CompuServe (Dial-up) AOL-owned	3.0
Road Runner (Cable) AOL-owned	2.4
AT&T Broadband (DSL)	1.4
AT&T WorldNet (Dial-up)	1.4
Verizon (DSL)	1.4
Comcast (Cable)	1.0
Cox (Cable)	1.0

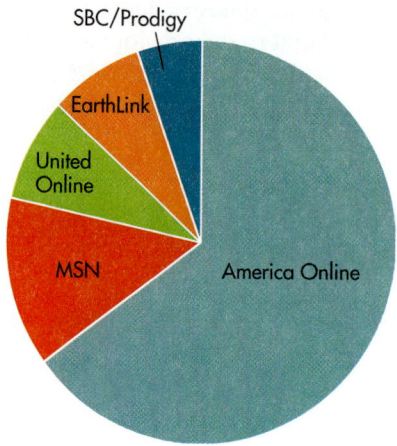

Figure 4.2.
AOL holds the largest market share.

Of course, the ISP that has the lion's share of the market at any given time can change. At this point, America Online (AOL) is in front (see Figure 4.2).

So that you can know a little bit about each of the big-name ISPs, we've included a quick synopsis for each:

AMERICA ONLINE (AOL)

America Online (AOL) is by far the largest ISP in the United States. It claims 26 million subscribers and has 17.5% of the total market share. The biggest advantages of this service includes content that's not otherwise available, a "buddy" system that lets you communicate in real-time with other AOL users, extensive parental controls, and ease of use. Drawbacks of this ISP include its heavy use of advertisements and spam. You can find out more about AOL on its Web site (*www.aol.com*).

MICROSOFT NETWORK (MSN)

Microsoft Network (MSN) is also a big player in the ISP game. It has the second largest numbers of subscribers (7.7 million), although the number is significantly less than AOL's. You can find out more about this ISP at its Web site (*www.msn.com*).

EARTHLINK

EarthLink became one of the biggest ISPs in the United States when it merged with MindSpring in 2000. EarthLink ranks high in customer satisfaction due to fast, reliable connections and a lack of advertising. According to its Web site, "We don't sell your personally identifying information or slam you with pop-up ads." You can find out more about this service at *www.earthlink.net*.

AT&T WORLDNET SERVICE

According to a *Consumer Reports* survey of 1,640 Internet users (September 2001), AT&T WorldNet Service ranked the best in customer satisfaction among dial-up users. The service has also won a number of other awards. You can find out more about this service at the company's Web site (*www.att.net*).

SBC/PRODIGY

SBC and Prodigy have had a partnership to provide Internet access. Recently, SBC Internet Services and Yahoo! joined forces to form SBC Yahoo! Dial. Still known to most people as Prodigy, this service includes a number of features, such as parental controls, a customized browser, and instant messaging. You can research this company at *www.prodigy.net*.

REGIONAL AND LOCAL ISPS

Instead of using one of the national ISPs, you may want to consider a regional or local one. For example, BellSouth (*www.bellsouth.com*), a regional ISP, tied for second place (with EarthLink) in customer satisfaction in *Consumer Reports*. Other regional and local ISPs may provide reliable service at a lower price than some of the major ISPs.

EVALUATE WHETHER OR NOT FREE ISPS ARE REALLY FREE

If you don't plan on spending more than a few hours per month online or are just looking for some ways to save money (and who isn't?) you may want to consider a free or discounted ISP. This type of ISP has traditionally provided a good value for many people, especially those who were just trying out the Internet or those who didn't want to spend a lot of money just to surf the Web or collect e-mail.

The most well-known free ISP is NetZero. Formerly, this service didn't limit the number of hours you could spend online. So you could surf at will, collect your e-mail, and generally enjoy your online time. NetZero is still a free service, but you're now limited to 10 hours of free access a month. This ISP has recently merged with Juno to form United Online (*www.unitedonline.net*). With the trend away from free access and toward discounted rates, it's unclear how long the United Online companies will be completely free (see Figure 4.3).

Like many other things in life that are provided at no cost, "free" Internet access has strings attached. One way or another, the service has to pay for its bandwidth, servers, and other costs, just like anybody else. Although free ISPs can be a viable option for some people, it's important to carefully evaluate the level of service you'll receive and the possible encroachments on your privacy.

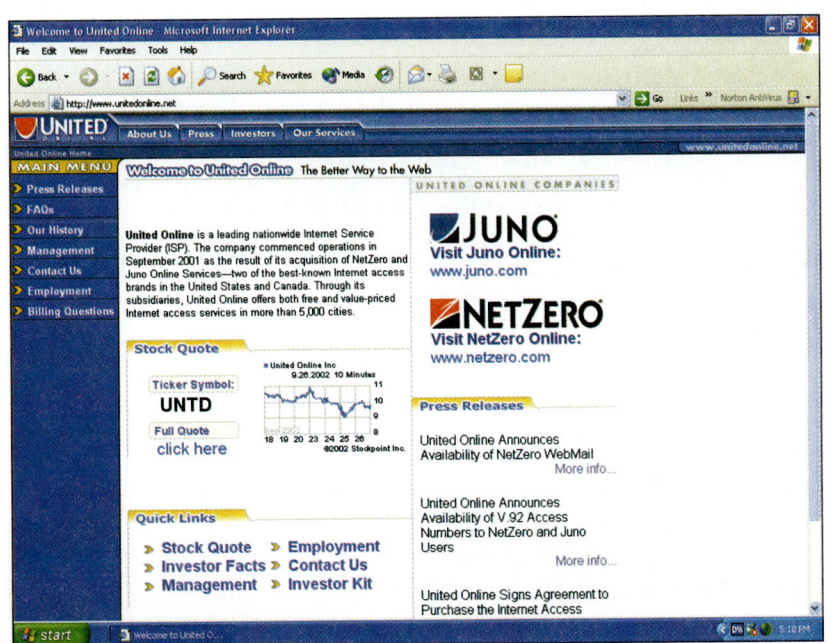

Figure 4.3.
You can cut your monthly ISP bills in half by using a discounted or free service.

ALERT!
If someone calls you (supposedly) from your ISP and starts asking you questions, see if you can call them back on the ISP's toll-free line. One recent scam involved calling an ISP's customers and then asking for their passwords, credit card numbers, and other personal information. A legitimate ISP won't call and ask you for this information.

ALERT!
Some free ISPs require that you fill out lengthy online forms when you sign up for service... and (you guessed it) they use this information to pitch products and services to you or they sell your information to marketing companies. Before you sign up for a free ISP, evaluate its privacy policy and determine whether the free Internet access is worth the possible infringement on your privacy.

Remember "free" television? Advertisers underwrite its costs; the same holds true for free ISPs. If you sign up for a free ISP, brace yourself to be bombarded with free banner advertisements, inundated with pop-up commercials, and for your e-mail box to quickly fill with commercial offers (spam). And if you send e-mail via the ISP's "free" service, an ad for the ISP will most likely display at the bottom of each and every message you send.

Some of the free ISPs also don't feel a strong obligation to provide seamless surfing for you; busy signals, poor reliability, and disconnects are relatively common. Additionally, some free services limit usage to 10 or 12 hours per month—hardly viable for a serious Internet user or a student who wants to conduct research. Of course, free services can go bankrupt as quickly as anyone else... and several of them *have* through the Internet's relatively short history. (Discounted ISPs, by the way, usually aren't plagued by the same problems as are the free ISPs. In fact, some of the discounted ISPs provide the same level of service as do the full-priced ISPs.)

Besides making money from commercial advertising, free ISPs use an age-old marketing ploy to get you to sign up for a paid-for service: the basic bait-and-switch. You sign up for the free ISP initially, but most "free" ISPs also offer a "platinum" or "gold" plan that gives you unlimited Internet access for about 50% less than regular ISPs. For example, Juno, one of the first free ISPs, offered free service initially. Even though the Juno Internet ride was bumpy at times (disconnects and slow speeds were common, as were ads), it was... well... free. The company recently began charging approximately $10/month for unlimited Internet access and quietly converting its "free" customers to a paid service. The bottom line? Even with its limitations (and advertisements), discounted or free ISPs provide a good alternative for those who plan to spend limited time online.

KNOW ABOUT ACCESSING THE INTERNET VIA COLLEGE AND BUSINESS NETWORKS

Instead of obtaining your own ISP account, you may be able to use the Internet through your school or college. The most obvious advantage is cost—you'll be able to access the 'net for free. However, there will be some limitations. You'll most likely be required to sign an **Acceptable Use Policy (AUP)**. An AUP is a set of rules that the school or employer requires you to follow if you use its Internet connections (see Figure 4.4).

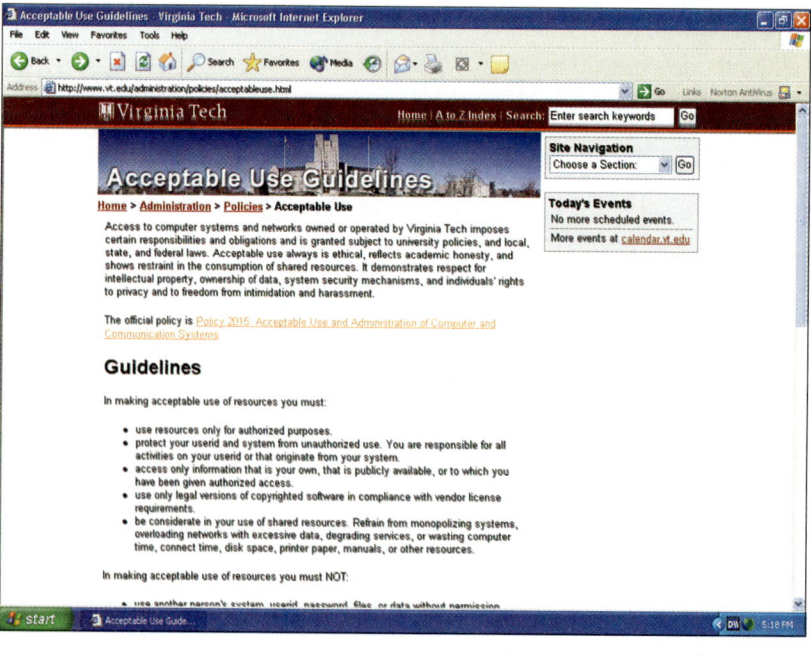

Figure 4.4.
Most universities require users to sign an AUP for Internet access.

Depending on your needs, the policy might hamstring you. For example, the policy may limit the number of hours you can use the Internet or prevent you from having multiple mailboxes for e-mail. If you sign an AUP at work, an employer usually reserves the right to monitor your e-mail messages and track the Web sites you visit. If you're uncomfortable with these limitations, you will probably want to set up your own ISP account.

Don't Forget...

- Carefully evaluate an ISP based on reliability, service, connections, and rates before signing up.
- There are advantages and disadvantages to most of the major ISPs. You should pick the one with the best mix of features, connection technology, and rates for your needs.
- Free and discounted ISPs offer Internet access at a minimal charge, but they might slam you with advertising or infringe on your privacy.
- Colleges, businesses, and libraries might provide you with free Internet access, but might not serve your needs as well as an ISP that you choose for yourself.

Check This Out

MULTIPLE CHOICE

1. Which of the following ISPs has the largest number of subscribers?
   a. AOL
   b. BellSouth
   c. EarthLink
   d. Prodigy
2. Which of the following should you evaluate when choosing a dial-up ISP?
   a. Rates
   b. Reliability
   c. Availability of local access phone numbers
   d. All of the above
3. Which of the following is a free ISP?
   a. EarthLink
   b. AOL
   c. MSN
   d. United Online
4. What is a potential drawback to using a free or discounted ISP?
   a. There is usually a limited number of hours you can use.
   b. Because the service's cost is underwritten by advertisers, you'll most likely have to regularly view online commercials.
   c. Frequent disconnects may be common.
   d. All of the above
5. Why might you want to pay for Internet access if you already have it free through your employer?
   a. The employer can view the contents of your e-mail messages.
   b. You may be limited in the amount of time you can spend online.
   c. You may be limited to a single mailbox.
   d. All of the above

MATCHING

a. metered rate
b. trial period
c. ISP
d. BSP
e. AUP
f. parental controls
g. advertisements
h. Juno
i. America Online
j. MSN

1. A few weeks or a certain number of hours that you can use an ISP without signing a contract
2. A way of pricing Internet access by the hour
3. Internet Service Provider
4. A set of rules governing how an employee or student can use the Internet
5. Broadband Service Provider
6. Software that you can use to limit which Web sites can be viewed or how long a person can stay online
7. Disadvantage of free ISP
8. An ISP owned by Microsoft
9. A free ISP
10. The ISP with the largest market share

Real Life

1. Look at the Web sites for several colleges or universities, including the one you attend. Locate and view the AUPs. Compare the policies, noting the similarities and differences. Develop a short chart that outlines them; then present it to a small group or your entire class.
2. Use The List's Web site (*www.thelist.com*) to research several ISPs in your area. Take a look at each ISP's Web site or call its customer service department to determine the features and rates for each.
3. Use the checklist provided in this chapter to interview personnel for at least two major ISPs. Compare the ISPs and develop a PowerPoint presentation or short written report that outlines your research. Additionally, if you're working in a class situation, report your findings to others in the class.
4. Compare the time, advertisements, and other features for free and discounted ISPs (such as Juno and NetZero). Determine which of these ISPs would best fit your needs.

I Spy: Privacy and Security Concerns

1. View the Web sites for the ISPs listed in this chapter and locate the privacy policy for each. Compare and contrast the privacy policies. Develop a chart that shows the differences and similarities for each.
2. Use the Web to research breaches of privacy by ISPs (such as selling of personally identifying information to marketing companies). Also, examine the privacy policies for several of the larger ISPs. Develop a report or a presentation of your findings.

SECTION Three
USING MAIL AND MESSAGING TOOLS

CHAPTER 5
MAIL AND MESSAGING SOFTWARE OVERVIEW

Key Terms

When you finish this chapter, you'll understand the following terms:

- encryption
- flaming
- Internet Message Access Protocol (IMAP)
- logging in
- mail client (e-mail client)
- mail server
- Multipurpose Internet Mail Extensions (MIME)
- Post Office Protocol, version 3 (POP3)
- Simple Mail Transfer Protocol (SMTP)

Chapter Objectives

After you complete this chapter, you'll

- Understand Why E-Mail is Popular... and Why It's Not
- Know How E-Mail Works
- Be Familiar with Common Mail Client Software
- Understand the Basics of Web-Based Mail Services

The Big Picture

It's been a long time since the days of the Pony Express. In fact, it even seems like an eternity since the days of postal-only mail! Nowadays, many people rely on electronic mail (e-mail) for communication rather than the traditional delivery systems, such as the United States Postal Service. In fact, some projections predict that people will be sending out 36 billion e-mail messages *each day* by the year 2005 (Source: IDC Research). From sending resumes and business proposals to getting Mom's chocolate chip cookie recipe or sharing photos of your beach trip. . . e-mail delivers messages quickly and inexpensively. And the Internet provides the grease to keep the mail moving. . . but how?

There are two main methods of sending and receiving e-mail over the Internet. The traditional approach involves using an e-mail program (also known as a **mail client** or **e-mail client**) in conjunction with your ISP.

The second main method you can use to work with e-mail involves utilizing Web-based mail services, such as Hotmail. When you use this type of service, you use your Web browser to send and retrieve messages.

In this chapter, we'll examine the advantages and disadvantages of using e-mail. Next, we'll turn our attention to understanding the way e-mail works. Finally, we'll take a look at the most popular e-mail client programs and Web-based mail services.

So take a look at your options regarding e-mail, and carefully weigh the pros and cons for each service or software product. By understanding the basics of how e-mail is transmitted and what type of client software and mail services are available, you can better manage your electronic communications.

Window on the Web

Due to its immense popularity and importance, e-mail is often referred to as the "killer application" of the Internet. This simply means that many people feel that it's the Internet's most useful application.

The first and most popular way to use e-mail is via a special program referred to as an e-mail client. One of the most popular e-mail clients is Microsoft's Outlook Express (see Figure 5.1). This software is included when you purchase Microsoft's Internet Explorer. In Chapter 6, E-Mail Basics, and Chapter 7, Beyond the Basics: Using E-Mail Safely and Effectively, you'll learn hands-on methods of working with e-mail by using this software as a springboard.

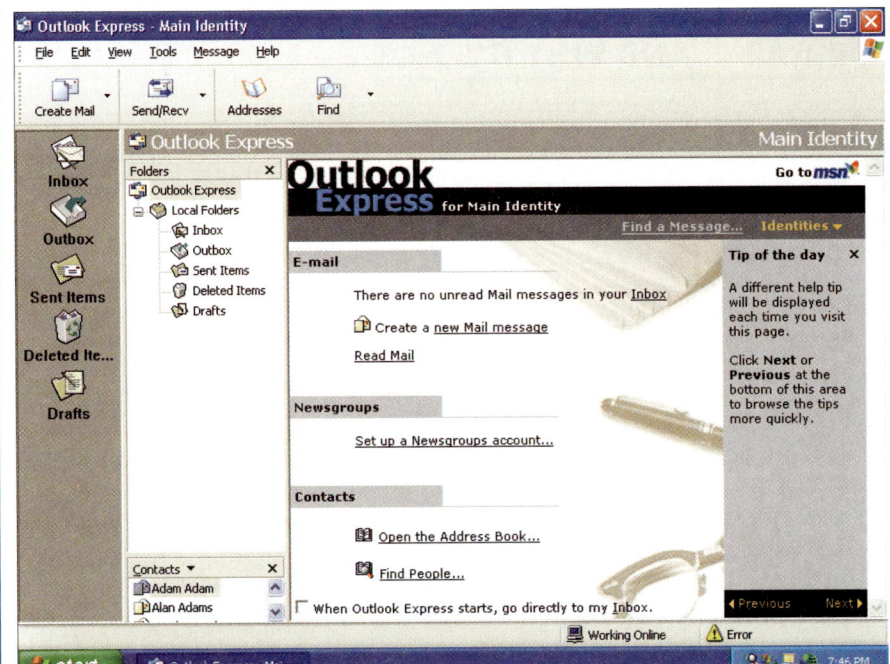

Figure 5.1.
Outlook Express is a popular e-mail client that you can use to send and retrieve electronic mail.

The Internet also provides another way to facilitate e-mail: via Web-based mail services, which enable you to send and receive mail using only your Web browser. When you use a Web-based mail service, you're not required to install or use e-mail client software. Besides the cost savings of not having to use a mail client, Web-based e-mail has another advantage: You can retrieve your mail from any computer in the world that has Internet access. This feature is especially helpful for people who travel a lot and for those who don't have a computer at home and consequently access the Internet through other locations (such as the library). Additionally, you can give out the address to a Web-based e-mail account more freely, which can help protect your client e-mail account from spam.

One well-liked Web-based mail service is Yahoo! Mail (see Figure 5.2). In this chapter, you'll learn about it and other popular and useful services.

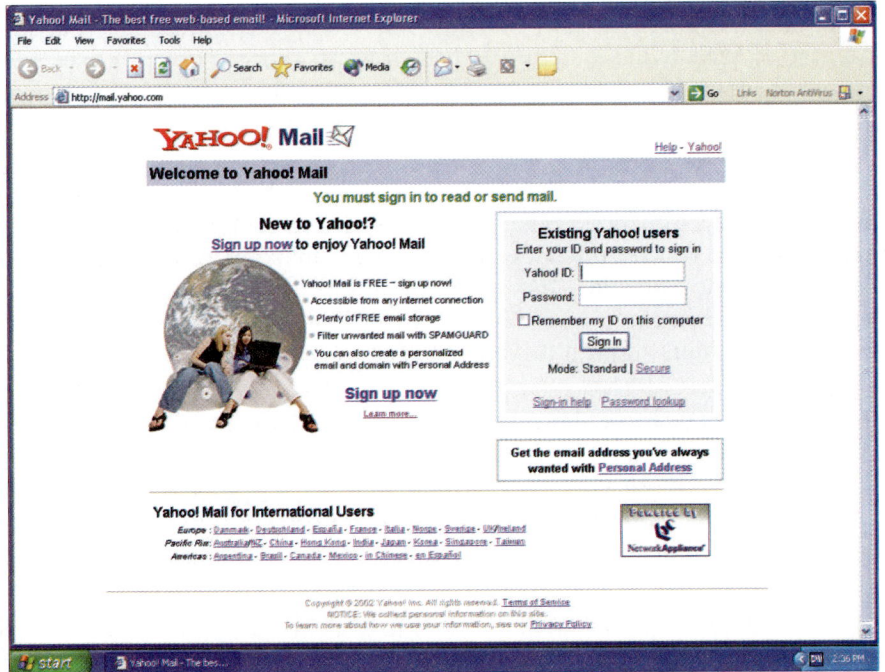

Figure 5.2.
Yahoo! Mail offers one of many popular Web-based mail services.

Let's take a look at the advantages and disadvantages of e-mail and then turn our attention to how e-mail actually works.

Window on the Web 75

UNDERSTAND WHY E-MAIL IS POPULAR ... AND WHY IT'S NOT

E-mail has the reputation of being the most popular Internet tool for a number of reasons. Here's a quick list of some of the most compelling reasons why this messaging system has grown so quickly:

- *E-mail is faster and more convenient to use than writing traditional paper-and-pen letters.* When you write a letter to send via the postal service, you need to complete several tasks (such as writing the letter, finding an envelope and stamp, addressing the letter, and placing the letter in the mailbox). In contrast, you can jot off an e-mail message, click the Send button, and you're done.
- *E-mail helps you better manage your time.* In comparison with making (or receiving) phone calls, e-mail offers convenience. You can retrieve and send messages at an opportune time. It also allows you to ponder your responses more than you can in a phone conversation.
- *E-mail is inexpensive.* After you initially incur the cost of Internet access and a device to send and receive your e-mail, using e-mail is basically free. The incremental cost of each message is almost nothing: it costs as little to send 1,000 messages as it does one. Additionally, you can send graphic or other mega files along with your e-mail—files that might cost a considerable sum to send in paper form via traditional delivery systems.
- *E-mail is speedy.* E-mail typically arrives at its destination in a matter of seconds, even if the recipient is halfway around the world. This speed is in sharp contrast to traditional postal mail (which is often referred to as "snail mail").
- *E-mail helps you stay organized.* If you've ever been overwhelmed by the paper clutter associated with traditional postal mail, you'll appreciate the inherent organization in e-mail client software. For example, you can use these programs to sort messages by date, subject, or sender.
- *E-mail lets you access your messages worldwide.* Depending on what software or Web-based system you use, you can retrieve or send mail from anywhere in the world. Postal mail, of course, can be retrieved only from your physical mailbox.

INSIDE TRACK

Netiquette is the general term that refers to using good online behavior no matter which Internet service is used. "E-mail etiquette" specially pertains to the informal rules governing electronic mail communications.

Of course, there's also a downside to e-mail as well. As you use it, keep the rules of courtesy, sometimes referred to as "e-mail etiquette," in mind. To help you understand which principles to follow, here are some of the things about e-mail that annoy people—and sometimes make them long for the days of paper-and-pen correspondence. As we cover the main abuses of e-mail, we'll give you some hints about how you *should* use e-mail.

- *Millions of messages.* Many people routinely get 50+ legitimate messages a day. To read, respond to, sort, or delete these messages takes time. Keep this in mind when you write or respond to messages from others, and make sure that your messages are purposeful.
- *Long-winded messages.* Be short, sweet, and to-the-point in your e-mail correspondence. Remember that many people receive several e-mail messages a day and don't really have time to wade through long, rambling messages. Additionally, include a topic or short description in the subject line of the message so that readers can tell at a glance what the message is all about.

- *Forwarded messages.* You probably know people who are on a joke-a-day mailing list and assume that you'd love to be privy to the same information. However, considering the volume of mail that most people receive, these forwarded messages are usually considered time-wasters. It's tough to tell your business associates or friends that you don't really want to receive this type of communication from them. However, if you're the one sending the messages, it's polite to ask whether the recipients really want this type of message sent to them. If they decline, honor their wishes.
- *Replying to everyone.* If you're responding to a group message, make sure that you actually mean to communicate with everyone on the e-mail list. When you click the Reply All button, you're sending your comments to everyone on the list. Don't annoy others (or cause embarrassment to yourself) by accidentally sending messages to multiple recipients when they are meant for private communication.
- *Bandwidth hogs.* Bandwidth hogs include e-mail practices that require a long upload or download time. For example, sending large attachments that the receiver didn't request can be annoying to them. Unnecessary formatting of e-mail messages can also take up time and bandwidth.
- *Flaming.* **Flaming** involves using criticism or insulting remarks in Internet communications designed to incite the recipients to anger. Flaming happens most often in newsgroups and bulletin boards as well as in e-mail messages. However, simple rules of courtesy should prevail in Internet communications just as in face-to-face ones.
- *Privacy issues.* If you address messages to multiple recipients, it's polite to prevent each person from seeing the others' e-mail addresses (unless, of course, they're working on the same project or have already shared contact information). To do so, type addresses in the Blind Carbon Copy (BCC) field. Another option? Learn to use distribution lists, which we cover in Chapter 7.
- *Spelling, grammar, formatting.* Avoid annoying others (or appearing unprofessional) by checking your spelling and grammar before sending the message. Additionally, don't type messages in all uppercase letters; doing so gives the impression that you're "shouting" at your readers. Finally, don't use excessive formatting, such as using bold, italic, and various fonts in your e-mail messages. The formatting takes more time to send over the Internet than does plain text. Additionally, your recipient may not have mail client software that can display formatted text correctly.
- *Abbreviations and smiley faces.* E-mail has lead to a proliferation of abbreviations, such as LOL for "Laughing Out Loud" and BTW for "By the Way." Use abbreviations and symbols faces sparingly, if at all. They can be misinterpreted by e-mail recipients.
- *Respect other people's privacy.* E-mail, by its very nature, is not considered private communication. Nevertheless, don't make it worse by forwarding messages sent to you to a third party unless you have permission to do so.
- *Spam.* Need we say more? If you've read the previous chapters in this book, you already know what a problem spam has become. The electronic version of junk mail, spam can clutter up your mailbox. Even worse, spam is one of many vehicles unsavory people can use to spread viruses. (By the way, we'll show you some ways to filter and ward off spam in Chapter 7.)

Now that you know a few of the positives and negatives about e-mail, let's take a look behind the scenes and find out how it works.

KNOW HOW E-MAIL WORKS

In its simplest form, electronic mail (e-mail) is the transmission of messages over a network, such as the Internet, from one location to another. You can think of it as the electronic form of the traditional mail delivery systems: In the same manner as you address a letter, write the message, and send it, you can do the same functions electronically. And in the same way as the United States Postal Service delivers your letter to the correct location, the mail server ensures that your electronic message gets to the recipient's mailbox.

As you recall from Chapter 1, How the Internet is Changing the World, the type of setup used for transferring information over the Internet is sometimes referred to as *server/client* architecture; in this case, the ISP's computer acts as a mail server and your PC steps into the role of the client. A **mail server** is a computer that receives your messages initially, and stores them until you use your personal computer to retrieve them. You can also use the mail server to send messages. Using the server/client system usually involves setting up your e-mail program so that it "knows" the location of the incoming and outgoing mail servers.

You probably already know that you need an Internet connection and an e-mail address to use e-mail. But, if you're like most people, you don't really understand how the system works. In this section, we'll walk you through the processes and discuss the protocols used to get e-mail from here to there.

ADDRESSING, SENDING, AND RECEIVING

E-mail travels around the Internet in a similar fashion to other data: It is broken down into small packets to flow smoothly through the Internet. These packets are transferred from one mail server to another and are then reassembled at the destination. The packets know where to go because each recipient has a unique e-mail address, which the sender places in the header section of the message (see Figure 5.3).

Ray Tomlinson developed the idea behind the e-mail address. In 1971, he sent the first e-mail message and quickly realized the necessity of specifying a unique address for each person. He came up with the now-familiar syntax for

Figure 5.3.
E-mail messages are set up with the address in the header area.

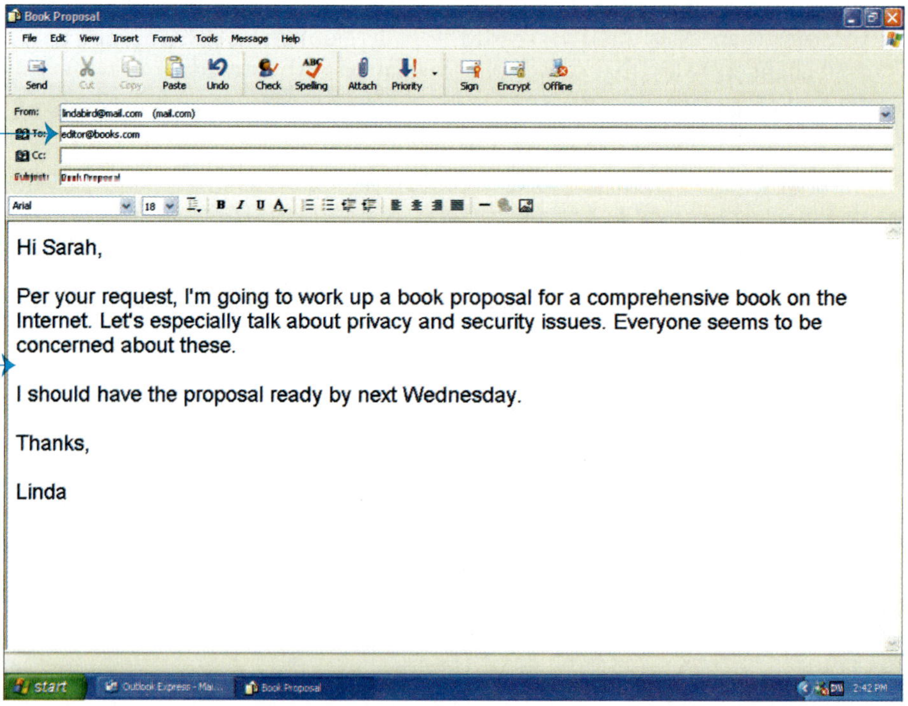

an e-mail address: username@domainname, such as lindabird@mail.com. The first part of the address—to the left of the at sign symbol (@) indicates the user's account name. The text to the right of the @ symbol indicates the domain name of the mail server. Where does the @ symbol come from? Actually, there's no real mystery to it. Tomlinson simply decided to use it to designate that someone was located "at" a certain location.

Think of the e-mail addressing system like this: You want to send mail to a family that lives at a certain location. The family consists of John and Betsy Jones and their daughter Heather. They live on Easy Street. In this case, EasyStreet is the domain in which the recipients are located; the username of each person is, well, their name. Furthermore, let's imagine that each addressee has a personal mailbox to keep the messages sorted and each recipient's separate from the others at the house. To send mail to Betsy, you'd address it to BetsyJones@EasyStreet; to her daughter, HeatherJones@EasyStreet, and so on. Betsy's mail would be delivered to her individual mailbox; Heather's goes into a totally separate one. One note: Because most of the time domain names can't accommodate spaces, you'd change Easy Street (with a space) to EasyStreet (without a space). In the same way, you indicate the person's name without a space between the first and last names, (although sometimes an underscore is used to separate the names).

The mail servers use the e-mail address to route the message to the receiving Simple Mail Transfers Protocol (SMTP) mail server. Once the message is delivered to the recipient's mailbox at the correct mail server, it remains there until the recipient connects to the mail server and downloads the message to his or her computer. From there, the recipient can use his or her e-mail client software to read, reply, or delete the messages.

SETTING THE STANDARDS

As you learned in Chapter 1, data is moved around the Internet by using certain standards and guidelines called protocols. Protocols are essential for moving data through the Internet because of the diversity between various platforms; conceivably, there can be an almost endless combination of hardware and software that can be used. To make sure that all the systems connected to the Internet can communicate with each other and share data, including e-mail messages, a set of standards (Transmission Control Protocol/Internet Protocol, TCP/IP) is required for transmitting data. In addition to TCP/IP, sending e-mail requires additional protocols for mail servers to communicate seamlessly with each other.

Post Office Protocol, version 3 (POP3) is the main protocol used for *storing* and *retrieving* messages from remote mail servers. Another less-used protocol that you'll encounter for storing and retrieving mail is **Internet Message Access Protocol (IMAP)**. The protocols responsible for retrieving e-mail, POP3, or IMAP work in conjunction with another protocol, **Simple Mail Transfer Protocol (SMTP)**. This protocol is responsible for *sending* messages. SMTP was originally designed to transfer text only.

INSIDE TRACK

Another protocol, **Multipurpose Internet Mail Extensions (MIME)**, is used to send graphic, sound, or other non-text files as e-mail attachments.

HEADS UP! In Chapter 1, we discussed that a Point of Presence (PoP) is an ISP's connection point to the Internet. Don't be fooled by the similarity of this acronym to the abbreviation for Post Office Protocol (POP). They're not the same at all!

When you send a message, your computer routes it to a SMTP mail server, which then sends the messages through the Internet to a receiving POP3 mail server. This type of mail server stores the messages until you use your e-mail client software to transfer the messages from the server to your computer system (see Figure 5.4).

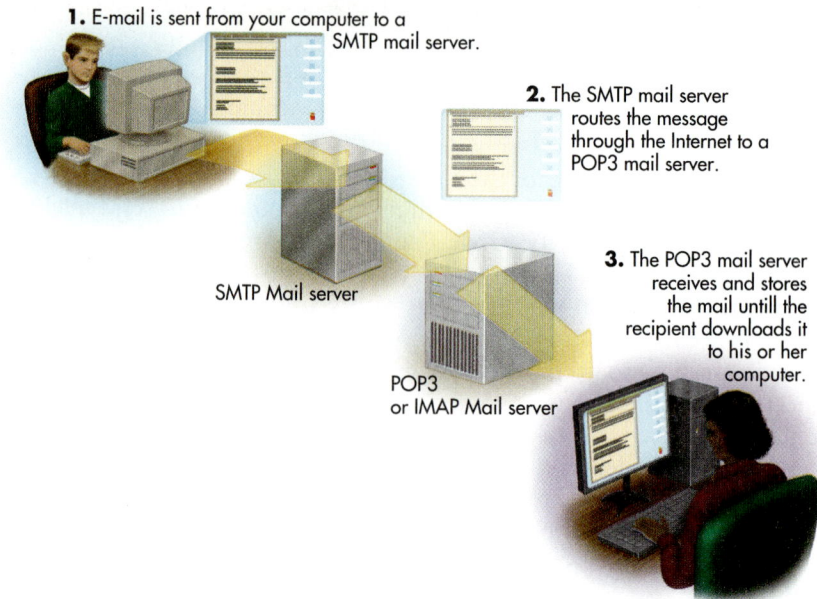

Figure 5.4.
How mail is sent over the Internet.

ALERT!
A username and password provide limited security for your e-mail messages. The security provided is not airtight, and (depending on many other factors) messages can still potentially be read by crackers or employers. We'll go over more about this subject in later chapters.

You can think of a mail server handing over your messages much like a fast food worker gives you your order at a drive-in window.

When you want to check your e-mail, you connect to the POP3 server by providing a username and a password, a process called **logging in**. Think of the combination of username and password as a key. Logging in provides a measure of security so that no one else can access your mailbox, much like a locked mailbox at an apartment building provides security for postal mail.

After your local computer connects to the POP3 server, your e-mail client software essentially "asks" the server if there are any new messages. If so, the files are transferred from the POP3 mail server to your machine. Simultaneously, the messages are usually deleted from a POP3 mail server.

The process of retrieving messages from an IMAP mail server to your local computer is similar to that of a POP3 server, except for an important distinction: In most cases, messages are not automatically deleted from an IMAP mail server, enabling you to manipulate the messages remotely (by sorting, for example). This means that you can leave your messages on an IMAP mail server; if you use POP3, the files are deleted from the mail server as they're transferred to your computer. You can decide which type of mail server to use based partly on how you want to manipulate and store your messages.

Now that you have a general idea of how e-mail is transported through the Internet, let's turn our attention to the software needed to download and manage your messages: the e-mail client.

BE FAMILIAR WITH COMMON MAIL CLIENT SOFTWARE

If you want to retrieve your mail from a POP3 or IMAP mail server, you need to tell your mail client software where to look for the messages, which you can do by configuring the mail client's settings. The exact steps will differ, depending on the software you use, but in general try to find a menu choice for Options, Settings, or Preferences. Sometimes, the POP3 and SMTP mail servers are actually located on the same machine and serviced by the same ISP. When this is the case, the settings for the mail server are typically indicated by the following commands: mail.domainname. You need to indicate both the incoming (POP3 or IMAP) and outgoing (SMTP) mail servers. For example, if you use EarthLink as your ISP, you will set up your mail servers similar to the way that's shown in Figure 5.5.

Using e-mail client software instead of a Web-based e-mail service has some advantages. The storage space for messages is limited only by the size of

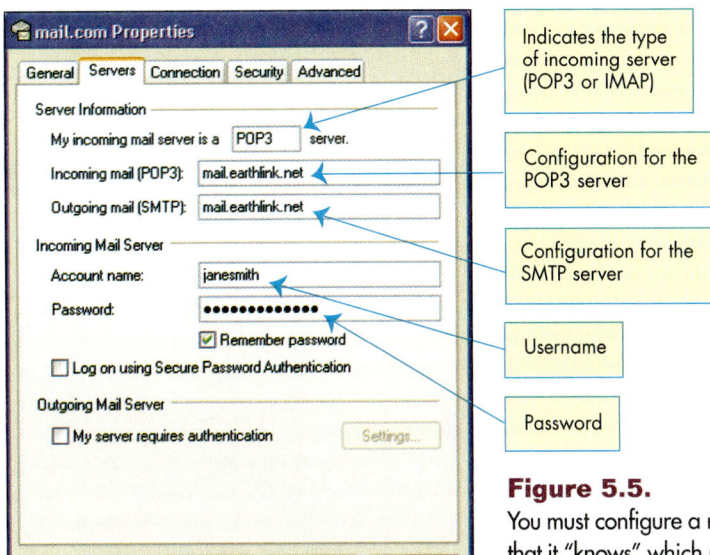

Figure 5.5.
You must configure a mail client so that it "knows" which mail servers are sending and receiving mail.

your hard drive, so you can conceivably keep messages for as long as you want. Client software lets you also manage your mail without being nagged by the advertisements that are so prevalent on Web-based sites. Additionally, the messages are kept on your personal machine instead of on a mail server. This gives you better control over renaming, sorting, and deleting messages than you have when you use Web-based services.

In later chapters, we'll go over how to use Outlook Express step-by-step. But there are a number of other e-mail messaging software programs available. Here's a rundown on the most popular:

INSIDE TRACK

Microsoft Exchange and Lotus Notes also include popular e-mail client software.

OUTLOOK

Outlook comes packaged with Microsoft's Office suite, although you can also buy it individually. This e-mail client includes calendar, appointment, task management, and scheduling features as well as comprehensive message handling tools, such as the capability to filter out spam. Outlook includes tools to help organize your e-mail messages, appointments, and other tasks (see Figure 5.6).

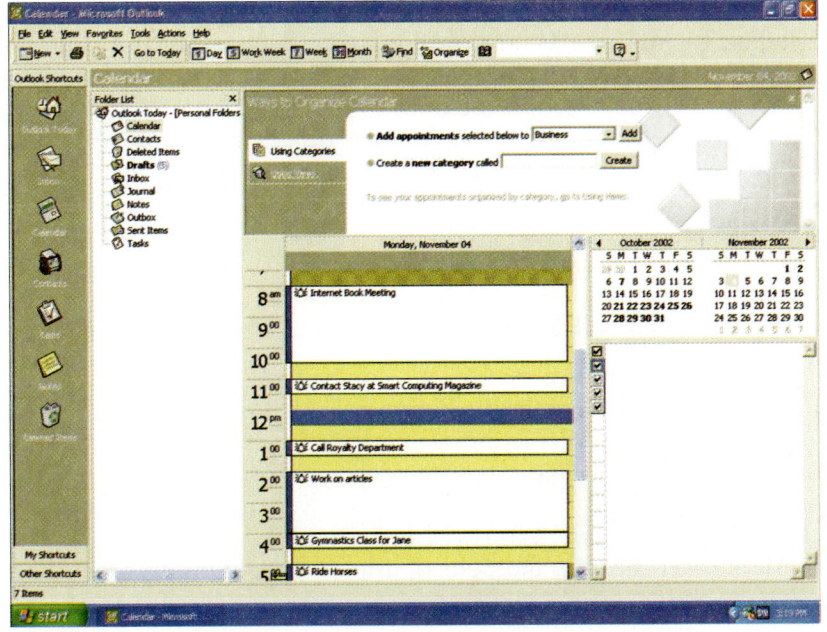

Figure 5.6.
Outlook helps you organize appointments as well as e-mail.

Be Familiar with Common Mail Client Software

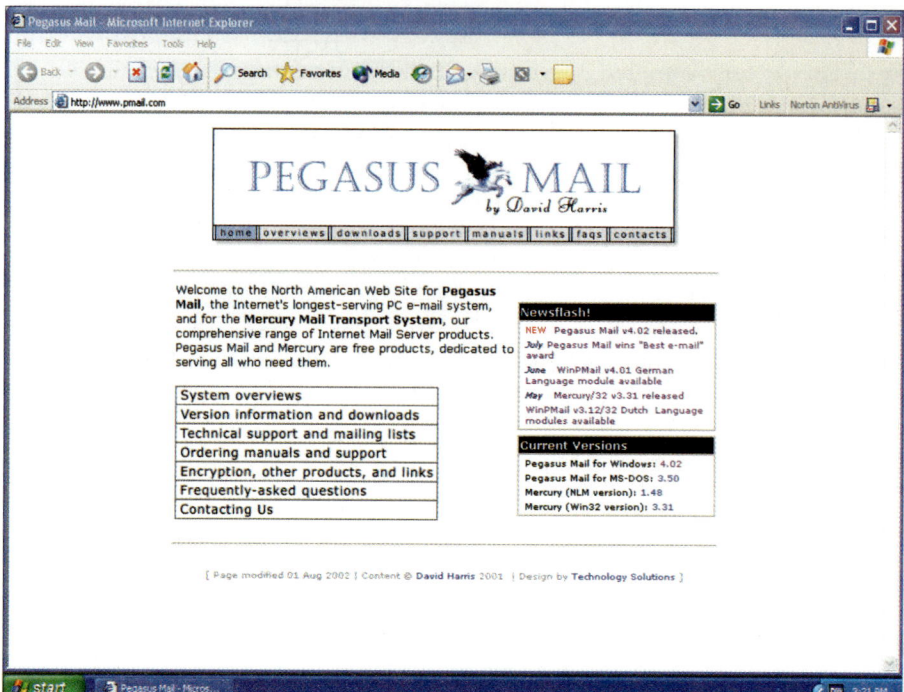

Figure 5.7.
Pegasus Mail is full-featured software that you can download for free.

PEGASUS MAIL

David Harris developed this full-featured e-mail client software and distributes this popular, well-written e-mail client software at no charge because he feels that communication should be free. Pegasus Mail has been one of the top-rated e-mail clients around for more than 10 years—an eternity in Internet time. You can find out more about this software and download it by visiting *www.pmail.com* (see Figure 5.7).

EUDORA

This e-mail client combines an attractive interface and high-end features with ease of use. This combination has helped Eudora gain a strong backing among savvy Internet users. The program also includes a few features that other clients don't have, such as a "MoodWatch" tool that helps you monitor incoming and outgoing mail for offensive language. Additionally, Eudora includes a tool that tracks the time you spend using e-mail and can even create charts of your usage patterns.

There are three options for obtaining this software, ranging from a free download to a paid-for version. Like many other "free" programs, the no-cost version includes a small, relatively unobtrusive advertisement. You can find out more about this client by taking a look at the company's Web site (*www.eudora.com*).

OUTLOOK EXPRESS

The Outlook Express e-mail client comes free with Microsoft's browser, Internet Explorer 6.0 (refer to Figure 5.1). It's a slimmed-down version of Outlook and includes basic messaging features: sending and retrieving mail, sorting messages, and so on. It arranges your information by using three separate panes to organize information. However, it doesn't include as many scheduling and calendar features as does Outlook.

We'll cover the nuts and bolts of using this helpful software in Chapters 6 and 7.

SOFTWARE TO MAKE E-MAIL SECURE

Sending e-mail is akin to sending an electronic postcard—almost anyone along the way can read it. Additionally, people can easily forward your messages to others, making e-mail anything but private or secure. To help out, a company called SafeMessage has developed a more secure way of sending e-mail. This system involves sending messages by using **encryption** and untraceable point-to-point messaging. (We'll talk more about encryption in Chapter 7; for now, it's enough to understand that it scrambles the message in a way that others can't read it unless they have a key to decode the message.) Additionally, SafeMessage doesn't leave copies of the message on mail servers, and sends you immediate confirmation that your message has been delivered. Best of all, delivered messages self-destruct after a preset amount of time, such as four days. SafeMessage even overwrites the area on the hard drive in which the file was located to prevent anyone from viewing the message. You can find out more about this product on the company's Web site (*www.safemessage.com*).

The bottom line? Choose the best e-mail client software for your needs and your pocketbook, learn how to use it well, and then enjoy the ease and speed of this form of communication.

UNDERSTAND THE BASICS OF WEB-BASED MAIL SERVICES

Instead of using client software in conjunction with SMTP and POP3 mail servers, you can set up a Web-based e-mail account. To use Web-based e-mail, you must first create an account with the service. You can then use your Web browser to view, send, and receive e-mail messages. In contrast to most mail client software, the storage location for Web-based mail is on the Web site's server, not your personal computer.

There are some advantages to using a Web browser for accessing e-mail. For starters, services like this are usually free (although, as you'll see in a minute, "free" e-mail typically has strings attached). Additionally, if you have a Web-based account, you can access your mail from anywhere in the world—all you need is an Internet connection and a browser. This is a definite advantage for travelers: As long as you can find a library or Internet café on the road, you can pick up your mail. Web-based accounts also provide you with an alternative address to give out if you want to protect the privacy of your client e-mail account. For example, when you're filling out online forms, it's strongly recommended that you *not* give out your regular e-mail address, or else you'll soon be "spammed" and junk mail will fill your mailbox. Using an alternative, Web-based account protects your main e-mail account from becoming overloaded with spam. . . and if the alternative mail account becomes too cluttered, you can just shut it down and get a new one.

Unfortunately, most Web-based e-mail services are bogged down by advertising or impose strict limitations on the features and service you can use. To use the premium services (such as more storage space in your mailbox), you must pay an additional fee. To show you the ups and downs of Web-based e-mail, we'll go through examples of some of the most popular services available.

MICROSOFT MSN HOTMAIL

Microsoft has offered Hotmail at no charge for a number of years. This service boasts a large number of users. Hotmail includes filtering against spam and anti-virus features. Additionally, Hotmail works with Outlook, which opens the door to other possibilities, such as displaying your Hotmail messages from

within Outlook or using Outlook to retrieve your Hotmail messages. For example, you might have Outlook at work, but want to use Hotmail to send and retrieve personal messages.

What is the downside of this service? There's a limit to the space in your mailbox of 2MB (or megabytes); exceed this amount and you'll find that Hotmail will automatically delete the oldest messages. Additionally, some people find the way Microsoft collects personal information to set up the mail account disconcerting. Another drawback is that you must log in at least once every 30 days or your account will be deactivated. Finally, the service continually badgers you to sign up for the paid service ($20/year), which includes more storage for messages and doesn't require you to log in periodically. You can find out more about Hotmail by visiting its Web site (*www.hotmail.com*).

YAHOO! MAIL

Yahoo! Mail is another free, popular Web-based service (refer to Figure 5.2). It provides 4MB of space, spam filters, virus checking, and other helpful features. Like most other Web-based services, Yahoo! Mail steers free users toward a paid service. Additionally, because it's underwritten by advertising, you'll feel like there's a billboard company on your computer. Despite these drawbacks, Yahoo! Mail is one of the most well liked Web-based e-mail services. You can find out more about Yahoo! Mail at *mail.yahoo.com*.

MAIL.COM

Mail.com provides a free Web-based service that includes a spacious, 10MB mailbox, which is much larger than most of the other Web-based services. This is probably enough space for most people unless you attach a lot of files. Another advantage is that you can choose from a wide variety of domain names, such as *consultant.com*, *usa.com*, *doglover.com* or *playful.com*.

However, if you sign up for this service, be prepared to be bombarded by advertising. Additionally, the Web pages display distressingly slowly due to the amount of advertising they include. And, like most other Web-based e-mail services, Mail.com pushes you toward its "premium," paid-for service. You can find out more about this mail service at *www.mail.com*.

MAIL2WEB

Mail2Web is a free, Web-based service that allows you to access your POP3 or IMAP accounts from the Web. Think of Mail2Web as a window to your existing e-mail client accounts.

For example, imagine that you're traveling and need to pull up mail that's normally sent to your Outlook Express mailbox (a POP3 account). Some of the Web-based mail services allow you to retrieve these messages, but charge

ON THE HORIZON

Many once-free Web-based e-mail services are now charging—at least if you want the premium features, such as the capability to retrieve messages from your POP3 mailbox or more storage space. It's possible that the time will come with these "free" services are so overladen with advertising that many users will abandon them in favor of using paid-for services.

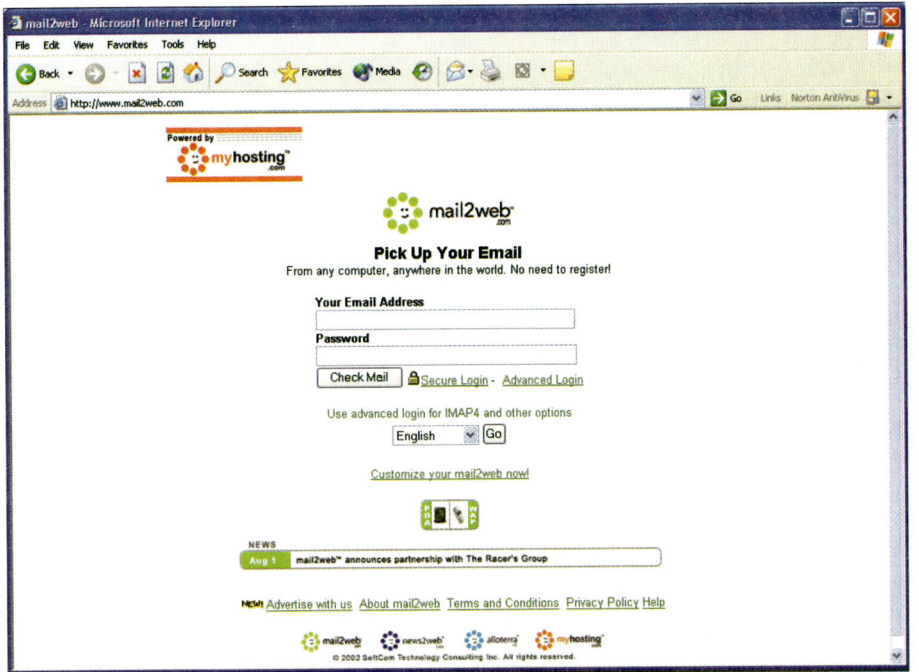

Figure 5.8.
Mail2Web is a free, Web-based service that allows you to access your regular POP3 or IMAP account.

for the service. One option is to use a site such as Mail2Web to view and reply to your messages.

Mail2Web doesn't download your messages; they remain on the server unless you specifically delete them or use your regular e-mail client to download them on your machine.

To access your account, you enter your e-mail address and password on Mail2Web's home page (*www.mail2web.com*). This allows you to view and respond to messages (see Figure 5.8).

So take a look at your options regarding e-mail, and carefully weigh the pros and cons for each service or software product. By understanding the basics of how e-mail is transmitted and what types of client software and mail services are available, you can better manage your electronic communications.

Besides Mail2Web, you can retrieve mail from a POP3 server via Web sites such as *www.worldroom.com*. The costs of operating these sites are usually underwritten by advertising.

Don't Forget...

- E-mail is one of the most important applications on the Internet.
- There are certain rules, or protocols, for the way mail is sent through the Internet so that it reaches the correct destination.
- You can use e-mail client software or a Web-based service to send or receive e-mail.
- A SMTP mail server typically handles outgoing mail.
- POP3 and IMAP mail servers manage incoming mail.
- A mail address is unique and is typically configured as username@domainname.
- The most well-known e-mail client programs include Outlook, Outlook Express, Pegasus, and Eudora.
- The most popular Web-based mail services include Hotmail, Yahoo! Mail, Mail.com, and Mail2Web.

Check This Out

MULTIPLE CHOICE

1. What does a SMTP mail server do?
   a. It manages incoming e-mail.
   b. It helps you to retrieve messages from a Web-based e-mail service.
   c. It sends e-mail.
   d. None of the above
2. What is an advantage of using a Web-based e-mail service?
   a. It usually provides you with ad-free e-mail.
   b. It's faster than e-mail client software at displaying messages.
   c. You can view and respond to messages from any location, as long as you have Internet access.
   d. All of the above are advantages.
3. What is an advantage of using e-mail client software over using a Web-based e-mail service?
   a. You can devote as much space on your hard drive as is necessary for storing messages.
   b. It usually provides you with ad-free e-mail.
   c. It typically includes many more features for handling your e-mail than does a Web-based e-mail service.
   d. All of the above are advantages.
4. Which of the following is a Web-based e-mail service?
   a. Yahoo! Mail
   b. Outlook
   c. Outlook Express
   d. Eudora
5. What is one of e-mail's advantages?
   a. Speed of communication
   b. Free/low cost after the initial purchase of equipment and Internet access
   c. It helps you to control your time.
   d. All of the above

MATCHING

a. mail client
b. Hotmail
c. Mail2Web
d. MIME
e. SMTP
f. POP3
g. Pegasus
h. Outlook Express
i. Outlook
j. mail server

1. A slimmed-down version of Outlook
2. An e-mail client that also includes robust scheduling and appointment tools
3. The protocol used for sending e-mail
4. The protocol used for retrieving and storing e-mail
5. A full-featured e-mail client developed by David Harris and distributed at no charge
6. The protocol used for attaching graphic and other large files to an e-mail message
7. The type of software loaded on an individual system that you can use to access POP3 or IMAP accounts
8. An Internet-based service that allows you to retrieve e-mail from existing POP3 and IMAP accounts
9. A popular Web-based e-mail service, sponsored by Microsoft
10. A computer that facilitates sending and receiving e-mail

Real Life

1. Research each Web-based e-mail service listed in this chapter to find out which features they include. Develop a table that compares the various e-mail services and then write a short report summarizing your findings. (Alternately, develop a PowerPoint presentation that explains the pros and cons of Web-based e-mail services and then present it to the class.)
2. Use the Web to research information about free e-mail services offered on the Internet. Also find reviews regarding Web-based e-mail services in online magazines. (Hint: Use `free e-mail` as your search text.) Using your research as a basis, compare these services with those listed in the chapter. Present your findings to the class or share them with a small group.

I Spy: Privacy and Security Concerns

1. Use the Internet to research the following issues and then discuss them with others in your class: What are the privacy issues surrounding the use of Web-based e-mail? Do you think Web-based, free e-mail services collect data as you set up an account and share it with companies that market various services and products? If so, is this a legitimate use by the e-mail services?

2. Some employers routinely monitor their employees' e-mail. Use the Internet to find out more about e-mail monitoring by employers and by the United States government. Discuss how surveillance by companies or the government can take away individuals' freedoms.

CHAPTER 6

E-MAIL BASICS

Key Terms

When you finish this chapter, you'll understand the following terms:

Address Book
attachment
header section
Plain Text
Rich Text
stationery

Chapter Objectives

After you complete this chapter, you'll

- Explore the Outlook Express Application Window
- Know How to Create an E-Mail Message
- Be Able to Format a Message
- Know How to Use Attachments
- Understand How to Receive a Message
- Know How to Reply to a Message and Forward a Message

The Big Picture

You already know that e-mail is one of the most important—if not *the* most important—Internet applications. In Chapter 5, Mail and Messaging Software Overview, we examined some of the most common e-mail client software and Web-based services. Now we'll turn our attention to using a specific program: Microsoft's Outlook Express 6.0. This common program comes packaged with Internet Explorer 6.0, so it's likely that you'll have access to it.

In this chapter, we'll guide you through the basics of working with this program, using step-by-step instructions. But even if you don't have this software, don't worry. You'll find that the principles used to work with almost all e-mail programs are similar. Because of this, you should be able to use the knowledge you gain working with Outlook Express to work with a variety of e-mail clients.

Window on the Web

Outlook Express provides a one-stop location for sending, receiving, and managing your e-mail messages. It does this by providing several folders, or categories, to keep your messages organized (see Figure 6.1).

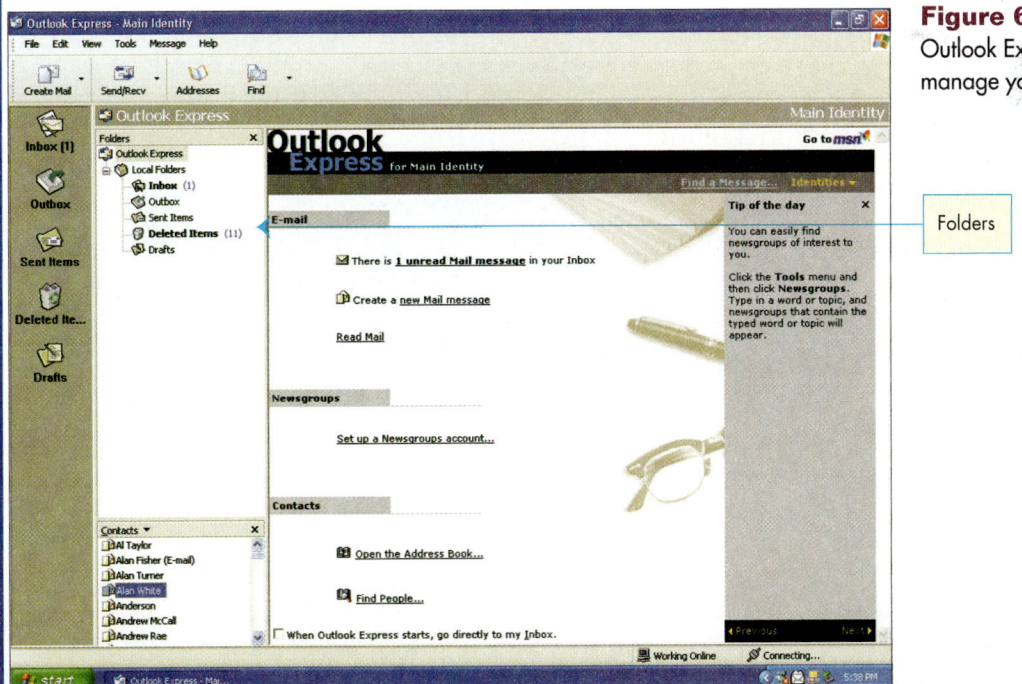

Figure 6.1.
Outlook Express helps you manage your e-mail.

Let's spend a few minutes learning the basics of e-mail, using Outlook Express as a springboard.

INSIDE TRACK

In Chapter 5, we discussed some of the common courtesies you should use when using e-mail. One of those courtesies involves checking your messages for spelling and typographical errors before sending them. To do this, choose Tools, Spelling in the message window. Any misspelled or mistyped words will be highlighted and a Spelling dialog box will display, offering you a variety of options for resolving the errors (such as to ignore the problem or correct it).

EXPLORE THE OUTLOOK EXPRESS APPLICATION WINDOW

The e-mail program interface provides a way for you, the user, to interact with the program. Outwardly, the Outlook Express program appears in an application window, much like other Windows programs. In the following activity, you'll learn the basics of starting Outlook Express and then take a quick tour of the main elements it includes.

ACTIVITY 6.1
To Explore the Outlook Express Application Window

① Click the Windows XP Start button.
   The Start menu displays (see Figure 6.2). (If you don't have this version of Windows and your screen looks slightly different, don't worry. The steps for launching Outlook Express are very similar, no matter which version of Windows you have.)

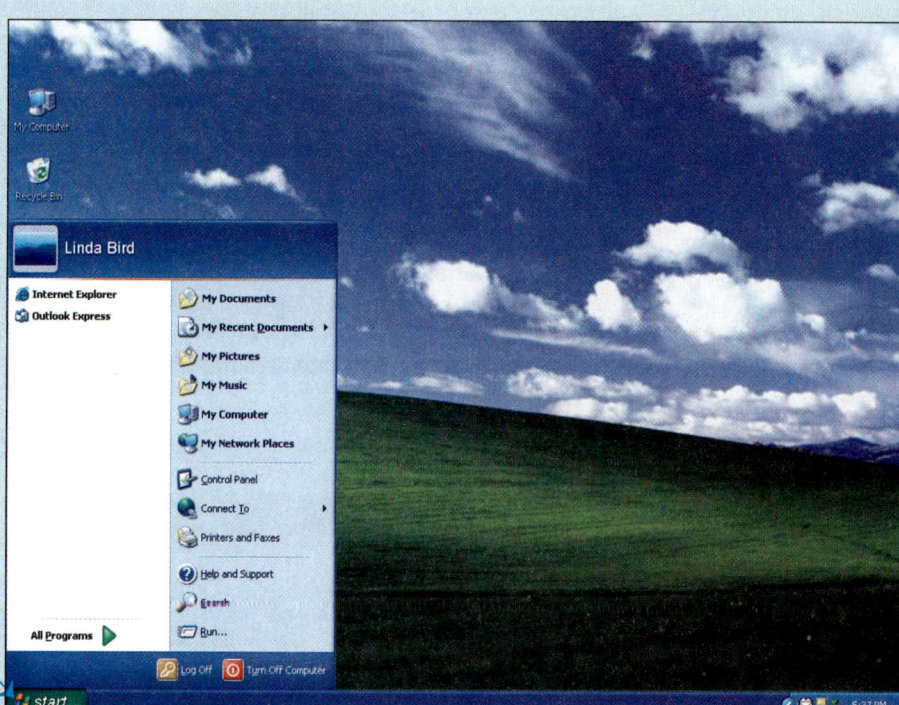

Figure 6.2.
You can launch Outlook Express via the Start menu.

Click the Start button to display this menu

② Click All Programs and then click Outlook Express on the All Programs list. (It's also possible that there is a shortcut icon on the desktop; if so, you can double-click the icon to start the program.)
   Either way you launch the program, Outlook Express displays in a window (refer to Figure 6.1).

> **HEADS UP!** If the Outlook Express application window on your computer doesn't appear the same as that shown in Figure 6.1, it's possible that some of the default elements that normally display in the Outlook Express window have been turned off. You'll learn in the next few steps how to ensure that your copy of Outlook Express is set up to match the figures in this book.

90   Chapter 6   E-Mail Basics

ACTIVITY 6.1
To Explore the Outlook Express Application Window

③ Click the Inbox folder icon.

Notice that the Outlook Express window includes many elements, including a menu bar, icons, separate window panes, and bars that help you work with the program (see Figure 6.3).

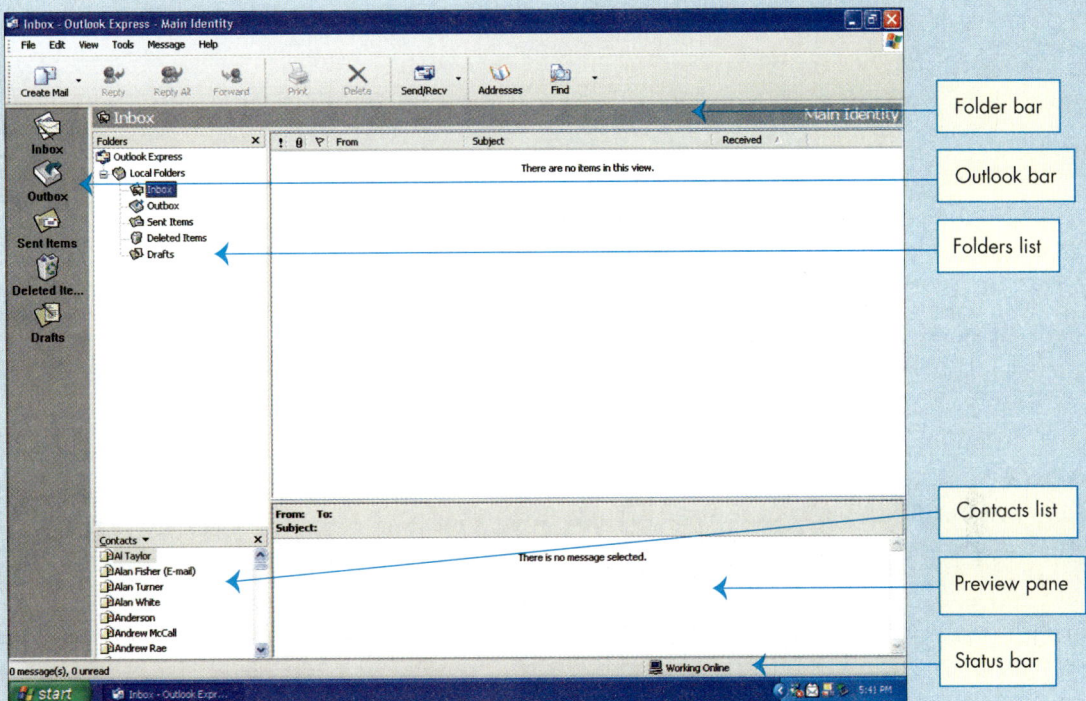

Figure 6.3.
Outlook Express includes several elements designed to help you manage your e-mail messages.

Most e-mail programs have similar features. For example, they universally store incoming messages in an inbox. Now try using a menu and customizing the way the Outlook Express window appears.

④ Click the View menu and then choose Layout.

The Windows Layout Properties dialog box displays (see Figure 6.4).

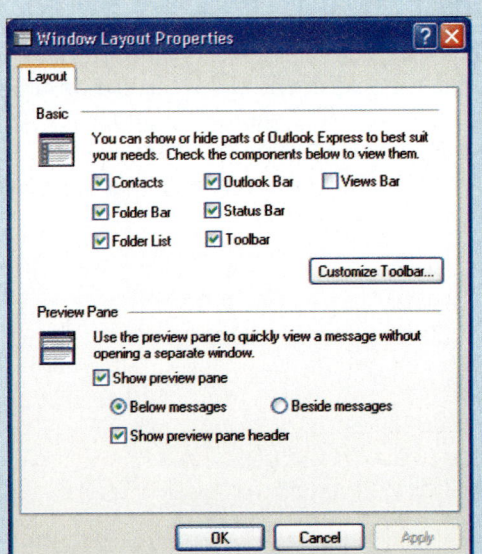

Figure 6.4.
Check or clear boxes to customize the way the Outlook Express window looks.

Explore the Outlook Express Application Window

ACTIVITY 6.1
To Explore the Outlook Express Application Window (Continued)

⑤ Make sure that the settings on your computer match those shown in Figure 6.4 and then click OK.

⑥ Click Outbox on the Folders list.
The messages that have been written but not sent are shown. (It's likely that this folder is empty.)

⑦ Click Inbox on the Folders list.
The contents of the Inbox display. The Inbox stores messages that others have sent you.

⑧ Keep Outlook Express running for the next activity, in which you set up and send an e-mail message.

HEADS UP! Before completing the next activity, you'll need an Outlook Express e-mail account. If you don't currently have an e-mail account (or are unsure whether or not you do), ask your instructor for help.

KNOW HOW TO CREATE AN E-MAIL MESSAGE

Creating an e-mail message is relatively straightforward: You open a new message form, indicate the recipient's address, enter a subject, type the message, and then send it. Of course, you can add a lot of bells and whistles by formatting the message differently or adding more recipients, but in its simplest form, that's all there is to it. Better yet, once you know how to create an e-mail message in Outlook Express, chances are good that you can use the knowledge you've gained to work with other e-mail programs as well.

ACTIVITY 6.2
To Create an E-mail Message

① In Outlook Express, click the Create Mail button.
A new message window opens and is layered on top of the main Outlook Express window. Notice that the message window includes text boxes that you can use to enter the recipient's e-mail address and what the message is about—the subject. The text boxes above the message area are collectively referred to as the **header section**, or simply **headers**. The window also includes a message area, a menu bar, and a toolbar (see Figure 6.5).

92 Chapter 6 E-Mail Basics

ACTIVITY 6.2
To Create an E-mail Message

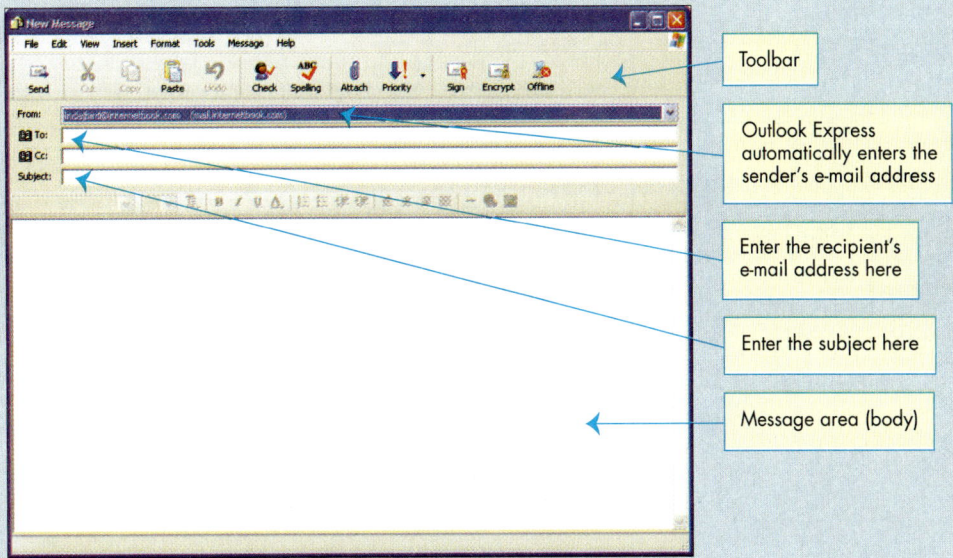

Figure 6.5.
Every new e-mail message is set up essentially the same.

HEADS UP! If the New Message window is too small for you to easily view the elements shown in Figure 6.5 or type your message, resize the window by dragging any of its borders.

INSIDE TRACK

If you're addressing multiple recipients, you can list the main recipient (or multiple recipients) in the To: text box. Alternatively, you can indicate one primary recipient in the To: text box and then place the remainder of the addressees in the carbon copy (Cc:) text box. Finally, you can send a blind carbon copy. This is handy when you want to send a copy of the message to someone, but don't want the other recipients to know that you're doing so. To display the blind carbon copy (Bcc:) box, choose View, All Headers in the message window.

❷ Click in the To: text box; then type an e-mail address for a friend (refer to Figure 6.5).

You can enter as many recipients in the To: text box as you want by typing a semicolon between each to separate them.

❸ Click in the Subject text box and then type Pizza.

This indicates the main topic for the message. It's important to designate a subject because doing so clarifies communication and encourages the recipient(s) to read the message. As you enter a topic in the *Subject* text box, the new Subject topic automatically replaces the *New Message* name on the title bar of the message window.

❹ Click in the message area and then type Hi. Don't forget to order pizza for the party tomorrow night!

Your message should appear similar to that shown in Figure 6.6.

ACTIVITY 6.2
To Create an E-mail Message (Continued)

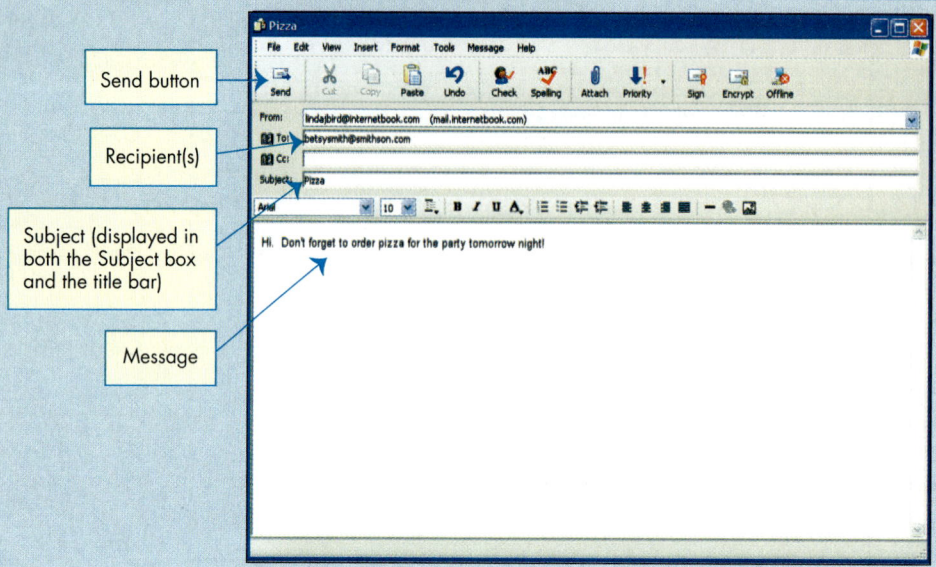

Figure 6.6.
Your completed e-mail message.

 ⑤ Click the Send button in the message window (on the Standard toolbar).

The message window closes and your e-mail is placed in Outlook Express' Outbox folder. Depending on how your program is set up, the message is either sent out immediately or when you actually click the Send/Recv button in the main Outlook Express window.

 **HEADS UP!** A Send Mail message box may appear when you click the Send button. If so, click OK to close it and then continue with the next step.

 ⑥ Connect to the Internet, if necessary, and then click the Send/Recv button on the toolbar.

The message is sent to the recipient.

⑦ Keep Outlook Express open for the next activity.

 INSIDE TRACK

You can also click the To button to open the Address Book; then double-click a recipient on the list. This is a more accurate way of entering recipient's addresses if the person is already listed in the Address Book. (An **Address Book** is a list of names and e-mail addresses that you can develop in Outlook Express or other e-mail programs. You'll learn more about how to work with the Address Book in Chapter 7, Beyond the Basics, Using E-Mail Safely and Effectively.)

94 Chapter 6 E-Mail Basics

BE ABLE TO FORMAT A MESSAGE

Tired of sending dull, listless-looking messages? You can easily apply formatting to text by using features such as bold and italic. Additionally, you can add **stationery**—a background pattern that emulates paper stationery—to your e-mail messages.

Outlook Express provides two main formatting options: Rich Text (HTML) and Plain Text. **Rich Text** is a universal way of formatting text originally designed by Microsoft that allows for formatting such as bold and italic. **Plain Text** is data that uses the American Standard Code for Information Interchange (ASCII). (ASCII uses a code that represents English characters as numbers.) Plain Text can be read and used by computers that use a variety of platforms, which makes it a universal way of exchanging data. However, it doesn't support formatting.

When you use Rich Text (HTML), you can apply formatting and backgrounds; when you use Plain Text, you can't. By default, the Rich Text option is chosen in Outlook Express, but you can switch between the options on the Format menu.

One caution: Messages that include formatting can become large in size and consequently take longer to send or receive. However, when you need to emphasize certain information, it's appropriate to add formatting to your message. In this activity, you'll experiment with some of the types of formatting you can use in an e-mail message.

INSIDE TRACK

In some e-mail client programs, there are more than two main formatting types. For example, in Outlook, you can use Plain Text, Rich Text, or HTML formatting. Outlook Express, on the other hand, combines Rich Text with HTML.

ACTIVITY 6.3
To Format a Message

① In Outlook Express, click the Create Mail button.

By default, Rich Text (HTML) formatting is turned on. However, to make sure that this setting hasn't been changed on your computer, we'll choose it from the Format menu. This ensures that you can easily follow the steps in this activity.

② In the message window, choose Format, Rich Text (HTML).

A toolbar with formatting options displays in your message window (see Figure 6.7).

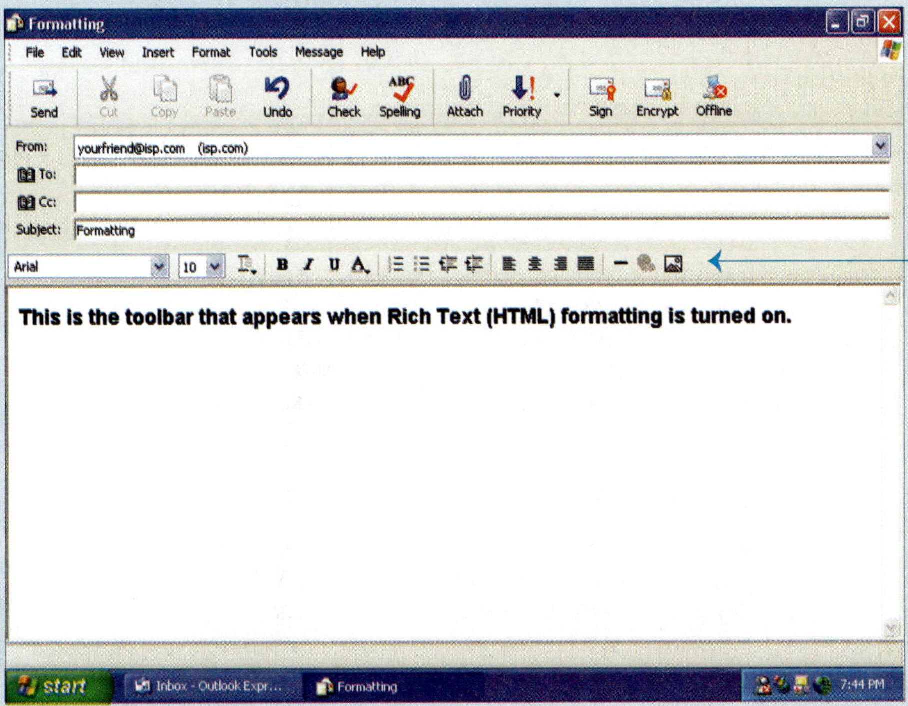

Figure 6.7.
Use various options to format your message.

ACTIVITY 6.3
To Format a Message (Continued)

3. Create an identical message to the one you developed in the previous activity (*Pizza*) and address it to a friend (or to yourself).

4. Click and drag over *Don't Forget* in the message area to select it; then click the Bold button on the formatting bar.

> **HEADS UP!** If the formatting bar isn't displayed, choose View, Toolbars, Formatting Bar from the message window's menu bar.

5. Choose Edit, Select All from the menu to select the entire message.

6. On the formatting bar, click the Font Size drop-down list arrow and then choose 18.
   All the text in your message is formatted using an 18-point font. Now try adding stationery.

7. Click outside the text to deselect it.

8. Point to Apply Stationery on the Format menu.
   A listing of available backgrounds is shown.

9. Click Clear Day on the displayed submenu.
   The stationery is applied to your message (see Figure 6.8).

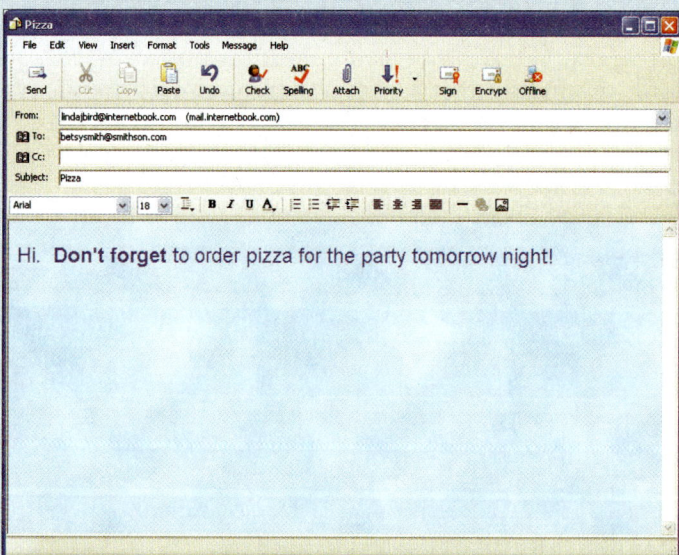

Figure 6.8.
Outlook Express includes several options for formatting your e-mail message, including adding background stationery.

Now take a look at what happens when you switch to Plain Text formatting.

10. Choose Format, Plain Text.
    A message displays, warning that you'll lose all the formatting you've added to the message.

ACTIVITY 6.3
To Format a Message

HEADS UP! It's possible that someone has turned off the setting that controls this message box; if so, the message does not display and the formatting is automatically removed.

⑪ Choose OK in the message box.
   The formatting is removed from the message.

⑫ Click the Send button in the message window; then click Send/Recv in the main Outlook Express window.
   When you click the Send button in the message window, the message is placed in the Outbox. When you click the Send/Recv button in the main window, the message is sent to the recipient(s) you indicated.

⑬ Keep Outlook Express open for the next activity, in which you attach a file to a message.

INSIDE TRACK

Retyping a similar message to multiple recipients can be tedious at best. Fortunately, you can copy and paste information—including text, addresses, or graphics—in Outlook Express by using the same type of methods you do for any e-mail program. To do so, select the text or object you want to copy and then press Ctrl+C. Click in the location where you want to paste the data (such as in another message) and then press Ctrl+V.

KNOW HOW TO USE ATTACHMENTS

Outlook Express, like most other current e-mail clients, allows you to attach files to an e-mail message. For example, you might want to send budget figures to a remote office, a report to your boss, or even a photo of a new puppy to your best friend. A file that is electronically linked and sent with an e-mail message is called an **attachment**. Almost any type of file can be attached to a message, including databases, graphics, spreadsheets, or text files. Just keep in mind that the size of the attached file will affect the speed at which the message is sent or received; larger attachments take longer to transmit than do smaller ones.

Outlook Express includes a straightforward method of attaching files to your messages. Let's take a look.

ALERT!

Keep in mind that e-mail is not 100 percent secure. Unless you use encryption, crackers or others can potentially open and view your messages.

ACTIVITY 6.4
To Use Attachments

1. In Outlook Express, choose Message, New Message from the menu.
   A new message window displays.

2. Create an e-mail message, using Figure 6.9 as a guide. Address the message to someone you know, but don't send the message yet.

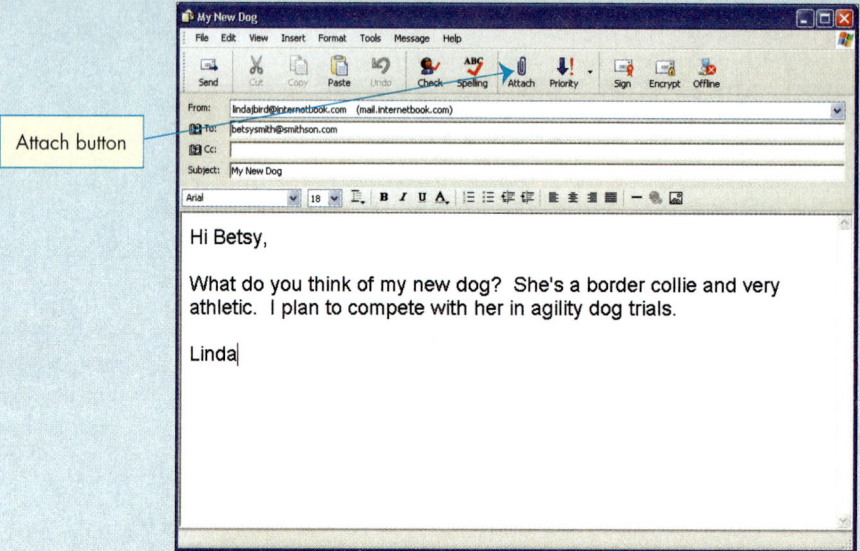

Figure 6.9.
Create this e-mail message.

3. Click the Attach button at the top of the message window (refer to Figure 6.9).
   The Insert Attachment dialog box displays (see Figure 6.10). You can use this dialog box to locate and select the file you want to attach.

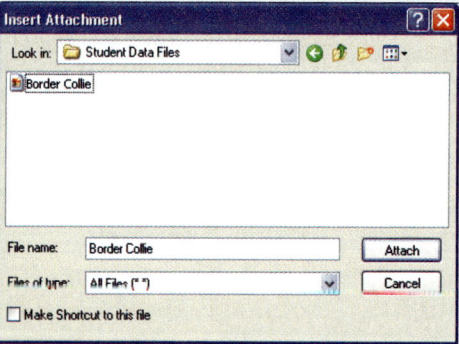

Figure 6.10.
You can attach files to an e-mail message.

4. Navigate to the drive and folder where the student data files for this book are located; then click the *Border Collie* file.

5. Press ↵Enter (or click the Attach button in the Insert Attachment dialog box).
   The Insert Attachment dialog box closes, and the attached file appears in the Attach text box (immediately below the Subject text box).
   Now indicate to the recipient that this message is extra-important. You can do this by adding a priority icon.

6. Click the Priority button's drop-down list arrow and then choose High Priority from the list.

ACTIVITY 6.4
To Use Attachments

A high priority icon appears above the message headers. Your completed message should appear and look similar to the one shown in Figure 6.11.

> **ALERT!**
> Never open a file attached to an e-mail message without first scanning it with an anti-virus program. This is especially true if you don't recognize the person who sent the message. However, even when you *do* know the sender, you should still scan the file before opening it because some viruses work by sending a copy of the malicious code to all the people in the Address Book of a computer they've infected. So your friend or acquaintance may be an unwilling partner in passing along a computer virus and not even know it. Fortunately, most colleges and business networks automatically scan attachments.

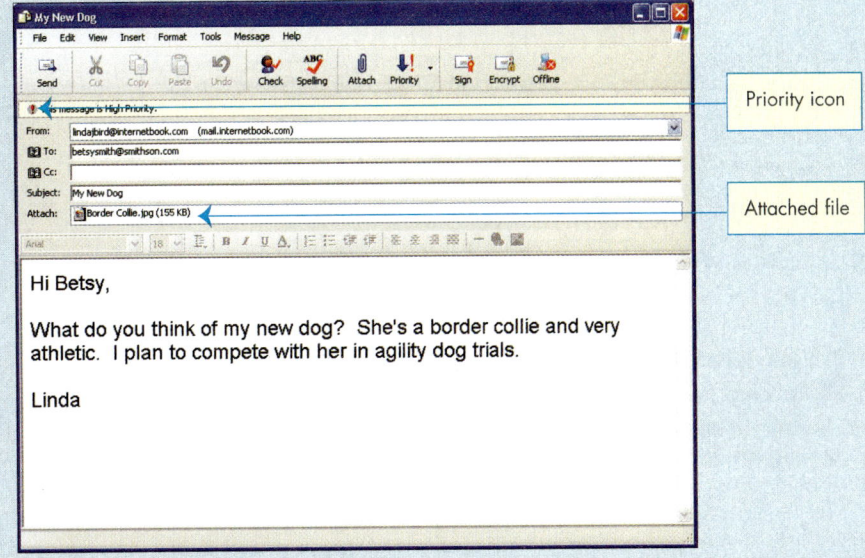

Figure 6.11.
You can attach files to e-mail and indicate the relative importance of the message.

> **HEADS UP!** Be careful not to indicate that your messages are high priority too often, or else people will start to ignore messages that are truly important.

 ⑦ When your message appears similar to that shown in Figure 6.11, click the Send button in the message window.

 ⑧ Choose Send/Recv in the main Outlook Express window.

⑨ Keep Outlook Express open for the next activity, in which you receive e-mail.

UNDERSTAND HOW TO RECEIVE A MESSAGE

Now that you're familiar with how to create, format, and send an e-mail message, you can see how easy it is to receive one.

ACTIVITY 6.5
To Receive a Message

① Ask a friend to send you a message similar to the one you developed in the previous activity.

 ② In the main window of Outlook Express, click the Send/Recv button.
A copy of the message appears in the Inbox. New messages are easy to spot because they appear using bold text (see Figure 6.12).

ACTIVITY 6.5
To Receive a Message (Continued)

INSIDE TRACK

If you leave a new message in the Inbox selected for at least five seconds, Outlook Express assumes that you've read the message, and the message no long appears in bold print. However, if you don't want Outlook Express to turn off the boldface so soon, you can change this setting. To do so, choose Tools, Options to display the Options dialog box. Click the Read tab. In the Reading Messages section, change the number of seconds in the *Mark message read after displaying for 5 seconds* box. Alternately, clear the check box. After you do so, Outlook Express won't remove the bold from new messages unless you actually open the message in its own window.

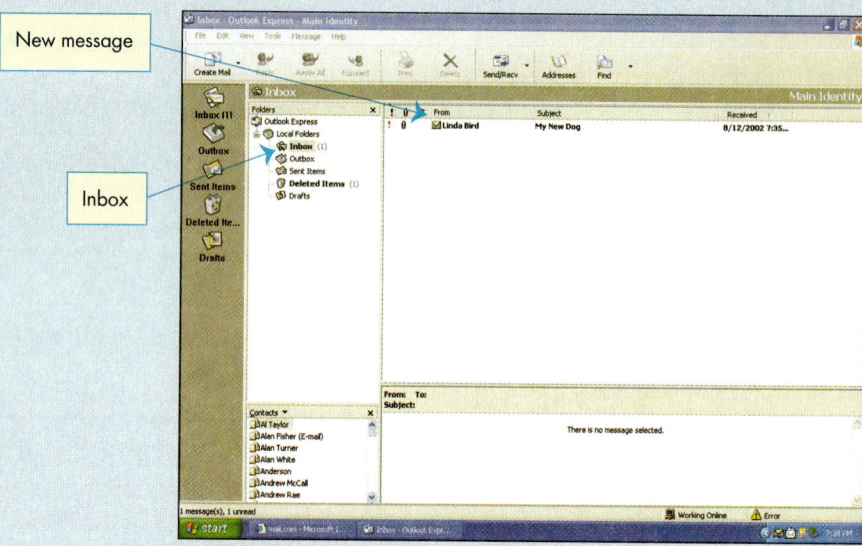

Figure 6.12.
Messages that you receive appear in the Inbox.

INSIDE TRACK

You can usually scan an attachment for viruses by first saving it and then scanning it. To do this, right-click the attached file and then choose Save As from the shortcut menu. In the Save Attachment dialog box, designate a location (such as the desktop) for the saved file. Next, right-click the saved file on the desktop or in a dialog box; then choose Scan for Viruses (or a similar command).

③ Double-click the new message (*My New Dog*) on the message list.
The message appears in a window, making it easier for you to read it.

④ If you have virus-checking software, use it to scan the attached file.

⑤ Double-click the attached file.
The file opens and the program responsible for displaying it is launched. For example, the Windows Picture and Fax viewer in Windows XP is used to display graphic files. In the same way, double-clicking an attached Excel worksheet causes Excel to be launched.

⑥ Close the window with the graphic.

⑦ Keep Outlook Express and the message window open for the next activity, in which you reply to the message.

INSIDE TRACK

You can view, reply to, or forward a message, even without opening the message window. To do this, single-click the message in the Inbox. A preview of the message appears in the Preview Pane below. With the message selected in the Inbox, you can click the Reply or Forward button. Also, keep in mind that clicking Reply sends an answer to only those listed in the From text box. If you want to simultaneously reply to everyone listed in the Cc: and Bcc: text boxes as well, you should click the Reply All button. This sends the message to everyone who originally received the message.

KNOW HOW TO REPLY TO A MESSAGE AND FORWARD A MESSAGE

Whenever you receive a message, you can reply to it with a click or two of the mouse. The ease with which you can reply to a message is one of the things that make e-mail so attractive and popular. In this activity, you'll send a quick reply to the message you received. You'll also see how to forward the same message to other recipients. (Although you wouldn't reply to messages you sent to yourself in real life, of course, going through the steps lets you practice for when you *really* want to answer messages.)

100 Chapter 6 E-Mail Basics

ACTIVITY 6.6
To Reply to a Message and Forward a Message

① In the open message window, click the Reply button.
   The message window appears, but this time with the sender's name in the To: text box. Additionally, a space appears that the top of the message area so that you can type a reply.

② Click in the blank area at the top of the message area and then type `Good looking dog!`

③ In the message window, click the Send button.

④ Click Send/Recv in the main Outlook Express window.
   You have sent a reply to a message; now try forwarding the message to another person.

⑤ Open the message window for the *My New Dog* message and then click the Forward button.
   The message window appears with a blank To: text box, which enables you to choose the recipient to whom you want to forward the message.

⑥ Enter the e-mail address for a friend (or your instructor) in the To: text box and then click Send.

⑦ Click Send/Recv in the main Outlook Express window.
   The message has been sent to the recipient's mail server.

⑧ Close any open windows, including Outlook Express.

Don't Forget...

- The Outlook Express application window includes a number of elements that help you create, send, organize, receive, and forward e-mail messages.
- Outlook Express provides a header section that includes text boxes for the sender, recipient(s), subject, and attachments.
- You can use commands in Outlook Express to create, format, and send an e-mail message. Fortunately, these processes are similar no matter what e-mail client program you eventually use.
- You can attach files, such as pictures or reports, to an e-mail message so that they are transported to the recipient at the same time as the message.

Check This Out

MULTIPLE CHOICE

1. What is considered to be the most significant application on the Internet?
   a. Games
   b. E-mail
   c. Chat rooms
   d. None of the above
2. Which of the following folders is included in Outlook Express?
   a. Inbox
   b. Outbox
   c. Sent Items
   d. All of the above
3. What is a file called that is linked to an e-mail message and sent to the recipient(s) along with the message?
   a. Web-based file
   b. Attachment
   c. Sent item
   d. Techfile
4. Which of the following is the best practice to follow when receiving an e-mail attachment—even from a person you know?
   a. Open the file immediately.
   b. Save the file to a disk; then open it later so the virus' payload will expire.
   c. Save the file to a disk, scan it with anti-virus software, and then open it.
   d. None of the above
5. Which of the following should you choose if you want to apply formatting, such as bold, italic, or stationery, to your message?
   a. Rich Text
   b. Plain Text
   c. No Text
   d. None of the above

MATCHING

a. blind carbon copy
b. Address Book
c. replying
d. virus
e. forwarding
f. anti-virus
g. Inbox
h. header section
i. Outbox
j. Rich Text

1. A file containing malicious code that can be attached to an e-mail message
2. A list of names and e-mail addresses that you can develop in Outlook Express or other e-mail programs
3. The folder that lists messages you've received from others
4. The type of software that you can use to check for dangerous e-mail attachments
5. The folder that shows messages that are ready to be sent
6. A response to an e-mail message that sends the message to a person other than the original recipient(s)
7. Responding to the original sender of an e-mail message
8. The area at the top of a message window that includes text boxes for the recipient and subject
9. A setting that allows you to use stationery and other formatting in an Outlook Express message
10. Sending a message to a person in a way that the other recipients don't know that the person is also receiving the message

Real Life

1. Spend a few minutes familiarizing yourself with Outlook Express' features. To do this, open Outlook Express and then choose Help, Contents and Index. If necessary, click the Show button (at the top of the window) and then click the Contents tab. Click each of the topics listed and then read the associated information. Practice using each feature you research. Create an outline (or PowerPoint presentation) that shows the basics of working with Outlook Express. Finally, use the outline or presentation to teach another person how to use an e-mail program.

2. Send several sample (test) e-mail messages (both with and without formatting) to a friend (both with and without attached files of various kinds). Ask your friend to reply to your messages. When you receive the replies, forward the message(s) to another recipient. Also, ask a student or friend to send you messages with attachments. Practice scanning the attachments for viruses before opening them.

I Spy: Privacy and Security Concerns

1. Use the Web to find out how viruses can be sent as e-mail attachments. You can use a search engine to find sites that cover this information or go to the Web sites for well-known anti-virus programs, such as McAfee (*www.mcafee.com*) or Symantec (*www.symantec.com*). Use the knowledge you gain to develop a prevention and contingency plan for small businesses that they can use to prevent infection from e-mail attachments.
2. Interview several students and instructors at your school to see if/when they have received e-mail with virus-laden attachments. Find out if they had anti-virus software installed on their system at the time and how effective the software was at preventing damage to their computer from the virus. If they didn't have anti-virus software installed, how did the virus affect their computer? What steps did they subsequently need to take to eliminate the virus and correct any damage to the computer? Finally, develop a chart or presentation that shows your findings and then present it to a small group or to your entire class.

CHAPTER 7

BEYOND THE BASICS: USING E-MAIL SAFELY AND EFFECTIVELY

Chapter Objectives

After you complete this chapter, you'll

- Have Explored the Advanced Options in Outlook Express
- Know How to Use the Address Book
- Know How to Find E-Mail Addresses and Contact Information
- Know How to Avoid Viruses and Virus Hoaxes
- Know How to Avoid Spam
- Understand about E-Mail Privacy in the Workplace

Key Terms

When you finish this chapter, you'll understand the following terms:

- blacklist
- contact
- directory service
- distribution list
- executable file
- workplace monitoring
- workplace privacy

The Big Picture

Just when you thought you were getting the hang of using e-mail, you realize that there's more to it than meets the eye. In fact, you begin to hear that there are a number of security and privacy issues surrounding the use of e-mail. You also have a sneaking suspicion that there are some advanced options that you can use to work with it more efficiently.

To use e-mail safely and effectively, it's helpful to understand the issues swirling around it and then know practical steps to take to protect your privacy and the security of your system. In this chapter, we'll go beyond the basics of simply using e-mail by examining how to use Outlook Express's advanced options. Keep in mind that even if you don't have access to Outlook Express, you'll find the features and options discussed in this chapter similar in almost any e-mail client program. We'll then go over ways to avoid spam, hoaxes, and viruses; and then wrap up by delving into some important issues, such as workplace monitoring and privacy.

Window on the Web

Outlook Express has many advanced features to help you work more effectively with e-mail. For example, the program includes options that help you filter your messages so that you aren't deluged with spam. It also includes settings to control the security level on your system (see Figure 7.1). As you work with Outlook Express, keep in mind that any e-mail program worth its salt will also have similar features for protecting your privacy and security.

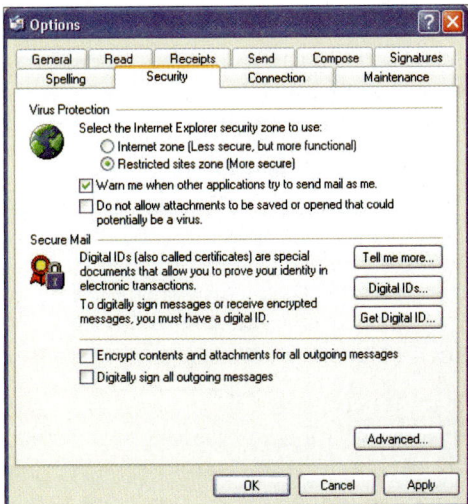

Figure 7.1.
You can change settings in your e-mail client to protect your privacy and security.

Sometimes, an e-mail client program's built-in settings aren't enough to ward off the malicious programming code associated with viruses. Because of this unfortunate fact, it's advisable to install (and keep-up-to-date) anti-virus software. It's also a good idea to set up the anti-virus software to scan your system every day (see Figure 7.2). Additionally, many anti-virus programs can be set to scan e-mail as it arrives on your system. This provides an additional layer of protection against malicious code because the anti-virus software can alert you to problems with individual messages before they can cause damage.

Figure 7.2.
Be safe... use anti-virus software to scan your system daily.

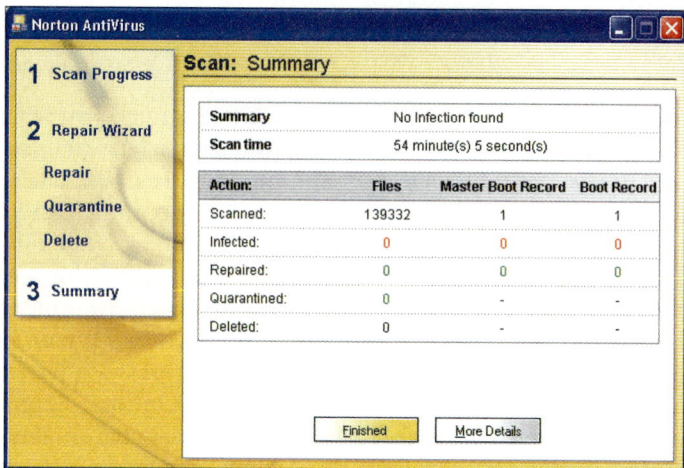

INSIDE TRACK

After awhile, you'll probably discover that you have a great number of e-mail messages in your Inbox. Luckily, the steps for managing your e-mail messages are similar, no matter which e-mail client you use. For example, to delete an old message (or spam), select the message in the Inbox and then press Del. To move a message to another folder, you can usually drag it from the list of messages to a folder in the Folder Bar or the Folder List. Finally, to print a selected message, click the Print button on the Toolbar; then choose Print in the Print dialog box.

EXPLORE THE ADVANCED OPTIONS IN OUTLOOK EXPRESS

You can customize Outlook Express so that it matches the way you work. To facilitate this process, the program includes a number of advanced settings, many of which are accessible through the Options dialog box. In this section, we'll look at some of these advanced features. Although we won't have time to go through *all* the settings that you can modify, we'll point you in the right direction and then show you how to research additional information on your own.

ACTIVITY 7.1
To Explore Advanced Options in Outlook Express

❶ Launch Outlook Express.

❷ Choose Tools, Options.
   The Options dialog box displays. This dialog box includes categorized information on individual pages. Like most other dialog boxes, you can click a tab to display the associated page (see Figure 7.3).

❸ Click the General tab, if necessary.
   The General page of the Options dialog box displays. You can change settings by checking or clearing the appropriate boxes. However, because there are numerous settings you can control in Outlook Express, you need an easy method to find out what each one does.

106 Chapter 7 Beyond the Basics: Using E-Mail Safely and Effectively

ACTIVITY 7.1
To Explore Advanced Options in Outlook Express

INSIDE TRACK

You can change Outlook Express's settings so that you can be notified when a recipient reads an e-mail message that you sent. You do this by requesting an electronic receipt from them. Here's how it works: When the recipient opens your mail, a message box displays and asks the person whether he wants to send a receipt. They can choose *Yes* or *No*.

To modify the program's settings so that a receipt request will accompany every message you send, choose Tools, Options; then click the Receipts tab. Check the box for *Request a read receipt for all sent messages* and then click OK.

④ On the General page of the Options dialog box, click the Help button (refer to Figure 7.3, if necessary); then move the mouse pointer to the middle of the dialog box.
The pointer changes appearance to a Help pointer.

⑤ Click the *Check for new messages every 5 minutes* box.
A ScreenTip displays, showing information related to the setting (see Figure 7.4).

 **HEADS UP!** Depending on your computer's settings, the number of minutes indicated in the *Check for new messages every x minutes* box may vary.

⑥ Move the mouse pointer to a blank area in the Options dialog box (in which there are no commands listed) and click.
The ScreenTip clears.

⑦ Using steps 4–6 as a guide, research several other commands in the Options dialog box.

⑧ When you're finished finding out about the advanced settings in Outlook Express, close the Options dialog box.

⑨ Keep Outlook Express running if you plan to complete additional activities.

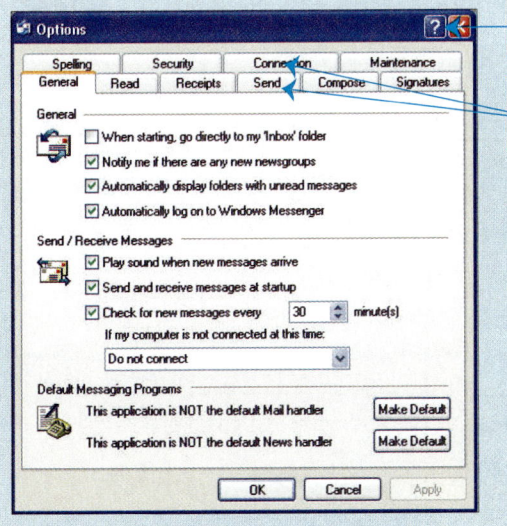

Figure 7.3.
The Options dialog box includes a vast number of settings that you can modify.

Figure 7.4.
Use the Help button to find out more about Outlook settings.

KNOW HOW TO USE THE ADDRESS BOOK

You can manually type in an e-mail recipient's e-mail address for each message you send. However, if you think you will be sending e-mail on a regular basis to that person, it makes sense to add her contact information to Outlook Express's Address Book. The *Address Book* is a file associated with your e-mail client program that is used to organize contact information. The contents of the file are displayed in an organized fashion in the Address Book window. You can add identifying information for a person, which Outlook Express stores as a **contact**. In this activity, you'll learn how to display the Address Book and add contacts to it.

ACTIVITY 7.2
To Use the Address Book

❶ In Outlook Express, click the Addresses button.
   The Address Book window displays. By default, this window lists the people who were previously added as contacts on your computer (see Figure 7.5).

 **HEADS UP!** You might find that your Address Book window displays names differently from the figures in this book. Not to worry. If this is the case, you can change the view settings so that your screen matches that shown in Figure 7.5. To do so, choose View, Details in the Address Book window. Then point the mouse to Sort By on the View menu and choose Name. Choose View, Sort By, Last Name. Finally, choose View, Sort By, Ascending.

❷ Click the New button in the Address Book window, and then choose New Contact on the drop-down list.
   The Name page of the Properties dialog box for the new contact displays (see Figure 7.6).

❸ In the First text box, type Angie; then press Tab twice to move the insertion point to the Last text box.

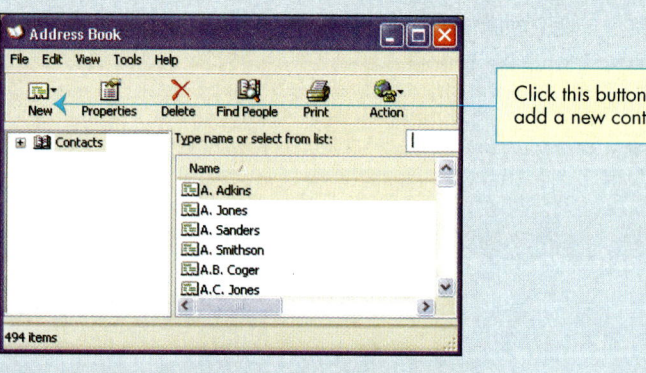

Figure 7.5.
The Address Book helps you organize contacts.

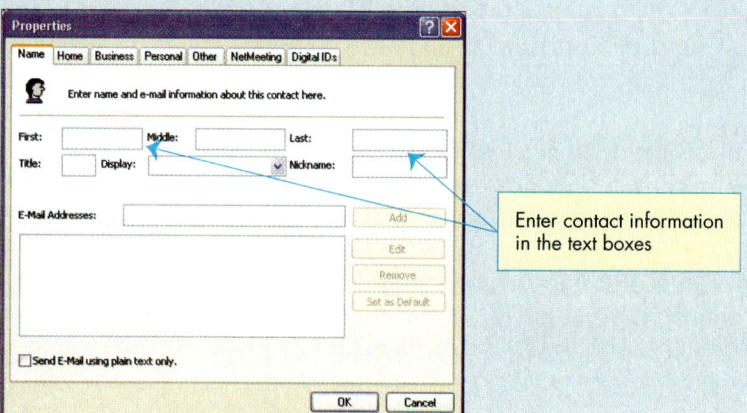

Figure 7.6.
It's easy to add a new contact to your Address Book.

Chapter 7 Beyond the Basics: Using E-Mail Safely and Effectively

ACTIVITY 7.2
To Use the Address Book

④ In the Last text box, type `Carpenter`; then press Tab four times to move the insertion point to the E-Mail Addresses text box.

⑤ In the E-Mail Addresses text box, type `angiecarpenter2003@hotmail.com`.

⑥ Click Add and then click OK to close the Angie Carpenter Properties dialog box.

The contact information for this person is added to the Address Book.

⑦ Using steps 2–6 as a guide, add the following contacts to the Address Book:

```
Andrew Johnson     andrewjohnson1865@yahoo.com
Angel Smith        angelsmith2003@hotmail.com
Betty Perry        bettyperry2003@hotmail.com
Bruce Jackson      brucejackson2003@hotmail.com
```

Now we'll edit one of the entries. This is often necessary when someone's e-mail address changes.

⑧ In the Address Book window, right-click the entry for Angie Carpenter and then choose Properties.

The Properties dialog box for Angie Carpenter displays so that you can make changes.

⑨ Click the Name tab in the Angie Carpenter Properties dialog box.

⑩ Click Edit and then change the e-mail address to `angiecarpenter2004@mymail.com` and press Enter. Click OK.

⑪ Close the Address Book window by clicking the Close button

⑫ Keep Outlook Express running if you plan to complete additional activities.

INSIDE TRACK

If you frequently send messages to a group of people, you can create a distribution list so that you can address them all at once. A **distribution list** is simply a list of names to whom you regularly send the same e-mail messages. To create a distribution list in Outlook Express, choose Tools, Address Book. In the Address Book window, click the New button and then choose New Group. Type a name for the distribution list in the Group Name box. Click the Select Members button. In the Select Group Members dialog box, double-click contact names to add them to the Members list. Finally, click OK (or the close button) in all dialog boxes and windows. To use your distribution list, click the button in any New Message window and then select the group in the Select Recipients dialog box.

KNOW HOW TO FIND E-MAIL ADDRESSES AND CONTACT INFORMATION

After you enter information in your Address Book, it's useful to know various ways to locate the data again. After all, you may eventually have several hundred entries in the Address Book, and scrolling through the list just to locate a person's address isn't always efficient or practical. In this activity, you learn a quick method of finding contact information in Outlook Express.

ACTIVITY 7.3
To Find Addresses and Contact Information

① In Outlook Express, choose Tools, Address Book.
The Address Book window displays.

② In the Address Book window, click the Find People button.
The Find People dialog box displays.

③ Click the Look in drop-down list and then choose Contacts or Address Book (if necessary).
The People page of the dialog box displays (see Figure 7.7). You can enter a contact's name in this dialog box and have Outlook Express locate the associated contact information.

ACTIVITY 7.3
To Find Addresses and Contact Information (Continued)

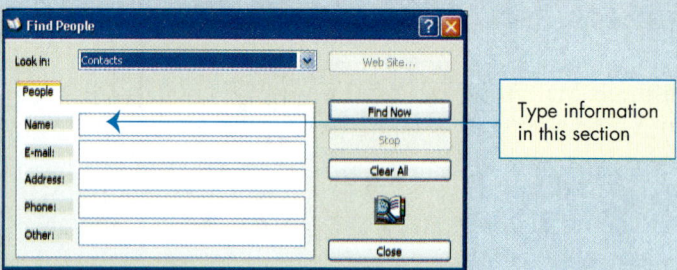

Figure 7.7.
You can use the Find People dialog box to locate a person's e-mail address.

INSIDE TRACK

You can also use options in Outlook Express to locate people on the Internet—not just those in your Address Book. That's because Outlook Express can access Internet directory services. A **directory service** is an Internet-based search tool that helps you locate people based on various criteria. The Outlook Express Address Book comes with built-in access to well-known Internet directory services.

To use a directory service from within Outlook Express, click the Find People button in the Address Book window. In the Find People dialog box, click the *Look in* drop-down list arrow and choose an Internet directory service (such as Bigfoot) from the list. Enter the person's name and then click Find Now.

④ Type Smith in the *Name* text box and then click *Find Now*.
Outlook Express lists all the people on your computer that have Smith as part of their name or e-mail address.

⑤ Double-click the listing for Angel Smith.
The information for this contact is displayed so that you can view or edit it.

⑥ Click Cancel to close the Angel Smith Properties dialog box.

⑦ In the Find People dialog box, right-click the entry for Angel Smith.
A shortcut menu displays.

⑧ Point to Action and then choose Send Mail from the submenu.
A new e-mail message window displays with the recipient's e-mail address already entered. This is a good alternative to use when you need to find a person's address and then send them a message. However, you don't need to actually send the message for now.

⑨ Close the New Message window.

⑩ Close the Find People dialog box and Address Book window.

⑪ Keep Outlook Express running if you plan to complete additional activities.

INSIDE TRACK

In Chapter 2, The Good, the Bad, the Ugly: Uses and Misuses of the Internet, we showed you some of the problems associated with malicious programming code and outlined the differences between viruses, Trojan Horses, and worms. If you need a quick refresher on these terms, take a minute to refer to Chapter 2.

KNOW HOW TO AVOID VIRUSES AND VIRUS HOAXES

You're already familiar with the threat that viruses can pose to your system's capability to function correctly and to your privacy. In this section, we'll examine the problem of viruses hidden in e-mail attachments in more depth than we have in previous chapters. We'll also run through some of the most common tricks that virus distributors use in their attempt to get you to open e-mail attachments. We'll tell you how to recognize virus hoaxes. Finally, we'll show you how to turn on the anti-virus features in Outlook Express.

RECOGNIZING VIRUS TRICKS

One of the first steps of protecting your system from becoming infected by a virus's malicious code is to recognize which e-mail messages might potentially be dangerous. As you know from Chapter 2, one of the most common ways of circulating a virus is via an e-mail attachment. When the attachment is opened, the associated virus is unleashed on your system. The virus's payload can have a wide range of effects, from relatively harmless (but annoying) to economically destructive. The following sections discuss some of the most frequently used schemes for tricking people into opening an e-mail attachment.

AN INFECTED DOCUMENT. This virus scam works by including an infected attached file. For example, Word or Excel files can include a macro virus yet appear relatively innocent. The message usually includes an alluring subject line or text, such as *Here's the important file you wanted, but don't show it to anyone else!* Additionally, the sender listed is usually someone you know (although, of course, the person probably didn't intend for his or her e-mail address to be used at all). Figure 7.8 shows an example of this type of message (see below).

A MISLEADING FILENAME. Clever virus writers can easily rename a file so that it appears to have a "harmless" file extension. By doing so, they hide the fact that the file actually contains an executable program. For example, files with extensions of .exe or .vbs are **executable files**, meaning that they perform an action when opened. Consequently, a file extension, such as .txt (for a text-only file) appears less dangerous. The file might also appear as a music or graphic file, masking the fact that it actually contains malicious code.

AN OFFER OF HELP. Some viruses are disguised as an offer to help. For example, someone might send you a message telling you that he or she received an e-mail from you that contained a dangerous virus. They attach a file to the message that supposedly will rid your computer of the virus . . . instead, it delivers a nasty payload upon opening.

A FAKE LINK. A worm or virus-laden e-mail attachment might appear as a Web link. Clicking the fake Web link will open the attachment, which can then replicate itself by sending messages to the contacts in your Address Book.

The bottom line? Be aware of the common methods used to encourage you to open dangerous attachments, and then act logically in response.

> **ALERT!**
> One way of helping to maintain the security of your e-mail communications is to use encryption. Encrypting a message involves running it through an encoder that uses an encryption key to change the characters. The person who receives the message must have the encryption key to decode it, or else the message will appear scrambled. Most e-mail programs include options that allow you to use encryption. For example, you can set up encryption in Outlook Express by choosing Tools, Options and then clicking the Security tab. Check the box for *Encrypt contents and attachments for all outgoing messages*.

RECOGNIZING VIRUS HOAXES

If you've read Chapter 2, you know that e-mail can be used to spread rumors, "warnings," and out-and-out lies. These rumors, commonly called *virus hoaxes*, are messages that warn of viruses and try to prompt the recipients to

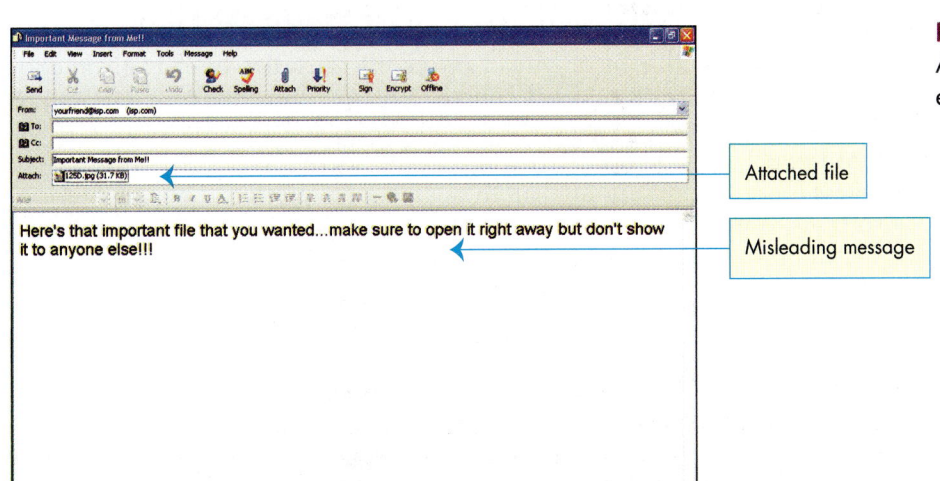

Figure 7.8.
An infected document sent as an e-mail attachment.

action—usually including instructions to send the message to as many others as they can. For example, one recent virus hoax warned recipients that they probably had a dangerous virus file on their computer and encouraged them to delete it. The truth? The file was actually part of the Windows operating system.

Although the hoax messages don't actually cause harm, they do waste time, resources, and energy. At the very least, the recipients have to take time to delete the messages; in many cases, they also spend time researching the validity of the claim. To further complicate matters, some virus hoaxes are originally harmless, but cybercriminals later attach malicious code to the hoax, turning the hoax into a real threat. The AOL4FREE situation is a good example. This was originally a hoax; later, a Trojan Horse program that deleted files on drive C: was attached to the message. The following is part of the text for the AOL4FREE message. This message includes many of the elements that are typical of hoaxes, such as a warning to "send the message to as many people as possible" and the idea that commercial anti-virus software can't detect the virus.

"Anyone who receives this must send it to as many people as you can. It is essential that this problem be reconciled as soon as possible. A few hours ago, I opened an E-mail that had the subject heading of 'aol4free.com.' Within seconds of opening it, a window appeared and began to display my files that were being deleted. I immediately shut down my computer, but it was too late. This virus wiped me out. It ate the Anti-Virus Software that comes with the Windows 95 Program along with F-Prot AVS. Neither was able to detect it. Please be careful and send this to as many people as possible, so maybe this new virus can be eliminated."

Most hoaxes are recognizable and include similar characteristics:

- They encourage the recipient to send the message "to as many people as you can." This is usually done under the guise of helping or warning friends and family members.
- The message usually warns of a very destructive virus.
- Sometimes the message indicates that none of the anti-virus software developers know about the virus or can stop it.

You can find out more about recognizing hoaxes by visiting the Hoaxbuster's Web site at *hoaxbusters.ciac.org*.

USING THE OUTLOOK EXPRESS ANTI-VIRUS FEATURES

Outlook Express, like most e-mail programs, includes built-in protection against some e-mail viruses. For example, you can change the program settings so that you can't open attachments that might potentially carry viruses. In this section, we'll show you how to control the anti-virus features in Outlook Express. Just keep in mind that the protection offered through Outlook Express is relatively slim, so you should have a full-fledged anti-virus program installed on your system.

ACTIVITY 7.4
To Use Outlook Express's Anti-Virus Features

1. In Outlook Express, choose Tools, Options.
2. In the Options dialog box, click the Security tab. The Security page displays (see Figure 7.9).

ACTIVITY 7.4
To Use Outlook Express's Anti-Virus Features

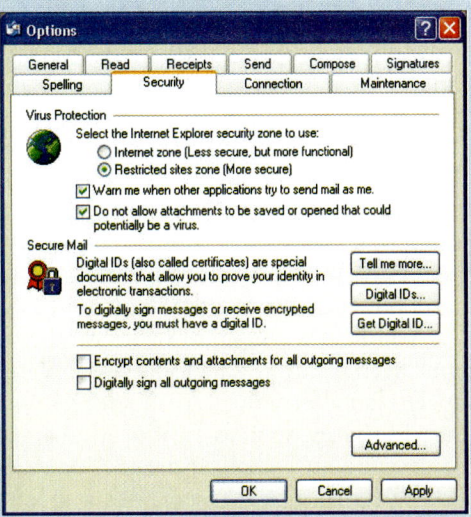

Figure 7.9.
You can turn on e-mail virus protection.

❸ Check the *Warn me when other applications try to send mail as me* box.
   This setting warns you if a virus tries to e-mail itself to people in your Address Book. Because this is a common way for viruses to spread, it's a good idea to turn on this setting.

❹ Check the *Do not allow attachments to be saved or opened that could potentially be a virus* box.
   This setting prevents attachments from being opened if they might contain malicious code.

❺ Close the Options dialog box.

❻ Exit Outlook Express.

KNOW HOW TO AVOID SPAM

As you learned in Chapter 2, spam is unsolicited e-mailed mass advertising. It's responsible for clogging up e-mail servers and personal mailboxes. This form of electronic junk mail can cause so much inefficiency and frustration that people sometimes completely abandon their e-mail accounts and create new ones. Most spam includes commercial advertising, typically for get-rich-quick schemes or second-rate products or services. Spam is particularly attractive for advertisers because the associated costs are paid for by the recipients and ISPs—not the sender.

But you don't have to watch helplessly as spam piles up in your Inbox. Instead, you can take action. First, check out some of the online resources related to e-mail abuse and spam. The Mail Abuse Prevention System (*www.mail-abuse.org*) and the Fight Spam on the Internet (*spam.abuse.net*) sites are particularly helpful. They explain a bit about how spam works and also include ways to report and prevent spam. When you report spam to these organizations, they are sometimes able to get the sender to stop mailing spam through negotiation. If that fails, the sender may be placed on a **blacklist**—a list of stigmatized persons developed for the protection of others. Individuals as well as network administrators can then use this blacklist to filter incoming mail. Additionally, some Internet Service Providers (ISPs) will even block messages from the offending party for you if the sender appears on the blacklist.

Next, change the settings on your e-mail program so that it automatically filters out junk mail. Most e-mail clients include the capability to do this by defining "rules" or adding filters. In Outlook Express, you prevent someone from sending you e-mail by blocking them. To do this, select any message from the sender in the Inbox and then choose Message, Block Sender. In the message box that displays, choose Yes to delete all the messages from the current folder; choose No to keep the message you've already received from the person. When you complete this process, the person is added to the Blocked Senders List, and any future messages you receive from the sender are automatically sent to the Deleted Items folder.

If you subsequently decide that you want to remove a person from the Blocked Senders List (and again receive mail from them), you can. To view and modify persons on this list, point to Message Rules on the Tools menu and then click Blocked Senders List (see Figure 7.10). Select a sender on the list and then click the Remove button. Choose Yes to confirm your action.

You have a couple of other ways to fight spam. One is to carefully protect your permanent e-mail address by giving it out only to good friends and family. Use an alternative e-mail address (such as those provided by the free Web-based services, such as Yahoo! Mail and Mail.com) whenever you are required to provide an e-mail address. For example, if you're signing up for a free newsletter on the Internet, use a secondary e-mail address. You can also use disposable e-mail addresses. For a small fee, a service, such as Spamex (*www.spamex.com*), allows you to set up disposable e-mail addresses. Mail to your "real" e-mail address will automatically be forwarded through the disposable address. If spam becomes a problem, you can discard the first disposable address and sign up for another one.

If despite your best efforts, spam is still piling up in your Inbox, you can delete it. To delete a single message, select it and then press Del. To select multiple adjacent messages, single-click the first spam message, press and hold Shift and then click the last spam message. Press Del to erase all intervening messages. If you want to select multiple non-adjacent messages, press and hold Ctrl while single-clicking the messages. Press Del when you're finish selecting the spam.

UNDERSTAND ABOUT E-MAIL PRIVACY IN THE WORKPLACE

Imagine that you're working for a less-than-optimal company, so you decide to look for new job. To facilitate your search, you use your company's e-mail system and Internet job sites. Imagine your surprise (and embarrassment) when

INSIDE TRACK

In addition to e-mail spam, there's another type of spam running rampant on the Internet: Usenet spam. Usenet spam is a message sent to 20 or more Usenet newsgroups. This type of spam ruins much of the usefulness of the newsgroups by overwhelming readers with advertising. You'll learn more about newsgroups in Chapter 13, Communicating via the Internet.

Figure 7.10.
You can add persons to the Blocked Senders List.

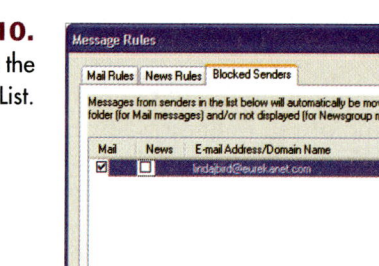

your boss calls you into his office a few weeks later, thumbing the stack of messages you wrote in your face... and letting you know that you're fired.

Some people don't have to imagine this situation. They've had something similar happen to them even though they thought that their personal e-mail communications were, well, private. To bolster their argument for **workplace privacy**, they relied on the Federal Electronic Communications Privacy Act (that's the law that forbids wiretapping and listening in to phone calls). This law, passed by Congress in 1986, protects the privacy of communications. However, the rulings in recent legal cases seem to indicate that these privacy rights don't extend to the workplace. Specifically, employees don't have privacy rights regarding e-mail usage when using their employer's system. This means that an employer can legally read an employee's messages. In fact, they can monitor overall Internet usage as well as e-mail communications, a practice sometimes called **workplace monitoring**.

This electronic surveillance makes many people uncomfortable. They feel they should have the right to privacy in all communications, even at work. However, employers defend their rights to monitor their employees based on three major concerns: productivity, sharing trade secrets, and liability. Companies feel they have the right to make sure their employees aren't spending working hours writing e-mail messages or needlessly tying up bandwidth instead of doing their job. Perhaps more importantly, inappropriate or illegal e-mail messages can be used as evidence in legal cases. This creates liability issues for the employer.

Imagine, for example, that two employees exchange a series of derogatory e-mails about a third co-worker. These messages can then be used in court to prove hostile work environment claims. This is exactly what happened when a sexual harassment lawsuit involving a subsidiary of Chevron Corporation settled for $2.2 million, partially based on e-mail evidence. In the *Owens v. Morgan Stanley & Co.* case, an e-mail was used as evidence for a race discrimination case.

Companies are not only monitoring e-mail, but also disciplining employees who use the system inappropriately. Dow Chemical recently fired 50 employees (and suspended an additional 200) for e-mailing offensive, pornographic, and violent material. One of the first cases involving electronic surveillance of e-mail, *Smyth vs. Pillsbury*, also involved disciplinary action for a worker. Smyth, a regional manager for Pillsbury, was fired after using the company e-mail system to send messages with unprofessional and negative statements. Smyth took the company to court over his firing, but lost. The court maintained that no employee has a reasonable expectation of privacy for communications sent over the company e-mail system. (You can find out more about this landmark case by running an Internet search on `Smyth vs. Pillsbury`.)

The bottom line? At this point, case law seems to indicate that an employer's business interests outweigh the privacy rights of an individual employee. However, from an ethical point of view, most people feel that companies should lay out the ground rules and clearly let employees know that their communications, including e-mail, aren't private. To protect their interests (and to act in an ethical manner) many employers are starting to set up and distribute policies regarding workplace monitoring and privacy.

ON THE HORIZON

Software has been developed that allows an employer to monitor employees' Internet usage. Not only does the software track how long a person has been online, but also which type of sites they visit. Some programs also include firewalls and filtering features to block dangerous or malicious Web sites.

Don't Forget...

- Outlook Express includes a number of advanced options you can use to customize the program to best fit your needs.
- Most e-mail clients include similar features to those in Outlook Express; if you have a different program, you can use Help to research the features.
- You can use the Address Book to organize information about your contacts.
- Outlook Express includes ways to find people in the Address Book and even on the Internet.
- Electronic junk mail (spam) is a growing problem, but you can use a variety of methods to minimize its impact.
- To prevent infection of your system, it's helpful to recognize the various types of viruses (and virus hoaxes) and to use anti-virus software and features.
- There are a number of issues surrounding workplace privacy. However, current case law seems to indicate that an employer's business interests outweigh the privacy rights of individual employees.
- In regards to workplace privacy, most people feel that companies should make it clear to employees that their communications, including e-mail, aren't private.

Check This Out

MULTIPLE CHOICE

1. Why do some companies monitor their employees' e-mail?
   a. To monitor productivity
   b. To make sure no illegal or offensive communications take place
   c. To make sure that trade secrets aren't being shared with others
   d. All of the above

2. How can you control spam?
   a. Use the message rules (filtering) features in your e-mail program.
   b. Give out a disposable e-mail address to everyone except selected friends and family.
   c. Report offenders to the spam Web sites.
   d. All of the above

3. You receive an e-mail message that informs you that a terrible virus has been unleashed on the Internet and that you should warn all the people in your Address Book. Which of the following have you most likely encountered?
   a. A virus
   b. A virus hoax
   c. Spam
   d. A filter

4. You find out that your boss has been monitoring your personal messages that you send using the company's e-mail system. If you protest, which is the most likely outcome?
   a. You'll be promoted because the company has no right to monitor your e-mail.
   b. Current case law is against you; previous courts have ruled that business interests outweigh employee privacy.
   c. You'll be put in charge of the Information Management Systems department so that you can monitor others.
   d. None of the above

5. Which of the following could indicate that a message is a hoax and not legitimate?
   a. It warns of a very destructive virus.
   b. It indicates that you should send the message to everyone in your Address Book.
   c. It indicates that even the major anti-virus companies don't know about the virus.
   d. All of the above

MATCHING

a. encryption
b. spam
c. virus
d. hoax
e. workplace monitoring
f. workplace privacy
g. Address Book
h. contact
i. executable file
j. Internet directory service

1. A central file in an e-mail program that you use to organize your contacts
2. Being able to have private communications at work
3. The identifying information for a person, such as an e-mail address
4. Scrambling e-mail communications
5. Commercial messages sent as a mass mailing to e-mail recipients
6. Malicious programming code
7. A fake message sent by e-mail
8. Electronic surveillance of employees
9. An Internet-based search tool that helps you locate people
10. A file that runs a program

Real Life

1. Because spam is a growing concern, many Web sites have been developed to help people prevent abuse of the e-mail system and deal with the problem. Use the following Web sites to research current legislation and active legal cases regarding spam: *www.emailabuse.org/legislation*, *www.abuse.net* and *www.spamlaws.com/us.html*. Prepare a short oral report to present your findings to the class or a small group. Alternatively, write a 1,000-word paper on the issue. Make sure to explain why spam is a problem, and include at least three ideas of how to control it.

2. Take a few minutes to become more familiar with Outlook Express's advanced settings. To do this, open the Options dialog box and then use the Help button to display ScreenTips for each setting in the dialog box. (If you use a different e-mail program, research its advanced options instead.) If your instructor approves, experiment by modifying some of the settings. When you're finished, change the settings back to the default ones for the program.

3. Interview the Human Resource or Information Managers at several companies to find out their policies regarding workplace monitoring. Find out if they track employees' communications, for what purpose, and to what extent. Also, ask them if they use Web-monitoring software. Finally, ask whether they have a written distributed policy regarding Internet and e-mail usage.

I Spy: Privacy and Security Concerns

1. Use the Internet to research information about the workplace monitoring of e-mail and Web usage. (Hint: Conduct searches using keywords, such as `workplace monitoring`, `workplace privacy`, `Smyth vs. Pillsbury`). Also, research Web-monitoring and filtering software, such as Websense, by looking at their Web site (*www.websense.com*).

2. Companies can not only monitor an employee's e-mail, but also their Internet usage. To help them out, they can secretly install software on the employee's computer that tracks Internet usage. What are the legal and ethical issues surrounding this type of tracking? Define the conflict inherent in workplace surveillance and research the associated issues. Break into two small groups and debate the issue: Have one small group look at the issues from the standpoint of the employer; the second group should take the side of the employee. After 10 minutes, switch sides.

SECTION CHAPTER

Four
GETTING AROUND THE WORLD WIDE WEB

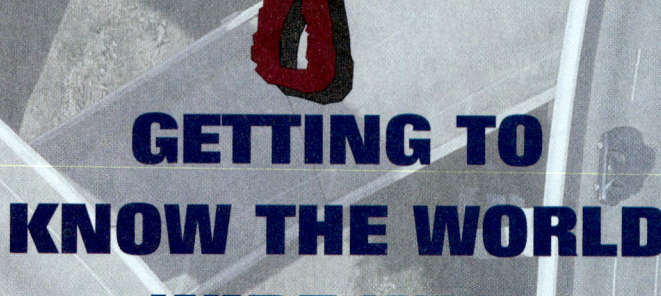

GETTING TO KNOW THE WORLD WIDE WEB

Key Terms

When you finish this chapter, you'll understand the following terms:

- browsing
- CERN
- domain name
- Domain Name System (DNS)
- Extensible Markup Language (XML)
- GET command
- Graphical User Interface (GUI)
- security hole
- Hypertext Transfer Protocol (HTTP)
- Internet Protocol (IP) address
- mirror site
- Mosaic
- name servers
- open standards
- patch
- proxy server
- root servers
- surfing
- top-level domain names
- Uniform Resource Locator (URL)
- upgrade
- Web server
- Whois
- World Wide Web Consortium (W3C)

Chapter Objectives

After you complete this chapter, you'll

- Understand Why the Web and the Internet are Not the Same
- Know About the Origins of the World Wide Web
- Understand How the Web is Administered by Web Servers
- Understand the Process of Getting Information from a Web Server to Your System
- Know the Basics of How Proxy Servers and Mirror Sites Work
- Know the Major Browsers in Use

The Big Picture

Unless you skipped all the other chapters in this book, you've already obtained some hands-on experience working on the World Wide Web and you understand that the Web is the friendly face that provides you with an easy-to-use way of accessing information from millions of Web pages. In fact, the World Wide Web (abbreviated WWW or Web) contains a seemingly endless stream of text, graphics, audio, video, and other data from computers and servers worldwide.

In this chapter, we'll expand on that knowledge. We'll look at the origins of the Web. Next, we'll go over the differences between the Internet and the Web, and explain how Uniform Resource Locators (URLs), Web servers, IP addresses, and domain names are set up. Finally, we'll show you where to find browser software and updates so that you're ready to surf the Web.

Window on the Web

The heart and soul of the World Wide Web are its hyperlinks. These links connect the documents and other objects that make up the Web and allow you to cross-reference information from one area of the Web to another. You can think of hyperlinks as the glue that holds the Web together.

Hyperlinks appear on a Web page as underlined (or highlighted) text, graphics, or other objects. You can click a hyperlink to access the associated Web document, object, or graphic (see Figure 8.1).

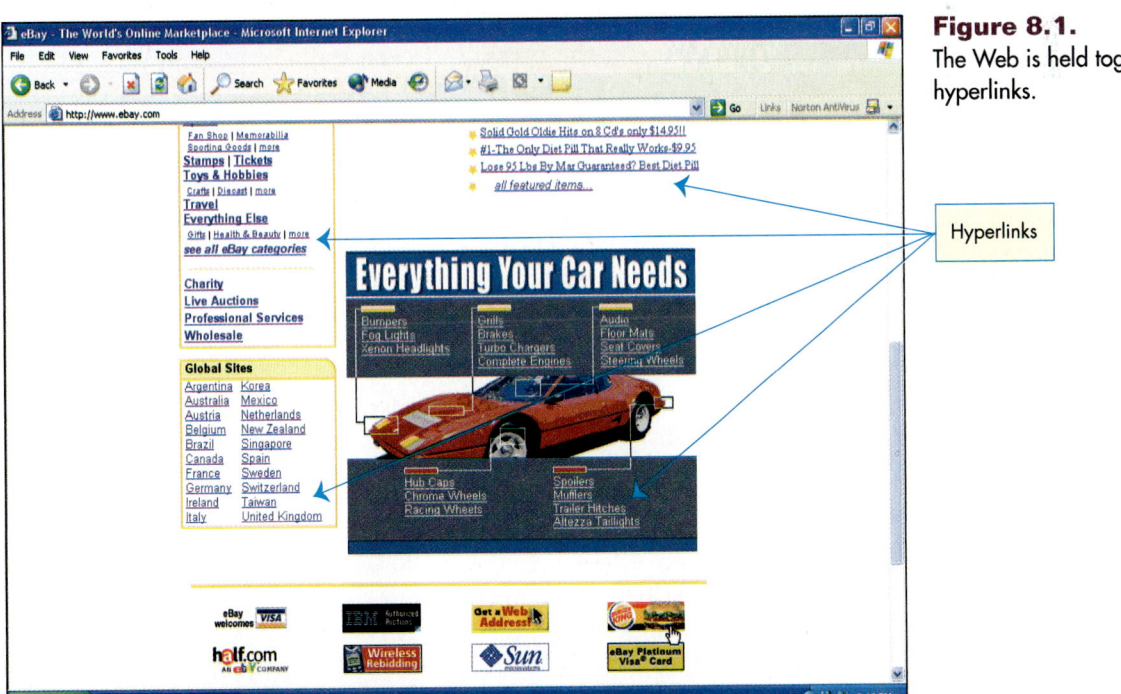

Figure 8.1.
The Web is held together by hyperlinks.

Fortunately, it doesn't take a complicated setup to access the Web: just an Internet connection and a special type of software, called a Web browser. This type of software is designed to interpret the coding behind the hyperlinks and to display the associated pages correctly. In this chapter, you'll learn where you can find this software; in Chapter 9, Surfing Basics, and Chapter 10, Beyond the Basics: Advanced Surfing, you'll learn advanced tips and tricks for using it.

Although there are several Web browsers from which you can choose, the most commonly used one is Microsoft's Internet Explorer (see Figure 8.2).

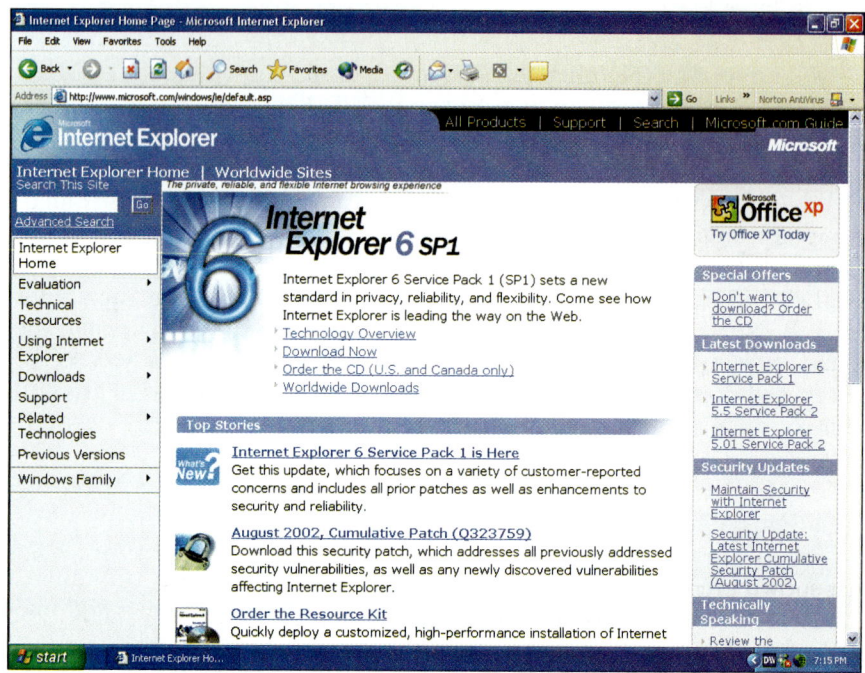

Figure 8.2.
Internet Explorer is a popular Web browser.

UNDERSTAND WHY THE WEB AND THE INTERNET ARE NOT THE SAME

Most computer users, the press, and even online businesses use the terms "World Wide Web" and "The Internet" interchangeably. Nevertheless, it is important that you understand that the Web is only a part of the larger Internet. The Internet includes many technical services in addition to the Web, such as Telnet, FTP (File Transfer Protocol), Gopher, and e-mail. It also includes the physical backbone, such as the cabling, computers, servers, routers, and wiring. (In Chapter 3, Necessary Equipment and Internet Connections, we discussed how the Internet's structure was set up. Chapters 5–7 covered mail and messaging tools. In Chapter 14, Pulling Information from the Internet, we'll cover some of the technical services such as FTP and Gopher.)

The Web has been vital to the popularity of the Internet because it provides a user-friendly way for people to view and interact with Internet content. Before the days of the Web, people needed to know and type a file's address on a specific server or wade through long complex menus before they could find the information they needed. Although experienced computer users were generally able to access Internet data using these methods, the average person usually found the text-based system confusing.

But all this changed when the Web arrived on the scene, with its system of hyperlinks and graphics. Suddenly, it was easy for any person with a reasonable computer background and mouse skills to view Internet content. Futhermore,

INSIDE TRACK

Web browsers, such as Internet Explorer or Netscape Navigator, provide a **Graphical User Interface (GUI)**. A GUI is an interface that allows users to interact with a program or data using graphical elements, such as icons or hyperlinks. Most people find that GUIs are more intuitive to use than pure text-based systems. This type of interface also allows the user to input data with a mouse in addition to (or instead of) a keyboard, opening up the computing world to those without keyboarding skills.

the person didn't have to know where to find the related information. Instead, he or she needed only to be able to recognize and click the links. This process of clicking hyperlinks to wander from page to page on the Web is referred to as **surfing** or **browsing**.

In addition to the heavy use of hyperlinks and the graphical interface, working on the Web differs from other Internet services in another way. Instead of the typical computer file hierarchical arrangement, the Web is set up similar to a spider's web. Following this analogy, Web users can wander at will from "strand to strand" (document to document or site to site).

Now that you understand the differences between the Web and the Internet, let's turn our attention to the origins of the World Wide Web.

KNOW ABOUT THE ORIGINS OF THE WORLD WIDE WEB

The Web had its beginnings in March 1989. Tim Berners-Lee thought of the idea so that members of the European Laboratory for Nuclear Research (**CERN**) could exchange data and collaborate on experiments. At that time, the Internet included a wide variety of platforms and ways of disseminating information, making it difficult to share data. This was a source of frustration for many, including Berners-Lee. As a result, he proposed the first system for the Web in 1989, and subsequently refined it with the help of Robert Cailliau in 1990. Berners-Lee finished the first browser/editor late in 1990 and called it WorldWideWeb (with no spaces). The system included a system of links to tie the documents together and enable the user to access them from any other document. By 1993, the browser/editor had been revised and appeared similar to that shown in Figure 8.3.

In 1993, two events occurred that dramatically affected the growth of the Web. First, the National Center for Supercomputing Applications (NCSA) at the University of Illinois developed the **Mosaic** browser software, the first browser to have a graphical user interface and a system of hyperlinks. The second event occurred in April; CERN announced that it would share Web technology (at no cost) with anyone who wanted to use it. By the end of 1993, the Web included approximately 500 servers, but was responsible for only 1% of all Internet traffic.

Things exploded in 1994, which became known as the "Year of the Web." Global conferences related to the technology were held, and the number of Web servers increased dramatically. Part of the Web's rapid growth resulted from the massive amount of attention the media gave to it.

INSIDE TRACK

You've probably never heard of Vannevar Bush. However, he may have been the first one to come up with the idea of a World Wide Web. In 1945, he wrote an article about a photo-electrical-mechanical device he called the Memex. This device would have had the capability to create and follow links between microfiche documents.

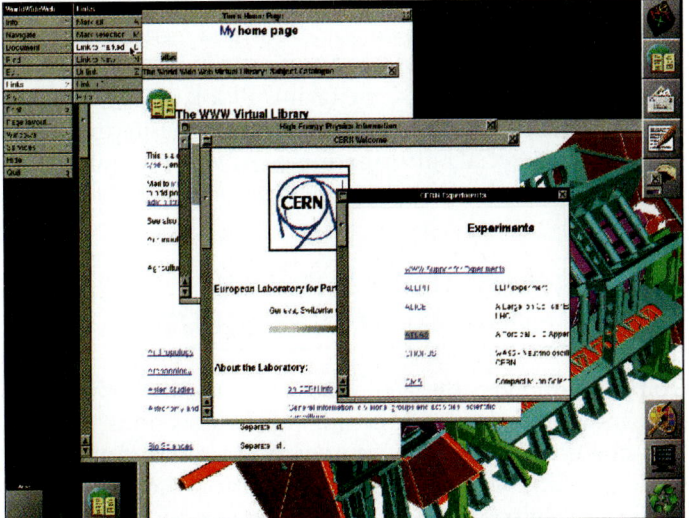

Figure 8.3.
Berners-Lee and Cailliau developed a system of accessing Internet documents and called the creation the WorldWideWeb.

Figure 8.4.
The idea of a global system connected by hyperlinks caught on quickly.

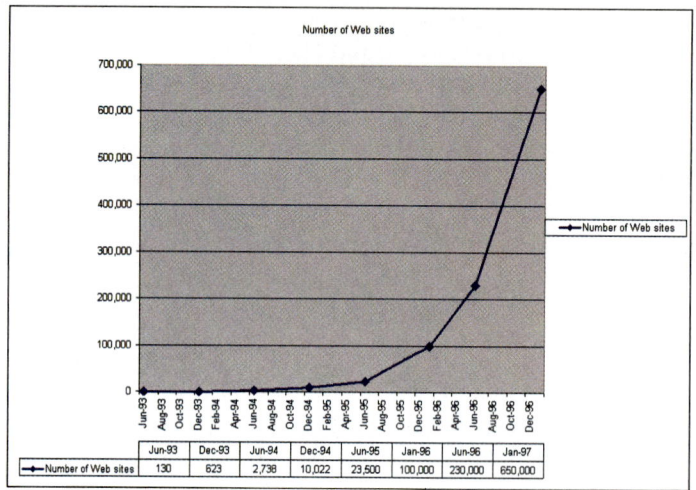

According to the Massachusetts Institute of Technology, the number of Web sites increased from 130 in June 1993 to 650,000 in January 1997 (see Figure 8.4).

Those involved in the Web's early development wanted to keep the Web from growing in a haphazard manner. To help set universal standards for developing Web pages, such as which languages should be used and how Web documents should be linked, a group of internationally based institutes and companies formed the **World Wide Web Consortium (W3C)**, headed by Tim Berners-Lee. The group's stated purpose is to promote Web technology, while maintaining open standards for new development. Using **open standards** simply involves making sure that the specifications and protocols are not proprietary and can be accessed by anyone.

ON THE HORIZON

The technology associated with the Web continues to evolve. Features related to security, multimedia, and online shopping are in the forefront. In fact, entire books on securing Web sites, e-commerce, and multimedia applications have been written.

W3C defines the set of rules that Web browsers and Web servers use to exchange data. This set of rules is referred to as **Hypertext Transfer Protocol (HTTP)**. The use of open standards and agreed-upon rules prevents single-handed control of the system by any particular group or government. You can find out more about W3C by taking a look at its Web site (*www.w3.org*).

So, where are we now? The Web continues to grow and expand. The number of commercial, informational, governmental, and personal Web sites increases daily. The Web has truly become a part of every day life.

UNDERSTAND HOW THE WEB IS ADMINISTERED BY WEB SERVERS

To put it simply... the Web is administered by Web servers. OK, it's not quite *that* straightforward. But in the next few sections, we'll go over the basics of how the Web works, beginning with its primary component: Web servers.

Physically, **Web servers** are similar to other Internet servers (such as FTP or Telnet). In contrast with the servers used for these other services, however,

ON THE HORIZON

Although HTML is the most commonly used language for developing Web pages, XML is being used more and more. **XML**, which stands for **Extensible Markup Language**, is promoted by W3C as a universal standard for developing Web documents.

Web servers use HTML-compatible software to distribute data. Web servers and browsers use HTTP as the protocol to communicate with each other—much like people use a common language to make sure they communicate properly. Let's look at the way servers and clients communicate and then delve into Web domain names and IP addresses.

SERVING UP THE DATA: CLIENTS AND SERVERS

The computers that make up the Internet can be categorized as either servers or clients. *Servers* are the machines that provide the services (such as distributing Web pages). *Clients* (user machines) are the computers that connect to the servers and receive information from them.

Here's an example: When you connect to Microsoft's home page, Microsoft provides a machine to service your request (the server). Your computer (the client machine) then uses a Web browser to accept and display a Web page. In this case, a *Web server* is facilitating the request. Need another example? A *mail server* "serves up" or distributes e-mail, whereas an *FTP server* provides FTP services. In each instance, the server sends the information to the client.

In real life, this situation isn't quite as straightforward because two (or more) servers can actually reside on the same machine. For example, a mail server and a Web server can physically exist on the same computer. To keep the information straight, each server uses a different port—a specific place for physically connecting to another device. Web servers typically use port 80, Telnet commonly uses port 23, and SMTP mail services use port 25.

Clients access the server when there's a specific purpose at hand, such as to collect e-mail. Because of this, they direct their request to the appropriate server and ignore the others that reside on the same machine: the e-mail application communicates only with the e-mail server, the Web browser talks with the Web server, and so on.

WHAT'S IN A (WEB) NAME?

OK, so the browser is connected to the Web server at the correct port. But how do the Web servers find the pages requested by the browser out of the millions available on the Web? This amazing feat is done through use of the Web page's domain name. Without the name, the Web server wouldn't have a clue about where to look to find the page the browser requests.

A **domain name**, sometimes known as a **Uniform Resource Locator (URL)**, is simply the Web site's address. It's set up following certain conventions, which helps everyone because the browsers know how to interpret the address and find the associated page. A typical Web address is *http://www.pearsoned.com*. The *http://* component of the URL indicates to the browser that the page you want is located on a Web server and should be transferred using the HTTP protocol. (In contrast, an FTP server would have the prefix *ftp://*.) The *www.pearsoned.com* part of the address lets the browser know exactly where the Web server is located. Sometimes the address also

INSIDE TRACK

Port numbers range from 0 through 65535. Ports 0–1024 are reserved for specific services. For example, the HTTP service uses port 80 by default. Although this isn't a strict requirement, most people stick with convention and use port 80 for their Web server.

includes reference to a specific document that you want the Web server to find. For example, the URL *http://www.pearsoned.com/higherEd.htm* includes reference to an exact document—*higherEd.htm*—within the pearsoned.com site.

There's only one hitch in this system. A name such as *www.pearsoned.com* is user-friendly to people, but not to machines. Because numbers are more easily interpreted by machines than text is, each Web site has a unique identifying number associated with it, just as you have a unique phone number that no on else in the world has. This not only makes it easier for the machines to process the information for a Web address, but also prevents duplicate Web sites. The unique number that is assigned to each Web site is called an **Internet Protocol (IP) address**. IP addresses are set up as a series of four numbers, each separated by periods. For example, a typical IP address might appear something like this: 215.47.62.132.

Created in 1972, the Internet Assigned Numbers Authority (IANA) was originally responsible for assigning a unique number to each site. By 1973, the IP addressing system became the universal standard. You could connect to a site by providing the numerical IP address of the Web site you wanted. However, as the number of servers on the system grew, this method became totally unworkable for most people. They simply couldn't remember long strings of numbers.

To help the situation, researchers at the University of Wisconsin developed the first name server, which eliminated the need for users to know the exact numbers associated with each IP address. The name server kept a list of IP addresses and the associated location of the files. In 1984, this evolved into the **Domain Name System (DNS)**. Thanks to DNS, it is no longer necessary to memorize or know the IP address for Pearson Education or any other Web site—you can just use its plain English name: *www.pearsoned.com*.

So here's how it works now: Each time you use a domain name, the DNS name servers convert the plain English name into something machines can read: the IP address. Think of the DNS system as a huge phone directory: Just as you can look up a person's name to find their unique phone number, so you can ask your browser to look up a domain name's unique IP address.

Obviously, each domain name has to be unique for this system to work. To ensure unique domain names, a system of domains, or groupings, was set up. **Top-level domain names** (sometimes called first-level domain names) include the well-known identifiers, such as .com, .org, .net, .edu, .mil, and .gov. Within each top-level domain grouping, there can be countless second-level domains. For example, within the .com top-level domain there are second-level names, such as *Microsoft*, *Pearsoned*, and *Yahoo*. They in turn produce unique names that are a combination of the top- and second-level domains, such as *Microsoft.com* or *Yahoo.com*.

Think of a top-level domain name as the last name for a large family and think of the second-level domain as the first name. When you're referring to people, the combination of the first and last name is unique and indicates a specific individual. In the same way, the combination of a top and second-level domain name represents a specific Web site.

Nowadays, the Internet Corporation for Assigned Names and Numbers (ICANN) takes responsibility for domain name system management, root server management, and the coordination of IP address assignments. If you want to register a domain name, you pay a fee to one of the many authorized registration services that ICANN oversees. These registration companies compete with each other, so their fees and services vary. Because ICCAN oversees the entire registration system, you can be assured that duplicate domain names are not registered. InterNIC is a Web site that was established to provide information to the public about the DNS. You can locate an ICCAN-accredited registrar that can assign domain names on InterNIC's Web site (see Figure 8.5).

INSIDE TRACK

Although most people think of URLs in reference to locating pages on the Web, they can actually specify any location on the Internet. The acronym they use at the beginning of the URL indicates the protocol that should be used. For example, *gopher://* specifies the gopher protocol, *ftp://* indicates File Transfer Protocol, and *telnet://* is used for Telnet sessions. You'll learn more about these Internet services in Chapter 14.

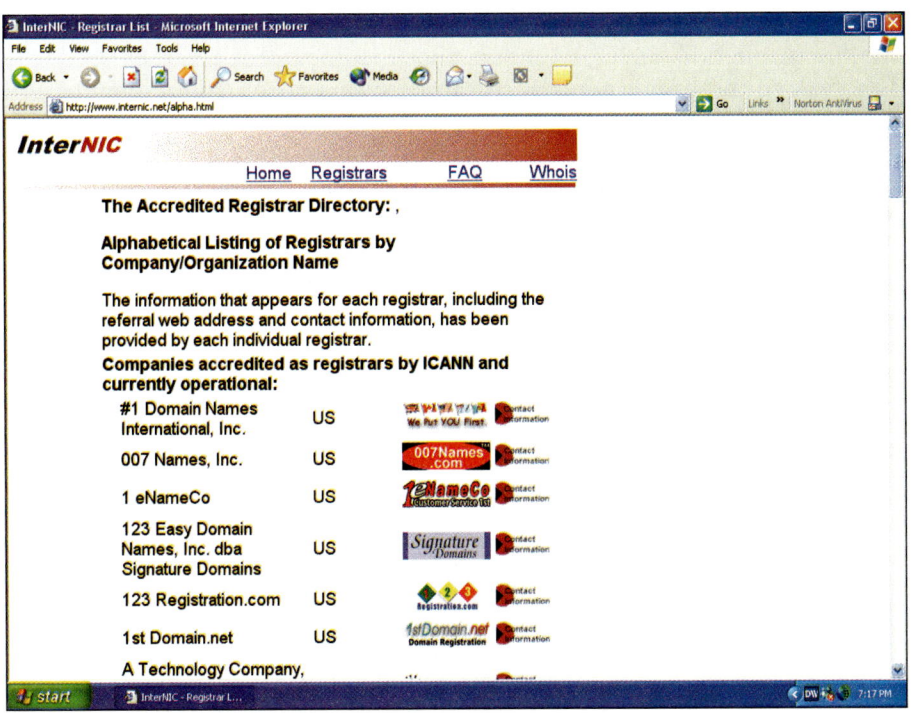

Figure 8.5.
You can sign up for a domain name by using an accredited registrar.

The DNS is maintained by thirteen special computers, called **root servers**, which are scattered around the world and contain duplicate information for all IP addresses. This information is usually updated twice daily because new domain names are constantly being registered. Additionally, so that the root servers aren't totally overloaded with requests to find IP addresses, numerous **name servers** (sometimes called *resolvers*) carry the load. Name servers translate domain names into IP addresses. The name servers include the same information as the root domain servers and help to spread the workload by handling the bulk of the requests.

UNDERSTAND THE PROCESS OF GETTING INFORMATION FROM A WEB SERVER TO YOUR SYSTEM

So, what actually happens when you click a hyperlink or type a URL? The associated document is "served up" by the Web server and transferred to your system. Just as you would tell a taxicab driver an address where you wanted to go, so you can enter a Web address, and your browser will take you to that page (or rather, bring the page to you) electronically.

Here's the process in a nutshell: You use your browser to request the Web page for a specific company (such as Pearson Education). Your browser "asks" a name server to convert the domain name (*www.pearsoned.com*) into an IP address. The name server can do a number of things at this point: fulfill the request because it knows the IP address, contact another name server to see if that server has a record of the IP address, or return an error message because the domain name doesn't exist. (The last possibility, by the way, is what causes an invalid page error message. If you're sure that the Web site does exist, you can always try retyping the URL because you may have accidentally entered the wrong address.)

Usually, the name server knows the IP address and hands it over to the browser. The browser then sends a **GET command** to the Web server in which the document is located. Just as its name implies, the browser uses the

INSIDE TRACK

You can find out the IP address and other related information for many Web sites by using the **Whois** command (as in "Who is. . ."). On InterNIC's Web site (*www.internic.net*) or any authorized registrar's site, click the *Whois* link and then enter the domain name. The corresponding IP address and registration information will display. However, Whois includes only the "generic" top-level domain names, such as .com and .net. If you can't locate the IP address using Whois, try the universal Whois registry at *www.uwhois.com*, which also includes top-level country code names (such as *us* for the United States).

INSIDE TRACK

By early 2001, there were more than 20 million registered domain names!

GET command to obtain files from the remote computer. The Web server searches through its directory until it finds the document and then sends the data back to the browser so that it can be displayed on your computer. Of course, this all happens behind the scenes. Most people aren't even aware of the process, but knowing about it helps you troubleshoot problems with Web pages and turns you into a more knowledgeable Internet user.

KNOW THE BASICS OF HOW PROXY SERVERS AND MIRROR SITES WORK

Many Web sites allow you to access their information from a single server. However, the Web servers for large popular sites (such as Yahoo.com) simply can't handle the sheer volume of requests of hundreds (or thousands) of browsers simultaneously. To handle this volume of electronic traffic, some sites use proxy servers and mirror sites. **Proxy servers** (also called *Web proxies* or *gateways*) act like electronic traffic cops by forwarding input to a different port. This process closes the straight route, simultaneously preventing crackers from learning a network's internal addresses and taking heat off of the main server. The proxy server then reroutes the request to the actual Web server or can handle the request itself. Exactly how the proxy server handles this information is determined by the software used by the proxy server and how the people in charge of the system (the network administrators) set up the system.

INSIDE TRACK

Mirror sites are not only used to even out browser traffic, but for backup and disaster recovery as well.

Another method that Web administrators use to prevent their servers from becoming overloaded by too many requests is to use a **mirror site**, which is an exact duplicate of the original site that is stored in another physical location. Some major sites (such as Microsoft's) automatically redirect browsers to a mirror site that then serves up the requested Web pages. (One indication that your browser has been routed to a different location is that the address shown in your browser differs from the one you entered.)

KNOW THE MAJOR BROWSERS IN USE

So far in this chapter, we've taken a look at the process of getting Web pages from their homes on Web servers to your client computer. The messenger responsible for carrying out this task (from your standpoint) is the Web browser software on your system.

INSIDE TRACK

Along with your computer's settings, the Web browser you use will determine how Web pages will appear on your monitor. For example, Web pages may display using different fonts or showing graphics slightly differently in Internet Explorer than they do in Netscape.

Fortunately, Web browsers are easy to install and use. In fact, Microsoft's Internet Explorer, the most-used browser on the market today, comes as a part of the Windows operating system. According to Microsoft, Internet Explorer 6.0 is included as one of the "core technologies" in its Windows 98/2000/ME/XP operating systems. If you have Windows installed on your computer, chances are good that you already have Internet Explorer (IE) available. You can find out if this software is loaded because the program's icon probably displays on the desktop (see Figure 8.6). Alternatively, you can look in the *Program Files\Internet Explorer* folder on your computer to see whether the executable file for the program exists. If Internet Explorer is installed on your system, you simply have to double-click the desktop icon to open the browser and connect to the Internet via your Internet Service Provider (ISP). You're ready to surf the Web.

If IE 6.0 is not installed on your system, you can download the program at no charge from Microsoft's Web site (see Figure 8.7). *Downloading* is simply the process of transferring files from the Internet to your computer

Figure 8.6.
Internet Explorer is distributed as part of the Windows operating system.

through your connection. Of course, you need an older version of Internet Explorer or another browser to access the Web site in the first place. If you don't have any browser on your system that you can use to access Microsoft's Web site, you can instead call Microsoft at 1-800-642-7676 to obtain the CD. Typically, there is a nominal fee charged to cover shipping and handling of the CD.

In addition to downloading a completely new version of the software from the Web site, you can also download **upgrades** (called *updates* by Microsoft). These upgrades may include new features or take care of problems with previous releases. For example, sometimes a problem with the security of a browser is discovered after the software has been released. This problem, which can be exploited by crackers, is often referred to as a **hole** or **security hole**. A **patch** is a minor upgrade specifically designed to fix this type of problem. Figure 8.7 shows one of Microsoft's pages for Internet Explorer, with links for downloading the program. In Chapters 9–10, we'll use Internet Explorer to work on the World Wide Web and show you some of the program's most important features; for now, just make sure that the software is installed on your computer.

Although Microsoft's Internet Explorer is the most commonly used program on the market, you may encounter other browsers and should at least have passing familiarity with them. Netscape Navigator (*www.netscape.com*) had the lion's share of the market before Internet Explorer arrived on the scene. The newest version of this software (Netscape 7.0) integrates several Web services that can help you conquer any Internet task. For example, this browser includes an instant messaging program, an e-mail/newsgroup reader, and a Web page editor. Opera (*www.opera.com*) also has a following. Opera's developers maintain that it is the fastest browser on the market. Mozilla (*www.mozilla.org*), which champions an open standard for browser development, is poised to grab at least some of the market. Finally, in December 2002, the W3C organization released a Web browser called Amaya (*www.w3.org/Amaya*) that you can use to view *or* create Web pages. You can learn more about the various browsers by exploring their respective Web sites.

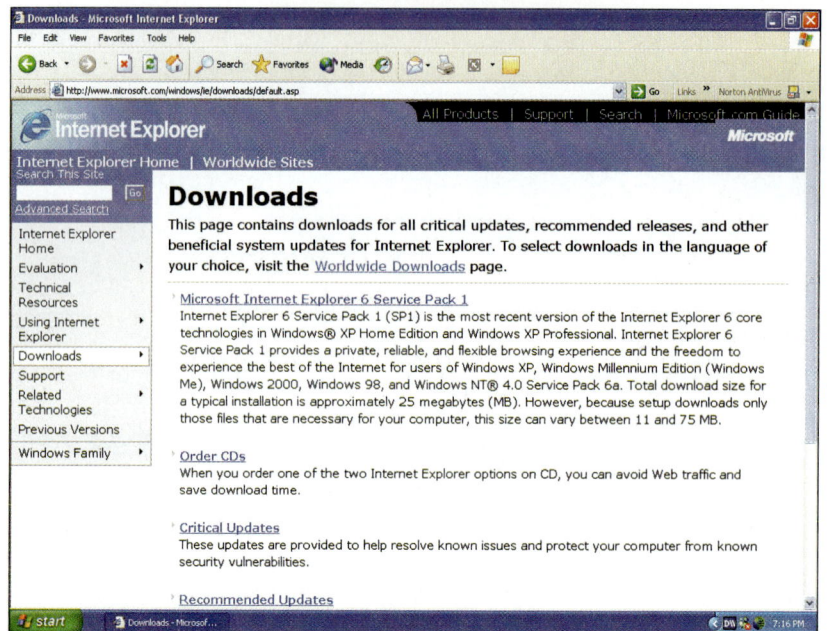

Figure 8.7.
You can download Internet Explorer at no cost from Microsoft's Web site.

Don't Forget...

- The Web and the Internet are not the same thing, although the terms are often used interchangeably.
- The Web is a recent development, exploding on the scene in 1994.
- Tim Berners-Lee was instrumental in the early development of the World Wide Web.
- W3C is a consortium whose purpose is to promote Web development and open standards.
- The servers on the Internet are set up specifically to provide a service, such as distributing mail or Web content.
- Web content is stored on Web servers, who distribute it via browsers to client computers.
- Each Web site includes a unique domain name.
- Top-level domain names include .com, .org, .net, .edu, .gov, and .mil. Within each top-level domain, there can be countless second-level domain names.
- Domain names are mapped to IP addresses so that computers can read them. The record of all the IP addresses and their corresponding domain names are kept on root servers, with copies on name servers.
- ICCAN oversees the authorized registrars for Web names.
- Mirror sites and proxy servers are often used to relieve the load from a site's main Web server.
- The protocol used for distributing Web content is Hypertext Transfer Protocol (HTTP).
- Currently, the most popular browser software program is Microsoft's Internet Explorer.
- You may need to update your browser if security or other programming flaws with the software are found.

Check This Out

MULTIPLE CHOICE

1. Who was responsible for developing the concept behind the World Wide Web?
   a. Tim Berners-Lee
   b. Robert Fulton
   c. Joseph Mozilla
   d. Sarah Cern

2. What is W3C?
   a. A specialized Web server
   b. The root server that keeps track of IP addresses and their associated domain names
   c. A consortium that recommends standards for using the Web
   d. The first browser (WorldWideWeb)

3. What is an IP address?
   a. The number that corresponds to a "plain English" domain name
   b. The protocol used for handling Web requests
   c. The address used by an International Port
   d. A domain name assigned by the International Protocol registrar

4. .com, .org, and .net are all examples of
   a. Proxy servers
   b. Security patches
   c. Top-level domains
   d. Web ports

5. Which browser is the most commonly used?
   a. Opera
   b. Internet Explorer
   c. Mozilla
   d. Netscape Navigator

MATCHING

a. DNS
b. 80
c. HTTP
d. GET
e. XML
f. WHOIS
g. registrar
h. open standards
i. WorldWideWeb
j. patch

1. The protocol used to distribute Web content
2. The command used by browsers to request files from a Web server
3. The first browser, developed by Tim Berners-Lee
4. The default port used by Web servers
5. A company authorized to assign domain names
6. Revised code for already-released software, often used to fix a security breach
7. Specifications that are publicly available
8. The command used to find out registration information about a domain name
9. The directory assistance for the Internet, responsible for looking up IP addresses
10. Extensible Markup Language

Real Life

1. Go to InterNIC's Web site (*http://internic.net*) and display the listing of registrars alphabetically. View the registration services and fees for at least 10 of the companies. Develop a chart that tracks the differences between their costs and services.

2. Think of a domain name that you want to have. Using the registration services, find out if the name you want is available for several of the top-level domains. For example, if you want to use *computer-wiz.com* but the name is already assigned, try *computer-wiz.org* or *computer-wiz.net*. Check the registration status of at least five different domain names.

3. Go to the Web site for the W3C organization and learn about its Web browser (*www.w3.org/Amaya*). Use the information you find to write a short report or develop a PowerPoint presentation about the major differences between Microsoft's Internet Explorer and Amaya. If time allows, present your findings to a small group or to your entire class.

I Spy: Privacy and Security Concerns

1. Use the Whois command to find out registration information on at least 10 different Web sites. Make a note of the information that is readily available for anyone on the Internet to access. In a small group, discuss the pros and cons for displaying this information.

2. Find out about the possible security issues surrounding the DNS. To do so, conduct a Web search using keywords, such as *domain name system* and *security*. Write a short report on your findings.

CHAPTER 9

SURFING BASICS

Key Terms

When you finish this chapter, you'll understand the following terms:

- Address bar
- AutoComplete feature
- drilling down
- dynamic HTML (DHTML)
- dynamic content
- Favorites list
- frames
- History list (History bar)
- keyboard shortcut
- Links bar
- metasearch engines
- offline
- portal
- search directory
- search engine
- spiders
- static HTML
- Web pages
- Web search site
- Web site

Chapter Objectives

After you complete this chapter, you'll

- Know How to Navigate the Web
- Be Able to Accurately Keep Track of Web Sites
- Know How to Use Search Tools
- Understand How to Get Around a Web Page
- Find Information on a Web Page
- Know How to Use Information Offline

The Big Picture

As you learned in Chapter 8, Getting to Know the World Wide Web, the Web is an important element of the Internet and is the service with which people are most familiar. However, even if you've spent a significant amount of time on the Web, don't skip this chapter. We'll start out by flying through the basics of getting around on the Web and then quickly move into several ways to make your surfing experience faster and more efficient. Learning useful techniques for navigating the Web will put you on the fast track to becoming a suave computer user—and help you enjoy your online time more as well.

Window on the Web

To locate the Web pages you want, you can run searches from within a browser (such as Internet Explorer). You can also use a variety of search engines and search directories. **Search engines** are software programs that help you find information on the Web. They do this by accessing large collections (databases) of Web data and documents. You'll get a chance to use some of the most popular search engines in this chapter. For example, one of the largest search engines currently in use is Google (see Figure 9.1).

In this chapter, you'll also learn some effective ways of using a specific browser: Microsoft's Internet Explorer. This browser includes a Standard Buttons toolbar, a menu bar, an Address bar, a Status bar, and

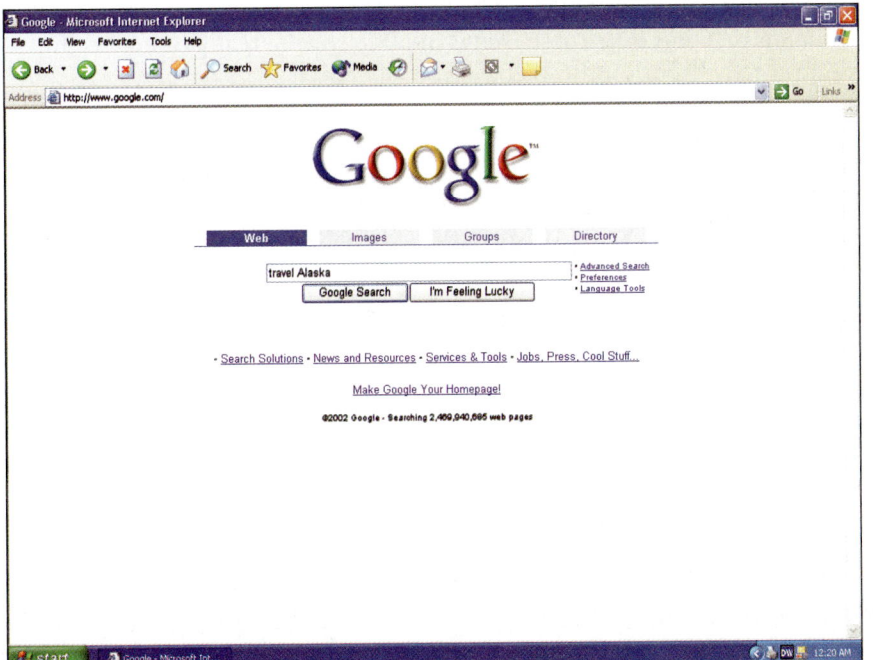

Figure 9.1.
Google is one of the largest and most popular search engines on the Web.

other screen elements that are similar to those found in other Windows programs (see Figure 9.2). Knowing how to use these elements correctly can dramatically increase your efficiency. To get you started, we'll familiarize you with a few of the ways you can use Internet Explorer to work more efficiently on the Web. (In Chapter 10, Beyond the Basics: Advanced Surfing, we'll expand on the information presented in this chapter.)

After you use a search engine or a browser such as Internet Explorer to find a Web site, you can tap into a number of techniques to find information on the page itself. To make the information useful when you're **offline**—not connected to the Internet—you can also save, print, or e-mail the page. Let's get going.

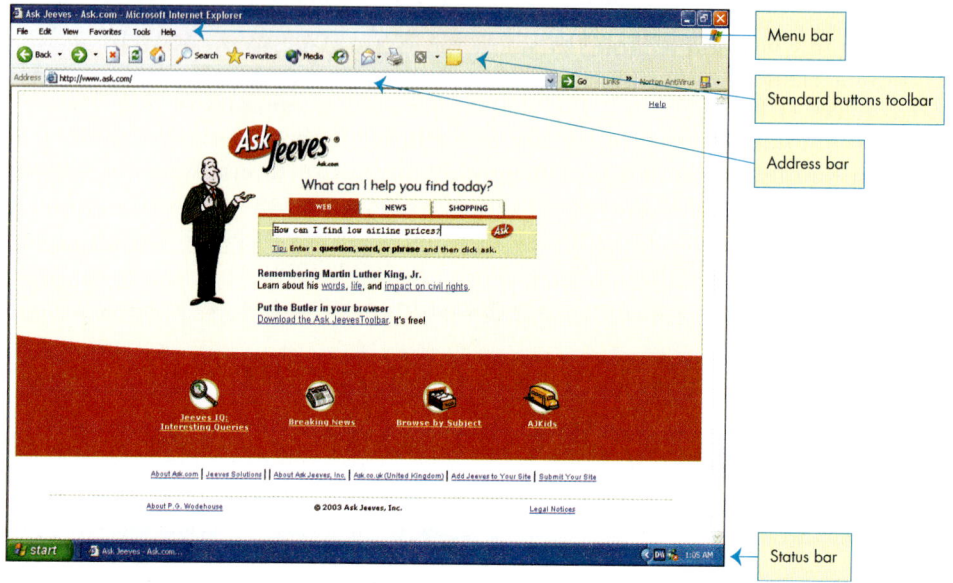

Figure 9.2.
Internet Explorer includes elements similar to those found in other Windows programs.

KNOW HOW TO NAVIGATE THE WEB

To get around the Web, you need a browser, such as Internet Explorer or Netscape Navigator. As you learned in previous chapters, the browser requests information from the Web server and then displays it in a graphical, user-friendly manner right on your computer. You'll also need an Internet connection via dial-up access, network, DSL, cable modem, or satellite. However, assuming that you have these things in place, you're ready to browse from one location to another on the Web.

Keep in mind that you're not actually traveling electronically through space, even though it might seem like it at times! Instead, at your request, the browser is displaying a series of Web pages on your system. **Web pages** are simply HTML documents; sometimes they are grouped together by hyperlinks into a **Web site** that's devoted to a particular purpose. For example, Microsoft's Web site includes a vast number of pages, all related to their main purpose, which is to provide information about Microsoft products and support.

In this section, we'll quickly go over some of the most commonly used ways to browse the Web. We'll also mention some inside tips to speed up your navigation. To do so, we'll use Internet Explorer as the sample browser. Why? Because it has the largest market share and chances are strong that you have access to it. So let's take a look at how to find the information you need on the Web.

USING URLS

In Chapter 8, you learned that URLs (Uniform Resource Locators), also called domain names, are used so that your browser will understand what type of document to retrieve and where it's located. URLs are also called Web addresses; just as you use a street address to locate a business or residence, so you can use Web addresses to find a Web site. The setup for most Web addresses is similar: They begin with *http://* to indicate that the Hypertext Transfer Protocol should be used; the *www.sitename.com* portion of the address indicates the location of the Web server in which the information is stored and the top-level domain (*.com* in this case). (Chapter 8 includes more detailed information about how URLs are set up if you think you would like a refresher on these concepts.)

Keeping these conventions in mind, let's look at how you can use the URL to find a specific Web site: First, locate the Address bar (see Figure 9.3). The **Address bar** is the area directly below the Standard Buttons toolbar in which you can enter the URL for the Web site you want to view. Next, type the Web site's URL in the Address bar of your browser and then press ↵Enter (or click the Go button). If all goes well, the Web site you want will be displayed; if you instead get an error message (such as *File Not Found*), try some of the troubleshooting methods covered in the next section of this chapter.

 INSIDE TRACK

If you see *https://* as part of a URL's name, it usually indicates that you're viewing a secure site (such as those set up for online shopping).

TROUBLESHOOTING ERROR MESSAGES

Running into error messages is relatively common when you're browsing the Web. Whenever you see an error message, such as *File Not Found* or *This page cannot be displayed*, it's possible that you've encountered a file that has been moved to another Web server or perhaps even been removed from the Internet. Because the Internet evolves and changes rapidly, chances are good that you'll eventually run into one of these Web site addresses that no longer works.

However, before you give up on finding a Web site, there are a couple of different things you can try. First, check to make sure you typed the address correctly—it's easy to miss a character in one of those must-be-letter-perfect URLs. Another glitch might be that the server where the files are located is temporarily "down." You can click the Refresh button to reload the page or

Figure 9.3.
Type a URL in the Address bar; then press ↵Enter or click the Go button to see the associated page.

Know How to Navigate the Web 133

just try again later. You can also try using the main domain name for the site—if *www.mysite.com/document* doesn't work, try using *www.mysite.com*. Finally, you can test to make sure that the problem is not within your system by accessing a mainstay Web site (such as Microsoft's). Because the sites for major corporations are almost always up and running, the problem might point to a problem on your computer if you have problems loading them.

REFRESHING YOUR DATA

OK, so you've located the Web site you want to view. In many cases, the pages at the site include exactly the same information each time you access it—the data returned by the source code for the page doesn't change. Web pages of this type are referred to as **static HTML**.

In contrast, many Web pages (especially those found on e-commerce sites or business sites) can change depending on the information you enter. For example, when you type in a Search box or an online form, the information shown on a page may change. **Dynamic content** is Web information that changes frequently, such as each time you access the site or in response to user input. Pages with dynamic content usually include static HTML as well as code that is capable of executing programs. This type of code is referred to as **dynamic HTML (DHTML)**.

INSIDE TRACK

Dynamic HTML includes static HTML programming code as well as other types of code that can run programs (such as JavaScript and cascading style sheets).

In addition to dynamic HTML code that can change a site's content "on the fly," many Web sites include data that is almost constantly modified by the people who maintain the site—sometimes as often as every couple of minutes. Imagine, for example, a weather or news site that only updated its information once a week! Of course, when you're using sites where the data changes frequently, you want to make sure that you're viewing the most current information. Here's how it works: Normally, after you've initially accessed a Web site, the data shown on your computer won't change even if the content on the Web server is modified. But you can easily update the screen you're viewing to make sure that it includes the most recent data. To do this, click the Refresh button (on Internet Explorer's Standard Buttons toolbar) or press F5. Either way, your browser will check the data on your system against that on the Web server and make sure you have the most up-to-date information.

TIPS AND TRICKS FOR ENTERING URLS

Of course, not only can it be a hassle to type URLs manually, but it's easy to accidentally type the wrong thing. To save you typing and to increase accuracy, most browsers include a number of keyboard shortcuts and other ways of quickly entering the address. A **keyboard shortcut** is a combination of keystrokes that you can use to perform an action in a program. Using a keyboard shortcut is sometimes faster than performing the same action by wading through menu commands or clicking the mouse. Keyboard shortcuts are handy to use if your mouse isn't working—or if you simply want to make your work on the Internet a little more efficient.

Here's an example: In Internet Explorer, you can press F4, which simultaneously highlights the address currently shown in the Address bar and opens a list of recently visited Web sites. You can use the keyboard arrows to move up and down the list of sites; when you locate the one you want, press ↵Enter.

HEADS UP! If the Address bar isn't displayed on your system, choose View, Toolbars, Address Bar from the Internet Explorer menu.

Chapter 9 Surfing Basics

You can also save time by typing the Web address without the *http://* element. This usually works because most browsers are smart enough to realize that you want a Web address and will automatically use the Hypertext Transfer Protocol. For example, you can type *www.domain.com* instead of *http://www.domain.com*. In many (but not all) cases, you can dispense with the *www.* portion of the address, too: try typing *domain.com* instead of *www.domain.com*. Want another great trick for entering addresses? If a name begins with *www.* and has a top-level domain of *.com*, you can enter just the site's name and then press Ctrl+Enter to add the *http://*, *www.*, and *.com* elements. For example, you can type coca-cola and then press Ctrl+Enter to complete the address and find the site. You can also select the text in the Address bar by pressing Alt+D; then begin typing the new URL.

As an alternative to using keyboard shortcuts, Internet Explorer has an **AutoComplete feature**. To use it, just start typing the URL in the Address bar and Internet Explorer will display all the recently visited Web sites that match your entry on a pull-down list. From the list, click the URL that you want.

Of course, you can't type a URL in the Address bar unless you know the site's name—and often you don't. That's where search engines and directories come to the rescue. But before you fire up a search engine, first try using logic to locate an address. In the case of major corporations, the name of the company and the Web site are almost always the same. For example, to locate Pepsi, simply type *www.pepsi.com*. Likewise, to locate Coca-Cola's site, type *www.coca-cola.com*.

 INSIDE TRACK

As handy as the AutoComplete list can be, some people prefer to delete its contents at the end of a work session, which protects their privacy and frees up disk space. To clear AutoComplete entries from the Address bar list, choose Tools, Internet Options. In the Internet Options dialog box, click the General tab (if necessary) and then click the Clear History button. Confirm your action by clicking Yes in the message box that displays. Finally, choose OK to close the Internet Options dialog box.

SCROLLING THROUGH VISITED WEB SITES

After you've been browsing online for a while, you may decide that you want to see a page you visited earlier in your work session. To scroll through the Web pages you've recently viewed, click the Back or Forward buttons on the Internet Explorer toolbar (see Figure 9.4).

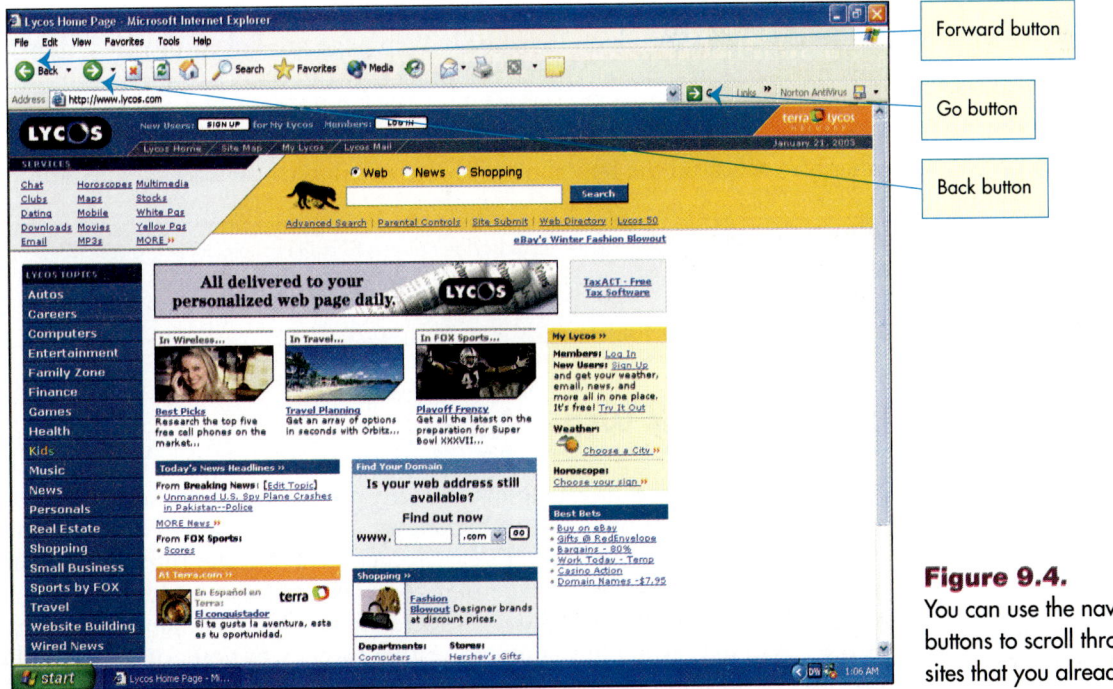

Figure 9.4.
You can use the navigation buttons to scroll through Web sites that you already visited.

Know How to Navigate the Web 135

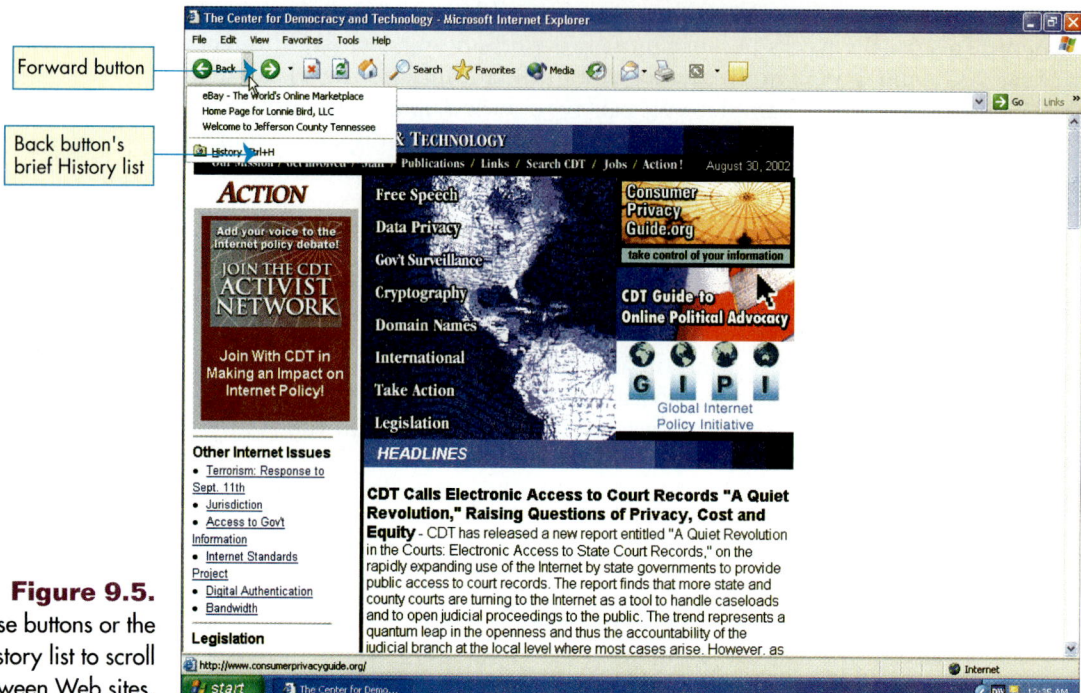

Figure 9.5.
You can use buttons or the brief History list to scroll between Web sites.

Alternatively, you can use the keyboard to scroll through recently viewed Web pages by pressing [Alt]+[←] or [Alt]+[→]. If you want to locate the page that you viewed several pages back, it is often quicker to view a brief list of sites you recently visited (sometimes called the *brief History*) instead of scrolling through individual pages. You can do this by clicking the Back or Forward drop-down list arrows and then clicking a site on the list (see Figure 9.5).

USING HYPERLINKS AND SHORTCUTS

Another way of finding Web pages and navigating between them is via hyperlinks. As you've already learned, hyperlinks can appear as text or graphics. Clicking a hyperlink will cause your browser to find and display the linked page.

You can identify which items on a Web page are linked to other sites by moving the mouse pointer over the object. If the object is a hyperlink, the pointer changes to a hand icon, and the hyperlink's Web address appears on the Status bar. The hyperlink is also usually underlined or shaded differently from other text. Click on the hyperlink to locate and display the associated page.

 **HEADS UP!** If the Status bar isn't displayed at the bottom of the browser window, choose View, Status Bar from the menu. You can also use the View menu to turn on or off other screen elements, such as toolbars.

 INSIDE TRACK

Internet Explorer includes a number of shortcut menus that you can display by right-clicking an area of the screen, an object, or a hyperlink. For example, you can right-click your Web page (not on a link) to display a shortcut menu with commands you can use for navigation, such as Back and Forward.

KEEP TRACK OF WEB SITES

Of course, using hyperlinks is old hat to many people. But hold on. We'll show you a couple of other ways to use hyperlinks more effectively. For one thing, you probably already know that it's easy to get "lost" on the Internet by wandering so much from page to page that you can no longer locate the original site. (Frankly, it's even easier to get distracted from your main *purpose* by clicking a series of interesting links until you either forget why you got online in the first place or simply run out of time!) To help you find a Web site again after some serious wandering, Internet Explorer includes a number of options. One of the best is to open a linked page in its own window, which keeps the original page open as well so that you can easily return to it. To do this, right-click the link and then choose Open in New Window. When you're finished using the second page, click its Close button to redisplay the original site.

BRINGING UP THE PAST

One effective method of finding Web sites you've previously viewed online is to use Internet Explorer's History list. The **History list** is simply the browser's way of keeping track of your most recently visited sites. This list is displayed in the History bar, which is a pane that you can display on the left side of the browser window by clicking the History button. (For all practical purposes, the terms *History list* and *History bar* can be used interchangeably.)

To view the History bar, click the History button on Internet Explorer's Standard Buttons toolbar. Alternatively, you can choose View, Explorer Bar, History from the menu or simply press Ctrl+H. After the History bar is opened, you can click on a Web site link to view the pages you visited at that site. You can display a specific page by clicking its link (see Figure 9.6).

You can also sort the sites you visited by date, by the ones you visited most often, or alphabetically by the site's name. To do this, click the View button at the top of the History bar and then choose the sort criteria, such as sorting By Date or By Site (refer to Figure 9.6). For example, you may have recently visited a site on travel and can't remember the name of the site, but you do know that it begins with the letter "T." By sorting the sites on the History bar alphabetically, you can quickly locate this site. When you're finished using the History bar, close it by clicking the History button or pressing Ctrl+H.

INSIDE TRACK

By default, Internet Explorer keeps track of sites you visited for the previous 20 days and includes them on the History list. However, if you're a confirmed Webbie and spend a lot of time online, you should consider reducing that number. Doing so saves disk space that would otherwise be devoted to tracking Web sites. To change the number of days to keep Web sites on the History list, choose Tools, Internet Options. In the History section on the General page, change the number of days to keep track of Web sites.

FINDING YOUR FAVORITES

Another way you can keep track of your favorite Web locations is to keep a running list of places that you specifically intend to revisit. In Internet

Figure 9.6.
The History bar provides an easy way to access pages you recently visited.

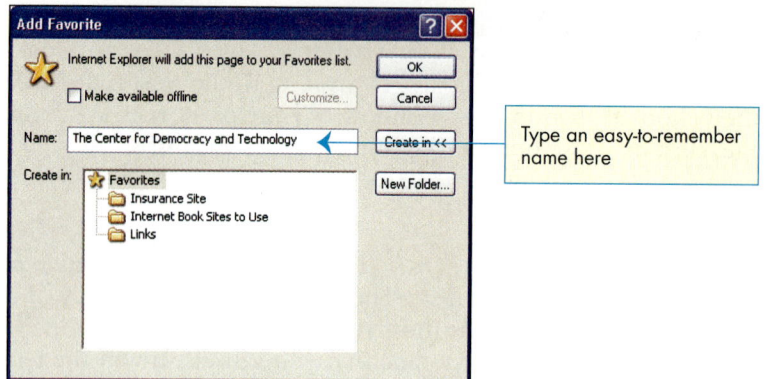

Figure 9.7.
You can easily add Web sites to the Favorites list.

Explorer, this list is called the **Favorites list**. It is similar to the History list in that it maintains shortcuts to Web pages. However, it differs because the History list is automatically developed by Internet Explorer, whereas the Favorites list includes only the sites you choose.

Because the Favorites list is so useful, Internet Explorer includes several ways to add sites to it. First, when you find a site that you want to return to, choose Favorites, Add to Favorites from the menu to display the Add Favorite dialog box (see Figure 9.7).

In the Add Favorite dialog box, click OK to add the site to the general Favorites list. When you do so, the newly added site appears at the bottom of the Favorites list. To add the site to a specific folder on the Favorites list, double-click the folder in the Add Favorite dialog box before clicking OK.

Another method of adding a Web site to your Favorites list is to right-click in a blank area of the page and then choosing Add to Favorites from the shortcut menu. Finally, you can use a keyboard shortcut, Ctrl+D, to add a site to the Favorites menu. This method is quicker than using the menu command because the site is automatically added to the list. Be aware, however, that there won't be any confirmation dialog box shown.

After you've added a Web site to your Favorites, you can use the list to locate the site again. To do this, click the Favorites menu. A listing of all the sites you've added to your Favorites appears below the Add to Favorites and Organize Favorites commands (see Figure 9.8). When you click a site on the list, your browser retrieves the appropriate file from the Web server.

Figure 9.8.
If you plan to revisit a Web site, you can add it to the Favorites list.

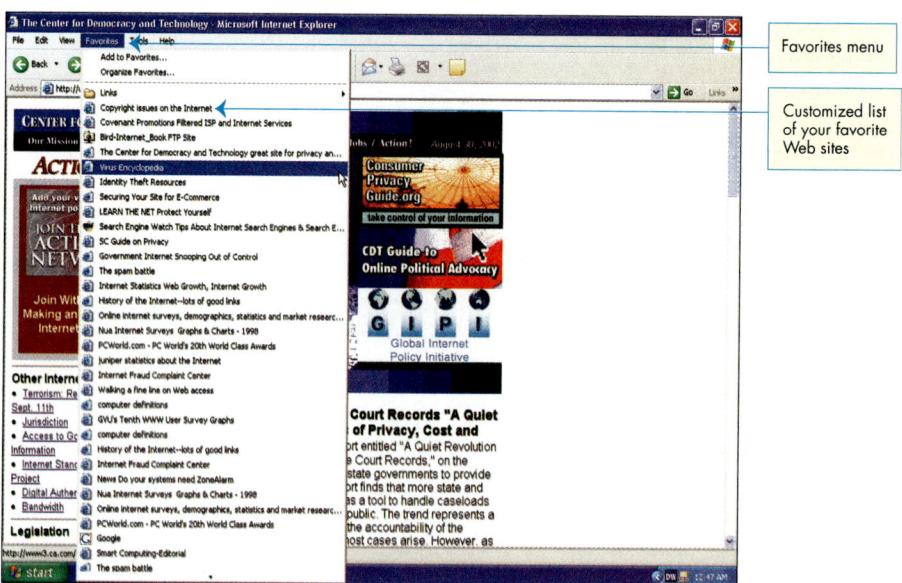

Chapter 9 Surfing Basics

Alternatively, you can click the Favorites button to display the Favorites bar. This bar displays in a pane on the left side of the browser application window, and includes the sites you've added to the list. You can click a site on the list to display it. Some people prefer to use the Favorites bar to using the Favorites menu. Why? Until you specifically close it, the Favorites bar is always displayed onscreen, which makes it easy to jump from site to site, just by clicking the links in the Favorites bar. The downside to using the Favorites bar is that it takes up space onscreen (which is why some people prefer to use the Favorites menu command).

CREATING WEB SHORTCUTS ON THE DESKTOP AND THE LINKS BAR

Another way to give yourself quick access to your favorite Web page locations is to place shortcuts to them on your desktop. To do this, display the Web page for which you want to create a desktop icon. Drag the Internet Explorer icon (the icon that appears to the left of the URL) from the Address bar to the desktop and then release the mouse. For example, if you have the page for *www.pepsi.com* displayed, you can drag the Internet Explorer icon to the desktop to create an icon for Pepsi's site. After you create a shortcut on your desktop, you can double-click the icon to start your browser and display the associated page.

Another way of relocating Web sites is to store them in the **Links bar**, which appears to the right of the Address bar. The Links bar is a good place to store your *most* frequently used sites because of its proximity to the Address bar. Compared with the Favorites list, the Links list usually includes only a handful of sites that you access most often. For example, you might want to include weather and news sites on the Links list if you check them frequently.

To add a Web site to the Links bar, drag the Internet Explorer icon from the Address bar to the Links bar and then release the mouse (refer to Figure 9.9).

INSIDE TRACK

If you spend much time on the Web, you'll quickly find that your Favorites list grows quicker than weeds on a hot summer day. To keep everything organized, choose Favorites, Organize Favorites from the menu to open the Organize Favorites dialog box. To create a folder in which to place related sites, choose Create Folder, type a name for the folder, and then press ↵Enter. You can also change a Web site's location on the list by dragging the site up or down or even by dragging it into a specific folder. To rename an entry on the Folder list in the Organize Favorites dialog box (perhaps to something you can more easily remember), select the item on the list and click the Rename button. Type a new name and press ↵Enter. Finally, to delete an entry from the list, select it and then press Del. In the Confirm File Delete message box that displays, choose Yes.

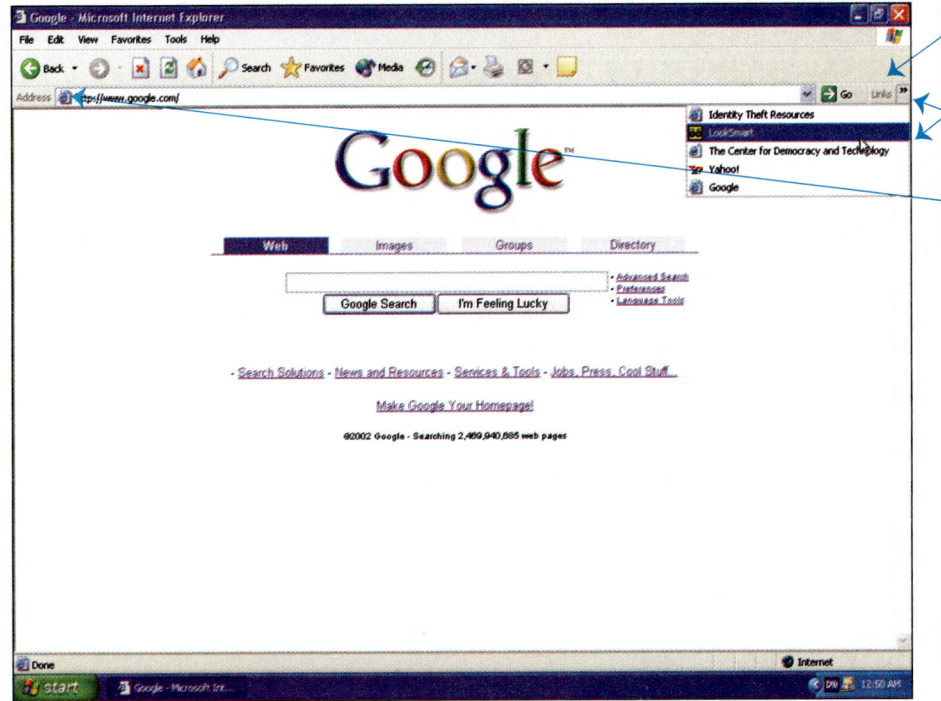

Figure 9.9.
The Links bar is a good place to store your most-visited sites.

You can also drag a hyperlink from a Web page to the Links bar. Alternatively, you can choose Add to Favorites from the Favorites menu and then save the page in the Links folder. After you add sites to the Links list, you can quickly display them by clicking the double arrows to the right of the Links bar and then clicking a site on the list.

> **HEADS UP!** If the Links bar doesn't appear in your browser window, choose View, Toolbars and then choose Links.

Now that you're familiar with the main methods of using Internet Explorer to find, display, and browse between Web pages, let's turn our attention to techniques of locating new sites.

KNOW HOW TO USE SEARCH TOOLS

You can use a wide variety of search tools to locate the information you want, including search engines and search directories. In this chapter, we'll go through the basics of using these tools; in Chapters 11 and 12, you'll build on this knowledge. A **search engine** is software that looks for data based on some criteria. It usually does so by searching through an indexed database of Web sites. Search engines pull up a listing of all the sites that include a topic or match the search criteria, but don't group them by subject. These search engines often collect data through the use of around-the-clock automated programs—called **spiders** or crawlers—that constantly search the text and coding of Web sites and then add the pages to their indexed databases. Two of the largest search engines are Google (*www.google.com*), shown in Figure 9.9, and AltaVista (*www.altavista.com*), shown in Figure 9.10.

In contrast to a search engine, a **search directory** is an organized collection of Web sites, categorized by subject. These directories are usually arranged in a hierarchical structure. For example, a search directory might

INSIDE TRACK

Search engines generally include three components: the site searcher (the spider), the index, and the software that presents the search results to the computer user.

Figure 9.10.
AltaVista and Google are two major players in the search engine game.

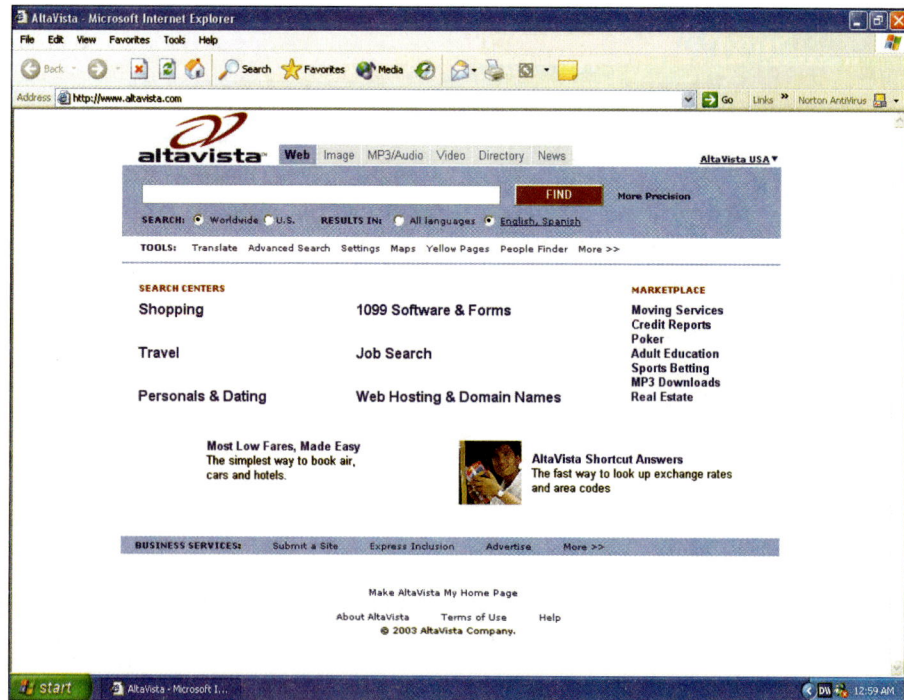

Figure 9.11.
Yahoo! is a search directory with information organized by content.

have a main category of *Pets*, which includes several subtopics, such as *Birds*, *Horses*, *Dogs*, and *Cats*. Each of the subtopics can potentially include its own set of subtopics: *Dogs* might include *Border Collies*, *German Shepherds*, *Poodles*, and so on. Real human beings, who have a say in what content will be included, organize search directories. One of the best-known search directories is Yahoo!, which is maintained by more than 100 editors (see Figure 9.11).

To help understand the difference between search directories and search engines, think of how a book is structured: A search engine is like the index in a book—the index entries are listed by topics with cross-references to the location where you can find the related data in the book. In contrast, a search directory is like a book's table of contents, with the data grouped by like subjects.

Let's take a look at a couple of related terms. A **Web search site** is simply a site that includes search engine capabilities. This term, which is used loosely, sometimes refers to sites that are technically directories. It can also refer to a portal site. A **portal** is a Web site that includes content and links to other sites as well as search engine capabilities. For example, some portals such as Yahoo! include free e-mail, chat rooms, travel and financial information, shopping, and a directory. As such, a portal serves as a starting point to other activities or destinations on the Web.

USING SEARCH ENGINES AND SEARCH DIRECTORIES: THE BASICS

Now that you understand the differences between search engines and directories, let's look at how to use them. Using a search engine involves simple steps: You display the Web site for the search engine and click in the text box provided. Type the topics (keywords) that you want to research; then click the *Go* or *Search* button that is usually located by the text box. The search engine finds sites that include your keywords and displays them in a list, sometimes with a brief description. You can then click a site on the list to display the page (see Figures 9.12 and 9.13).

INSIDE TRACK

Most people think the terms *search engine* and *Web search site* are the same thing. Technically, however, the term *search engine* refers to the software used, whereas *Web search site* is the site's physical location on the Web. In practical terms, however, the terms can be used interchangeably. In this book, we'll generally use the term *search engine*.

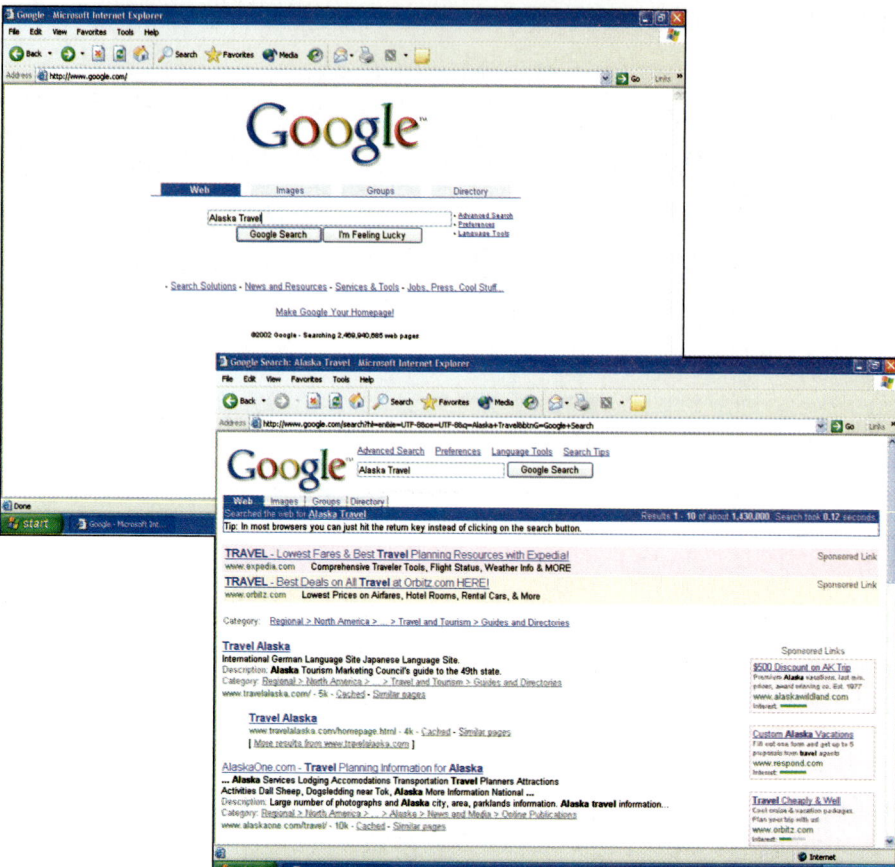

Figures 9.12 & 9.13.
Enter topics (keywords) in the text box provided... and the search engine finds related Web pages from its indexed database.

Because search directories are set up in a hierarchy, the technique for finding a Web site with them is slightly different from that used by search engines. Instead of entering keywords in a text box, most people use directories to browse through the related topics until they find what they want. You can work your way through the directory structure by clicking the links to display a subtopic; click on a subtopic to display *its* subtopics, and so on. This process is sometimes called **drilling down**. Most search directories indicate your location in the hierarchy so that you don't get too lost (see Figure 9.14).

The line between search directories and search engines is becoming more and more blurred. Search directories, such as LookSmart (*www.looksmart.com*), often include a text box you can use for searches *and* topical directories (see Figure 9.15); Google, technically a search engine, also includes a directory listing.

CONDUCTING MORE EFFECTIVE SEARCHES

Due to differences in the way that databases are set up and the way a search is conducted, search engines often produce different results from each other. This can be a good thing because if you can't find the information you need by using one search engine, you can try employing another.

There's an even more efficient method that you might want to consider, however. Instead of relying on just one or two search engines, try using one of the **metasearch engines**. These jumbo search engines look through multiple databases simultaneously, eliminating duplicate listings as they do so. One of the best-known metasearch engines is MetaCrawler, located at *www.metacrawler.com* (see Figure 9.16); another is Dogpile (*www.dogpile.com*).

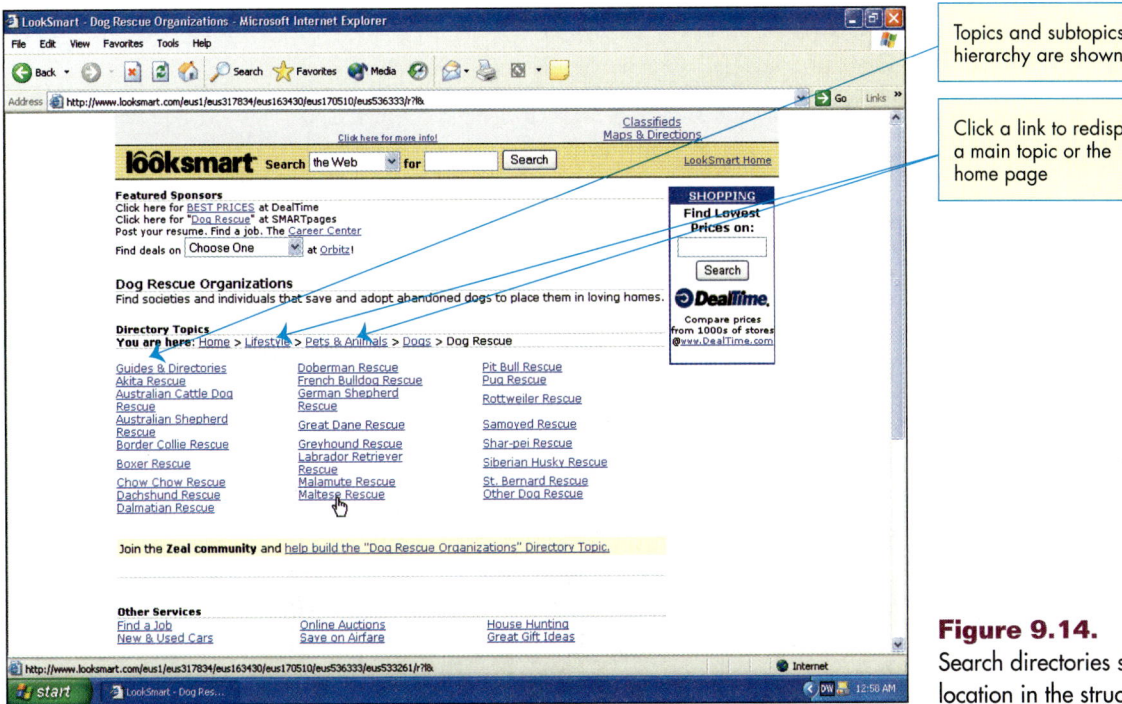

Figure 9.14.
Search directories show your location in the structure.

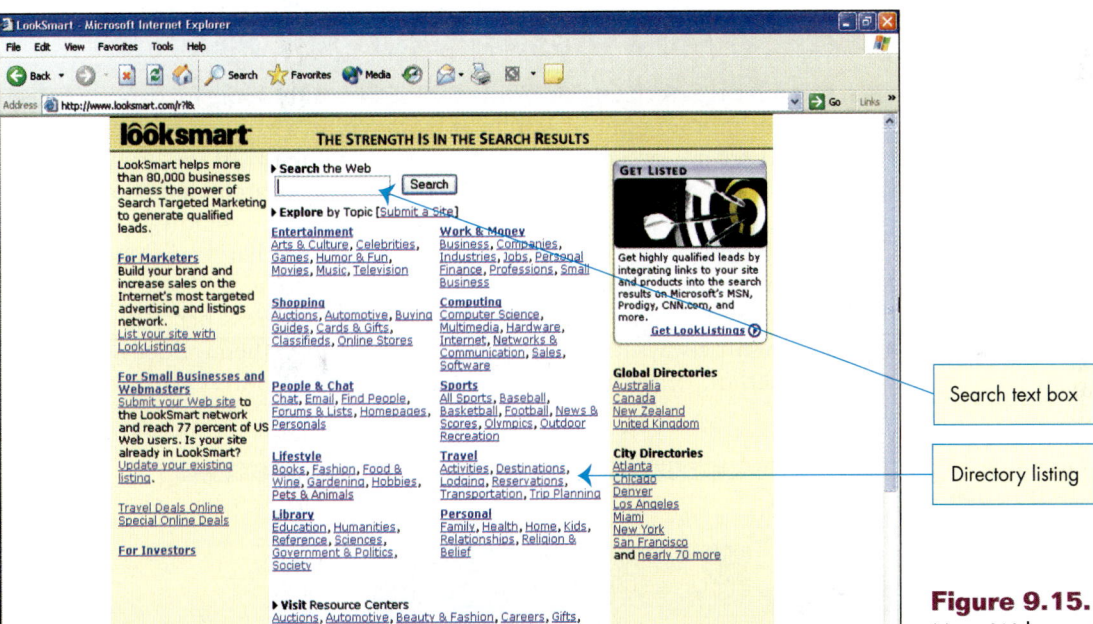

Figure 9.15.
Many Web search sites include search capabilities as well as a directory listing.

 **ON THE HORIZON**

You'll probably be hearing soon about the Semantic Web, which is an idea thought of by Tim Berners-Lee and promoted by the W3C group. The Semantic Web would let users search by meaning, not only specific words.

Know How to Use Search Tools 143

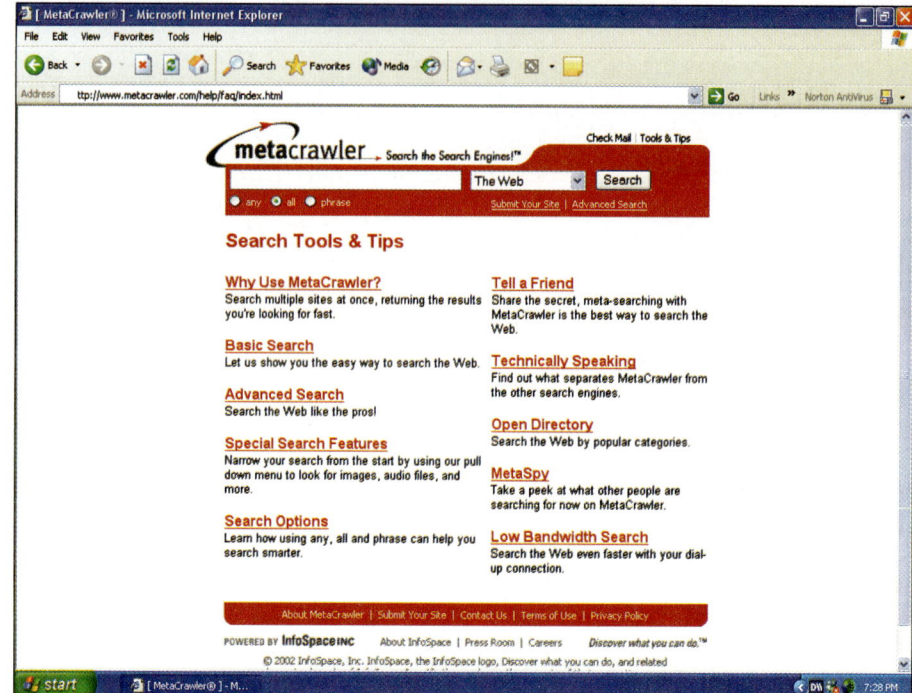

Figure 9.16.
Use a metasearch engine to simultaneously use multiple search engines.

SEARCHING FROM WITHIN INTERNET EXPLORER

Even though the search engines, directories, and other tools are extremely useful, you have another option: searching from within a browser such as Internet Explorer. There are two main ways to launch searches from the browser. First, you can click the Search button, which launches the Search Companion in the Search bar (a pane) on the left side of the application window (see Figure 9.17). Furthermore, you can type a topic in the Search bar's text box and then click Search (or press ↵Enter).

You can also search from Internet Explorer's Address bar. Although this method doesn't always locate the Web site you want, when it does, it provides a speedy method of finding a Web site. To use the Address bar for a search,

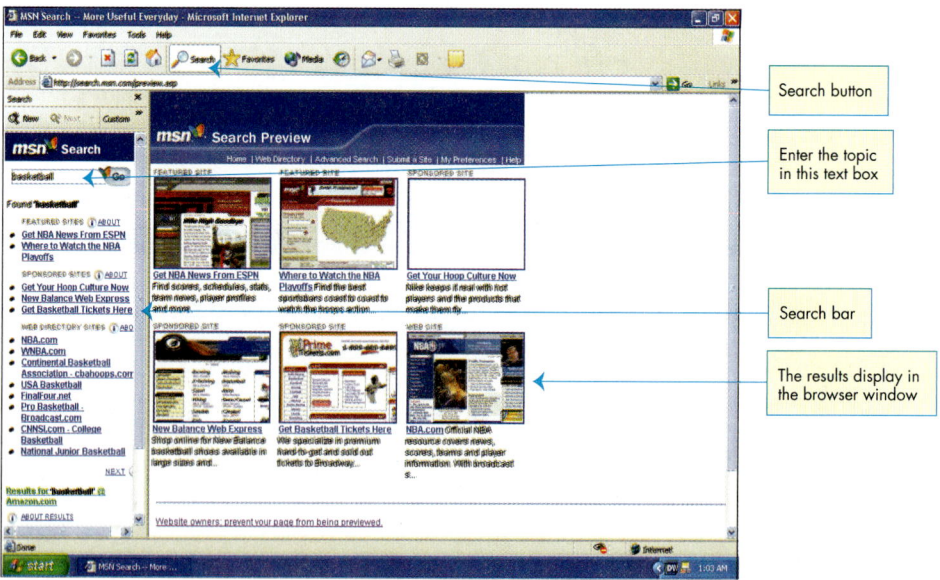

Figure 9.17.
You can use Internet Explorer's built-in search features to find information.

simply type the keyword in the Address bar and then press ⏎Enter. Internet Explorer will display the "most likely site" and show the other matches in the Search bar.

You can control how the searches you conduct from the Address bar operate. For example, you can indicate that the browser should display only a listing of related sites in the application window instead of going to the "most likely site." To change settings, choose Tools, Internet Options. In the Internet Options dialog box, click the Advanced tab. Scroll through the list to the *Search from the Address bar* section. Choose the option you want before closing the dialog box (see Figure 9.18).

Armed with these methods of finding just the site you want, you're ready to learn about methods of getting around an individual Web page quickly—and in the next section, we'll show you how.

UNDERSTAND HOW TO GET AROUND A WEB PAGE

OK, so you've found just the Web site you want. You can now read the entire thing top-to-bottom, click a hyperlink to go to another page, read it, and so on. It can be very helpful to know additional methods of moving within a Web page. Table 9.1 lists a few keyboard shortcuts that can help you get around.

INSIDE TRACK

If you're not sure which option you want in a dialog box, get some help. To do this, click the Help button (in the upper-right corner of the dialog box) and then click a command or option in the dialog box. A ScreenTip will display with an explanation of the option.

INSIDE TRACK

Many Web sites use **frames**, which is a method of coding a Web page to lay out the information into two (or more) independent sections. Technically, using frames is like loading multiple Web pages within the same browser screen. Frames can be used to organize the information on a Web page, such as including a listing of hyperlinks. You can then click a hyperlink in one frame to display the associated information in another one. So that they will display correctly, frames usually require the viewer to have a current browser (such as Internet Explorer 6).

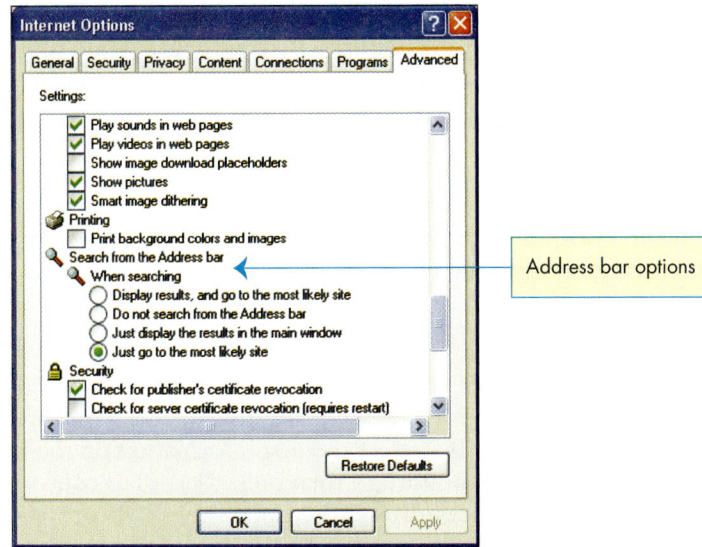

Figure 9.18.
You can control how searches you run from the Address bar operate.

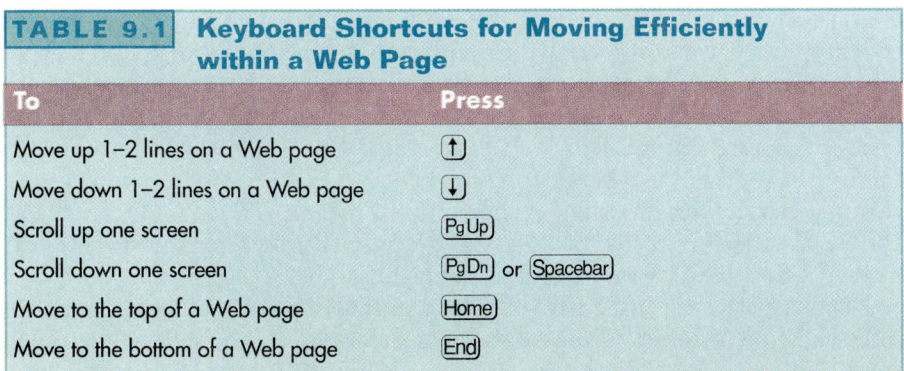

TABLE 9.1	Keyboard Shortcuts for Moving Efficiently within a Web Page
To	**Press**
Move up 1–2 lines on a Web page	↑
Move down 1–2 lines on a Web page	↓
Scroll up one screen	PgUp
Scroll down one screen	PgDn or Spacebar
Move to the top of a Web page	Home
Move to the bottom of a Web page	End

INSIDE TRACK

One quick method of moving through a Web page is to use the mouse's scroll wheel.

FIND INFORMATION ON A WEB PAGE

After you display a Web page, you're presented with the task of finding the specific information you want to find. For example, some sites include long lists of items for sale—lists that can continue for several pages. Instead of scrolling (and reading) the entire page, you can use the Find feature to quickly jump to the information you want. This is also helpful when you want to find a specific name or topic. To use this feature, click in the frame where you want to look for the information and then choose Edit, Find (or press Ctrl+F) to display the Find dialog box. Enter the text you want to locate in the Find what box and then press Enter.

Some Web sites also include a site-specific Search feature to help you locate data on their pages. Even though each site is set up a bit differently, here's a general technique you can use: Type the word or phase you're looking for in the Search box provided and then press Enter. A listing of associated documents (hyperlinks) within the site is displayed.

You can also browse incognito to protect your online privacy by using an anonymous browsing service, such as Anonymizer (*www.anonymizer.com*) This service—and others like it—help to protect your privacy. They do this by hiding the IP address of your computer, disabling pop-up windows, and disabling cookies. All of these measures help ensure that your online movements won't be traced.

KNOW HOW TO USE INFORMATION OFFLINE

Although it's useful to read through Web pages while online, it's likely that you'll forget the bulk of what you read. Instead, you can use the information offline by employing a few simple techniques to save, print, or even e-mail the data. Putting the information in a form that you can use offline also frees up your phone line (if you have dial-up access) and keeps you from being chained to the computer. So instead of spending hours staring at a computer screen, you can copy, save, or print Web site data and then read it while relaxing in your armchair or at the beach.

SAVING WEB DATA

If you want to save Web page data, you have several options. First, you can simply copy the data from the browser window into a word processing program, such as Word. To do this, select the text information on the Web page by dragging over it with the mouse and then press Ctrl+C to copy it to the Clipboard. Open your word processor and then press the keyboard shortcut for pasting the data: Ctrl+V. Alternatively, you can select the text and then right-click within the selection. On the shortcut menu, choose Copy. Right-click in your word processor and then choose Paste. Don't forget that you are not limited to copying text; you can also copy the graphics and hyperlinks that are on a page.

Another way to keep information handy for later use is to save it as a file on your system. Display the Web page and then choose File, Save As from the browser's menu. In the Save Web Page dialog box, indicate the location for the file. In the Save as type section, you can save all the coding, graphics, and text associated with the site by choosing *Web Page, complete*. Alternatively, choose *Text File* from the Save as type drop-down list to retain only the text from a Web site. Click Save to finish the process.

You can also save just a site's graphics, such as a picture or logo. To do so, right-click the picture to display a shortcut menu; then choose Save Picture As (or Save Image As). In the Save Picture dialog box, choose a location, filename, and file format before clicking Save.

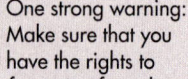

ALERT!

As you work on the Web, keep in mind that the sites you visit may place cookies on your system without your knowledge. As you remember from Chapter 2, The Good, the Bad, the Ugly: Uses and Misuses of the Internet, cookies are text files that a Web site stores on your computer so that it can "remember" who you are. Although some cookies (such as those at e-commerce sites) serve legitimate business purposes, many are used solely to gather marketing information. You can disable cookies on your system, although doing so will probably mean that some Web pages don't display as you expect. To do so, choose Tools, Internet Options. On the Privacy page, use the slider to indicate which cookies you're willing to have placed on your computer. Click OK to close the Internet Options dialog box.

ALERT!

One strong warning: Make sure that you have the rights to copy the information from the Web site. Much of the data on the Web is copyrighted; other information can be copied for personal, but not commercial use.

146 Chapter 9 Surfing Basics

PRINTING AND E-MAILING WEB PAGES

Printing a Web page is handy so that you have it as an offline reference. If you already copied the data to a program, such as Word, you can simply choose File, Print in that program. However, you can also send a Web page directly from the Web to the printer. To do so, display the Web page and then choose File, Print from the browser's menu. In the Print dialog box, click the Print button.

There are some drawbacks to printing Web pages, however. Printing a Web page as it appears onscreen can be slow and often includes graphics, colors, and even advertisements that you don't really need. These can significantly slow down printing as well as waste paper and ink or toner. Fortunately, many Web pages include a *Printer Friendly version* link. You can click this link to print the site's text *without* all the associated graphics.

Another problem with printing Web pages is that many college labs charge for each page you print. To avoid printing (and paying for) unnecessary pages, indicate which ones you want in the Page Range section of the Print dialog box. Alternatively, you can select only the text you want on the page (such as a paragraph) and then press Ctrl+C to copy it to the Clipboard. Display a blank document in a word processing program such as Word and then press Ctrl+V to paste the data. You can then print the text from within the word processing program.

Finally, you can easily e-mail a Web page to a friend or business associate. Display the Web page and then point to Send on the File menu. Choose *Page by E-mail* on the submenu. The page will be included in the body of an e-mail message. Finish the process by adding the recipient's e-mail address in the To text box and then clicking Send.

You can also e-mail an individual graphic. For example, imagine that you want to send a particularly funny cartoon to a friend (assuming, of course, that you have the ethical and legal rights to use the cartoon). You can right-click the cartoon and then choose *E-mail Picture* from the shortcut menu. In the *Send Pictures via E-Mail* dialog box, choose the size of graphic that you want to send. Click OK to simultaneously close the dialog box and place the graphic in a new e-mail message window. Finish the process by indicating the recipient's e-mail address in the message window and then clicking Send.

You should now be armed with a number of tips and tricks that can help to put your online Web time into high gear. Welcome to the Web.

INSIDE TRACK

You can quickly determine how a Web page will print by first previewing it. To do this, display the Web page and then choose File, Print Preview. You'll be able to see how the printed Web page will appear. You can also look at the Print Preview toolbar to see how many sheets of paper it will take to print the page.

Don't Forget...

- You can navigate on the Web by entering the specific URL for the site in the Address bar, clicking hyperlinks, using keyboard shortcuts, or using AutoComplete.
- You can keep track of Web sites you visit by using a variety of methods, including using the Favorites list.
- Search engines and search directories are not the same.
- Search engines are specialized software programs that read indexed databases and display the results to Web users.
- Search directories are set up in an organized fashion by real people.
- Some of the best-known search tools include Google, Yahoo!, and AltaVista.
- Metasearch engines retrieve information from multiple databases simultaneously.
- Internet Explorer includes a feature that you can use to conduct searches from within the program.
- You can use a variety of keyboard shortcuts to move efficiently within a Web page.
- You can use the Find command to locate specific information on a Web page.
- You can save and use Web page information offline.
- You can print or e-mail a Web page's text or objects (such as graphics).

Check This Out

MULTIPLE CHOICE

1. What is one difference between a search engine and a search directory?
   a. The search engine is an indexed database; the search directory is created by editors and based on categorized content.
   b. Using a search directory is always faster than using a search engine.
   c. The search engine is developed by real people; a search directory uses entries that a spider program finds.
   d. There is no difference between them.
2. Which of the following lists includes sites that the user specifically adds?
   a. Favorites
   b. History
   c. Places
   d. My Places
3. How can you make a Web site available so that you can find it again?
   a. Press Ctrl+D.
   b. Place it in the Links bar.
   c. Drag a link for it onto your Windows desktop.
   d. All of the above
4. Which of the following can you do to organize your favorite Web sites?
   a. Rename them.
   b. Group them by topic in a folder.
   c. Delete the ones you no longer use.
   d. All of the above
5. After you locate a Web page, you can
   a. Print it.
   b. E-mail it.
   c. Save it to your system.
   d. All of the above

MATCHING

a. URL
b. Web page
c. Address bar
d. History bar
e. Keyboard shortcut
f. AutoComplete
g. Search engine
h. Metasearch engine
i. Search directory
j. Portal

1. A Web site that includes content and links to other sites as well as search engine capabilities
2. Specialized software that can search indexed databases of Web sites
3. A combination of keystrokes that you can use to perform an action in a program
4. The location in a browser window in which you can enter a URL
5. An Internet Explorer feature that shows a list of all the Web sites you've *recently* visited whenever you start typing an entry in the Address bar
6. A search tool that is developed by people and organizes topics in a hierarchical structure
7. A search tool that scans several search engines simultaneously
8. A listing developed by your browser of the sites you visited in the last 20 days
9. A site's address, sometimes called the domain name
10. A document on the Web that you can use a browser to display

Real Life

1. Use the following search engines: AltaVista (*www.altavista.com*), Google (*www.google.com*), AllTheWeb (*www.alltheweb.com*), Excite (*www.excite.com*), HotBot (*www.hotbot.com*), and MetaCrawler (*www.metacrawler.com*). Use each engine to run searches on the following words: Travel, Pets, Computers, and Sports. Compare the speed of the search and the results each engine produced. Develop a chart that shows the results of your research.
2. Use main search directories, such as LookSmart (*www.looksmart.com*) and Yahoo! (*www.yahoo.com*) to find information on the same topics listed in Real Life Activity #1 (Travel, Pets, Computers, and Sports). Compare the method and results with that in Real Life Activity #1.
3. Spend time working with the Favorites list and Links bar. Add several Web sites to each; then use the list and bar to locate the sites again. In the Favorites folder, create subfolders and move some of your sites into the subfolders. Finally, delete the sites from the Favorites list and the Links bar.
4. Using the information in this chapter as a guide, practice using Internet Explorer's shortcuts for entering URLs. Also, practice various methods of scrolling through Web sites.
5. Find a Web site on Internet privacy and security issues. Save the Web page to your hard drive, print it, and e-mail it to a friend.

6. Internet Explorer provides a way to share your Favorites list between multiple computers: Choose Import and Export on the File menu, which launches the Import/Export Wizard. Use Internet Explorer's Help system to find out more about this feature; then practice transferring the Favorites list from one computer to another using the wizard.

7. Some of the sites you'll encounter on the Web may not be legitimate or may contain erroneous information. Discuss some ways that you can determine whether or not a Web site includes accurate information with others in your class. If time allows, develop a short checklist that you can use to evaluate Web sites for accuracy.

I Spy: Privacy and Security Concerns

1. Go to Anonymizer's Web site (*www.anonymizer.com*). Explore the information included on the site and the list of features included in the program. If available, use the site's "Snoop test" to find out what crackers know about your system. For example, depending on your system's configuration, snoopers may be able to see what you copied to the Clipboard. If possible, complete the Snoop test on several different systems and then develop a report that compares the differences.

2. Research the privacy and security issues related to Internet Explorer. To do so, open Internet Explorer and then choose Help, Contents, and Index. If necessary, click the Show button. Click the Index tab to display that page. On the list, find and read the information about *privacy* and *security*. Summarize your findings in a short oral report that you can present to a small group or to your class.

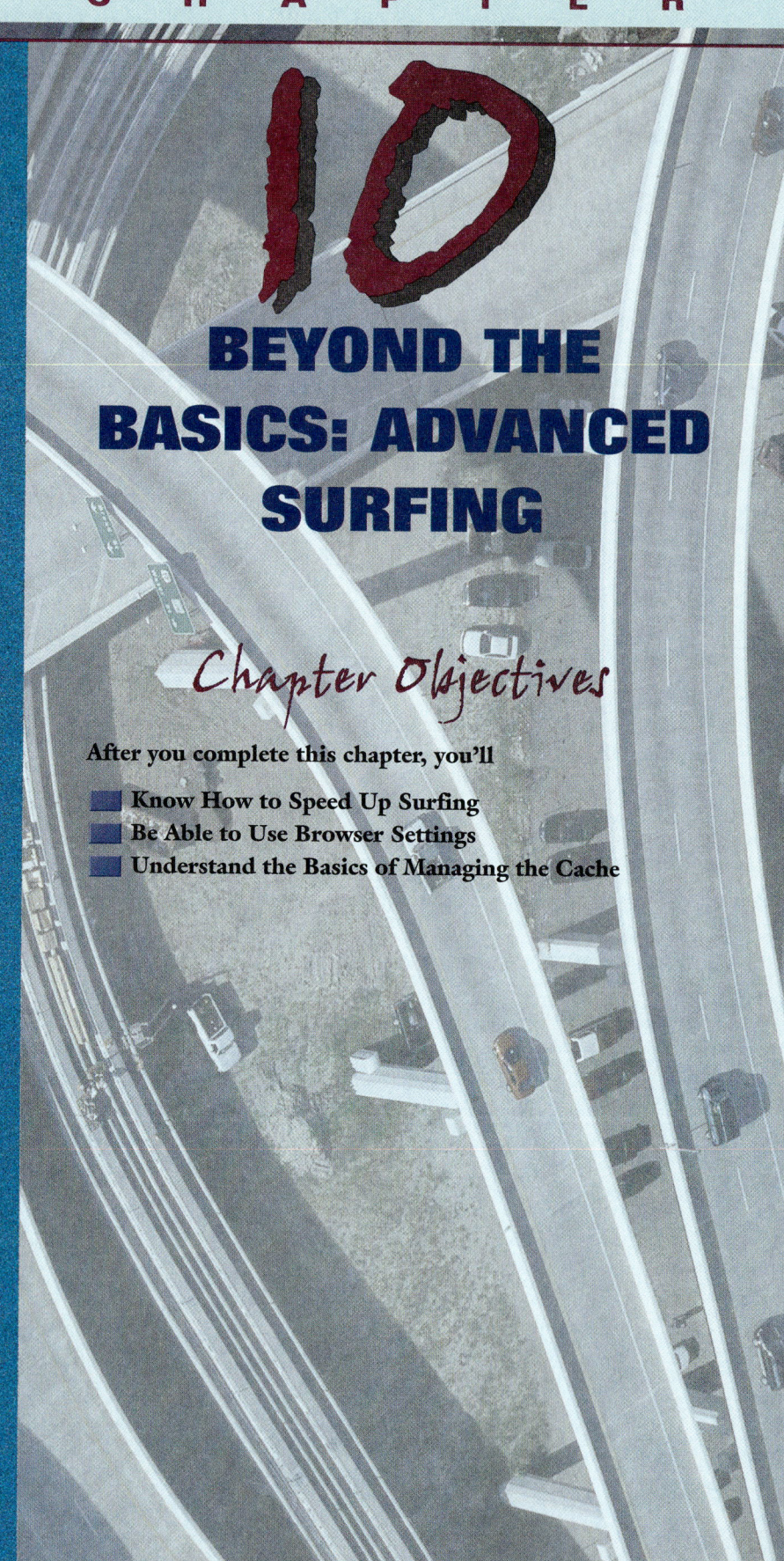

CHAPTER 10

BEYOND THE BASICS: ADVANCED SURFING

Key Terms

When you finish this chapter, you'll understand the following terms:

- active content
- active window
- ActiveX
- ActiveX controls
- applets (Java applets)
- cache
- Java
- JavaScript
- referrer
- session
- start page (home page)

Chapter Objectives

After you complete this chapter, you'll

- ■ Know How to Speed Up Surfing
- ■ Be Able to Use Browser Settings
- ■ Understand the Basics of Managing the Cache

The Big Picture

You probably know many people who can browse the Web using the basic features in search engines and directories. However, when it comes down to it, the majority of them only scratch the surface in terms of getting around effectively and becoming *really* knowledgeable Web users. It's not that they don't want to work more quickly on the Web. They just don't know the inside tips and tricks that more savvy users do.

But you're not doomed to that fate—at least not if you go through this chapter. By reading it, you'll learn ways to dramatically increase surfing speed, squash online commercials, change browser options, keep malicious code at bay, and manage your system's cache.

Window on the Web

In this chapter, we'll focus on techniques to work more efficiently on the Web. For example, one way to streamline your work is to open multiple windows in your browser (see Figure 10.1). Opening multiple browser sessions allows you to cross-reference the information from various sites—a technique that's particularly useful if you do much research. It also helps you download Web pages in a hopscotch fashion because you can view one window while the other is downloading; then switch windows and repeat the process.

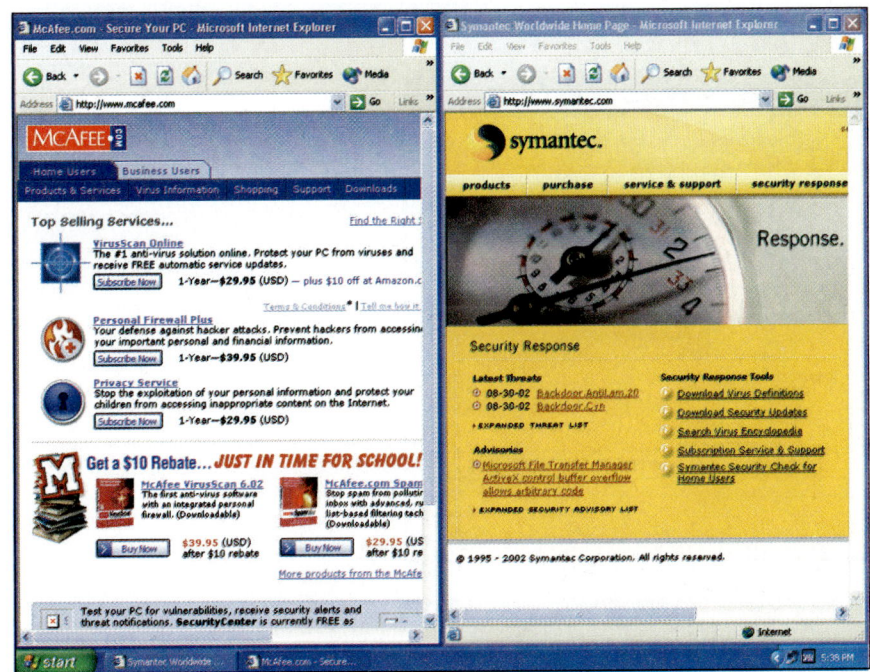

Figure 10.1.
You can sometimes operate more efficiently on the Web by opening multiple windows in your browser.

In this chapter, you'll also learn how to speed up browsing. For example, you can speed up your browser's retrieval of Web pages by turning off Internet commercials. These online commercials are heavily laden with graphics and multimedia features that take system resources to load (see Figure 10.2). Turn them off and you should see an increase in browser speed.

Another way to more effectively manage your online sessions is to regulate the cache: the place where Web pages are stored on your system. The cache stores the pages, graphics, sounds, and URLs of the online sites you visit on your hard drive. If you request the page again, the browser doesn't have to download everything from scratch again. Because the computer can display items on the hard drive much more quickly than those it has to download from the Internet, using a cache speeds up your online work. And, as you'll see in this chapter, you can change the cache settings in your browser (see Figure 10.3).

By now, you probably realize that you can tap into advanced features to better manage your online time. Let's explore some practical ways to do this.

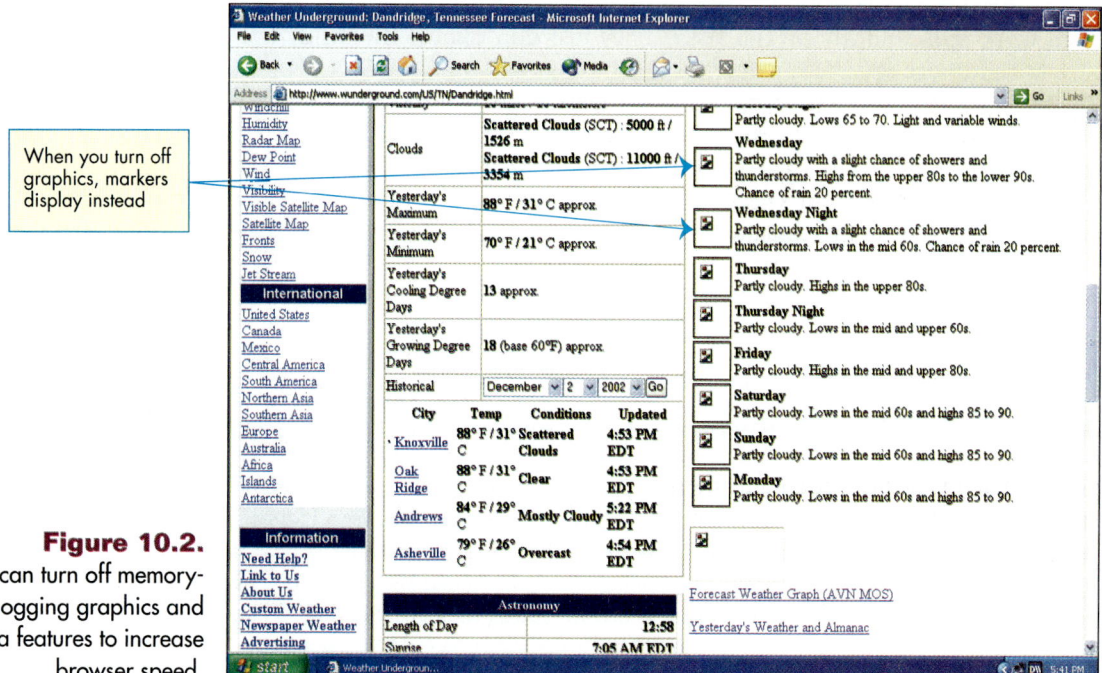

Figure 10.2.
You can turn off memory-hogging graphics and multimedia features to increase browser speed.

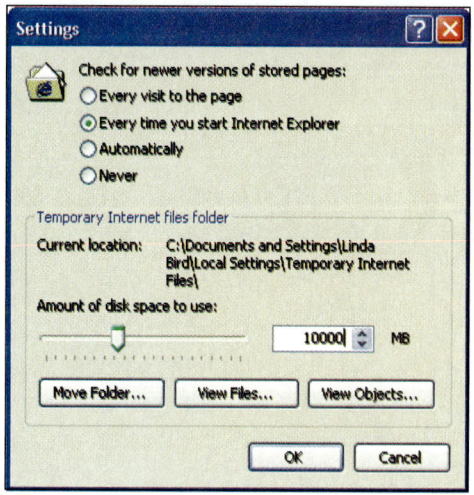

Figure 10.3.
You can control how your system handles retrieved Web pages.

KNOW HOW TO SPEED UP SURFING

If you've spent very much time browsing the Web, it's probably happened to you. You view several pages on a subject, such as how to buy a car or tips when traveling to the beach. Pretty soon, you notice that a number of extra additional windows are open as well as the main browser window. Additionally, your system is running more slowly. Guess what? Every time you viewed a page, a pop-up advertisement opened as well, zapping system resources, such as memory (see Figure 10.4).

Or perhaps this sounds familiar: You request a Web page on a particularly interesting topic ... and then wait ... and wait ... and wait ... after a while the page finally displays, but by then you're out of time to read it. But don't let online advertisements, unwanted graphics, or other problems slow you down. Instead, you can use the techniques covered in this section to make your browsing sessions faster and more efficient.

USING MULTIPLE BROWSER SESSIONS

One way to better manage your time on the Web is to run multiple browser sessions, each in its own window, within Internet Explorer. This is handy when you need to compare the information on various Web sites or if you want to see them simultaneously. Being able to view multiple Web sites at the same time is also useful for times when you want to keep a window open for a particular Web site, but use a second window to wander freely to other sites. For example, imagine that you're evaluating anti-virus software. You can open several windows, each with product information from a different company.

Each browser window you use operates independently of any others that are open. Each time you open and then close a browser window, you've run a **session**. When you have more than one browser window open, you're technically running multiple browser sessions.

Figure 10.4.
Each extra window or pop-up advertisement can eat up system resources.

The easiest way to do this is to start more than one copy of Internet Explorer. For example, you can double-click the Internet Explorer icon that (by default) is on your Windows desktop to launch the first session; then double-click the icon again to start a second session. (Alternatively, you can choose Internet Explorer from Windows' Start menu.)

Like other Windows' programs, each time you open a program, an associated button is placed on the Windows taskbar. You can switch between these open windows by clicking the appropriate taskbar button. Whichever program you select becomes the **active window**, and it appears on top of the others (see Figure 10.5).

INSIDE TRACK

Instead of clicking taskbar buttons with the mouse, you can switch between open programs by using a keyboard shortcut: Press and hold down Alt and then press Tab repeatedly to scroll through the open program until the one you want is selected in the task manager window. Release both keys, and the selected program will become the active window.

There are other ways to initiate multiple browser sessions than to launch Internet Explorer from the desktop or Start menu, however. Display Internet Explorer in the active window and then press Ctrl+N to create a duplicate browser session. In the newly created window, you can click a link or enter an address in the Address bar to view another site. Repeat this process for each Web site you want to view.

You can also view all the open browser windows at once: right-click the Windows taskbar and then choose *Tile Windows Horizontally* or *Tile Windows Vertically* from the shortcut menu (see Figure 10.6).

You can also resize and move the browser windows just as you do other Windows programs. Finally, when you're finished with a browser window, clear it by clicking its Close button or simply press Ctrl+W.

USING MULTIPLE BROWSERS

By now, you know that Internet Explorer holds the largest portion of the browser market share. In fact, most computers (notably, those that use a recent version of Windows as the operating system), come with Internet Explorer preinstalled. However, many Web-savvy users recommend installing Netscape's browser on your machine in addition to Internet Explorer. This allows you to use them simultaneously to surf the Web. How? Simply open different Web sites in each browser window. For example, while you're waiting

Figure 10.5.
You can freely switch between multiple Internet Explorer browser sessions.

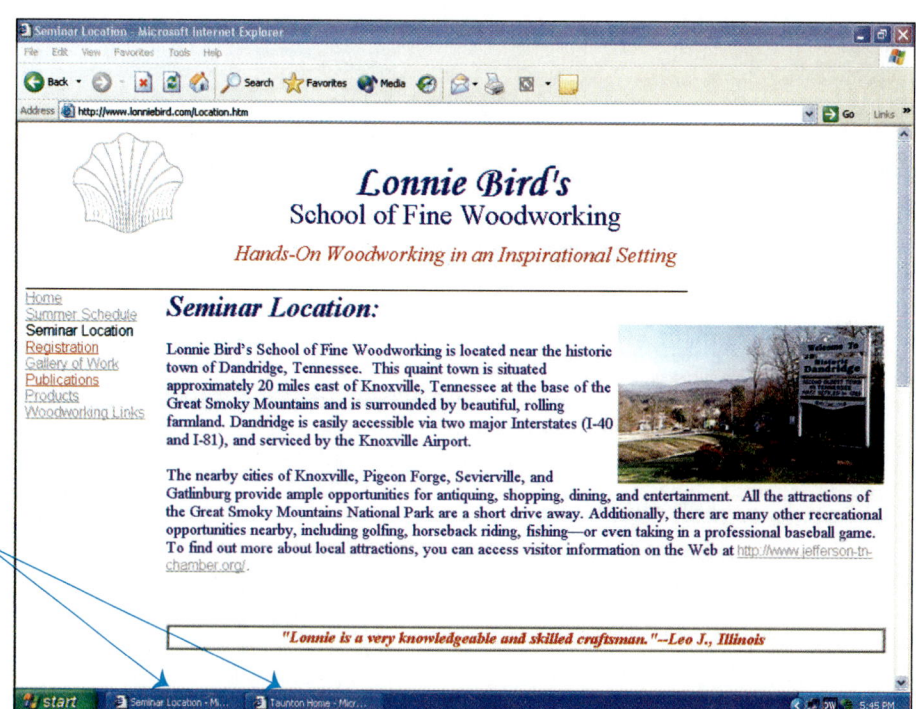

Click a taskbar button to switch to its program

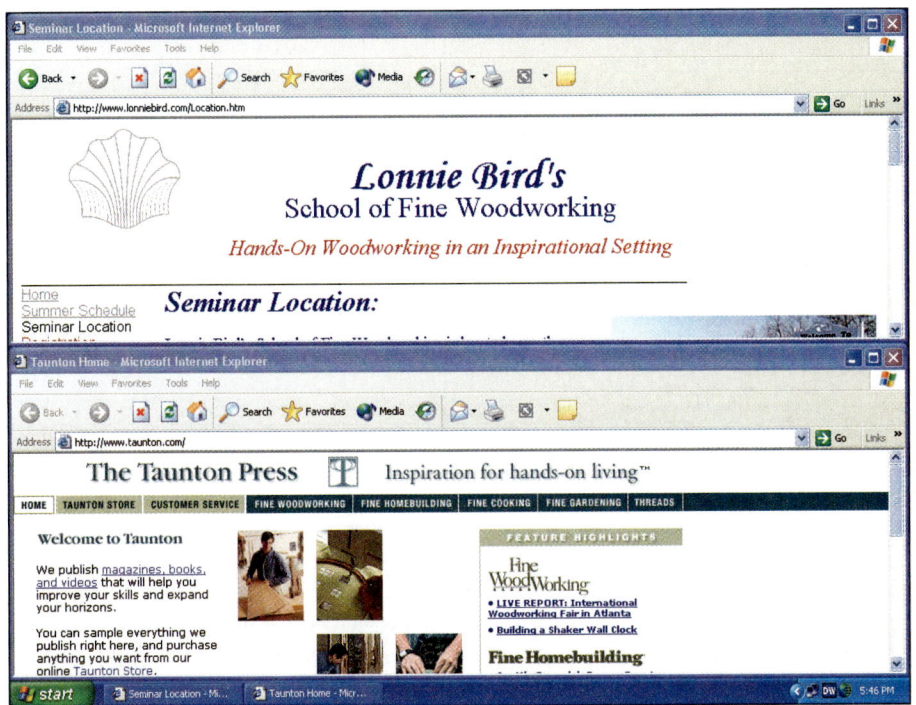

Figure 10.6.
You can tile open windows so that you can view multiple Web sites simultaneously.

for a Web site to load in Internet Explorer, you can view another site in Netscape and then repeat the process. By keeping two different browsers downloading information in a hopscotch fashion, you'll maximize your online time. Additionally, some Web sites look better in one browser than the other. Because of this, having both browsers installed on your system maximizes your chances of seeing the Web site formatted in a graphically pleasing (and readable) manner.

Here's how to use multiple browsers: After you've loaded both Netscape and Internet Explorer on your system, launch each program from the Windows Start menu. In each browser window, open the Web sites you want to view. It's as easy as that.

Are there any drawbacks to a dual-browser system? Just a couple. Although tapping into the strengths of multiple programs works for more experienced Web users, some people feel that they would rather learn just one software program well and then use it exclusively. And having two browsers on your computer takes up more disk space than does a single program, of course. But if these shortcomings don't bother you, take a serious look at this technique.

DISABLING GRAPHICS AND MULTIMEDIA

Many Web sites are underwritten by advertising, just as television and radio are supported by paid commercials. But even if you're sympathetic to this principle, you probably don't appreciate having your entire online experience slow to a crawl as banner advertisements march across the page or flash in Las Vegas-style neon colors. Conversely, a sure way to speed up the display of your favorite Web pages is to squash these ads.

So...how do you eliminate these Internet commercials? Most online ads are simply graphics, so if you modify your browser settings to suppress the display of graphics, you'll generally eliminate the ads as well. To turn off graphics in Internet Explorer, choose Tools, Internet Options, and then click the Advanced tab. You'll notice a long list of settings for the program. Scroll

 **INSIDE TRACK**

Internet Explorer has strong merits, including an almost universal usage and strong support. And even though it's lost some of its market share, Netscape still has a reasonable following. However, you might want to consider looking beyond these two heavyweights to a third option: Opera. Available as a downloadable program on Opera's Web site (*www.opera.com*), this company claims that Opera loads Web pages faster than other browsers. The difference is marginal if you have broadband, but is marked if you still have dial-up access (and a sluggish system).

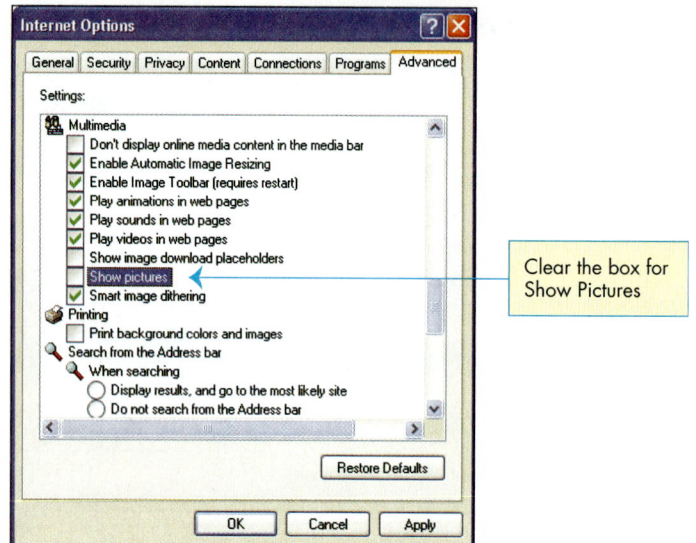

Figure 10.7.
Turn off the display of Web page graphics, and you'll simultaneously turn off most online commercials.

downward through the list until you find the Multimedia section. Clear the *Show Pictures* check box and then click OK (see Figure 10.7).

When you turn off the display of graphics, a graphic icon in a box will appear to mark the location of the picture on Web pages. If you decide that you want to view a picture on a Web site, right-click within the border that indicates the graphic's location and then choose Show Picture from the shortcut menu (see Figure 10.8).

INSIDE TRACK

Although you can eliminate the bulk of online commercials by turning off pictures (graphics), some advertisements include videos, animations, or sound files. To rid yourself of these *and* speed up the display of Web pages, choose Tools, Internet Options, Advanced. In the Multimedia section, clear the appropriate boxes.

BLOCKING ADVERTISEMENTS

If you want a more permanent solution for turning off those slow-loading online commercials, consider using ad-blocking software. Ad-blocking software is a utility that essentially acts as a wall between your browser and the out-

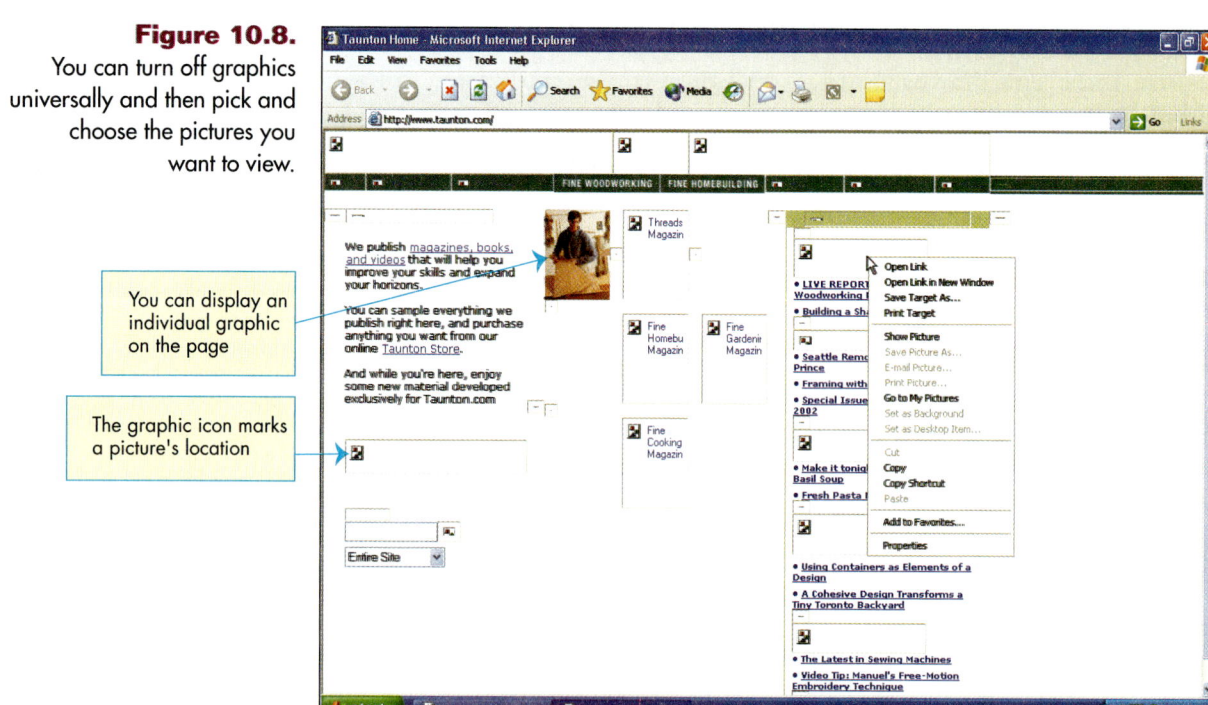

Figure 10.8.
You can turn off graphics universally and then pick and choose the pictures you want to view.

156 Chapter 10 Beyond the Basics: Advanced Surfing

side world—you don't even see the ads because they never even get to your computer.

Most of the ad-blocking programs can be downloaded from the Web. Even though some companies charge a small fee for the software, you may feel the money is well-spent. Not only will blocking ads speed up your surfing experience, but also some of the ad-blocking programs increase your online privacy as well by blocking cookies and clearing the browsing history.

Some ad-blocking programs are also able to block referrers. A **referrer** is used to track your online movements and then share that information with advertisers. Here's how it works: When you click an ad or hyperlink on a site, the browser sends along the URL of the page you were originally viewing (the referral site) along with the request. This information helps advertisers to track your online movements.

When you enter keywords in some search engines, referrers can also be used by advertisers to send your search text to advertising agencies. These agencies then custom-design advertisements for the next site(s) you view. For example, if you type *insurance* as the keyword in some search engines, you may soon find yourself viewing a number of ads related to buying insurance.

So, if you decide that ad-blocking software is worth the money, where should you look? On the Web, of course. One of the best-rated ad-blocking programs is AdSubtract (*www.adsubtract.com*), shown in Figure 10.9. This program includes well-respected ad-blocking and privacy features. Another useful utility you can consider using to block ads and crush cookies is Internet Junkbuster (*www.junkbusters.com*). Internet Junkbuster can be downloaded for free.

SURFING DURING OFF-TIMES

Internet traffic can be almost as bad as that found during rush hour in a major metropolis. If you have a choice, browse during off-times. This will ensure that pages load faster, and you'll probably enjoy your online time more as a result. The busiest times are usually late afternoon, evenings, Saturdays, Sunday after-

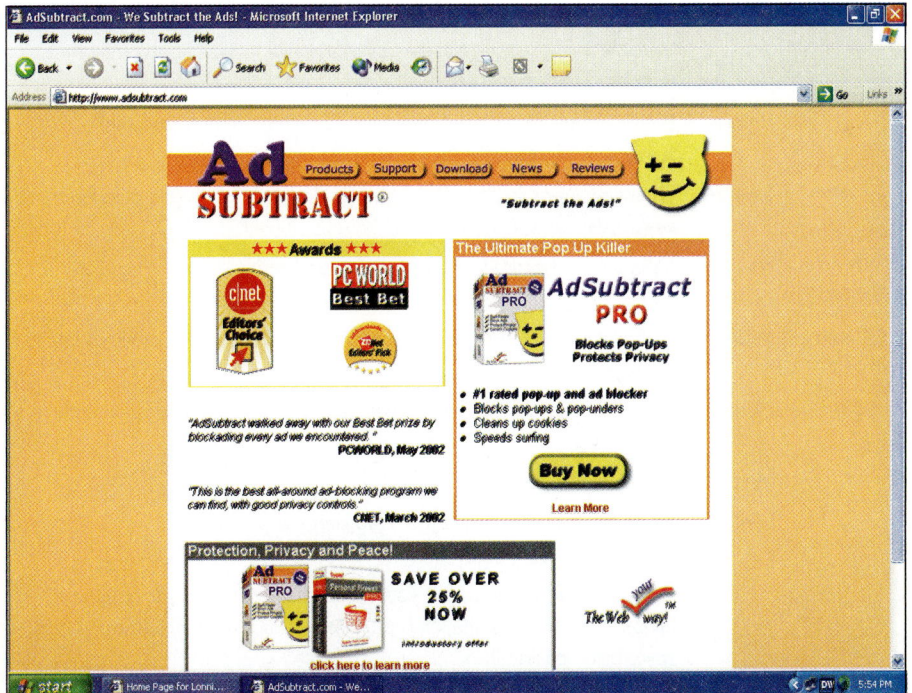

Figure 10.9.
Ad-blocking software stops a variety of annoying ads from getting to your computer.

noons, and holidays. Consequently, the Web is less-traveled late at night or early in the morning.

A related idea is to make sure that you sign up with an Internet Service Provider that has enough connections to accommodate everyone who signs up for the service. If not, you may find yourself having difficulty even *getting* online during peak times if you have a dial-up connection. (For a review on choosing an Internet Service Provider, see Chapter 4, Internet Service Providers.)

BE ABLE TO USE BROWSER SETTINGS

Internet Explorer includes a number of options and settings that can make your online experience more enjoyable. In this section, we'll cover some of the most useful ones.

USING THE STANDARD BUTTONS TOOLBAR

In Chapter 9, Surfing Basics, you learned how to use the main buttons on Internet Explorer's Standard Buttons toolbar, including Forward, Back, Search, History, and Favorites. But you can use other buttons on the toolbar as well, which will allow you to operate at a more advanced level. Table 10.1 shows a listing of the buttons and the main purpose for each.

INSIDE TRACK

If you're really serious about speeding up your Web experience, make sure that you have the best equipment and Internet connection you can get. Also, make sure that your computer system has plenty of Random Access Memory (RAM). Increasing the memory on your system may make Web pages display snappier than almost any other system upgrade (except for switching to broadband, of course).

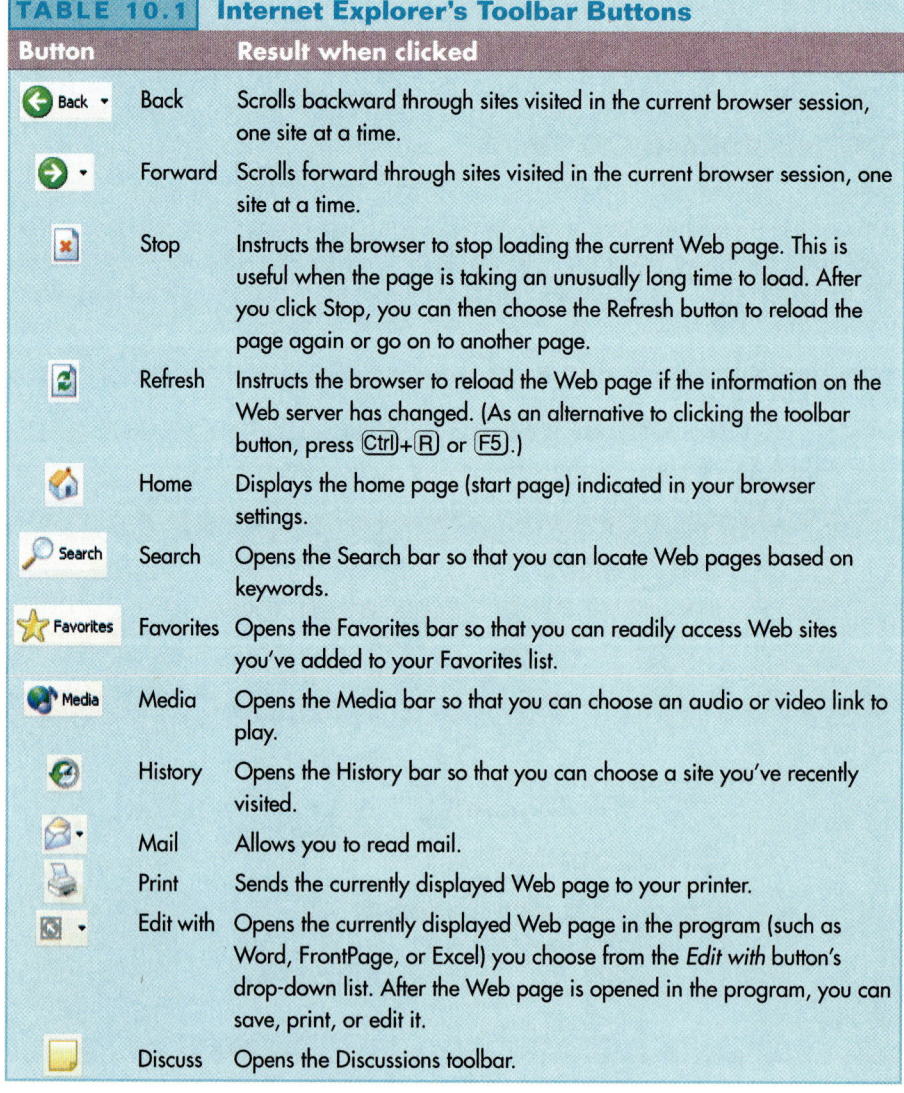

TABLE 10.1	Internet Explorer's Toolbar Buttons
Button	Result when clicked
Back	Back	Scrolls backward through sites visited in the current browser session, one site at a time.
Forward	Forward	Scrolls forward through sites visited in the current browser session, one site at a time.
Stop	Stop	Instructs the browser to stop loading the current Web page. This is useful when the page is taking an unusually long time to load. After you click Stop, you can then choose the Refresh button to reload the page again or go on to another page.
Refresh	Refresh	Instructs the browser to reload the Web page if the information on the Web server has changed. (As an alternative to clicking the toolbar button, press Ctrl+R or F5.)
Home	Home	Displays the home page (start page) indicated in your browser settings.
Search	Search	Opens the Search bar so that you can locate Web pages based on keywords.
Favorites	Favorites	Opens the Favorites bar so that you can readily access Web sites you've added to your Favorites list.
Media	Media	Opens the Media bar so that you can choose an audio or video link to play.
History	History	Opens the History bar so that you can choose a site you've recently visited.
Mail	Mail	Allows you to read mail.
Print	Print	Sends the currently displayed Web page to your printer.
Edit with	Edit with	Opens the currently displayed Web page in the program (such as Word, FrontPage, or Excel) you choose from the *Edit with* button's drop-down list. After the Web page is opened in the program, you can save, print, or edit it.
Discuss	Discuss	Opens the Discussions toolbar.

If you want to explore more ways to use Internet Explorer—including these toolbar buttons—more effectively, choose Help, Contents and Index.

SETTING THE HOME PAGE

You've probably noticed that when you initially start a browser session, the same Web site is shown each and every time. This page is referred to as the browser's **start page** (or the **home page**). This is also the page that displays if you click the Home button on Internet Explorer's toolbar.

 **HEADS UP!** Don't be confused by the overlapping terminology associated with *home page*. This term is used in two ways: as the main page for a Web site and as the page that automatically displays when you start your browser software. When it's used in the latter context, it's sometimes referred to as the *start page*.

Unless you deliberately change it, your browser typically displays the home page for the company that manufactured your computer, your browser, or your ISP. For example, if you bought your system from ABC Computer Company, the start page will probably display its Web site. This is tantamount to viewing a commercial message every time you start a browser session. Not only is being forced to view a particular Web site annoying, but it can also take more time to start your Web session. That's because many manufacturers' Web sites are so heavily laden with graphics, animations, and commercial messages that they can significantly delay your browser's launch.

Waiting for a commercial-ridden default start page to display each time you connect to the Internet can be like trudging through the mud on an early spring day. To rev things up, you can instead use a quicker-loading site for your start page. For example, in Chapters 21–22, you'll develop a Web site of your own, and you may prefer to have it display when you start a browser session instead of the default. Alternatively, you can display a blank page when you start a Web session, which ensures an even faster startup for your browser. If you're not particularly concerned about the speed at which the browser launches, you can specify a portal site (such as Yahoo!) for your start page.

To change the Web site that is used as the start page, choose Tools, Internet Options and then click the General tab. In the *Address* text box, type the URL for the page you want to use as your start-up page. If you want to instead use a blank site, click the *Use Blank* button (see Figure 10.10).

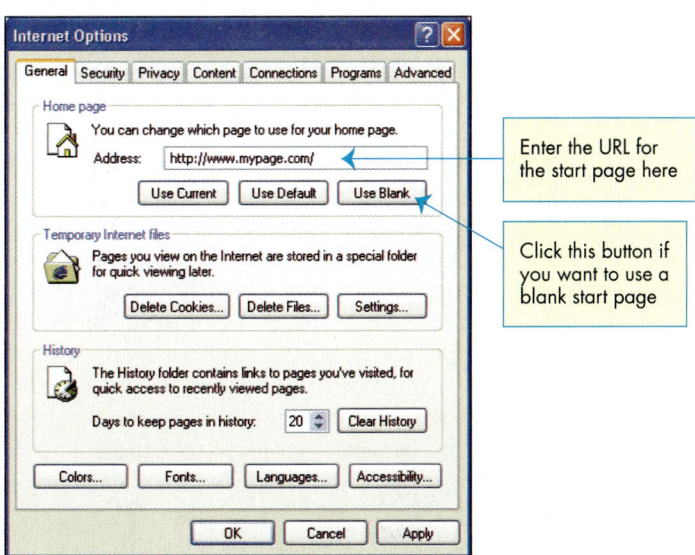

Figure 10.10.
You can indicate which site you want to use as the start page.

An even faster way to change the start page in your browser is to first display the Web page you want to use. Drag the Internet Explorer icon from the Address bar to the Home button and then release the mouse. Choose Yes in the Home Page dialog box to confirm your action.

One final note: If you're currently using a college or business network to access the Internet, you may not have a choice of the browser's start page. Instead, network administrators often use the organization's Web site as the start page.

MANAGING ACTIVEX CONTROLS AND JAVA

You've already seen that you can accelerate the speed at which you surf the Web by turning off graphics, animations, and advertisements. Another way to increase speed and (more importantly) to protect your system from malicious code is to set your browser so that it doesn't download ActiveX controls and Java applets without your approval.

INSIDE TRACK

You can change the display options in Internet Explorer to help you better view Web page content. For example, you can change the size of the onscreen font, which is especially helpful if a Web page has tiny text. To do this, point to Text Size on the View menu; then choose the font size on the list. You can also quickly hide or view all screen elements (except for the Standard Buttons toolbar) by pressing F11 to toggle between Normal and Full Screen views.

You'll learn more about ActiveX controls, Java, and JavaScript in Chapter 18, Beyond the Basics: A Closer Look at Security Issues. For now, however, realize that these technologies can be used to include dynamic content on a Web page. Dynamic, or **active content**, can be used to make a Web page interactive. For example, you might be able to play a game or run an animation on a Web site that was developed using Java, JavaScript or ActiveX technologies.

But even though these technologies can be used to make Web pages interactive and more interesting, there are potential dangers associated with them, especially ActiveX and Java. Why? Because ActiveX and Java can potentially load malicious code on your computer.

Java is an object-oriented programming language used to create applications; mini-applications created using Java are called **applets** (or **Java applets**). In contrast, **JavaScript** is a scripting language that is used to create active content (such as animations) on Web pages. Even though JavaScript includes many of the features of Java, it cannot create standalone applications and is therefore considered less of a risk to the security of your system.

ActiveX is a proprietary Microsoft technology that lets Web developers build a wide variety of applications and content into a Web page. **ActiveX controls** are the actual components on Web pages that run these applications. ActiveX is extremely versatile and runs on a variety of computer configurations. It can also be used for almost any action—from performing a useful function to deleting all the files on your hard drive.

Although much of the Web content developed using Java applets or ActiveX controls can be used to enhance a Web site, the same technologies can also be used to place malicious code onto your computer. ActiveX controls can be embedded in a Web page and then downloaded by an ActiveX-compliant browser (such as Internet Explorer). This can potentially turn a Web page into a dangerous mini-program with nasty code that can run on your computer. For example, you might download a game from a Web site. Unbeknownst to you, the game is simply used as a carrier for a Trojan horse program. In this way, ActiveX controls can create a back door for viruses and other malicious code. The same technology that lets honest people develop animations and helpful programs using ActiveX can also open the door to dangerous code.

You can use the Security Settings dialog box (shown in Figure 10.11) to specify which Java applets and ActiveX controls you want to download to your computer. To access this dialog box, choose Tools, Internet Options to open the Internet Options dialog box and then click the Security tab. You can then indicate how you want Internet Explorer to handle Java and ActiveX in two ways: You can use the preset security levels or you can customize the individual items on the list.

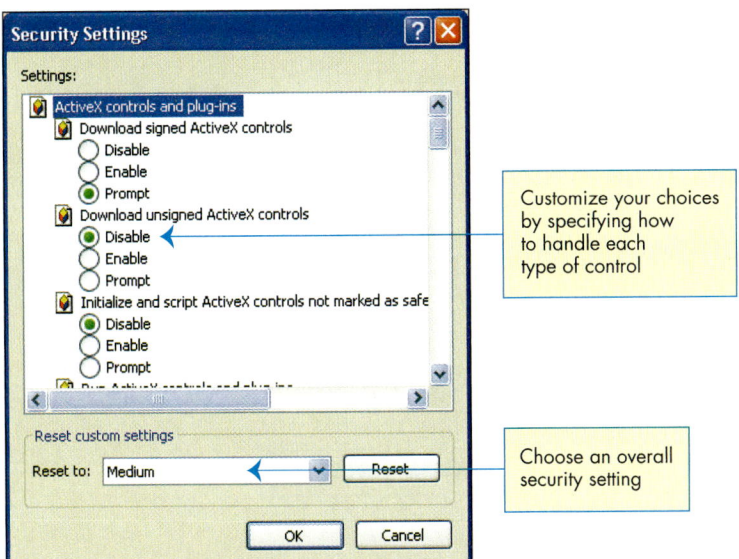

Figure 10.11.
You can decide which ActiveX controls are downloaded to your system and which ones to completely disable.

Internet Explorer includes four preset security levels: *Low*, *Medium-Low*, *Medium*, and *High*. Each preset security level automatically matches the settings to the level of security that meets your needs. Logically, the *Low* level allows you to view the most applets and animations, but it is also the riskiest because it lets through the controls that allow these components to work. On the other hand, the *High* level affords you the most protection from unwanted malicious code, but you probably won't be able to interact as well with Web pages that have active content. In fact, some Web pages won't display at all if you have the security level set to High.

To change the security level, click the *Reset to* drop-down list arrow in the Security Settings dialog box (refer to Figure 10.11) and then choose a level from the list. Click the Reset button and then choose Yes in the warning box to confirm your action. Choose OK in the Security Settings and Internet Options dialog boxes.

The second way of setting security is to specify how you want to handle each type of ActiveX control and Java applet. Display the Security page of the Internet Options dialog box and then click the Custom Level button. In the Security Settings dialog box, you'll notice options for each control or applet: Prompt, Enable, or Disable. In general, choose *Prompt* if you want Internet Explorer to get confirmation from you before downloading ActiveX controls. To have Internet Explorer automatically download any ActiveX control without getting your OK, choose *Enable*. To completely turn off the program's capability to download this type of control, choose *Disable*.

UNDERSTAND THE BASICS OF MANAGING THE CACHE

The Web **cache** (pronounced *cash*) is the storage place on your hard drive and memory where your browser temporarily stores Web pages you've recently visited. The cache speeds up your browsing experience because instead of having to download all the elements of a page whenever you revisit or refresh a page, the browser just checks in the cache. If the elements are already stored in the cache, the browser displays them. This increases browsing speed because your program doesn't have to continually reload information across the entire Internet.

Although the cache can be useful, it's even more efficient if you know how to manage it. For example, there's a relationship between cache size and browsing. If you increase the cache size, you'll probably find that your browser

ALERT!
Don't rely solely on the security settings included in Internet Explorer to keep you from all harm. Instead, make sure that you have a firewall installed on your system as well. ZoneAlarm (*www.zonealarm.com*) provides a free firewall program that is suitable for most home users.

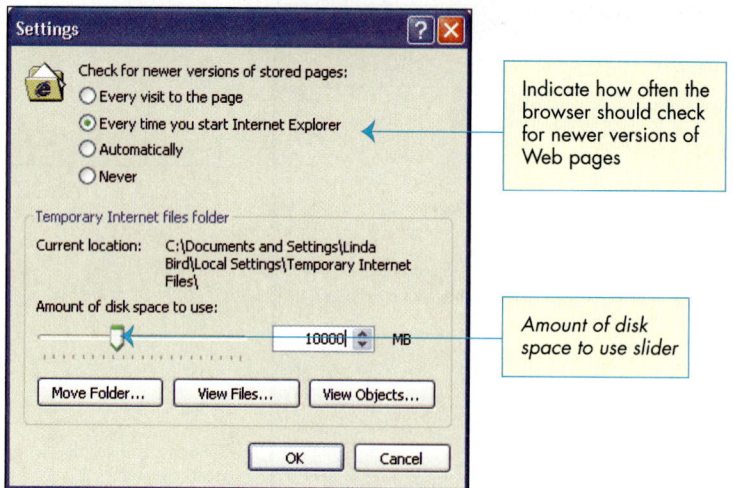

Figure 10.12.
You can manage your system's cache.

sessions are smoother and faster. However, if you devote more space to the cache, it can gobble up too much room on the disk. Additionally, because the cache is essentially a history of everywhere you've surfed lately, any nasty cracker that gains access to your system can investigate where you've been, infringing on your privacy.

Fortunately, it's easy to specify the amount of space you want to devote to the cache. In Internet Explorer, choose Tools, Internet Options. In the *Temporary Internet files* section on the General page, click Settings. This displays the Settings dialog box, complete with four options for controlling the cache (see Figure 10.12).

Here's how the cache options work. There's a direct correlation between the amount of verification required and the speed of browsing. For example, if you choose *Every visit to the page*, you'll be assured of having the latest and greatest information available. However, the time Internet Explorer takes to verify all the text and elements on a page may overshadow the slight increase in accuracy. If you choose *Every time you start Internet Explorer*, the information is confirmed just once per browser session. *Automatically* is the default option, and it is a good choice for most people. It checks for newer versions of a page, based on your browsing habits and the site's content. For example, it determines how often to check for current content based on how often the Web page has previously been modified. For example, if you use this option, Internet Explorer would "know" to get current content for news and weather sites, but not to update the information from a site on World War II history very often. Finally, if you choose *Never*, Internet Explorer won't bring in the most up-to-date information, but you will browse very quickly. This setting is most appropriate for people who use Web sites with static content. Don't forget—no matter which cache option you choose, you can always update a Web page manually (instead of using the cached information) by clicking the Refresh button or by pressing F5.

You can also change the amount of disk space devoted to the cache. A rule of thumb is to dedicate at least 10MB (or 5%–10% of your hard disk) to the cache. To do this, drag the *Amount of disk space to use* slider to a higher or lower number in the Settings dialog box. After you finish changing options in the Settings dialog box, choose OK in the Settings and Internet Options dialog boxes.

Another way to manage the cache is to clear it out using the Security tab of the Internet Options dialog box (see Figure 10.13). For example, if you share a computer and don't want others to know what sites you've surfed, you can automatically delete the files at the end of each browser session.

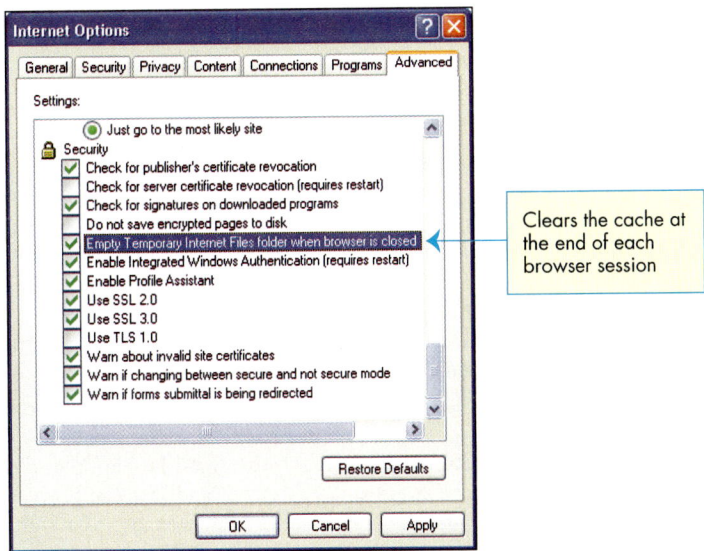

Figure 10.13.
To protect your privacy, you can remove all temporary Internet files from your computer.

To clear your cache file to protect your privacy or to free up more space on your computer, follow these steps:

1. Choose Tools, Internet Options to display the Internet Options dialog box.
2. Click the Advanced tab and then scroll down the *Settings* list to the Security section.
3. Check the box for *Empty Temporary Internet Files folder when browser is closed*.
4. When you're finished, click OK to close the Internet Options dialog box.

So the next time you fire up your browser and start working on the Web, remember these methods for navigating more smoothly and efficiently. You'll be glad you did.

Don't Forget...

- You can speed up browsing on the Web in various ways, such as disabling graphics, blocking out online advertisements, and surfing at times when other people generally are not online.
- You can launch multiple browser sessions, each in its own window.
- To view Web content in various ways, it's sometimes helpful to use multiple browsers such as Internet Explorer and Netscape.
- Alternative browser programs, such as Opera, may display Web content differently or faster than Internet Explorer.
- You can use Internet Explorer's toolbar buttons to perform a variety of useful actions.
- You can reset the page that your browser displays upon startup.

- Internet Explorer includes options that you can use to change display settings, such as font size.
- ActiveX controls and Java applets are used to provide active content on Web pages, enhancing the browsing experience for many people.
- There are security risks associated with downloading ActiveX controls and Java applets from Web pages, including the possible introduction of malicious code on your system.
- Internet Explorer includes security settings to help you manage the way ActiveX controls and Java applets are handled.
- You can manage the way the Web cache manages temporary Internet files.

Check This Out

MULTIPLE CHOICE

1. You change the cache settings in Internet Explorer so that your browser verifies the contents of each Web page in the cache against the Web server's copy before displaying it on your computer. What is the likely result?
   a. Browsing will be speeded up.
   b. Browsing will be slowed down.
   c. There won't be any difference in the browsing speed.
   d. None of the above

2. What is an advantage of viewing a page with ActiveX controls?
   a. The page is potentially more interesting because it can include active content.
   b. Trojan horses can be downloaded to your computer.
   c. It reduces the security risk to your computer.
   d. The page will display more quickly on your computer than a page without ActiveX controls.

3. Which of the following is true regarding Internet Explorer's settings?
   a. You can change the security settings to High, Medium, Medium-low, or Low.
   b. You can change the amount of disk space devoted to the cache.
   c. You can determine the browser's start page.
   d. All of the above

4. Which of the following is true regarding ActiveX and Java?
   a. ActiveX and Java are the same.
   b. ActiveX and Java can both add active content and more functionality to a Web page.
   c. Neither ActiveX or Java poses any significant security hazards.
   d. ActiveX and Java were both developed by Microsoft.

5. Which of the following can speed up Web browsing?
   a. Blocking online advertisements
   b. Turning off graphics and multimedia features
   c. Increasing your computer's memory
   d. All of the above

MATCHING

a. Java
b. ActiveX
c. JavaScript
d. active content
e. cache
f. active window
g. ad-blocking
h. session
i. applet
j. start page

1. Storage place on your hard drive and RAM where your browser keeps copies of Web pages you've visited
2. Scripting language used to develop active content for Web pages
3. Mini-program developed using Java
4. Proprietary technology developed by Microsoft that can be used to create dynamic content for Web pages
5. Opening and closing a browser
6. The page that displays when you first launch your browser
7. Dynamic content on a Web page, such as animations or games
8. The window that appears on top of the others on your Windows desktop
9. Object-oriented programming language
10. Software used to block online commercials

Real Life

1. Explore Internet Explorer's settings. To do so, choose Tools, Internet Options to display the Internet Options dialog box. Display the General page of the dialog box and then click the Help button (in the upper-right corner of the dialog box). Click the first option on the General page and read the associated ScreenTip. Repeat this process for each option listed in the Internet Options dialog box.

2. Conduct an experiment to see if you can significantly speed up browsing.
   a. First, clear the Web cache on your system. Open your browser and view 20 different Web pages. Keep track of the URLs for each (because you will use the same sites for the second part of your experiment) and track the total time it took all 20 pages to display.

b. Next, clear the Web cache again and close your browser. Reopen it to start another browser session. Use settings in Internet Explorer to turn off graphics and multimedia features. View the same 20 Web pages that you did in the first part of the experiment, again keeping track of the total time it took the pages to load. How did the time compare?

c. Repeat the experiment using more (or different) Web pages. Remember to clear the cache and change Internet Explorer's settings between the *a.* and *b.* parts of the experiment.

d. What conclusions can you draw from the experiment? Use a chart (perhaps in PowerPoint or Excel) to illustrate your findings and then present them to a small group or your class.

I Spy: Privacy and Security Concerns

1. Conduct a Web search on *ActiveX controls*. Because this is a Microsoft technology, make sure to check out non-Microsoft Web sites as well as Microsoft's Web page. After you conduct your research, write a two-page report that includes the following information: a brief description of ActiveX technology and its advantages and disadvantages (including security risks).
2. Interview at least three Web-savvy people. Find out if they've ever encountered any malicious code from ActiveX controls. If so, what happened?

Also, conduct research on the Web by using keywords such as *security, ActiveX controls, Java applets,* and so on. Take notes on what you learn.

Review the information you gathered from the interviews and your research. Use it to develop a list of security measures that you can implement for home or small business use. Share your information via e-mail with a few friends and family members.

SECTION Five
RUNNING EFFECTIVE INTERNET SEARCHES

CHAPTER 11
SEARCH BASICS

Key Terms

When you finish this chapter, you'll understand the following terms:

- conceptual query
- hit
- keyword
- natural language query
- query
- ranking
- results page
- robots
- search engine optimization
- search engine positioning
- search expression
- sponsored links

Chapter Objectives

After you complete this chapter, you'll

- Know How to Generate Search Engine Results
- Understand How to Use Keywords to Query Search Engines
- Know How to Use a Web Directory
- Know How to Use a Combination Search Engine/Web Directory
- Be Able to Use a Natural Language Search Engine
- Know How to Use a Metasearch Engine

The Big Picture

By now, you realize that the Internet is akin to a huge electronic city, full of information on almost every conceivable topic. In the same way that real cities have libraries for information, shopping centers for buying stuff, and restaurants for hanging out and communicating with others, so the Internet has places to do the same types of things—electronically, of course.

Naturally, the trick to using the Internet effectively is to be able to quickly find the information you need in this huge electronic city. After all, you don't want to wander around the Internet for hours any more than you want to get lost in a large city. To help you out, we'll show you some great ways to quickly locate the data you need.

In this chapter, we'll show you how to run effective searches. First, you need to understand the difference between browsing and searching: Technically, you navigate from one Web page to another by following links when you *browse*; you enter keywords in a search engine and ask the search engine to display a list of pages that match the keywords when you *search*. Searching provides a more pinpointed approach than does browsing.

Think of it this way: Imagine that you go into a large mall, looking for a particular pair of shoes. You could wander around the store until you found the shoe area—akin to browsing on the Internet to locate the information you want. You'd probably eventually find the shoes, although it would probably take awhile. (In the balance, however, you'd probably see some interesting sites along the way!) The second method would involve going directly to the information desk and asking where the shoes are located; then proceeding unswervingly to the shoe department. This would be a more focused approach to finding the information you need, and it is analogous to running an Internet search based on keywords.

In the past couple of chapters, we showed you how to browse more quickly and efficiently on the Web. In this chapter, we'll show you how to use the various types of search tools to locate exactly the information you need. Along the way, you'll gain lots of hands-on practice using the Internet.

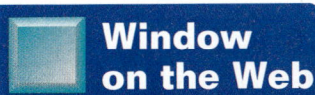
Window on the Web

The Web has numerous search engines that you can use to find data. These engines, which include software that search large databases of Web information, vary in the number of sites they include and how they organize their data.

INSIDE TRACK

In case you forgot, a *search engine* is a general class of programs that searches documents for keywords and then displays a list of documents in which the keywords are found. The term is often used to describe systems such as AltaVista that help users look for documents on the Web.

One of the most straightforward ways to use a search engine is to use a word or phrase that represents the topic you want to find out about, such as *vacation* or *music*. A topical word that you use in a search is called a **keyword**. You can use search engines such as Google to find information by keyword (see Figure 11.1).

In this chapter, you'll become familiar with some of the most popular and useful search engines. We'll not only go over the largest and most popular, but also introduce you to the less-familiar Web directories, natural language search engines, and metasearch engines.

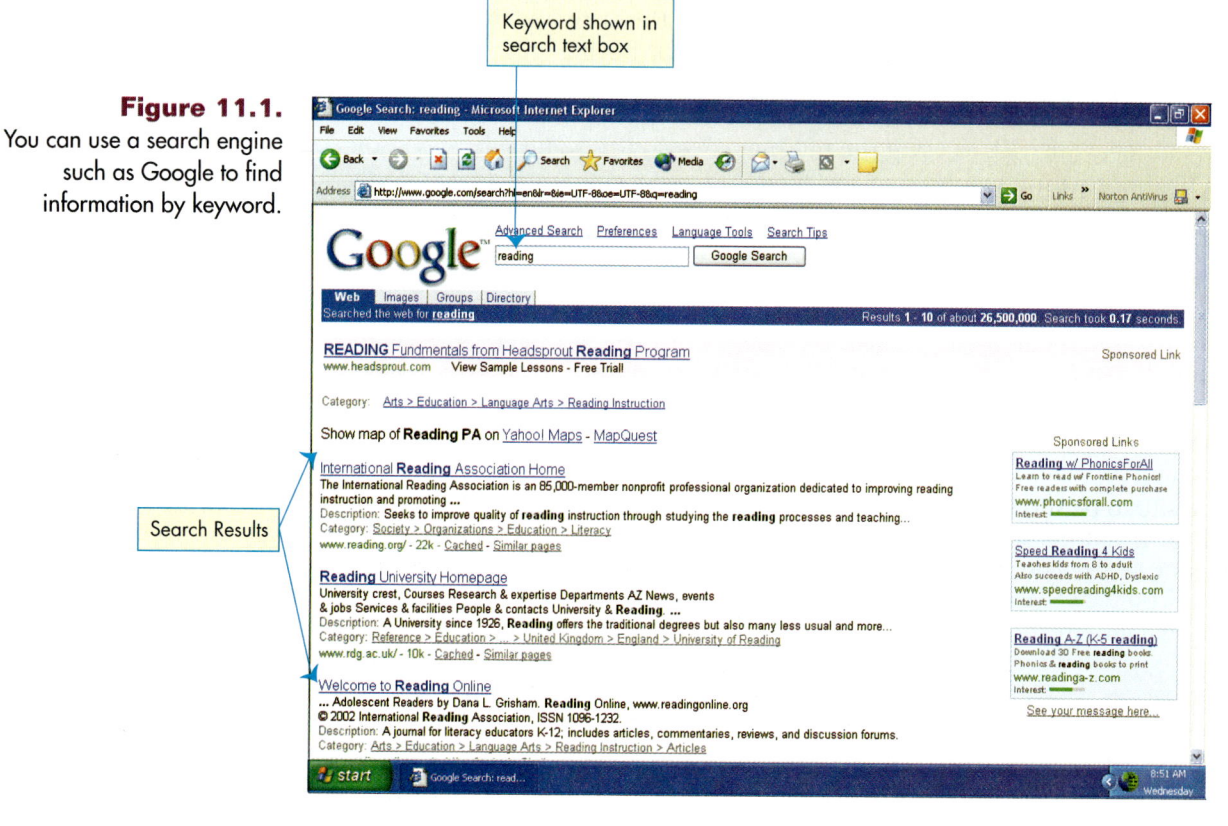

Figure 11.1.
You can use a search engine such as Google to find information by keyword.

KNOW HOW TO GENERATE SEARCH ENGINE RESULTS

Although there are various ways to use search engines, the most common method involves running a search based on keywords (topical words). When you enter keywords or a question in the search engine, your entry is called a **search expression**. The process of typing the search expression in an engine and then "asking" the search engine to generate results is called a **query**.

As you conduct your search, the search engine looks through its database of pages and then displays the results. A **results page** is a listing of Web pages that include the keyword(s)—each Web page that matches the query is called a **hit**. Every query can potentially produce several thousand (or even million) hits. Depending on the search engine, the results page listing might also include a brief description of each hit. More importantly, each of the hits includes a hyperlink that you can click to view the associated page.

A group of hits that is highlighted or set apart from the rest is usually found at the top of the results page. These Web sites don't get there by chance. Instead, these **sponsored links** or "sponsored matches" are usually paid advertisements. Companies pay to have their Web site positioned at the top of the list in hopes that the link's location and visibility will entice people to click it.

Beneath the sponsored links, the search engine typically displays Web sites in order of relevancy to the keywords, from the most to least relevant. The positioning of a Web page on the results page is called a site's **ranking**.

Keep in mind that where the page appears in the ranking will vary, depending on which search engine you use. That's because each search engine taps into a different method of determining relevance. For example, some search engines determine ranking by the number of times a keyword appears on the site; others decide the ranking by the number of links to and from the page from other Web sites.

You should also realize that search engines examine only their own databases. Each search engine uses its own methods and standards for generating the results. That's why you can end up with differing results when you use multiple search engines.

In short, the search engines differ in the results generated because they

- use different Web robots (spiders) to collect information
- choose different Web pages to index
- interpret search expressions differently
- store a different amount of text from a Web page in the database

A basic search using one of the major search engines can easily produce thousands of results—which is why businesses consider it so critical for their Web site to be shown near the top of the first page. In fact, several studies have shown that Internet users have a low tolerance for wading through multiple pages of results, and generally view only the first page or two before running another query.

Those who develop Web pages commercially know a variety of methods they can use to make sure that their page appears near the top of the list. The way businesses structure their pages and submit the site to the search engines has the biggest influence on their ranking. Strategizing Web pages for the most online exposure is called **search engine optimization** or **search engine positioning**. (You'll learn more about positioning your Web page in Chapter 23, Publishing to the World Wide Web.)

Finally, as you learned in Chapter 9, Surfing Basics, search engines rely on automated programs to constantly crawl on the Web to find new pages and remove outdated ones. As you learned in Chapter 9, these automated programs are called spiders. They're also known as Web **robots** (bots for short). Because the search engines are constantly updated with the data that the bots find, they can include millions (or even billions) of Web sites in their database. At the time of this writing, for example, Google boasted that it had 3,083,324,652 Web pages in its database. Let's take a look at how you can use keywords to wade through those pages to find the ones you want.

UNDERSTAND HOW TO USE KEYWORDS TO QUERY SEARCH ENGINES

Now that you understand the general concepts related to using keywords in search engines (and know why the results can vary from one search engine to another), you're ready to run a few searches. If you use a limited number of keywords in a query, you'll probably find that running a search is easy and straightforward.

INSIDE TRACK

Search engines each have their own clearly defined set of rules and procedures for how Web sites should be indexed, called algorithms. Because of the difference in algorithms, different search engines can potentially produce different results for the same keywords.

INSIDE TRACK

There are some online libraries and search engines that are specifically devoted to helping you find academic information. Start by visiting the Search Engine Colossus site (*www.searchenginecolossus.com*) and then clicking the Academic link. You can also try Northern Light at *www.northernlight.com* or the Online Computer Library Center (OCLC) at *www.oclc.org*.

INSIDE TRACK

Most of the time, you'll have a pretty good idea of which words to use as keywords. However, if you're not sure which words to use, here's a technique you can employ. First, write the sentence down in plain English, such as, "Are there any dinner theaters in New York City?" Next, circle the words that portray the main concepts. In this example, you'd circle *dinner*, *theaters*, and *New York City*. Usually you'll get better results by using root words— so, in this case you'd use *theater* instead of *theaters*. One final hint: If you don't get the results you want using the exact keywords, try entering synonyms that are more general or more specific. In the previous example, you could substitute the keyword *plays* or *Broadway* for *theater* to generate different results.

In the next activity, you'll use keywords to query two different search engines. You'll get some hands-on practice conducting searches. You'll also see how the results differ from one search tool to another—even when you use the same keywords for each query.

ACTIVITY 11.1
Using Keywords to Query Search Engines

1. Open Internet Explorer and make sure that your computer is connected to the Internet.

2. In the Address box, type the URL for HotBot (www.hotbot.com) and then click Go. The home page for HotBot is displayed.

3. Type travel in the search box and then click the Search button.
   A listing of Web pages that include the keyword *travel* are shown. Notice that HotBot begins the listing with sites that it calls "Sponsored Links." Companies generally (though not always) pay the search engine company for this privilege of being listed at the top of the search results (see Figure 11.2).

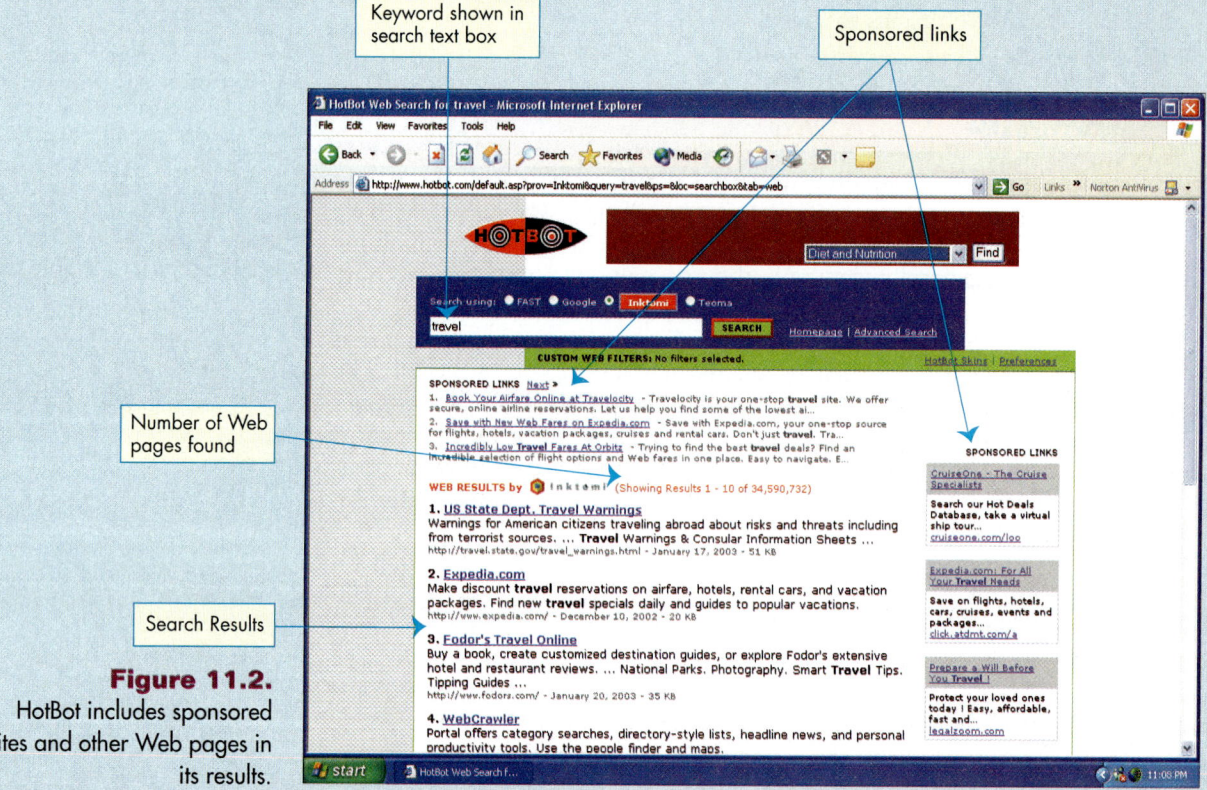

Figure 11.2.
HotBot includes sponsored sites and other Web pages in its results.

4. Type www.google.com in Internet Explorer's Address box and then click Go.
   The home page for Google is displayed.

5. Type travel in Google's search box and then click the Google Search button.
   Listings of Web pages that include the keyword *travel* are shown. Notice that a completely different set of Web pages is shown on Google's results page from those on HotBot's, though this search engine also displays sponsored links (see Figure 11.3).
   Now experiment to see how adding another word to the search expression affects the results.

ACTIVITY 11.1
Using Keywords to Query Search Engines

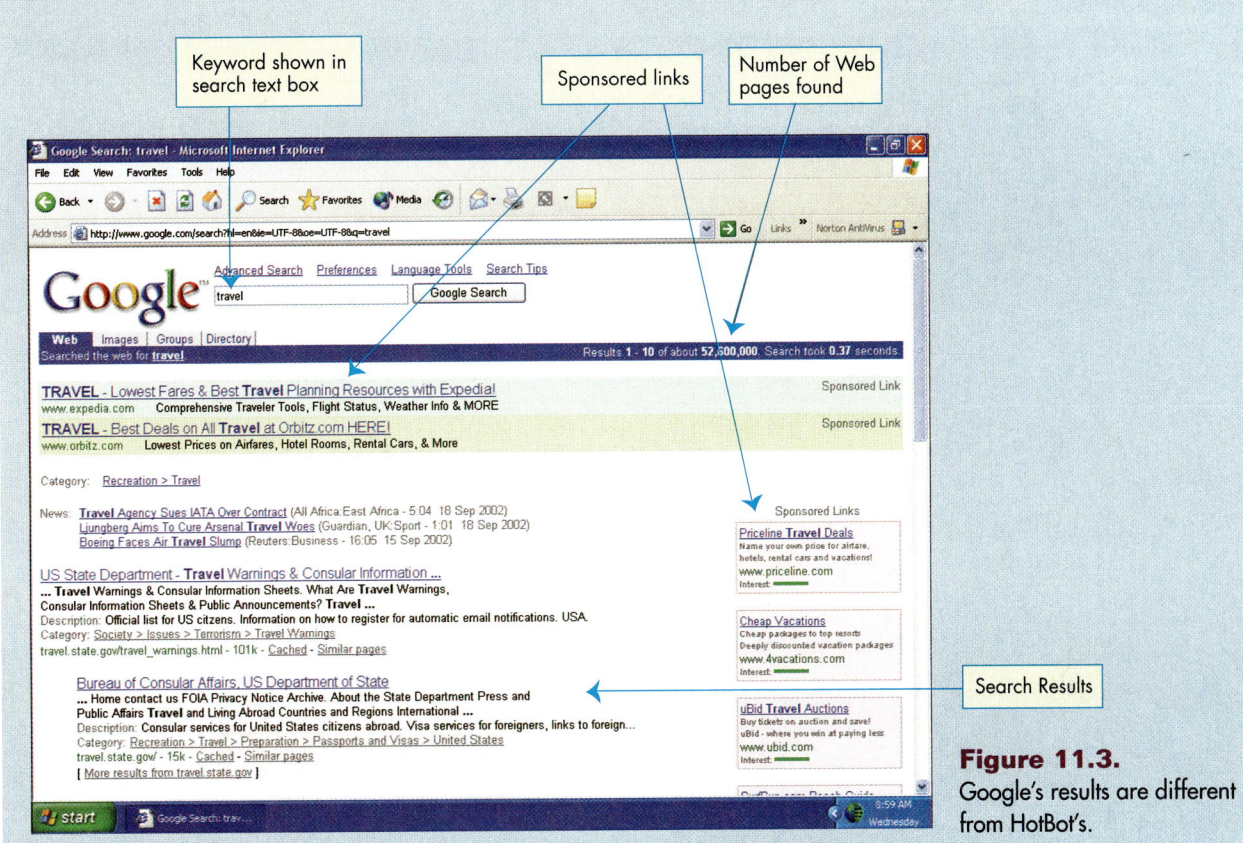

Figure 11.3.
Google's results are different from HotBot's.

⑥ Type `travel student` in Google's search text box and then click the Google Search button (or press ⏎Enter).

Google searches for both keywords, and display sites that include them at the top of its results. Notice that the results differ from those shown when you only used a single keyword (*travel*). Some search engines (such as Google) find sites with all the keywords entered; others simply look for any of the keywords.

⑦ Scroll to the bottom of the Google page.

Notice that this page of results is only the first of many (see Figure 11.4). You can display the next page of results by clicking its link.

⑧ Click the number **2** to display the next page of hits.

⑨ Click the browser's Back button (on the toolbar) to redisplay the first page.

⑩ Click a link for a Web page of your choice.
The Web page displays.

⑪ Leave Internet Explorer open if you plan to complete more hands-on activities in this chapter.

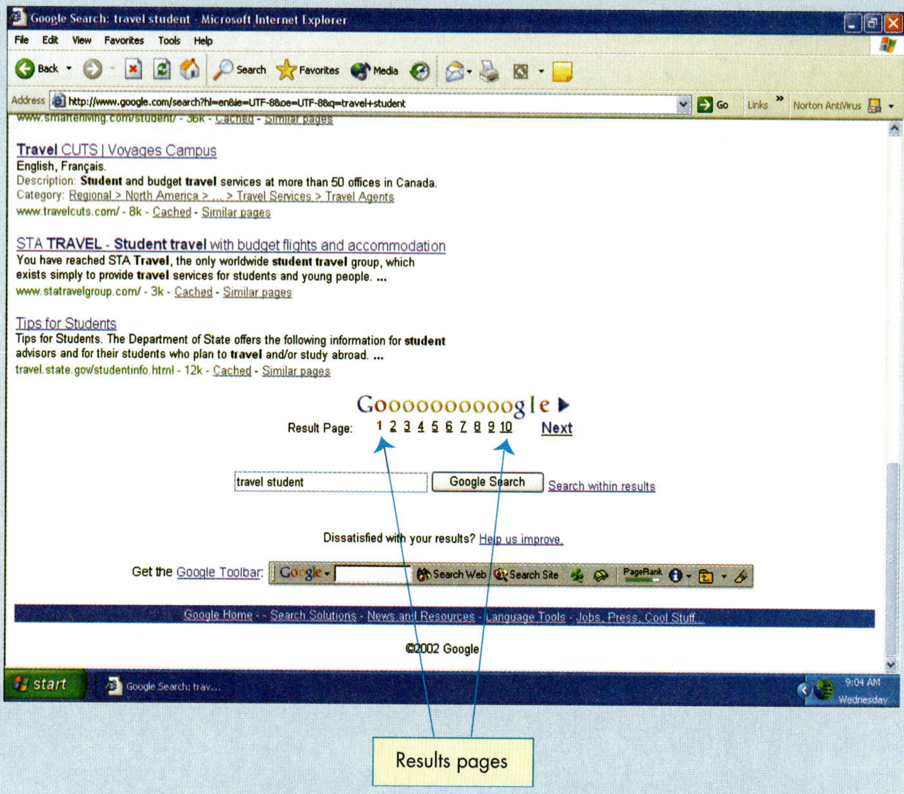

ACTIVITY 11.1
Using Keywords to Query Search Engines (Continued)

Figure 11.4.
The search results can include many pages of hits.

INSIDE TRACK

Google has a couple of useful features. First, if you enter a keyword in Google's search text box and then click the *I'm Feeling Lucky* button, the search engine will automatically display the top-ranked site in this search engine's database for the keyword.

Second, you can prevent Google from displaying "adult" sites in the results by using the search engine's built-in filter. To activate the filter, click the Preferences link on Google's home page. In the SafeSearch Filtering area, click the option button for Use strict filtering and then click the Save Preferences button.

KNOW HOW TO USE A WEB DIRECTORY

In their purist form, search engines index words in Web pages and then add them to their databases. They do this by employing automated programs, such as Web robots. In contrast, real people (a whole group of them, usually) develop Web directories and decide which Web sites should be added to the directory. Additionally, directories are organized by main topic and subtopics—this is sometimes called a hierarchical structure. You find information by drilling down levels in the hierarchy until you locate the topic you want. (*Drilling down* refers to successively clicking links to access subcategories.) You continue to do this through the subcategory levels until you find the Web site you want.

In this activity, you'll drill down through directory levels to locate data in one of the best-known Web directories, Yahoo!.

ACTIVITY 11.2
Using a Web Directory

1. Make sure that Internet Explorer is open and your computer is connected to the Internet.

2. In the Address box, type the URL for Yahoo! (www.yahoo.com) and then click Go (or press ⏎Enter).
   The home page for Yahoo! is displayed.

3. If necessary, scroll down the Yahoo! page until you see the Web Site Directory (see Figure 11.5).

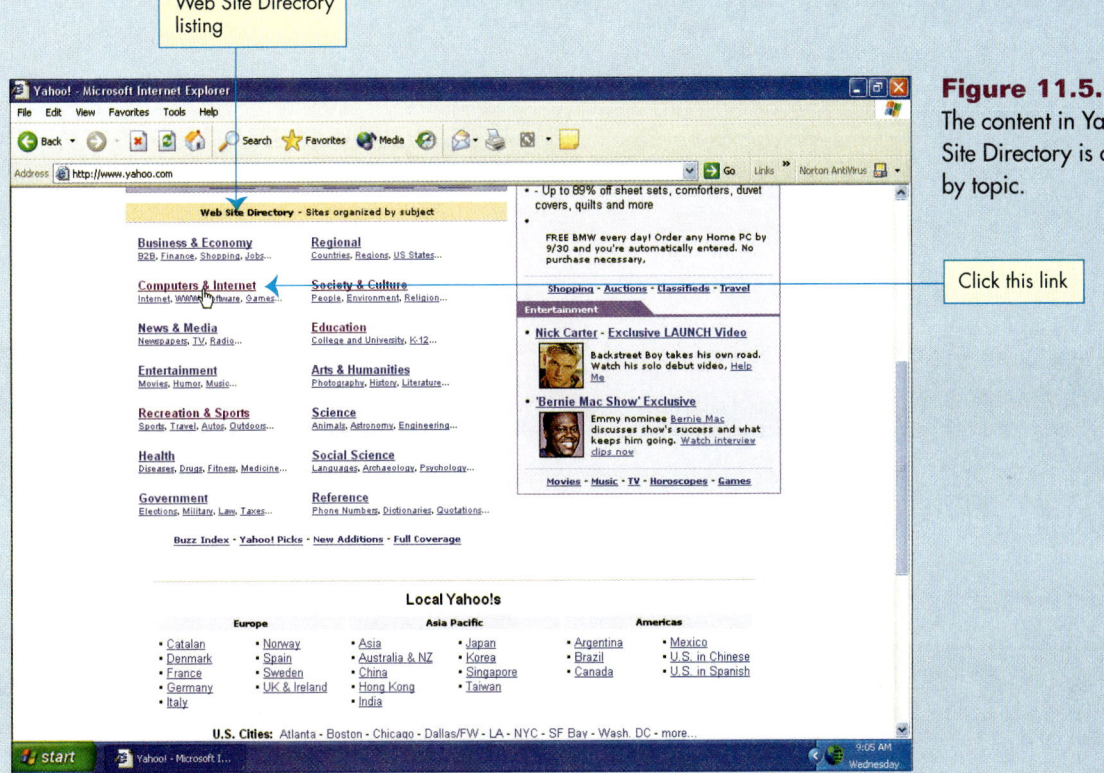

Figure 11.5.
The content in Yahoo's Web Site Directory is organized by topic.

4. On the Web Site Directory, click *Computers & Internet*.
   The subcategories for the main topic (*Computers & Internet*) are shown. Notice that each one lists the number of further subcategories it includes (see Figure 11.6).

5. Click the *News and Media* subtopic.
   A listing of subtopics for News and Media displays. Additionally, a listing of actual Web sites shows in the bottom part of the window. You can click one of these sites to jump to it (see Figure 11.7).

6. If you want, click on further categories or Web sites and view their contents.

7. Leave Internet Explorer open if you plan to complete more hands-on activities in this chapter.

ACTIVITY 11.2
Using a Web Directory (Continued)

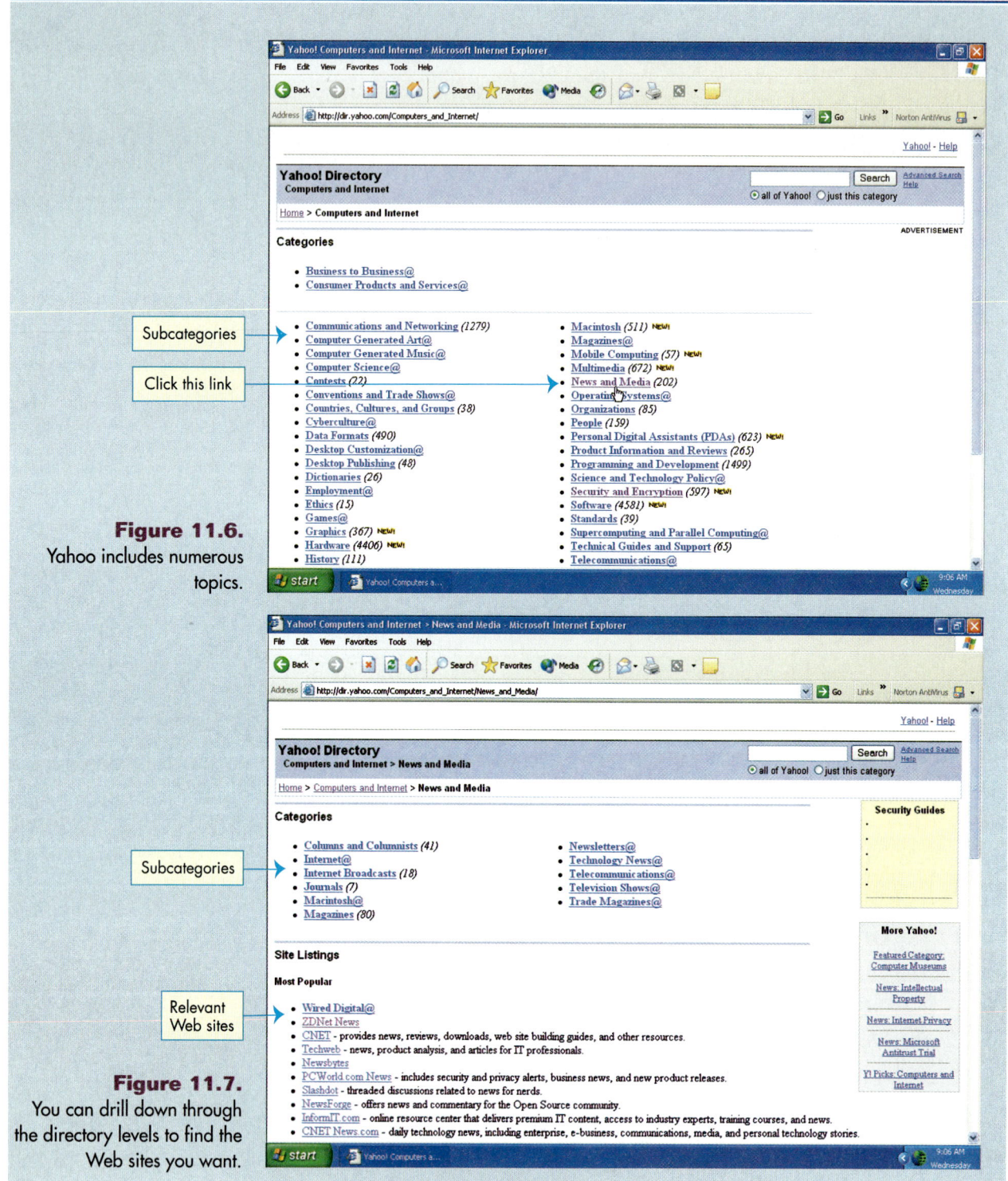

Figure 11.6.
Yahoo includes numerous topics.

Figure 11.7.
You can drill down through the directory levels to find the Web sites you want.

KNOW HOW TO USE A COMBINATION SEARCH ENGINE/WEB DIRECTORY

Although search engines and Web directories started off as separate entities, in some cases they've been combined so that you can access both on the same site. For example, even though Yahoo! is technically a Web directory, you can also conduct searches on the site. In the next activity, we'll take a quick look at how easy it is to switch between search engine and Web directory capacities if they're available on the same site.

ACTIVITY 11.3
Using a Combination Search Engine/Web Directory

1. Make sure that Internet Explorer is open and your computer is connected to the Internet.

2. In the Address box, type the URL for Yahoo! (www.yahoo.com) and then click Go (or press ⏎Enter).
    The home page for Yahoo! is displayed. You are now already familiar with the process for drilling down through levels of information in Yahoo! Web Site Directory; now try using Yahoo as a search engine.

3. Click in the Search text box at the top of the Web page, type skiing and then click the Search button.
    Yahoo! shows categories from its directory as well as a listing of Web pages (see Figure 11.8). In this sense, Yahoo gives you the best of both worlds.

4. Leave Internet Explorer open if you plan to complete more hands-on activities in this chapter.

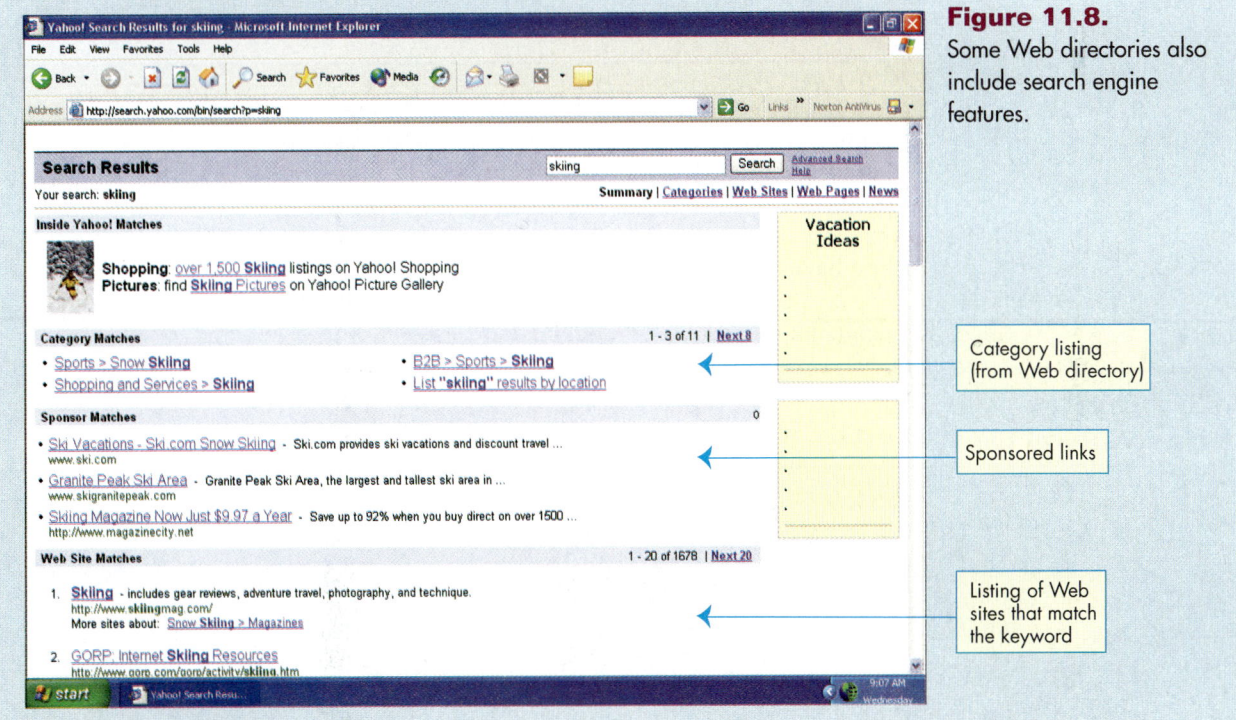

Figure 11.8.
Some Web directories also include search engine features.

BE ABLE TO USE A NATURAL LANGUAGE SEARCH ENGINE

Most search engines conduct exact keyword searches: You plug in the word and the engine shows you everything that matches that keyword, regardless of how it is used. However, a few search engines, sometimes called natural language search engines, can perform concept-based searches. A **conceptual query** is one in which the search engine returns only Web pages that are relevant to the topic, even if the words don't precisely match your keywords. Let's say, for example, that you type in the keyword *horse*. An engine that can run concept-based searches will also bring up sites that include words such as *equine*, *mount*, and so on. On the other hand, a standard search engine will bring sites on horse breeds and horse trailers, but will also list sites containing the terms *Trojan Horse* and *charlie horse*.

How do concept-based search engines do it? Some of the search engines use human editors to evaluate Web sites for inclusion in the search results. Additionally, they also have software that examines Web pages to determine the context in which a word is used. To use our previous example, if a page with the word *mount* also had words such as *saddle* and *bridle*, the search engine would categorize it differently from a page that combined *mount* with words such as *climb* and *view*.

Two well-known concept-based search engines are Excite (*www.excite.com*) and Ask Jeeves (*www.askjeeves.com*). Ask Jeeves is popular because not only can Ask Jeeves determine the most relevant Web sites by conceptual-based searching, but it can also "interpret" natural language questions. A **natural language query** is one that's written as a full sentence by using the same language that you might use if you were conversing with a real person. Being able to use natural language queries makes the Internet more approachable for some people.

HEADS UP! Some of the "adult" sites will include almost anything in their keywords so that they will get hits. Because of this, it's a good idea to use Internet filtering software, such as CyberPatrol (*www.cyberpatrol.com*), which blocks such sites.

Yet another advantage of Ask Jeeves is that it automatically includes a built-in filter so that you don't accidentally stumble across Web sites with "adult" content. Assuming that the default filters are in place, Ask Jeeves displays a warning message and doesn't show questionable sites without your permission. Although no filter is bulletproof, any filter can be helpful, especially if you have children with access to the Internet.

In the next activity, you'll work with Ask Jeeves to see how a natural language query works.

ACTIVITY 11.4
Using a Natural Language Search Engine

1. Make sure that Internet Explorer is open and your computer is connected to the Internet.

2. In the Address box, type the URL for Ask Jeeves (`www.askjeeves.com`) and then click Go (or press `Enter`).
   The home page for Ask Jeeves is displayed (see Figure 11.9).

3. Click in the text box at the top of the Web page and then type `Why is the sky blue?` Click the Ask button.
   Ask Jeeves displays a listing of relevant Web sites. Now try another search.

4. Click in the text box at the top of the Web page, and then type `Where can I go snowboarding?` Click the Ask button.
   Ask Jeeves displays a listing of relevant Web sites related to snowboarding. Before we leave this search engine, let's take a look at one more useful feature that Ask Jeeves includes: the capability to display up-to-the-minute news stories related to your search.

5. Click the News Results tab at the top of the Web page.
   Ask Jeeves displays a listing of links to news items about snowboarding (see Figure 11.10). Ask Jeeves updates these news stories every few minutes.

ACTIVITY 11.4
Using a Natural Language Search Engine

⑥ Leave Internet Explorer open if you plan to complete more hands-on activities in this chapter.

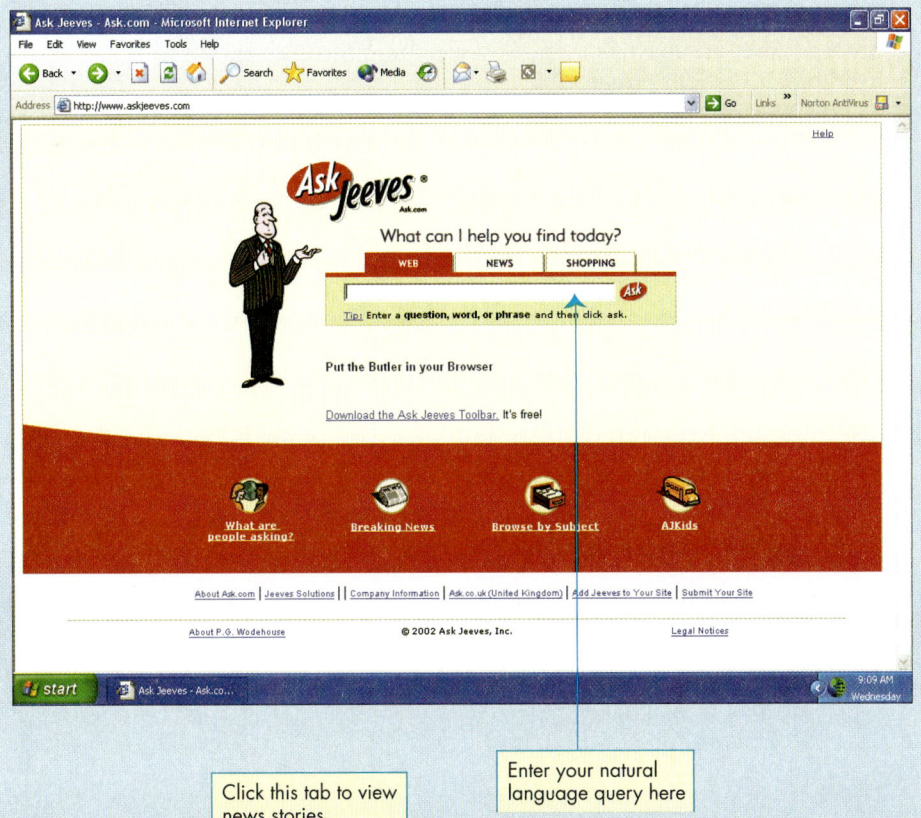

Figure 11.9.
You can use Ask Jeeves to find Web pages using keywords, concepts, or even by simply asking a question.

Enter your natural language query here

Click this tab to view news stories

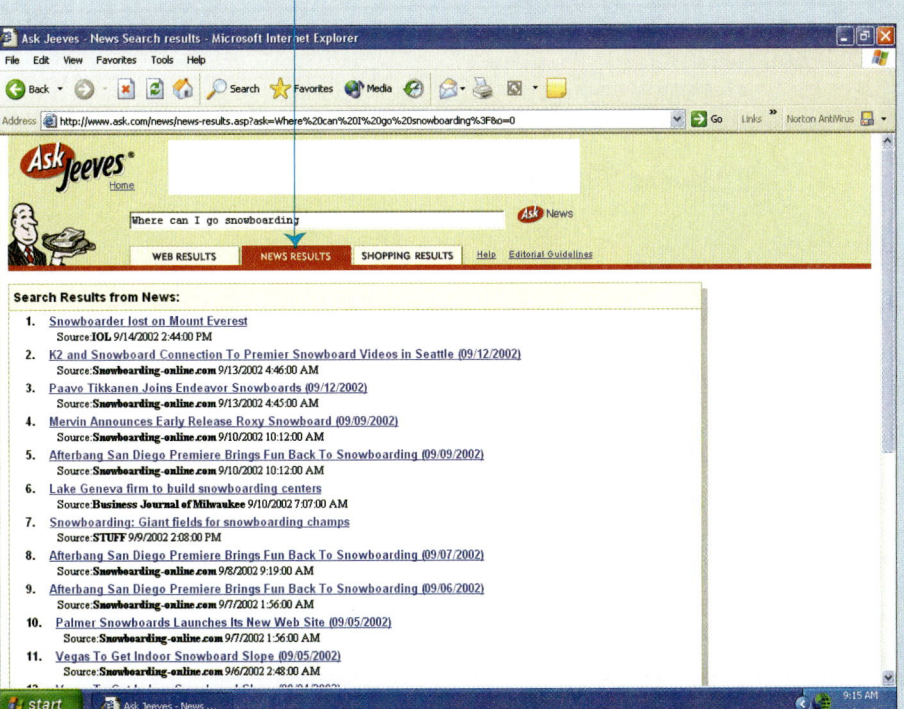

Figure 11.10.
Ask Jeeves shows current news topics related to your question or topic.

Be Able to Use a Natural Language Search Engine   177

KNOW HOW TO USE A METASEARCH ENGINE

Instead of combing through engines and directories individually, you can use a metasearch engine to query several simultaneously. The metasearch engine then displays the top matches on a single page. They do this by using software to break down a query in a way that's compatible with each engine's search criteria. Metasearch engines don't store information in their own database. Instead, they are masters at quickly searching through the existing databases of search engines and directories.

InfoSpace (*www.infospace.com*) is the leader in metasearching because it owns both Dogpile (*www.dogpile.com*) and MetaCrawler (*www.metacrawler.com*). Another metasearch engine that has gained popularity as "the mother of all search engines" is Mamma (*www.mamma.com*).

In the following activity, you'll try your hand at using another well-known metasearch engine: WebCrawler.

ACTIVITY 11.5
Using a Metasearch Engine

1. Make sure that Internet Explorer is open and your computer is connected to the Internet.

2. In the Address box, type the URL for WebCrawler (`www.webcrawler.com`).
   The home page for WebCrawler is displayed.

3. In the text box at the top of the Web page, type `fitness equipment`. Click the Search button.
   WebCrawler displays a listing of relevant Web sites. Notice that the search engines and Web directories that it examines are shown at the top of the results (see Figure 11.11).

4. Run additional searches on WebCrawler if you want. Close Internet Explorer when you're finished.

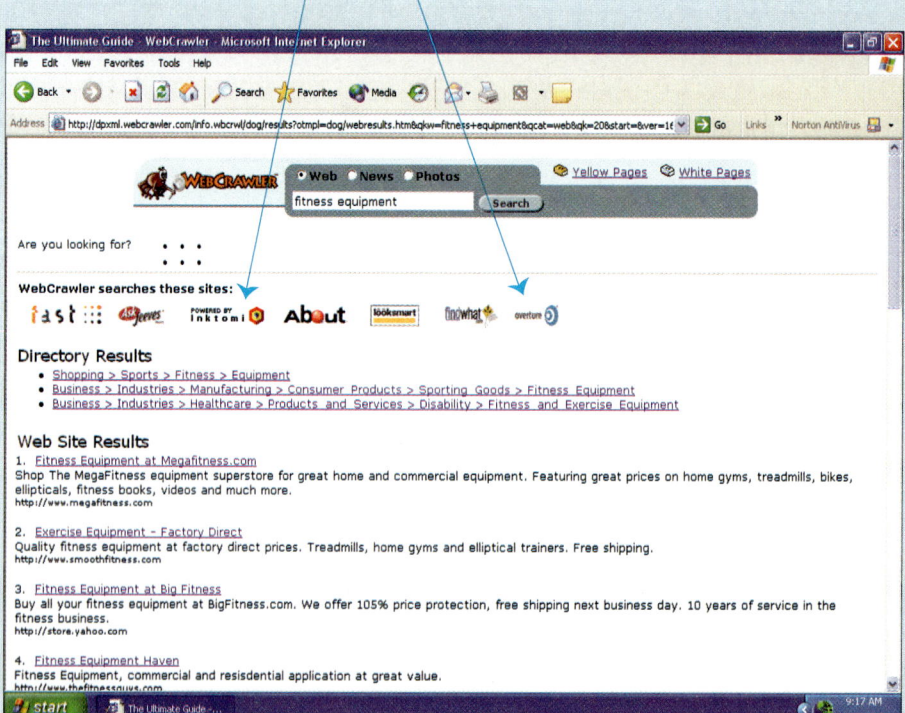

Figure 11.11.
A metasearch engine pulls results from several search engines and directories.

Chapter 11 Search Basics

ON THE HORIZON

Search engines are continuing to get both smarter and easier to use. Within the next couple of years, data visualization technology (the process of representing abstract scientific or business data as images) will probably be in place so that you can display your search results much more graphically.

Don't Forget...

- You can conduct a simple search by entering topical words (called keywords) in a search engine.
- Search engines are developed and maintained differently from Web directories.
- Because of the way they locate and index data, different search engines will usually return somewhat different results from each other.
- Some search sites now include both search engine and Web directory capabilities.
- Natural language search engines search by concepts in addition to keywords.
- Metasearch engines collect data from a number of search engines and directories.

Check This Out

MULTIPLE CHOICE

1. What is the main difference between a Web directory and a search engine?
   a. A Web directory includes more sites than does a search engine.
   b. A Web directory includes sites added by people; a search engine relies on Web robots to add the sites.
   c. A Web directory is harder to use than a search engine.
   d. All of the above

2. Which of the following is the best example of a natural language search engine?
   a. Yahoo!
   b. Google
   c. Ask Jeeves
   d. AltaVista

3. Why do different search engines usually return different results?
   a. They index the data differently.
   b. They use different robots to find the data.
   c. They include different amounts of Web page text in their databases.
   d. All of the above

4. What does a metasearch engine do?
   a. Scans your system regularly for viruses
   b. Acts as a firewall against malicious code
   c. Searches a maximum of five search engines, one-by-one
   d. Searches several search engines simultaneously

5. What is a difference between browsing and searching?
   a. Your system is safe from hackers when you browse, but not when you conduct a search.
   b. You can use a filter when browsing, but not when searching.
   c. Searching usually produces more targeted results than browsing because you generate a hit based on the keyword(s) you choose.
   d. All of the above

MATCHING

a. hits
b. keyword
c. natural language search engine
d. ranking
e. bot
f. search engine positioning
g. sponsored link
h. query
i. natural language query
j. relevancy

1. Where a Web site appears on the results page
2. An engine that displays Web pages relevant to a topic, even if the words don't precisely match your keywords
3. A link that is displayed at the top of the results page because the company pays to have it shown in that location
4. An automated program that searches the Web for new or updated changes
5. Structuring a Web page and submitting it to sites so that it appears at the top of search engine results
6. A topical word you include in a search
7. Phrasing your query as a plain English question
8. Web pages that match your keywords, usually displayed as a link on a results page
9. A general term that means asking a search engine a question
10. How closely a result matches your query

Real Life

1. Use keywords and the following search engines to conduct searches: Google (*www.google.com*), AltaVista (*www.altavista.com*), HotBot (*www.hotbot.com*), and Excite (*www.excite.com*). First, run a search on each engine using the keyword sports. Then run a second search using the keywords sports equipment. Finally, run a search using the keywords running sports equipment. Note the difference in the number and type of hits generated by each engine.
2. Use Google (*www.google.com*) to conduct similar (but not identical) searches and then compare the results. Pay attention to the number of hits for each search and what type of sites are returned. Also notice whether the sponsored links change when you modify the search expression. Use the following search ideas to get started:

   - First search for books running and then search for running books. Was there any difference?
   - Search for computer; then search for security. Finally search for computer security. How did the results vary?
   - Search for the keyword college; then search for scholarship. Combine the keywords to search for college scholarship. Next, run a search with the keywords college scholarship private school. Finally, mix up the order of the keywords and determine whether the keyword order affects the results.

I Spy: Privacy and Security Concerns

1. Conduct searches on several of the major search engines by using your name as the keyword. (If necessary to generate relevant hits, add other information about yourself, such as where you live, your college major, and so on.) Look at several of the sites on the results pages to see what information about you is on the Web. Next, use the same search engines to conduct searches using the name of someone you know that has local or regional prominence, such as a college football player or minor league baseball player. Finally, conduct searches using the name of a well-known person. What are the implications of having so much online information readily available on people? Are there any ways to protect your identifying information or keep it from being listed in a directory?
2. Take a look at each search site's privacy policy. Also, determine which search engines have built-in filters and research how to set the filters.

CHAPTER 12

BEYOND THE BASICS: SEARCHING SEAMLESSLY

Key Terms

When you finish this chapter, you'll understand the following terms:

AND
Boolean logic
deep Web
logical operators
mathematical operators
NEAR
NOT
OR
precedence
surface Web
wildcard character

Chapter Objectives

After you complete this chapter, you'll

- Know How to Use Operators in a Search
- Know Some of the Advanced Search Engine Options
- Have Used Some of the Specialized Search Sites

The Big Picture

How can I find a pet python? Where is Timbuktu? Can I afford that trip to Hawaii? And how will I ever get that technology report done by Monday?

Questions like these are what inspire people to run Internet searches—they want to know something. But most people also quickly find that the Web is too unwieldy to wade through without some help.

That's where search engines come in. They sort through the available Web pages and pull out the ones with the topics you really need. As you learned in the last chapter, this is an inexact science, and many of the hits produced by a search aren't very helpful.

In this chapter, we'll look at some advanced techniques you can use to generate search results that better match what you want to find. You'll learn how to combine keywords with logical and mathematical operators to produce more exact results. We'll also take a tour of some of the specialized search sites you can use to find specific types of information, such as those that help you find people, library resources, or jobs.

Window on the Web

As you learned in the previous chapter, the Web includes a number of search engines you can use to locate information. But the simple keyword searches you did in the previous chapter only scratch the surface of what you can do with search engines. By learning a few additional techniques, you can generate much better results—hits that more precisely fit the information you had in mind.

In this chapter, you'll also get a chance to visit some specialized search sites. You'll learn how to use these sites to do things like find an old classmate, get a new job, or read the latest news. For example, one well-known job search site is CareerBuilder at *www.careerbuilder.com* (see Figure 12.1).

Figure 12.1.
Specialized search sites help you find information—such as how to get a job.

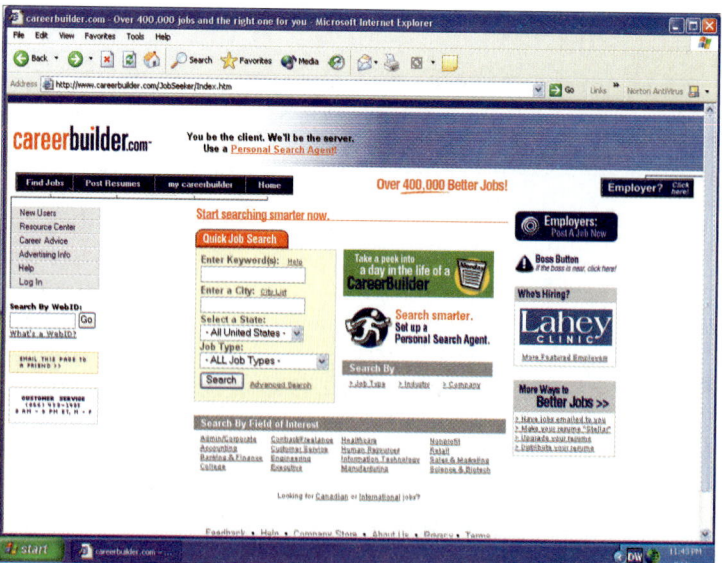

182   Chapter 12   Beyond the Basics: Searching Seamlessly

You'll also get a taste of how you can conduct research online that enables you to tap into a wealth of information. As we go through the chapter, you'll see a number of sites that you'll probably want to access in the future.

After you complete the chapter, you'll be much more search-savvy and able to locate almost any information you want. So spend a few minutes learning how to construct effective search expressions and successfully wield search tools.

KNOW HOW TO USE OPERATORS IN A SEARCH

There's one search technique that will help you more than almost any other to run better searches: Boolean logic. Don't let the austere sounding name scare you off. **Boolean logic** boils down to using four different operators—AND, NOT, OR, and NEAR—in conjunction with keywords or terms.

These Boolean operators are also called **logical operators** because they specify the logical relationship between elements. Take a look at some of the most common Boolean operators:

- **AND** is used to make sure that the keywords joined by the AND operator are *all* present on a hit page. For example, entering `Horse AND Show` narrows the search results to horse competitions while simultaneously eliminating sites for buying horses, horse equipment, and television shows. You're not limited to using only two keywords separated by AND, either; you can specify as many keywords as you want, separating each with the AND operator. For example, you can enter `Horse AND Pony AND Show` to make your search more precise. From this, you can see that using AND is a great way of limiting the number of hits to only those pages that include data for your purposes.
- **OR** is used to specify that *either* of the words can be present on a page. For example, entering `Germany OR France` returns pages that include one or the other of the search terms, but not necessarily both.
- **NOT** is used to eliminate pages with a certain word. For example, entering `Horse NOT Pony` returns only sites that include *horse* as a keyword, but eliminates any that used *pony*. Another example? `Beach NOT Bums` yields sites that are about the *beach*, but excludes those that also include the word *bums*.
- **NEAR** is a useful Boolean operator, but is not supported as often by search engines as are AND, OR, and NOT. NEAR is used to tell the search engine to look for pages that include both terms within a specified proximity to each other (usually up to 10 words apart). For example, if you want to locate information on mulching plants, you can enter `plants NEAR mulch`, which returns hits in which the words *plants* and *mulch* are within 10 words of each other. Obviously, this effectively eliminates Web pages that include both keywords in arbitrary locations on the page.

You can also use mathematical operators in place of the Boolean operators. **Mathematical operators** are symbols used to perform an operation on a value. The most common mathematical operators that you'll use for Internet searches are the plus (+) and minus (-) signs, which are analogous to the AND and NOT Boolean operators. Entering `NOT Pizza` and `-Pizza` in a search engine will generate the same results. Similarly, `Hamburger AND Fries` will produce the same hits as does `Hamburger +Fries`. Note that when you use the mathematical operators, the symbol must be placed next to the keyword *without* a space. The better you understand logical operators, the better you'll be able to use them to pinpoint helpful data.

INSIDE TRACK

George Boole, a 19th-century mathematician, developed Boolean logic. This logic is still used in computer programming and algebra today.

USING THE AND, OR, AND NOT OPERATORS

Now that you understand a little about using Boolean operators, try utilizing them in some searches.

ACTIVITY 12.1
Using the AND, OR, and NOT Operators

1. Open Internet Explorer and make sure that your computer is connected to the Internet.

2. In the Address box, type the URL for AltaVista (`www.altavista.com`) and then click Go.
   The home page for AltaVista is displayed. Now, imagine that you want to find out about water skiing (but want to eliminate sites that talk about snow skiing).

    **HEADS UP!** Make sure to type Boolean operators, such as AND, in all caps.

3. Type `water AND skiing` in the text box; then click the Find button.
   A listing of Web pages that include both keywords is shown. This is a good example of using the AND logical operator. Now try performing the same search using a mathematical operator.

    **HEADS UP!** When you use the plus and minus mathematical operators, don't leave a space between the operator and the keyword.

4. Delete the text in the search text box; then type `water +skiing` and click Find.
   The same hits display. Now try using OR in a search expression.

5. Delete the text in the search text box; then type `Germany OR France`. Click Find.

6. Scroll through the page of results.
   Notice that the hits can include either Germany or France. Some of the pages include both search terms, even though the Boolean search expression you used doesn't require it. Now try using NOT. In AltaVista, you combine the NOT operator with AND.

7. Delete the text in the search text box and then type `Europe AND NOT France`. Click Find.

8. Scroll through the list of hits, noticing that using NOT eliminated pages on France that also included the keyword *Europe*.

9. Leave Internet Explorer open if you plan to complete more hands-on activities in this chapter.

 **HEADS UP!** Not all search engines support all the Boolean operators. For example, some search engines support AND, NOT, and OR, but do not support NEAR. If the search engine you like to use doesn't support these operators, it may include "Advanced Search Options" that you can instead use to narrow your search.

LIMIT RESULTS BY USING MULTIPLE KEYWORDS AND BOOLEAN OPERATORS

You can couple multiple keywords and Boolean operators to limit the hits to just the information you actually need. For example, imagine that you want to go on a cruise to see the castles along Germany's Rhine River. Furthermore, you want to find tours with special pricing for students. Instead of conducting a general search for the keyword *Germany*, you can set up a search expression that limits the results to only student tours of this type. Let's take a look.

ACTIVITY 12.2
Limiting Results by Using Multiple Keywords and Boolean Operators

1. Open Internet Explorer and make sure that your computer is connected to the Internet with the AltaVista Web site (*www.altavista.com*) displayed.

2. Select any text that already displays in the search text box and then type `Germany`. Click Find.

   The pages that include hits about Germany display. Also, notice that the search engine generated several million hits for this keyword. Now try adding more keywords to limit the number and increase the quality of the hits.

3. Replace the text in the search text box with the following expression: `Germany AND castle AND Rhine AND river AND cruise AND student AND group AND tour`. Click Find.

   The number of hits is a much more manageable at 200 or so (see Figure 12.2).

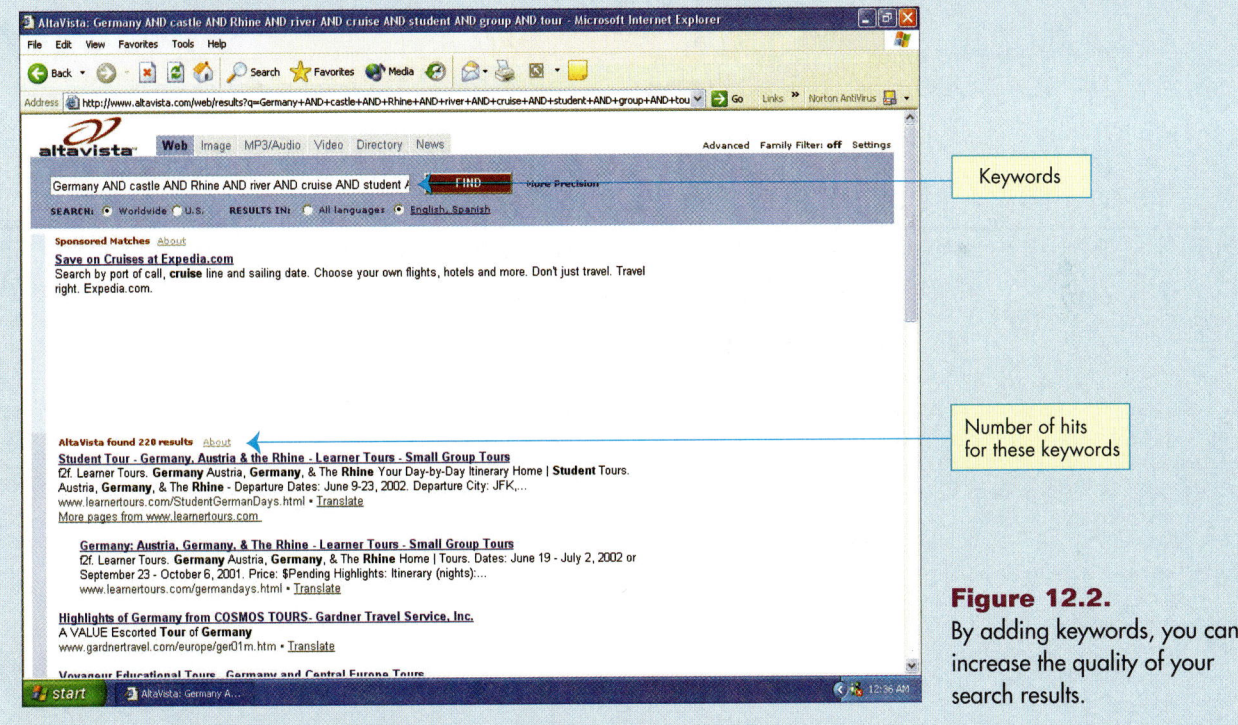

Figure 12.2.
By adding keywords, you can increase the quality of your search results.

4. Leave Internet Explorer open if you plan to complete more hands-on activities in this chapter.

LIMIT SEARCHES BY USING QUOTATION MARKS

INSIDE TRACK

Precedence is a component of an operator that indicates when it will be evaluated in a formula. Operators with high precedence (such as those used for multiplication and division) are completed before those with lower precedence (such as addition and subtraction). However, you can change the order of precedence for a search expression by placing parentheses around part of the expression. When you do, operations within the parentheses will be completed first.

Most search engines include another useful way of limiting your searches: surrounding the search phrase that you want by using quotation marks around it. This feature limits the hits to just those pages that have an exact match for the phrase. For example, if you want to only find Web sites on Abraham Lincoln, you could enter "Abraham Lincoln" as the search text. Constructing the search expression in this manner would eliminate sites that included the famous Jewish patriarch Abraham or Lincoln cars. Likewise, placing Gettysburg Address between quotation marks ("Gettysburg Address") produces results different from the results of typing the search expression without them.

In this activity, you'll see how to use this technique to limit the search results. You'll also find out where to tap into a handy reference of Boolean operators within AltaVista.

ACTIVITY 12.3
Limiting Searches by Using Quotation Marks

1. Make sure that Internet Explorer is open and the Web site for AltaVista is displayed (*www.altavista.com*).

2. Select any existing entry in the search text box and then type "Abraham Lincoln". Click Find.

   The search engine returns results with *Abraham Lincoln*.

3. Clear the entry in the search text box, type "George Washington" AND "Valley Forge", and then click Find.

   The results are confined to pages that include both *George Washington* and *Valley Forge* (see Figure 12.3).

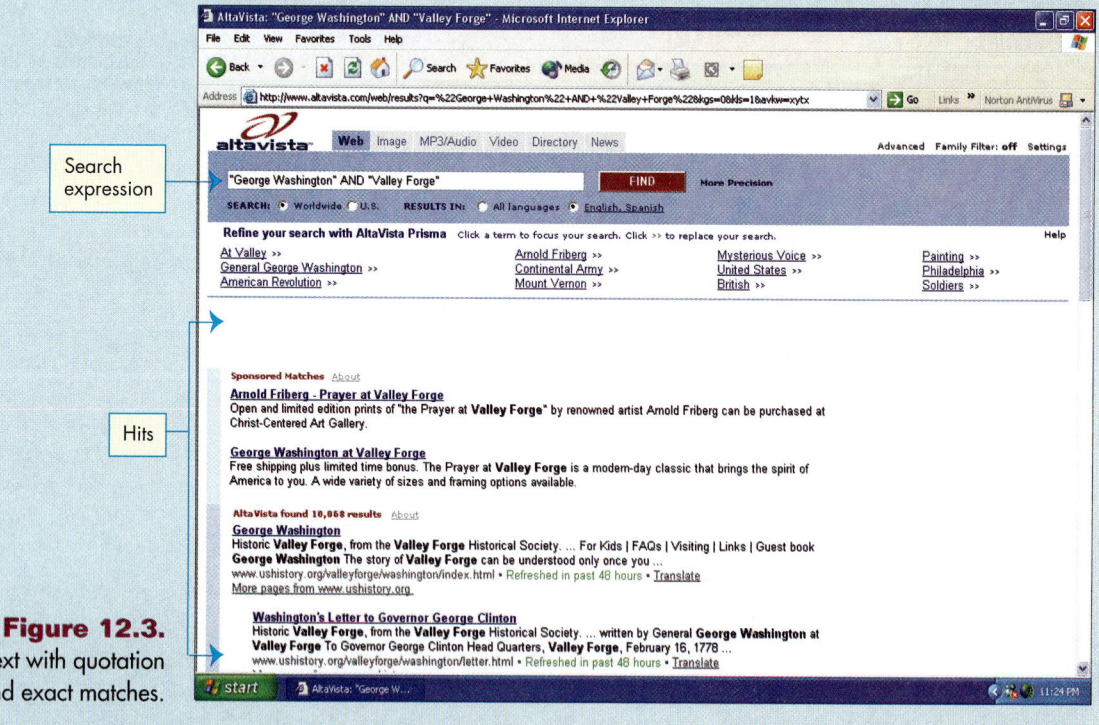

Figure 12.3. Surround text with quotation marks to find exact matches.

4. Redisplay AltaVista's home page.

ACTIVITY 12.3
Limiting Searches by Using Quotation Marks

5 Click the *Advanced Search* link, located in the Tools section (below the search box). The Advanced Web Search page is displayed. Notice that this page includes a number of options related to setting up your queries (see Figure 12.4).

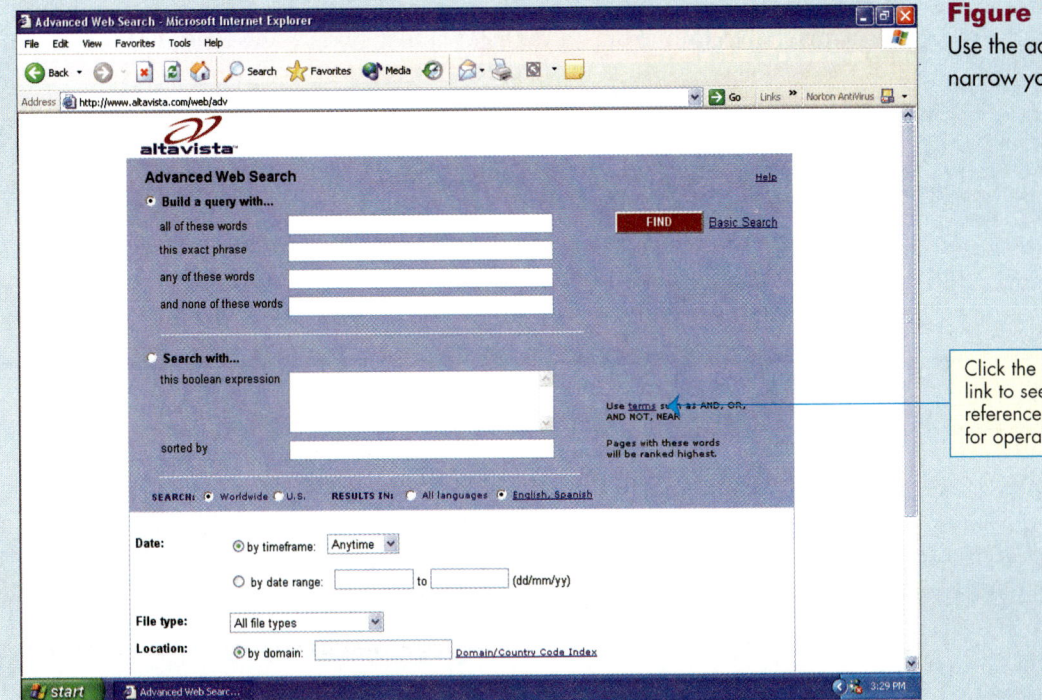

Figure 12.4.
Use the advanced options to narrow your search.

Click the *terms* link to see a reference page for operators

6 Click the *terms* link (refer to Figure 12.4).
A reference page for working with logical operators is shown (see Figure 12.5).

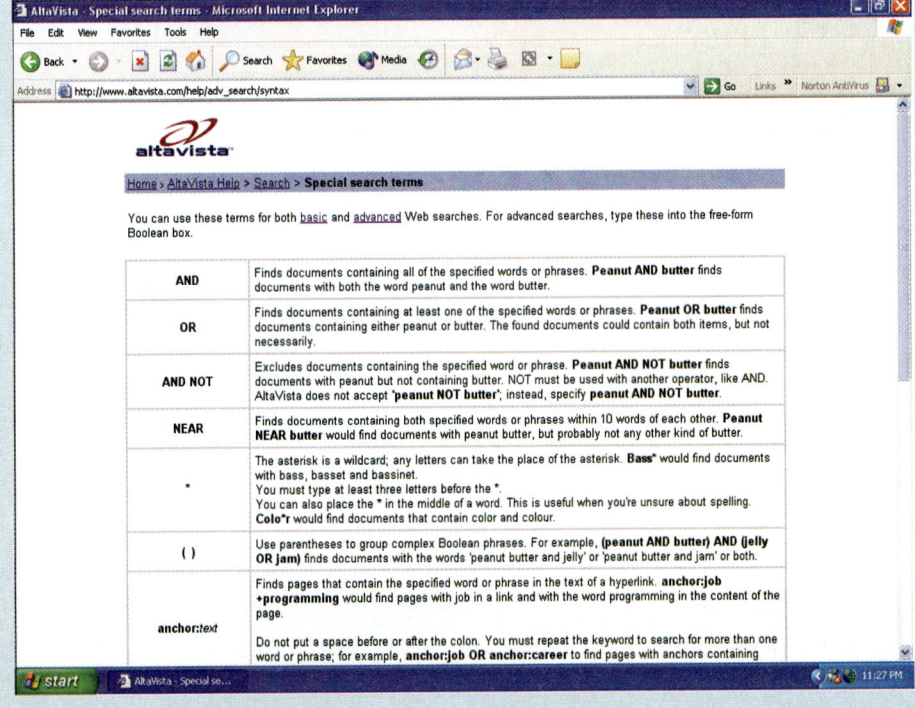

Figure 12.5.
Confused about logical operators? Most search engines offer assistance.

7 Read over the information shown on AltaVista's reference page.

8 Leave Internet Explorer open if you plan to complete more hands-on activities in this chapter.

Know How to Use Operators in a Search 187

INSIDE TRACK

AltaVista includes other helpful options for advanced searches: Use *like* to find words similar to the specified Web URL; use *link* to find pages that have links to the URL. For example, if you want to find sites related to privacy issues, you could type `like:www.epic.org` in the search text box to find pages similar to those at the Electronic Privacy Information Center. Likewise, if you wanted to list the pages that were linked to the site (for future reference or to find similar pages), you could enter `link:www.epic.org`.

KNOW SOME OF THE ADVANCED SEARCH ENGINE OPTIONS

Most of the larger search engines include additional advanced search capabilities. Depending on the search engine, they include options such as searching by world region, the date the site was modified or created, and so on. You can usually find out about the advanced search features for a search engine by clicking the Help button. In the next activity, you'll get a taste of using some of the advanced features in Google. As you go through the activity, keep in mind that these features are similar to those found in other major search engines (such as AltaVista).

ACTIVITY 12.4
Using Advanced Search Engine Features

1. In Internet Explorer, type the URL for Google (www.google.com).

2. On Google's home page, click the Advanced Search link (located to the right of the search text box).
   The Advanced Search page of the Web site is displayed (see Figure 12.6).

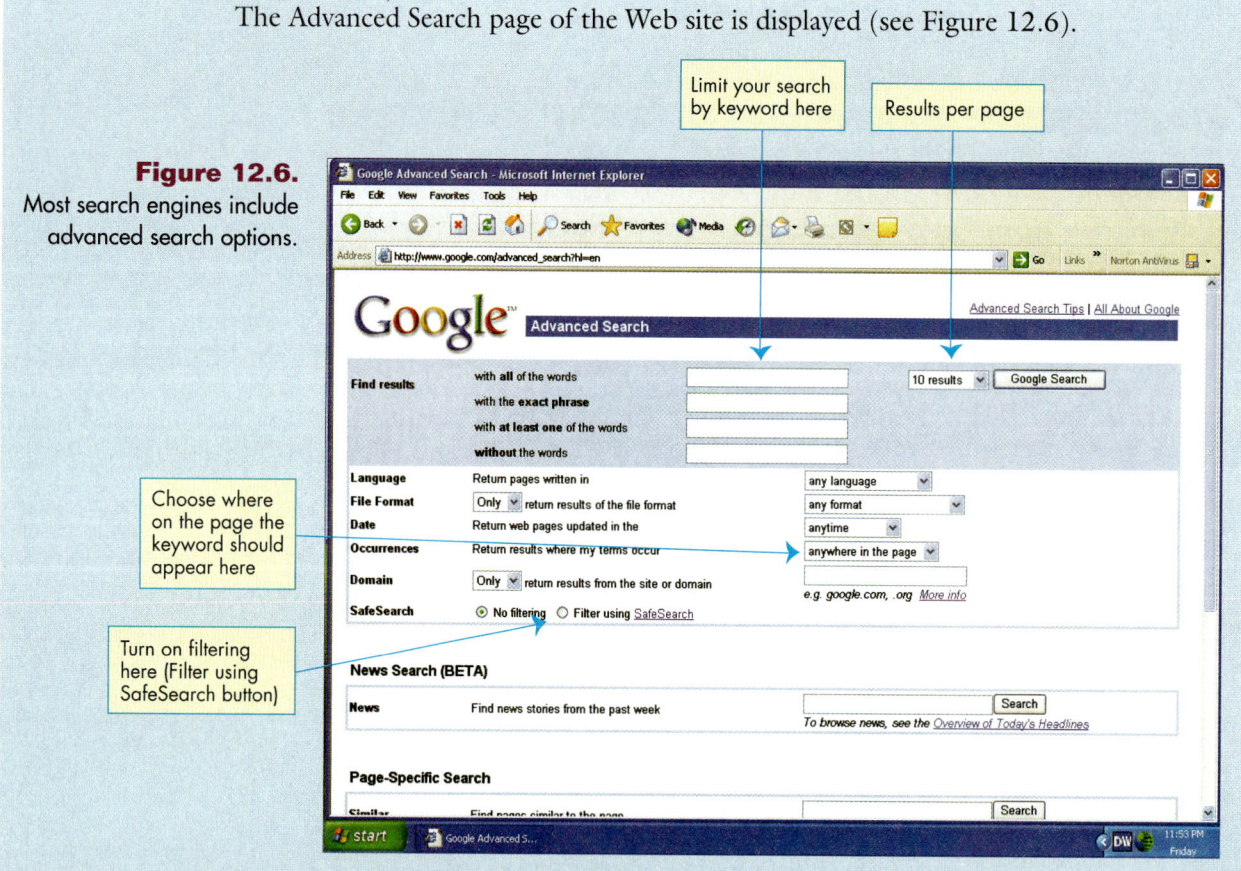

Figure 12.6.
Most search engines include advanced search options.

3. In the *with all of the words* box, type `Alaskan Cruises`.

4. Click the results per page drop-down list arrow and then choose 100 results (refer to Figure 12.6).

188 Chapter 12 Beyond the Basics: Searching Seamlessly

ACTIVITY 12.4
Using Advanced Search Engine Features

⑤ In the SafeSearch area, click the *Filter using SafeSearch* option button.

Your screen should appear similar to that shown in Figure 12.7.

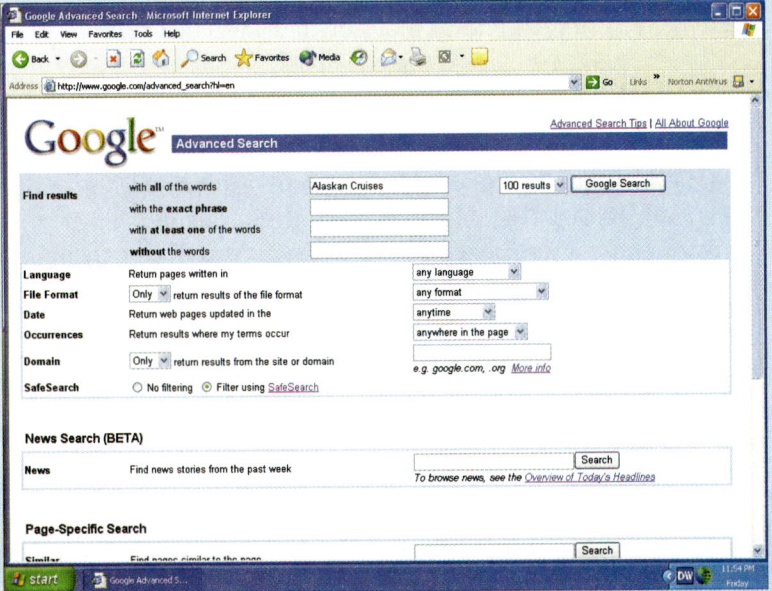

 INSIDE TRACK

Some of the search engines are case-sensitive; others are not. If the search engine is case-insensitive, you'll see the same results no matter what capitalization you use. In this activity, you use Google, which is case-insensitive, so it really doesn't matter if you type `Alaskan Cruises` or `alaskan cruises`.

Figure 12.7.
By changing options, you can limit which (and how many) hits are shown.

 HEADS UP! Most search engine sites are constatnly being upgraded and changed. Because of this, you may see slightly different options from those shown in Figure 12.7. If so, just choose similar options to those used in this activity.

⑥ Click the *Google Search* button.

The results show only those sites that adhere to the search expression you indicated: sites that include *Alaskan Cruises* (see Figure 12.8).

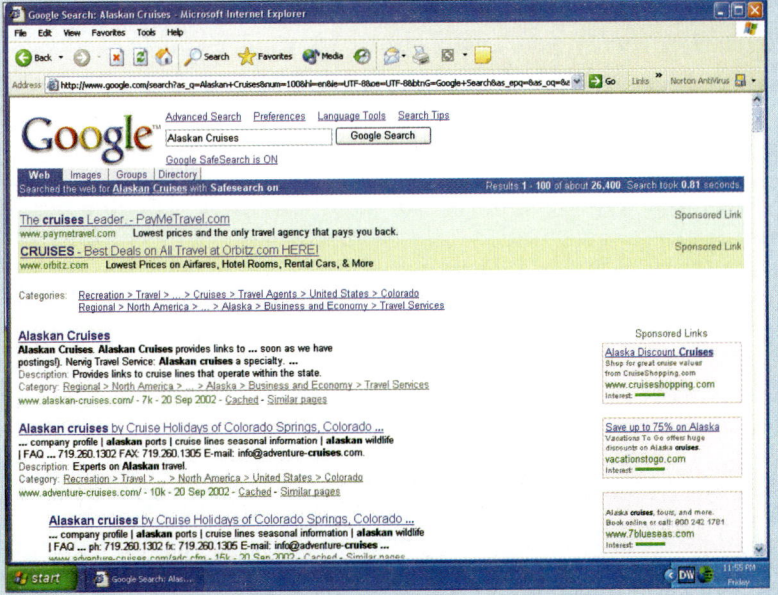

 INSIDE TRACK

A **wildcard character** is a special type of character that you can use in a search expression to make the search more general. The most common wildcard character is the asterisk (*), which represents any type or number of characters. For example, entering `com*` in a search expression might yield results with words such as *computer*, *composition*, or *command*. Wildcard characters are typically used when you don't know the complete word or phrase or when you don't know how to spell a keyword.

Figure 12.8.
Restrict hits by using the advanced search options.

⑦ Leave Internet Explorer open if you plan to complete more hands-on activities in this chapter.

Know Some of the Advanced Search Engine Options 189

USE SOME OF THE SPECIALIZED SEARCH SITES

INSIDE TRACK

There's a large portion of the Web that's not indexed by general search engines. This information, called the **deep Web**, consists of dynamic Web pages and databases. The deep Web is sometimes called the "invisible Web" because it consists of a vast amount of content that's inaccessible to conventional search engines. Specialized search tools can dig into the deep Web; general search engines tend to more easily locate information on the **surface Web** because it consists mainly of static Web pages. BrightPlanet, a company that specializes in search technologies, estimates that the deep Web may contain *500 times* more content then does the surface Web. (If you want to find out more about the deep Web, take a look at BrightPlanet's Web site at *www.brightplanet.com*.)

Instead of using the general search engines such as Google or AltaVista to find information, you can use the tools found at specialized search sites. The specialized search tools can help you find online resources about distinct topics, such as politics, science, technology, or entertainment. They more effectively target information about a topic because they index data only on these subjects. In contrast, general search engines index the material found at a wide variety of Web sites and don't focus on any particular topic.

For example, you can find specialized search engines for most academic disciplines, professional careers, and hobbies. These specialized search engines pull their information from Web sites, online professional journals, and abstracts—all of which are related to the main topic. Additionally, specialized search engines usually index more pages at each Web site than do the general search engines, which provide better depth of coverage for the topic at hand.

You can use a specialized search engine if you need detailed or highly specialized information on a topic. For example, imagine that you want to learn about a particular medical condition, such as rheumatoid arthritis. Although a general search engine such as Google would probably return a number of hits related to arthritis, you'd probably also see quite a few pages that weren't closely related to this topic. In this case, you would probably find better quality information using the medical search engines on a site such as the National Library of Medicine (*www.nlm.nih.gov*).

You'll probably eventually develop an affinity for particular search sites, especially those related to your profession. For example, if you're a computer guru, you'll most likely want to tap into specialized Web sites for computer information and reviews, such as CNET (*www.cnet.com*); if you're a real estate agent, you'll soon discover how useful a site like Realtor.com (*www.realtor.com*) can be. Medical personnel (or anyone who is sick) may want to take a look at Medsite (*www.medsite.com*); legal buffs and professionals will head for FindLaw (*www.findlaw.com*) or LawGuru (*www.lawguru.com*). If you want to find out more about specialized search engines, including information about some of the largest and most popular, take a look at SearchAbility's Web site (*www.searchability.com*).

Obviously, we can't show you all the possibilities that exist for specialized Web sites (although Appendix B includes a list of helpful Web sites). But in the following activity, you'll get a chance to search a couple of them.

ACTIVITY 12.5
Using Specialized Search Sites

① In Internet Explorer, type the URL for the OneLook Dictionaries Web site (`www.onelook.com`).

The Web page for the OneLook Dictionaries site displays. This site has words from more than 800 dictionaries. You can use the site's built-in search feature to find multiple definitions for a word (see Figure 12.9).

> **HEADS UP!** If you have trouble accessing the OneLook Dictionaries site, try finding definitions on an alternative dictionary site, such as yourDictionary (*www.yourdictionary.com*) or the Merriam-Webster site (*www.m-w.com*).

② In the *Word or pattern* text box, type `Internet` and then click Search.

A list of dictionaries that include a definition for the word are displayed.

190 Chapter 12 Beyond the Basics: Searching Seamlessly

ACTIVITY 12.5
Using Specialized Search Sites

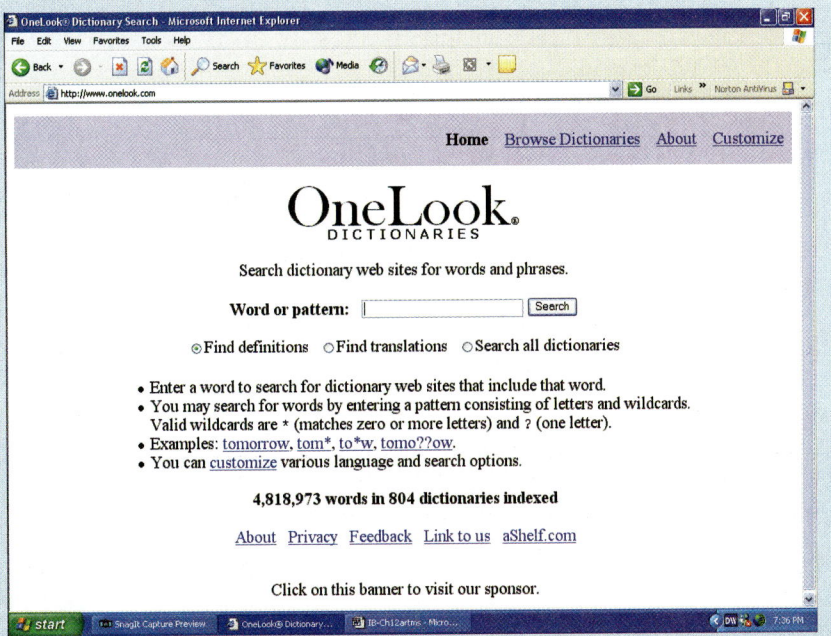

Figure 12.9.
The OneLook Dictionaries site accesses multiple dictionaries at once.

❸ Click the link for *Internet* or *internet* for any of the dictionaries shown on the list.

The definition for *Internet* is shown. If you want, find the definition for other words. When you're finished, proceed with the next step in the activity.

❹ In the Internet Explorer Address box, type the URL for Peterson's, a site that you can use for finding a college or scholarship (www.petersons.com).

If you want, spend a few minutes exploring this site. When you're finished, proceed with the activity.

❺ In the Internet Explorer Address box, type the address for Yahoo's PeopleSearch (http://people.yahoo.com) as shown in Figure 12.10.

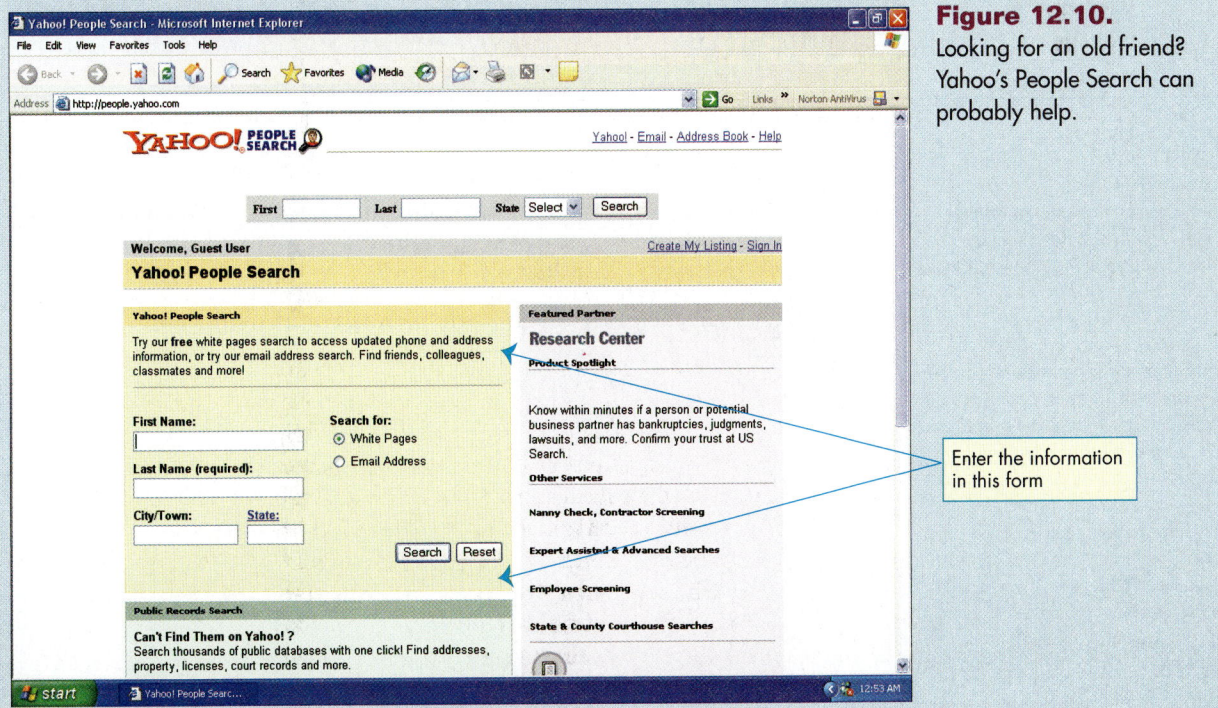

Figure 12.10.
Looking for an old friend? Yahoo's People Search can probably help.

Use Some of the Specialized Search Sites

ACTIVITY 12.5
Using Specialized Search Sites (Continued)

INSIDE TRACK

There are other specialized search engines you can use to locate people. For example, you can use www.peoplesearch.net or www.peoplesearch.com.

❻ In the form provided, enter the name for an old friend or someone you're trying to locate, including the state in which they reside. Click the *Search* button.

The results are displayed on a list.

❼ Type www.zdnet.com in Internet Explorer's Address box and then click Go.

The Web site for ZDNet is shown. This site includes a wealth of information about the latest technology (see Figure 12.11). If you want, explore the ZDNet site for a few minutes. When you're finished, proceed with the next step in the activity—using a library site.

Figure 12.11.
ZDNet is a good place to start if you're interested in the latest computer technology and news.

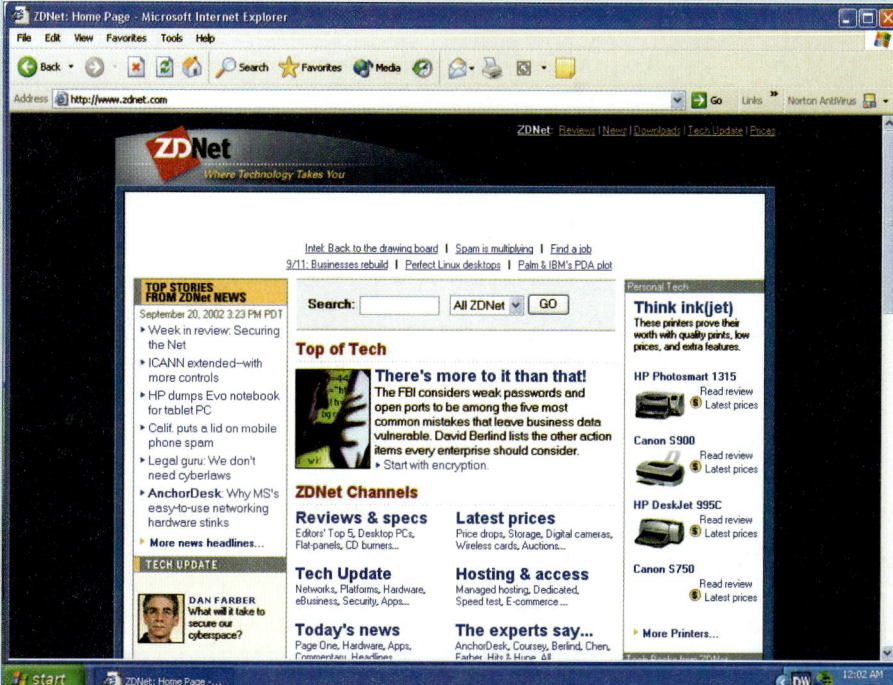

INSIDE TRACK

There are a number of job search sites on the Web, including CareerBuilder (*www.careerbuilder.com*) and HotJobs (*www.hotjobs.com*). These sites have career-related information, including huge, searchable databases of current job postings. You can also post resumes on the sites. But beware. At least one of the job search sites (Monster at *www.monster.com*) has allegedly tracked those who post resumes on their site for sharing identifying information with third parties, such as advertisers or training organizations. This information could also be used for identity theft. Before posting your resume, evaluate the privacy policy of the organization and weigh the advantages and disadvantages carefully.

❽ Type http://infomine.ucr.edu in the Internet Explorer Address box and then click Go. (Note: Don't type *www* as part of the address.)

The Web site for INFOMINE is shown. This site, which is maintained by the University of California, is essentially a huge online library (see Figure 12.12). If you want, follow some of the links on the INFOMINE site or conduct a site search.

❾ Leave Internet Explorer open if you plan to complete the end-of-chapter activities.

ACTIVITY 12.5
Using Specialized Search Sites

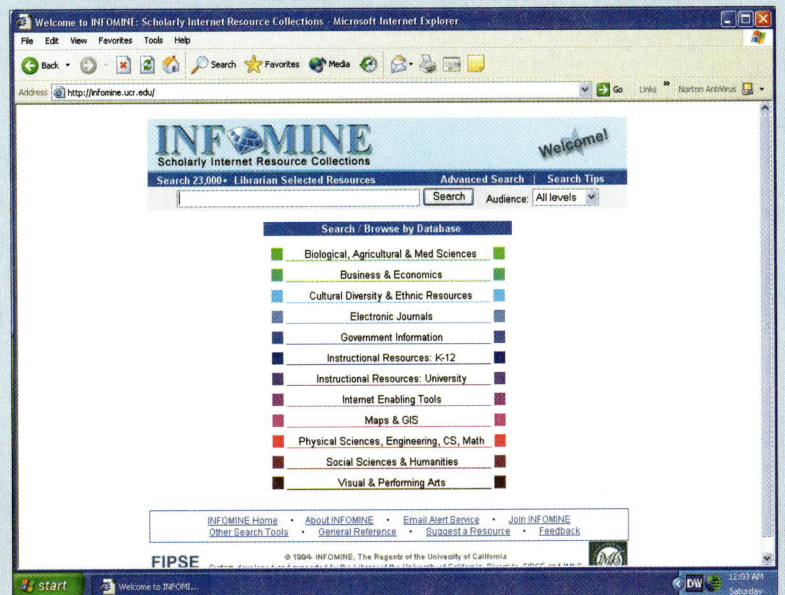

Figure 12.12.
Take a library tour—online style.

Don't Forget...

- You can use logical and mathematical operators in searches to generate more-specific results for your needs.
- You can use the AND, OR, NEAR, and NOT operators to limit searches.
- You can find exact matches for a search expression by enclosing the phrase within quotation marks.
- Many of the major search engines include support for Boolean operators as well as a number of other advanced search options.
- Wildcard characters can be used to make a search expression more general.
- The Web includes a host of specialized search sites, including online libraries, job search, and industry-specific sites.

Check This Out

MULTIPLE CHOICE

1. Which of the following search expressions would generate sites about bird watching?
   a. bird NOT watching
   b. "bird watching"
   c. GO TO bird watching
   d. All of the above

2. Which of the following characters is the wildcard character most supported by search engines?
   a. Asterisk (*)
   b. Minus (-)
   c. Period (.)
   d. Ampersand (&)

3. AND, OR, and NOT are all examples of
   a. search engines
   b. operators
   c. specialized search sites
   d. online libraries

4. Which of the following can you set using advanced search engine options?
   a. The number of hits to display per page
   b. Filtering
   c. The date on which the Web site was created or modified
   d. All of the above

5. Which of the following is an example of a specialized search site?
   a. PeopleSearch
   b. ZDNet
   c. CareerBuilder
   d. All of the above

Check This Out   193

MATCHING

a. AND
b. OR
c. NOT
d. NEAR
e. plus sign (+)
f. asterisk (*)
g. minus sign (-)
h. search expression
i. logical operator
j. Boolean

1. This is also known as a Boolean operator
2. A character used to make a search term more general
3. The combination of keywords and operators
4. Used in a search expression the same way as the AND operator
5. Logic on which some computer programming is based
6. Used in a search expression the same way as the NOT operator
7. Logical operator that is used to specify that *either* of the words can be present on a page
8. Includes pages in which the keywords are in close proximity to each other
9. Is used to make sure the two words joined by them are *both* present in search results
10. Excludes pages if they include certain keywords

Real Life

1. Research how to use the advanced search options in each of the following search engines: Google (*www.google.com*), AltaVista (*www.altavista.com*), HotBot (*www.hotbot.com*), and Lycos (*www.lycos.com*). Next, think of your favorite hobby or class at school and choose keywords related to it. Using these keywords and search engines, conduct several advanced searches. Compare the results you get with each search engine and develop a table or chart that outlines your findings. Based on the advanced options, which search engine do you feel will best fit your needs?

2. Go to each of the following specialized search sites listed in this chapter and spend time looking over the information included. If time allows, also take a look at the following sites. Make sure to run searches on each site to locate specific information.

- Consumer information: *www.consumerworld.org*
- Map and driving directions: *www.mapquest.com*
- Cars (including used): *www.kbb.com*

3. Use the Web to find out more about how search engines work, how to run Boolean searches, and which features are included in each search engine. Start with *www.searchenginewatch.com* and *www.searchengineshowdown.com*. Run searches to locate additional sites. Develop a research paper or a PowerPoint presentation based on your findings.

4. Search for your ideal job using the job search sites listed in this chapter, such as CareerBuilder (*www.careerbuilder.com*), HotJobs (*www.hotjobs.com*), and Monster (*www.monster.com*). Compare the services provided by each of the services, how easy they are to use, and the privacy policies each embraces.

I Spy: Privacy and Security Concerns

1. There have been allegations that some of the specialized search sites (especially job search sites) collect identifying information from people who visit the sites. This information is then used for tracking the person or is shared with advertisers. Spend some time researching this issue. Start at the Web site for the Privacy Foundation (*www.privacyfoundation.org*) and follow the links about the privacy practices for Monster.com. Then use your advanced search skills to research this issue in more depth.

2. Conduct several searches, using various search engines and settings, to research Internet security and privacy issues. Find out about the issues surrounding the people search sites and determine whether there are infringements on privacy inherent in these sites. Develop a short oral presentation or a written report that outlines your findings.

SECTION SIX
TAKING CONTROL OF THE INTERNET

CHAPTER 13
COMMUNICATING VIA THE INTERNET

Key Terms

When you finish this chapter, you'll understand the following terms:

- buffer overflow
- Bulletin Board System (BBS)
- chat
- chat room
- digest
- instant messaging (IM)
- Internet Relay Chat (IRC)
- forum
- LISTSERV
- lurking
- mailing list manager (MLM)
- messaging client
- moderated group
- Netiquette
- NetMeeting
- newsgroup
- postings
- real-time
- thread
- unmoderated group
- video conferencing
- whiteboard

Chapter Objectives

After you complete this chapter, you'll

- Know About Instant Messaging
- Understand the Basics of Using Chat
- Know About Newsgroups and Bulletin Board Systems
- Know About LISTSERV and Mailing Lists
- Understand the Trends Associated with Real-Time Conferencing

The Big Picture

Communication. That's what it's all about, right? Fortunately, the Internet is set up to facilitate many forms of communication. In fact, you're already familiar with one of the most popular types of communication on the Internet: e-mail.

But there's more. Instant messaging, chat rooms, bulletin boards, bulk mailing lists, and newsgroups provide additional ways to bolster your enjoyment of the Internet. Video conferencing can be used to collaborate on business projects or for taking a college course.

In this chapter, we'll go over some great ways to use the Internet as a springboard for communicating with others. We'll cover how each of the major communication services works, point you in the right direction for finding and using each service, and then help you avoid some of the related security and privacy pitfalls.

Window on the Web

The Web has a host of services you can use to communicate with others. Take, for example, **instant messaging (IM)**—and some of the other forms of online communication, such as chat—in which you can communicate with friends by typing messages that are sent and replied to via the Internet in real-time. In reference to computers, the term **real-time** means that computer systems are able to process inputted information immediately. In other words, people can view and react to the data right away. That information is updated immediately, which provides speedy feedback or gratification to the users and has catapulted this type of communication to its current level of popularity.

A **messaging client** is simply the type of software installed on a personal computer and used to facilitate real-time communication on the Internet. One of the most popular and well-known instant messaging clients is America Online's Instant Messenger (see Figure 13.1).

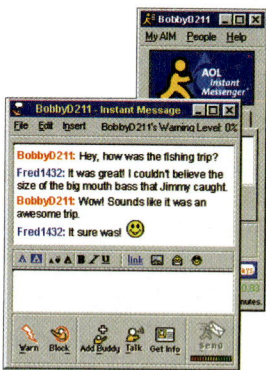

Figure 13.1.
America Online's Instant Messenger provides quick, real-time communication.

196 Chapter 13 Communicating via the Internet

Another way to communicate using the Internet is chat (electronic style, that is). **Chat** is an interactive, online discussion on a particular topic, usually with a group. To participate, you access an electronic **chat room** and then type your message. A chat room, of course, is nothing more than a specialized Web site or other virtual space that allows you to broadcast your messages to everyone who is also accessing the same location at that time. Chat is similar to instant messaging in that it provides immediate communication; it differs in that with chat you converse with a group of people, most of whom you probably don't know.

If you're looking for another way to communicate online with an entire group, try tapping into a newsgroup (see Figure 13.2) or to post and read messages on an Internet bulletin board. You can also join a mailing list or an electronic newsletter, which allows you to read and send messages to an entire group of people at once about a specific topic.

By the end of the chapter, you'll know about the myriad of ways that people are using the Internet to communicate with others and be in an informed position to decide which ones you want to use.

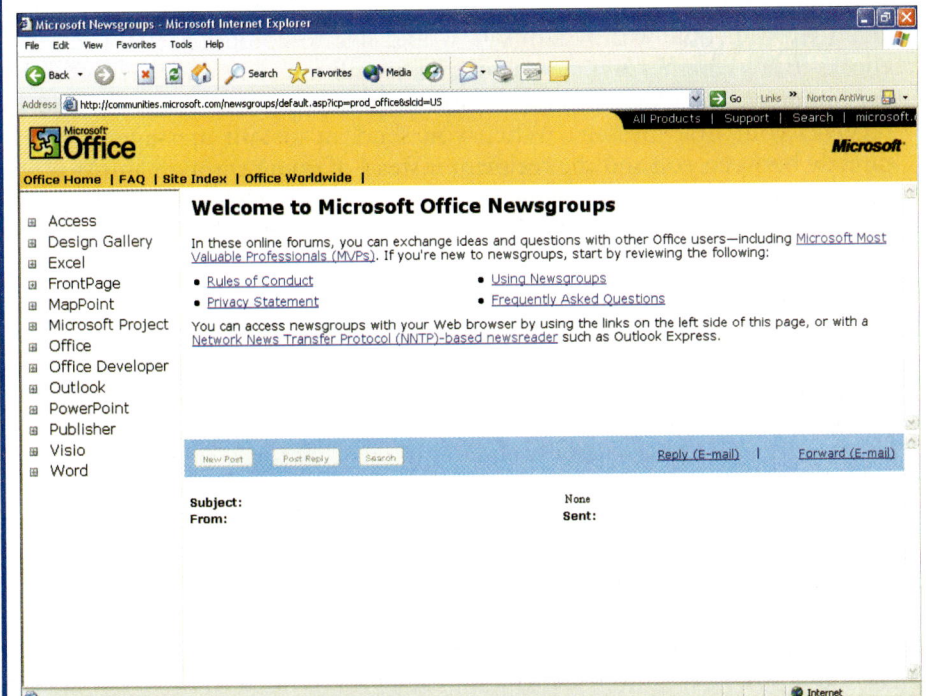

Figure 13.2.
You can tap into newsgroups to find out information about a particular topic.

KNOW ABOUT INSTANT MESSAGING

If you're a typical 21st-century person, you want information delivered to you at the speed of light. You don't want to wait for people to return phone calls or answer e-mail messages; you use a cell phone so that you can make calls whenever it's convenient instead of having to wait.

If this describes you, you're probably also a fan of instant messaging services on the Internet—or will be soon. Because messages are sent and received in real-time, instant messaging gives you quick access to anyone who you want to communicate with—providing, of course, that they're online at the same time and have the same instant message tool available. In this section, we'll cover how instant messaging works, some of the messaging clients that are available, and the rise of IM's popularity. We'll wrap up by discussing security and privacy issues surrounding instant messaging.

HOW INSTANT MESSAGING WORKS

So, what exactly is instant messaging? Picture it as the electronic version of the notes you passed in school between a classmate and yourself. It's just a bit more sophisticated because it's done electronically over the Internet—and usually with people in far-flung locations.

If you haven't experienced instant messaging yet, it's probably just a matter of time before you do. Furthermore, your transition into using instant messaging will be smoother if you know which IM programs are available and how IM operates. And even if you're an experienced IM user, understanding a little about how it works will help you use it more effectively.

First, let's take a quick refresher course on client-server architecture. Remember our discussion of clients and servers in Chapter 1, How the Internet is Changing the World? Guess what? There are instant messaging clients and servers, too, logically called IM clients and IM servers. When you open your IM client and log in, your IM server is able to authenticate your identity. Your IM client software then sends your information to the IM server. This information consists of things such as your computer's IP address and a list of people with whom you would like to communicate. The server checks to see whether anyone on your list is online and notifies them that you are online as well. After the IM session is initiated, you're ready to send (or receive) your first message. When you send an instant message, it travels directly between you and the recipient instead of going through an IM server. In this way, it's similar to talking to someone on the telephone. Finally, when you log off, the IM client lets the IM server know, who then in turn informs people on your list.

Before you begin to use IM, you need to make sure that you have an IM client loaded on your system. One of the most popular clients is AOL Instant Messenger (AIM), available at no cost on AIM's Web site (*www.aim.com*). You can also download other IM clients, such as ICQ (*web.icq.com*) or Yahoo! Messenger (*messenger.yahoo.com*) from the Internet. (We'll cover a little more about available IM messaging tools later in this chapter.)

 You weren't able to set up contact lists within instant messaging to control who was able to send you messages? Without contact lists in place, think of the possibilities for Internet stalkers or other nasty people to use instant messaging against you!

After you install the IM client software you want to use on your system, your next step is to set up a list of people with whom you want to communicate. This list is usually called a *buddy list, contact list* or a *friend list*. It's important because it controls who can send you messages. This prevents IM from becoming a free-for-all in which anyone can interrupt you at any time by sending you a message.

You can send a message to the people on your list anytime you're both online. When you send a message (or one is sent to you), a small window containing the note opens on your desktop so that you can enter a reply. You can keep sending notes back and forth as long as you want and as long as you're both online.

MESSAGING CLIENTS

The most popular instant messaging clients currently on the market include AOL Instant Messenger (AIM), ICQ (for "I seek you"), MSN Messenger, and Yahoo! Messenger. Although each of these services varies in the features they include, they all provide good service according to a recent CNET survey (*www.cnet.com*). Best of all, these services are free. If you want to use instant messaging, you can sign up for a service, download the software, and then take whatever other steps are necessary to develop an account and buddy-type of list. You can find out more about each of the services by visiting their respective

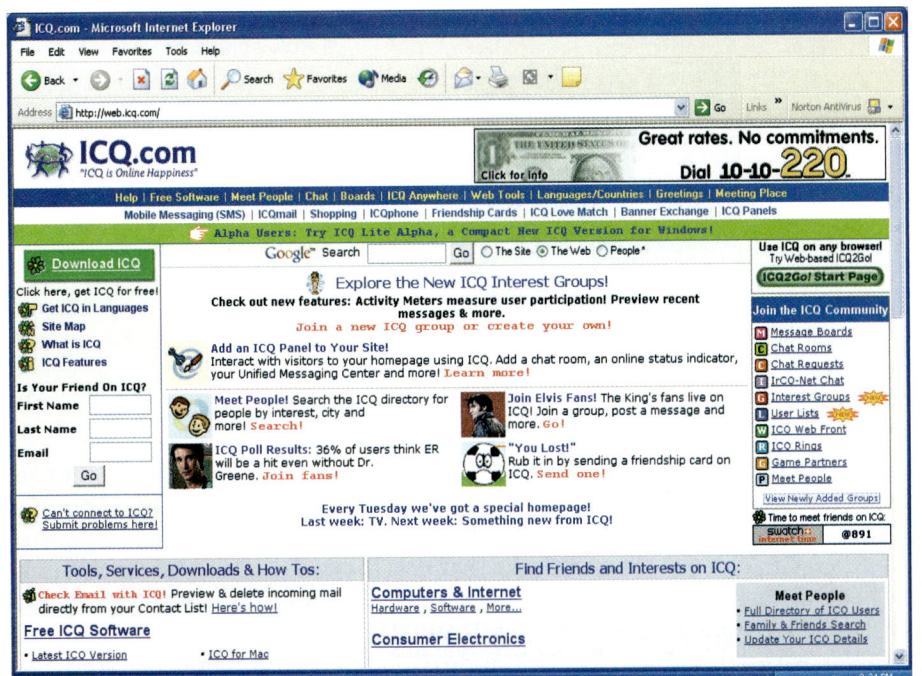

Figure 13.3.
ICQ claims that 120 million people around the world use its program to communicate.

Web sites: AIM (*www.aim.com*), ICQ (*web.icq.com*; see Figure 13.3), MSN Messenger (*messenger.msn.com*), and Yahoo! Messenger (*messenger.yahoo.com*).

A note of caution: If you sign up for an instant messaging service, you'll probably be asked for a good deal of personal information, including your name and e-mail address. You can either ignore these fields in the online form you use to sign up because most IM clients require only your e-mail address. Alternatively, you can be "creative" with your answers by entering only your initials—or even your pet's name. Either approach will protect your privacy better than handing over contact information without a blink.

THE RISE OF INSTANT MESSAGING'S POPULARITY

Instant messaging has had a marked gain in popularity over the past few years. A Nielsen//NetRatings survey in December 2002 indicated that more than 27 million people use AOL's Instant Messaging service; MSN's and Yahoo's messaging applications were used by 22.7 and 15.6 million users, respectively.

Instant messaging is also gaining prominence in the workplace. IM's popularity in the workplace is related to its efficiency: You can use it to get quick answers about a project or to remind people of an upcoming meeting.

Despite the usefulness of IM and its increasing acceptance in the workplace, most of the people who tap into this online resource are young. College students, for example, comprise the highest percentage of those groups using

 **INSIDE TRACK**

Windows Messenger is the IM client that comes as part of Windows XP. Windows Messenger is essentially the same as MSN Messenger, with the addition of a few new features.

ON THE HORIZON

There's a new instant messaging application that connects users from all of the major messaging services (Yahoo!, MSN, AOL, and ICQ) together. Dubbed *Trillian*, this messaging tool is rapidly gaining users.

You can download the basic version of Trillian at no cost or download the Pro version for about $25 from Cerulean Studio's Web site (*ceruleanstudios.com/trillian*).

Figure 13.4.
Statistics indicate that instant messaging is popular among young people.

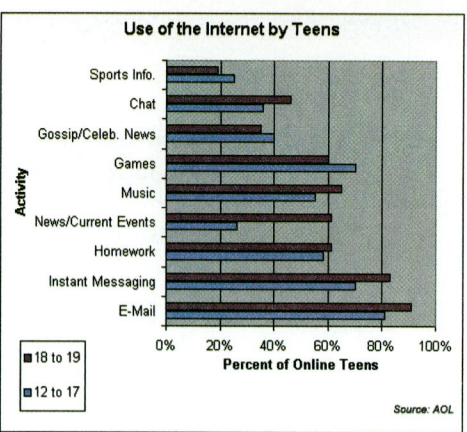

instant messaging: On an average *day*, 28 percent of online college students use it, compared with 12 percent of the general Internet public (Pew Internet & American Life study, September 2002). According to the same study, the *total* percentage of college students that use IM is 72%, compared with only 44% of the general Internet population. Another study (this one by the Nielsen//NetRatings group in August 2002) showed that IM was especially popular with young people, with approximately 11.5 million children and teenagers using IM in July 2002. This amounts to one-fourth of the total IM population during that month. Finally, an AOL study in January 2002 indicated that 83% of older teens (18–19 years of age) use IM.

The graph in Figure 13.4 shows the popularity of instant messaging, chat, and e-mail among American teenagers (source: AOL subsidiary Digital Market Services, Inc.).

SECURITY AND PRIVACY CONCERNS

Unfortunately, like many Internet tools, there are security issues to keep in mind when using instant messaging. Most IM clients don't have the same level of security in place as do other forms of online communication (such as e-mail). For example, many of the IM clients don't offer encryption. Because of this security deficiency, there have been cases in which a person's instant messaging identity was stolen by a cracker, who then sent nasty messages to people on the buddy list in the person's name. The cracker sometimes also threatened to continue the activity unless the person sent them money. This type of incident, although still rare, reveals some of the potential problems of IM. There are other security holes in IM as well. For example, clicking a link to a Web site in an ICQ message from a cracker can potentially allow the cracker to gain control of the user's computer. Some IM clients also create a problem with the **buffer overflow**. The problem arises when the buffer (an area of memory used for storing messages) is flooded with more characters than it can handle. A cracker can overwhelm a field (such as an address bar) with too many characters. An attacker could potentially hide an executable code in the extra characters that would give him control of the computer.

Because of the security risks, some organizations are beginning to use secure IMs that operate internally within their organization, behind a firewall. This type of service allows employees to use IM for collaboration, but keeps information securely within the company. If you're a member of the general public who simply wants to use IM to talk with friends across the country, you'll have to determine the level of security risk that you're willing to tolerate. To find out about the latest vulnerabilities in the IM client you're considering, check out CERT's Web site at *www.cert.org/advisories* (see Figure 13.5).

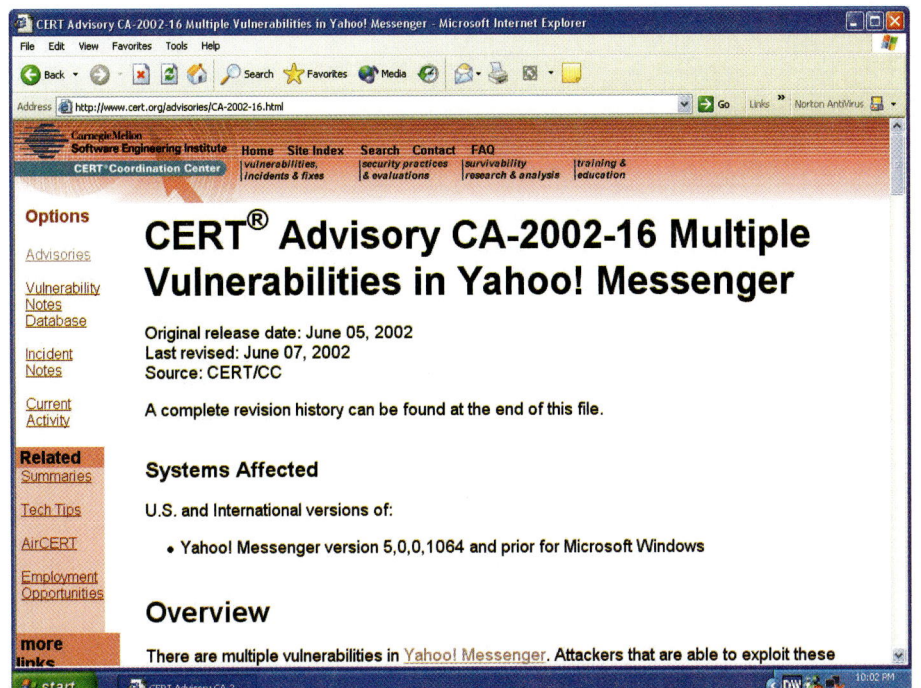

Figure 13.5.
Use the CERT Web site to find out about current security holes in the IM client you want to use.

UNDERSTAND THE BASICS OF USING CHAT

Another real-time service available on the Internet is chat. Chat is a generic term that describes an online activity in which Internet users enter virtual spaces (chat rooms) and communicate in real-time. The Internet areas or Web sites that sponsor these virtual spaces often follow the metaphor of the chat room by giving them names of rooms in a house or library (such as "The Study" or "The Rec Room"). Imagine yourself entering the room and sitting down to converse with others. Chat rooms are available on individual Web sites, from AOL and other ISPs, and via the Internet Relay Chat (IRC) system.

Currently, all you need to participate in chat is to create an account on a site that sponsors chat rooms and log in. In some cases, you might also need to download specialized software. It's that easy.

After you set up an account, you're ready to chat. You and others can exchange notes by typing them on the keyboard and sending them to the chat room. All the messages are displayed in a specialized chat window that everyone can read and respond to in an ongoing discussion.

Some chat rooms now also support multimedia functions, so that you can talk with (or even see) the other people in your chat room. Of course, this requires additional hardware, such as speakers, microphones, and video cameras. It also generally entails using a broadband connection because the bandwidth required for multimedia applications is much greater than for text-based ones. However, as the number of people with broadband connections increases, it's likely that the number of multimedia chat rooms will rise proportionately.

One place that you can go to chat is iVillage (*www.ivillage.com*). There are a number of chat rooms, you can sign up for an account by filling out a short form that doesn't require you to provide a lot of identifying information shared, and you don't have to download specialized software. After you create the account, you can log in, view which chat rooms have participants, and then jump into the discussion (see Figure 13.6). Most chat sites are set up in a similar way.

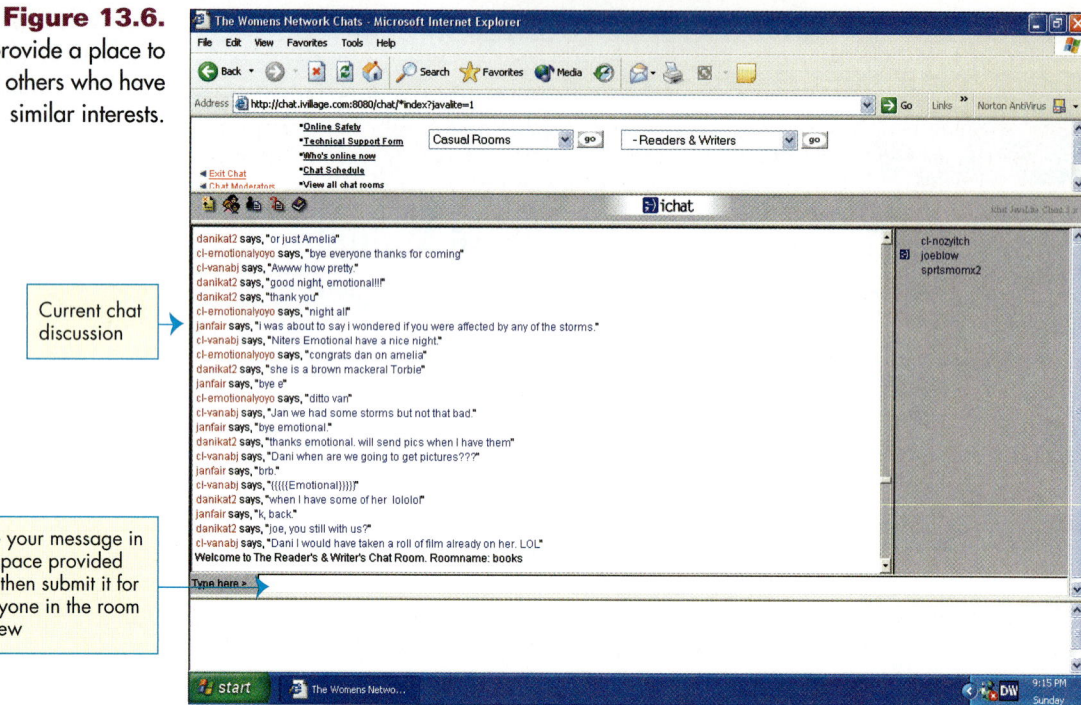

Figure 13.6.
Chat rooms provide a place to network with others who have similar interests.

Current chat discussion

Type your message in the space provided and then submit it for everyone in the room to view

Finally, you should know that **Internet Relay Chat (IRC)** is a system for chatting that uses a certain set of rules and conventions as well as client/server software. IRC was one of the first ways that people could connect with other Internet users and exchange written notes, live and in real-time. If you're interested in using IRC, you'll need an IRC client (specialized software that you can download for free) and an IRC server. After you're set up, you can connect to the IRC server and join a channel (discussion group).

KNOW ABOUT NEWSGROUPS AND BULLETIN BOARD SYSTEMS

Think about your next vacation to some exotic spot. You *can* research lodging, restaurants, and area attractions via Web pages, but if you really want to know the inside scoop, you can also head to a newsgroup.

A **newsgroup** is an Internet discussion group that includes a bunch of articles, or postings, on a topic. Contrary to the name, newsgroups don't necessarily talk about current news. Instead, a newsgroup is simply a collection of online conversations about almost any topic imaginable.

HOW A NEWSGROUP WORKS

Newsgroup users discuss subjects by posting messages, conducting online conversations, and sending e-mail messages—either to the entire group or to an individual. Messages submitted to a newsgroup are called **postings** or articles. Despite their name, these messages aren't articles from a real publication; they're simply notes from one user to the entire newsgroup. A collection of follow-ups on a posting, sequentially ordered by date, is called a **thread**. Depending on the topic, there can be zero to many follow ups to a particular message, each grouped in a threaded discussion. A new series of messages is started when a user posts a question or message to the newsgroup community. People can respond to the main message by submitting their own postings.

> **ALERT**
> Be careful what you tell others in a chat room. Because people can sign up anonymously, they can easily disguise their true intentions. For example, pedophiles have masqueraded as children in kids' chat rooms and then tried to meet the other participants in person. Others may try to find out your contact information to harass you or to steal your identity. To avoid problems, don't share personal information, including contact information. Additionally, carefully consider the dangers of actually meeting someone you encountered in a chat room face-to-face. The safest solution is to turn down requests for such a meeting. If you decide to go, however, take another person with you.

Unlike instant messaging and chat, newsgroup postings and responses aren't necessarily read in real-time. And newsgroup postings are kept on a server and archived so that they can be viewed at a later time; chat discussions vanish when everyone leaves the virtual chat room and IM messages don't go through the server. There is also another difference between newsgroup postings and IM: Postings in a newsgroup can be viewed by anyone who has the necessary setup, whereas IM communications are private.

FINDING A NEWSGROUP

If you're interested in newsgroups, you're in luck: The Internet is packed full of them. One of the most popular newsgroup collections is Usenet, which currently boasts more than 100,000 groups. Usenet groups are organized by topic and arranged in a hierarchy. As you probably recall from earlier chapters, this means that each topic includes a number of subtopics. Newsgroups typically have common prefixes, such as *rec* for recreation, *sci* for science topics, and *soc* for social issues. A typical newsgroup name would include this prefix and then indicate the main topic for the group, such as *rec.pets*, which would be a discussion about pets in the recreation category.

Until recently, you needed a program called a newsgroup reader to read and post information in a Usenet newsgroup. A newsgroup reader allowed you to read information in a newsgroup in the same way that a browser enabled you to view Web pages. Now Outlook Express and other e-mail clients include a newsgroup reader; you can also download newsgroup readers. In times past, you also needed to subscribe to the newsgroup to post messages.

But things have changed. Nowadays, you can access any of the Usenet articles (and archived postings for the past 20 years!) through Google. To access these postings, go to Google's home page at *www.google.com* and then click the tab for Groups. You'll see a listing of groups similar to that shown in Figure 13.7.

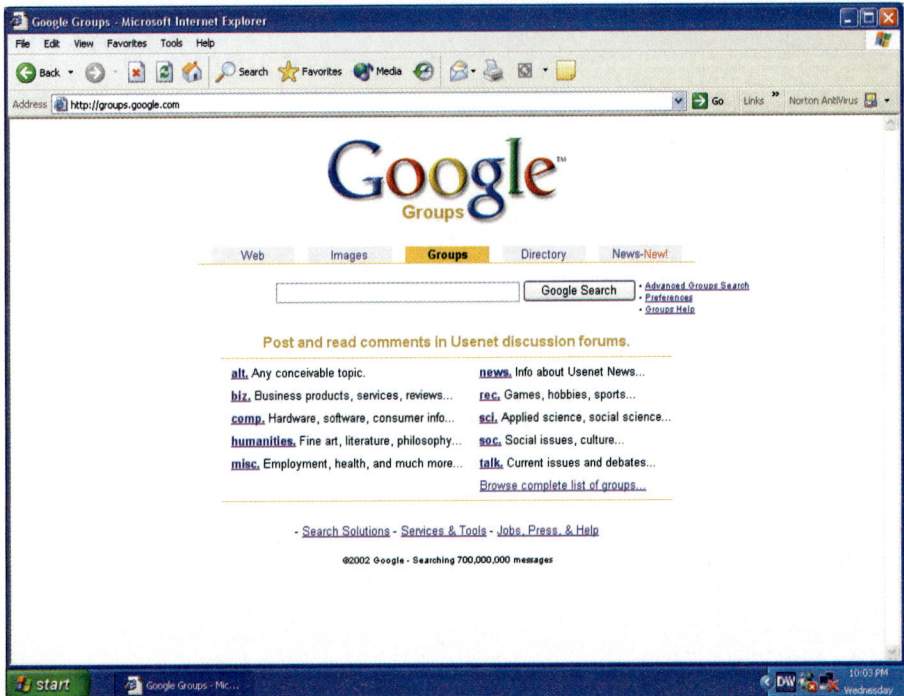

Figure 13.7.
You can access the Usenet groups via Google.

>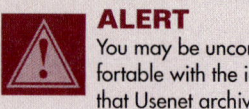
> **ALERT**
> You may be uncomfortable with the idea that Usenet archives postings for 20 years (including the one with the bad comment about your best friend's hairstyle). Fortunately, you can remove your old postings from the archive. To find out how to do so, display the Google Groups page, and then click Google Groups Help.

You can click on a main group (such as *sci*) to view the subtopics it includes (see Figure 13.8).

If you drill down through the Google groups, you'll eventually see that each of the subgroups lists current postings (see Figure 13.9).

KEEPING CONTROL: MODERATED AND UNMODERATED GROUPS

Newsgroups can be either moderated or unmoderated. A **moderated group** has an administrator who reviews the messages before posting them; in an **unmoderated group**, anything goes.

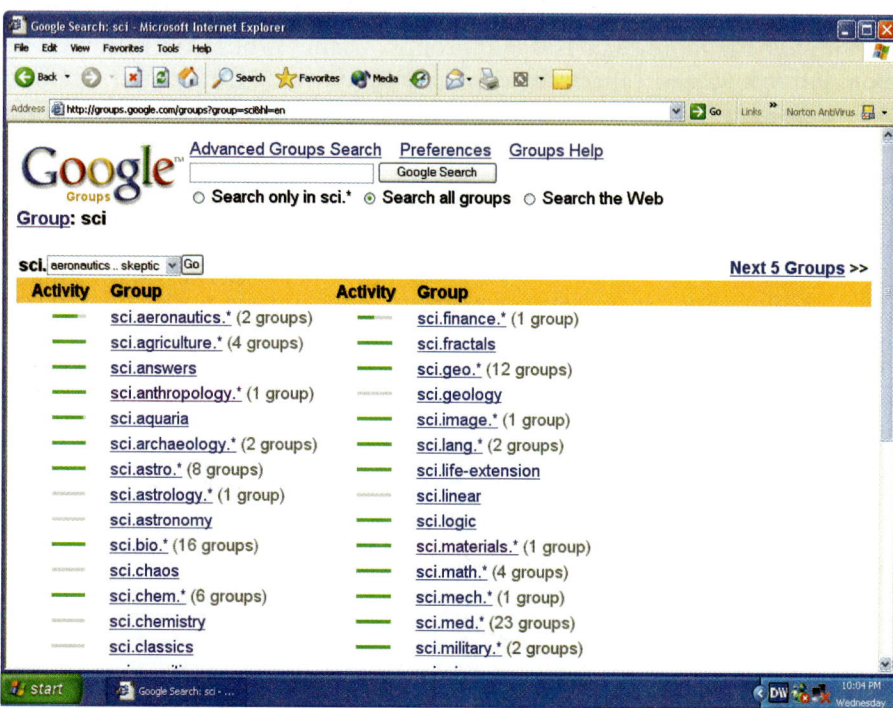

Figure 13.8.
Each main group (such as *sci*) includes a number of subtopics.

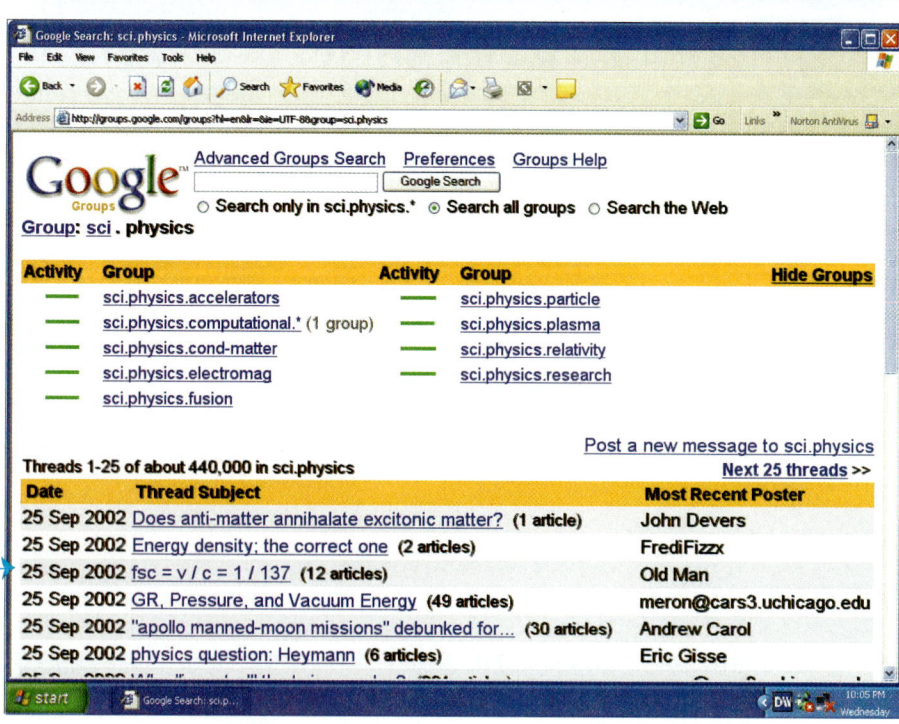

Figure 13.9.
Each subgroup includes a number of messages.

Unfortunately, Usenet and related newsgroups have been abused by spammers, who use the service to post advertisements to the masses and to harvest e-mail addresses. This abuse, combined with the rise of real-time communications and Internet bulletin boards, has caused a decline in newsgroups over the past few years.

BULLETIN BOARD SYSTEMS

A **Bulletin Board System (BBS)** is a computerized version of the cork bulletin boards that you might see in a public place, such as a grocery store. Just as people can leave messages, share information, and advertise on a physical bulletin board, they can also do the same things electronically. Internet bulletin boards are similar to newsgroups in that they focus on a particular subject, accept postings, and use threads to keep the main messages and follow ups together. Many Web sites include their own bulletin boards (**forums**) which are dedicated to the site's purpose.

Bulletin board systems were widely used in the days before the Internet was easily accessible. Instead of accessing the Internet, you would dial into the BBS. This use has widely been replaced by Internet-based message boards and forums.

KNOW ABOUT LISTSERV AND MAILING LISTS

Distributed (or bulk) mailing lists are similar to newsgroups in that they focus on a particular topic or purpose and deliver information to a group. However, they differ from newsgroups because they use automated lists to distribute information via e-mail instead of an Internet site. Additionally, distribution is limited to the individuals on the list. Electronic newsletters are often distributed in this manner. However, people can't respond to electronic newsletters although they can respond (to either an individual or the entire group) to a distributed mail message.

To participate in an automated bulk mailing list, you first subscribe to the list. After you subscribe, all the messages distributed via the list are automatically broadcast to everyone on the list and appear in your mailbox. Some lists include an option for you to receive a digest form of all the messages that were broadcast within a certain amount of time (such as one day). A **digest** is a compilation of the messages that are placed in one e-mail message. Many people like this option because they find it more convenient to scan through one long digest message than to receive multiple short messages throughout the day.

Most of these lists are open to the public, but some are restricted by the administrator. For example, if you're working on a project with others at work, but you are all located in remote locations, you could use a distributed mailing list to collaborate on the project. By its very nature, a list for this purpose would need to be restricted.

The traffic and activity associated with the distributed mailing list is automated and managed by specialized programs called **mailing list managers (MLMs)**. One of the earliest mailing list managers was **LISTSERV**. This software was originally developed for an IBM mainframe network called BITNET, but it is still in widespread use today. LISTSERV is marketed by L-Soft International. Even though LISTSERV refers to a specific commercial product, many people use the term in a generic way to refer to any mailing list server. Another frequently used program is Majordomo.

You can find lists to join by taking a look at the list directories on the Internet. Try Yahoo! Groups (*groups.yahoo.com*) or Topica, which maintains

Figure 13.10.
Click L-Soft's catalog link (CataList) to find mailing lists.

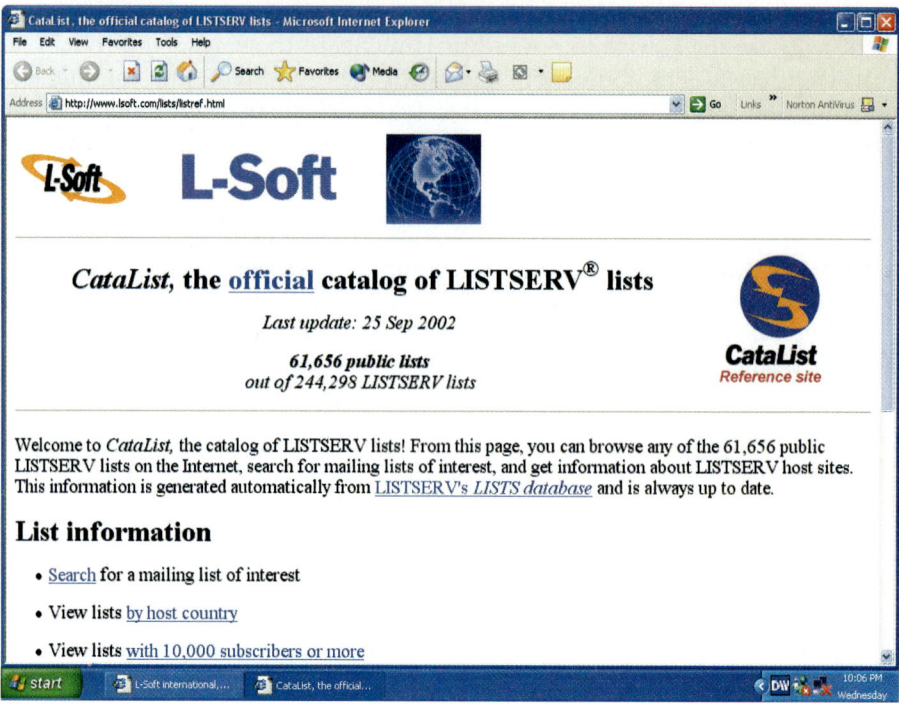

more than 90,000 lists (*www.topica.com*). L-Soft, the developers of LIST-SERV, also maintain a catalog of lists on their site at *www.lsoft.com* (see Figure 13.10).

After you subscribe to a mailing list or newsletter, it's usually best to read the messages for awhile before jumping in with your own comments. This practice is called **lurking**. If you want to make sure to mind your Ps and Qs, spend a few minutes looking at the practical lists of do's and don'ts at List-Etiquette.com (*www.list-etiquette.com*).

If you can't find a list that is a good match for your interest, or you simply want to start a list for a specialized group (like the Banana Eaters Club you were involved with in high school) you can start your own—for free. To do so, you can go to a site that specializes in mailing lists, such as Yahoo! Groups (*groups.yahoo.com*) and click the link for *Start a new Group*. Be aware, however, that to set up the group you'll have to fill out the typical online form that probes for marketing information and contact information. Having a free, Web-based e-mail account to use for setting up a list is a good plan to help protect your privacy.

INSIDE TRACK

If you decide that the online communications discussed in this chapter are for you, you should keep in mind that respect and good manners apply online just as much as they do in face-to-face communications. **Netiquette** refers to using proper manners in online communications. You can find out more about Netiquette at *www.getnetiquette.com*.

UNDERSTAND THE TRENDS ASSOCIATED WITH REAL-TIME CONFERENCING

So far, chat and other forms of real-time communication have been primarily text-based: Users typed their messages to communicate with others instead of using multimedia technologies, such as audio (voice transmissions) and video (visual images). The biggest reason why audio and video technologies are not used more frequently is because most people don't have the broadband connections that they need to use them.

However, the recent trend toward using broadband may pave the way for real-time conferencing via audio and video, especially in the business world. The hardware is already in place or can be installed at a low cost: Practically all new computer systems are well-equipped with speakers and a microphone that allow for audio transmissions. If you want to use video conferencing, you can also buy an easy-to-install video camera (WebCam) that plugs directly into your computer via a USB port for about $75. The main thing that prevents people from using audio and video real-time conferencing is narrowband Internet connections. Technology is in place for people to use this type of conferencing via the Internet; as soon as it becomes more affordable, it will most likely become extremely popular.

VIDEO CONFERENCING

Video conferencing is simply holding an online meeting between multiple participants in different locations by using a network (such as the Internet or an intranet) to transmit audio and video data. Each person has a computer with a video camera, microphone, and speakers. This type of setup lets participants speak to and see each other as the images and audio are transmitted via the microphone, speaker, video camera, and monitor.

To use video conferencing, you need specialized video-conferencing software, such as Microsoft's **NetMeeting**. NetMeeting is included in most of the Microsoft Office Programs (such as Word, PowerPoint, and Excel) and in Internet Explorer. NetMeeting supports voice, chat, a whiteboard, and application sharing. A **whiteboard** is analogous to the laminated whiteboard that you might see in a corporate conference room. Electronically, it appears in a window on the monitors of everyone in a video conference, so that they can share ideas by writing or drawing on it. Application sharing is what the name indicates: sharing files (such as a PowerPoint presentation) with others in the conference, which allows users in various locations to collaborate on projects. If you want to learn more about NetMeeting, see Microsoft's official Web site at *www.microsoft.com/windows/netmeeting* (see Figure 13.11).

As you can probably guess, NetMeeting is primarily used by businesses so that end users can collaborate on projects. Another well-known software product that allows for video conferencing functions is CUseeMe. If you want to find out more about this software, check out the CUseeMe's Web site at *www.cuseemeworld.com*.

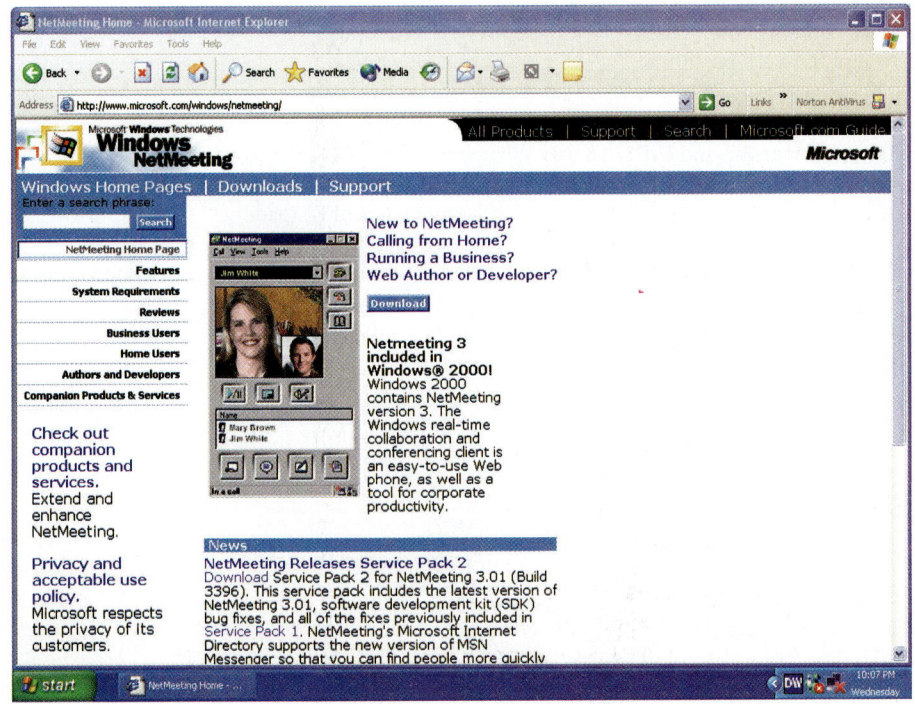

Figure 13.11.
NetMeeting helps you collaborate via the Internet.

Don't Forget...

- The Internet can be the medium for many types of communication, including instant messaging, chat, bulletin boards, forums, mailing lists, newsgroups, and video conferencing.
- Real-time communication, such as instant messaging, provides immediate feedback for those who use it.
- Instant messaging is growing rapidly in popularity, especially among teenagers and college students.
- Increasingly, businesses are using instant messaging so that employees can communicate and collaborate on projects.
- Chat is a popular online activity that takes place in real-time.
- Be cautious about what personal information you share in a chat room.
- Newsgroups discuss topics via submitted messages that appear sequentially in a thread (instead of in real-time).
- Usenet has more than 100,000 newsgroups; there are other newsgroups available as well.
- Newsgroups have been abused by spammers in recent times, which has lead to a decline in using this type of communication.
- Mailing lists focus on a particular topic or purpose and distribute it to a group.
- LISTSERV is a well-known mailing list manager; some people use the term in a generic way to refer to all distributed mailing lists.
- Most electronic newsletters are distributed via mailing list managers.
- NetMeeting (bundled with Microsoft Office and Internet Explorer) is the most common tool for video conferencing.
- Real-time conferencing, complete with audio and video capabilities, is becoming more prevalent as the number of people who use broadband increases.

Check This Out

MULTIPLE CHOICE

1. What is one difference between chat and IM?
   a. Chat is private; IM communication is not.
   b. Chat doesn't take place in real-time; IM does.
   c. IM communication is private; chat is not.
   d. Chat uses a buddy list to limit communication to a certain group of people; IM is broadcast to any Internet user who is online at the time.

2. What is the difference between a newsgroup and IM?
   a. IM takes place in real-time; newsgroups typically do not.
   b. IM is similar to an Internet bulletin board; newsgroups send communications to people only via an electronic mailing list.
   c. IM communication is public; newsgroup postings are limited to people on your buddy list.
   d. IM and newsgroups are the same thing.

3. Which of the following groups of people would probably use IM the most?
   a. Kids under 5 years of age
   b. College students
   c. Senior citizens
   d. All of the preceding groups would use IM the same amount.

4. What is true regarding newsgroups?
   a. Some of them have become unusable because of the large amount of spam.
   b. They are organized by topic.
   c. They include moderated and unmoderated groups.
   d. All of the above

5. Which of the following is *not* an IM client?
   a. AIM
   b. BBS
   c. MSN Messenger
   d. ICQ

MATCHING

a. BBS
b. buddy list
c. real-time
d. LISTSERV
e. chat
f. posting
g. buffer overflow
h. chat room
i. thread
j. moderated

1. Virtual space or specialized Web site in which you can chat
2. Message posted to a newsgroup
3. Bulletin board system
4. Messages and communication are updated immediately
5. Mailing list manager program
6. A list of contacts from whom you will accept real-time messages
7. A group where the articles are first reviewed by an administrator before they are posted
8. Real-time communication that takes place in a virtual space with a group of people
9. Sequential listing of articles
10. Security breach that exists in some IM clients

Real Life

1. Explore the groups at Google (*www.google.com*). Drill down through several of the main groups (such as *sci*, *news*, or *rec*) to see what types of subtopics they include. If time allows, take a look at the articles for several of the groups. Notice which discussion groups tend to have spam associated with them.
2. Explore several online forums. Begin your search at the Tech Support Forums (*www.computer-forums.com*) and the Search Engine Forums (*www.searchengineforums.com*). Use your abilities to use the search engines to find other forums with topics of interest to you.
3. Sign up for an instant messaging service, such as Trillian, and download the appropriate software (available at Cerulean Studio's Web site; *ceruleanstudios.com/trillian*). After you sign up, establish a contacts list and then use the messaging tool to communicate with others.

I Spy: Privacy and Security Concerns

1. Conduct several Internet searches to find out more about the security issues associated with IM clients. Determine if there are more or less security vulnerabilities with IM clients developed especially for the workplace than those used by the general public (such as AIM and ICQ). Write up a brief report that outlines your findings.
2. There have been numerous stories in the news of minors being asked to meet face-to-face with people they have "met" in a chat room. In fact, a Girl Scout Research Institute survey (March 2002) indicated that 30% of the teenage girls asked had been harassed in chat rooms. Pose some solutions to this problem. (Hint: Start by taking a look at the Web site for Media Awareness Network at *www.media-awareness.ca/eng/webaware/parents/safe/pchat.htm#risks*, and the Annenberg Public Policy Center's site at *www.appcpenn.org*).
3. Discuss ways in which you can protect your privacy when using chat and IM or when signing up for electronic newsletters or mailing lists. Develop a presentation (in PowerPoint, if you have access to that program) that outlines the main ways to do this. Give the presentation to a small group or to your entire class.
4. What are some of the issues related to real-time communication in terms of nuisance, intrusion, and loss of productivity? Use the Internet to research and find examples of these problems and then discuss your findings with your class.

CHAPTER 14

PULLING INFORMATION FROM THE INTERNET

Key Terms

When you finish this chapter, you'll understand the following terms:

- Adobe Acrobat Reader
- Anonymous FTP servers
- archive
- freeware
- FTP client
- FTP server
- Gopher
- MP3
- nag screens
- Portable Document Format (PDF)
- self-extracting archive
- shareware
- trialware
- updates
- wallpaper
- WinZip
- ZIP file

Chapter Objectives

After you complete this chapter, you'll

- Understand the Types of Information You Can Download
- Copy Information from a Web Site
- Save an Entire Web Page
- Download Files from a Web Page
- Understand the Basics of FTP
- Download an FTP Client

The Big Picture

The Internet includes a wealth of information. And even though all that great information is available online, sometimes you want it right on your very own computer. Take, for instance, a particularly great photo, clip art image, music file, game, or program that you found. You can use these types of files much more readily on your own system than you can if they're on a Web site. Spell checkers, games, educational activities, browsers, e-mail clients, audio files... they're all available, and they're free or offered at a minimal cost in many cases. As long as you have the rights to place a copy of it from the Internet onto your computer, you're free to do so. The process of transferring a file from the Internet to your system is called *downloading*.

In this chapter, we'll show you the logistics of getting files from the Internet onto your system. We'll go over how to copy programs, videos, music files, graphics, and documents. To do so, you'll use the two main download methods: using a simple copy-and-paste operation and employing an FTP client. We'll also warn you of the dangers associated with indiscriminately downloading files without first putting safeguards in place.

Window on the Web

Even in the early days of the Internet, you could copy information onto your system, but it wasn't as simple as it is at present. Then, to find the information to download, you had to wander through text-based menus or know a file's exact locations on a remote server. Nowadays, there is a host of Web sites that specialize in downloadable content and files, such as CNET's *Download.com* site (see Figure 14.1).

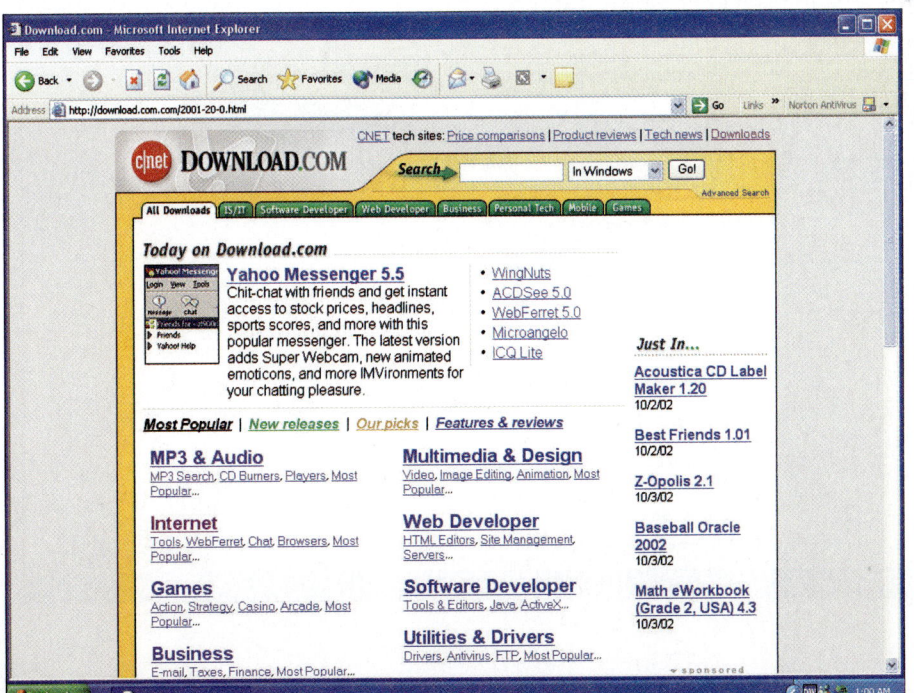

Figure 14.1.
Many sites include a variety of programs and files you can download.

Another popular site you can access to download files is Jumbo! (*www.jumbo.com*). This site organizes downloadable files by topic. For example, Figure 14.2 shows some of the business applications you can download from the site.

When you download a file or program from a Web site, the process that you will most likely use to transfer files is *File Transfer Protocol (FTP)*. File Transfer Protocol is the set of standards and rules used on the Internet to send and receive files. Unlike e-mail (which sometimes has trouble transferring huge files), it can handle large files with ease and speed.

To transfer files using FTP, you need an FTP client and an FTP server, just as you need a Web browser to "serve" you files from a Web server or a mail client to bring you files from a mail server.

Figure 14.2.
Jumbo! offers many downloadable programs and files.

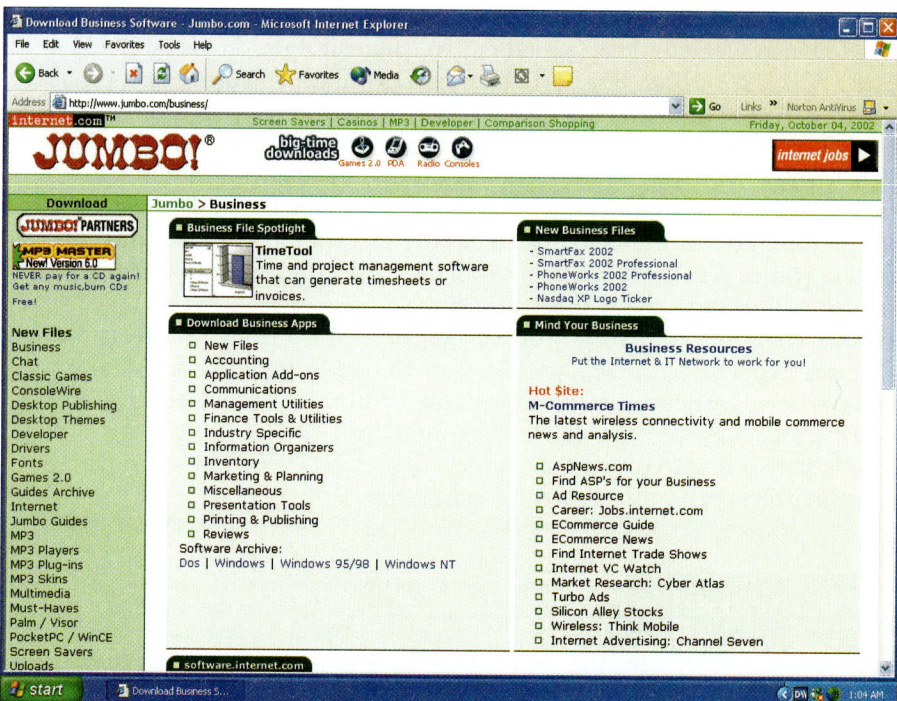

Figure 14.3.
Transferring files frequently? Get an FTP client.

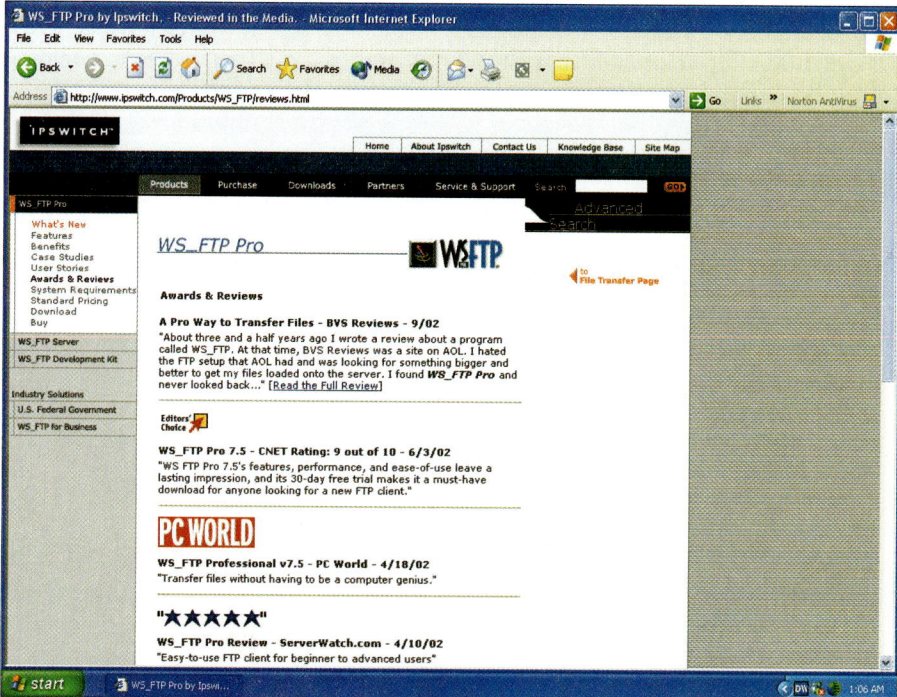

212   Chapter 14   Pulling Information from the Internet

The **FTP client** is software that resides on your local computer; the **FTP server** stores and transfers the files. Although the most common Web browser (Microsoft's Internet Explorer) has a limited FTP client built into it, you may want a full-featured FTP client, such as WS_FTP if you plan to frequently transfer files (see Figure 14.3).

In this chapter, we'll go through the various ways that you can use to download files from the Internet. We'll also discuss the best ways to protect your system from the security issues associated with this process. By the end of the chapter, you'll have a much better idea of how you can more effectively tap into the online resources available.

UNDERSTAND THE TYPES OF INFORMATION YOU CAN DOWNLOAD

The ability to pull files from the Internet opens the door to using them on your computer. But this doesn't just help individuals to be able to play music files or use a cool new screensaver. Being able to download files also helps companies because they can quickly distribute information or programs via the Internet. For example, Microsoft (among others) regularly places software fixes (called patches) on its Web site to help take care of problems in the software or to plug security holes. Anti-virus programs, such as Norton AntiVirus, post updated virus definitions almost daily. You can go to its Web site and download these definitions so that your anti-virus software will recognize new viruses.

HEADS UP! If you're operating on a network that has security measures (such as a firewall) installed, you may not be able to download files from the Internet. If you're blocked from doing this, you can instead read through the chapter and learn the main concepts. Also, see if you can find a personal system that you can use to practice downloading files.

Want another example? Imagine that you just bought a new digital camera. The company might distribute the user manual as a downloadable file instead of printing it. Additionally, the company probably has software for the camera that is available online. The technical support team might maintain a series of troubleshooting articles online that you can use in case of problems. Support team members might even have a rebate form that you can download from the company's Web site. By posting downloadable files on the Web, they can save both the company and the customer considerable time and effort.

Here are a few more scenarios from the business and collegiate world that demonstrate how helpful it can be to transfer files via the Internet:

- An automobile manufacturer that wants to send engineering drawings from one facility to another
- An ISP that wants its customers to be able to download new software
- A publisher who wants to transfer manuscripts to authors for editing
- Consultants who want to send contracts and other documents to clients
- A life insurance company that wants to transfer current data to field agents
- Students who transfer assignments to their professors via university servers

You can readily see that there are many practical uses for transferring files across a network, such as the Internet. But you may be wondering which *types* of files are transferable. The answer? Almost any. Let's go over some of the most common types of files that are sent and received over the Internet.

TEXT DOCUMENTS

Text documents include those containing text, such as those found in online libraries or research Web sites. Some of these documents can be downloaded and viewed by using **Adobe Acrobat Reader**, a free downloadable program that allows you to view a variety of documents. Adobe Acrobat Reader uses **Portable Document Format (PDF)** files. PDF is a universal format that preserves the fonts and colors of any document, no matter which platform or application was originally used to develop it.

 HEADS UP! Before you start downloading or copying information from the Internet, *make sure* that you have the right to use it. Some of the information is copyrighted—and copying it may be illegal. The recording industry in particular, is cracking down on illegal copying of music files and videos. If a copyright symbol is used on a Web site (or if the site includes explicit information about how its data can and can't be used) it's a good bet that the information is copy-protected

AUDIO AND MUSIC FILES

The most common type of music file shared via the Internet is in MP3 format. **MP3** is a digital format that is the current standard for sharing music files across the Internet. Sharing music files between users has been greatly facilitated by use of peer-to-peer file sharing software. You'll learn more about the copyright issues associated with this practice in Chapter 16, Beyond the Basics: Taking Advantage of the Internet's Multimedia Capabilities.

IMAGES, PHOTOGRAPHS, AND CLIP ART

 The Internet is a treasure trove of free photographs and clip art images that you can copy for your use. Many Web sites allow you to use their images at no cost. For example, Microsoft maintains the Design Gallery Live Web site, from which you can pull clip art or video images at *dgl.microsoft.com* (see Figure 14.4). Additionally, you can use a variety of other sites on the Internet, such as *www.freefoto.com*, to locate free photographs and other images.

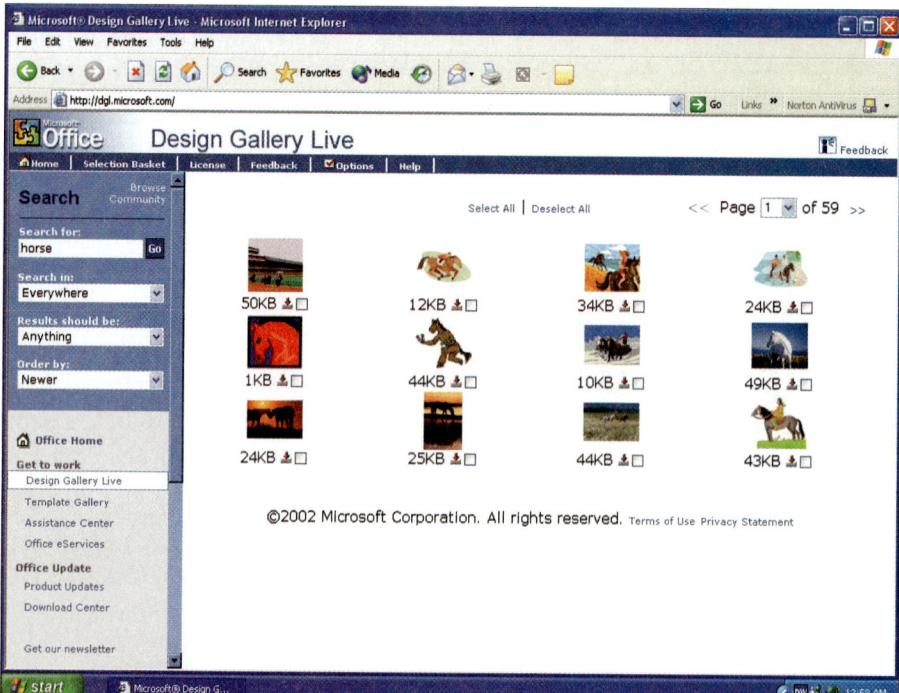

Figure 14.4. Microsoft lets you download images from the Design Gallery Live.

COMMERCIAL SOFTWARE PROGRAMS, PATCHES, AND UPDATES

You can download a variety of software programs from the Internet, such as complete copies of commercially available software. Because there is a cost for this software, you usually enter your credit card number on the vendor's online site and can then download the program. Many software companies offer incentives, such as a lower price, to encourage people to download their software from the Internet. In addition to downloading a complete program, most commercial software companies allow you to download *patches* (fixes for software problems) and **updates** (which include new or improved features). Microsoft, for example, regularly posts updates and patches for its products on its Web page (see Figure 14.5).

TRIALWARE

Besides downloading commercially available software online, you can also download an evaluation copy for software that you are considering purchasing. This type of software is sometimes called **trialware**. It usually is a complete version of the program, but one that will work only for a limited time (such as 30 days). If you don't purchase or uninstall the software at the end of the trial period, some programs automatically become partially disabled, stop working, or keep displaying **nag screens**, pop-up windows that remind you to register the product. Figure 14.6 shows the Web site (*nct.digitalriver.com/0001*) from which you can download a trial copy of Norton AntiVirus.

SHAREWARE AND FREEWARE

Shareware is software that is copyrighted and distributed on a free-will donation basis. To receive full support and documentation, users are typically required to pay a small fee. **Freeware**, as its name implies, is software that is available at no cost. Keep in mind, however, that it is copyright-protected, so you can't resell it or pass it off as your own.

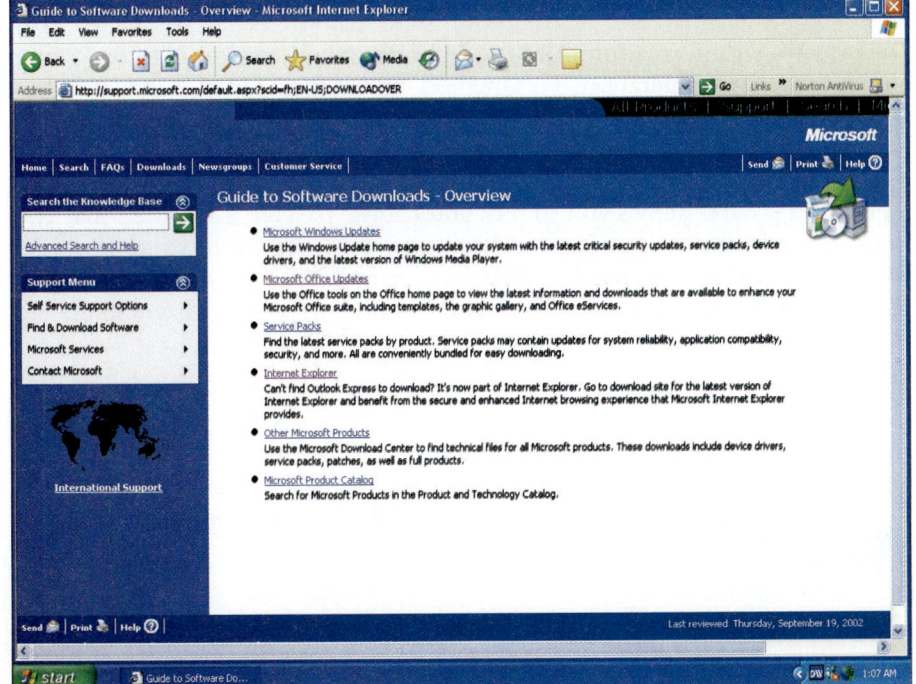

Figure 14.5.
Download updates and patches from Microsoft's Web site.

Understand the Types of Information You Can Download

Figure 14.6.
Some companies will let you download a trial copy of their software and use it for a limited time.

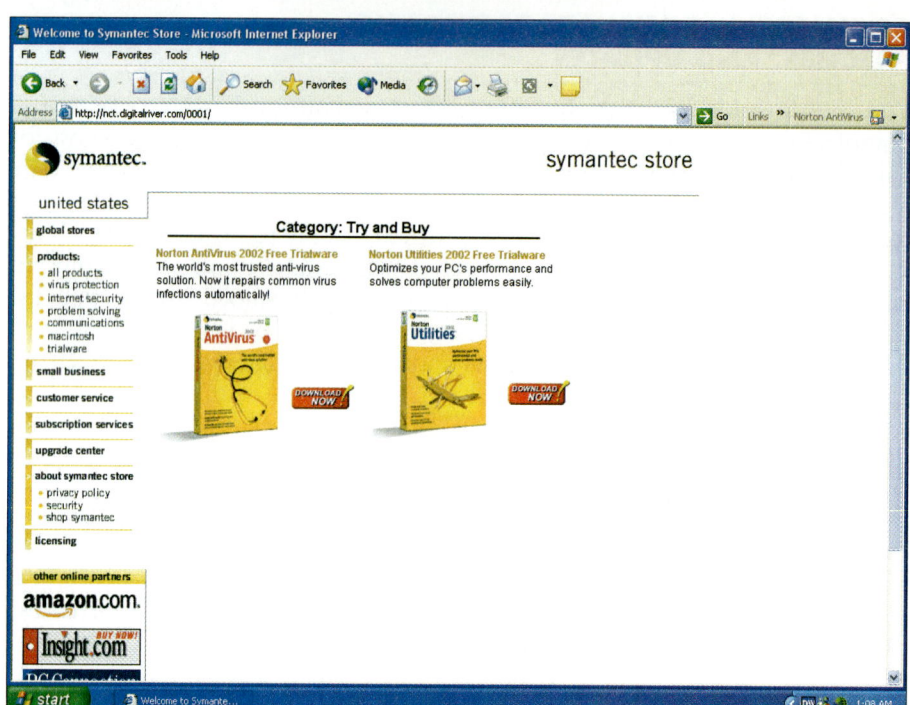

 **ALERT!**
Beware of freeware. Although most people who distribute freeware have legitimate and ethical reasons for doing so, others have shady motives. Sometimes they want to use their free software to unleash viruses on your system. Because of this, you should always virus-scan freeware files that you download before opening them.

Not only is there a wide variety of files that you can pull from the Internet, but there are also multiple ways to get it from remote Internet servers to your own system. You can use a simple copy-and-paste operation, download the information from a Web site (a process that sometimes uses FTP), or install and use an FTP client. Throughout the remainder of the chapter, you'll see firsthand how to use these methods to pull information from the Internet.

COPY INFORMATION FROM A WEB SITE

One way to get information from the Internet to your system is to use a simple copy-and-paste operation. This method works especially well if you want to copy data from a Web site because such sites are graphical in nature and easy to navigate. In contrast with downloading entire files, you can also use this method to download specific text or a graphic from a Web site to your computer. This process allows you to pick and choose parts of a Web site that you want to use in the future, without having to copy the entire page. If you're copying information from other Web sites, make sure that you have the rights to do so. With that in mind, we'll show you how to copy text, graphics, and links from the Web to your computer.

 INSIDE TRACK

In the early days of the Internet, transferring files wasn't as seamless as it is now. Many people used **Gopher**, an application developed at the University of Minnesota (and named after its mascot), which helped to organize files on the Internet. Gopher was a subject-based, menu-oriented guide that helped you find and retrieve Internet files. Although Gopher is still in use, it has been largely replaced by the graphical interface used on most Web pages and modern search engines.

 Everyone could copy and paste any information, music, or video files they wanted? What do you think would eventually happen to the recording and publishing industries?

Chapter 14 Pulling Information from the Internet

COPYING TEXT FROM A WEB SITE

If you've ever copied and pasted information using desktop computer programs, such as Excel and Word, you should have a pretty good idea about how to copy and paste information from a Web page. Fortunately, the procedure is almost exactly the same: To copy text, first select it by dragging over it. After you select the text to copy, choose Edit from the menu bar and then choose Copy. If this option isn't available (and it often isn't), you can instead press the universal keyboard shortcut for copying: Ctrl+C. (You can also right-click within the selected text to display a shortcut menu and then choose Copy.) Next, open the program into which you want to place the copied information and choose Edit, Paste. Again, if the menu command is unavailable, you can use the standard keyboard shortcut for pasting (Ctrl+V) or right-click where you want to place the text and then choose Paste from the shortcut menu.

COPYING GRAPHICS AND OTHER OBJECTS FROM A WEB SITE

The procedure for copying pictures or other graphics isn't too different from that used for copying text. To copy a picture from a Web page, right-click the graphic to display a shortcut menu and then choose Copy. Right-click in the document where you want to place the picture and then choose Paste from the shortcut menu.

Instead of using a simple copy-and-paste operation to place a graphic within another document on your computer, you can save a graphic, such as a photo or logo, as a complete file on your system by using one of the graphic file formats, such as GIF, JPEG, or BMP. You'll again use the shortcut menu: On the Web page, right-click the picture to display a shortcut menu; then choose Save Picture As. In the Save Picture dialog box, choose a location, filename, and file format before clicking Save (see Figure 14.7). We'll cover file formats in much more detail in Chapter 15, Working with Various File Types and Plug-Ins

You can also plaster a picture from a Web site on your computer's desktop. **Wallpaper** is a term that refers to the background used for your Windows desktop. To use a Web graphic as the background desktop image, right-click the image and then choose Set As Background from the shortcut menu. If you tire of the wallpaper graphic, repeat the process with a different online picture.

Now that you know how to copy bits and pieces of a Web page, let's examine how to save a Web page in its entirety.

INSIDE TRACK

If you're having trouble dragging over the exact text you want, click at the beginning of the selection and release the mouse. Hold down ⇧Shift, and then click at the end of the selection—all the intervening text will be selected.

INSIDE TRACK

After you save a graphic from the Web to your computer, you can use it in other programs, such as Word or PowerPoint. To do this, open the program and then choose Insert, Picture, From File. Locate and select the file in the Insert Picture dialog box and then click Insert.

INSIDE TRACK

Finally, you can send a picture directly to your printer without actually saving it. For example, you might want to print an online photo of your favorite movie star or a beautiful scene without saving it forever on your computer. To do this, right-click the picture and choose Print Picture from the shortcut menu. In the Print dialog box, confirm your print settings and then choose Print.

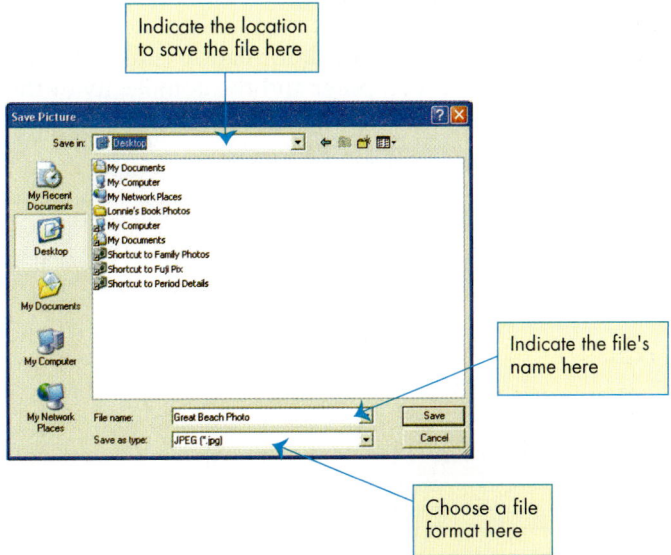

Figure 14.7.
You can save pictures, such as photos or logos, to your personal computer.

SAVE AN ENTIRE WEB PAGE

Imagine this scenario: You just spent several hours on the Web, running searches and clicking hyperlinks, and you *finally* found that elusive piece of information. Suddenly, it strikes you: How in the world can you save the page for later?

If this sounds familiar, you probably already realize the value of being able to save Web-based information permanently so that it doesn't disappear into cyberspace the second you walk away from your computer. Fortunately, you can take advantage of Internet Explorer's built-in commands for saving the entire page, including all links and graphics or for saving just the text (which, of course, creates a smaller file, but with less information and fewer pictures).

The process you use to save an entire Web page is similar to saving a document in almost any Windows program. First, display the Web page and then choose File, Save As on the Internet Explorer menu to open the Save Web Page window. Click the *Save in* drop-down list arrow and locate the folder in which you want to save the page. Type a descriptive name for the Web page. Next, click the *Save as type* drop-down list arrow and choose the type of file format you want to use for the file (see Figure 14.8).

Here's where things get a bit sticky. You should choose the format type that you want to use later to view the page. For example, to save all the files associated with the Web page so that you'll be able to see all of the graphics, frames and style sheets, choose *Web Page, complete* from the *Save as type* drop-down list. When you choose this option, the associated files (including .gif files) are automatically saved in a separate folder.

You can also save just the current HTML page, which saves the information on the current Web page, but doesn't save the associated files. To do this, choose *Web Page, HTML only* on the *Save as type* drop-down list. Finally, you can save only the text on the Web page by choosing (what else?) *Text File* from the list. When you finish setting the file's name and format, click Save.

After it's saved, you can open and view a Web page by finding it on your system. For example, you can double-click the My Computer icon on the desktop and then locate the file. Double-click it to open it.

Instead of using Internet Explorer to save a Web page, you can copy and paste the entire thing into another program, such as Word or FrontPage. After you paste the whole page into the application, you can save it as you would any other. To copy the entire page, first display the Web page you want to save; then right-click in the background area of the page. Choose Select All from the shortcut menu to select all the text, graphics, and links (see Figure 14.9).

After you select all the items on the page, right-click a second time and choose Copy from the shortcut menu. Next open the program (such as Word) in which you want to place the information and choose Edit, Paste. Depending on the speed of your computer and the complexity of the Web page, you may

INSIDE TRACK

You can send a saved Web page to a friend via e-mail. To do this, locate the saved Web page file in My Computer or Windows Explorer. Right-click the file; then choose Send To, Mail Recipient. Enter the person's e-mail address in the window that displays and then click Send.

INSIDE TRACK

To quickly select an entire Web page (including text and graphics), you can also press Ctrl+A instead of using the Select All command.

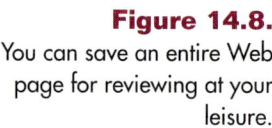

Figure 14.8.
You can save an entire Web page for reviewing at your leisure.

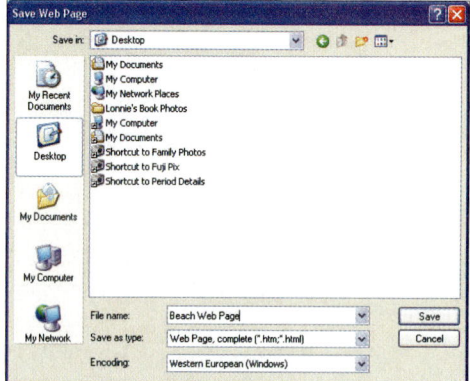

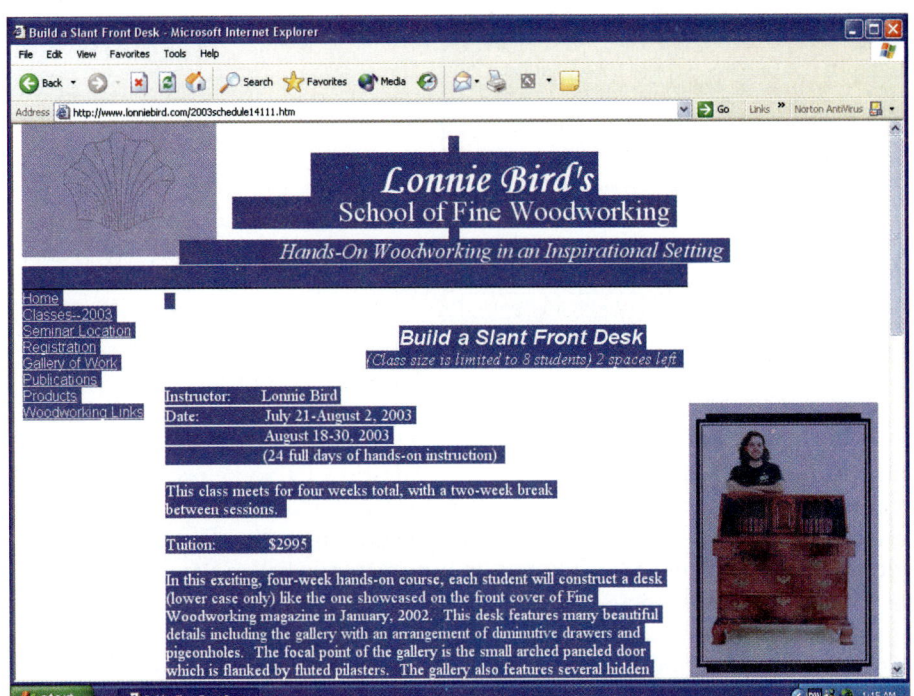

Figure 14.9.
Select all the text, objects, and links on a page before copying it.

have to wait while the information is pasted. After the data is finally pasted into Word, you'll see that the graphics and text shown mirror the original Web page's. You'll also notice that the links are active (and that pressing Ctrl while clicking them will activate the associated Web page).

Now you just need to save the file in your program as you would any other file—by using the Save As command. In Word, for example, choose File, Save As, which opens the Save As dialog box. Choose a name and location for your file and then click Save. That's it! Because the Web page is saved in your chosen program, you can open, close, and print the file just as you would any other document. (For example, to print the document, choose File, Print to display the Print dialog box and then click OK.)

Now that you know how to use the Copy, Paste, and Save As commands to save information from the Internet to your computer, let's turn our attention to other methods of transferring files from the Internet, such as WinZip and FTP.

DOWNLOAD FILES FROM A WEB PAGE

Downloading files, including software, from a Web page isn't as difficult as many people think. In fact, the process has become more or less standardized, so you'll have a good idea of how to work through the process after you download files a few times. For the most part, you're required to do very little during the entire download because FTP (or a similar process) handles the whole thing. Your contribution is to indicate a location in which to save the file and then to scan the file for viruses before opening it. That's about it.

First, you should understand that many of the files transferred and downloaded via the Internet are in a compressed form called an **archive**, or **ZIP file**. A ZIP file may contain several files, "squishing" them into a smaller space than they originally occupied. Using a ZIP file helps significantly when transferring data over the Internet because it is smaller than the same files when they are unzipped. Consequently, most files available for downloading *are* archived (ZIP) files.

ALERT!
When you download files, you need to keep an eye out for viruses. How? First, don't download files from Web sites that have dubious authors or look suspicious. Second, always make sure to save and scan the downloaded files before opening or running them. You can't be too careful.

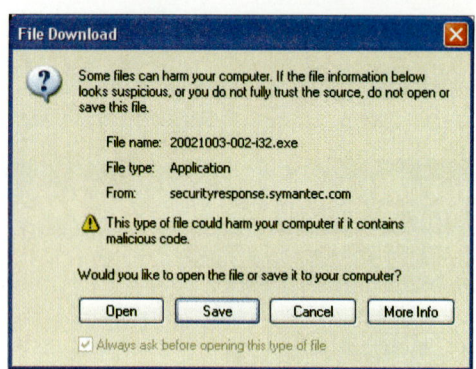

Figure 14.10.
Save a file to your computer and scan it for viruses before opening it.

A program called **WinZip** allows Windows users to work with archived files using the familiar graphical interface. Additionally, some program files distributed as downloadable files are self-extracting archives. A **self-extracting archive** is a compressed file that includes program files. You first download the file and then double-click it to start an automated installation of the program or extract the zipped files.

With this in mind, imagine that you've found a Web site with software or files that you want to download (such as the update for the virus definitions on your computer). Click the link that represents the file you want to download. This is usually as simple as clicking a button that says *Download Now!*

As soon as you click the button or link, the File Download dialog box displays. This dialog box includes a generic warning that the downloaded files might contain malicious code (see Figure 14.10). Even if you trust the source of the file, it's a good idea to save the file and then scan it with your anti-virus software before opening it.

After you click *Save* in the File Download dialog box, the Save As dialog box opens so that you can choose a file location. (People who regularly download information from the Internet usually create a folder into which they place all the downloaded software and files to make them easier to find.) Specify a folder location, click Save, and the file(s) are then transferred to your computer. When the file is completely copied to your computer—a process that can take anywhere from a few seconds to a few hours, depending on the size of the file—your browser displays a message that the download is finished. Close this message box by clicking the Close button. After the process is complete, you should scan the downloaded files for viruses. The exact steps for scanning a file depend on the anti-virus software that you use. However, the following steps usually work: Right-click the file you want to examine for viruses and then choose *Scan With* from the shortcut menu. If the downloaded file doesn't contain any viruses, your anti-virus program will display a message indicating this. Finally, to open the files or program, double-click the icon.

UNDERSTAND THE BASICS OF FTP

Before you use File Transfer Protocol (FTP) to actually download a file, you should understand a little bit about it. FTP is a set of rules and standards used for transferring files from one computer to another. Like most of the transfers that occur on the Internet, FTP requires a server and a client. The **FTP client** is used to download files from the **FTP server** to a computer or to upload files from a computer to a server. Because of its capability to transfer large files between systems, FTP is extremely useful.

Internet Explorer does have limited FTP capacity built into it, but its features are restricted. If you want a full-featured FTP client, you should instead consider using FTP client software, such as Ipswitch's WS_FTP client or CuteFTP.

FTP sites include *ftp* as the host name in the URL, such as *ftp://ftp.cdc.gov*. You can search for FTP sites by going to the Web site for FTPFind (*www.ftpfind.com*) and then conducting a keyword search—just as you would when using a Web search engine.

There are two main types of FTP servers: Anonymous servers and servers on which you need an account and password. **Anonymous FTP servers** are set up to distribute files or programs to the public. Because of this, an account isn't needed: the identification used for logging on is the word "anonymous," and the password is your e-mail address. In contrast, some FTP servers are set up for a specific purpose and limit access by allowing only people with a specific account id and password to transfer files. For example, some companies set up FTP sites that they use to transfer files between offices in various locations.

INSIDE TRACK

If ftp is used as part of the Address (URL) in your browser, it's usually a sign that your computer is being connected to an FTP server, not to a Web server. FTP differs from HTTP because it delivers the entire contents of a file (or several files) to your computer, whereas HTTP only transfers a Web page's contents into the browser for viewing purposes.

You can use FTP to transfer files between computers as long as four conditions are met:

1. Your computer (called the "local host machine") has an FTP client or Internet Explorer installed and is connected to the Internet.

2. The machine you're connecting to (called the "remote host machine") has FTP server software installed and is connected to the Internet.

3. You know the correct ftp address to use to connect to the FTP server.

4. You have an account and password that you can use to access the server, or else it is an anonymous FTP server.

That's FTP in a nutshell. Now let's see how to download and install the full-featured FTP client.

DOWNLOAD AN FTP CLIENT

You've already seen that you *can* download and transfer files using the FTP features that are built into Web browsers, such as Microsoft Internet Explorer. However, you'll be able to complete your file transfer much more quickly if you use a full-fledged FTP client. In this activity, you'll download a trial version of a well-known FTP client.

 **HEADS UP!** If you're working through this book as part of a college-level class, make sure that you have permission to download software and other files from the Internet before proceeding with the next activity (*Downloading an FTP Client*). If not, read through the steps carefully, study the figures—and practice on your own personal system.

ACTIVITY 14.1
Downloading an FTP Client

1. In Internet Explorer, click in the Address text box and then type www.ipswitch.com. Press ⏎Enter.
   The home page for Ipswitch displays (see Figure 14.11).

2. Click the link for *File Transfer/WS_FTP* (refer to Figure 14.11).
   A page displays so that you can choose to download either an FTP client or FTP server (see Figure 14.12). Notice that you can download an evaluation version of the software before buying it. Like most trialware, this client is fully functional, but only for a limited time.

ACTIVITY 14.1
Downloading an FTP Client (Continued)

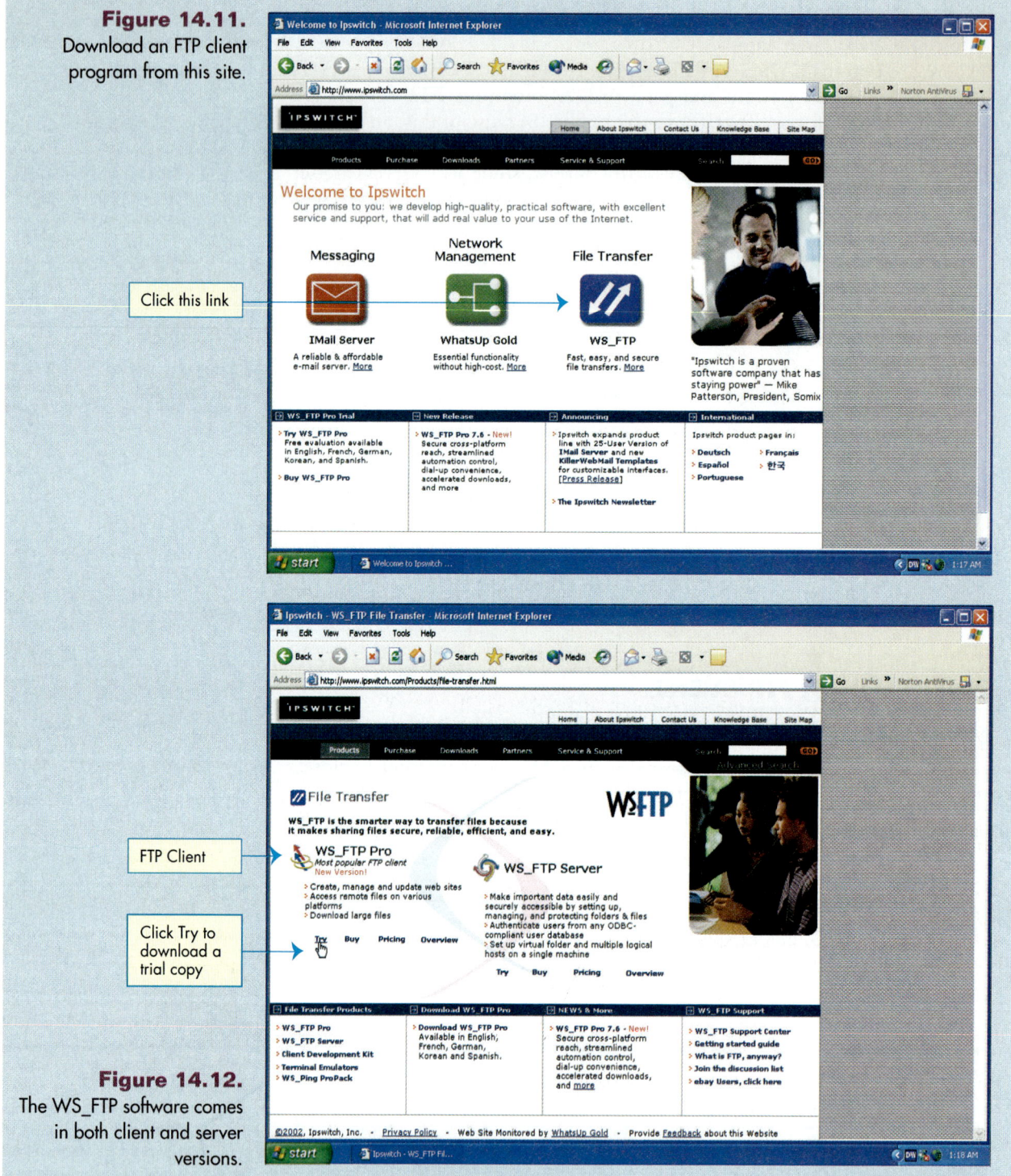

Figure 14.11. Download an FTP client program from this site.

Figure 14.12. The WS_FTP software comes in both client and server versions.

③ Click the *Try* link for WS_FTP Pro.
A page with a short form displays (see Figure 14.13).

④ Enter your e-mail address, User Type, and Country. If you don't want to receive electronic newsletters, check the appropriate box; then click *Next*.
A screen with various locations from which you can download the software displays.

ACTIVITY 14.1
Downloading an FTP Client

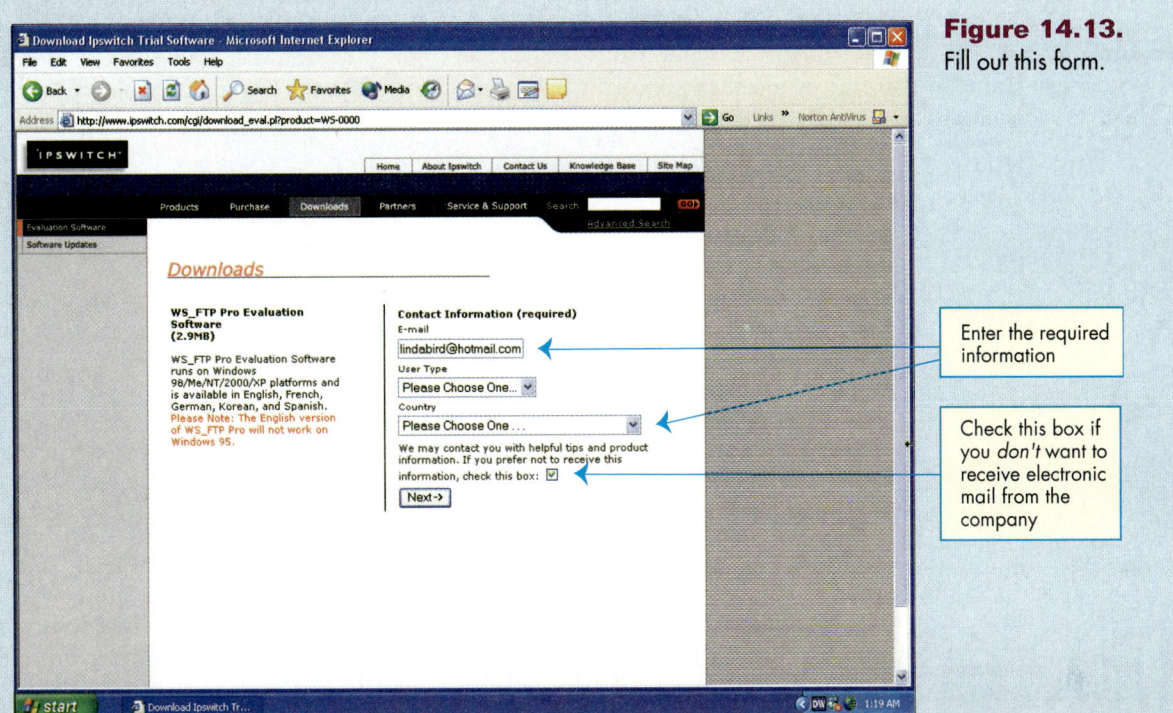

Figure 14.13.
Fill out this form.

Enter the required information

Check this box if you *don't* want to receive electronic mail from the company

 Click a link (*English v7.6*) from any of the locations listed.
    A File Download dialog box displays. By default, Internet Explorer displays this dialog box any time you download software as a general warning that the software might include malicious code. It's advisable to save the file and then scan it with anti-virus software before opening it.

6 Click the *Save* button.
    The Save As dialog box displays so that you can indicate a location to save the file.

7 Indicate a location in the Save As dialog box, then click Save.
    The file is downloaded (see Figure 14.14). "Behind the scenes," FTP is being used to transfer the program to your computer. When the download is complete, an icon for the new file will appear on your desktop or in the folder that you indicated.

> **ALERT!**
> Registration forms like this one are good places to use secondary or blind e-mail addresses (at least, if you don't want to share your primary one). If you use your primary e-mail address, you risk being placed on a variety of electronic mailing lists.

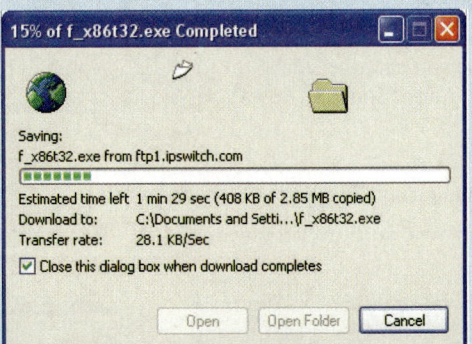

Figure 14.14.
FTP often handles the downloading process.

8 Scan the icon for the program with an anti-virus program. (For example, if Norton AntiVirus is installed, you can right-click the icon and choose Scan with Norton AntiVirus from the shortcut menu.)

Download an FTP Client 223

ACTIVITY 14.1
Downloading an FTP Client (Continued)

⑨ If the anti-virus program indicates that the downloaded file doesn't contain any malicious code, you can double-click the icon to install the software.

⑩ After the software is installed, you can open and use it. The FTP client should appear similar to that shown in Figure 14.15.

Figure 14.15.
The WS_FTP program includes a Windows interface.

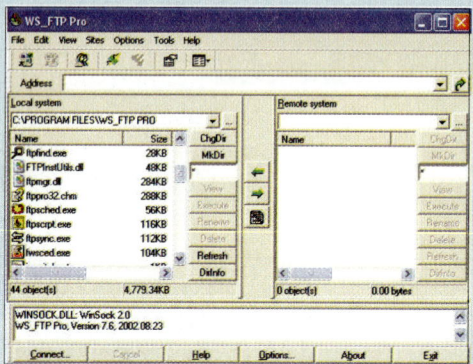

⑪ Close any open windows, including the one for the WS_FTP client program.

INSIDE TRACK

If you want to learn more about using an FTP client, such as WS_FTP, go to an associated Web site (*www.ftpplanet.com*). This site includes tutorials and support for the product. If you want to practice using ftp to transfer files, you can find a list of ftp sites at *www.ftpfind.com*.

That's it. Armed with these methods and techniques for pulling information from the Internet, you can now tap into the wealth of programs and files for which the Internet is famous.

Don't Forget...

- The Internet includes a wealth of files and information you can download, including software, games, graphics, and music.
- You need to make sure that you have the legal right to copy and use any file or information you download from the Internet.
- The fastest way to transfer large files is to use FTP. FTP requires an FTP client and an FTP server.
- You can download commercial software, trialware, shareware, and freeware.
- Downloading is a uniform and straightforward procedure. However, you need to indicate the location in which you want to save your files and scan the downloaded files for viruses before opening them.

- You can use copy and paste commands to copy text or objects from a Web page to your computer.
- You can save an entire Web page as a file on your computer.
- To save time and space, files are routinely transferred as ZIP or archived files.
- Depending on how it's set up, you may be able to access the files on an FTP server without having an account.
- You can download and use an FTP client such as WS_FTP.

Check This Out

MULTIPLE CHOICE

1. You want to display a picture you found on the Web on your computer's desktop. Which of the following is the best method for transferring the file to your system?
   a. Copying and pasting it as a shortcut
   b. Downloading the file using an FTP client
   c. Using the Set as Background command from the shortcut menu
   d. Clicking the Download Now button on the Web site

2. Which of the following is the best way to transfer a large file from a remote office to your company's corporate headquarters?
   a. Gopher
   b. Shareware
   c. FTP
   d. HTTP

3. What is the main advantage of using trialware?
   a. You can evaluate the software before buying it.
   b. It may contain viruses.
   c. The company charges you only a nominal amount per day to try it.
   d. All of the above

4. What is a potential disadvantage of using shareware or freeware?
   a. It can possibly include malicious code.
   b. It sometimes contains adware.
   c. If you don't buy it, nag screens may regularly display on your computer.
   d. All of the above

5. What is an advantage of using FTP?
   a. You can easily transfer large files, such as entire programs.
   b. Most Web browsers include the capability to handle FTP.
   c. FTP allows you to transfer files between a variety of platforms.
   d. All of the above

MATCHING

a nag screens
b ZIP
c PDF
d anonymous FTP
e patch
f MP3
g wallpaper
h shareware
i freeware
j WinZip

1. Programs for which you register on an honor system basis; usually have a nominal cost associated with registering
2. Programs that are distributed at no cost
3. A Windows program used to compress files
4. An account is not necessary to transfer files
5. Fixes security problems with software
6. Digital file format for music files
7. A format that makes it easy to view files, no matter what software was used to develop them
8. Desktop background
9. Remind you to register for software regularly
10. A compressed file or files

Real Life

1. Many works posted on the Internet are protected by copyright laws. To find out more about copyright issues, go to the United States Copyright Office Web site (*www.lcweb.loc.gov/copyright*) and click the Copyright Basics link. Next, run a few searches to research the Digital Millennium Copyright Act (DMCA), which was passed in 1998. Develop a list of "dos" and "don'ts" regarding copying information from the Internet.

2. Explore the various types of files that are available for downloading. To do so, go to Download (*www.download.com*), Microsoft's Download Center (go to *support.microsoft.com* and then click the Download Software link), and Jumbo! (*www.jumbo.com*). Develop a list of the types of software and files that you can download from the Internet and give an example of who might use each (such as a small business owner, parent, college student, and so on).

I Spy: Privacy and Security Concerns

1. Research the issues surrounding the use of Napster-type programs to exchange music and video files (perhaps without the consent of the copyright owner). Develop two papers or speeches: one that defends the rights of the recording artists and copyright owners; the other that takes the side of Internet users who want to freely exchange creative works without the explicit permission of the copyright holders. If time allows, hold an in-class debate regarding these issues.

2. Many of the programs that assist in file sharing between users will search your entire hard drive to locate MP3 or video files. Additionally, some of them do not close when you exit the browser; as long as you have an active connection to the Internet, the software can search your system. Discuss the privacy and security implications of this practice.

3. Some "free" downloadable programs include adware or spyware that can then be used to display advertisements or track information about your browsing habits. Use the Web to research this issue; then discuss it with others in your class. (Hint: Start by taking a careful look at the popular KaZaA software, which allows file sharing between users. The program's Web site is *www.kazaa.com*; also examine other Web sites, such as CNET's Download.com, which discuss this software.)

4. Develop a list of best practices to use when downloading software (especially freeware or shareware) from the Internet. For example, you might want to list safeguards, such as running a virus scan on all downloadable files before using them, and so on. (Hint: Run Internet searches using keywords such as `best practice download files`.)

CHAPTER 15

WORKING WITH VARIOUS FILE TYPES AND PLUG-INS

Key Terms

When you finish this chapter, you'll understand the following terms:

- Animated GIF
- codec
- Digital Audio Tape (DAT)
- digital media
- Extensible HyperText Markup Language (XHTML)
- file extension
- file format
- Graphics Interchange Format (GIF)
- graphics file
- HTML tag
- JPEG
- Macromedia Flash Player
- Macromedia Shockwave Player
- MOV
- MPEG (Moving Picture Experts Group)
- multimedia
- Notepad
- plug-in
- QuickTime
- RealOne Player
- Rich Text Format (RTF)
- Text (TXT)
- Tagged Image File Format (TIFF)
- VoiceXML
- Waveform (WAV)
- Windows Media Player
- Windows Media Audio (WMA)

Chapter Objectives

After you complete this chapter, you'll

- Be Familiar with Common File Types
- Examine the Main File Types
- Know About Common Plug-Ins

The Big Picture

Most people agree that it would be a boring world indeed if you could see things only in black-and-white still pictures instead of in living, moving colors. Imagine if ice cream came in only one flavor or if everyone had to wear gray clothes...things just wouldn't be the same, would they? Likewise, the Internet would be useful but somewhat dull if it was able to handle only one file type and displayed everything in text without graphics, colors, animations, or music.

But in fact, the Internet (especially the Web portion of it) is rich with enhancements, partly because Web browsers, such as Internet Explorer, support many file formats or types. And if the browsers don't recognize a file type, they can use a special program called a plug-in to work with the data contained in the file.

A **file format** is the way a file stores information. The program used to develop the document and the way the data is stored determine the file format. **Plug-ins** (sometimes called add-ins) are software programs that are tightly integrated with a main program, such as a browser. Plug-ins extend the capabilities of the browser so that it can work with a wider variety of file types. For example, there are plug-ins for playing music, video clips, animations, and other multimedia applications. **Multimedia** refers to the simultaneous use of multiple forms of media to communicate, such as combining text, audio, video, graphics, and animations.

In this chapter, we'll go over the main file types you'll encounter when you browse on the Web. That way, you won't be confused the next time someone mentions that they're sending you a "JPEG," "ZIP," or "MP3" file. We'll also help you learn which file type is used by which program, so that you can match them up and use them appropriately. Along the way, we'll warn you about the security and privacy issues that you might want to watch for.

We'll then turn our attention to the most common add-ins currently available and show you how they can enhance your browsing experience on the Web. We'll even point you to the Web sites from which you can download these add-ins if they're not already installed on your system. After you complete the chapter, you just might feel that a brave new world—one rich with multimedia and animations—has been opened up for you.

INSIDE TRACK

Originally, the term *plug-in* referred to programs used to enhance Netscape's browser; *add-in* was the term used for Microsoft's products. However, the line between the terms has become increasingly blurred. At this point, the terms are more-or-less used interchangeably.

The computing power of most up-to-date systems, coupled with multimedia programs and players, makes working on the Web a multisensory experience: The next time you're working on that term paper or major project for work, you can listen to the radio or other music on your system (see Figure 15.1).

Although add-in programs are sometimes used to display multimedia content, they can be used for other purposes, too. For example, Adobe Acrobat Reader allows you to view files—including graphics, fonts, and colors—just as they were created and laid out in their original program. In a sense, Acrobat

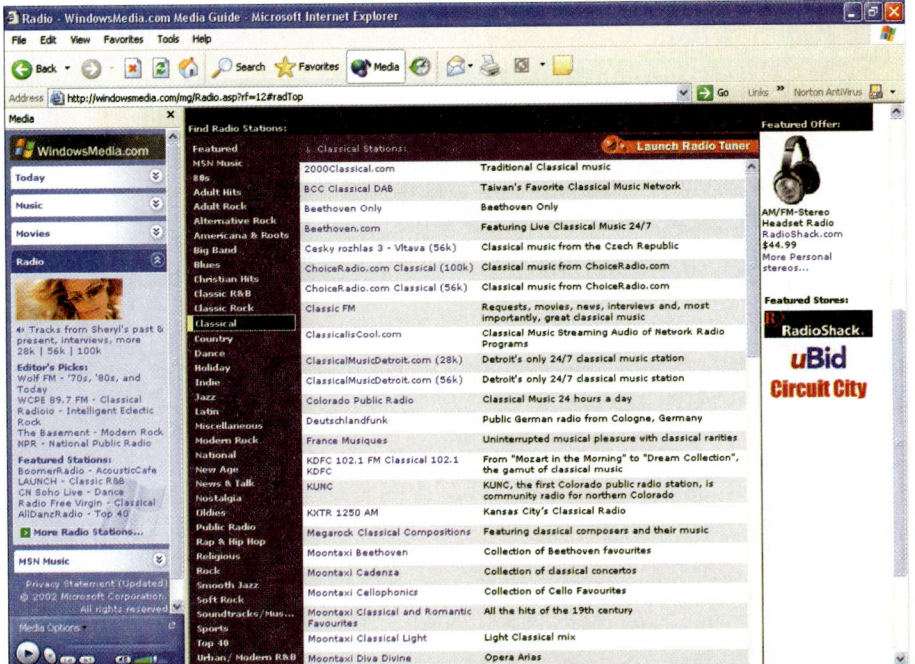

Figure 15.1.
Working on that research paper or browsing on the Web? Listen to radio programs via Windows Media Player at the same time.

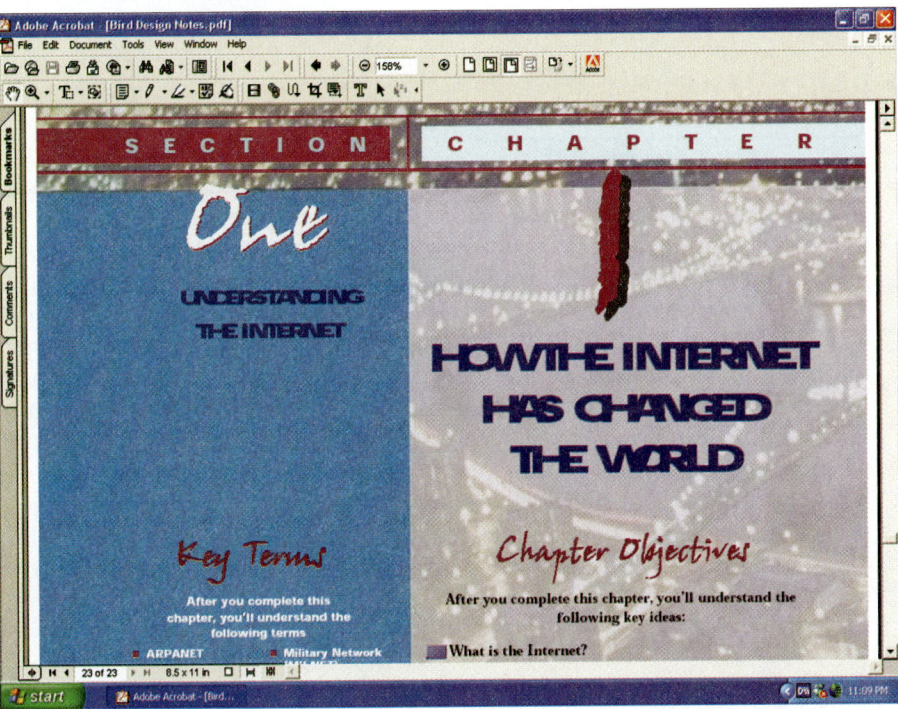

Figure 15.2.
Adobe Acrobat Reader allows you to view files as they were originally created, including graphics and fonts.

Reader makes a level playing field between various computers, operating systems, and programs by creating a way to view files, no matter what combination of technologies was used to develop them (see Figure 15.2).

   You can usually find all these great plug-ins on the individual Web sites of the companies that developed them. However, you can sometimes make your downloading experience a one-stop experience by going to a mega download site such as CNET's *Download.com*. Sites like this have links to several browser plug-ins in one central location (see Figure 15.3).

Window on the Web   229

Figure 15.3.
Go to a Web site from which you can download several plug-ins at once.

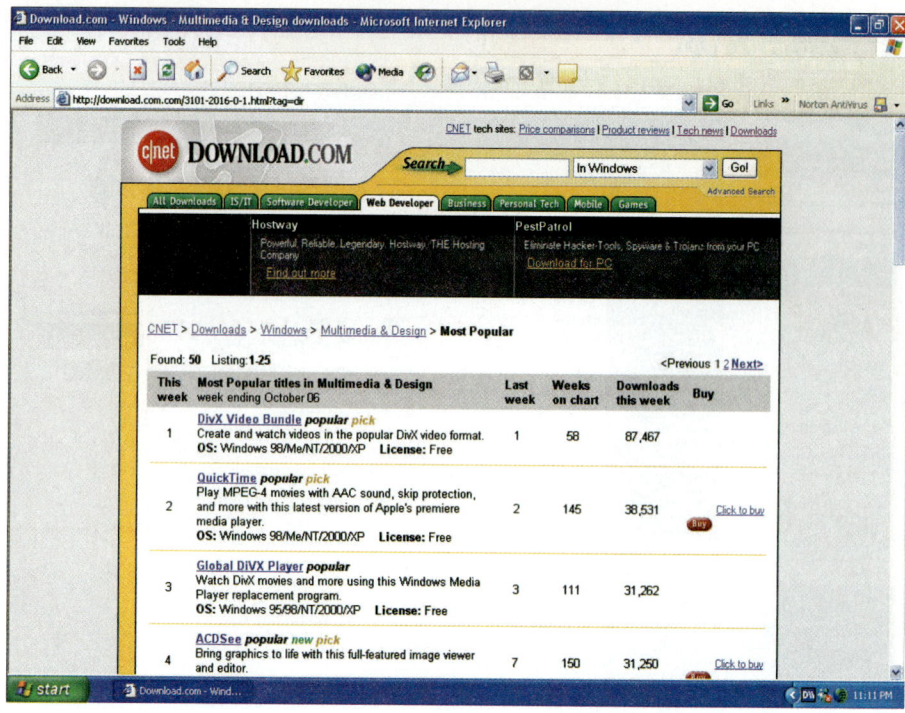

BE FAMILIAR WITH COMMON FILE TYPES

Most browser software can operate just fine and make your journey through the Web almost seamless all by itself. But once in awhile (especially if you visit multimedia-rich sites), you'll encounter a file that your browser doesn't recognize and can't really use. That's when you'll benefit by downloading a browser plug-in.

Before we look at how to download and use the most common plug-ins, it's helpful to understand how your browser recognizes the various file types or formats. Here's how it works: When you click a link that points to a Web page, your browser asks the Web server to find the page. But the Web server usually doesn't send just one page; it "serves up" a number of files that make up the elements on the page. For example, the main files might have the page's text, written in HTML. Additionally, each graphic, object, and element is passed from the Web server to the browser as a separate file. Your browser's job is to reassemble all these parts onscreen so that you can view a complete Web page.

> **HEADS UP!** It's likely that there is variation between which plug-ins are available on the computers at your school, home, and business. If you don't have a particular plug-in available (and can't download it because you're blocked by a firewall), just read through the chapter and familiarize yourself with the main concepts.

INSIDE TRACK

Most plug-ins have corresponding development software that helps Web designers develop content for the associated plug-in. For example, designers use Adobe Acrobat to develop Web content; to view the content, you use the Adobe Acrobat Reader plug-in.

But the browser doesn't wait until all the files are available before it begins to download the Web page on your screen. Instead, it begins to display the page whenever the files arrive from the server. Text-based files generally arrive and are downloaded well before graphical files. This is especially evident if you have a slower (dial-up) connection. (If you have a high-speed connection, it will probably seem that the entire page displays at once.)

Today, Web pages can include a wide variety of file types, HTML, pictures, audio and music files, video clips, animations, and so on. As each file arrives from the Web server, your browser needs to recognize the data and display it properly.

Most of the time, a browser, such as Internet Explorer, *does* know how to handle the various files that make up a Web page. It does this (in part) because each file type has a different extension. A **file extension** is represented by the last three (or four) characters of a file's name—the part to the right of the period. This extension represents the data type used by the file and the program was used to develop it.

Think of a file extension as a file's last name: Just as your last name groups you with others in your family, so a file extension groups it with other similar files. File extensions are important because the Windows operating system (and browsers such as Internet Explorer) use them to determine which program or plug-in should be employed to read the file. Table 15.1 includes a few of the file types that you'll probably encounter in your travels on the Internet:

Table 15.1 only scratches the surface because there are literally thousands of file types in use. If you're curious about some of the other file types currently used, you can visit one of the Web sites specifically devoted to listing them. Here are some sites to get you started: *www.stack.com*, *www.ace.net.nz/tech/TechFileFormat.html* and *extsearch.com*.

INSIDE TRACK

In the days of DOS (Disk Operating System) and Windows 3.1, extensions were limited to three characters. At this point, there's no particular reason to stick with three characters, but old habits are hard to break. Even though programmers can use more than three characters for a file's extension, it's rare to see it.

TABLE 15.1	File Extensions Commonly Encountered on the Internet
File Extension	**Typical Use**
ASP	A Web page generated as an Active Server Page.
AVI	An abbreviation for Audio Video Interleave, this format is used to create and view short movies. Files that use this format tend to be large, necessitating a fast Internet connection to view the videos.
EXE	A file that executes code; usually a program file. Although usually used for legitimate purposes, this type of file *can* contain malicious code.
GIF	An abbreviation for Graphics Interchange Format, which is a graphical format commonly used on the Web for simple artwork and line drawings.
HTM or HTML	A Web page formatted in HTML (HyperText Markup Language).
JPG or JPEG	An abbreviation for Joint Photography Experts Group, which is a graphical format commonly used for photography quality images.
MPG	The file type associated with the Moving Picture Experts Group (MPEG) files, this is one of the current standards for storing and transmitting digital video across the Internet.
MP3	The current standard for storing and transmitting music in digital format over the Internet. Because MP3 files are smaller than WAV audio files, they are more easily shared across a network.
MOV	A file format used by Apple Computer's QuickTime. MOV files can be video clips or still images.
PNG	An abbreviation for Portable Network Graphics, this is a high-quality graphics format. This file format is approved by the W3C group as a replacement for GIF files.
PDF	An abbreviation for Portable Document Format, which is a file generated by Adobe Acrobat or Adobe Acrobat Reader.
RM	An abbreviation for RealMedia files.
RTF	An acronym for Rich Text Format, developed by Microsoft. It's designed as a universal standard for exchanging text-based documents between different software programs.

TABLE 15.1	File Extensions Commonly Encountered on the Internet (continued)
File Extension	Typical Use
SWA	An abbreviation for a Shockwave file.
TIF	An abbreviation for Tagged Image File Format, which is a high quality, but large graphic format. It can be used universally on different types of computers and platforms.
TXT	A file format used for documents that are text-only. Because these files don't have special characters for formatting, they can be read by most text-based programs (such as word processors) and HTML editors, such as FrontPage.
VBS	A script (mini-program) file created using Visual Basic for Applications. Although usually used for legitimate purposes, this type of file can contain malicious code.
WAV	An abbreviation for waveforms, which is a digitized audio file format. Files that use this format are larger than MP3 files.
WMA	An acronym for Windows Media Audio, this is a digital audio file format.
ZIP	A compressed archive file, usually created by PKZip (or its graphical, Windows-based cousin, WinZip).

EXAMINE THE MAIN FILE TYPES

Now that you have a general idea of the types of files that might be used as you browse the Web and transfer files via the Internet, we'll look at a few of the most important ones in more depth.

TEXT FORMATS

Although they don't pack the punch that the multimedia files that you'll see on the Web do, words convey thoughts in ways that pictures can't. Most of the text that you see on a Web page is produced by HyperText Markup Language (HTML). As you learned in earlier chapters, HTML is the programming specification that Web developers use to set up Web pages. Programmers who are familiar with HTML can create Web pages by writing the appropriate code. However, many people instead prefer to use an HTML-editing program, such as Microsoft's FrontPage. HTML-editing programs enable people to develop Web pages using the familiar Windows interface instead of developing the code from scratch. (You'll learn more about using FrontPage in Chapters 21–22 of this book.)

In addition to the text on Web pages, you also have a few other text-based formats that you should know about: **Text (TXT)** and **Rich Text Format (RTF)**. Files saved in text (TXT) file format contain only characters, spaces, and punctuation. These files can be read by any word processor or mail program on the market. Even Windows has a small text editor built into it (called **Notepad**) that is designed to work with text-only files. Because of the fact that text files can be used universally, they're practical even if they are boring. One side benefit of a limited text-editing program such as Notepad is that you won't accidentally add formatting characters to documents that need to remain text-only.

Rich Text Format (RTF) files trade universality for formatting. They include limited formatting features—such as bold and italic typefaces—but the files can't be read by as many programs. Don't count on being able to tap into high-end features, such as charts or tables, in a Rich Text Format file. To do that, you need a full-blown word processing application, such as Microsoft Word.

INSIDE TRACK

Many companies now require you to post your resume in plain text. This enables them to view it no matter which program you used to develop it.

WEB PAGE FORMATS

As you already know, Web pages are typically saved using HTML, a markup language. As such, pages created for use on the Web usually have HTML or HTM extensions. The actual display of the page, such as the colors used and the placement of tables and graphics, is controlled by hidden HTML tags—the tags appear in the code text for the page, but are not displayed by the browser that reads the page. An **HTML tag** is a code that gives instructions for formatting or actions—instructions used in laying out a Web page and setting up links. Typical code for a Web page would consist of text encompassed by tags.

Figure 15.4 shows how a Web page appears when displayed by Internet Explorer. Figure 15.5 gives you an idea of how the associated HTML code (including tags) appears when viewed in Notepad. (In Chapters 19–22, you'll learn more about HTML when you develop your own Web page.)

A related Web page file format you'll see increasingly more often is XML (Extensible Markup Language). XML is similar to HTML, but more flexible because it allows programmers to custom-design tags so that they can more effectively link their page with other locations on the Web. For example, XML supports links that point to multiple documents—an HTML link can reference only one destination. A variation of the XML format, **VoiceXML**, will make it possible for people to communicate with Web servers by talking over the phone. VoiceXML combines XML with voice recognition technology, which would allow people to check e-mail and Web-based information (such as sports scores or the weather) via the phone.

Because it supports more advanced technology, some people want to see XML supplant HTML as the standard Web-formatting specification. An intermediary programming language, **Extensible HyperText Markup Language** (**XHTML**), is providing a bridge between HTML and XML.

INSIDE TRACK

If we've sparked your interest in this formatting language, find out more by going to the World Wide Web Consortium's (W3C) site at *www.w3c.org*.

GRAPHIC FILE FORMATS

Of all the services on the Internet, the Web in particular is graphically oriented. Its rich look is due in large part to the images displayed on the pages.

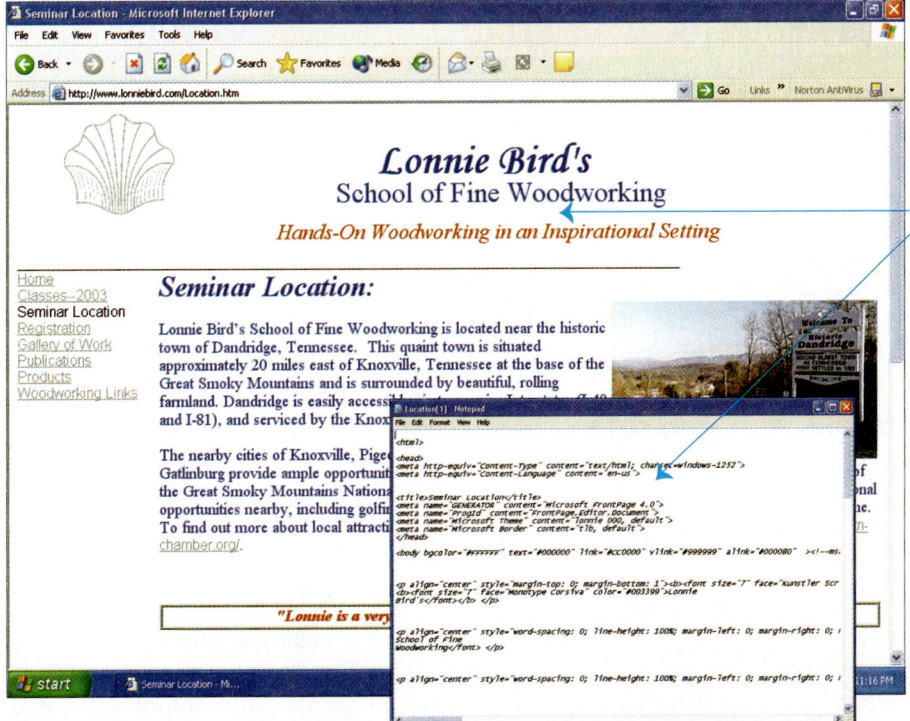

Figure 15.4. and 5
The Web page displayed in a browser. The HTML code is used to create the Web page.

Examine the Main File Types   233

Some of the elements are generated by the HTML code (which you'll learn a little more about when you create your own Web page later in this book). However, most of the graphics you view on the Web are inserted as objects that use one of several graphic file formats, such as those with extensions like TIF, TIFF, GIF, and JPG. A **graphics file** is a file that includes only images such as paint program files, scanned images, photographs, clip art, or other electronic art. Graphics files are generally edited by using drawing- or photography-editing programs. Small add-in drawing programs are also sometimes included as part of other programs. For example, Microsoft's Office programs include a built-in drawing program, called OfficeArt, which allows you to perform limited graphic editing.

GIF (**Graphics Interchange Format**) files are commonly used on the Web. This format is useful for Web applications because it supports a limited number of colors (256) and looks good on a variety of computer platforms. The limited number of colors reduces file size, which results in Web pages that display more rapidly. Because the number of colors is restricted, the GIF file format is best used for images that include large sections of the same color, such as cartoons, logos, graphics, and simple line art.

Animated GIF files are what the name implies—a series of GIF files that are shown in rapid succession to give the illusion of movement. These animations are sometimes used for online advertisements. However, because the animations consist of multiple individual images in a sequence, the size of animated GIFs can make a Web page display slowly.

In contrast with the 256-color limitation of GIFs, **JPEG** files (with an extension of JPG or JPEG), support 16 million color variations. Consequently, the JPEG format works well for scanned photographs and other artwork that require color gradients and variations. Think about a photo of the ocean: At first glance the image might appear to only have a couple shades of blue, but upon closer examination you'll probably realize that it actually is made up of many variations of blue, gray, green, and other colors. Because of its capability to correctly display these color variations, JPEG is best used on the Web when accurate portrayals of color or depths of perception are important. Another important aspect of the JPEG file format is that it can compress images so that the resultant file will be smaller and load more quickly when used on a Web page. JPEG does this by taking advantage of the limitations of the human eye; it reduces image quality slightly, which results in a smaller file, yet the difference can't be detected by the naked eye. Because these small color variations aren't noticed, a compressed JPEG file effectively trades image quality for smaller file size.

You'll occasionally see TIFF files (with an extension of TIF or TIFF) on the Web. **TIFF (Tagged Image File Format)** files can be displayed on a variety of computer systems, which increases their usability. This type of file format is also high quality and can use a variety of color combinations or black and white without losing that quality. However, this type of file is typically larger in size than JPEG files, so TIFF graphic files are used less on the Web than are JPEG files.

INSIDE TRACK

You may be familiar with the bitmap file format, with an extension of .bmp. This file format is used by some Windows programs, such as Paintbrush. However, bitmap files are not typically used on the Web because they tend to store graphics inefficiently and take up more storage space than necessary. If they are used on Web pages, they can make the page display more slowly than other types of graphic files.

MEDIA FILE FORMATS

So far, you've learned that Web pages display text or graphic files. But there's more. A typical home computer is also able to handle multimedia, such as digitized audio (sound) and video. Digitized audio and video are called **digital media**.

Digital audio is sound that has been created, stored, and transmitted as a series of 0s and 1s (binary numbers) instead of as analog sound waves. In practical terms, this means that sound files, including your favorite song, can be reproduced and listened to on computerized systems. More importantly, digi-

INSIDE TRACK

You can tell which type of graphic file format is used on a Web site. To do this, right-click the image and then choose Properties on the shortcut menu, which displays the Properties dialog box for the graphic. The file type (and other information) is shown in the dialog box.

tized sound doesn't wear out over time. In contrast, the old vinyl records wore out a little bit each time the needle passed over the record's grooves; tapes also degraded slightly each time you listened to them. But digitized sound eliminated this drawback and could be reproduced or copied almost endlessly.

However, before audio files could be easily transmitted over the Internet, a few technologies had to be put in place. Without them, the large size of audio files (and slow Internet connections) kept these files from being exchanged efficiently online. To work around this problem, companies worked hard to develop compression methods (called **codecs**) that would reduce file size without compromising sound quality. In 1992, a technology was developed, called **MPEG (Moving Picture Experts Group)**, which could accurately compress a digital audio file to 1/12 of its original size without losing quality. However, the technology didn't initially take over the market, as you might expect it would, because Microsoft incorporated a competing technology (**WAV**, for **waveform**) into the Windows 95 operating system multimedia tool: the Windows Media Player. **Windows Media Player** is a program used for playing sounds and video on Windows operating systems. Primarily because of name recognition, Microsoft's WAV became the consumer standard for audio files during that time period. Even today, most multimedia players can play WAV sounds. However, files that use the WAV format are not compressed, so they take up a lot of storage space and can't be transferred over the Internet as quickly as files that use newer technology, such as MP3.

Another technology that competed with MPEG's initial acceptance was RealPlayer (developed by RealNetworks and now called **RealOne Player**), a technology that could almost simultaneously record, compress, transfer, decompress, and play sound (and video) files. The WAV and RealOne Player technologies were used more than MPEG until the late 1990's. But after MP3 players (to play the MP3 sound files that use the MPEG technology) were commercially developed, this technology quickly caught on. You'll learn more about RealNetworks in Chapter 16, Beyond the Basics: Taking Advantage of the Internet's Multimedia Capabilities.

So where are we today as far as audio file formats are concerned? The main file format used for music files nowadays is MP3 (short for MPEG-Audio Layer 3). This technology, which compresses sound and movie files, has taken over as the current standard for transmitting and downloading digital sound and video files across the Internet. Its rise to prominence is due partly to the creation of a Web site devoted to downloading MP3 files—appropriately named MP3.com (see Figure 15.6). You'll learn more about MP3 in Chapter 16.

The WAV and RealOne Player formats are also still in use, but are feeling some competition from other technologies. For example, Microsoft's **Windows Media Audio (WMA)** technology is being marketed by Microsoft as an alternative to the MP3 audio format. Files created with WMA technology have sound quality similar to MP3 files, but take up less disk space. One way Microsoft has gained market share with WMA is to make it the default file format for the Media Player that ships with Windows.

At present, Windows' Media Player—as well as most third party players, such as MUSICMATCH Jukebox (see Figure 15.7)—can play MP3, WAV, WMA, and other audio files.

The same technology that was useful and exciting for music enthusiasts who wanted to download and exchange music files was unsettling for the recording companies because the technology allowed computer users to easily duplicate copyrighted recordings of their favorite artists. Furthermore, when peer-to-peer file music sharing programs such as Napster reached the Internet, the recording industries were seriously worried—worried enough to take legal action against Napster. Through court rulings, they were able to effectively close Napster down, but there are still many other programs and music file sharing Web sites online.

INSIDE TRACK

A peer is simply a computer on a network that operates at the same level as another computer. A peer-to-peer relationship is one in which you have two computers on a network (such as the Internet) sharing files between each other's hard drives. As you learned in Chapter 2, The Good, the Bad, the Ugly: Uses and Misuses of the Internet, Napster's software was used to share MP3 files between two computer users' hard drives. This software had been downloaded at least 70 million times before the site was effectively shut down.

Figure 15.6.
MP3.com is a popular Web site from which you can download MP3 files.

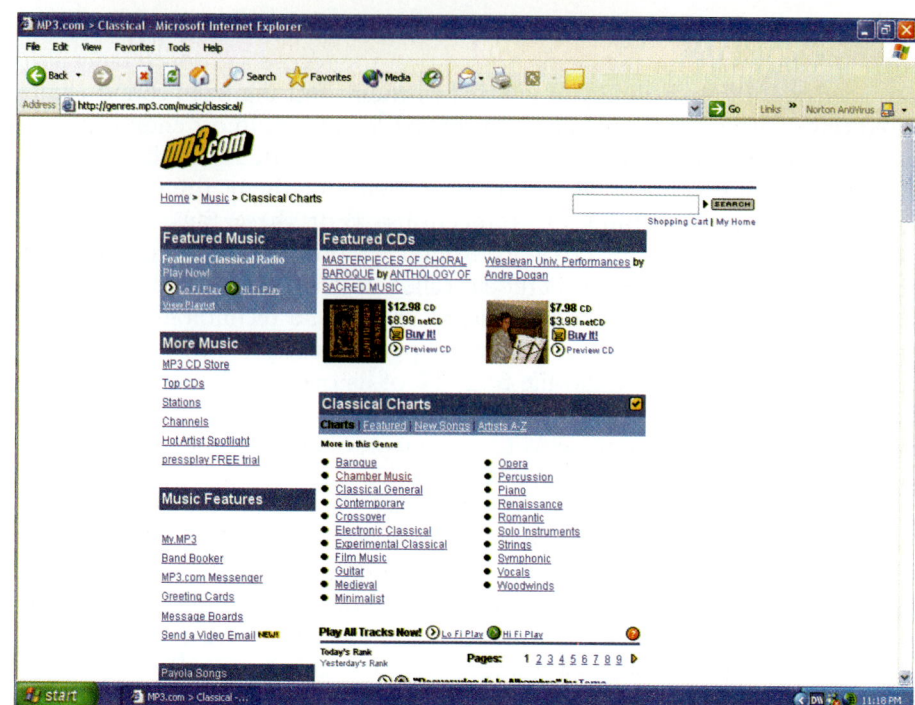

Figure 15.7.
MP3 Players, such as MUSICMATCH Jukebox, have become very popular for playing digitized audio files.

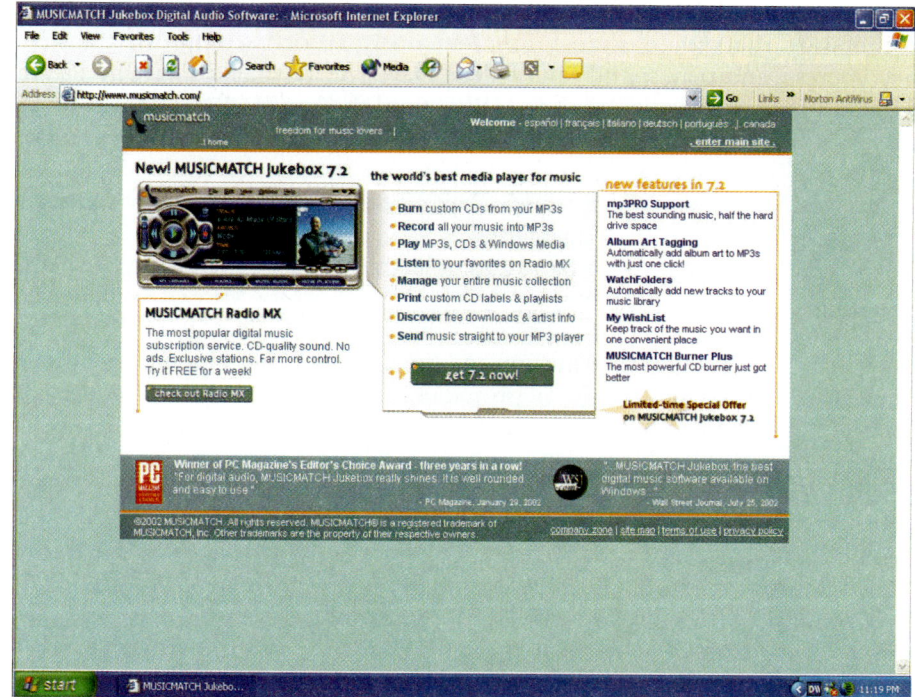

ON THE HORIZON

New technologies for using audio files online are still being developed with vigor. MP3 players have become commonplace accessories, and new compression technologies are being created, such as MP7. You'll learn more about some of the new technologies in Chapter 16.

Like audio, the format for video has been digitized and transformed from earlier formats. Digital video (sometimes called digital capture) refers to converting analog signals into a digital format and then storing them on some type of mass storage device. It does this by converting the video signal to machine-readable numbers.

Even though it was theoretically possible to create digitized video images in the early 1990s, the process for doing so was costly and complicated for the average home user. Because of this, it wasn't until the late 1990s that the hardware and software necessary for digitizing video were affordable and user-friendly enough to enter the consumer market in force.

A common digital medium is **Digital Audio Tape (DAT)**, which is a type of magnetic tape used to store digital video. The cartridge used for DAT is small—only a little larger than a credit card.

Camcorders are now developed that store and use both analog and digital images. Digital video (DV) camcorders store images on digital medium, such as DAT. Additionally, video-editing programs allow the average person to achieve professional-looking results. These camcorders can also be connected to either your computer or your television, which gives the users great flexibility in how they will use video: on a Web site, to edit and send to another person, or to just view. Most likely video, like audio, will continue to take advantage of cutting-edge technology. (You'll learn more about digital video and streaming media in Chapter 16.)

PORTABLE DOCUMENT FORMAT

Adobe Acrobat, developed by Adobe Systems, Inc., uses the Portable Document Format (PDF). The Adobe Acrobat Reader allows anyone to view files using this form (with the PDF file extension). You can download Adobe Acrobat Reader for free from the company's Web site (*www.adobe.com*).

Adobe's technology is largely responsible for standardizing the format of documents on the Internet. This is because it doesn't matter what program a file was developed in; you can use the Reader to view it without having the original application on your computer.

PDF is widely used—so widely used that many people include a link to Adobe's site on their own sites to facilitate the viewing of files on their sites. You can click this link, download the Reader, and then return to the original site to view the documents. Because Adobe Acrobat Reader is a mainstay plug-in on the Internet, you'll learn where you can download it later in this chapter.

COMPRESSION FILE FORMAT

Although there are several compression file formats, such as those used to compress music and video files, most people immediately think of ZIP files when they consider this type of format. ZIP files allow users to compress (zip) and later decompress (unzip) files. The reduced file size of zipped files helps when you want to store and transfer files.

The first ZIP files were based on Phil Katz's DOS-based program PKZip (which now has a Windows interface and is called WinZip). As you've probably guessed, the file extension for ZIP files is ZIP. You can download this popular software from WinZip's Web site at *www.winzip.com* (see Figure 15.8).

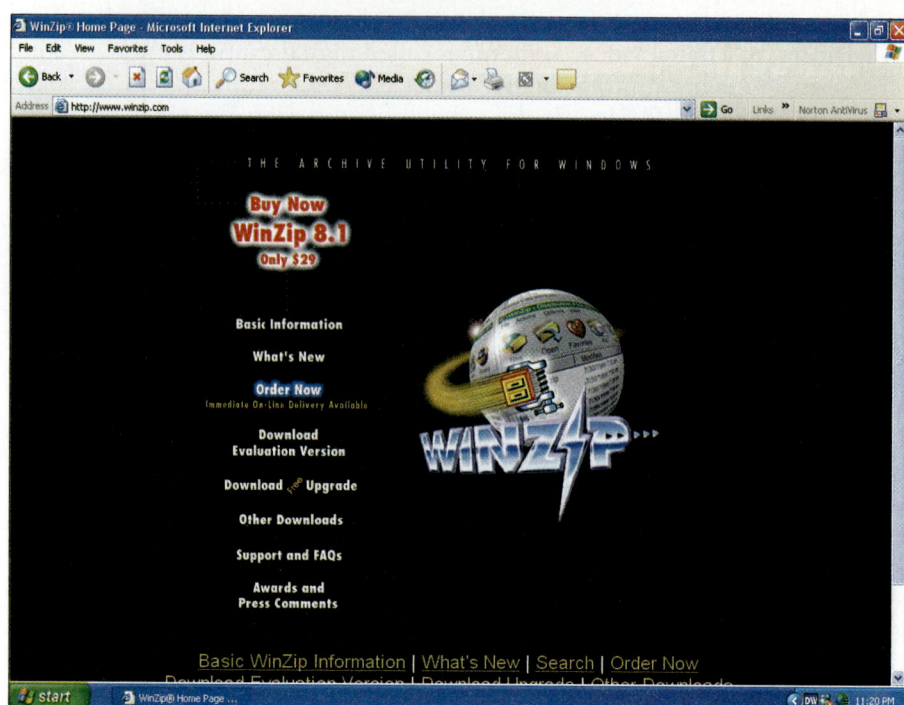

Figure 15.8.
Download this useful program and then use it to compress your files.

KNOW ABOUT COMMON PLUG-INS

Now that you're familiar with the various file extensions, you're ready to turn your attention to some of the common plug-ins that work with browsers to display Web content. These add-ins, as we've already mentioned, are necessary to use for displaying or using certain types of content. In this section, we'll go over the most commonly used plug-in programs. Along the way, we'll point you in the right direction in case you want to download a couple of them.

For the most part, however, you don't need to worry about downloading all the plug-in programs you need ahead of time. Instead, just start using the Internet; more than likely, you'll eventually run into a data type that your browser can't handle. When that happens, just spend a moment or two downloading the necessary add-in. The associated Web page will usually include a link that you can click to access the appropriate site and do so. With that in mind, let's look at some of the most common and popular plug-in programs.

INSIDE TRACK

You can try out the full version of several of Adobe's products. However, most of the free tryout software does not allow you to save, print, or export the files you create.

ADOBE ACROBAT READER

You already know that Adobe creates a product (Adobe Acrobat Reader) that allows you to view files with the PDF file format. Now it's time to expand your knowledge regarding the other products this company produces, most notably the full version of Adobe Acrobat. The full version enables you to create PDF files. Additionally, the full version lets you create and edit PDF files for use on the Web. For example, it includes features that help you convert your Microsoft Office documents to PDF; display documents on any system, no matter what hardware or software is used; and use security features that prevent others from changing your PDF files.

In contrast, the free downloadable Acrobat Reader is used just to view files. You can download this reader by going to Adobe's Web site (*www.adobe.com*) and then clicking the Downloads button (see Figure 15.9).

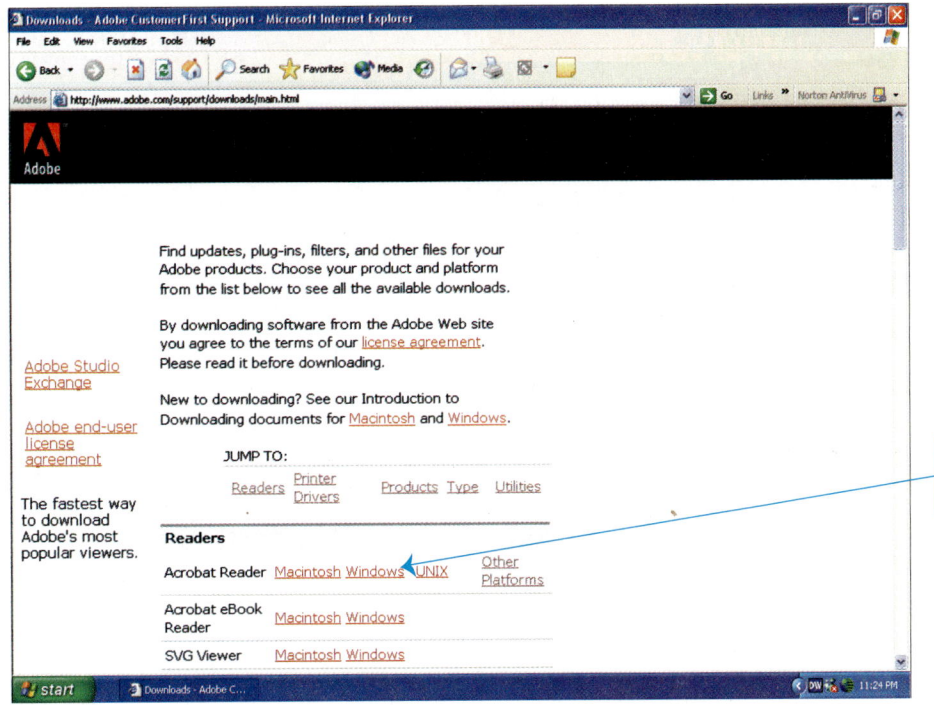

Figure 15.9.
You can download Acrobat Reader for free from the company's Web site.

MACROMEDIA FLASH PLAYER AND MACROMEDIA SHOCKWAVE PLAYER

The **Macromedia Flash Player** (Flash for short) is a plug-in developed by (who else?) Macromedia. Flash is a programming technique that shows movies and animation on Web sites—at least as long as the user has downloaded the proper plug-ins for the browser. This is probably one of the most popular plug-in programs used today.

The advantages of using Flash include its capability to work on a variety of hardware and software platforms. Because Flash can be used for images, sounds, and videos, it is a good choice for multimedia applications.

Fortunately, it's easy to find and download Flash—it's even free. Just go to Macromedia's Web site (*www.macromedia.com*) and then click the Get Macromedia Flash Player button (see Figure 15.10).

Shockwave Player, also developed by Macromedia, is great for playing multimedia games, product demonstrations, and interactive learning programs. For example, you can play animated games, such as online puzzles. Some browsers have Shockwave Player built in, but if not, you can download the Shockwave Player from the downloads page of the company's Web site (*sdc.shockwave.com/shockwave/download*).

Want to try your hand at working with some Macromedia Flash and Shockwave content? Visit The Discovery Channel (*www.discovery.com*) to see Flash animations and the Lexus Radical Contest (*www.radicalcontest.com*) to play with Shockwave and create your own commercial. Keep in mind that if your Internet Explorer security settings are configured to block ActiveX Controls, you may not be able to view all the animations. (You'll learn much more about ActiveX controls in Chapter 18, Beyond the Basics: A Closer Look at Security Issues.)

INSIDE TRACK

Macromedia sells its development tools, including Macromedia Flash, to Web designers. The Web content they develop using this software is viewed by the associated plug-in—Flash Player—which you can download at no cost. Additionally, because Flash Player is sometimes built into browser software, you may not even need to download it.

ALERT!
Any time you download an application from the Internet, you take a risk that the program will also include malicious code. Although you're generally safe when you download programs from reputable sites such as Macromedia's, even these companies might have security breaches in their software despite their best efforts. Always remember to scan your downloads for viruses.

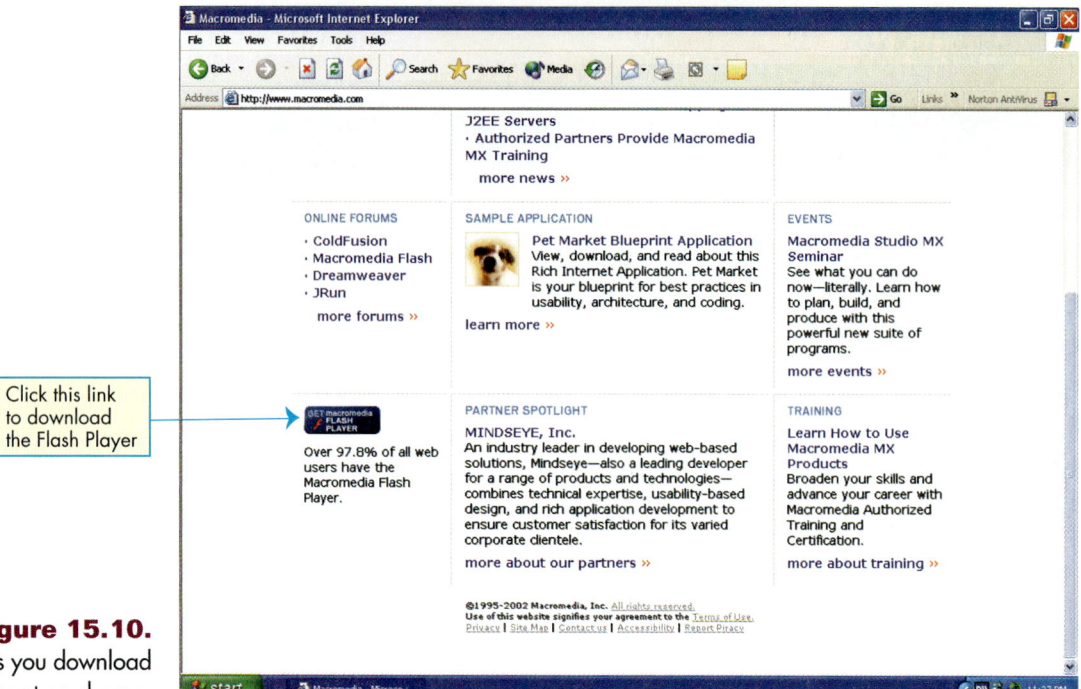

Figure 15.10.
Macromedia lets you download its Flash Player at no charge.

INSIDE TRACK

QuickTime Pro is the development software used to develop QuickTime content for the Web.

INSIDE TRACK

If you want to see both QuickTime and Macromedia Flash in action, visit the Sydney Opera House's Web site (*www.soh.nsw.gov.au*).

QUICKTIME

QuickTime is a technology that was originally developed by Apple Computer for Macintosh systems. This technology is used for storing sounds, graphics, and movie files. In fact, it can handle more than 200 kinds of media. QuickTime is adept at handling various types of media files.

The typical file extension for QuickTime files format is MOV (and less commonly, QT). Even though QuickTime was originally designed for Macintosh computers, it's subsequently been developed for Windows systems as well.

Like most multimedia plug-ins, this software includes a free downloadable player; if you want to tap into Web authoring tools, you need to buy the complete version, which is called QuickTime Pro. If necessary, you can download QuickTime Player from Apple's Web site (*www.apple.com/quicktime*). You can also view QuickTime media content on Apple's Web site (see Figure 15.11).

By now, you have a grasp of the main file formats, extensions, and plug-in programs that you'll encounter on the Internet. Together, these plug-ins provide a rich, graphical, and multimedia experience on the Web—an experience that people could only imagine just a short time ago. And if you really like multimedia, we'll delve even more into working with this technology in the next chapter.

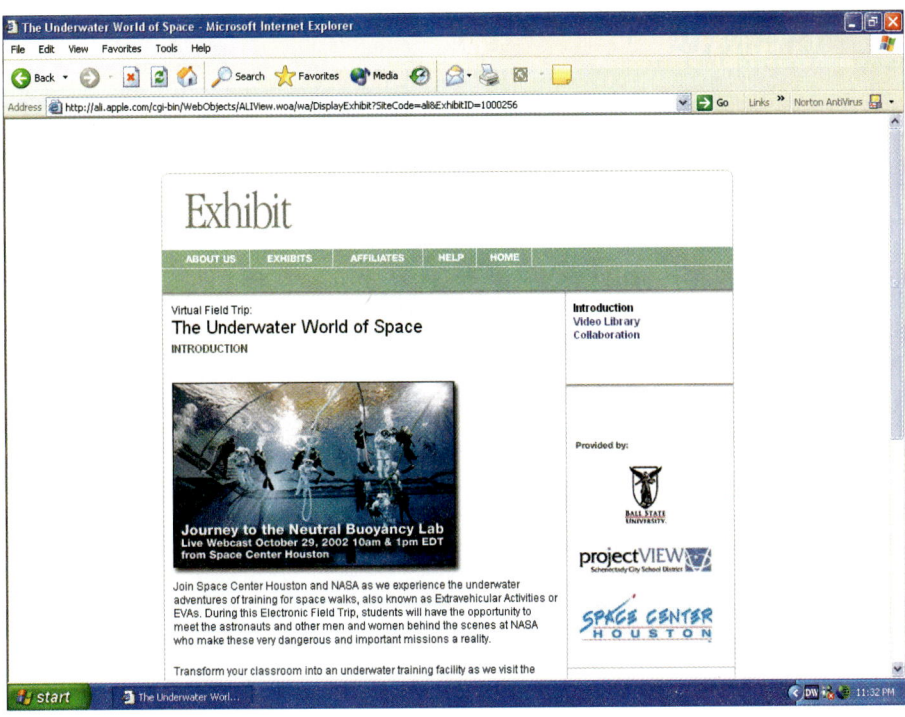

Figure 15.11.
Take QuickTime for a spin on Apple's Web site.

Don't Forget...

- Plug-ins (add-ins) can significantly increase your browser's functionality and your enjoyment of the Web.
- A file format is the way data is stored in a file.
- There are a wide variety of file types that are used on the Web.
- A file's extension gives a clue to what type of data it includes.
- The mainstay on most Web pages is still text, enhanced with graphics and multimedia.
- As technology advances, multimedia applications and plug-ins are increasing in use on the Web.
- HTML, XML, and XHTML are common Web page formats.
- Text-based files, which can be viewed in Notepad, usually include file formats such as HTML, TXT, or RTF.
- Graphic file formats can include GIF, JPEG, and TIF formats.
- The current compression techniques enable users to more easily send digital audio and video files over the Internet. However, this has raised copyright issues and caused conflict between everyday computer users and the recording industry.
- MP3 is the de facto industry standard for digitized music files. To play these types of files, you need an MP3 player.
- Adobe's PDF file format allows users to share files between diverse computer platforms.
- Macromedia Flash Player, Macromedia Shockwave Player, and QuickTime are very popular plug-ins.

Check This Out

MULTIPLE CHOICE

1. Which of the following is *not* a graphic file format?
   a. TXT
   b. GIF
   c. JPG
   d. TIF
2. Which of the following programs is best to use if you want to accurately view documents created in a different program?
   a. ShockFlash
   b. Notepad
   c. QuickTime
   d. Acrobat Reader
3. Which of the following had to be in place before sound and music files could be easily shared on the Internet?
   a. Everyone had to have broadband access who wanted to share the files.
   b. Compression schemes had to be developed.
   c. QuickTime had to be developed for the Windows environment, not just for Macintosh computers.
   d. All of the above
4. Which of the following graphic file formats are most commonly used on the Web?
   a. MOV and DOC
   b. TXT and RTF
   c. GIF and JPG
   d. MP3 and AVI
5. What is MP3?
   a. A digitized audio format
   b. An antivirus software program that prevents music files from carrying viruses to your computer
   c. A graphics file format that supports 10 million color variations
   d. A text-editing program included in Shockwave Player

MATCHING

a. JPEG
b. Flash
c. HTML tag
d. digital audio
e. file extension
f. Notepad
g. plug-in
h. GIF
i. multimedia
j. codec

1. Sounds that have been digitized
2. The same as an add-in; a peripheral program that you can use to enhance your browser's functionality
3. A code that gives instructions for formatting or actions—instructions used in laying out a Web page and setting up links
4. A graphics file format that supports 16 million colors and color variations
5. A text-editing program included in Windows
6. Developed by Macromedia, this add-in displays animations
7. The three digits following the period on a file's name, denoting the type of data the file uses
8. A technology used to encode and decode (or compress and decompress) data, especially audio and video
9. A graphics file format that supports only 256 colors
10. Using more than one medium at the same time

Real Life

1. Visit several of the Web sites mentioned in this chapter. If possible, download the plug-ins mentioned (such as Flash Player, Shockwave Player, QuickTime, and Acrobat Reader). Then run a few searches on topics in which you are interested and view the associated Web pages. Do any of them use plug-ins? If so, see if you can identify which one is used.

2. Internet Explorer includes plug-ins that are built right into the software. Go to Microsoft's Web site (*www.microsoft.com*) and find out which technologies are included in the browser. Develop a list of these technologies; then compare it with the previous versions of Internet Explorer.

I Spy: Privacy and Security Concerns

1. Any time you download programs from the Internet, you take a risk of introducing malicious code on your system. The risk is less when you're downloading software from the Web sites of reputable companies. Conduct some research on the Web to see whether there are any security problems associated with the plug-ins listed in this chapter. Write a short one-page report that details your findings.
2. Internet Explorer includes options that you can use to change its security levels. Spend a few minutes using the Help system in Internet Explorer to find out how to modify security settings. Next, go to a Web site (or several Web sites) that you know include multimedia content, such as Flash animations. Revisit the same sites using High and Medium security settings. *If your instructor allows*, visit the same sites using Low security settings. From your experience, what are the security issues associated with viewing active content on the Web? Develop a PowerPoint presentation or a short oral report that outlines your experience and research.

CHAPTER 16

BEYOND THE BASICS: TAKING ADVANTAGE OF THE INTERNET'S MULTIMEDIA CAPABILITIES

Key Terms

When you finish this chapter, you'll understand the following terms:

- buffer
- CD burner
- compression schemes
- Content Scrambling System (CSS)
- DeCSS
- downloadable media files
- encoder
- Helix DNA platform
- Helix Universal Server
- perceptual compression
- pull technology
- push technology
- static media
- streaming media
- technical compression
- Universal Serial Bus (USB)
- voiceovers
- Web cam
- Webcasting

Chapter Objectives

After you complete this chapter, you'll

- Understand Streaming Media
- Know About Some of the Technologies Used for Streaming Media
- Know About Webcasting and Web Cams

The Big Picture

In the early days of the Web, people were thrilled to view any kind of graphic in addition to text. However, this situation quickly changed as technologies were developed that used multimedia, including movies, music, and **voiceovers** (voice transmitted at the same time as music or video). Media were converted into digitized forms and compressed into smaller file sizes so that these types of files could be more easily shared online. After these technologies were developed, people were no longer content to just view text. They wanted more interesting Web sites—and they got them.

In the last chapter, you learned the essentials of how browsers handle various types of files, including multimedia. Now you're ready to dig much deeper. In this chapter, we'll cover cutting-edge topics, such as streaming media and associated technologies and trends. Next, we'll turn our attention to seeing how Web cams and Webcasting work. Sprinkled throughout the chapter, we'll mention a few of the copyright issues associated with using multimedia applications on the Web. So turn on your speakers (but not *too* loud!), and we'll take a spin through some of the current multimedia applications.

Window on the Web

As you learned in the previous chapter, there are many types of multimedia files that your browser can automatically download and display on your computer, such as videos, audio, and animations. Videos may include movie trailers (clips), news clips, and even made-for-Internet shows; audio files can include sounds, music, books on tape, speeches, and presentations. The plug-in programs installed on your system—either those built-in to your browser's technology or plug-ins you previously downloaded—determine which media items you can view. However, assuming that you have the browser and add-in programs in place to view any multimedia content you might encounter on the Web, the door is open to check out the multimedia files at sites such as the ones shown in Figure 16.1 and Figure 16.2.

Figure 16.1.
Some Web sites include more than one type of digital media.

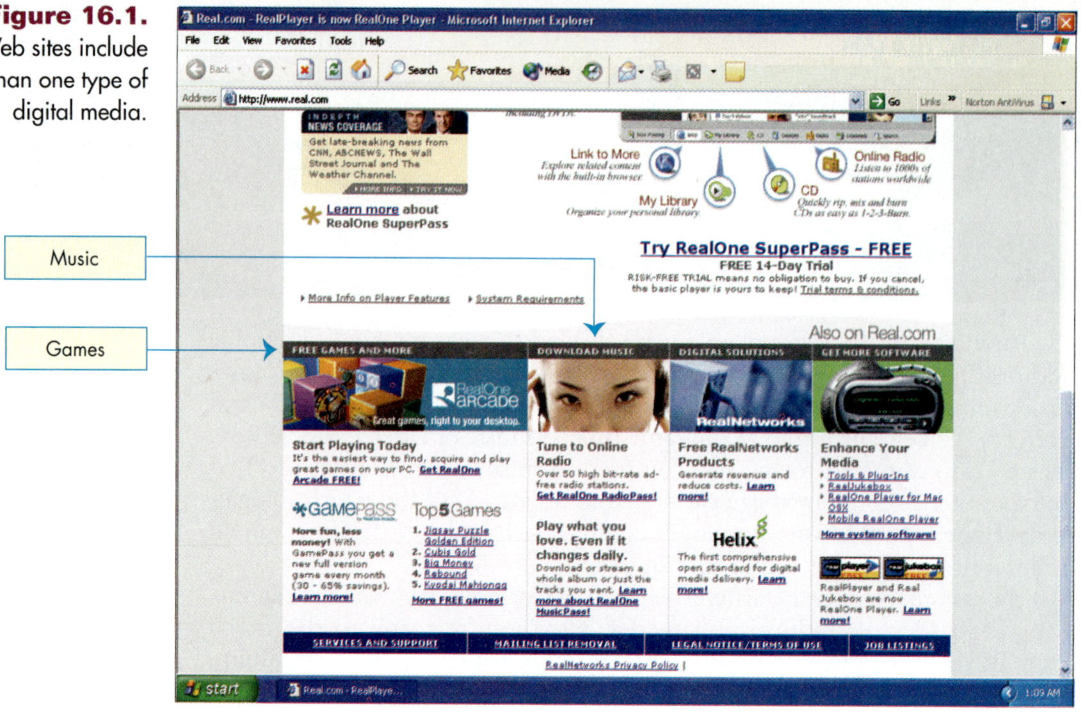

Figure 16.2.
Assuming that you have the connection speed, computer system, and plug-ins to do so, you can view a variety of audio and video files.

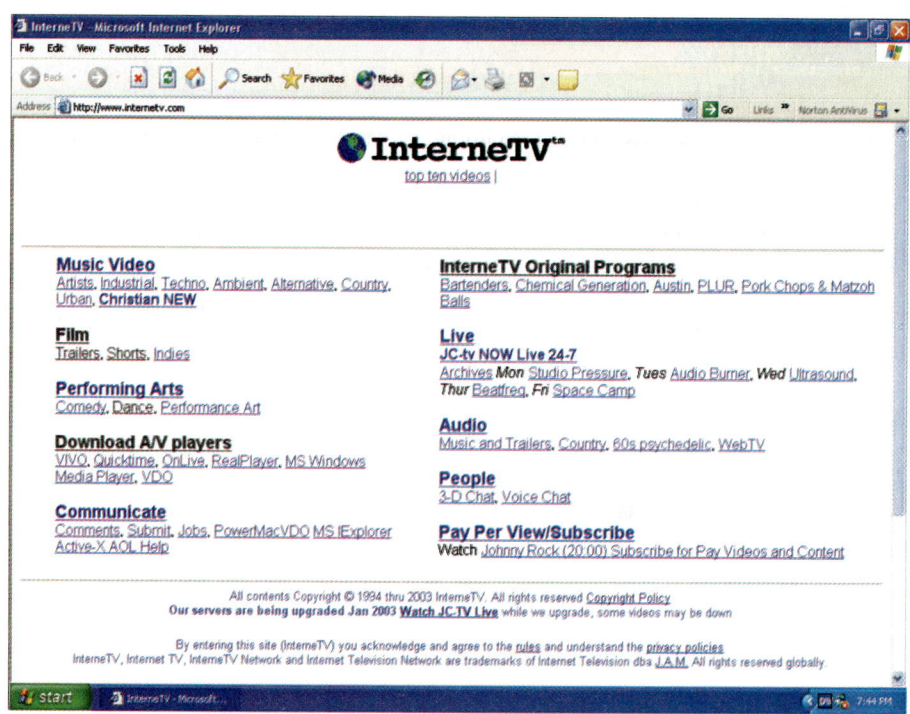

To work seamlessly with online media, several technologies need to be put in place in addition to plug-ins, such as the increased use of broadband and uniform methods of creating and delivering digital content. One of the main leaders in creating technology and content for online multimedia usage has been RealNetworks. This company's vision includes delivering television and radio-like programming on the Internet. They also developed the Helix Universal Platform, which they propose as a standard way of distributing media files over the Internet (see Figure 16.3). We'll talk more about this company and its developments and impact on multimedia later in this chapter.

Both Webcasting and Web cameras take advantage of streaming media to distribute their content over the Internet. A **Web cam** is a small digital camera that connects to your computer system and transfers what-

Figure 16.3.
RealNetworks, one of the leaders for delivering online digital media, has been developing a way to deliver digital media using virtually any system.

ever image is captured on the camera to the Internet. Web cams allow Internet users to interact face-to-face if a small digital video camera is connected to each user's system, and these systems are connected to the Internet. Another use for digital cams is to transmit and post updated, (almost) real-time photos from a particular location to the Internet. For example, resort sites can show real-time photos that depict the current weather conditions at a travel destination (see Figure 16.4).

Online multimedia relies on a variety of underlying technologies that are changing almost daily. In the midst of those changes, online digital media is rapidly gaining popularity. In this chapter, you'll see why.

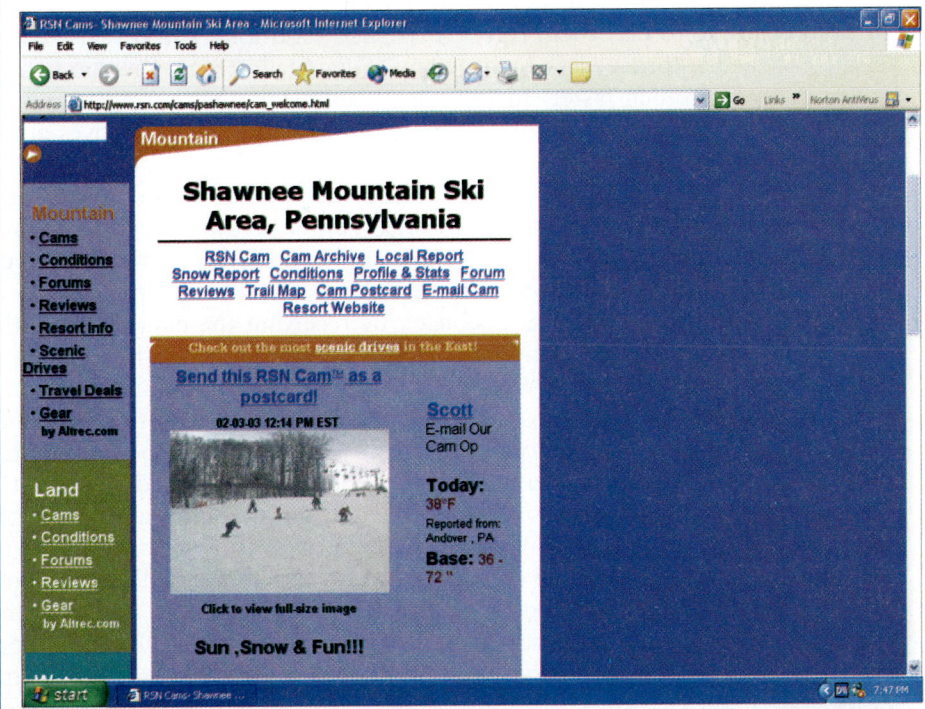

Figure 16.4.
Web cams can be used for promotional purposes, such as showing real-time photos for vacation destinations.

Window on the Web

UNDERSTAND STREAMING MEDIA

There are a number of technologies that are currently revolutionizing the way we view multimedia on the Web. One of the most interesting and compelling is *streaming media*, media that is sent in a continuous flow to your computer. Here's a brief synopsis of how it works:

Streaming media is a technique used to transfer media, especially audio and video, over a network in a way that the receiving computer can process it continually. Streaming media stands in direct opposition to downloadable media files. **Downloadable media (static media) files** are those that must be completely downloaded from the Internet before you can play them. For example, let's say that you want to use a sound effect (such as clapping) stored as a WAV file on a Web site. The file must be downloaded from the Internet to your computer in its entirety before it will begin to play. Until the streaming media technology was in place, this was the main way people shared audio and video files on the Internet. Downloading a small WAV file sound effect wasn't too time-consuming or resource-draining for most systems, but as media files grew and people demanded more online multimedia bells and whistles, downloading large media files wasn't practical. The sheer size of these files limited how many sounds and videos were transmitted because most people didn't want to spend hours downloading them.

Streaming media differs from static media because it plays data as it downloads it to your computer in a continuous flow. As soon as the first data arrives on your system, the application responsible for handling it can begin to use it without having to wait for the entire file to be downloaded.

You can think of the difference between static (downloadable) and streaming media this way: Imagine that you're waiting in a long line to register for classes at your college. To get into the room where you register, you must file, one at a time, through a narrow hallway. Furthermore, let's say that *no one* can register for any classes until *everyone* in the line has proceeded into the room. After everyone in the line has finally arrived in the designated location, you can then begin to register. Slow and somewhat frustrating, right? In the same way, downloading media files in their entirety from the Internet to your system before beginning to play them can be extremely laborious. But if registration at the college can proceed as each person individually enters the room, the entire process is much faster. In the same way, media that is transferred in small, manageable pieces (streamed) instead of as entire chunks arrives at its destination much more quickly.

Streaming makes working with online media files easier and faster. However, for streaming to work well, the computer that is receiving the data has to be able to collect it and then send it as a continuous flow to whatever program is processing the data and converting it to sound or videos. This system works best if the computer is constantly receiving the data at a slightly faster rate than the server is sending it, which allows it to hold the extra data momentarily in a buffer. The **buffer** is an area of memory used for temporarily holding data that's in transit from one device to another. The use of a buffer keeps one device or system from slowing down the other, especially if the devices operate at different speeds. In the case of streaming media, when it's ready for more data, the browser can pull data from the buffer and give it to the media application (such as Windows Media Player) to process.

Ideally, your system will be able to download streaming media at a steady rate, but this doesn't always happen. If the streaming data doesn't arrive from the Internet rapidly enough, the audio or video will appear jerky or even stop temporarily while waiting for more information to arrive. Because of this, the faster your Internet connection and the more computing power your system possesses, the better streaming media will work for you.

Not surprisingly, the rise of streaming media (and downloading media files in general) corresponds with the increased use of broadband. For example, a Jupiter Media Matrix/Jupiter Research survey in October 2002 indicated that 39% of broadband users in Europe use their high-speed connections to swap music files; only 18% of European dial-up users did so.

With the rise of streaming media, you might be thinking that there's not a place for *downloading* media files anymore. However, if a file is downloaded, you can save it permanently on your system. So even though downloading a media file is slow, the result can be worth the effort.

Now that you understand the difference between static and streaming media and the advantages of each, let's examine the technologies used for streaming media.

 In October 2002, the Jupiter Research survey warned the recording and music industry that they needed to offer viable alternatives to the illegal file-swapping services on the Internet soon or they would likely lose the opportunity to convince users to pay for legitimate online music-swapping services. What if the recording industry is *not* successful in doing this?

KNOW ABOUT SOME OF THE TECHNOLOGIES USED FOR STREAMING MEDIA

Streaming media has become a reality for the many computer users in the last few years because of the convergence of several technologies. The concurrent development of browser plug-ins, media servers that can handle any type of file, file-compression technologies, media players, and broadband all contributed to the rise of streaming media. Let's take a look at these technologies and see how they played a part in helping to create a more interactive and interesting multimedia world.

COMPRESSION SCHEMES (CODER/DECODERS)

In Chapter 15, Working with Various File Types and Plug-Ins, we introduced you to the concept of compression schemes. Called codecs (an acronym for COder/DECoder), these **compression schemes** decrease the size of media data to convert it into a more Internet-friendly package that could be readily transmitted online. Compression schemes do this by removing non-essential data from the digital files, such as colors a human eye can't see or sounds the human ear can't hear.

First, let's take a quick moment to differentiate between file formats and codecs. Codecs act on the file formats (such as an MPEG video clip) to compress and decompress the data. For the most part, each file format has a specific codec that works on it, although some codecs work well on multiple file types. Codecs are essential for transmitting video files because video is a ravenous disk storage eater; even a second of uncompressed digital video can require as much as 3.5MB of storage space. The exact process used by each codec varies, but the bottom line is essentially the same: They maintain overall quality while reducing file size to something workable.

Although it's beyond the focus of this book to delve too deeply into compression schemes, you should realize that there are many ways to "squeeze" a file into a smaller package without sacrificing quality—some technical and some perceptual. A **technical compression** technique might be used to eliminate unnecessary duplicate information. Digitized files represent their data by binary numbers: a series of *1s* and *0s*. If a file includes a long sequence of these, a technical compression scheme might be able to represent the same data with a single character.

On the other hand, **perceptual compression** eliminates audio and visual signals that humans can't normally detect, anyway. For example, some of the color nuances in a video can be eliminated and no one will be the wiser. Why? The human eye just can't pick up as many subtle variations as can a computer.

Another way videos are compressed is by eliminating duplicate frames. Videos are actually a series of frames, or still images, that are shown in rapid succession to create the illusion of movement. The number of frames per second (fps) shown dictates how smoothly a video clip plays. Eliminating frames (or duplicate information on the frames) has proved to be a good method of compressing video clips.

Video producers have a balancing act every time they edit clips: They can reduce the size of their files by eliminating some of the frames, but the motion will appear jerky if they chop out too many frames.

The best-known codec for video of all is MPEG, which achieves a high compression rate for video by storing only changes from one frame to another, instead of the entire frame. In Chapter 15, we mentioned that MPEG is the acronym for Moving Picture Experts Group, the internationally based group that defines standards for digital video. There are three main MPEG standards currently in use: MPEG-1 (used for video CDs), MPEG-2 (used for DVDs) and MPEG-4 (used for audio standards, including MP3).

Another well-known technology is DivX. The DivX technology is based on MPEG-4, but improves on it to make the compression even more efficient. If you want to find out more about this codec, you can visit DivX's Web site at *www.divx.com*.

If you're interested in the technology and products associated with codecs, take a look at some of the codecs currently on the market: Sorenson Media (*www.sorenson.com*), those at RealNetworks (*service.real.com/main.html*; see Figure 16.5), the H.261/H.263 codecs, and Compression Technologies, Inc., which produces the Cinepak codec (*www.cinepak.com*).

Codecs are used on audio files, such as MP3s, just as they are on video files—and for the same reasons. For example, codecs used for MP3s can elimi-

INSIDE TRACK

Producers of commercial DVDs originally prevented illegal copying of their disks by scrambling the information on them. To do this, they used a **Content Scrambling System (CSS)**, which is simply a method of encrypting the content. However, a **DeCSS**, which is a computer program capable of descrambling this content, was soon developed. Because it's now possible to use DeCSS to copy DVD videos without a loss of quality, groups such as the Motion Picture Association of America (MPAA) argue that the technology may lead to copyright infringements because people can use it to copy the movies.

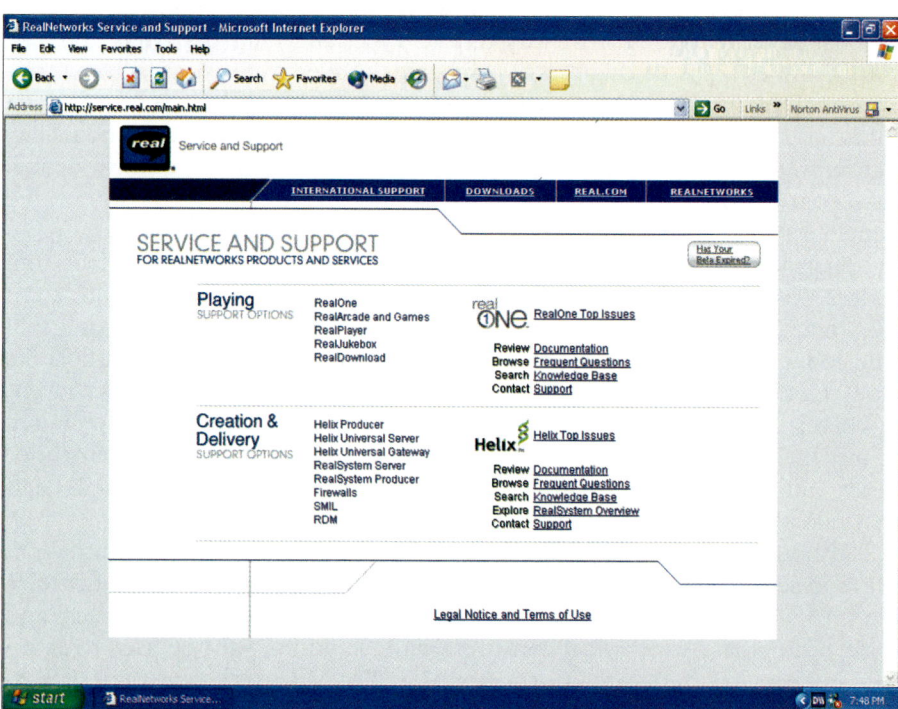

Figure 16.5.
You can find out more about RealNetworks service and products on their Web site.

nate sound waveforms on a recording outside of hearing range for most people, effectively reducing the file size enough for file swapping and other Internet transfers.

If you want to use a codec to get your video ready for Web use, you can. In fact, you can probably use a free or inexpensive codec to do so. For starters, try Ligo's Indeo codecs (*www.ligos.com*) and MPEG-4 (*mpeg4ip.sourceforge.net*). Furthermore, chances are good that the Windows operating system on your computer already includes a handful of basic codecs that you can use for video and audio. If you have Windows XP, Professional Version, you can view which codecs are already installed by performing the following steps:

1. Choose Start, Control Panel.
2. Click Sounds, Speech, and Audio Devices.
3. Next, click the Sounds and Audio Devices link.
4. In the Sounds and Audio Devices Properties dialog box, click the *Hardware* tab.
5. Click a device (such as Audio Codecs) and then choose Properties.
6. In the Audio Codecs Properties dialog box, click the Properties tab, and you can view a list of installed codecs for your system (see Figure 16.6).

 **INSIDE TRACK**

Most computer systems now come with CD burners. A **CD burner** is simply a drive that can copy ("burn") data or music to a CD that is capable of reading and writing (CD-RW). Because it's quite easy to reproduce data, the increased use of CD burners raises copyright issues.

MEDIA PLAYERS

If you want to view online media, your browser needs to know how to handle the file format the media uses. Some of the technologies necessary to work with the various file types are built into the browser (especially in Internet Explorer); others you need to download as special add-in programs. Here's a quick recap of how this works: Assuming that the correct plug-in is installed, when you click a media file link on a Web site, your browser quickly checks to see if you have the appropriate player or plug-in for that type of file. If so, the media is streamed to your computer. Streaming players read the data as it is coming in. This is long before the remainder of the file arrives—much as people might start to read ticker tape before the entire message is received.

In Chapter 15, you saw that you needed various plug-ins to use different file formats. For example, to work with multimedia file formats, you usually need a media player. Like the name implies, a player is responsible for playing video and audio files. The main media players on the market today are

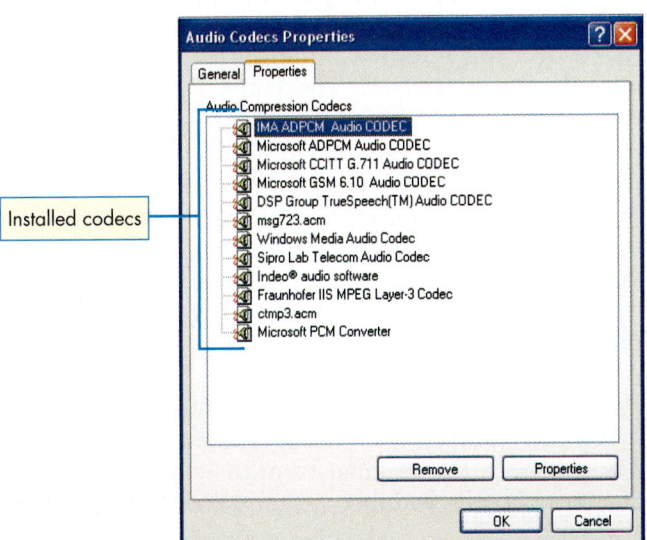

Figure 16.6.
You can check to see if you already have some codecs on your system.

RealNetwork's RealOne Player, Windows Media Player, and Apple's QuickTime Player. At this point, RealNetwork's RealOne Player can play any type of media file; Windows Media Player is more limited in the types of media files it can handle.

MEDIA ENCODERS

Most people begin working with online media by using a player to view or listen to it. Although media players are great if all you ever plan to do is view or listen to Web content (and there's nothing wrong with that!), you might eventually decide to create streaming multimedia yourself. For example, you might want to include a video as part of a personal Web site or for a product demonstration on a business Web site. If you work for the human resource department of a business, chances are good that you might also use streaming media to develop training videos to distribute over an intranet. To create streaming media, you'll need a special type of software that prepares your media files for Web use, called an encoder. An **encoder** is a special software tool that breaks a media file into smaller, readable packets that can be streamed to a player.

The encoding process usually includes four main parts. First, the performance is recorded and *captured*, which is simply sending it to a computer so that it can be edited. Editing can involve several processes, such as eliminating extra frames from a video clip or sounds from a music file that the human ear can't hear. This reduces the file size while still maintaining overall quality. Next, the edited file is encoded into a stream. Finally, the encoded file is uploaded to a Web server for distribution to the world.

Each of the main media players (such as RealOne Player and Windows Media Player) has a corresponding encoder: RealNetworks' Helix Producer Plus prepares files to be used by RealOne Player; Microsoft Windows Media Encoder is used to develop Windows Media Player files. As you might expect, the companies that create these encoding tools don't give them away as readily as they do the media players. For example, at the time this book was written, RealNetworks' Helix Producer Plus will set you back about $200.

STANDARDIZING THE DIGITAL MEDIA PLATFORM

RealNetworks has spearheaded the effort to standardize the way digital media are distributed and played on the Internet through its development of the Helix DNA platform, or system. Standardizing the development and distribution of digital media improves the speed and ease at which this media is transferred over the Internet. Additionally, users can then install a single plug-in instead of multiple ones. The **Helix DNA platform** is a set of technologies that can be used for developing, distributing, and playing digital media content. It consists of three parts: the Helix DNA client (to play digital media content), the Helix DNA encoder (to edit and encode the content), and the Helix DNA server (to distribute the content). The Helix client is universal, meaning that it will work with any type of media data on any computer system. In the same way, the Helix server (sometimes called the **Helix Universal Server**) can work with 11 different operating systems and a wide variety of platforms (see Figure 16.7).

One of the reasons that the Helix client and server are universal is because RealNetworks opened up its source code for these technologies and worked with other companies and independent developers to develop the platform. *Source code* is the original form in which a computer program is written. Sharing this code with people outside the company enables Helix to be devel-

INSIDE TRACK

According to the Helix Community's Web site (*www.helixcommunity.org*), Helix DNA was named after DNA (deoxyribonucleic acid); just as DNA controls the structure and purpose of each living cell, so Helix DNA code is the building block for standardized media created using Helix technologies.

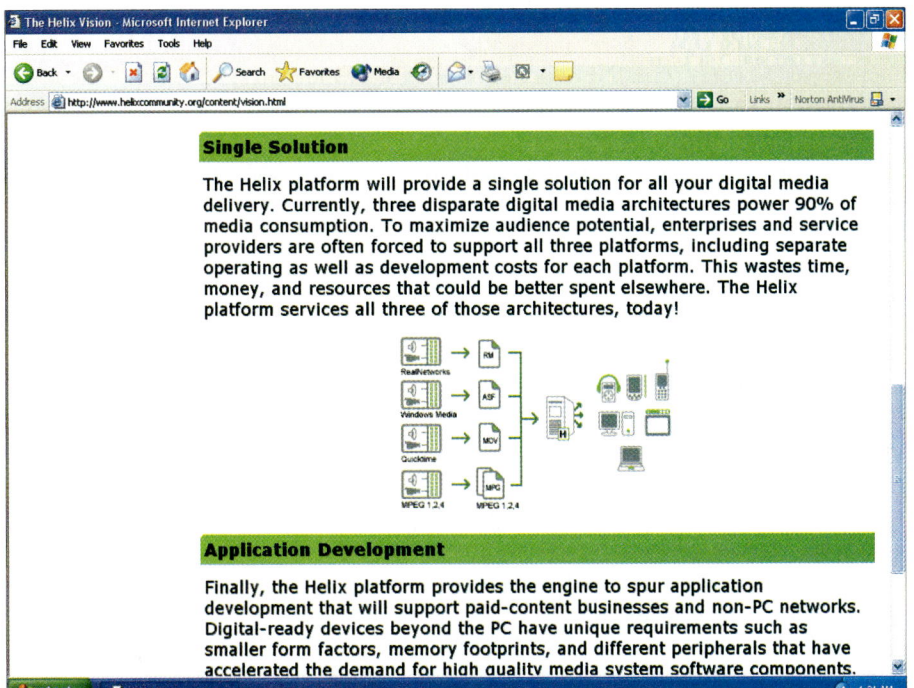

Figure 16.7.
The Helix Universal Server can handle any media file format.

oped so it can seamlessly distribute media content almost anywhere on the Internet. Distributing Helix's source code also helps RealNetworks compete with Microsoft, who is trying to make their proprietary Windows Media Player the de facto standard for digital media delivery.

What does RealNetworks hope to gain from all of this? Most likely, they are hoping to make a profit by charging for the actual content that can be viewed using these technologies. Additionally, RealNetworks is not giving away everything related to Helix: Organizations that want to use the Helix Universal Server will pay licensing fees.

As of early 2003, RealNetworks and Microsoft were gearing up for a battle over which company will eventually emerge as the leader for working with online digital media. According to statistics, streaming media using RealNetworks is offered on the majority of Web sites: approximately 54,000. (In contrast, media using Apple's QuickTime technology is on 16,500 sites, and Microsoft's Windows Media Player is used on 14,000.) In spite of these numbers, RealNetwork's dominance in this area might be changing. A Nielsen//NetRatings survey indicated that the Windows Media Player audience grew at a rate of 21% during a six-month period in 2000, whereas the RealNetwork user base increased only 2%. The rollout of the Helix platform and opening of its source code in late 2002 by RealNetworks and the almost simultaneous release of Windows Media Player, version 9, are sure to make this battle of the titans interesting.

KNOW ABOUT WEBCASTING AND WEB CAMS

So, what's in store for streaming media? With things on the Internet changing almost daily, it's hard to say. But some trends are emerging, such as requiring users to pay for online video and audio content, Webcasting, and an increase in sophisticated multimedia technologies. In this next section, we'll specifically focus on the use of Webcasting and Web cameras for delivering media over the Internet.

WEBCASTING

As you just learned, RealNetworks has been a pioneer in distributing the technology and content for online digital media. They've also been at the forefront of Webcasting. **Webcasting** is an Internet technology that some Web sites use to broadcast information, such as radio or video programming. Webcasting is similar to television broadcasting, except that it uses the Web to stream the media content to the viewers. The idea behind Webcasting is for the sponsoring business to develop unique content for its Web site (such as news or sports videos) and then charge users a monthly fee to access it.

For example, RealNetworks lets Internet users download their Helix-based RealOne Player at no charge, but then requires Internet users to subscribe and pay a monthly fee to access most of the video and audio data on their site. Because RealNetwork's content offerings include programming that was traditionally in the realm of television, such as sports, savvy Web users are watching the content via the Internet instead of over the airwaves. Even if you don't sign up for the service, you can use the RealOne Player to view content from any other Web site that includes digital media. Although it is still in its infancy, Webcasting will most likely become mainstream as more sophisticated technologies are put in place.

INSIDE TRACK

Webcasting relies on push technology to transfer information. **Push technology** is when a server sends information to a client without the client requesting it. E-mail is an example of push technology; you receive messages when the sender "pushes" them to you. Browsing on the Web is a **pull technology** because the client browser has to request a Web page before the server will send it.

ON THE HORIZON

According to a study by Pew Internet Research, those using broadband tend to do more (and more sophisticated) online activities per day than do dial-up users. The same research indicates that broadband users spend more time interacting with multimedia content online, and simultaneously watch television less. In fact, 37% reported that they watch television less since they started using broadband. Because there is a strong movement toward using broadband connections, all of this adds up to good news for developers of streaming media applications.

WEB CAMERAS

Web cameras (Web cams) are gaining popularity because they allow people to transmit real-time pictures and short films over the Internet. A Web cam is a small digital camera that connects to the users' computer so that the pictures can be posted to the Web. For the most part, people use Web cams to take real-time pictures of the area or people in the vicinity of the computer.

USES FOR WEB CAMERAS. Web cameras can be used for surveillance, videoconferencing, Webcasting, or creating a Web cam site. A Web cam site involves focusing a camera on an object or scene and then uploading images at regular intervals to the Web site. Some typical Web cam sites are those that show tourist sites, zoos, dorm rooms, city streets, offices, childcare centers, college campuses, and so on (see Figure 16.8).

Web cams can also be used in conjunction with instant messaging, videoconferencing, and chat so that the participants can view each other while they talk. They can also be used for security purposes, such as to monitor activity at a construction site or in an office.

THE CAMERA'S HARDWARE. A Web camera, which is a fairly basic peripheral, includes a lens, circuit board, software, and cable to connect the entire thing to a computer, although some have a few more bells and whistles. Formerly, Web cams used the main computer's memory and power. However,

Figure 16.8.
Web cams can be used to see regularly updated images.

newer models have their own internal memory and rely on batteries for power so that they can also be used as a standalone digital camera.

Originally, Web cams were connected to the PC by using the parallel or serial port, which resulted in a poky data transfer. Today's Web cams instead use a **Universal Serial Bus (USB)** connection because this port comes standard on most systems.

Digital cameras for Internet use vary greatly in price. An inexpensive Web cam that you purchase to show your parents your newest hairstyle (or perhaps how many pizza containers are laying around your dorm room) will probably cost well under $75. Logitech manufactures a popular line of Web cams called QuickCams. Like most Web cams, these cameras look a little bit like space aliens (see Figure 16.9).

In contrast, an Internet all-weather digital camera that is capable of being connected to a network and producing streaming video will cost $1,500 or more (see Figure 16.10). This type of camera is typically used for surveillance and security.

INSIDE TRACK

The Web camera has an interesting (and practical) origin. In 1991, the University of Cambridge Computer Lab had a single coffeepot (money was tight) that was shared by several people. It was located in the "Trojan Room," which was located some distance from the lab. Rather than discovering that the coffeepot was empty after a long walk to get coffee, the researchers came up with a solution: They pointed a camera at the pot and then connected it to a computer. Being clever, they wrote a program that grabbed and transmitted images of the pot three times a minute to the laboratory. From this humble beginning, the Web cam was born. (This coffeepot, by the way, was sold on eBay in 2001 for $4,780 to a German magazine. You can still view the famous machine online in its new home at *www.spiegel.de/static/popup/coffeecam/cam2.html*.)

Figure 16.9.
Web cameras are simple but useful peripherals.

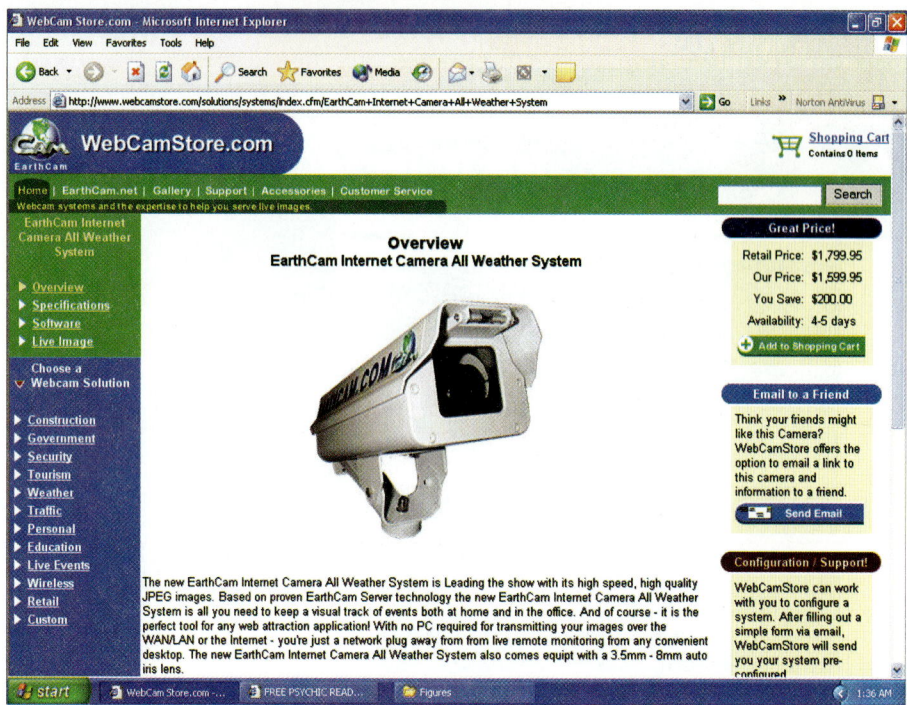

Figure 16.10.
Web cameras vary in power and price.

 What are the privacy implications of using Web cameras in the workplace? At a school? In a daycare facility? In public locations?

The technology associated with Web cams, like other forms of digital media that is transmitted via the Internet, is constantly changing. In the near future, you can expect better transmission rates at lower prices. Also, as more people use broadband, the quality of the images transmitted should improve. Finally, the continued drop in price for Web cams, coupled with the capability to quickly connect to home computer systems via a USB port, are expected to help Web cameras become standard equipment for most people.

Don't Forget...

- Digital media and associated technologies continue to grow at a rapid pace in popularity and sophistication.
- Streaming media differs from static (downloadable) media in significant ways, including the speed at which it is transferred over the Internet.
- The online media that you can view depends on your browser and the plug-ins available on your system.
- Various compression schemes (codecs) and technologies are currently being used. These enable streaming video and audio files to be shared via the Internet.
- Led by RealNetworks, there is a movement toward using a universal standard for viewing and listening to digital media, represented by the Helix DNA platform.

- Media players typically have a corresponding encoding tool used to prepare files for Internet use.
- The trend toward using broadband connections is predicted to impact the use of online digital media.
- Some Web sites are now charging subscription fees if you want to view their media content.
- Webcasting is an Internet technology that some Web sites use to broadcast information, such as radio or video programming.
- There are a number of uses for Web cameras, including surveillance, communication, and publicity.

Check This Out

MULTIPLE CHOICE

1. Which of the following companies has been considered the leader in digital media?
   a. EarthLink
   b. MP3.com
   c. RealNetworks
   d. Open Source, Inc.

2. For which of the following could you use a Web camera?
   a. Giving a short speech to classmates from the comfort of your room
   b. Showing your mother your new puppy
   c. Posting pictures of the weather outside your room so that your friend in another town can see them
   d. All of the above

3. What is the main difference between streaming and static media?
   a. Static media uses CSS; streaming media uses DivX.
   b. Static media uses technical compression; streaming media does not.
   c. Static media uses push technology; streaming media uses pull technology.
   d. Static media is fully downloaded before it plays; streaming media begins to play as soon as part of the data arrives on the client computer.

4. Which of the following technologies is probably the *least* worrisome to the president of a movie studio?
   a. CD burner
   b. DeCSS
   c. Broadband
   d. DivX

5. Which of the following technological advances were necessary for streaming media to become viable for the average Internet user?
   a. Compression schemes to reduce audio and video file size
   b. Narrowband Internet connections
   c. Virus-checking software
   d. All of the above

MATCHING

a. technical compression
b. buffer
c. open source
d. perceptual compression
e. push technology
f. burner
g. compression scheme
h. encoder
i. Web camera
j. streaming

1. When a server sends information to a client without the client requesting it
2. Making a media file smaller by leaving out sounds that aren't audible to the human ear
3. A drive and software that can copy data to a CD-RW
4. Using various compression techniques to convert a file to an Internet-friendly size
5. A software tool that can break a media file into smaller readable packets so they can be streamed to a player
6. A technique used to transfer media over a network so that the client can continually process it
7. Sharing programming code with developers
8. A digital device you can use in videoconferencing or for surveillance
9. Eliminating duplicate information in a media file
10. An area of memory used for temporarily holding data that is being transferred from one device to another; typically used when the devices process data at different rates

Real Life

1. The Digital Millennium Copyright Act (DMCA) became law in 1998. This act has implications for distributing and reproducing copyrighted material on the Internet, including music and video files.

    Use your Internet search skills to find out the provisions of this act. Also, conduct research (and personal interviews, if time allows) to outline and substantiate the views of the typical Internet user and the recording/publishing industries regarding the DMCA. Make sure that you can define and defend each side's views on the issues surrounding this act.

    Finally, discuss the topic as a small group in your class and/or write an analytical paper on the topic. Alternatively, present an oral report to your class about the DMCA.

2. If possible, download and use RealNetworks' RealOne Player, Apple's QuickTime, and Microsoft's Windows Media Player to display streaming media. After spending a few minutes getting used to how each player operates, play the content from three different Web sites in each player. Develop a chart that shows the similarities and differences between the players. If time allows, conduct a short survey of your classmates to find out which player they prefer and why.

3. Visit the Web sites for RealNetworks (*www.real.com*) and the Helix Community (*www.helixcommunity.org*). Research the concept of open sourcing. Develop a report that details the pros and cons of open source for the company who owns the code, for competing companies, and for the larger Internet community. From your findings, why do you think RealNetworks decided to share its source code via the Helix platform? How might this decision affect its efforts to keep its market share in the digital media arena and keep Microsoft at bay?

I Spy: Privacy and Security Concerns

1. Discuss the privacy concerns associated with the use of Web cams. For example, should people know that cameras are being used in their workplace, in a public location, or at a school? Why or why not? (Hint: To help with your research, visit the KinderCam Web site at *www.kindercam.com*.)

2. Visit several Web cam sites that show city street scenes or public places. Discuss the implications of using this type of technology in these locations.

SECTION SEVEN: PRIVACY AND SECURITY ISSUES

CHAPTER 17: BEYOND THE BASICS: A CLOSER LOOK AT PRIVACY ISSUES

Chapter Objectives

After you complete this chapter, you'll

- Understand How Lack of Privacy Can Lead to More Control by Others
- Understand Data Snooping and How Others Can Track Your Activities
- Know About Government Surveillance and Control Issues
- Understand Privacy Issues in the Workplace
- Understand Children's Online Privacy Rights
- Understand Privacy Issues Related to Biometrics
- Implement the Best Practices for Protecting Your Privacy

Key Terms

When you finish this chapter, you'll understand the following terms:

- best practices
- biometrics
- Carnivore Diagnostic Tool (Carnivore)
- Children's Online Privacy Protection Act (COPPA)
- computer monitoring software
- cyberslacking
- cybersurveillance
- data snoops
- Echelon
- Employee Internet Management (EIM)
- facial recognition technology
- hostile work environment
- Freedom of Information Act (FOIA)
- keylogger program
- Magic Lantern
- sniffer
- universal view software
- workplace surveillance

The Big Picture

Keylogger programs. Spyware. Carnivore. Surveillance. Iris scanners.

It sounds mysteriously like something from a James Bond spy movie, doesn't it? But in fact, this is the Internet world of the 21st century. Information about yourself might not be as private as you think—at least if you live like most Americans, and not on a desert island. In fact, the more you use your computer or tap into newer technologies such as broadband, the greater your exposure to breaches in privacy and security.

In the early chapters of this book, we introduced you to some of the privacy issues swirling around the Internet. And because these issues affect just about anything you might do with the Internet, we interspersed privacy and security concerns throughout the subsequent chapters.

At this point, you have a solid foundation in understanding how the Internet works, how it's used in a myriad of ways, and some of the cutting-edge technologies that are emerging. You should also have a heightened awareness of privacy and security issues. Because you're turning into a knowledgeable Internet user (some might even say a *guru*), you're poised to understand these complicated issues at a more advanced level. In this chapter and the next, you'll get your chance.

Window on the Web

Lately, it seems everyone is concerned about privacy. There's substantial evidence to prove that privacy concerns are growing almost as rapidly as the Internet itself! In fact, a simple Internet search on the words `Internet privacy` will probably yield a host of Web sites devoted to the topic. One of the best is the Electronic Privacy Information Center's Web site at *www.epic.org* (see Figure 17.1).

Figure 17.1.
Concerned about your online privacy? Privacy advocates can help you find out more about topics ranging from workplace surveillance to biometrics.

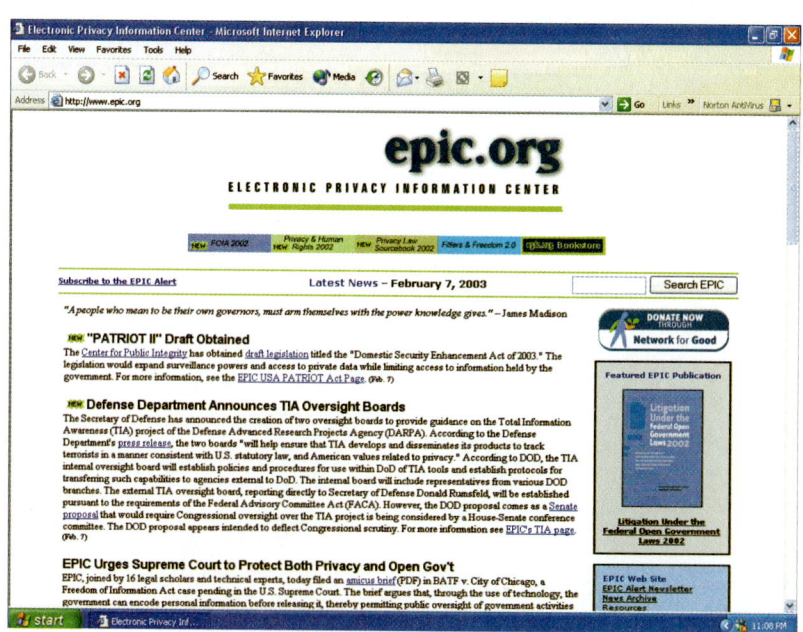

260 Chapter 17 Beyond the Basics: A Closer Look at Privacy Issues

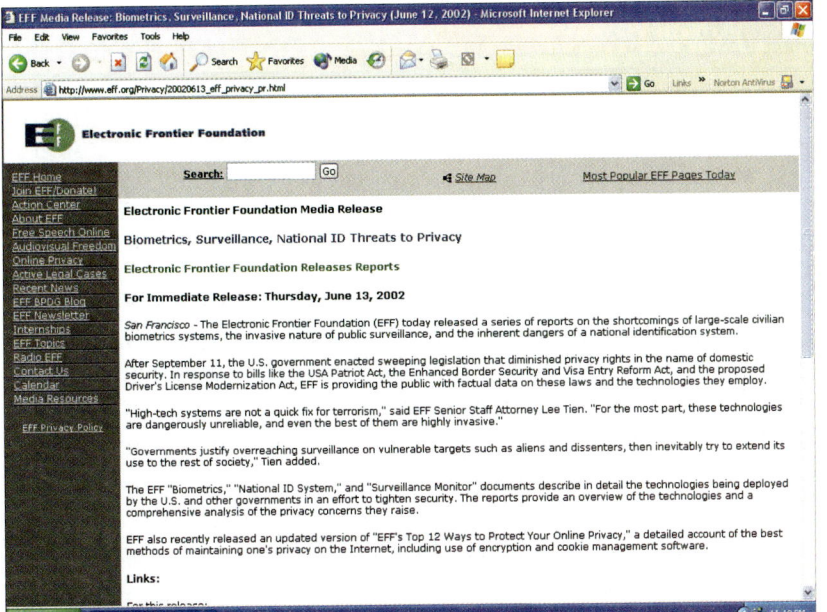

Figure 17.2.
Watchdog organizations can provide helpful information about protecting your privacy.

Another site that includes helpful information, including current news and a list of ways to protect your privacy, is the Electronic Frontier Foundation. This site's privacy pages begin at *www.eff.org/Privacy/20020613_eff_privacy_pr.html* (see Figure 17.2).

If you're concerned about privacy, you're not alone. Not only are private citizens becoming increasingly uneasy about the lack of online privacy, but responsible companies are also putting policies and practices into place to build trust. One place you can find out more about privacy policies is on the Online Privacy Alliance's Web site at *www.privacyalliance.org* (see Figure 17.3).

We'll focus on privacy issues in this chapter and scrutinize security problems in the next. There will be some overlap between the two—for example, a virus might install a spyware program on your computer (which compromises security) to find out which Web sites you're visiting (an encroachment on privacy) or to completely trash your system (another security breach). Either way—if the practice infringes on your privacy or disrupts security—you'll want to be aware of these issues and determine the best ways to prevent problems.

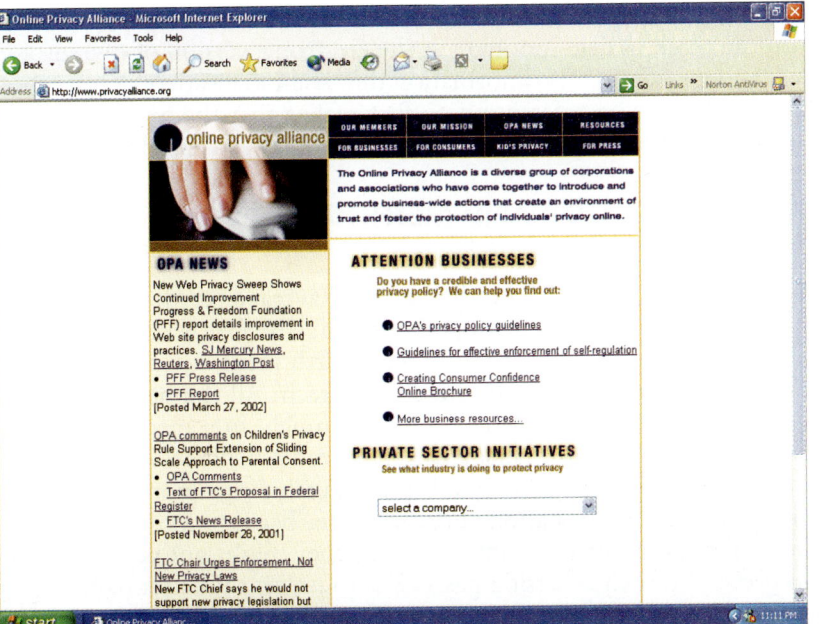

Figure 17.3.
Some organizations are taking strides toward respecting and protecting people's privacy.

Window on the Web

UNDERSTAND HOW LACK OF PRIVACY CAN LEAD TO MORE CONTROL BY OTHERS

In George Orwell's famous classic, *1984*, the government ("Big Brother") controlled every aspect of the lives of the main characters: Winston and Julia. One way it did this was by using technology to constantly track people's movements. The gross infringements on personal privacy resulted in extreme control by "Big Brother." In this case, knowledge (of information about a person) *was* power.

Unfortunately, the same relationship (between knowing personal information about a person and then leveraging the knowledge against them) has the potential to take place today. If a Web company knows intimate details about your marketing preferences, it can control (or attempt to control) your purchasing habits. If an unscrupulous person hacks your credit card number, that person can control your finances. If the government knows personal information about you, it has leverage in controlling you as well.

Although infringements on personal privacy aren't exactly new, the ease with which the Internet can be used to track a person's movement and gather information about him or her makes it more commonplace than ever. Additionally, the open and freewheeling atmosphere associated with the Internet has led many people to be less-than-cautious about the information they're willing to share.

But things are changing. As awareness of the problems with privacy surface, people are becoming more proactive in protecting their privacy. If you, like others, are increasingly uneasy about these infringements, you can take specific measures to protect yourself.

Your first step is to understand how data snoops operate and what information others can find out about you. In the next section, we'll examine the methods and issues related to how (and why) they do it.

UNDERSTAND DATA SNOOPING AND HOW OTHERS CAN TRACK YOUR ACTIVITIES

Data snoops are people who try to use technology to gain access to personal information so that they can use it for their own gain. For example, an identity thief would snoop to learn your credit card and bank account numbers. In fact, you can think of data snooping as the electronic version of eavesdropping.

Snoops can find the information they want in a variety of ways, both illegal and legal. Your best defense is to first realize that the practice is taking place and then put some measures in place to protect yourself. Let's see how.

THE TECHNOLOGY AND METHODS USED FOR DATA SNOOPING

There are three main methods that your average, garden-variety data snoop can use to find out information about you. The first is direct access, a process so ordinary that it doesn't even seem worth mentioning—except that it's so common. Direct access is decidedly low-tech: All the person has to do is sit down at your computer when you're at lunch, in a meeting, or attending a class. The unscrupulous person can then read e-mail messages or take a look at other information stored on your system, including reports, papers, and financial or medical information. Furthermore, because most people don't even take this type of intrusion into account, they might not put measures in place to prevent it, such as setting passwords to prevent unauthorized access.

The second way that intruders can find out information about you is by tracking your online activity. This is usually done with the help of computer monitoring software. **Computer monitoring software** can track your actions, including your Web browsing history, your e-mail messages, and your keystrokes. This information can then be consolidated into a report that's sent (without your knowledge) to the person who installed the computer monitoring software in the first place. Computer monitoring software is usually unobtrusive, and isn't always detected by virus scanning software. Because of this, it can potentially operate in the background for a long time without your knowledge, quietly collecting and transmitting personal information.

Computer surveillance software includes spyware, adware, and keylogger programs. Each of these programs works like an electronic spy that resides on your computer. Spyware is software that's designed to operate quietly in the background, eavesdropping on the actions and activities you perform on the computer. This information can be transmitted back to whoever was responsible for installing the spyware—such as your employer, a Web site, or a marketing company. Adware is software that specifically tracks your online usage and sends the information back to the marketing company, who then channels appropriate advertisements to you. A **keylogger program** is specialized software that records each key pressed on a computer; then sends the information back to the person who installed the program. This can yield valuable information for the hacker, such as credit card numbers, company reports, trade secrets, or financial data.

Imagine, for example, that you download a free software utility that helps you organize your MP3 files. Unbeknownst to you, the person who distributed the software packaged a hidden keylogger program with the utility, which was automatically installed at the same time. The next day, you decide to order some books online, using your credit card to do so. The keylogger program records all your keystrokes and sends the information back to the person.

A Web bug is an electronic surveillance tag that can be as small as one pixel by one pixel. Web bugs are usually disguised as invisible (transparent) GIF files on a Web page that can be used to track your movements or report information, such as the IP addresses of the people who view the site.

Another way that your online movements can be tracked is through the use of sniffers. A **sniffer** is a software or hardware tool that monitors data packets on a network. (Packet sniffers, by the way, refer to sniffers that operate on networks that use the TCP/IP protocol.) Sniffers are often used for legitimate reasons; in fact, companies use sniffers to make sure that messages are being processed correctly and everything is working on the system. In these cases, sniffers are helpful—they're used to monitor and fix network problems. However, crackers (*cr*iminal h*ackers*) can monitor and track legitimate sniffers so the crackers can steal information from a network. These sniffers can expose information on your network, including Plain Text passwords. The most straightforward way to deal with this vulnerability is to use encryption software to scramble (encrypt) all the data sent or received by the network.

The last method of tracking online movements that we mention here is the use of cookies. A cookie, as you probably recall from Chapter 2, The Good, the Bad, the Ugly: Uses and Misuses of the Internet, is a small file placed on your computer by a Web site when you visit it. The file includes information used to track passwords, the pages you've viewed, items placed in your online shopping cart, and so on. Although some cookies are used to make subsequent visits to a Web page more convenient, many cookies are employed to track your online surfing habits, compile them into a profile, and then market products or target the ads you see accordingly.

INSIDE TRACK

There's another type of computer monitoring software that is being used to track the computer activities of employees. We'll discuss this type of tracking tool later in the chapter.

INSIDE TRACK

BugBear, which was malicious code distributed widely on the Internet beginning in late September 2002, included a keylogger program that could transmit information back to the cracker.

INSIDE TRACK

Remote access tools and software allow you to tap into a computer from a remote location. For example, you might use remote access to log on to your work computer or server from home. Although remote access can be extremely useful, it's critical that you use passwords, firewalls, and other defensive measures to protect the privacy and security of your information and system.

THE DATA SNOOPS

So, who are these people who take such an interest in your life and electronic movements? Some might be people you actually know, but who have a stake in tracking you. For example, your boss might be interested in knowing whether you're stashing resumes on your hard drive or sending them out via company e-mail. An employer might also want to confirm that you're not involved in any actions that will trigger a harassment lawsuit and aren't wasting work time surfing the Web. If you're a good student, others at school might be interested in tapping into your computer to get their hands on your latest term paper. Parents might want to track which sites their children are viewing or the content of their e-mail messages.

The government also feels that it has a vested interest in following the online movements of suspected criminals in the name of national defense. Due to the Patriot Act, which passed Congress in October 2001 (and the general mindset in America since September 11, 2001), most citizens seem to be more tolerant of this type of monitoring than in the past. People still have misgivings, however, and watchdog privacy groups are quite vocal in stating their concerns about the practice of government surveillance.

ALERT!
Wireless networks (those that transmit data over public airwaves) are becoming increasingly cost-effective, so they are gaining in popularity. However, if you use one of these networks, make sure that you put strict security measures in place—or your private information might not stay private.

Companies are also interested in tracking your movements or accessing data so that they can determine your buying patterns and market the products or services to you that you are most likely to purchase. Although this type of monitoring is not malicious in nature, many people don't like the idea of their online activities being watched.

Another category of people who might potentially want to spy on your data or activities are crackers, who are people who steal or use private information with malicious intent. They might want to steal your identity, credit card number, or other personal information; vandalize your data; embarrass you by sending personal messages to everyone in your e-mail address book; or use your system to launch attacks against other computer systems—and that's just for starters.

To protect your privacy from these individuals, follow the "Best Practices" checklist toward the end of the chapter.

KNOW ABOUT GOVERNMENT SURVEILLANCE AND CONTROL ISSUES

Even in the days of the Revolutionary War (and before), the government relied on spies to find out information about people they wanted to track. But with the advent of the Internet, government surveillance has become increasingly high-tech. There is even a new term associated with this type of electronic monitoring: **cybersurveillance**. In this section, we'll discuss some of the ways that the United States government can track people on the Internet and the issues related to this practice. Along the way, we'll point you to some helpful Web sites in which you can find out more information.

CARNIVORE

Carnivore—even the name sounds mysterious. We introduced you to this surveillance tool in Chapter 1, How the Internet is Changing the World; now you're ready to learn more details about it. The full name is **Carnivore Diagnostic Tool** ("Carnivore"), a software surveillance system developed by the FBI that allows government agents to intercept and collect data transmitted over the Internet or another network. No one really knows *exactly* how it works (except for the FBI agents who developed it). The FBI defends this secrecy, maintaining that the technology used for Carnivore and its exact implementation must be kept secret so that terrorists and criminals can't come up with methods of blocking it.

Although Carnivore's exact technology is shrouded in secrecy, the basic concept behind it is straightforward: The system filters Internet data transmissions (such as e-mail messages) and pulls out only those that match predefined criteria. For example, the system can be used to collect messages to a known terrorist or those containing certain topical words. Figure 17.4 shows the FBI's illustration of how the Carnivore program works.

Although many people are concerned about the idea of using Carnivore to watch online transmissions, the FBI maintains that only messages that meet criteria indicated in a lawful warrant are gathered; the rest of the messages that pass through a network are ignored. The FBI also has guidelines for the type of search warrant that can be issued. For example, the search warrant—for specific criminal activities—must be authorized by a high-level Department of Justice official. The FBI further defends the practice of electronic surveillance because of its role in helping to put criminals behind bars: According to the FBI's Web site (*www.fbi.gov/hq/lab/carnivore/carnivore2.htm*), "Electronic surveillance has been extremely effective in securing the conviction of more than 25,600 dangerous felons over the past 13 years."

Of growing concern to privacy advocates is the fact that the government may use surveillance increasingly since the terrorist attacks on September 11, 2001. For example, the powers given to the FBI for electronic surveillance were expanded through new guidelines issued by Attorney General John Ashcroft in May, 2002.

The secrecy surrounding Carnivore makes it both interesting and unsettling for many people, especially privacy advocates. Groups such as the Center for Democracy & Technology (*www.cdt.org*) and the Electronic Privacy Information Center (*www.epic.org*) have been especially outspoken about Carnivore. If you want to find out more about the viewpoints put forth by these organizations, you can visit their Web sites.

Although privacy groups have been the most vocal about Carnivore's secrecy, some Internet Service Providers (ISPs) are unhappy with Carnivore as well. Here's why: The government has required ISPs to install the software on their systems and then prevents the ISPs from sharing this information. This worries ISPs, which don't like the government to force them to install an unknown or untested technology on their sophisticated systems. In fact, EarthLink, one of the largest ISPs in the nation, took the matter to court in an effort to avoid installing the surveillance device because the Carnivore tool didn't work with part of EarthLink's system in Pasadena, California—causing

INSIDE TRACK

A report published in October, 2002 by the Pew Internet Project (*www.pewinternet.org*) showed that approximately half of all Americans (45%) think the government should be able to monitor people's e-mail and Web activities; slightly more (47%) opposed such surveillance. However, a majority of *Internet* users opposed government monitoring. (Source: Pew Internet Project)

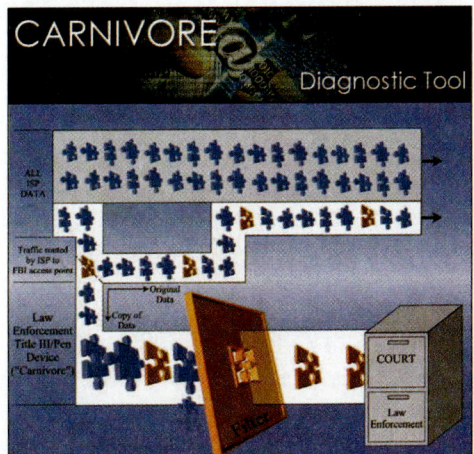

Figure 17.4.
Carnivore helps the FBI catch the bad guys by intercepting data.

some of the ISP's servers to crash. EarthLink also voiced concerns over the possible intrusion of their users' privacy by Carnivore. EarthLink and the government eventually reached an agreement in which the ISP would supply the documents requested by the government authorities, but didn't have to install the software on their systems. You can view a list of which ISPs are "Carnivore-free" (and which probably are not) as well as further information on Carnivore at the StopCarnivore Web site (*www.stopcarnivore.org*).

MAGIC LANTERN

Magic Lantern, another FBI electronic surveillance project, is even more mysterious than Carnivore. Because the program is (apparently) still under development, the FBI won't say much about it. However, it appears that Magic Lantern is similar to a keylogger program and is installed on the suspected criminal's computer via a worm or Trojan horse that's e-mailed to the person or physically installed by an agent or by using common hacker techniques to break in to the system via the Internet. The theory is that Magic Lantern can be used to read encrypted e-mail and documents.

You're probably thinking that a good, up-to-date antivirus software program should stop Magic Lantern in its tracks—and you're right. To work around this "problem" the government has reportedly tried to persuade antivirus companies (such as McAfee) to create virus definitions that will ignore Magic Lantern. Whether or not this will actually happen is anyone's guess.

INSIDE TRACK

Echelon is yet another government-maintained electronic surveillance system. The system, which was reportedly developed several decades ago, was designed to monitor international communications. It's also effective at eavesdropping on cellular phone conversations, satellite transmissions, and radio signals. Because it monitors *international* communications, privacy advocates seem less disturbed by Echelon than they do by Carnivore and Magic Lantern.

Privacy advocates are less concerned about Magic Lantern than they are about Carnivore because Magic Lantern is much more selective about the information it gathers. Instead of filtering everyone's messages, Magic Lantern targets a specific identified individual.

If you want to find out more about Magic Lantern, don't look on the FBI's Web site. You won't find any information. However, conducting an Internet search on `magic lantern fbi` should yield a few matches.

There are other government electronic surveillance projects about which almost nothing is known. These projects have names such as *Cyber Knight* (which includes Magic Lantern) and *Dragon Net*. The **Freedom of Information Act (FOIA)** was used by the Electronic Privacy Information Center (EPIC) to reveal some of the data about these projects to the public. You can find out more about these surveillance projects and the FOIA on the Electronic Privacy Information Center's Web site (*www.epic.org/privacy/carnivore*).

OTHER GOVERNMENT DATA SNOOPING TECHNIQUES

Although Carnivore and Magic Lantern attract interest and concern, you might not be aware that the government tracks some of your other online activities as well. Technically, these tracking procedures are not data snooping, but they can represent an infringement on your privacy nevertheless.

For example, some government agencies, such as the FBI, the Department of Labor, and the Department of Health and Human Services, collect information about you each time you visit their sites. They track information, including how long you visit the site, your ISP, and which pages you viewed. Additionally, they sometimes use cookies so that they can determine how often you visit the site. Although the government doesn't share this information with businesses, it's still collected. This mirrors the practice of many businesses that track how often you visit their sites.

266 Chapter 17 Beyond the Basics: A Closer Look at Privacy Issues

The government is also interested in your financial transactions and can track them using computer technology called FinCEN (Financial Crimes Enforcement Network). This database was set up in 1990 under the United States Department of the Treasury. Each time you make a sizable transaction (usually more than $10,000), it is registered in a computerized log. The government then checks this against your other financial data to determine if it's consistent with legal or illegal activity. Such tracking causes additional concerns for privacy groups. (If you're interested in finding out more about this practice, run an Internet search on `FinCEN`.)

UNDERSTAND PRIVACY ISSUES IN THE WORKPLACE

Using the Internet to check personal e-mail, look at the news or weather, play games, download MP3s, or conduct other non-work related activities is an everyday occurrence for many. This practice, which is known as **cyberslacking**, is a growing problem for many organizations. For example, an eMarketer study in September, 2000 indicated that more than 70% of the working online population had accessed the Internet for non-business uses at least once. The IDC, a research group, also reported in 2002 that 30–40% of Internet usage during working hours wasn't business-related.

The combination of misusing work time and computer resources for these activities hasn't gone unnoticed by employers. In Chapter 7, Beyond the Basics: Using E-Mail Safely and Effectively, we told you a little bit about workplace monitoring, also called workplace surveillance. **Workplace surveillance** is the practice of monitoring employees electronically, especially tracking e-mail and Internet usage. We also mentioned that the legal cases (so far) have come down on the side of the employer. Courts have ruled that an organization's interest in protecting trade secrets, maintaining their reputation, deterring criminal behavior, or avoiding liability problems outweigh the privacy rights of an individual employee. Let's take a closer look at why—and how—organizations monitor the Internet usage of their employees.

REASONS WHY ORGANIZATIONS TRACK EMPLOYEES

Organizations have various reasons for implementing workplace surveillance. For example, they may be concerned that Internet usage during work hours will lead to lower productivity. Additionally, they may be worried that employee actions will lead to liability or harassment lawsuits. The following list outlines the main reasons why businesses use surveillance, according to the American Management Association:

- *Performance Review.* Surveillance can be used to help managers evaluate how well employees are doing their jobs. (How many times have you heard the prerecorded message that a phone call might be recorded for "quality-control purposes?")
- *Legal Compliance.* Some industries, such as banking and finance, are tightly regulated. Recording the online actions of employees might help to legally protect the company and/or the customer.
- *Legal Liability.* Companies feel a need to monitor the activities of employees to prevent hostile workplace environment or sexual harassment lawsuits.

- *Productivity.* Organizations want to control the use of time and computing resources during working hours, knowing that the misuse of these resources costs the company money.
- *Protection of Company Information.* Businesses usually have a significant amount of time and money invested in a product, service, or idea. They have a vested stake in making sure this information isn't shared with competitors.

Because of these concerns, an increasing number of businesses and government agencies are monitoring their workers. Of the 40 million Americans with Internet access at work, greater than one-third (14 million) are constantly monitored, according to a study published by the Privacy Foundation in July 2001. Furthermore, the survey only took into account *continuous* surveillance; it's likely that even more workers are subject to random ("spot-check") monitoring. Another survey conducted by the Society of Human Resource Management indicated that more than 70% of organizations monitor their worker's Internet activities. The biggest problem with employee surveillance, according to privacy advocates, is the fact that businesses aren't required to tell their workers that they're being watched. This controversy—not informing employees that they're being tracked—offsets the privacy rights of an employee with the business interests of an employer.

Despite these concerns, the American Management Association survey in 2000 indicated that approximately 88% of employers *did* tell their workers that their Internet and e-mail activities were under surveillance. However, this notice might involve only a paragraph or two in the employee handbook—something that privacy experts feel is inadequate. At the minimum, they feel that a message should display on a user's computer at startup, reminding employees that they might be watched.

But whether or not an employee is informed about it, electronic surveillance of Internet-related activities can lead to discipline (or dismissal) if the employer feels that the employee's online actions are inappropriate. For example, in February 2002, R.R. Donnelly disciplined 100 people in an Illinois facility for misusing e-mail. The Privacy Foundation also reports that many well-known companies, such as Xerox, Dow Chemical, and the New York Times, have fired or disciplined employees for inappropriate Internet or e-mail usage.

The American Management Association's 2000 Survey on Workplace Monitoring and Surveillance reported the following breakdown related to disciplinary action for misuse of e-mail or the Internet (see Table 17.1). Disciplinary incidents will probably increase in proportion to the number of companies that are using workplace surveillance to track employees' actions.

The Privacy Foundation maintains a Web site with information related to its Workplace Surveillance Project at *www.privacyfoundation.org/workplace/job_loss*. This site includes information on current technologies used for mon-

TABLE 17.1	Disciplinary Actions for Misuse or Personal Use of Internet Technologies (Source: American Management Association)	
	E-mail Misuse	Internet Misuse
Any disciplinary action	44.8%	41.9%
Informal reprimand or warning	22.3%	19.7%
Formal reprimand or warning	29.6%	26.1%
Dismissal	16.0%	17.4%

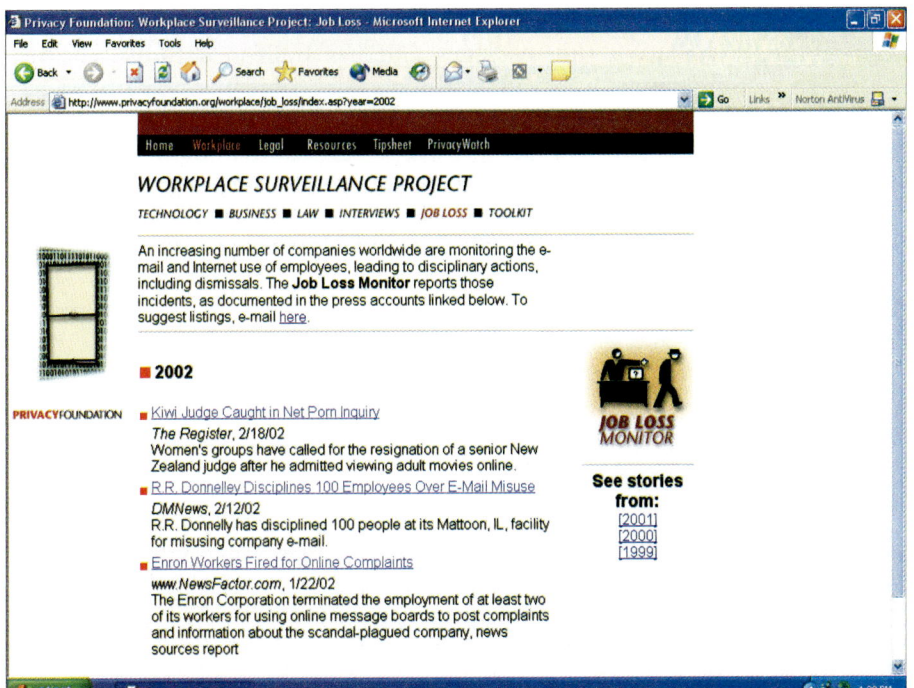

Figure 17.5.
Find out more about workplace surveillance at the Privacy Foundation's Web site.

itoring, statistics on the number of businesses using surveillance, and stories about those who have lost jobs (see Figure 17.5).

HOW ORGANIZATIONS MONITOR INTERNET USAGE

There are several commercial products currently on the market that companies can use for surveillance. The most frequently used product for Internet monitoring is Websense; MIMEsweeper is used most often for e-mail monitoring (see Figure 17.6).

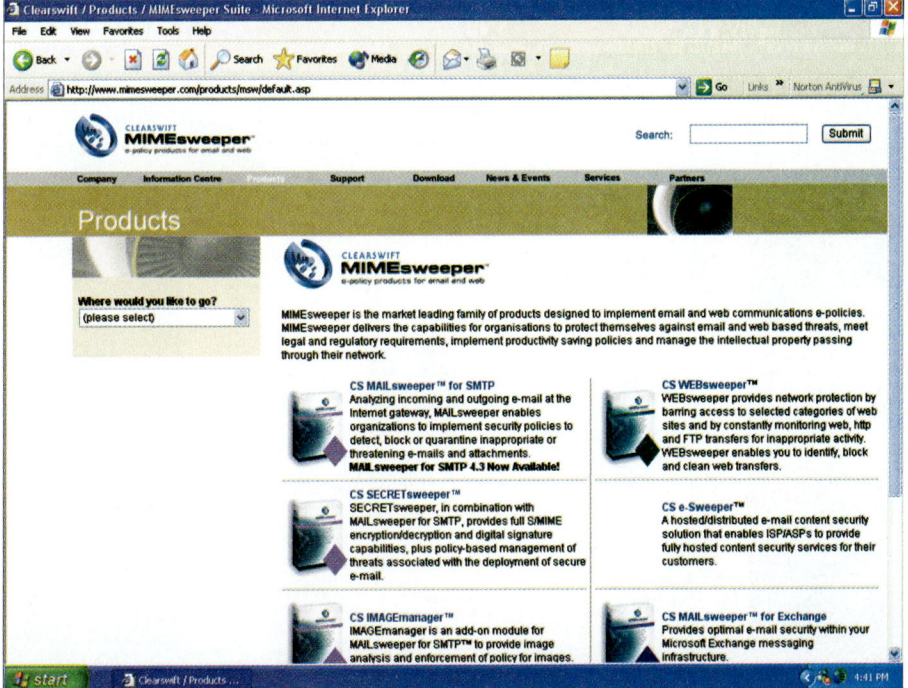

Figure 17.6.
Products such as MIMEsweeper have been developed to monitor employee e-mail.

MIMEsweeper monitors e-mail messages for inappropriate content. It can also be used to encrypt the messages and has built-in security features. Businesses that use this software can determine what content is "inappropriate."

Websense, by its own admission, allows managers to "transparently monitor, manage, and report traffic slowing from internal networks to the Internet." According to Websense's Web site, more than 17,500 companies and government agencies use their product to manage 6.6 million employees. Some of the clients include such well-known names as Pepsi, Shell Oil, Compaq, Ralston Purina, IBM, American Express, and the United States Army. If you're interested, you can find out more about this product on the company's Web site at *www.websense.com* (see Figure 17.7).

According to the Privacy Foundation, the low cost of the technology is fueling the growth of employee surveillance. For example, it costs only $9 per employee for the United States Army to monitor an employee per year. This is generally considered a cost-effective move because the cost of implementing the technology can potentially add up to significant savings in recovered employee productivity. For example, if a company with 6,000 employees recovers only 15 minutes/day/person (and the employees are paid an average of $17/hour), the savings will add up to more than $25,000 per day.

A type of software that is loosely related to Websense (although it's not designed for employee-surveillance per se) is AltaVista's AV Enterprise Search. This software is based on AltaVista's Internet search engine; but differs from the Internet search engine in that it helps people in a corporation search for information within the company. This software can be a useful business tool because it allows workers to find information they need in e-mails or the laptop computers of other employees. **Universal view software**, such as AV Enterprise Search, can be set up to exclude certain folders or areas of a user's hard drive so that others can't access sensitive or confidential information. Corporate information management rules determine which files on a system can be accessed, preventing people from gaining unlimited access to a worker's hard drive. Although it wasn't designed as a tool to monitor employees, universal view software has implications for an individual's privacy rights because others may be able to access personal data.

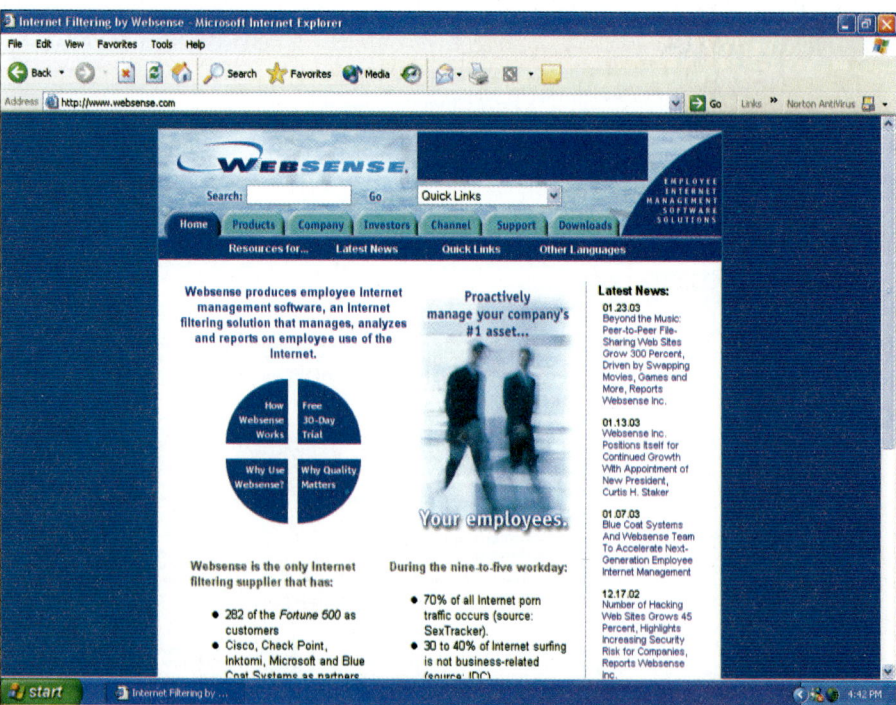

Figure 17.7.
Websense is a tool that many organizations use to watch workers' Internet usage.

FastTrack by Fatline is another surveillance software program that allows for universal search capabilities but can also be used to monitor activities. This software differs from other employee monitoring software in that employees can monitor each other's activities in addition to the surveillance done by management. This technique uses employee peer pressure as a means of encouraging people to be productive and to avoid viewing inappropriate or productivity-wasting Web sites.

Besides the possible privacy infringements, the use of monitoring tools like AltaVista's AV Enterprise Search and Fatline's FastTrack might cause internal security leaks if they are set up carelessly. For example, it would be possible for a determined employee to use the software to find out company salaries or other confidential information if controls are not in place. Additionally, there is some concern that the use of these types of programs could potentially lead to "hostile environment" lawsuits.

The full AMA report is available online at *www.amanet.org/research/pdfs/monitr_surv.pdf*. The Privacy Foundation makes its report available at its Web site (*www.privacyfoundation.org/workplace*).

INSIDE TRACK

A **hostile work environment** is one in which the behavior of others has the effect of significantly interfering with a person's work by creating an intimidating or offensive workplace setting. Although the term "hostile work environment" originally referred specifically to sexual harassment, the meaning has since broadened to include other situations as well, such as a co-worker who hassles you about your religion or personal beliefs.

ON THE HORIZON

As the number of employees who have Internet access grows, organizations will increasingly implement surveillance software. In fact, a new industry has sprung up, called **Employee Internet Management**  **(EIM)**, which develops software for this market and strategies to monitor employees. The EIM market is projected to grow at a compound annual growth rate of 55%, to more than $560 million by 2004.

UNDERSTAND CHILDREN'S ONLINE PRIVACY RIGHTS

Just as today, Web sites from 1995–2000 increased in number and variety. What changed after 2000 was the regulation of sites designed specifically for children. Here's why: Some Web sites are designed primarily for children, both in content and in layout. As you can imagine, some of them have been developed for legitimate purposes; others exist mainly to collect identifying information on kids or their families. This data could then be used to specifically market products to children, find out identifying information about them or their families, or (even worse) stalk or abuse them.

To protect the rights of children, especially those under 13 years old, the United States enacted a law in April, 2000 called the **Children's Online Privacy Protection Act (COPPA)**. This law stipulates that Web sites that target children under 13 years old must follow certain guidelines. For example, these sites must post a privacy policy, obtain parental consent before collecting personal information about kids, allow parents to review the information they collect, and let parents revoke their consent.

COPPA affects sites that are specifically geared toward children. For example, a site on coding in XML doesn't technically have to adhere to COPPA because most kids aren't using the technology to design Web pages. However, Yahooligans (*www.yahooligans.com*) and other kid-oriented sites are required to carefully follow the guidelines (see Figure 17.8).

If you're interested in learning more, take a look at KidsPrivacy (*www.kidsprivacy.com*), a site partially sponsored by the Federal Trade Commission. The KidsPrivacy site offers helpful information regarding COPPA and children's privacy rights (see Figure 17.9).

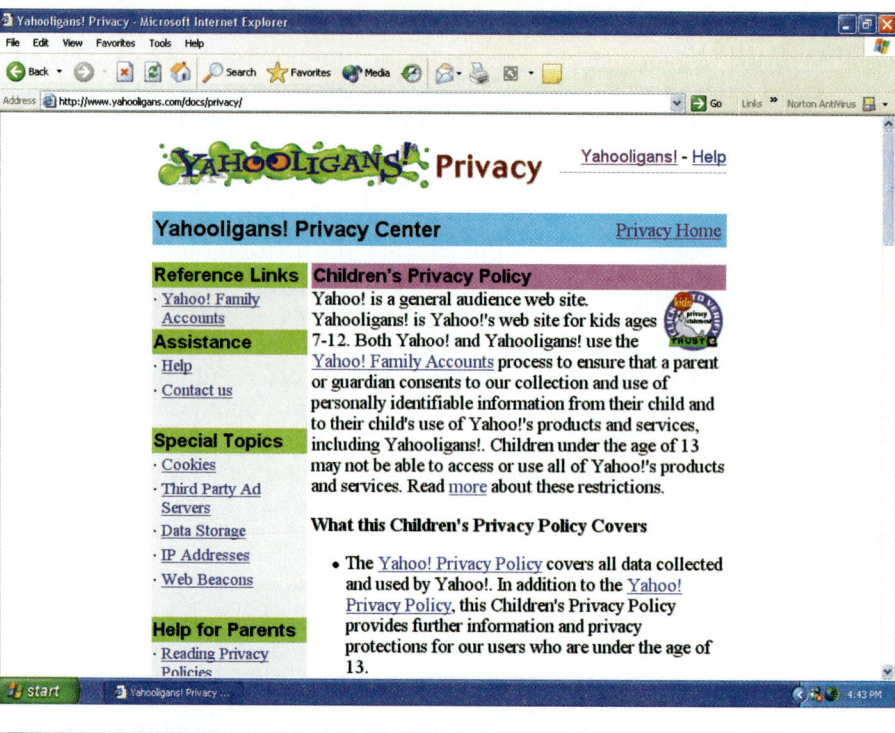

Figure 17.8.
Sites marketed specifically to children must have tight privacy policies in place.

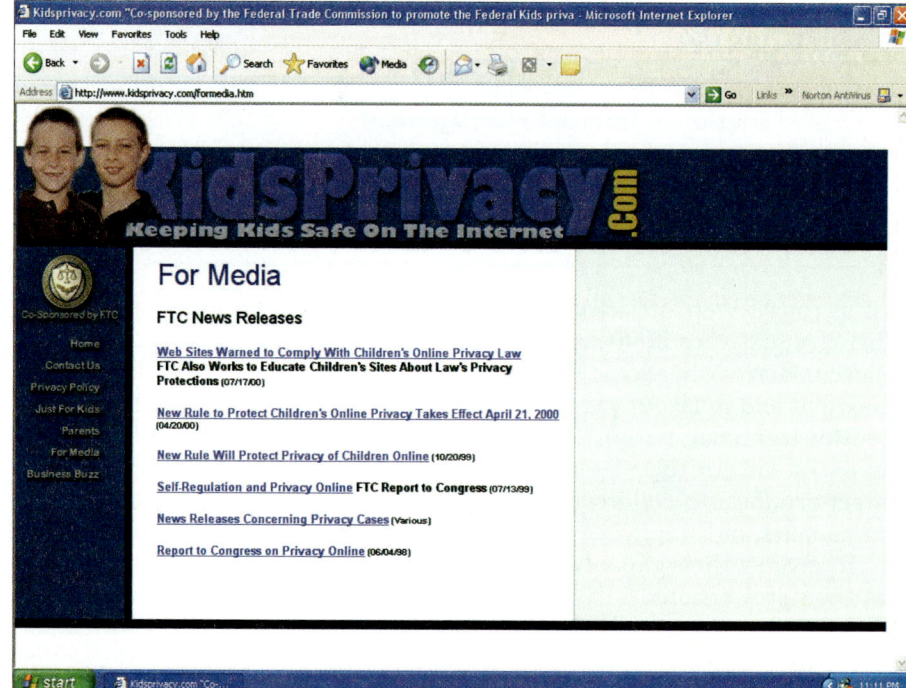

Figure 17.9.
Find out more about COPPA on the KidsPrivacy site.

UNDERSTAND PRIVACY ISSUES RELATED TO BIOMETRICS

Biometrics definitely smacks of Big Brother—and it's on the rise. **Biometrics** is the technology that computers can use to identify people based on unchangeable biological information. Although biometrics can be effectively used for security, it can also infringe on personal privacy when it is misused.

The oldest biometrics technology in use is fingerprinting. However, this technology (which has now evolved into fingerprint scanning) is rapidly being joined by a number of others, some of which privacy advocates consider invasive. In this section, we'll take a quick look at the biometric technologies that are being developed (or are already being implemented) and discuss the impact on the privacy rights of individuals. We'll also point you to Web sites in which you can find out more about this emerging technology.

FINGERPRINT SCANNING

The idea of using fingerprints to identify an individual has been in practice (especially for the purposes of law enforcement or for verifying a person's identity) for more than 100 years. However, new technologies are now being used to record and verify fingerprints, including fingerprint scanning. For example, one method analyzes electromagnetic impulses to map out the fingerprinting pattern.

This technology can be used to secure computer systems from unauthorized users. For example, you can connect a small device to the USB port of a computer and then place your finger in a "reader" that uses fingerprint scanning to grant or deny access to the system. Fingerprint scanning can help to prevent unauthorized access to computers, but may simultaneously unsettle those concerned with privacy. You can take a look at some of these devices on the Web sites for companies who manufacture them, such as Identix's BioTouch USB Fingerprint Reader at *www.identix.com* and the U.are.U Pro fingerprint scanner at *www.digitalpersona.com* (see Figure 17.10)

HAND AND PALM RECOGNITION TECHNOLOGIES

Hand and palm recognition systems use technologies similar to that used for fingerprinting. These systems operate by having people place their hand on a scanning surface and then recording the hand's characteristics, such as the size and shape and the vein patterns on the back of the hand. Identification based on hand recognition is not considered as reliable as fingerprinting because there are fewer unique characteristics. This technology is probably best used when coupled with other identification, such as photo IDs.

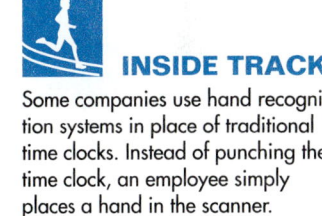

INSIDE TRACK

Some companies use hand recognition systems in place of traditional time clocks. Instead of punching the time clock, an employee simply places a hand in the scanner.

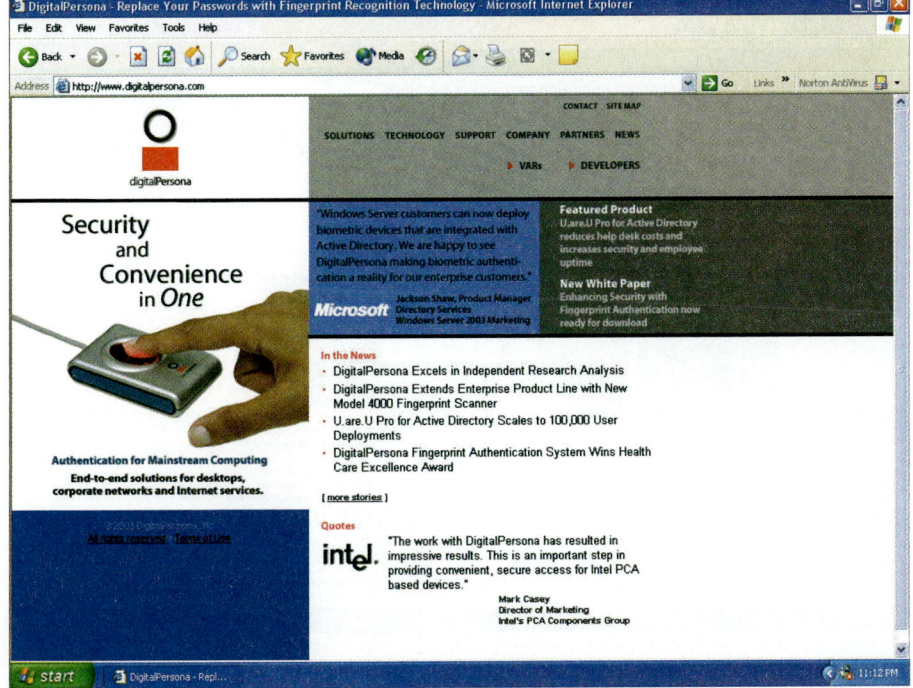

Figure 17.10.
Fingerprint scanners can be used to prevent or grant access to computer systems.

EYE SCANNING TECHNOLOGIES

Eye scanning technology, including iris scanning, is emerging as a reliable technology for identification. In the same way that each person has a unique fingerprint, so individuals each have a unique iris pattern. Testing has shown that iris recognition is the most reliable form of biometrics you can use to authenticate a person's identity, with a failure rate of only 1 in 200,000. The technology is lowering in price at a time when the 9/11 terrorist attacks have caused some people to look more closely at technologies that were formerly too expensive or difficult to implement.

FACIAL RECOGNITION TECHNOLOGIES

The last main biometrics technology that's being rolled out is facial recognition. In fact, you may have heard about this technology being used at the 2001 Super Bowl Game or in public places such as the Virginia Beach Boardwalk. **Facial recognition technology** uses hardware and software to scan a crowd and then converts specific characteristics of each face into digital form. This information is crosschecked against the profiles of known terrorists and other criminals.

Face recognition isn't nearly as reliable as iris scanning, but it is attractive to security experts because it is noninvasive and can be done without detection. Identix has developed FaceIt, one of the best-known facial recognition systems. If you want to find out more about this biometric company's technologies and how they can be used in a variety of settings, take a look at their Web site, located at *www.identix.com* (see Figure 17.11).

You may also want to take a look at Viisage's Web site at *www.viisage.com*. Viisage offers an affordable facial recognition software program that can be coupled with a Web cam to grant or deny access to a local computer.

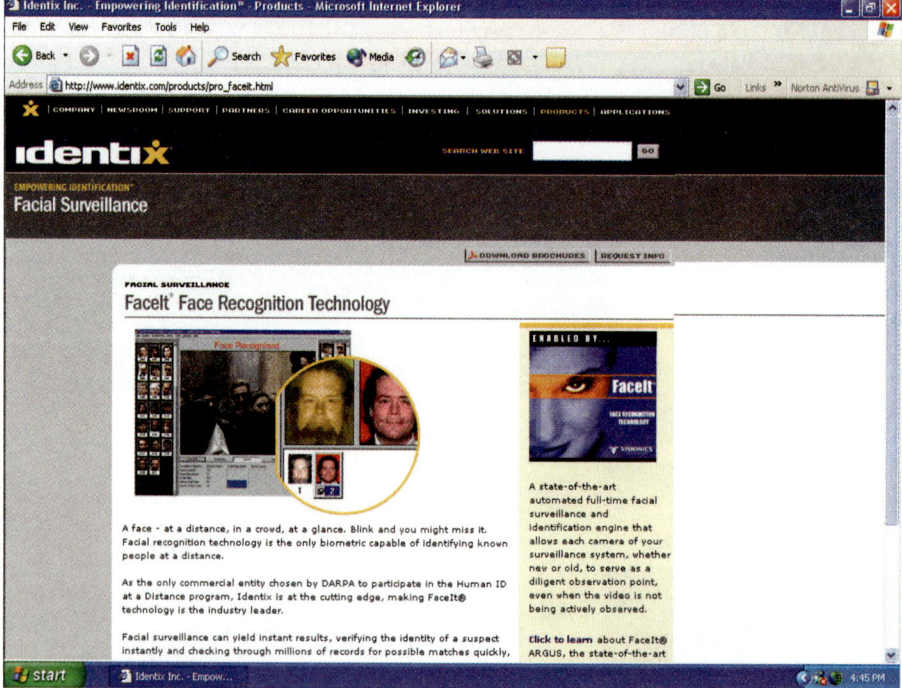

Figure 17.11.
Several companies have been developing face recognition technology.

CONCERNS ABOUT BIOMETRICS

There are several concerns related to the use of biometrics: First, the surveillance techniques have already led to more government control and a lack of personal privacy; second, that people will be falsely identified because the technology is not foolproof; and third, that surveillance can take place without the knowledge of those being tracked. The Electronic Privacy Information Center raises the following concerns in regards to biometric technology:

- *Storage of information.* Where and how should the data be stored? Who should have access? How long will it be retained?
- *Vulnerability.* What safeguards will be in place to prevent theft or abuse of the compiled data?
- *Failure Rates.* What failure rate in collecting the data is acceptable? What are the issues related to false positives and false negatives? How will the rights of the persons falsely accused be protected?
- *Constitutional Rights.* What constitutional protections are in place related to this technology? Will the technology trample on constitutional rights?
- *Authenticity.* What is considered authentic information? Can anyone corrupt the data?
- *Linking and Consolidating.* Will the data gained via biometrics be consolidated with other database information? For example, can biometric information be linked to medical or financial information—or even spending habits? Will the information be shared with government agencies, private companies, or both? What limits and protections will be in place to protect peoples' privacy?
- *Cultural Climate.* What are the societal and governmental implications of a society in which every person's activities can be tracked?

As technology—both on- and offline—evolves and merges, these types of issues will come more and more into the forefront of the debate.

IMPLEMENT THE BEST PRACTICES FOR PROTECTING YOUR PRIVACY

Just as Hansel and Gretel in the fairy tale left breadcrumbs to mark their trail, so you potentially leave digital breadcrumbs just about every time you visit a Web site, send e-mail, or download an MP3 file. Some of the data stays on your computer; other information is transmitted to others, often without your knowledge. Although you might not care about some of the information you send (probably not that many people care about the e-mail to your friends about the pizza party Friday night), it's a good idea to maintain control over who gets to know details about your life and surfing habits.

Best practices are optimal strategies and tactics that professionals agree work well in a particular situation. In this case, there are certain best practices that you can follow to help to protect your privacy. Although they aren't bulletproof, these practices will help ward off most data snoops—better than simply doing nothing, anyway.

CHECKLIST FOR EVALUATING ISPS
BEST PRACTICES FOR E-MAIL PRIVACY

✔ *Use different e-mail addresses for different purposes.*

It's a good plan to get a free e-mail address that you can use to register at various sites, keeping it separate from your main e-mail address. On the same note, get and use a personal e-mail address that you can access from work instead of using your work e-mail address to send or receive personal messages.

✔ *Use encryption software.*

Unless you use this type of software to "scramble" e-mail messages, anything you write is about as private as a postcard from Jamaica. Don't forget to be careful about the messages you write. They can be stored forever on someone else's computer, kept on mail servers, or even forwarded to your old boss or girlfriend. One encryption program you can download at no charge is PGP, which stands for Pretty Good Privacy at *www.pgpi.org*.

✔ *Ignore and Delete Spam.*

Conventional wisdom is to delete spam rather than replying to it or trying to unsubscribe. Responding to spam only confirms to the sender that you are a person who opens spam.

✔ *Delete old messages.*

This sounds pretty self-explanatory, but messages (or other files) that are sent to the Deleted Items folder in your e-mail program are not really gone...neither are those in the Recycle Bin on your Windows desktop. So make sure that you use methods that completely erase these files.

✔ *Use an Anonymous Remailer.*

This service works by sending your messages to a special server (a remailer) that removes all traces of the origin of the message and then sends it to the recipient. Some anonymous remailers combine encryption with remailer capabilities for even more privacy.

✔ *Install and update antivirus software.*

This prevents viruses, worms, and any other nasty code (such as keylogger programs) from compromising the security of your system or your privacy.

BEST PRACTICES FOR SURFING

✔ *Install a firewall.*

This prevents Trojan horses, keyloggers, and other nasty code from getting access to your system. Additionally, firewalls usually "ask" for your permission to let programs already on your system access the Internet via a message box. This can alert you to the fact that adware or spyware is eavesdropping on you. (We'll talk more about firewalls in Chapter 18, Beyond the Basics, A Closer Look at Security Issues.)

✔ **Control cookies.**

As we mentioned in previous chapters, you can change your Internet Explorer security settings to prevent many cookies from being automatically placed on your computer. You can also use third-party software, such as Cookie Crusher (*www.thelimitsoft.com/cookie*), to control these files (see Figure 17.12).

✔ **Be anonymous.**

You can prevent your activities from being monitored by using a tool that disguises your identity, such as the Anonymizer software (*www.anonymizer.com*).

✔ **Read the Privacy Policy on Web sites.**

Most legitimate Web sites (especially those that require you to fill out a form) include a Privacy Policy that explains what the company intends to do with the data they gather. If an ISP promises to maintain your privacy and then fails to do so, they are guilty of violating the Federal Trade Commission's (FTC) fair trade practices. The FTC has taken action against ISPs that have violated this practice. Read the policy and make sure that you're comfortable with the intended use of your personal data—or else find another Web site to visit and use.

So even though American society is not quite like Orwell's *1984* society yet, some of the privacy issues we now face are reminiscent of this prophetic novel.

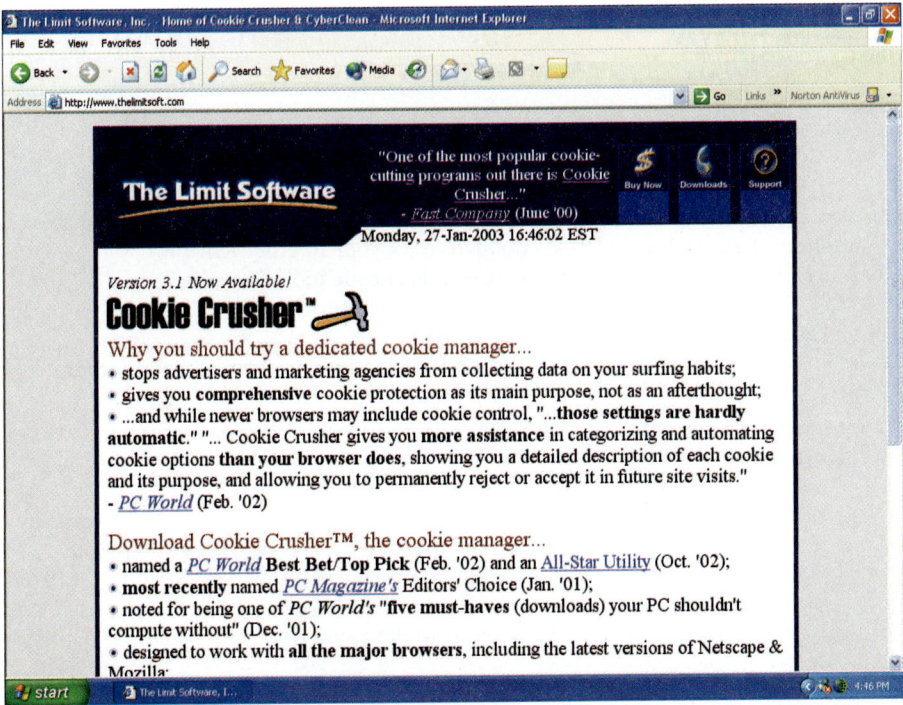

Figure 17.12.
Use cookie management software to control cookies.

Don't Forget...

- Privacy issues have increased in magnitude and complexity because of the ease with which information travels on the Internet.
- Many privacy organizations and advocates are vocal about limiting access to personal information and protecting personal privacy.
- The more information an organization or agency has about you, the more it can potentially exert control over you.
- Many people have traditionally been casual about the amount and type of information they share online, although they are becoming increasingly concerned with privacy issues.
- Data snoops can use a number of methods to get data from your system, most of them not very legitimate (or even legal).
- Computer monitoring software, including adware and spyware, can be used to track your online activities.
- Keylogger programs can compromise both privacy and security by transmitting information about each keystroke to others. These programs can be spread by worms or viruses, or installed by a cracker.
- The government has the tools to conduct cybersurveillance of American citizens, including Carnivore and Magic Lantern. Additionally, law enforcement officials have been given more latitude to conduct surveillance than they possessed before September 11, 2001.
- An increasing percentage of people are being monitored while at work to ensure that they're engaging in legitimate and non-productive Internet and e-mail activities.
- The increase in workplace monitoring is driven by the affordable cost of implementing surveillance technologies.
- If workplace surveillance shows misuse of e-mail or the Internet, it can lead to disciplinary action or even termination.
- Privacy experts feel that employees should, at the very least, be informed that their actions are being monitored electronically.
- Children under 13 years old have specific privacy rights that are guaranteed under the Children's Online Privacy Protection Act (COPPA).
- Biometrics is an up-and-coming technology that can be used to authenticate a person's identity. However, privacy advocates are very concerned about the use of biometrics, especially face recognition technology, in public locations.
- There are a number of things you can (and should) do to guard your privacy.

Check This Out

MULTIPLE CHOICE

1. Which term is related to the new practice of having employees electronically monitor each other's actions?
   a. Adware
   b. Freedom of Information Act (FOIA)
   c. Universal view software
   d. Magic Lantern
2. Which of the following is a government program that privacy groups are concerned about?
   a. KeyLog
   b. Carnivore
   c. Herbivore
   d. Pretty Good Knight
3. Which of the following is a current biometric technology?
   a. Facial recognition
   b. Retina scanning
   c. Hand scanning
   d. All of the above
4. Which of the following is the government capable of doing to track your Internet activities?
   a. Use a diagnostic tool to monitor e-mail
   b. Track which visitors have accessed a government Web site
   c. Install a keylogger program on your system
   d. All of the above
5. What is a likely result of a keylogger program being installed on your computer?
   a. Your antivirus software will be disabled.
   b. You won't be able to type on your keyboard anymore because the software jams ("logs") it.
   c. All the e-mail messages in your inbox will be deleted.
   d. None of the above

MATCHING

a. best practices
b. keylogger
c. COPPA
d. workplace surveillance
e. EIM
f. Carnivore
g. biometrics
h. Websense
i. Echelon
j. cyberslacking

1. Software industry related to workplace monitoring
2. The practice of monitoring the Internet use of employees
3. A commercial software product used to track the Internet usage of employees
4. Tactics and strategies used to achieve a particular result
5. Using a person's physical characteristics for tracking and identification
6. Engaging in non-productive (or counter-productive) online activities while at work
7. A diagnostic tool developed by the government that filters information in an attempt to find criminal activity
8. An act that protects children's right to online privacy
9. Records keystrokes without your knowledge
10. Electronic surveillance tool that monitors international communications

Real Life

1. Chances are there is a substantial amount of information about you already online. To find out what others can find out about you, visit the following Web sites, making sure to conduct searches for your name on each: *Search Engines:* Google (*www.google.com*), AltaVista (*www.altavista.com*). *Online Telephone Directories:* Switchboard (*www.switchboard.com*), Yahoo! PeopleSearch (*people.yahoo.com*), WhoWhere from Lycos (*www.whowhere.lycos.com*), and Classmates (*www.classmates.com*). If you've been in the military, check out *Military.com*. You can also look at your college's Web site. Additionally, check the archives of your local newspaper or local government sites.

    What (and how much) information was available online about you? If there is erroneous information on the Internet about you, what can you do to remove it?

2. There have been sweeping changes in many privacy laws since September 11, 2001, both in the United States and in the European Union (EU). Use the privacy Web sites listed in this chapter to find out more about how the law and public mindset regarding privacy have changed. After you conduct your research, write a paper that outlines your findings.

3. LinuxSecurity (*www.linuxsecurity.com*) maintains a Web site packed with links to current news articles about privacy and security. Read at least 12 articles related to privacy over the period of the past two years, making sure that the articles are from different months. Start with the oldest article and finish with the most current. What trends do you see regarding privacy? Are there new laws or technologies that might impact personal privacy? If so, what? Take notes and then discuss the issues with your classmates.

4. The United States government is increasingly interested in using biometrics for identification and tracking of citizens and those crossing our borders. Read the government's perspective on this issue (and others) at the Government Computer News Web site (*www.gcn.com*). Next, conduct an Internet search using both the words `biometrics` and `privacy`. Use the information you find to develop a list of pros and cons regarding the use of biometrics to identify and monitor United States citizens. If your instructor indicates, also write a paper that explains your findings.

5. The World Wide Web Consortium has developed the Platform for Privacy Preferences Project (P3P). Go to the Web site for W3 (*www.w3.org/P3P*) and find out more about this initiative. How would this standard help protect privacy of Internet users?

I Spy: Privacy and Security Concerns

1. In September 2002, President Bush's administration proposed a National Strategy to Secure Cyberspace (known as NSSC) as part of the Homeland Security bill. This bill allows for establishment of a centralized facility to gather and analyze Internet traffic for security threats. To ward off protests by privacy advocates, the draft copy of the plan also included the appointment of a "privacy czar" to oversee this surveillance.

    Use the Internet to conduct research and determine the current status of the Homeland Security Bill, the National Strategy to Secure Cyberspace, and related legislation. Then write an analytical paper that discusses the balance between security and privacy. In what way does an increase in security potentially infringe on personal liberty? Does liberty always mean less security? Why or why not?

2. Privacy.net (*www.privacy.net*) maintains an interesting and interactive Web site. For example, you can view a demonstration on how ad tracking works by registering on a fictitious Web site; then see how your activity is monitored across other Web sites in the fabricated network, linked to your e-mail, and to your identity. You can also run a demonstration to see what information about your system is revealed.

    Visit this Web site and run several of the demonstrations available; then read the articles on ways to protect your privacy. (Note: If you're operating from behind a firewall, you might not be able to conduct the entire test.) Take notes as you work through the activities and read the information on this site; then develop your own "best practices" checklist for protecting your privacy online.

3. Philip E. Agre in the Department of Information Studies at the University of California has penned an interesting and thoughtful essay about the dangers and implications of using face recognition systems in public places, entitled, "Your Face Is Not a Bar Code: Arguments Against Automatic Face Recognition in Public Places."

    Read Professor Agre's essay at *dlis.gseis.ucla.edu/people/pagre/bar-code.html*. Write a paper that summarizes his main points; then discuss whether you agree with his conclusions and why. To back up your ideas, make sure to include factual information from Web sites maintained by privacy groups, biometric companies, and government agencies.

CHAPTER 18

BEYOND THE BASICS: A CLOSER LOOK AT SECURITY ISSUES

Chapter Objectives

After you complete this chapter, you'll

- Understand the Importance of Internet Security
- Understand the Main Types of Internet-Based Attacks
- Understand the Potential for Damage from Mobile Code: Java, JavaScript, VBScript, and ActiveX
- Know Ways to Prevent Malicious Code from Executing
- Understand the Importance of Using a Firewall
- Know How to Create Strong Passwords
- Know the Best Practices for Conducting Safe E-Commerce
- Implement the Best Practices for Security

Key Terms

When you finish this chapter, you'll understand the following terms:

- attack tools
- attacker
- back door
- blended threats
- CERT
- Code Red
- critical infrastructures
- cross site scripting
- cyberterrorism
- Denial of Service (DoS)
- Distributed Denial of Service (DDoS)
- hash
- Internet worms
- intruder
- Java
- JavaScript
- Macro viruses
- mobile code
- password
- password cracker
- Remote Administration Trojan (RAT)
- retrovirus
- reverse engineering
- sandbox
- Script worms
- scripts
- security incident
- security vulnerability
- self-propagating
- spoofing
- virus definition
- Visual Basic Scripting Edition (VBScript)
- zombie

The Big Picture

You probably wouldn't think of leaving for a three-week vacation without locking your home, especially if you live in the middle of a high-crime section of town. Neither should you leave your computer system unprotected against malicious people and code. Instead, you should secure your computer and your data using the same care that you do to safeguard your home and possessions.

But what does securing your computer involve? Securing your computer refers to protecting data and programs so that unauthorized users can't access or compromise them. These security measures can range from password-protecting your computer to the complex hardware and software technologies that corporations use to safeguard their networks.

Unfortunately, some people don't take security risks seriously, especially those with home systems or small business networks. For example, some users casually browse the Internet without adequate antivirus measures and firewalls in place. Meanwhile, crackers and other bad types are actively searching for vulnerable computers—those without these security measures.

In previous chapters, you learned about some of the misuses of the Internet. You found out the essentials of how crackers operate, about malware (*mal*icious soft*ware*), and the importance of installing antivirus software. In this chapter, we will take a more in-depth look at some of the main security risks and at the kinds of attacks that cybercriminals have launched against major organizations and agencies, and how even your personal computer can be commandeered to launch attacks.

To prevent you from becoming tangled in a maze of security issues, we'll cover the best practices for safeguarding your system. You'll learn how to use antivirus software, firewalls, secure passwords, and filtering software to do so. You'll also find out how to better control Java, JavaScript, and ActiveX controls that are associated with many Web sites.

Armed with this information, you can better protect your home or small office computer. You'll also become more aware of the security issues at large that can pose a danger to the Internet. Along the way, we'll point out helpful Web sites so that you can learn even more about security issues. And who knows? Maybe you'll become so interested in security issues that you'll want to become an information security specialist. Believe us. There *will* be a need for people like you.

Window on the Web

The Internet has so many Web sites devoted to Internet security that it is easy to become overwhelmed by the sheer quantity of them. We'll help you sift through the available information to locate unbiased sites that will give you some sound strategies for protecting your system. For example, to help you understand the importance of the issues surrounding Internet security, you can view the

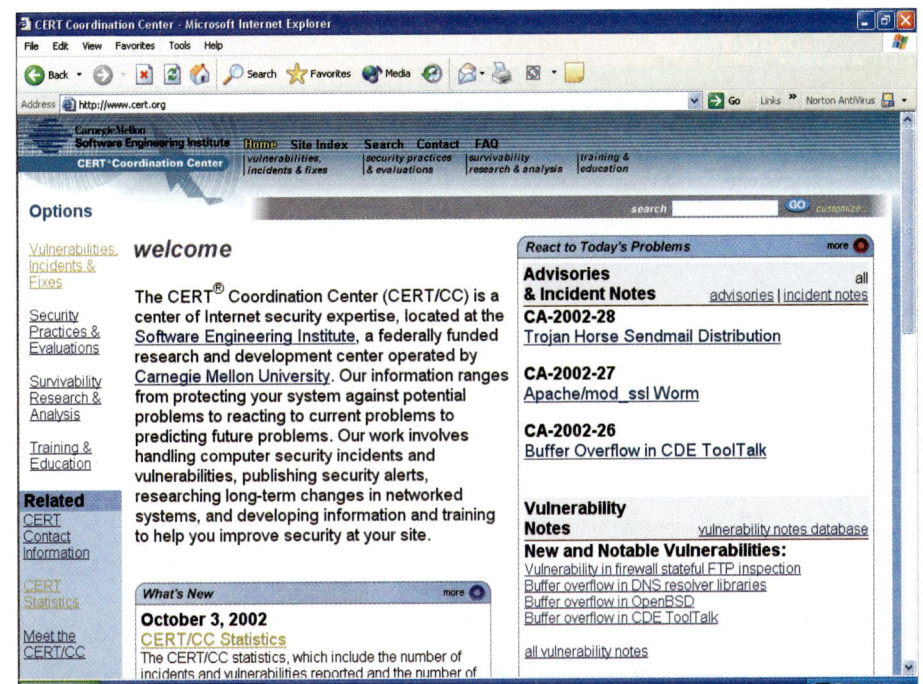

Figure 18.1.
Concerned with security issues? Start with CERT's site.

CERT (Computer Emergency Response Team) site at *www.cert.org*, created by the Carnegie Mellon University's Software Engineering Institute (see Figure 18.1).

In this chapter, you'll also learn about the various types of malicious code that can enter your system if you don't have tight security measures in place. To understand the main types of Internet attacks and how to prevent them, you can look at the Web site for the Computer Security Resource Center, maintained by the National Institute of Standards and Technology. Its Web page on viruses at *csrc.nist.gov/virus* includes beneficial information as well as a number of links to other sites (see Figure 18.2).

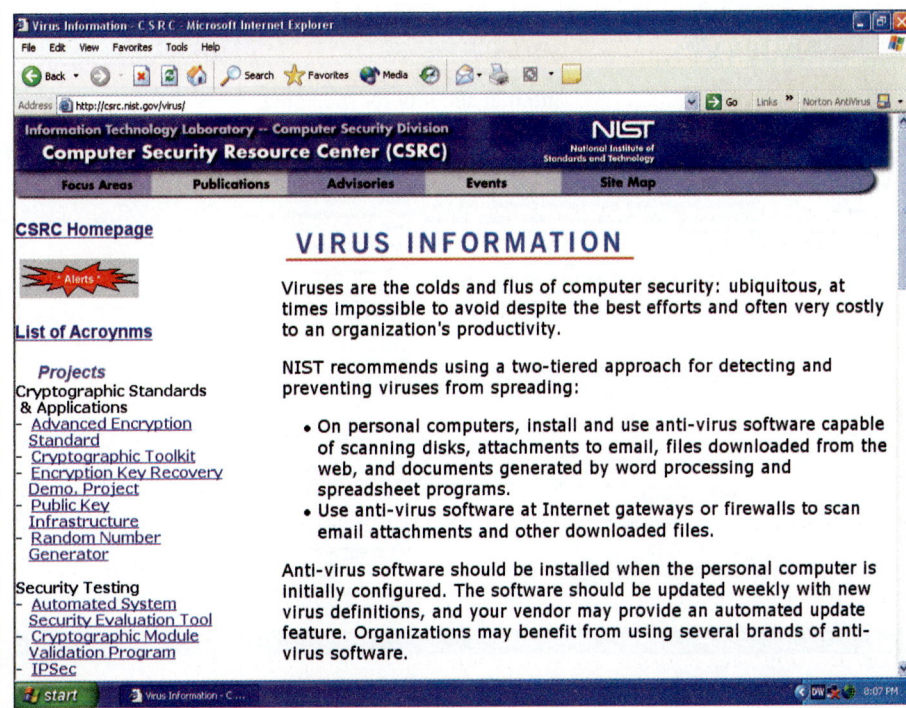

Figure 18.2.
Find out more about viruses at the Computer Resource Security Center's site.

Window on the Web 283

Figure 18.3.
Use the government's site to find out about security issues and how to best defend against Cybercrime.

We'll also examine some of the issues related to cybercrime. To find out more about cybercrime, check out the United States Government's Web site at *www.cybercrime.gov* (see Figure 18.3).

After we discuss the current security threats running rampant on the Internet, you'll learn some of the best practices for security, which span both the corporate world and home systems. For example, you'll learn how some companies, such as Symantec (developers of Norton AntiVirus software) produce products and updates to ward off malicious code (see Figure 18.4).

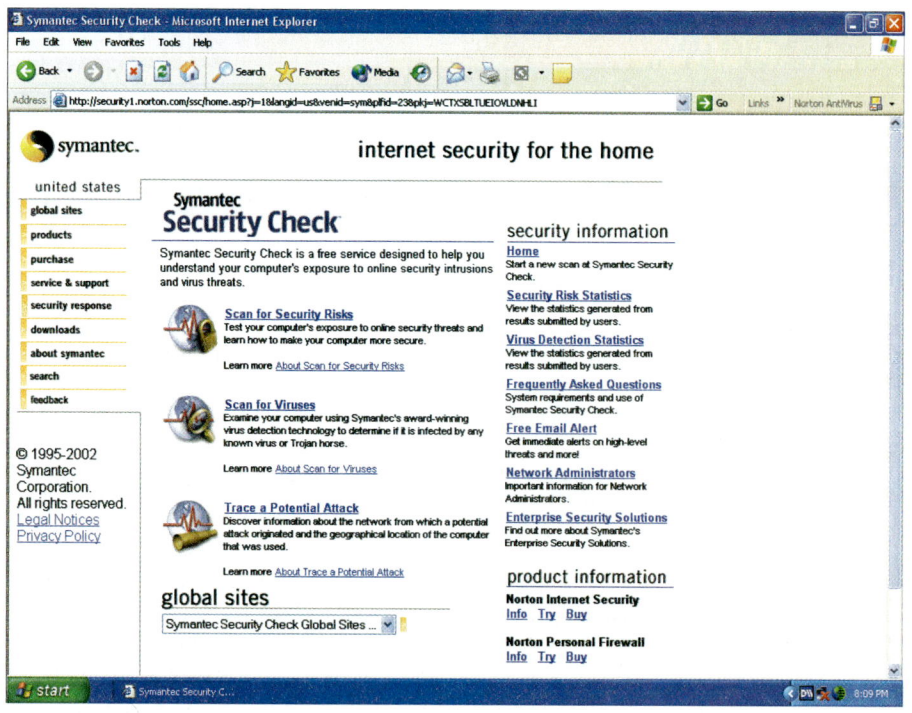

Figure 18.4.
The Symantec Web site contains tools to help you run a security check on your system.

284 Chapter 18 Beyond the Basics: A Closer Look at Security Issues

UNDERSTAND THE IMPORTANCE OF INTERNET SECURITY

Vulnerabilities. Threats. Holes. Exposures. No matter what term you use to describe them, the result is the same: There's a security opening in the way that your network or individual computer is set up—and it could allow malicious code to enter and wreak havoc. Your first step to secure your computer system is to find out how computer systems can be compromised. In this section, we'll acquaint you with some of the common terms related to Internet security and then show you why you should be concerned.

A **security vulnerability** (or hole/breach) is a deficiency in the hardware or software of your system that allows others to view, steal, or compromise the integrity of your data. A person who breaches the security of a computer system to gain unauthorized access is called an **intruder** or **attacker**. (*Crackers* are those who develop malicious code to cause security problems; whereas an *intruder* or *attacker* might develop code or simply reuse existing code to gain access.)

Picture an ancient walled city encircled by a dangerous enemy. Imagine that the wall is tall and strong everywhere...except for one small break. If the enemy finds that hole, it doesn't really matter that the rest of the wall was strong. In the same way, your entire computer system needs to be secured, or else the bad guys will be sure to find and exploit the weak spot.

If a weakness in your system occurs, cybercriminals can attack it via viruses, worms, Trojan horses, ActiveX controls, scripts or by using a host of other attack mechanisms. Any of these attacks can potentially cause your data or system to be compromised.

The exact nature and extent of the problems caused by security breaches vary as widely as does the malicious code used to launch an attack. Some codes might simply cause a minor inconvenience or drain system resources; others might completely trash your system. Some security problems might be so subtle that you don't even realize that your system has been compromised. For example, a security hole can allow a cracker to install a keylogger program and then spy on you by quietly recording every keystroke.

INSIDE TRACK

There have even been security breaches at software giants such as Microsoft. For example, in October 2002 an intruder hacked into Microsoft's site for beta (pre-release) software. According to Microsoft, the intruder didn't access the source code for the products, but the mere fact that this company's systems could be hacked was disconcerting.

FINANCIAL LOSSES DUE TO INTERNET SECURITY BREACHES

There are many instances of malicious code bringing an entire business network to its knees, causing significant loss of income. An April 2002 study co-sponsored by the Computer Security Institute (*www.gocsi.com*) and the FBI showed that 90% of the respondents, which included big corporations and government agencies, reported security incidents within the previous year. An additional 80% also admitted that their organizations incurred financial losses due to the incidents, with the financial losses estimated at more than two million dollars per incident. Approximately 67% of this loss was due to theft of proprietary data; the remainder of the loss was from financial fraud. The financial loss can span a variety of categories, as shown in Figure 18.5.

Although the losses might not be as great as those in large businesses, home users can experience losses as well. If a $2,000 system is trashed or your financial records are stolen, you probably won't consider it a minor loss. And in some ways, home computers can be more at risk than corporate or school networks. At home, it's tough to duplicate the security that a business can implement for its system, a fact that the intruders know quite well. Even if you don't have valuable information stored on your computer, a cracker might still want to gain control of your system and use it as a springboard to launch attacks against other systems. This effectively masks the true origin of the attack and forces you to provide the computing resources for the attack without your knowledge.

INSIDE TRACK

Corporations do their best to put airtight security in place. But even in corporations, people can expose systems to attacks, however unintentionally. As an example, one company had a secure network set up, including a strong firewall. But an employee dialed out to the Internet directly by using his phone modem so that he could access his AOL account, creating a hole in the firewall that opened up the entire company's network to intrusion.

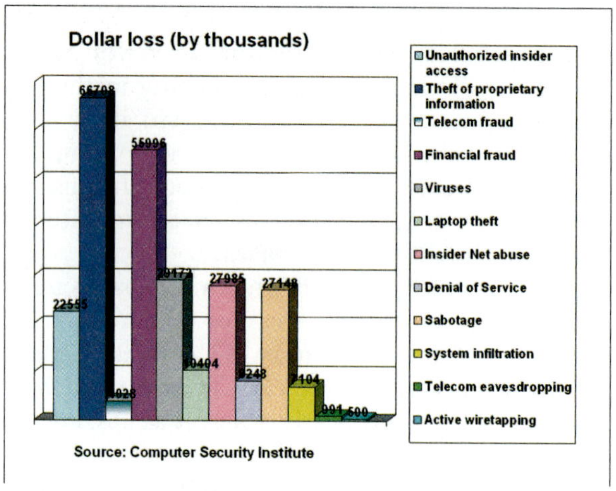

Figure 18.5.
Financial losses from cyberattacks can add up (*Source: Computer Security Institute*).

KNOW ABOUT RECENT DEVELOPMENTS IN INTERNET SECURITY THREATS

There's no doubt that Internet security incidents are on the rise. A **security incident** is an event that is believed to have a negative effect on a system's security or performance. In fact, according to statistics on CERT's Web site, the number of security incidents has steadily increased since 1988. This is clearly shown in Figure 18.6: In 1988, there were six security incidents reported to CERT; in the first three quarters of 2002 an astounding 73,359 were reported. Additionally, the Internet Security Systems, a company that specializes in helping businesses safeguard their networks, reported that there was a 65% increase in the security vulnerabilities reported for the third quarter of 2002 over the third quarter of the previous year (2001).

Several factors have contributed to the increase in security incidents. First, attack tools have become progressively more automated. **Attack tools** include the code and techniques cybercriminals use to exploit security holes via the Internet. Before 2000, the attacker had to physically launch attacks. Now, the attacker can program the malicious code to relaunch itself, a process that is called **self-propagating**. Because they are automated, an attack at one point on the Internet can quickly spread worldwide. For example, **Code Red**, a self-propagating worm, multiplied at such a rapid rate in 2001 that it spread worldwide in less than 18 hours.

Figure 18.6.
In the past few years, the number of security incidents has increased at an alarming rate.

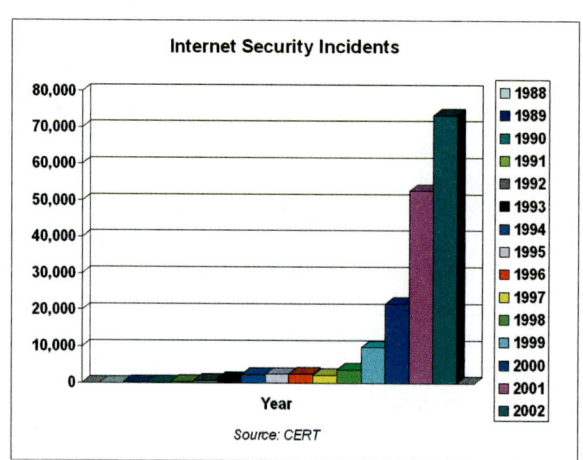

286 Chapter 18 Beyond the Basics: A Closer Look at Security Issues

The attack tools have not only become more automated, they've also become increasingly more sophisticated. For example, attackers have been able to coordinate tools to simultaneously attack multiple systems and different locations on the Internet since 1999. Other modifications to the attack tools have given crackers the ability to attack systems more effectively than in the early days of the Internet. Some of the automated attack tools can modify their behavior randomly or in response to the actions of the victims. Additionally, the tools can also be modular, which simply means that they can swap out parts of the malicious code. These technologies allow the attack to constantly change behavior, making it harder for antivirus software companies to quickly come up with effective antivirus products.

Another factor that has contributed to the number of Internet security issues is the rise of broadband services, such as DSL and cable modem. Because computers that use broadband are constantly connected to the Internet, there's a greater opportunity for intruders to attempt to attack a system. Furthermore, a computer that uses broadband always has the same IP address, whereas those that use dial-up access are assigned a different address each time they make a connection. The combination of technologies that makes high-speed access appealing to Internet users also makes it an attractive target for crackers and intruders.

Crackers attempt to locate open ports by employing automated tools that continually roam the Internet, testing the security of all open connections. When it finds a security hole, such as an open port for a broadband computer that's not protected by a firewall, the cracker has an opportunity to gain control over the system. Think of an unprotected port as an open window in a high-crime area; if the bad guys look long enough, they can probably locate this vulnerability and take advantage of it. Once inside the system, they can probably do as they please.

There's another factor that has contributed to the severity of attacks: Security vulnerabilities in commercial software are being discovered more quickly than in the past. If the vulnerability is a hole in a computer's security, the code that will fix the problem is a *patch*. However, software vendors need time to develop the corresponding patch after a software-based security problem is discovered. Obviously, if the bad guys find the hole before the patch is available, they can exploit the vulnerability. Furthermore, some commercial software programs have become so complex that it's difficult to find *all* the vulnerabilities before releasing the product to the public. As an example, at least one security problem was discovered in a Microsoft product five years after the program was initially released!

Another factor? The huge variety in the type of operating systems, hardware, and software used by Internet users also presents multiple security risks. It's estimated that there are more than 500 million Internet users, each with a slightly different computer configuration. And each system can potentially have its own vulnerabilities.

To add to the mix, an ever-increasing number of people are using the Internet, some of whom don't even realize that they need to put security in place. Finally, there's more knowledge among the cybercriminal community and a large body of existing malicious code on which to base new malware.

After reading this section, you're aware that there are serious Internet-based security issues and that they're on the rise. Now, we'll turn our attention to some of the types of attacks being launched via the Internet.

UNDERSTAND THE MAIN TYPES OF INTERNET-BASED ATTACKS

The attacks on corporate and home security systems can be as varied as the people who dream them up. Many of these attacks can affect both home computers and large networked systems. However, some intruders tend to target businesses, whereas others take aim at home users. Let's take a look at the most common types of attacks and then sort out which usually aim at large businesses and government agencies and which target home systems.

DENIAL OF SERVICE ATTACKS

One specific type of attack that uses the Internet as a conduit and a target is Denial of Service. This type of attack is typically targeted at businesses, though the attack can affect home systems as well. A **Denial of Service (DoS)** attack is one in which a resource on the Internet, such as a server or a Web site, experiences impaired function because the attackers launch a coordinated attack that overwhelms the target with so many bogus requests that the system can't handle them all. The most common type of DoS attack has the effect of preventing Internet users from accessing the target Web site. This can result in a huge financial loss to an organization whose business is Internet-dependent.

As you may recall, information is sent over the Internet as *data packets*. Flooding an Internet resource, such as a Web server, with too many of these packets can cripple it. The more coordinated the attack, the greater the number of sites that will be affected as the data overload bogs down Internet traffic similar to the way that rush hour can cause a traffic jam on a busy interstate.

The Internet's strength—its connectivity—is also its downfall in the case of DoS attacks. This vulnerability is because the Internet is made up of limited resources; there are only so much bandwidth, processing power and storage capacity available. If a DoS attack consumes too many of these resources, service is disrupted and a Web site can be disabled. Furthermore, Internet security is interdependent; every computer on the Internet can potentially communicate with any other connected to it. So even if your system is secure, other computers on the Internet probably aren't, which can put your system at risk. Even the best efforts to thwart DoS attacks might not completely succeed, so computer security experts are dedicated to limiting their occurrence and impact.

The most common Denial of Service attack is the **Distributed Denial of Service (DDoS)** attack. This type of attack originates from a variety of locations. Here's how it works: The perpetrator of a DDoS uses a "master" computer to control multiple client computers for the attack. First, the cracker gains control over a single computer by exploiting its security holes. The intruder then uses the compromised computer to invade other systems. Finally, the intruder can tell the controlled systems to launch attacks against a specified target with a single command.

Large commercial Web sites, such as CNN, can be a magnet for DDoS attackers, who might consider disabling the servers of such a large organization as a challenge. Early in 2000, a single cracker did attack CNN—as well as Yahoo!, Amazon, Charles Schwab, and eBay—reportedly costing each organization "millions."

The computers at the University of California in Santa Barbara were among the many that were commandeered to launch the attack. Eventually, it was found that the perpetrator was a 15-year-old Canadian nicknamed "Mafiaboy," who allegedly boasted about the crime in chat rooms frequented by crackers. Later evidence suggested, however, that Mafiaboy simply copied the methods of other more-sophisticated cybercriminals. Nevertheless, the ease with which the sites were rendered inaccessible was unsettling to most people, especially the security personnel for the affected organizations.

Due to their size and prominence, commercial Web sites are a tempting target for DDoS attackers. But political tensions between countries can also be the motivation for cybercriminals to launch attacks. In May 2001, the United States White House experienced a DDoS attack, which was believed to be

INSIDE TRACK

A Denial of Service attack is abbreviated DoS. Don't confuse this acronym with the one for DOS—a text-based operating system used in the early days of personal computers.

ALERT!

In September and October 2002, the "Slapper" worm affected Web servers that were using a particular type of software. Though this worm didn't directly affect home systems, antivirus experts worried that it was being used to create a network of infected hosts and that these hosts would be used as an attack platform for future DDoS attacks.

from Chinese crackers who were upset about the increase in tensions between the two countries.

Even political differences *within* the United States can lead to DDoS attack. For example, the Recording Industry Association of America's Web site experienced two DDoS attacks during the summer of 2002. These attacks were likely in retaliation to a controversial bill introduced in the House of Representatives by Rep. Howard Berman. This bill would allow RIAA to launch a Denial of Service attack against anyone they felt was trading music illegally; speculation is that music fans were taking revenge by doing the same type of thing to RIAA's Web site. In conclusion, no matter what people's motivation is for launching them, DDoS attacks will most likely continue.

POTENTIAL ATTACKS AGAINST CRITICAL INFRASTRUCTURES

INSIDE TRACK

In October 2002, there was a DDoS attack against the 13 main (root) servers that manage global Internet traffic. During the attack, seven of the servers did not respond to legitimate Internet traffic; two others failed intermittently.

One type of potential attack that concerns the United States Government is an attack against **critical infrastructures**, such as banking, energy, telecommunications, transportation, or public utilities. The government is worried that a well-coordinated attack by terrorists or other cybercriminals could knock out a piece of the country's infrastructure.

An attack against the Internet's infrastructure is called **cyberterrorism**. To prevent widespread damage from this type of attack, government agencies are putting security measures in place. Like other government agencies, the Federal Bureau of Investigation (FBI) has understandably become increasingly concerned about the integrity of the nation's infrastructure. Because of these concerns, the FBI established the National Infrastructure Protection Center (NIPC) at *www.nipc.gov* in a joint partnership with private industry. The Center's mission is to prevent and respond to any cyberattacks on the nation's infrastructures, including the Internet. Congress also passed a bill in October 2002 that included 880 million dollars for implementing cybersecurity measures.

To help with the overall effort necessary to secure the Internet, the government wants individuals to better secure their personal systems. Because the Internet connects vast numbers of computers, securing your own system will help to protect the overall Internet infrastructure. Securing private computers prevents viruses and other malicious code from traveling through the Internet as quickly or causing as much harm as they would otherwise. To help users protect their computers, the government recently established the Stay Safe Online Web site at *www.staysafeonline.info*. This site includes information and practical steps for securing home systems and links to a number of other Internet security sites (see Figure 18.7). It also includes a self-test you can take to evaluate the security of your personal computer system.

COMMON ATTACKS ON HOME SYSTEMS

Many Internet-based attacks affect both home and business systems. However, home computers often fall victim to intrusions that corporate security would carefully guard against. After all, most businesses shield their computer systems by using high-end security software, preventing physical access, and through the vigilance of a full-time Information Technology (IT) staff.

But if you're like most home computer users, you probably don't have an entire department watching out for security issues on your system. Instead, you have to do it yourself. But a lack of resources, such as an industrial-strength firewall and an IT staff, isn't the only reason why home users tend to be more at risk than businesses. CERT reports that most home computers use the Windows operating system and Microsoft software, both of which are

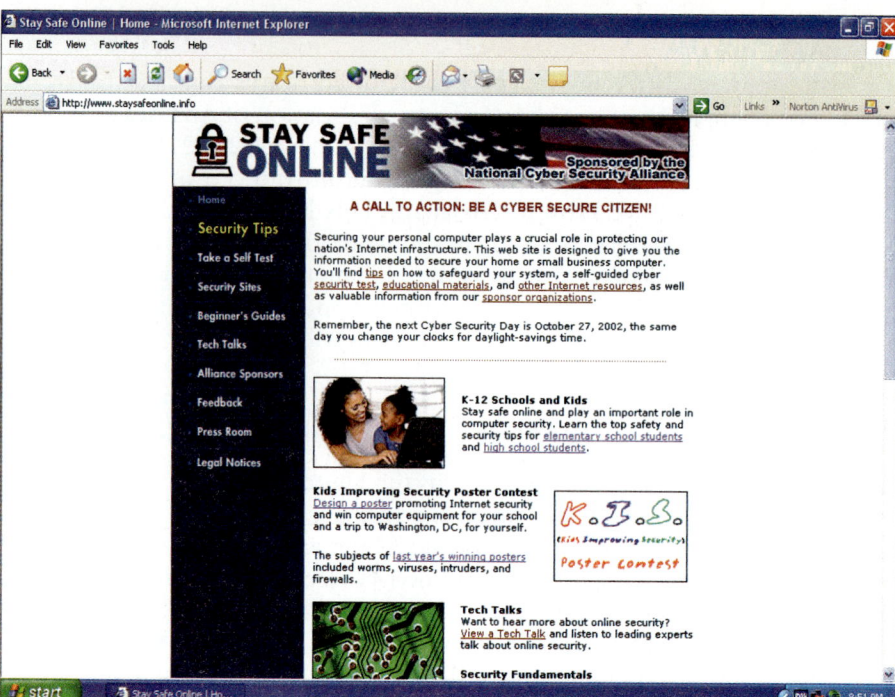

Figure 18.7.
Learn more about personal cybersecurity on the Stay Safe Online Web site.

attractive targets for intruders. This is because Microsoft software has had some security problems in the past, and it is perceived as more vulnerable than some other software companies. With that in mind, let's look at some of the most common techniques cybercriminals use to take aim at home systems.

One typical method is to use social engineering to install Trojan horses or other vicious code. As you probably recall from Chapter 2, The Good, the Bad, the Ugly: Uses and Misuses of the Internet, *social engineering* is the practice of using trickery to convince people to do something they wouldn't otherwise do, such as opening an e-mail attachment. Cybercriminals do this by using alluring messages in e-mail subject lines. This practice can be combined with e-mail spoofing. **Spoofing** is using deception to make it appear that a message is from a different source than the one who actually sent it. Spoofing is often done so that a person will open an attachment (which could contain a Trojan horse) or reveal confidential information. For example, a spoofed e-mail might claim to be from your ISP, requesting your password. A spoofed message might also ask for your credit card number "for billing purposes." The important thing to remember is to verify any communication with the company that allegedly sent the e-mail.

INSIDE TRACK

Although back door programs are generally considered sinister, some remote administration applications are deliberately programmed into software. Some operating systems, for example, include ways that the software's programmers can remotely install updates via the Internet.

If the social engineering *is* successful and the recipient opens an e-mail attachment, a Trojan horse program can be unleashed on the computer, with a variety of effects. A common use for the Trojan horse is to enable the cracker to install a back door or administration program. A **back door**—sometimes called a **Remote Administration Trojan (RAT)**—is a security hole deliberately left on a system so that another can access it. Back door programs typically allow the intruder to gain control of the victim's computer. A computer that is under the remote control of an intruder without the knowledge of the computer's owner is called a **zombie**. A zombie can then be used to launch DDoS attacks on other systems. Obviously, beyond the fact that you don't want your system used for criminal activity, your computer might become so bogged-down in processing data during an attack that you can't use it yourself.

At the end of this chapter, we'll give you a checklist of best practices for safeguarding your system, which includes ways to secure your computer against e-mail spoofs and social engineering. However, your best defense against this type of deception is awareness and common sense. For now, we'll look at a more insidious way that attackers can compromise the security of your system: mobile code.

UNDERSTAND THE POTENTIAL FOR DAMAGE FROM MOBILE CODE: JAVA, JAVASCRIPT, VBSCRIPT, AND ACTIVEX

Another way an attacker can gain control of your system or introduce malware is via mobile code. **Mobile code** is programming code that others write and embed in an HTML document. When your browser loads the Web page, mobile code is downloaded and executed by your browser. Mobile code gets its name from the fact that it can be passed from one system to another in this way. Java, JavaScript, and ActiveX are all examples of programming languages or technologies that can be used to create mobile code.

In many cases, mobile code can be useful and enhance your Internet experience by providing dynamic and interactive Web pages. For example, you might use an interactive Web page to determine the cost and availability of lodging for your next vacation or to register online for a college course. However, attackers can also use mobile code to run malicious code on your computer. Because there are security issues associated with it, we'll examine the basic differences between the three main tools used to develop mobile code (Java, JavaScript, and ActiveX) and then give you some practical ways to guard against associated security breaches.

TYPES OF MOBILE CODE

Java is a full-blown programming language developed by Sun Microsystems. Because Java is designed to run on any size or type of computer platform, it's heavily used to develop Web applications.

Not to be confused with Java, **JavaScript** is a scripting language developed by Sun and Netscape. Although it shares many of the characteristics of Java, JavaScript was developed independently of Java. **Scripts**, such as those created with JavaScript, are mini-programs that can be embedded in HTML Web documents. Like other forms of mobile code, scripts are essentially a double-edged sword: They can make a Web page more interesting and interactive, but they also carry the risk that malicious code will be introduced to your system.

Visual Basic Scripting Edition (VBScript) is similar in function to JavaScript. Like JavaScript, VBScript is used to create dynamic Web pages. VBScript was developed by Microsoft for use with Internet Explorer and can work with ActiveX.

ActiveX is a set of technologies developed by Microsoft. *ActiveX controls* are a specific way of implementing these technologies. These technologies allow the developer to develop dynamic Web sites with forms, interactive multimedia, and games. ActiveX also permits developers to connect desktop applications to the Web. For example, a developer can use ActiveX to create a Web site in which users can view an Excel workbook or a Word document—right from within their browser. In fact, Web sites developed using ActiveX sometimes look more like a computer program than a static document. To produce this level of usefulness and interactivity, however, ActiveX controls need to have access to many (or all) parts of a user's computer system—a practice that concerns some people.

ActiveX differs from the other mobile codes because of the unfettered access it has on your computer. Java and JavaScript operate on your system in

INSIDE TRACK

The term *sandbox* is coined after the children's sandbox you might see in a playground. In the same way that a child's sandbox confines where kids can play, a computer sandbox limits the area in which the code can "play."

a **sandbox**, a protected area in computer memory in which the code can "play" without causing damage to the computer. Operating in a sandbox prevents the code from executing in the system at large because it doesn't have access to the entire computer. Confining the program's execution to a limited area makes the code less dangerous, but also less functional.

In contrast, ActiveX controls aren't confined to a sandbox; they can operate freely throughout your system. This freedom gives them a greater potential to introduce malicious code on a system, so Java and JavaScript are considered "safer" than ActiveX controls.

CONTROLLING MOBILE CODE

Most browsers, including Internet Explorer, include support for mobile code. In fact, the default settings might automatically execute these codes without asking you for confirmation. Fortunately, you can tweak your browser settings to turn off mobile code, such as ActiveX or JavaScript. Alternatively, you can modify the settings so that your browser will prompt you whenever a Web document containing mobile code is about to execute on your system. You can then determine whether you want to download the mobile code within your browser.

Unless you use mobile code on a regular basis to enhance your browsing experience, you might want to completely disable it. To do this in Internet Explorer, follow these steps:

1. Choose Tools, Internet Options.
2. Click the Security tab to display the Security page and then click the Custom Level button.
3. In the Security Settings dialog box, choose Disable (or Prompt) for each type of mobile code.
4. When you're finished, click OK in each of the open dialog boxes (see Figure 18.8).

You can also disable VBScript. This prevents vulnerabilities that may be introduced by cross site scripting. **Cross site scripting** is a process in which scripts (mini-programs) can be included as malicious code in a hyperlink on a Web page; when the hyperlink is clicked, the malicious code can be executed automatically by your browser. Your best way of avoiding problems associated with cross site scripting is to disable your operating system's capability to automatically execute scripts. You'll lose a little functionality in the process, but you'll surf more safely.

When you remove the operating system's capability to understand how to handle VBScripts, you simultaneously prevent this type of file from being

ALERT!
If you don't want to disable scripting, you should be aware of some other ways scripting can be used to spread malicious code. For example, it can be embedded in a link contained in an e-mail message to you. When you click the link, the associated Web page (which might be faked) can execute the dangerous script on your computer. If you leave scripting turned on, don't click links in e-mail messages if you don't recognize the sender. Instead, type the URL in the Address bar from scratch.

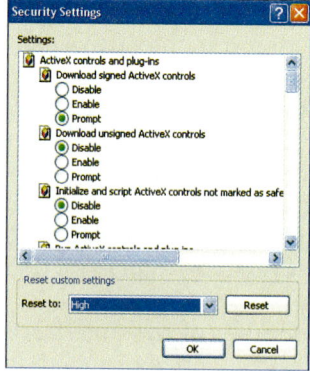

Figure 18.8.
You can change settings in your browser, depending on how you want to handle mobile code.

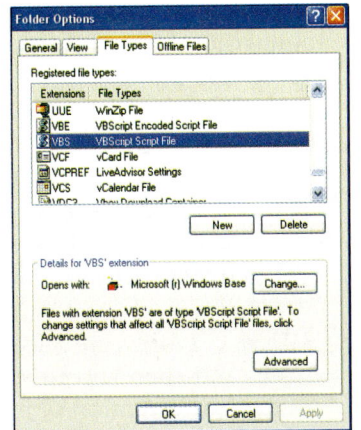

Figure 18.9.
It's a good idea to disable the automatic execution of scripts on your computer.

opened—with or without your consent. To disable VBScripts in Internet Explorer, follow these steps:

1. Right-click the Windows Start button and then choose Explore.
2. In the Start Menu window, choose Tools, Folder Options to open the Folder Options dialog box.
3. Click the File Types tab to show a list of the file types your system "knows" how to handle (see Figure 18.9).
4. Scroll down the list to find VBS Scripting and then single-click to select it.
5. Click Delete and then confirm your actions by choosing Yes in the message box that displays.
6. Choose OK in all open dialog boxes.

Mobile code can be handy, but it is also risky. Just make sure that you understand the hazards associated with running it on your system and use all security measures you can.

KNOW WAYS TO PREVENT MALICIOUS CODE FROM EXECUTING

Several years ago, most computer viruses were spread via floppy disks that were physically transferred from one user to another. Now they're developed with sophisticated features and at an ever-increasing rate, using the Internet to spread globally in a matter of hours.

In Chapter 2, we introduced you to the security issues related to malicious code, including viruses, worms, and Trojan horses. In this section, we'll quickly review how these scourges of the Internet spread and find out how antivirus companies help you in the war against this dangerous code. Along the way, we'll give you tips on how you can secure your own system against malware.

MALICIOUS CODE AND HOW IT SPREADS

Question: Which spreads faster: a worm or a Trojan horse? If you said the former, you're right. In fact, viruses, worms, and Trojan horses all represent malicious programming code that can cause a variety of effects on your computer. However, the exact mechanism they use to spread and how rapidly they proliferate all vary, a fact you probably recall from Chapter 2. However, if you need a quick refresher, here's a brief rundown of how each of the main types of malware is spread:

- *Trojan horse.* If you're familiar with Greek mythology, you probably understand how this type of malicious code got its name: by masquerading as something else. A Trojan is a program that hides its destructive nature by pretending to be something else, such as a useful utility. Keep in mind that Trojan horses don't replicate themselves, which sometimes limits their damage. Instead, they usually rely on user interaction to be unleashed.
- *Virus.* A virus is a program that invades your computer without your knowledge, infects files, replicates, and then spreads to another computer. Usually, the virus also drops a payload, which causes a variety of effects, from annoying to damaging.
- *Worm.* Worms are self-contained programs that execute a payload, replicate, and then spread to other computers. Because they don't require human intervention to propagate, they tend to spread rapidly throughout the Internet. Some of the main types of worms include **Internet worms** and **Script worms**. Internet worms usually spread via e-mail, but also have the capability to self-activate and spread through security holes in operating systems and networks. They can also spread via Internet Relay Chat (IRC). Script worms are those that are created and executed using a scripting language, such as VBScript.
- *Macro virus.* **Macro viruses** use the internal programming language of an application to spread malicious code. One of the first known macro viruses was WM/Concept, which spread through corporations via shared Word documents. Like other malicious code, macro viruses can cause a variety of effects from simple annoyances to widespread damage.
- *Blended threat.* Blended threats are becoming an increasingly common occurrence on the Internet. **Blended threats** are hybrids, or combinations, of two types of malicious code and can include characteristics of each. Because they use multiple methods to spread and exploit Internet vulnerabilities, they can spread very rapidly. They typically cause harm in a variety of ways. For example, they can launch a DDoS, deface Web servers, or install Trojan horse programs. They can also strike from more than one location and propagate by using multiple methods. For example, a blended threat might spread via an e-mail worm *and* by adding script into an HTML file. Blended threats typically spread without the intervention of humans and use automated tools to scan the Internet for vulnerable computers and systems.

The nature of malicious code has changed over the past few years. According to Kaspersky Labs, developers of the Kaspersky antivirus software, the main virus threat in 1995 was from boot sector viruses—the kind that was spread via floppy disks. By 2001, the main security problems arose from worms (see Figure 18.10).

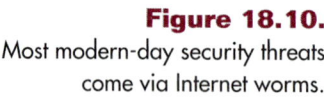

INSIDE TRACK

Some computer viruses disarm antivirus programs so that the malicious code can't be detected or removed. A virus that acts in this way is called a **retrovirus**. BugBear, one of the nastiest worms unleashed in 2002, was considered a retrovirus because it actively worked against antivirus software.

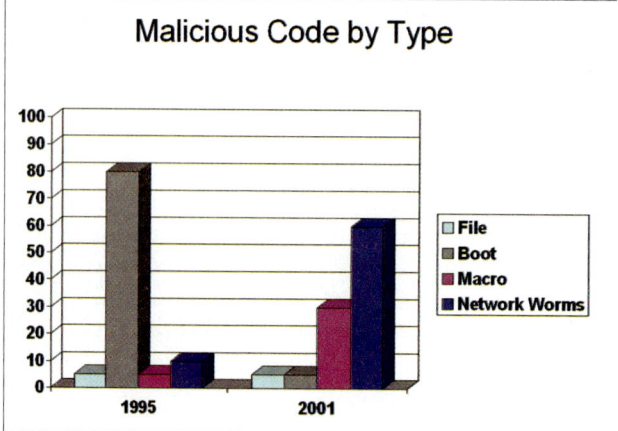

Figure 18.10.
Most modern-day security threats come via Internet worms.

Although the sophistication and number of viruses have increased over the past few years, we have some good guys on our side. Casually called "Virus Hunters," these are high-tech policemen who work hard to neutralize the effects of viruses by quickly developing antivirus tools. In the next section, we'll see how they do it.

HOW ANTIVIRUS COMPANIES HELP YOU WARD OFF MALICIOUS CODE

You may have wondered how antivirus software companies, such as McAfee and Symantec, keep ahead of the malicious code that threatens to run out of control on the Internet. In a nutshell, they do it by constant vigilance and concentrated effort. Here's how.

First, all the major antivirus vendors have teams of people stationed around the world, which helps them instantly respond to any virus that raises its ugly head. Each of the antivirus research teams is composed of software engineers who monitor the Internet 24 hours a day, seven days a week. They can evaluate and dissect malicious code; then quickly create a product to counteract it.

Besides watching diligently for suspicious activity on the Internet, these around-the-clock research teams rely on a global network of customers, administrators, and other techies who alert the teams about possible problems. The first sign of trouble is typically in the form of e-mail sent by someone in this global network. Immediately, the antivirus team uses sophisticated automatic virus detectors to determine if the code is similar to any other malware. If the team finds a match for the code, an antidote for it is developed and posted on the company's Web site as an antivirus update.

If a match is not found, the team must instead use a variety of methods to determine the nature of the virus. They can see if the malicious code operates in a manner similar to other, known viruses. If the code isn't easily identifiable using these techniques, the antivirus engineers can use reverse engineering to determine how best to neutralize a virus. **Reverse engineering** is a process in which a person takes something (such as code) apart to figure out how it works and then reassembles it. This term also refers to decoding a program so that you can use the technology to create another product. After an antivirus product is developed to defuse the threat, it is known as a **virus definition**. If the threat is severe enough, press releases will also be issued to spread the word quickly about the virus.

ASSESSING THE THREAT: RATING SYSTEMS FOR MALICIOUS CODE

 INSIDE TRACK

Malicious code that has been unleashed on the Internet and is rapidly spreading is said to be "in the wild." In contrast, viruses that exist "in the zoo" are those that have been created in antivirus lab settings.

The antivirus companies assign a risk level to every threat or piece of vicious code. Symantec, for example, gives category levels from 1 (no real problem) to 5 (sound the alarms). The risk level is assigned based on the number of infections, the rate of the spread, the distribution, and the possible damage.

 **ON THE HORIZON**

Unfortunately, crackers are constantly developing new types of malware. For example, malicious code might be embedded in files that most people consider safe. Recently, it was found that an Internet worm was embedded in Adobe Acrobat PDF files. Users were offered a chance to play a game; if they clicked on the link, they activated the worm... all of which begs the question, "What will they think of next?"

W32.BugBear and W32.Klez.H, two of the worst threats in 2002, were placed in category 4. Thankfully, most of the malicious code that appears daily on the Internet is placed in category 1. In fact, Symantec maintains that although it receives virus reports at a rate of seven to ten per day, it rates only one incident every six to eight weeks as high risk (see Figure 18.11).

McAfee also rates viruses based on the potential damage and rate of spread. If you want to see a graphical map of which viruses have spread the most in the last 30 days, take a look at McAfee's Web site at *www.mcafee.com* (see Figure 18.12).

BEST PRACTICES FOR PROTECTING YOURSELF FROM MALICIOUS CODE

Be careful out there. It's a word of warning to everyone who's on the Internet, especially in relation to the malicious code that seems to be everywhere nowa-

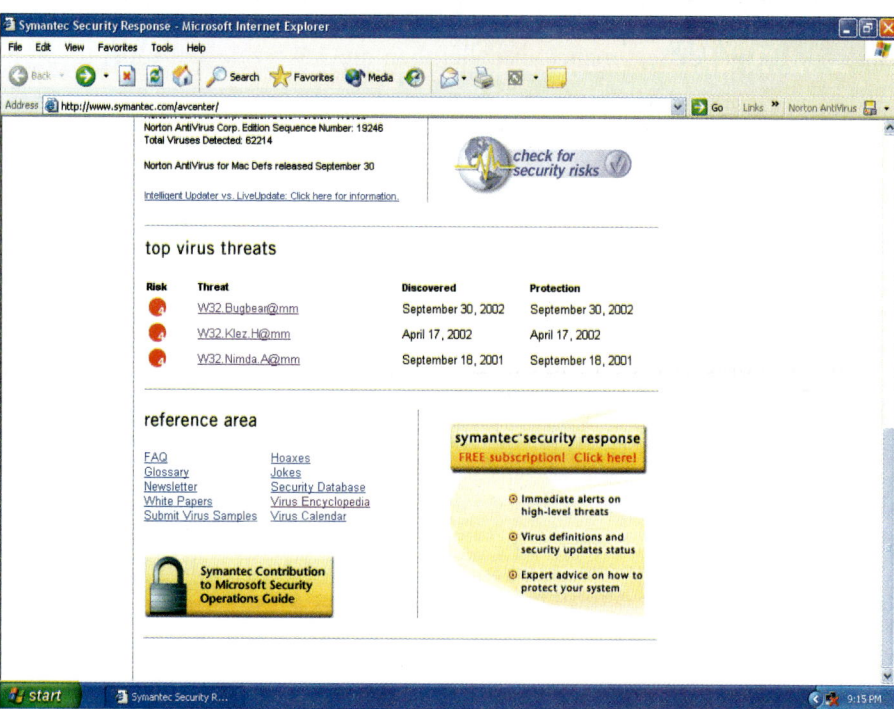

Figure 18.11.
Symantec rates threats from viruses on a scale of one through five.

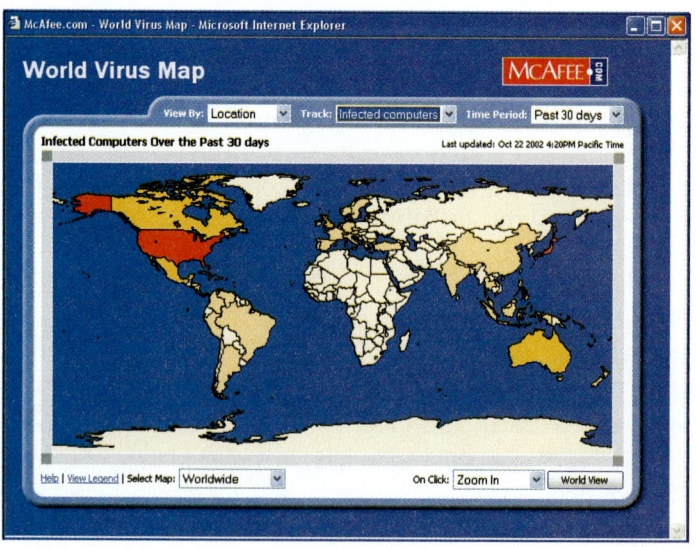

Figure 18.12.
The McAfee Web site includes a visual representation of worldwide security threats.

296 Chapter 18 Beyond the Basics: A Closer Look at Security Issues

ON THE HORIZON

At the time of this printing, there are only three of them, but the potential is there to develop more. We're talking about Personal Digital Assistant (PDA) viruses. Even though the threat from a PDA being infected with malicious code is very small, most experts feel that PDAs and cell phones will be the next target for crackers.

days. Here are some best practices you can implement to protect yourself from the inevitable times when you'll brush up against malicious code.

- Understand how viruses operate and how they spread. (That's why you're reading this book, right?) But even if you feel that you understand all about malware, keep up your guard. You can never be too vigilant in protecting your system from dangerous code.
- Make sure that you configure your system for maximum safety. For example, we already told you how to disable scripting on your system and how to control cookies. If you have antivirus software installed on your system (and you should), you can also modify its settings to medium or high security levels. Additionally, change your e-mail settings to provide maximum security.
- Be on the lookout for ways that crackers might try to send you bad code. For example, you should be suspicious—very suspicious—of e-mail messages that are poorly worded or generic. As usual, don't open attachments from people you don't know. Even if you recognize the sender, save the attached file to disk and then scan it with your antivirus software before opening it. You never know if someone has hijacked your sender's address book or commandeered his computer.
- Limit your online exposure. You can do this by disconnecting from the Internet whenever you're not actually using it. Along these lines, you need to be especially careful if you're using a computer that hooks to the Internet via a broadband technology. These connections are "always on" whenever the computer itself is booted up. So if you're not planning to use the system at 4:00 am, turn it off, which will simultaneously disconnect your computer from the Internet, too.
- Don't go it alone. Install a good quality commercial antivirus program and then keep it up-to-date. But it's not just enough to install the software initially. It's important to download the new virus definitions *at least* once a week so that your system can "recognize" dangerous-looking code. It doesn't hurt to keep an eye on the company's Web site for virus alerts, either. If the company issues a warning, it's time to download the appropriate virus definition—even if it's not time for your weekly update. In addition to downloading the latest virus definitions, make sure to scan your system regularly for viruses. Finally, install a top-notch firewall program so that hackers can't access open ports on your system and compromise security...something that we'll talk about next.

INSIDE TRACK

Because macro viruses can reside in the macro programming language of applications such as Word and Excel, make sure that you change the Security Settings in Microsoft Office to High. To do this, choose Tools, Options in either program. In the Options dialog box, click the Security tab and then click the Macro Security button. Choose High in the Security dialog box and then click OK in both of the open dialog boxes.

INSIDE TRACK

You might want to sign up to be on your antivirus software company's mailing list. The main advantage is that it will be sure to let you know if a high-alert virus is running around in the wild.

UNDERSTAND THE IMPORTANCE OF USING A FIREWALL

A *firewall* is a piece of hardware or software that protects your computer from cyberintruders. Think of a firewall as a large Rottweiler guard dog that sits at the front door of your house. If the dog is properly trained to repel intruders, no bad guys will gain access to your house; and if they do, it's a sure bet they won't get out again. In the same way, a firewall blocks cybercriminals so they can't intrude on your system.

To guard a home system, install a personal firewall. Personal software firewalls to protect home systems can be obtained from Symantec (Norton Personal Firewall) or from ZoneAlarm Labs (*www.zonealarm.com*) (see Figure 18.13).

Windows XP also includes a built-in firewall, called the Internet Connection Firewall. However, the Windows XP firewall is not turned on when you install the system; instead, you must specifically activate it. Additionally, there is a security hole in Windows XP. To prevent problems, download the latest patch that is available at Microsoft's Web site (*www.microsoft.com*).

Additionally, if you have an always-on broadband connection, you might also want to purchase a hardware firewall. The cost will set you back about $100, but adds a second layer of protection. If you're working on a business or school network, you're probably already protected by multiple layers of firewall. Just make sure that *some* kind of firewall is in place, no matter where you're using the Internet.

KNOW HOW TO CREATE STRONG PASSWORDS

Chances are good that you'll need to enter a password to access a network account that connects to the Internet. Additionally, if you work in a business setting, sign up for free e-mail, or order products online you'll generally need to establish one.

A **password** is simply a string of characters that you enter so that you can access a network, online service, or Web site. Think of a password like the key to your house—it allows entry to something. Crackers want to get their hands on your passwords, just as they would any of your important information. After they have a password, they have keys to the kingdom in a sense.

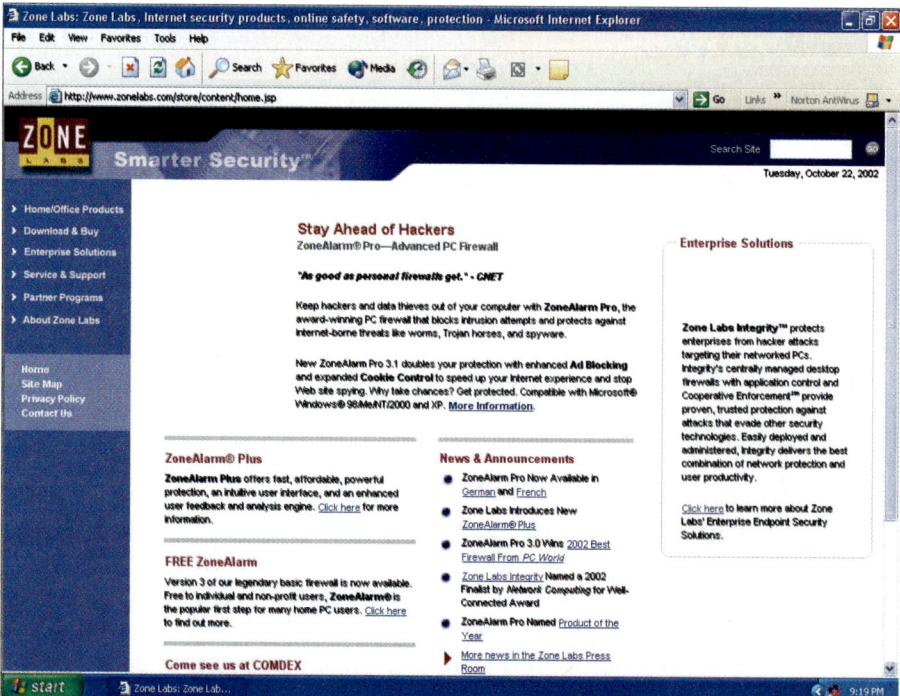

Figure 18.13.
Even personal systems need to use a firewall against cyberintruders.

But despite warnings by Internet security experts, most users don't take the trouble to create secure passwords. It's not difficult to create a good password, but there are a few things to keep in mind: Your mission is to create a cryptic enough password that the cybercrooks will never be able to guess it or decipher it using automated tools. In this section, we'll let you know some of the ways that crackers can find out passwords and then how to use that information to create a secure one.

PASSWORD TRICKERY

Because a password is a valuable piece of information, criminal minds have thought of many ways to wrestle the information from Internet users. One of the longest-standing methods is to use deception to convince a person to willingly give up their password. For example, a cracker might redirect Internet traffic from a legitimate commerce-driven Web site to a faked copy. If the copy exactly mirrors the original, the Internet surfer might be tricked into entering a password and even financial information, such as a credit card number.

Another way for cybercriminals to obtain passwords is by sending spoofed e-mail messages, supposedly from the administrator at the user's ISP. As a twist on this ploy, they might even call you and ask for your password over the phone. If the criminal can sound convincing enough, people just might be fooled into giving out the information the criminal wants.

GUESSING AND CRACKING

If a cracker can't trick you into revealing your password, he moves to the next level: guessing. This isn't as laughable as you might imagine. There are more passwords like "password" and "123" than you might think. And if these don't work, chances are strong that the password includes the person's last name, spouse's or child's name, pet's name, birthday, or license plate number.

If the cybercriminal can't guess the password, he can pull out all the stops and use a specialized program called a **password cracker**. Just as you expect, password cracker application programs use a variety of techniques until they determine a password.

INSIDE TRACK

Not all password cracker programs are used illegally. Corporate information technology administrators also use these programs to determine forgotten passwords.

One way the crackers do this is by examining the password's underlying hash pattern. A **hash** pattern is a scrambled, numeric equivalent of the word. It's generated when your password is transformed by software into a shorter, fixed-length value. For example, a password of *LetMeIn* might be changed into a hash value of *1234*.

A *dictionary-based password cracker* uses words from the dictionary to try to match the hash pattern to known words. Some dictionary-based password crackers also create hybrid forms of known words or add incremental numbers to words. For example, *dog* might become *dog01*, *dog2*, and so on. Crackers can also apply mutation filters, which convert a word to a similar form, such as *hassle* being converted to *ha55le*.

A *brute-force password cracker* tries every possible password until it finds a match. Brute-force password crackers owe their success to their extreme speed. Some brute-force programs can check as many as 100,000 passwords per second!

CREATING SECURE PASSWORDS

Before telling you how to create a secure password, we'll go over a few things *not* to include. It's a bad idea to use your own name, an account name, your initials or those of people you know, or common words or names. In fact, avoid using real words of any kind because they're already in some password cracker dictionary program somewhere. Names of famous places, music groups, actors, television shows, or other things related to popular culture are

INSIDE TRACK

Most companies require their employees to change passwords every 30–60 days. This is probably a good practice for home computer users to follow, too.

off-limits, too. Phone numbers, license plate numbers, or the name of your school? Not a good idea. Also, avoid using sequences on the keyboard (such as *asdf* or *qwerty*) or words that are simply spelled backwards: The crackers know all about these methods.

So, what's left? Well, one way to create a secure password is to use a combination of upper- and lowercase letters, numbers, and symbols to make a password harder to crack. To remember the sequence, think of a sentence that makes sense to you, but hopefully won't to a cracker. For example, "My dog, Sadie, cost 200 dollars and is very nice!" could be distilled down to "MdSc200daivn!"

Think about using passwords that are at least eight characters long. Also, avoid placing the number at the beginning or the end of the password because some password cracker programs might use incremental techniques, which would crack the password more quickly.

If you're still not totally convinced that coming up with a secure password is worth the effort, take a look at this: Imagine that a cybercriminal is intent on discovering your password, and is using a program that guesses passwords at a rate of 100,000 per second. Under these conditions, any eight-character, lower case-only password could theoretically be cracked in approximately three weeks. However, if you instead created an eight-character password that has a mix of upper- and lowercase letters, numbers and symbols, it would take the cracker *two years* to figure it out.

There are a couple of other safe practices to follow as well. Create different passwords for each account (yes, we know that's a lot to remember), and don't attach a sticky note to your computer with a list of them, either. If your operating system or a Web site offers to "remember" your password for you, decline the offer. It could open up security holes as well.

Now that you've developed a secure password, bring it along for the next section. We're going shopping online, but safely and securely.

KNOW THE BEST PRACTICES FOR CONDUCTING SAFE E-COMMERCE

Online shopping is big business. Just how big is hard to judge, but some feel that it's gaining in popularity as sites such as Amazon expand their offerings. To purchase items online, you typically need to enter credit card information and send it to the merchant via the Internet, along with other identifying information. Obviously, this can introduce some serious security risks if you're not careful. To help you shop safely, we've developed a list of best practices to use when engaging in this activity.

- *Know the privacy policy.* Before ordering a product online, it's a good idea to acquaint yourself with the merchant's privacy policy. This helps you make an informed decision about what might happen to your personal information. If you're not comfortable with the way the data will be used, find another place to buy the product.
- *Erase digital footprints.* Erase cookies and clear the Internet history and temporary files before making your next purchase. This process gives unscrupulous marketers less opportunity to trace your browsing habits.
- *Protect your e-mail address.* Provide a free, Web-based e-mail address on any forms that you're required to fill out, not your main e-mail address. This keeps spam out of your personal mailbox.
- *Don't send confidential information via e-mail.* Never, ever send confidential information, especially credit card numbers, via e-mail. E-mail is

not a secure way to send data over the Internet because the data can be read or stored anyplace along the way.

- *Keep good records.* Print a copy of the online receipt that the merchant provides and keep it until you receive the product.
- *Protect your mailing address.* Because online merchants may share your data, you may want to consider renting a private mailbox at your post office or a service, such as Mail Boxes, Etc., just for Internet deliveries. This is especially the case if you regularly buy items online.
- *Check it out.* Before purchasing from an online merchant, make sure that the company is reputable. You can find out by going to the Better Business Bureau's Web site (*www.bbb.org*).
- *Go with SSL.* Don't shop at Web sites unless they use Secure Sockets Layer (SSL). SSL encrypts your data before transmitting it over the Internet to keep it secure. Web sites that use SSL usually advertise it. Additionally, you can usually identify a site that uses SSL because of the closed lock icon that appears in the Windows Taskbar. Additionally, the Web address should begin with *https://* instead of *http://*, indicating a secure site.
- *Expect the worst.* Assume that the credit card number you use for online purchases may be stolen. Because of this, you may want to use a separate card for shopping on the Internet, one with fraud protection.

IMPLEMENT THE BEST PRACTICES FOR SECURITY

So you have a choice: Either completely disconnect from the Internet or implement the best practices for security. Because most of us find the Internet useful, we'd opt for the latter choice. If so, here's a safety checklist you can use to ensure that you're doing everything in your power to keep your system and data secure.

✔ *Install, run, and update antivirus software.*

Need we say more? Because there are an estimated seven to ten new viruses per day unleashed on the Internet, it's critical to protect your system with a commercial antivirus program. After initial installation, most experts recommend conscientiously updating the virus definitions on your computer every week and scanning your system daily.

✔ *Install any software patches.*

Check the Web site of software vendors, such as Microsoft (*www.microsoft.com*), to see if there are new patches that should be downloaded and applied (see Figure 18.14).

ON THE HORIZON

A new concept in online commerce is the use of electronic wallets, which are designed to be more convenient than entering your information at each shopping Web site. An e-wallet keeps track of your identifying information and credit card numbers, storing the information on your hard drive or a secure Web site. When you want to make a purchase, you simply access the e-wallet instead of re-entering the information at each merchant's site. However, the security of e-wallets is still open for debate. Additionally, some people feel that the services might infringe on your privacy by tracking your purchases and then using the data for marketing purposes.

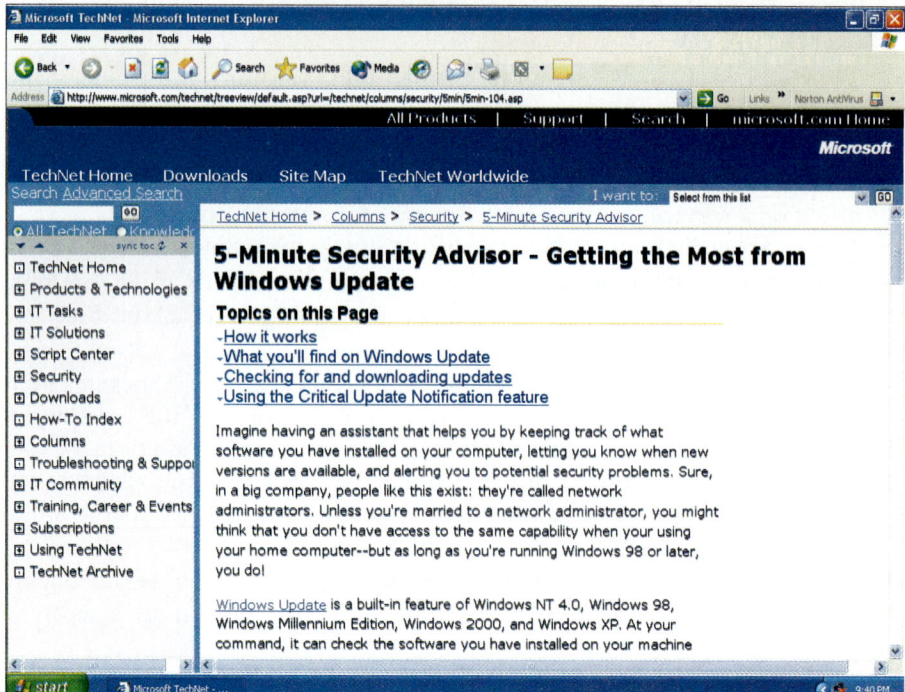

Figure 18.14.
Install program patches, usually available on your software vendor's Web site as a free download.

✔ *Build a (fire) wall.*

Keep sufficient software and hardware firewalls on your system to ward off cybercriminals.

✔ *Disable or control mobile code.*

Instead of letting ActiveX controls and VBScript run unfettered on your system, turn off these technologies. At the very least, modify your settings so that you're prompted when either type of code is about to execute.

✔ *Use filtering software.*

Filtering helps control what actually arrives at your computer. This helps to manage dangerous, offensive, or inappropriate content that some Web sites contain. Although filtering by itself won't ward off malicious code, it can prevent you from accidentally accessing sites that are used for cross site scripting schemes. There are a number of popular filtering programs available to you, such as CyberPatrol at *www.cyberpatrol.com* (see Figure 18.15) and We-blocker (*www.we-blocker.com*).

✔ *Use e-mail encryption.*

To maintain privacy and security, use an encryption program for sending e-mail.

✔ *Create secure passwords.*

If you use the "rules" we outlined in this chapter, you'll have passwords that are difficult for any cracker or automated tool to decipher. And finally...

Figure 18.15.
Use filtering software to block cross site scripting schemes and to avoid viewing offensive or inappropriate content.

✔ *Use common sense.*

Coupled with technologies such as antivirus software and firewalls, this is one of the best ways to stay safe while using the Internet.

So now you know how to lock the door and stay secure—even if you do reside in the high crime world of the Internet.

Don't Forget...

- As the Internet matures, security for both personal and business systems has become a major issue.
- Security incidents have risen dramatically in number from the Internet's infancy until present.
- Attackers and intruders are using increasingly more sophisticated tools to attack systems.
- Breaches in security have cost companies, organizations, and individuals millions of dollars.
- The United States government is concerned about Internet security because of possible attacks against critical infrastructures.
- One common form of Internet attack is a Distributed Denial of Service (DDoS).
- Social engineering and spoofing can be combined with attack tools and malicious code.
- Intruders are interested in home systems so they can commandeer them in DDoS attacks or pull confidential information from them.

- Mobile code, such as Java, JavaScript, and ActiveX can be used by crackers to introduce malicious code to your system.
- ActiveX is considered more risky than Java and JavaScript because it doesn't operate in a limited area of the computer.
- Cross site scripting can be used to place malicious code on your system.
- Malicious code can use a variety of methods to infect computer systems.
- You can best prevent malicious code from executing on your system by taking preventative measures, such as installing antivirus software and firewalls.
- Antivirus software companies are strongly proactive in fighting malicious code.
- Creating a strong password is part of your overall plan of implementing security.
- Online commerce can be conducted safely if you're careful to follow the best practices.

Check This Out

MULTIPLE CHOICE

1. Which of the following is true of Internet worms?
   a. Internet worms are more prevalent than boot sector viruses.
   b. Worms generally spread more rapidly throughout the Internet than do Trojan horses.
   c. Worms can be part of a blended threat.
   d. All of the above
2. Compared with 1995, why are there more security concerns nowadays?
   a. There are more people using the Internet.
   b. Attack tools are more sophisticated.
   c. There is a more established group of crackers.
   d. All of the above
3. Which of the following would be a "best practice" for Internet security?
   a. Update virus definitions regularly.
   b. Install a firewall.
   c. Change your password once a month.
   d. All of the above
4. Which of the following examples of mobile code causes the most security concerns?
   a. ActiveX
   b. ZoneAlarm
   c. Java
   d. JavaScript
5. Which of the following represents the most secure password?
   a. Cat
   b. RaSclgwa6a10yo!
   c. Password
   d. Chicago01

MATCHING

a. back door
b. sandbox
c. DDoS
d. security
e. spoofing
f. self-propagating
g. blended threat
h. password cracker
i. firewall
j. zombie

1. Overwhelming an Internet resource so that it can't be used
2. Program used to decipher passwords
3. Capable of spreading by itself without human intervention
4. Deception used to make it appear that an e-mail message comes from a known sender
5. A protected, limited area of the computer in which Java and JavaScript can be executed
6. Using a combination of methods and technologies to compromise the security of other systems
7. Creating a security hole so that other programs can be installed
8. Hardware or software used to protect your computer from intruders
9. A computer that is commandeered and then used in a DDoS attack
10. Putting safeguards in place to protect computer systems

Real Life

1. They send shivers down the back of every knowledgeable Internet user. With names like LoveLetter, Melissa, Sircam, Bantrans, Nimda, and Klez, these pieces of malware have done more than their share of damage. They're the worst of the worst. As a knowledgeable Internet user, you owe it to yourself to be familiar with them. After all, if you understand a little bit about how these spread and the damage they do, you'll probably be more alert for other bad code as well.

   To familiarize yourself with these threats, find out about the most damaging malicious code. To do so, use Symantec's Expanded Threat List and Virus Definition page (*www.symantec.com/avcenter/vinfodb.html*) to conduct research. Then write up a paragraph on each of the top 10 pieces of malware. Make sure to include information about how the malicious code spreads and the payload that each delivers.

2. Use the Internet to find out how companies are using a variety of methods (firewalls, physical security, and so on) to secure their computer systems. Then interview the Information Technology (IT) staff members at three local companies or at your school to find out how they handle Internet security, including what's currently being done and what could be improved. Write a three-page paper that discusses your findings and then present it to the class.

3. View each of the following sites to see some of the seals of authenticity that you might encounter on the Internet: *www.bbbonline.org*, *www.truste.org*, *www.webassured.com*, *www.pwcbetterweb.com*, *www.privacybot.com*, and *www.verisign.com*. Find out how these organizations verify the authenticity of a site and how you can tell whether a Web site is valid or not. Develop a short presentation or paper that outlines your findings.

I Spy: Privacy and Security Concerns

1. Look at Symantec's Web site, especially the pages related to Security Response. Spend a few minutes looking over the threat list at *www.symantec.com/avcenter/vinfodb.html*, which includes the most current threats. Also, spend a few minutes looking through portions of the virus definition dictionary. Notice that the threats are listed by type, such as virus, worm, or Trojan horse. Also note that the name for the malicious code usually indicates the type of threat, such as *backdoor* or *mm* (for mass mailer worm). Using Excel or graph paper, develop a bar chart that shows the worst security threats by type (virus, worm, or Trojan horse).

2. Interview three Information Technology (IT) professionals, such as your school's computer network administrator or IT personnel at local companies. Ask their opinions about the safety and functionality of ActiveX controls and JavaScript. Next, spend time online researching these technologies and how they're used. Finally, write a report or create a PowerPoint presentation that outlines your findings. Present your information to a small group or to your entire class.

3. Go to Symantec's Web site (*www.symantec.com*). Find out how antivirus software can block and/or quarantine viruses on your system. Also, learn how to submit suspicious code you encounter on your computer to Symantec or another antivirus company. Share your findings with the class.

SECTION Eight
CREATING A WEB SITE

CHAPTER 19
DESIGNING A GREAT WEB SITE

Key Terms

After you complete this chapter, you'll understand the following terms:

- authoring
- hierarchy
- information architecture
- online presence
- scalability
- switching
- usability
- Web page developers
- Webmaster

Chapter Objectives

After you complete this chapter, you'll

- ■ Understand Some of the Reasons for Creating Web Pages
- ■ Understand the Main Types of Web Sites
- ■ Know the Basics of How Web Sites are Developed
- ■ Understand Design Considerations

The Big Picture

By now, you're probably eager to create your own Web pages. After all, although it's great to be able to get around the Web seamlessly, you're probably ready to develop your own Web site at this point in your Internet career.

In this chapter, you'll learn the essentials of designing and developing a working Web site. You'll find out what elements on a Web site make it more appealing and easier to navigate for visitors. You'll also see that it's important to think about these issues because it's very easy for Internet users to stop viewing your site if they can't readily find the information they need.

In the next few chapters following this one, you'll actually get a chance to create Web pages, using Microsoft FrontPage to do so, and then see how you can transfer the pages from your system to the Internet. Along the way, you'll probably discover talents and interests you didn't realize you had—and have a lot of fun as well.

Window on the Web

If you've worked through the previous chapters in this book, you've spent quite a bit of time online viewing various Web sites. You've also probably noticed a big difference in the layout and design of various Web sites. The variance in structure and design translates into sales—or a lack of sales—for online businesses. But even if the total sum of your interest lies in developing a one-page Web site so that you can use it to post your resume, it's still important to understand Web design issues. Why? Because if your Web page takes a long time to display, is unattractive or is poorly laid out, visitors at your site won't stick around long enough to view your resume or other content.

First, it's particularly important for the site's home (start) page to be laid out in an attractive manner with information that's easy to locate. That's because the start page essentially acts as a gateway for the rest of the site. For example, the professionally designed Web site in Figure 19.1 (*www.skdesigns.com*) is well-designed, with the appropriate balance between text, graphics, pleasing colors, and a great-looking design.

Figure 19.1.
Well-designed Web sites balance graphics and content.

On the other hand, the Web site shown in Figure 19.2 (*www.embassyworld.com*) includes far too much text, too many links, and an extremely confusing navigation scheme. Additionally, the site's purpose is unclear: is it to sell cigars or to help you locate an embassy?

Too many graphics, garish colors, and hodgepodge designs are also a turnoff for most Web visitors. Figure 19.3 shows a personal Web page with text that fades into a noisy background.

In this chapter, we'll give you some key principles for designing top-notch Web sites. Keeping these ideas in mind as you work on your Web pages will prevent you from falling into the traps many novice Web authors do. Not only will you learn how to develop a professional-looking site, but hopefully you'll enjoy the process, too. After all, the full-time Web developers shouldn't have *all* the fun!

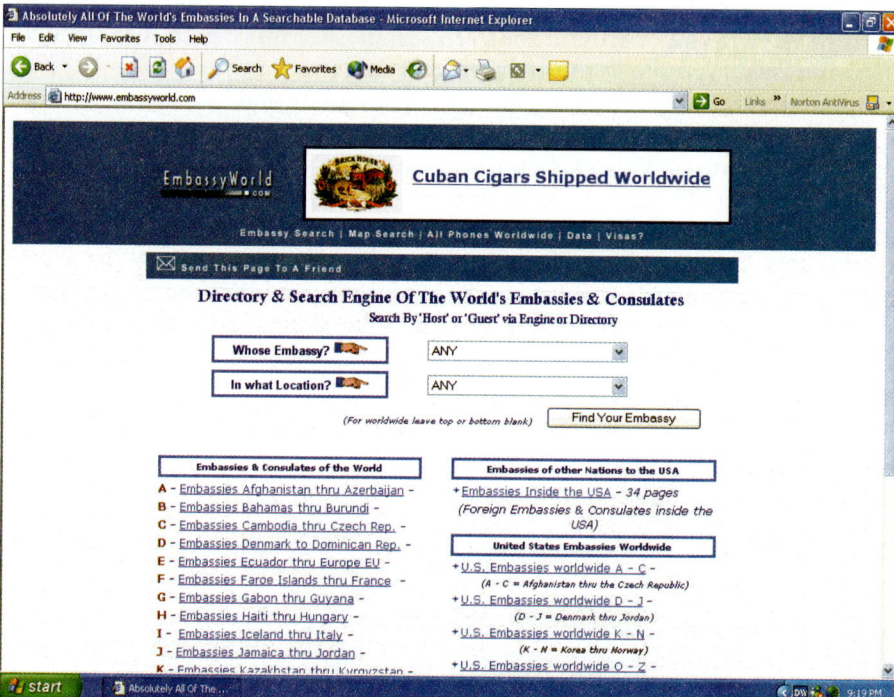

Figure 19.2.
You'll lose Web visitors if your site's purpose and method of navigation are unclear.

Figure 19.3.
Make sure that your text is readable.

UNDERSTAND SOME OF THE REASONS FOR CREATING WEB PAGES

By now, you realize that the World Wide Web is a part of everyday life in the United States. Most of us spend at least a few minutes every day on the Web to find information, such as the news or weather.

But perhaps you're not content to simply be a consumer of the Web, viewing pages others have created. Instead, you might be ready to develop your own Web site. But changing from simply being a Web surfer to an Internet designer does take some effort and know-how. However, learning how to create and manage Web sites can have multiple benefits. For example, you'll

- Develop practical skills that you can potentially use in getting or keeping a job.
- Learn how to use a Web page editor, such as FrontPage.
- Write some HTML code from scratch.
- Be able to use the Web as a worldwide forum for your ideas.

When you're finished, you'll have a working Web site that you can post on the Internet. Best of all, developing Web pages helps you better understand how pages are tied together and how the Internet works.

Before we get into the nuts and bolts of designing a Web page, let's take a brief tour of the main types of Web sites that are being developed and why each one exists.

UNDERSTAND THE MAIN TYPES OF WEB SITES

Web sites run the gamut from simple, single-page text documents to complex e-commerce shopping sites. Simple Web sites are usually developed by individuals so that they can post their resumes or tell others about their interests. In contrast, a large business usually has an entire team of Web designers working on a complex, dynamic site that includes hundreds of pages and secure online shopping. Web sites for small businesses usually fall somewhere in-between these two extremes in terms of size and complexity. For example, a small business' Web site might consist of information on its products, but not include secure shopping functions.

For businesses small and large, an **online presence** (meaning a Web site) is certainly expected. It's also just about essential, at least if the organization hopes to remain in business or generate sales outside of a local market. Where else can a business potentially gain millions of global customers at a cost that's significantly cheaper than traditional forms of advertising?

Although online shopping is a major element of corporate Web sites, there are many other valid reasons for a business to have a Web site. Companies use Web sites to test new markets, products, and services. Companies can also use a site to provide customers with 24/7 technical support. Not only is this practice cost-effective for the business, but it can mean a quicker response for the customer as well. Additionally, a Web site can provide a conduit for customer feedback or the timely release of information. For example, antivirus software developers post virus definitions on Web sites almost daily.

But the value of having a Web site isn't just confined to individuals, small businesses, and large corporations. Most educational institutions also maintain a Web site that includes information about courses, majors, faculty members, and activities. Some also include interactive features that you can use to sign up for on-campus classes or even take an online course.

KNOW THE BASICS OF HOW WEB SITES ARE DEVELOPED

Although you'll learn how to create a Web site step-by-step in later chapters, it is important to understand the basics before you begin. To give you a preliminary look at the process of Web site creation, let's look at the following:

Web page developers (sometimes called *designers* or *content managers*) are responsible for creating attractive and easy-to-use Web pages. Most large organizations hire professional Web page developers. These people are usually specialists in e-commerce, production, programming, or graphic design. However, smaller companies and colleges often use in-house personnel. For example, a small college might assign the job of developing its Web site to the same person who keeps the network running.

The actual process of developing a Web site is called **authoring**. To create a Web site, you add text, graphics, animations, hyperlinks, and other elements to a series of Web pages. After formatting and laying out the objects as you see fit, you send the files to a Web server. As you recall from Chapter 14, Pulling Information from the Internet, many large files are transferred over the Internet via File Transfer Protocol (FTP). This is the same method typically used to send Web pages that you develop from your computer to a Web server. The Web server in which the pages will be stored is called the *host*. Whenever someone types the URL for your Web site in their browser, the Web server responds to the browser's request and sends the appropriate files to the Internet user's system. At that point, the user can view your page on their system.

Even after the Web pages are initially developed and posted on a Web server, your job isn't finished because most Web pages require periodic maintenance, generally because the content on the pages needs updating. For example, when a company has new information to include on its Web site, the Webmaster changes the data on the Web pages and then resends it to the Web server.

Webmasters and content managers develop and edit the Web sites using a variety of software tools. However, Hypertext Markup Language (HTML) code is used "behind the scenes." HTML is considered the language of the Web because it represents the standard protocol Web servers and clients use to communicate. You'll learn more about the various tools and methods you can use to develop Web pages in Chapter 20, Tools You Can Use to Create a Web Site.

INSIDE TRACK

The person in a company who is in charge of maintaining the content and functionality of a Web site is called the **Webmaster**. However, this term is used rather loosely and it sometimes refers to anyone who is involved with the creation or management of a Web site.

UNDERSTAND DESIGN CONSIDERATIONS

When you develop a Web site, your mission is to create a functional and attractive Web site that loads quickly, is user-friendly, and accomplishes your organization's goals. But before you can create this type of Web page, you need to figure out your action plan. If you don't plan properly, you're likely to end up with a disjointed, unorganized, or jumbled mess.

A little planning up front will help you create a well-designed Web site. But what constitutes a well-designed Web site? We'll give you some guidelines to keep in mind when you develop your Web site.

THINK GOALS AND MARKET

Your first step in development is to determine the goals for your Web site. Is it to generate sales, share information, or post a resume? Next, determine the target audience for the site, based on age, interests, and other demographic information. Are you appealing to jazz buffs or lovers of classical music? People who hike in the mountains or those who frequent shopping malls?

The site's objectives and audience should drive much of the content, layout, and formatting for the site. For example, a Web site that you develop to share your MP3 collection will probably have more splash and color than one aimed at convincing prospective employers that you're perfect for working in a white-collar environment.

THINK USABILITY

It's also critical to consider how usable a site will be for your target audience. Sometimes, site developers are so technically minded that they forget how "real" people will use the site. To illustrate this, how many times have you wandered aimlessly around a Web site, looking for the information you need, but the designer accidentally forgot to include it (or buried it so deep that it was difficult to locate)? Or perhaps the links were so cryptic that it was hard to navigate the site?

One of the main reasons that Web sites—even those developed by major companies—fail is because they don't take into account the site's **usability**—how easy it is for real people to interact with the site to perform tasks. Usability is important because it's so easy for site visitors to click over to the competition if they don't like your site or can't easily find data.

Make it tough for users to find information, overload the site with glitzy graphics and animations that annoy the visitor, or construct slow-loading pages, and you'll quickly realize how a poor design can translate into sluggish sales. Other things that might cause visitors to leave your site include registration forms, pop-up advertisements, garish color schemes, and confusing navigation systems.

Changing over from one supplier or vendor to another is called **switching**. In the physical world, switching from one store to another requires a significant effort for the buyer; consequently, most of us will grit our teeth and stick with the situation even if the checkout line is long and the salesperson is rude. After all, it will cost us time and effort to switch stores. But the switching costs on the Web are negligible. All we have to do to find and switch to a competitor is to click another site or run a quick search on Google or AltaVista. And if a site sticks a pushy survey in our face, we're liable to leave the site—and fast. Only easy sites that provide an enjoyable experience will get the attention. Ever heard of survival of the fittest? Well, on the Web, it's survival of the easiest.

There's an entire industry built around analyzing and restructuring Web sites for usability. But you don't have to become a usability expert to design a decent Web site. Instead, think analytically about why people use Web sites in the first place: To get information or accomplish a task. Anything that you place on your Web site that supports this is advantageous; extraneous things that don't have a direct bearing on your objectives will not. For example, you might think a trumpet call that plays when people arrive at your site is exciting, but if it doesn't support the main focus of the site, get rid of it.

People usually go online to do a specific task, such as to buy a book, check out the latest news, or register for a course. It's your job as a Web designer to create elements on your Web page that support these functions in the easiest, most minimalist way. For example, if your site's purpose is to promote vacation rentals of beach houses, your site should include features that make it easy to locate and sign up for rentals. In short, if you want to be a good Web site designer, you need to be able to analyze human behavior and think how people will best interact with your site; then take that analysis and find ways to make it easy for them to get around the site in a way that will achieve the site's goals.

INSIDE TRACK

An inexpensive way to conduct usability testing is to invite testers over for pizza; then let them spend a couple of hours wandering around your Web site. Watch how they interact with the site and with your competitors' sites. Ask the testers for their feedback on how you can improve your Web site. At least one usability expert feels that you can conduct effective usability testing with just five people—and that might cost only a few pizzas.

Figure 19.4.
Some of eBay's popularity is due to its usability: People can accomplish what they set out to do.

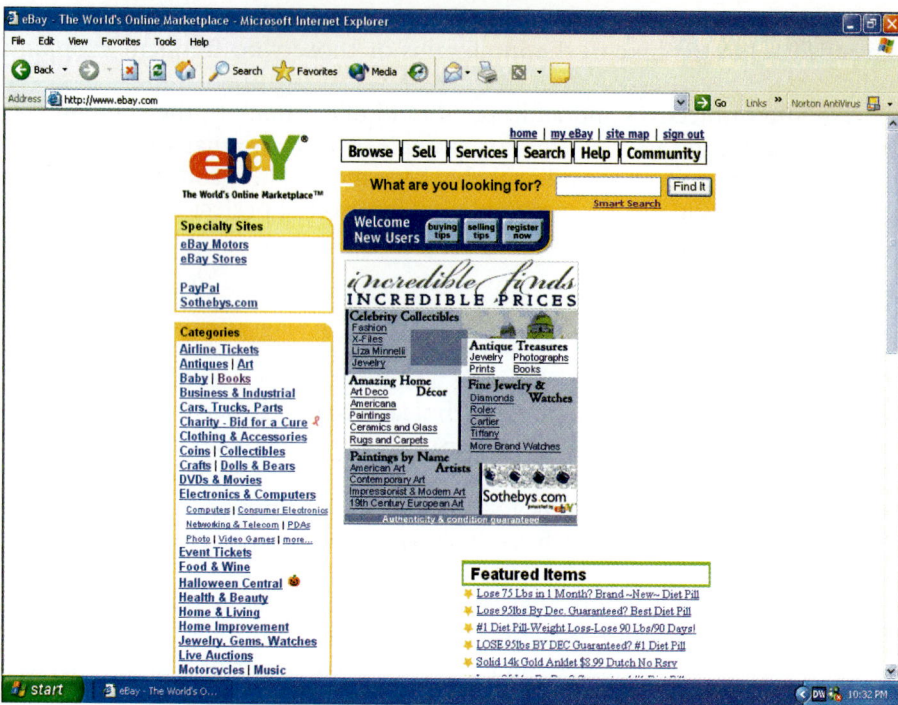

Jared Spool, a usability expert and author of a book on Web site usability, indicates that the bottom line is whether a site's visitor is successful at finding the wanted information. In Spool's estimation, this only happens an average of 42% of the time. He also thinks that some of the best-designed sites include those for Dell (*www.dell.com*), eBay (*www.ebay.com*; see Figure 19.4), and Amazon (*www.amazon.com*).

To help you more carefully evaluate usability issues, go to the Web. We'll give you a listing of more Web sites on Web usability in the end-of-chapter exercises, but if you want a head start, take a look at the Usable Web's site (*www.usableweb.com*), which includes a vast number of links.

THINK STRUCTURE

You won't have to work on the Web for long before you'll come across a Web site that is badly structured. No matter where you wander on the site, you just can't locate the information you needed. Sooner or later, you may even become so frustrated with the site that you abandoned it altogether. Unfortunately, this problem is common, partly because the Web has grown at such a rapid rate.

In fact, many Web sites have been thrown together with no thought to how things should be laid out. But Webmasters and designers are increasingly realizing the importance of **information architecture**, organizing and structuring data so that it's easy for users to find and Webmasters to maintain.

Although you can technically create a single-page Web site, most of the time you'll include multiple levels of information on a site. Most Web designers recommend diagramming the way you want your pages to relate to each other before getting too deep into the actual design. Here are some general guidelines to keep in mind as you plan your information architecture:

- *Think like your visitors will think.* Organize your content in a way that end-users will find meaningful. Because you're familiar with your organization, you might include industry-specific information that visitors don't really care about. (For example, how many sites have you visited lately just to see the company's organizational chart?) On the other hand, you might forget to include essential information because it seems too basic or easy. If possible, have "real" users that represent your target market give you input on how to structure the site and what content to include.

- *Get rid of extra routes.* By now, you probably realize that there are a vast number of ways to get to the same place on a Web site. As a designer, it's tempting to include links to and from every little bit of information on your site. But this approach can confuse your users. Instead, try including only the main ways that most people will use to navigate your site.

- *Trim away the excess.* Don't include so many facts about your products or services that people will get bogged down with irrelevant information. Because Web pages are visual in nature, most people don't like to wade through detailed text. Narrow down your content to the best stuff and get rid of the rest.

- *Plan for the future.* Although you're designing your Web site today, think about what might happen tomorrow. Most professional designers do this by setting up their Web sites for scalability. **Scalability** is the capability to easily adjust to changing conditions by modifying the size or configuration. For example, if you're working for a company that plans to introduce new products in the near future, it's good to structure the Web site to account for the expansion.

Most of the time, you'll use a **hierarchy** for your Web site. A hierarchy is a tree-like setup that begins with a single point, or root, that describes the most general characteristic of the topic. This topic is then divided into branches that contain increasingly more specific information. For example, if your Web site were about sports equipment, the root might be labeled *Sports*. Some of the branches from the Sports root might include *Football, Baseball, Basketball*, and so on.

If you use a hierarchical structure like this, use the home page as a table of contents to the other pages on the site, providing links to important subcategories. Most of the time, a Web site will include at least two levels: the home page and the linked pages. Commercial Web sites for large organizations are significantly more complex than that. Additionally, each of the pages on the site should link back to the home page so that people can easily return to it at any time. Figure 19.5 shows a diagram of a simple Web site, with the home page linking to each of the pages on the second level of the hierarchy.

THINK CAREFULLY ABOUT THE HOME PAGE'S DESIGN

The structure and design of the home page is critical to the success of your Web site—it is usually the most important page in a site. Because of this, it needs to be attractive, to be easy to navigate, and to load quickly. If not, people will go to your competitor's site. After all, it's usually only a couple of mouse clicks away.

A well-used analogy is to think of the home page as a store's front entrance. If a storefront of a physical ("brick-and-mortar") store isn't appealing and functional, it won't attract customers. In the same way, a site's home page needs to be attractive and inviting to attract customers. The following is a list of guidelines for designing the home page—keep in mind that the same principles can be used throughout the entire Web site:

- *Keep it quick.* The home page should load quickly—within 10 seconds—and steer visitors toward other information via links. But don't include

 INSIDE TRACK

Don't include so many graphics or animations that your home page takes longer than 10 seconds to load on a computer with 56K dial-up access. If you create a slow-loading Web page, chances are strong that your potential customers will stop loading your site and switch to your competitor's.

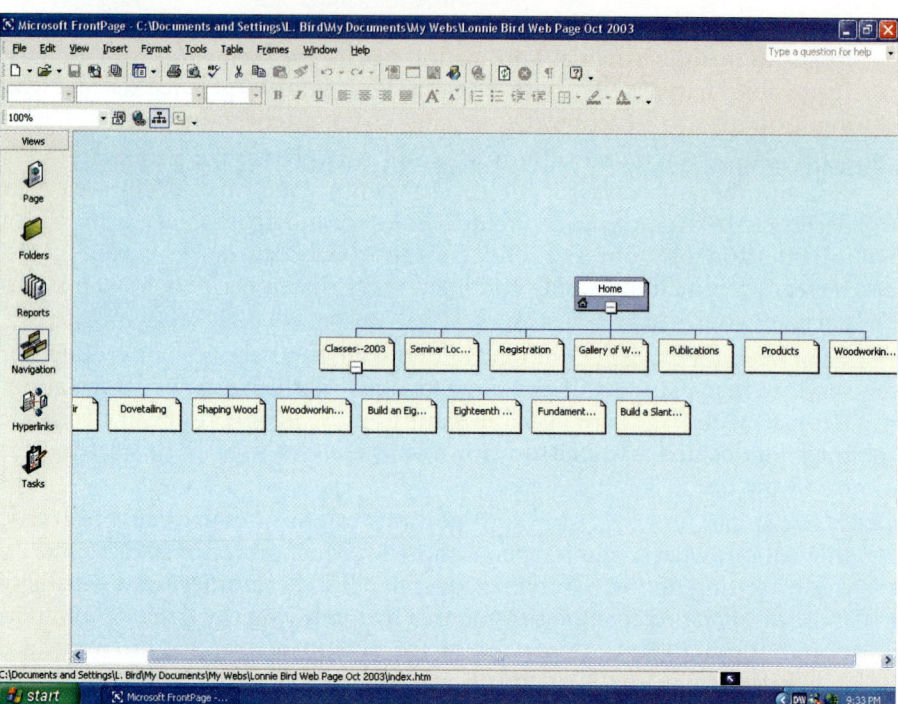

Figure 19.5.
The home page acts as a table of contents and usually links to each secondary page on the Web site.

everything about your business on the home page. Besides boring your visitors, it will make the page load more slowly.

- *Keep it interesting.* The home page should include the business's name, a logo or other carefully selected graphics, a brief synopsis of the business, and links to main categories and contact information—but not much more. Make sure that the content is presented interestingly enough to keep your visitors' attention. Figure 19.6 shows an example of a professionally designed Web site that includes the necessary information, a sprinkling of graphics, and clearly defined hyperlinks.

- *Keep it simple.* Keep the information on the home page short and snappy, yet interesting enough that visitors will stay at your site. Mirror this concept throughout your site: It's better to have more pages with well-written and thought-out content than a few long boring ones. (Web designers refer to this as building a deep site with short pages.) But don't just condense the content. Keep the design elements clean as well. For example, keep the background simple and the number of fonts and graphics to a minimum.

- *Keep it short.* Everything that you want visitors to see on your home page should be clearly visible on an average-sized computer screen when the page first loads, without having to scroll down. If you decide to include more information on the home page than will fit on most computer screens, limit it to one scroll sequence. Not only does a home page with a lot of data take a long time to load, but it is harder to navigate and view the information.

- *Keep it attractive.* First impressions are important. Keep the home page aesthetically pleasing. A good design will support your content; a bad one will detract from it.

- *Keep it consistent.* Common fonts, bullets, logos, backgrounds, and color schemes tie a site together. Changing the look and feel of each of the pages in a Web site might show that you know how to use your Web page editor to modify these elements, but it doesn't show that you understand design. Instead, mirror the home page's logo, color scheme, and fonts throughout the site to create a unified look.

ALERT!
If you're designing a personal Web site, carefully consider what identifying information you plan to include. If you're not comfortable sharing personal information, such as your home phone number or address with the entire world, consider using a secondary e-mail address or a remailer.

314 Chapter 19 Designing a Great Web Site

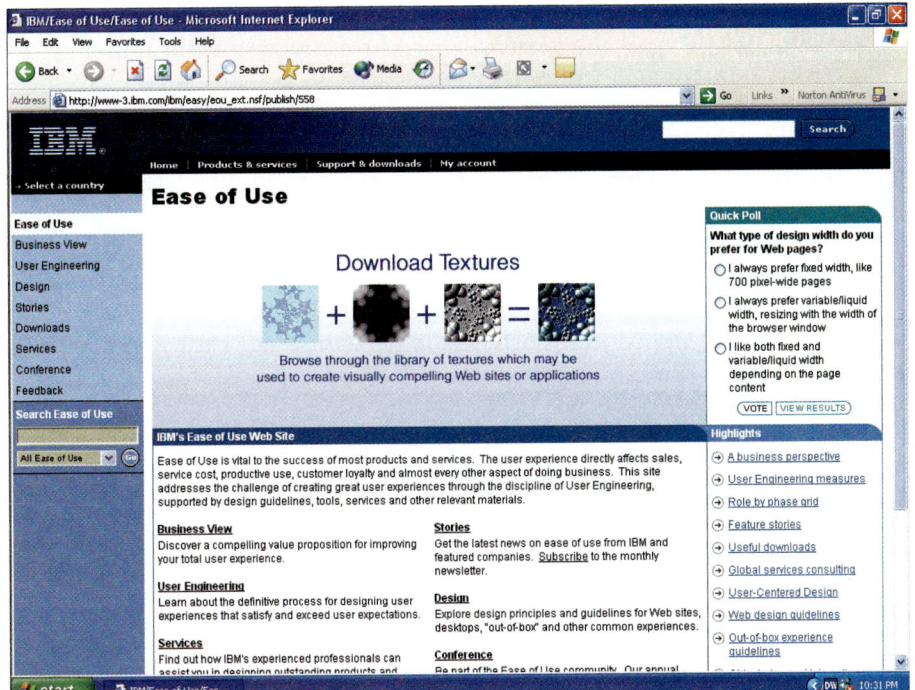

Figure 19.6.
Professionally designed Web sites make it easy to find the information you need.

- *Keep it navigable.* Visitors should be able to easily locate links and buttons they can use to visit other pages on your site. Hyperlink text should also clearly indicate to what information the link points. Visitors to your site should always know where they are, where they came from, and where they can go next.

- *Keep it error-free.* Unless you're adept at using multimedia plug-ins, such as Flash and Shockwave, don't include them on your site. Usability gurus maintain that 90% of users will abandon a site if even one error message displays. And don't forget to make sure that the site is free from other kinds of errors as well—such as grammatical and spelling errors.

- *Keep it free of excessive multimedia.* Yes, many people like music and animations. But others find them annoying or simply don't have the bandwidth to support downloading videos, music, and animations. If you want to include these elements on your site, don't make them automatically pop up when the visitor displays the home page. Instead, give your visitors a choice of whether or not they want to view multimedia content by providing links to them.

- *Keep it readable.* Make sure that the text doesn't fade into the background color you've chosen or isn't so small that it's not easily readable.

- *Keep it original.* Relying heavily on predesigned templates can make your Web site look like a cookie-cutter version of many others on the Web. (In Chapter 20, you'll design a Web page in FrontPage by using one of the program's templates. However, we'll show you how to modify the design so that it looks more original and avoids this pitfall.)

- *Keep it slim in terms of graphics.* Sure, you have to include some limited graphics on your home page. But don't let them clutter it up. A rule of thumb is to include only GIF and JPEG files because they can retain the essential look of the image without slowing down the page's loading. The total size of the graphics on each page shouldn't exceed 20K so that it will load quickly.

INSIDE TRACK

Many Web servers call up GIF files in groups of four. Because of this, it's a good plan to limit GIFs to four or fewer per page. This prevents multiple server calls for GIFs, ensuring that your pages will load briskly.

- *Keep it honest.* Don't copy elements, graphics, or content from other sites unless you have the written, express permission of the author to do so. Although copying from other Web pages is easy, unless you have permission, it's not honest (not to mention illegal).
- *Keep it free from counters, advertisements, and scrolling text.* Counters are used to track how many visitors have viewed your Web site. However, most professionally designed sites don't include them, so they give the appearance of being amateurish. And advertisements and scrolling text tend to annoy site visitors.

That's it. By keeping your goals, usability factors, and basic design principles in mind, you should be able to create an appealing, useful, and easy-to-navigate Web site.

Don't Forget...

- You can gain valuable skills and insights from developing a Web page.
- Web sites vary in purpose and complexity.
- Web sites are used commercially for a wide variety of purposes, such as providing technical support, disseminating information, and testing new markets and products.
- For businesses, it's important to have a Web site—and one that's usable for the average Internet visitor.
- The process for developing Web pages, although not complicated, should be well-thought-out.
- Webmasters are the people in charge of maintaining the content and functionality of a Web site.
- You can use a variety of Web-creation tools to develop a Web site, all of which use HTML.
- When designing a Web site, you need to think about the target audience, usability, structure, and scalability.
- A well-designed, usable Web site translates into more visitors who stay longer at the site—and who end up coming back again.

Check This Out

MULTIPLE CHOICE

1. Which of the following is a good practice when you're designing the home page?
    a. Using as many fonts and colors as possible
    b. Limiting graphics to those that support the site's main purpose
    c. Including several pages of detailed information about your company
    d. All of the above
2. Which of the following might cause most visitors to leave your Web site?
    a. A slow-loading page
    b. A complicated navigation system
    c. A JavaScript error message
    d. All of the above
3. Learning the basics of designing a Web site might be advantageous so that you can
    a. Gain a better understanding of how the Web works.
    b. Learn marketable skills.
    c. Share information with a global market.
    d. All of the above
4. What is the multiple-level structure that most Web sites use to organize information called?
    a. Brick-and-mortar
    b. Authoring
    c. Hierarchical structure
    d. Scalability
5. Which of the following can potentially slow down the loading of a page?
    a. Large graphic files
    b. Flash animations
    c. Music
    d. All of the above

MATCHING

a. information architecture
b. authoring
c. online presence
d. scalability
e. HTML
f. usability
g. host
h. switching costs
i. Webmaster
j. brick-and-mortar

1. Organizing and structuring data so that it's easy for users to find and Webmasters to maintain
2. The Web server in which the Web pages for a site are stored
3. The person responsible for creating and/or maintaining a Web site
4. A physical business, with buildings such as stores, offices, or warehouses
5. The capability to easily adjust to changing conditions by modifying the size or configuration
6. The effort, time, or money required to use a different vendor
7. Developing a Web page using HTML tools to do so
8. The language of the Web
9. How easy it is for a visitor to find his or her way around a Web site
10. Having a Web site

Real Life

1. One of the main principles of Web site design is to make your site easy for real people to use. To find out more about usability issues, go to the Usable Web's site (*www.usableweb.com*). Follow the links from this site to read at least 10 articles on usability and user testing. Use the information you find to develop a written report on how to increase the usability of a Web site.

2. Conduct an Internet search to find Web sites about your favorite hobby. Using the sites you find as examples, develop a list of 10 Web sites that are well-designed and usable for the average person. Indicate why you feel each site on your list illustrates good design and usability. Next, develop a list of five Web sites that have design, structure, or usability problems, and why each site is being included on the list. Develop an oral presentation on good and poor Web design, using the sites you found as examples. If your classroom has the necessary technology in place (an overhead projection system connected to the Internet), use it to show the actual Web sites as you give your presentation.

3. Visit CNET's site on planning and designing Web sites (*builder.cnet.com/webbuilding/0-3881.html*). Read the articles in the sections on site design and usability. Next, run an Internet search to find out about the laws regarding Web site accessibility. Determine which elements can make a Web site accessible to those with disabilities. Consolidate your findings into a presentation; then give it to your class.

4. Interview the Webmasters at three businesses, agencies, or colleges to find out how they develop Web sites. Ask if they conduct usability testing. If not, determine why. If appropriate, ask if they want you to be a usability tester for their site on a volunteer basis. Write or give a short report of your experience as a tester.

5. You can learn a great deal about design and usability by analyzing professionally designed Web sites. View sites of at least five major companies. Write down the design principles and usability features that you notice on the sites and then think about how you can incorporate many of the same features in Web sites you develop.

6. Usability experts have designed several sites on the Web that include examples of good and bad Web sites. To see some of these examples, go to *www.saturnfolios.co.uk/usability/examples.html*. This site includes a brief description of "what's wrong" with the indicated Web sites and then provides a link so that you can view the site first-hand. Follow the links on this site to view these Web sites, which illustrate common problems with Web sites.

I Spy: Privacy and Security Concerns

1. Many sites are set up so that users can't access the information unless they register, using an online form. Imagine that you're the Webmaster (content manager) for a site that is designed in this way. Discuss this practice from a Web design standpoint. Do you feel that it supports a site's purpose, or is it an infringement on visitor's privacy? Give reasons for your answer.

2. Because of the security issues associated with ActiveX controls and other plug-ins, some users won't visit Web sites that use these technologies. If you were in charge of designing a Web site for a small business, would you include these technologies? Why or why not? What is the balance between usability and security for the site's visitors? Write a report or create a presentation that outlines and defends your ideas.

CHAPTER 2.0

TOOLS YOU CAN USE TO CREATE A WEB SITE

Key Terms

After you complete this chapter, you'll understand the following terms:

Web page editor
Web host
What You See Is What You Get (WYSIWYG)
markup tags

Chapter Objectives

After you complete this chapter, you'll

- Know About Using Web Page Editors
- Know About Using Free Web Creation Tools
- Understand the Basics of Using HTML Markup Tags

The Big Picture

You're ready. You know all about determining a Web site's purpose before beginning to create it. You also clearly see why you should include only content and elements on a Web page that support the site's underlying objectives. Site usability? Super important. In fact, you recognize that it's a higher priority than all the multimedia bells and whistles you could ever dream up.

Now that you've learned the essentials of designing a Web site, you should be ready to dig in and start working on the site. But which software tool should you use to do it? Where do you start? And what about HTML?

Sure, there are many choices available. But don't worry. In this chapter, we'll show you some of the options you can use to create a Web site. You'll learn that you can use commercial Web editor programs, such as Microsoft's FrontPage, or free software tools readily available on the Web. You'll also see that you can develop Web sites from scratch by using Hypertext Markup Language (HTML)—and it's easier than you might think. Finally, you'll begin to understand the relationship between how a Web page displays and the underlying HTML that creates it. After you're armed with the information in this chapter, you'll be ready to roll up your sleeves and start developing your own Web site.

Window on the Web

A casual glance at a Web site won't reveal which program was used to develop it. However, in previous chapters we explained that HTML is used to specify the structure and layout of Web pages, using markup tags to do so. HTML is the language of the Web, the protocol used to develop and maintain Web pages. Interestingly enough, you *can* view the HTML markup tags for most Web pages. Seeing the relationship of the HTML tags to the displayed Web page will give you a better understanding of how HTML works. To view the HTML tags on a Web page, right-click near the top of the page and then choose View Source from the shortcut menu (see Figure 20.1).

You have a wide choice of tools that you can use to create Web-ready pages. You can always develop the pages in Hypertext Markup Language (HTML). However, unless you're technically minded, you may not want to spend the time necessary to learn HTML markup tags. Instead, you can use one of the most popular options: a Web page editor. A **Web page editor** (sometimes called simply a Web editor) is a program that lets you create Web pages by interacting directly with the software's interface. The most well-known Web page editor is Microsoft's FrontPage (see Figure 20.2).

Another option is to use free Web creation software. Here's how you get your hands on it: To maintain a Web site, you need a **Web host**, which is the business that provides the equipment and services necessary to store and service the Web files and act as your Web server. (You'll learn about finding and evaluating a Web host in Chapter 23, Publishing to the World Wide Web.) To help you develop files for your Web site, most Web hosts include free software tools that you can use to prepare the HTML files. Furthermore, just like a commercial Web editing program, you don't have to know HTML. Instead, these tools are usually simple programs that walk you through a step-by-step process to create your Web pages. One Web hosting service that provides a free tool (called Click-n-Build) to help you develop your Web site is EarthLink. You

Figure 20.1.
You can view the underlying HTML markup tags for a Web page.

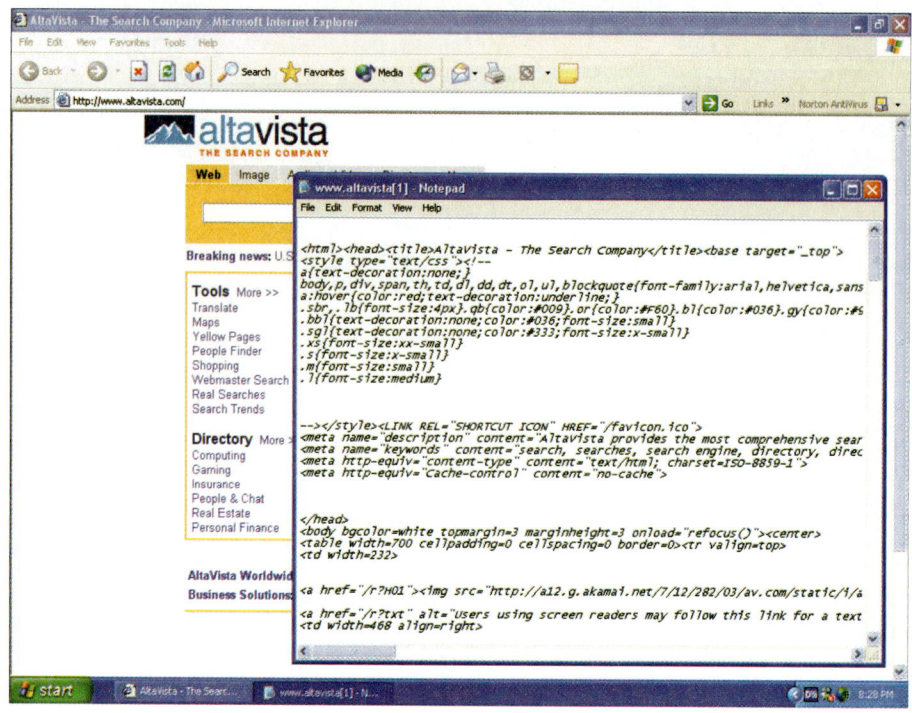

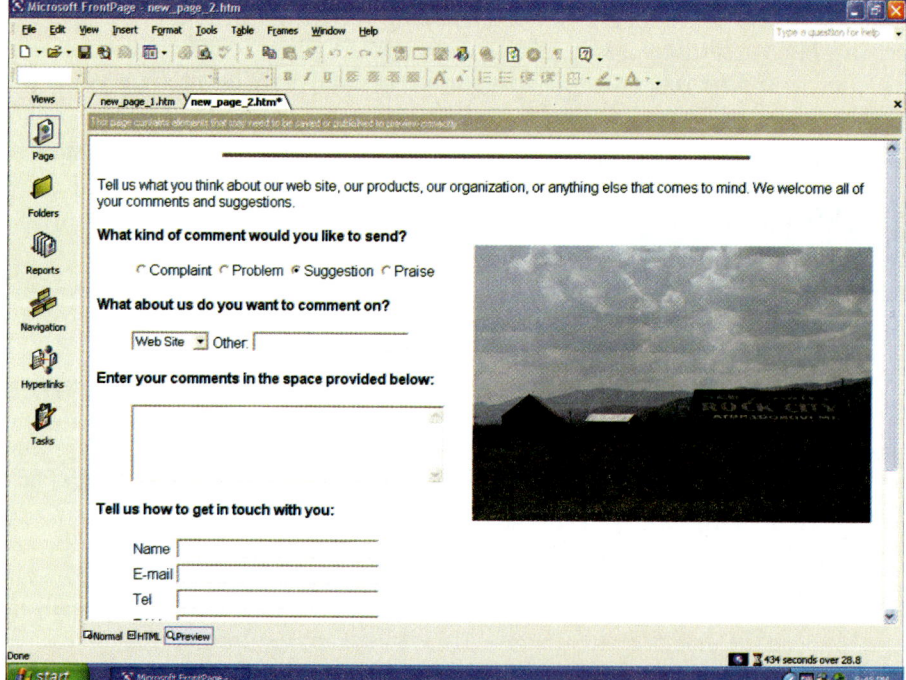

Figure 20.2.
Microsoft FrontPage is an easy to use, visually based Web editing program.

can view EarthLink's home page at *www.earthlink.net*; you'll find this company's information on Click-n-Build at *www.earthlink.net/home/tools/clicknbuild* (see Figure 20.3).

Finally, if you are technically minded, you can learn to develop pages by developing them directly in HTML instead of using a Web page editor or a free software tool. Teaching you how to use all the HTML markup tags is beyond the scope of this book. However, we'll show you a couple of examples of tags and tell you a little bit about how HTML works.

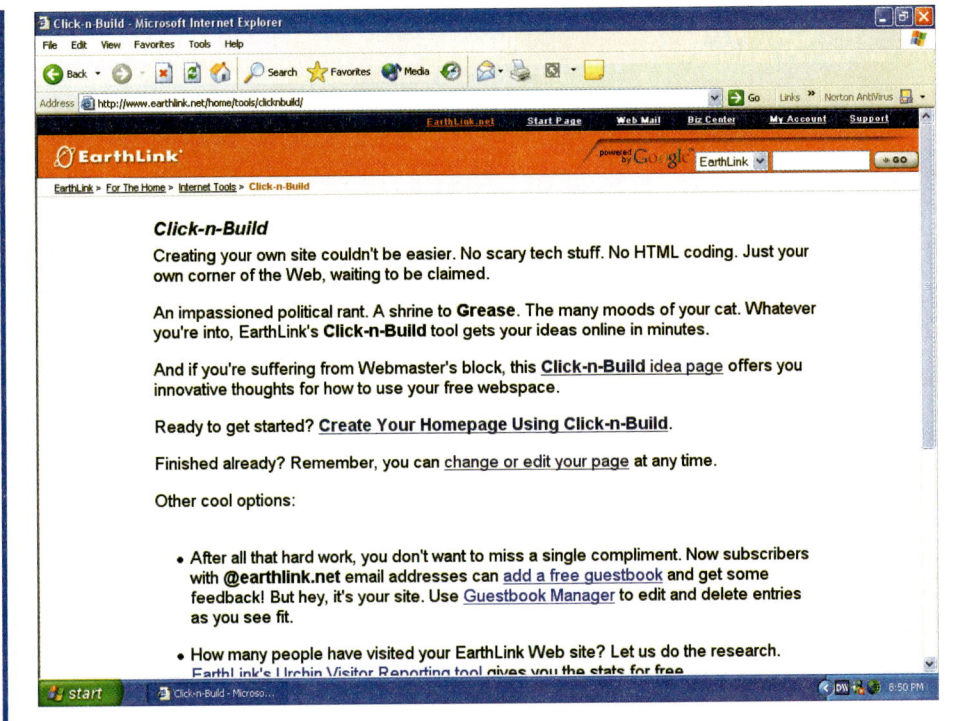

Figure 20.3.
EarthLink, like most Web hosts, provides free software that you can use to develop Web pages.

KNOW ABOUT USING WEB PAGE EDITORS

Although HTML is always used "behind the scenes" to develop Web pages, you don't have to interact directly with this language to author a Web site. Instead, you can use a Web page editor, such as Microsoft's FrontPage. This program lets you develop your Web pages by using the familiar Windows interface, the mouse, and menu commands.

For those who don't have the time or interest required to learn HTML, a program such as FrontPage is a great way to quickly develop Web content. As you'll see when you begin to work with the program, you *can* interact directly with HTML within FrontPage if you want. However, the easiest option for most casual computer users is to bypass the technicalities of HTML and create pages visually and by using familiar mouse and menu commands.

FrontPage and other similar commercial Web editors let you see how your completed document will appear while you're working on it. This feature is commonly called **What You See Is What You Get (WYSIWYG)**. Whatever you create on the screen visually by using the menus and mouse is mirrored "behind the scenes" in HTML code, but you don't ever have to deal with the language unless you really want to. For those that do, FrontPage's interface allows you to switch quickly from one view to the other (see Figures 20.4 and 20.5).

Macromedia also sells Web development software: Dreamweaver MX (*www.macromedia.com/software/dreamweaver*). This software is more expensive than FrontPage and has a steeper learning curve. However, it's a popular option among businesses and individuals who want to develop more complex Web sites (see Figure 20.6).

The last Web editor we'll mention is Adobe GoLive. You can find out more about this Web development tool at Adobe's Web site (*www.adobe.com/products/golive*).

In Chapter 21, Using FrontPage to Develop a Web Site, you'll learn the step-by-step process of how to create Web pages using FrontPage. For now,

INSIDE TRACK

Another option for developing a Web site is to create it in a Microsoft Office program, such as Word or PowerPoint.

If you're already familiar with Word or PowerPoint and have limited needs for a Web site, using Office applications might be a good choice. To do so, first develop your document or presentation as usual and then choose File, Save as Web Page. In the Save As dialog box, indicate a filename and location and then choose Save. The pages will automatically be saved using HTML and ready to be published to the Web.

Although this process is straightforward, you might eventually feel constrained by the lack of flexibility inherent in using these programs for this purpose.

Figure 20.4.
Normal view provides you with a WYSIWYG version of your Web page—showing you exactly what it will look like on the Web.

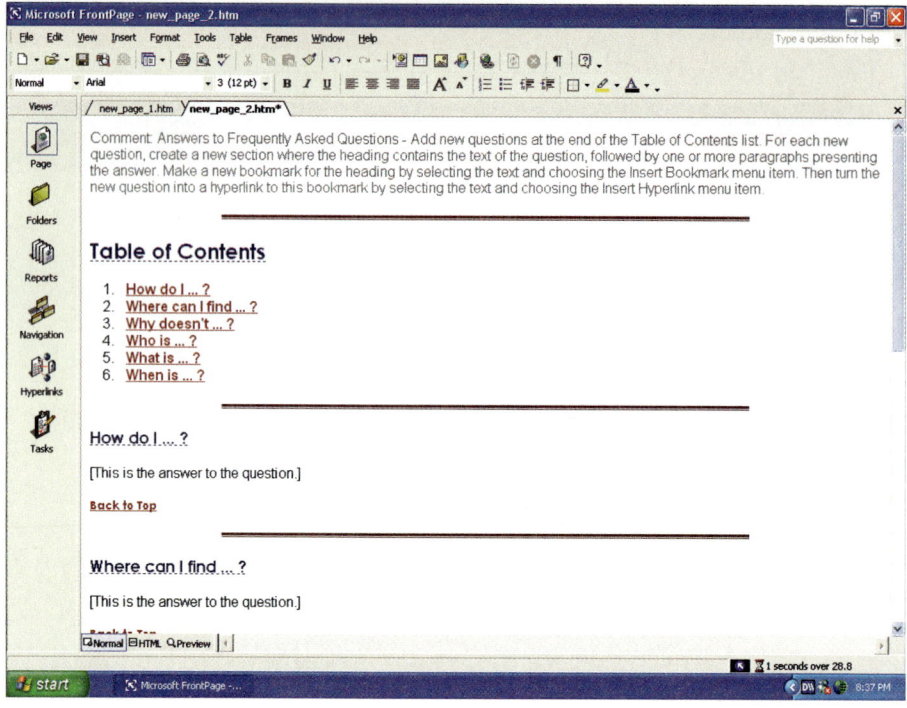

Figure 20.5.
FrontPage also lets you work directly with the HTML markup tags using HTML view.

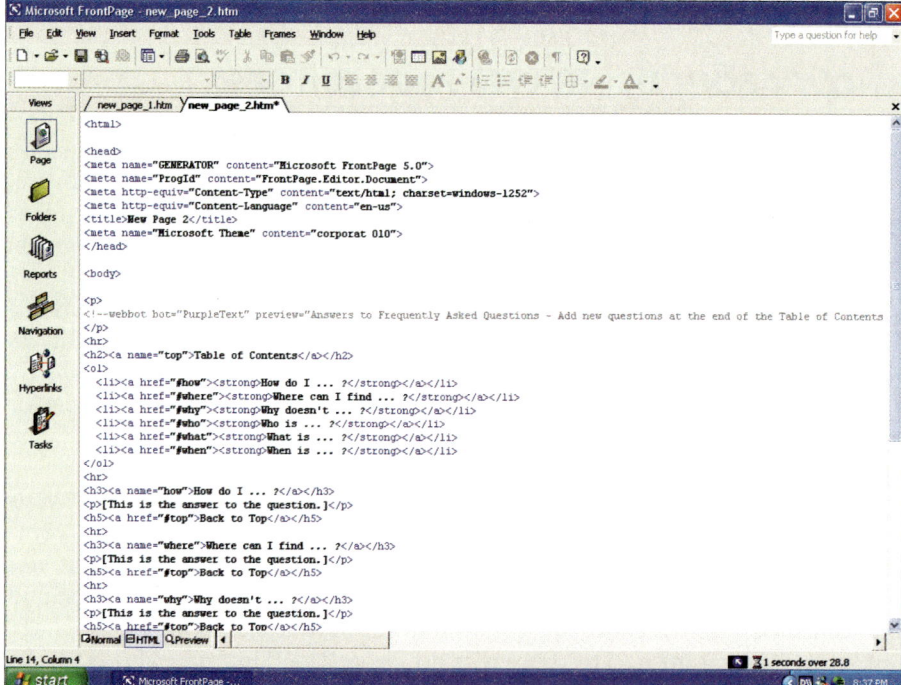

we'll explore the Web site creation tools that are readily available on the Internet from Web hosts.

KNOW ABOUT USING FREE WEB CREATION TOOLS

Instead of using a commercial Web editing program, such as FrontPage, to create a Web page, you can use a simple Web page creation tool. There are a number of these available for use on the Internet.

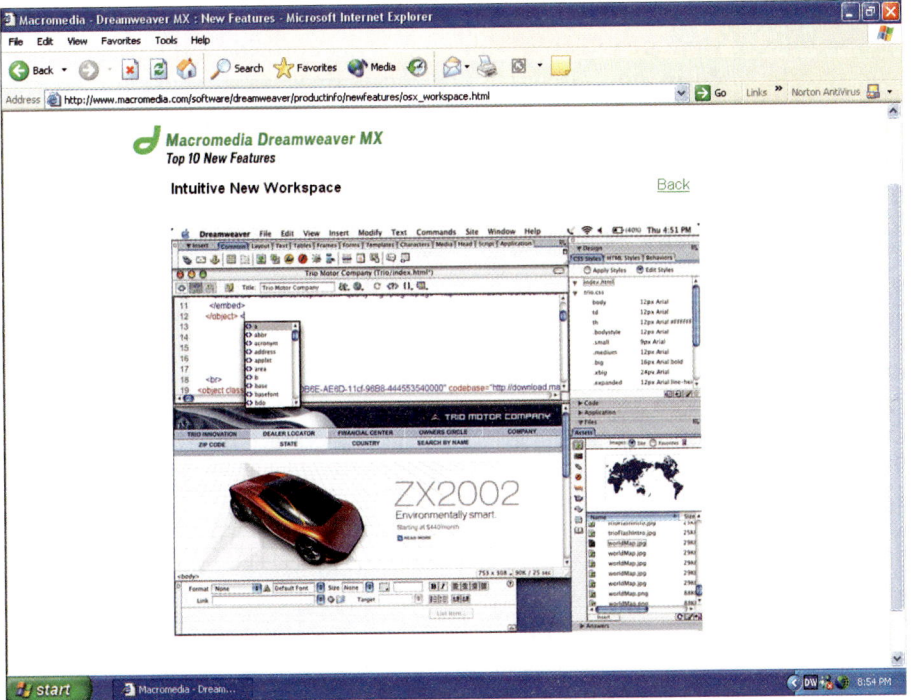

Figure 20.6.
Macromedia's Dreamweaver is a strong Web creation tool, although it might require more up-front learning time than does FrontPage.

The good news is that these software tools are typically free, especially if you've signed up to use a specific Web host. The Web host will provide the software so that you can quickly develop your site. Like Web editing programs, most free tools also include *templates*, which are professionally designed documents that include preset backgrounds, fonts, and other formatting associated with the document (see Figure 20.7). These free software programs are usually easy to use; however, they support limited features and formatting compared with full-blown software, such as FrontPage.

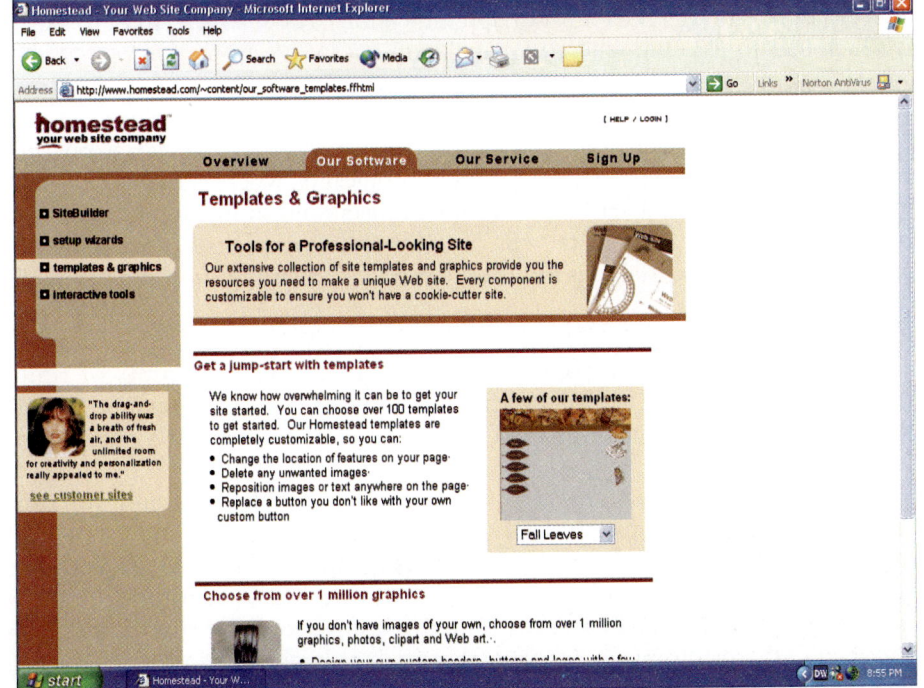

Figure 20.7.
Free Web creation software is designed to help novices quickly create Web sites.

Know About Using Free Web Creation Tools 323

For people who don't want to learn HTML or even a full-blown Web page editor, the free software most Web hosting services provide is the way to go. If you're interested in finding out more about these free tools, conduct an Internet search using `Web host software` as keywords.

UNDERSTAND THE BASICS OF USING HTML MARKUP TAGS

Hypertext Markup Language (HTML) is the universal language of the Web because it's used to develop Web pages. HTML is a markup language, not a true programming language. Programming languages have a set of rules that programmers use to write computer applications, using an artificial language (a code). A programming language can perform logic and make decisions; HTML can do neither. However, Web developers can use HTML markup language to create Web pages resplendent with text and images that anyone can view, no matter what type of computer or browser they use. They do this by entering plain text in an editor; then surrounding the text with HTML markup tags that specify how the text should appear on a Web page. Because HTML is used uniformly on the Web, pages developed using it can be displayed in a variety of browsers.

INSIDE TRACK

If you want to view a list of common HTML tags, look at the following Web sites: *www.w3schools.com/html/html_primary.asp*, and *hotwired.lycos.com/webmonkey/reference/html_cheatsheet*.

For those with an interest in working with HTML, developing Web pages directly in it might be appealing. To do so, use a simple text editor, such as Notepad or Word, to enter the text that you want on your Web site. You then insert the **markup tags** that control the structure and design of the text or graphical elements. The markup tags tell the browser how to format and display the text. There are literally hundreds of these tags, but most simple Web pages include only 20 or 30, which are relatively easy to learn. Think of HTML as stage directions that tell the browser which props to use, what to say, and how to say it. If you're good at memorizing detailed information and visualizing results without seeing them, using HTML tags to develop a Web page might be for you.

INSIDE TRACK

Some HTML tags work fine, even if you don't include the closing tag. However, it's a good idea (and strongly advocated by the World Wide Web Consortium) to get in the habit of including paired opening and closing tags as you develop your HTML Web pages. This makes existing HTML pages compatible with XHTML, the up-and-coming standard, which requires paired tags.

Happily, HTML is not as difficult to learn as are many languages because the markup tags are typically plain English words (such as *BLOCKQUOTE*) or abbreviations (such as *P* for a paragraph indication). All you really have to learn is which tags to use, and where to place them.

HTML markup tags typically appear in pairs; the opening and closing tags surround the text to which they apply. Brackets are used to differentiate between the plain text that you want to appear in the browser from the markup tags. The opening tag is included in brackets, whereas the closing tag includes brackets and a slash. The following example shows some text with opening and closing brackets: *<B>The Web is an interesting place to hang out.</B>*. In this case, the tags indicate that bold formatting should be applied to the text.

ALERT!

If you notice references to *doubleclick* in the View Source window, most likely the page includes advertising or Web tracking by DoubleClick. (If you need a refresher on the dangers of DoubleClick, see Chapter 2, The Good, the Bad, the Ugly: Uses and Misuses of the Internet.)

A basic understanding of how HTML tags work can be extremely helpful as you develop your Web pages. We won't spend great amounts of time working in HTML, but we will briefly view some HTML code on an existing Web page. After that, we'll use HTML to develop a short Web page from scratch.

Viewing HTML tags that already exist on a page is helpful because you can see how it relates to the page's display, which gives you a better understanding of HTML and helps you learn the markup language. It's also helpful because you might come across a great-looking table or title and wonder how the Web developer set it up. By analyzing the underlying tags, you can learn a great deal about HTML. Additionally, viewing the markup language is uncomplicated because Internet Explorer includes a built-in command to do so.

 **HEADS UP!** If the View Source command is not active on the shortcut menu, right-click near the top of the Web page, outside of any graphics or other symbols. If this doesn't work, choose Source from Internet Explorer's View menu.

To view the underlying HTML tags, right-click on a Web page to display a shortcut menu. Choose View Source from the shortcut menu to display HTML for the page (see Figure 20.8). Notice that the *<HTML>* tag at the beginning of the page indicates that this is an HTML document; the *<HEAD>* tag indicates the title and other information located at the beginning of the page. Any text encompassed by *<BODY>* tags is used for the main part of the page. The *<P>* tag indicates the beginning of a new paragraph.

Besides viewing the tags and coding from existing Web pages, you can also work directly in HTML. Practice using HTML might help you understand it better, so we're going to give you a chance to try your hand at it.

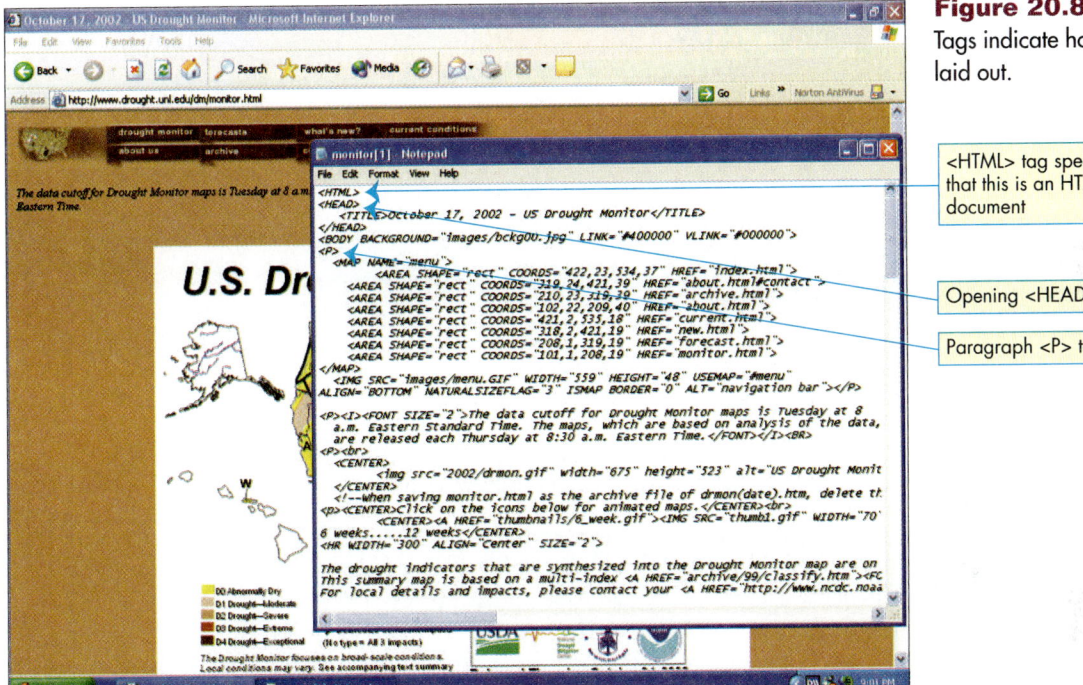

Figure 20.8.
Tags indicate how the page is laid out.

ACTIVITY 20.1
Creating a Simple HTML Document

1. Click the Start button, and then choose All Programs, Accessories, Notepad.
   The Notepad window opens. You can type text directly into this editor and then add HTML markup tags. It really doesn't matter if you enter the markup tags in upper- or lowercase (though FrontPage creates them in lowercase by default.)

2. In the Notepad window, type <HTML> and then press ←Enter.
   This indicates to a browser that the document is using HTML.

3. Type the information in Figure 20.9 into the Notepad window:

4. In Notepad, choose File, Save.
   The Save As dialog box displays. By default, Notepad documents are saved as text files. You need to change the settings so that your document is saved using the HTML file format. (Files saved using HTML can use either the HTML or HTM extension; in this exercise, we'll use HTML.)

Understand the Basics of Using HTML Markup Tags 325

ACTIVITY 20.1
Creating a Simple HTML Document (Continued)

Figure 20.9.
Enter this information in your text editor.

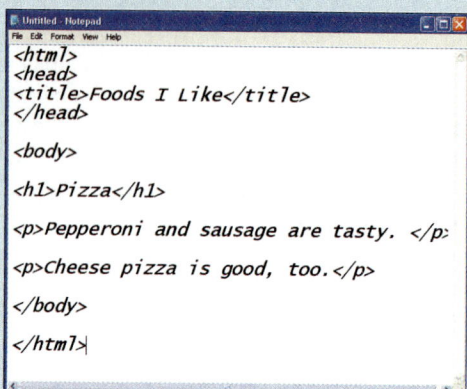

 **HEADS UP!** It's important to specify that you want to save the file using the All Files option, and type `html` for the extension. If you don't, Notepad will save the file using its default file format (TXT).

5. In the Save As dialog box, click the *Save as type* drop-down list arrow and then choose All Files.

6. In the File name box, type `Pizza.html`.

7. Specify the location indicated by your instructor for saving your file; then click Save.
   Notepad saves the document using HTML file format.

8. In Notepad, choose File, Exit.
   Notepad closes, and now you're ready to view your document in a browser. Keep in mind that the file isn't available to people on the Internet at this point. The file is still in the location you indicated (such as on the hard drive or a network drive) because you haven't uploaded it yet to the Web. (Uploading is simply copying the files to a location on the Internet, such as a Web server.)

9. Open Internet Explorer; then choose File, Open from the menu.
   The Open dialog box displays.

10. Click the Browse button in the Open dialog box; then navigate to the drive and folder where your *pizza.html* file is located.

11. Double-click the *pizza.html* file and then click OK in the Open dialog box.
    The HTML file opens; however, instead of displaying the underlying HTML code, the browser shows the *results* of the code, including the formatting.

12. From the Internet Explorer's window, choose View, Source.
    A second window opens so that you can view the HTML tags for the file (see Figure 20.10).

13. Close all open windows, including Internet Explorer.

ACTIVITY 20.1

Creating a Simple HTML Document

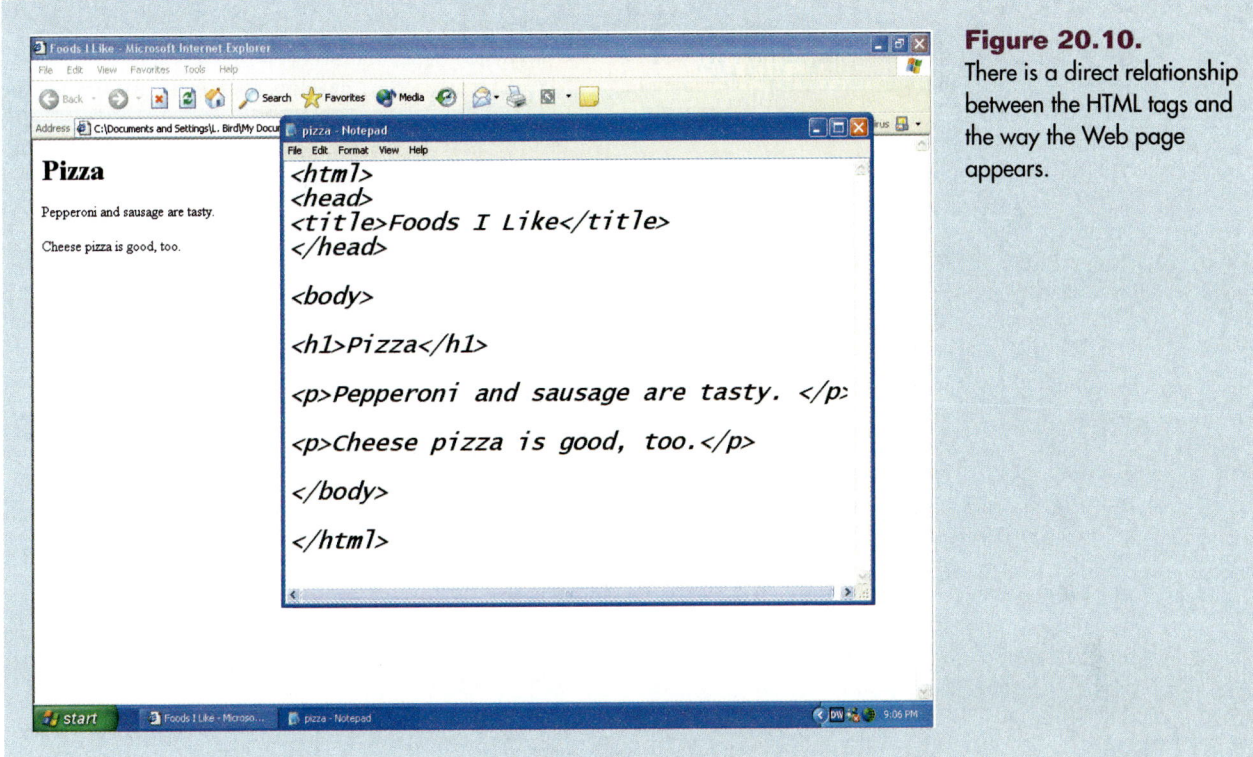

Figure 20.10.
There is a direct relationship between the HTML tags and the way the Web page appears.

It's that simple. Now you should have a basic understanding of the various tools that you can use to develop a Web site. You're primed to go for the gold: Developing your own Web site…and in the next chapter, you'll do just that.

Don't Forget…

- You can use a variety of Web creation tools to develop HTML documents for the Web.
- All Web documents use Hypertext Markup Language (HTML) so that they can be viewed on any type of computer and by using any type of browser.
- Web page editors, such as FrontPage, include many features and are generally easy to use.
- Free Web creation tools typically offer more limited features than do commercial Web development software programs, but are extremely easy to use.
- You can develop pages for Web use by entering text in a text editor, such as Notepad, and then inserting HTML markup tags where necessary.

Check This Out

MULTIPLE CHOICE

1. Which is probably the best choice to use if you're a computer novice and want to create a very simple, one-page Web site?
   a. Dreamweaver
   b. FrontPage
   c. HTML
   d. Click-n-Build

2. Under which of the following conditions are you most likely to receive a free Web creation tool?
   a. You signed up for a Web hosting service and the host is providing the software at no extra charge.
   b. You fill out an online registration form.
   c. You write to Adobe and ask for a free copy of GoLive.
   d. None of the above

3. You want to work directly in HTML. Which of the following programs would you most likely use to do so?
   a. Click-n-Build
   b. Notepad
   c. PowerPoint
   d. Outlook Express

4. Which of the following is true regarding HTML?
   a. It is used to develop documents for use on the Web.
   b. Text in HTML is encompassed by an opening and a closing tag.
   c. <HTML> is the tag used at the beginning of the document.
   d. All of the above

5. What does the <P> tag in HTML indicate?
   a. The start of a new paragraph
   b. A page break
   c. That the current page should be printed
   d. None of the above

MATCHING

a. FrontPage
b. markup tags
c. EarthLink
d. Dreamweaver
e. Notepad
f. Web host
g. Hypertext Markup Language
h. <BODY>
i. WYSIWYG
j. <B>

1. Directions your browser uses to display a Web page
2. Tag used to apply bold to text
3. A text editor you can use to develop HTML pages
4. Macromedia's Web page editor
5. The universal "language" of the Web
6. The general name for a business that you pay to store your Web pages
7. A major ISP that also hosts Web sites
8. A Web page editor marketed by Microsoft
9. A type of software where you view the graphical result of commands in a window
10. The HTML tag used for the main section of a Web page

Real Life

1. Understanding how HTML works is useful, even if you plan to use a Web page editor such as FrontPage. To gain a better grasp of HTML, view the source code (markup tags) for five different Web pages. Note the similarities and differences that you see in the tags. Next, copy the code from one of the View Source windows into Notepad. Save the newly created Notepad file as *sample.html*. For additional practice and to reinforce the concepts you've learned, view the file and the HTML code in your browser. When you're finished, close the browser.

2. Use the Internet to compare the Web editing software commercially available, including FrontPage (*www.microsoft.com/frontpage*), GoLive (*www.adobe.com/products/golive*), and Dreamweaver (*www.macromedia.com/software/dreamweaver*). What are the strengths and weaknesses of each program? Develop a chart that identifies the pros and cons of using each program. Also indicate for what type of user each program would be most helpful.

I Spy: Privacy and Security Concerns

1. Use the View Source command to look at the source code for the home page for the following Web sites: Expedia (*www.expedia.com*), Amazon (*www.amazon.com*), eBay (*www.ebay.com*), Geocities (*www.geocities.com*), AltaVista (*www.altavista.com*), CNN (*www.cnn.com*), and USA Today (*www.usatoday.com*). What are the privacy and security implications of being able to view HTML for these sites?

2. Redisplay HTML for the sites listed in the previous question; then check for DoubleClick ads. To do this, choose Edit, Find in the source code window. In the Find dialog box, type `doubleclick` and then click Find Next to highlight the first occurrence of a DoubleClick advertisement. Use this method to locate all incidences of DoubleClick for the home page of each Web site. Develop a chart that shows your findings.

CHAPTER 2.1

USING FRONTPAGE TO DEVELOP A WEB SITE

Key Terms

After you complete this chapter, you'll understand the following terms:

cell
child page
Hyperlinks view
link bar
list
modes
Navigation view
Page view
parent page
Reports view
shortcut menu
table
theme
Web
wizard

Chapter Objectives

After you complete this chapter, you'll be able to

- Start FrontPage and Create a Simple Web Site
- Enter and Edit Text on a Web Page
- Switch Between the Normal, HTML, and Preview Panes
- Develop a List and a Table
- Apply a Theme
- Revise and Create Hyperlinks
- Create an E-Mail Hyperlink
- Examine a Link Bar's Properties
- Change a Web's Structure
- Test Your Web

The Big Picture

Unless you totally skipped the last couple of chapters, you know how to determine the main purpose of your Web site and the software tool you want to use to develop it. Now you're ready to gain some practical experience at creating a Web site. In real life, you'd be able to choose the exact software or tools you want. In this book, we'll make the decision for you: You'll use FrontPage.

Why should you use FrontPage? Because it's so popular that the chances of encountering it again in a business situation are great. Having a fundamental knowledge of the software is a marketable skill. FrontPage is also well-supported by Microsoft, which means that there's a wealth of information available on how to use the program. Furthermore, the program includes some built-in tools that can help you quickly create a Web site.

Window on the Web

Even if you only have a basic understanding of FrontPage, you can still have a working personal or business Web page. That's because FrontPage includes some built-in tools that help you quickly construct an operational Web page.

In this chapter, you'll work with these built-in features to quickly create a personal Web site. These tools enable you to set up the overall structure and organization of the site, complete with some sample text. The simple personal Web site you develop will have a home page linked to several second-level pages (see Figure 21.1).

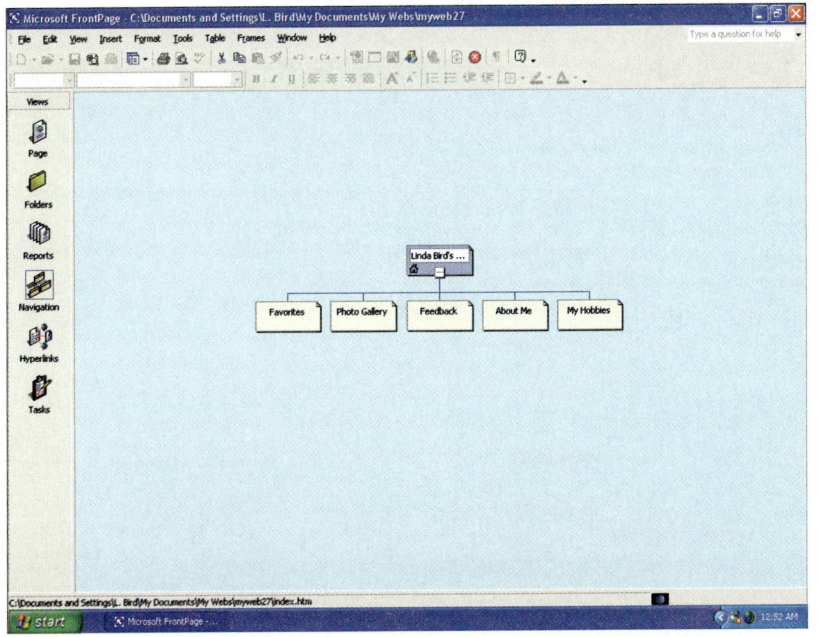

Figure 21.1.
FrontPage comes with several built-in tools you can use to develop the Web's structure.

Window on the Web

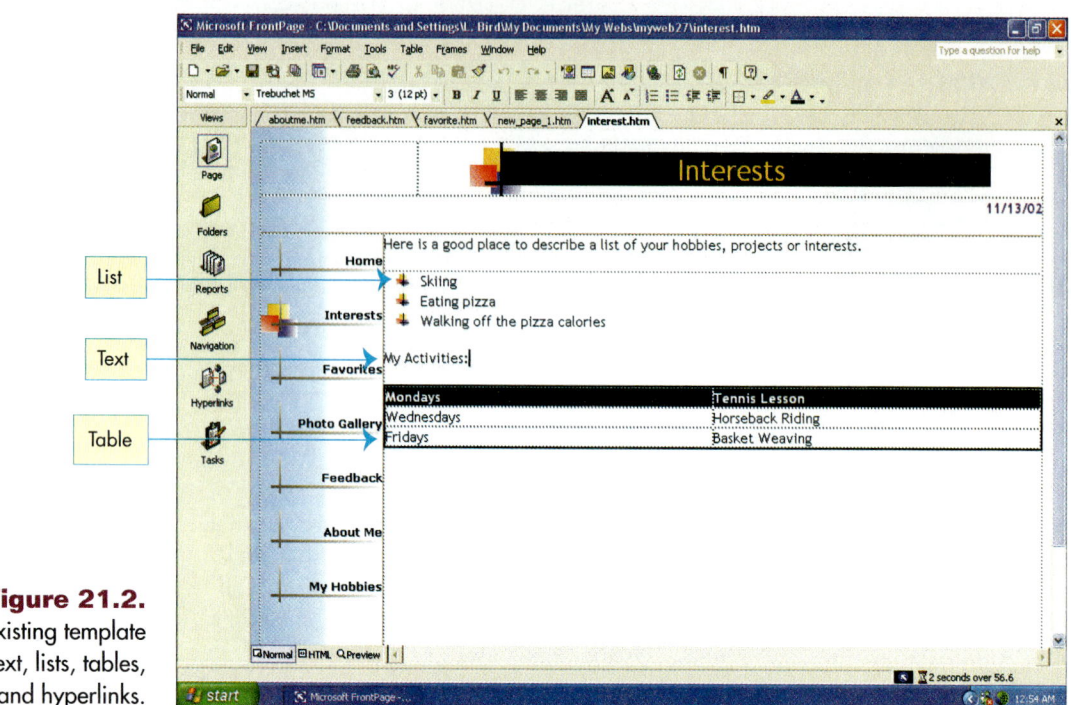

Figure 21.2.
Build on an existing template by adding text, lists, tables, and hyperlinks.

After you initially set up the structure for the Web site, you'll replace the sample text by entering, editing, and formatting the text on the pages. You'll also learn how to create lists and tables and to manage hyperlinks. Additionally, you'll apply an overall formatting scheme to the Web to change its look (see Figure 21.2).

Finally, FrontPage includes a feature that lets you test the look and feel of the Web site before actually uploading it to a Web server (see Figure 21.3). You'll be able to see how your Web site operates by viewing it in either FrontPage or in a browser.

When you're finished with the chapter, you'll have a good start on using FrontPage's essential features. In the next chapter, you'll build on the foundation by adding graphical features to your Web pages. The bulk of the material for these two chapters is hands-on, so make sure your computer is up and running, grab your mouse, and let's get going.

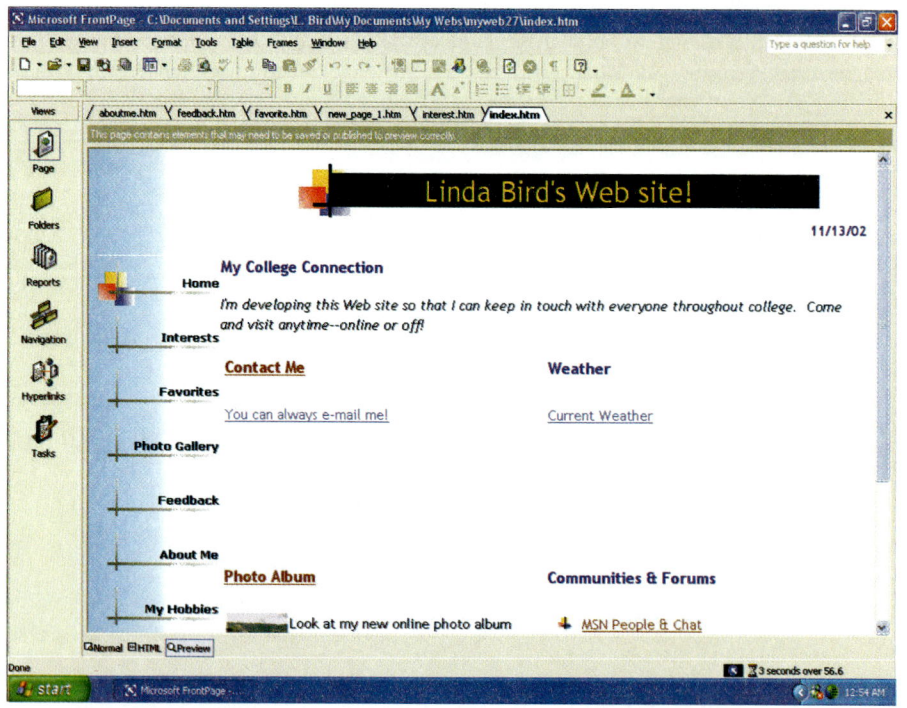

Figure 21.3.
FrontPage lets you preview the way your Web site will look on the Internet.

START FRONTPAGE AND CREATE A SIMPLE WEB SITE

FrontPage 2002 is a graphical Windows program. As such, it's designed to look and feel similar to other Microsoft Windows' applications. It's also launched in the same way: By choosing it from the Start menu or the Windows' desktop.

HEADS UP! Before beginning the activities in this chapter, make sure that FrontPage is installed on your system. If you need assistance in verifying that the program is installed, ask your instructor.

FrontPage considers a **Web** to be a collection of pages that can be used to make up a Web site. Each Web is organized as a series of folders and files. Because a Web site can consist of a number of graphics, links, HTML documents, and other associated files, a FrontPage Web can easily grow to hundreds—or even thousands—of files. Keeping these files grouped in a Web folder is the best way to keep them from becoming scattered throughout the computer.

After you launch the program, you can use FrontPage's built-in features to quickly set up the overall structure of your Web site. Most of the time, you'll either use a template or a wizard to do this. Templates and wizards are helpful because they provide the structure and sample content for the Web site. You can then customize the Web site by either revising or replacing the text or restructuring the site. Although the end result—a structured Web with sample text—is the same whether you use a template or wizard, they differ in the process used to create the Web. Wizards give you more choices as you set up the Web because they present you with several screens of options before creating the site. In contrast, a template sets up the Web pages in the same way every time, without asking for user input. You can also create a Web completely from scratch, but using a template or wizard is usually more efficient because it gives you a base on which to build.

In this activity, you'll launch FrontPage and then use a wizard to create a simple Web. You'll also examine the various FrontPage views.

ACTIVITY 21.1
Starting FrontPage and Creating a Simple Web Site

① In Windows, click the Start button, and then point to All Programs.

② Click Microsoft FrontPage on the All Programs submenu.
FrontPage launches and displays onscreen. Notice that many of the screen elements are similar to those used in other Windows programs (see Figure 21.4).

HEADS UP! If the Views Bar isn't shown on your screen, choose View, Views Bar.

③ If the task pane isn't displayed on your screen, choose View, Task Pane from the menu. Next, you'll create a new Web using a wizard.

④ In the *New from template* section of the Task Pane, click the link for *Web Site Templates*.
The Web Site Templates dialog box displays. You can double-click an option in this dialog box to automatically create a Web with the structure, formatting, and sample content already in place. You can then customize the Web by replacing the sample content and formatting with your own (see Figure 21.5).

ACTIVITY 21.1
Starting FrontPage and Creating a Simple Web Site (Continued)

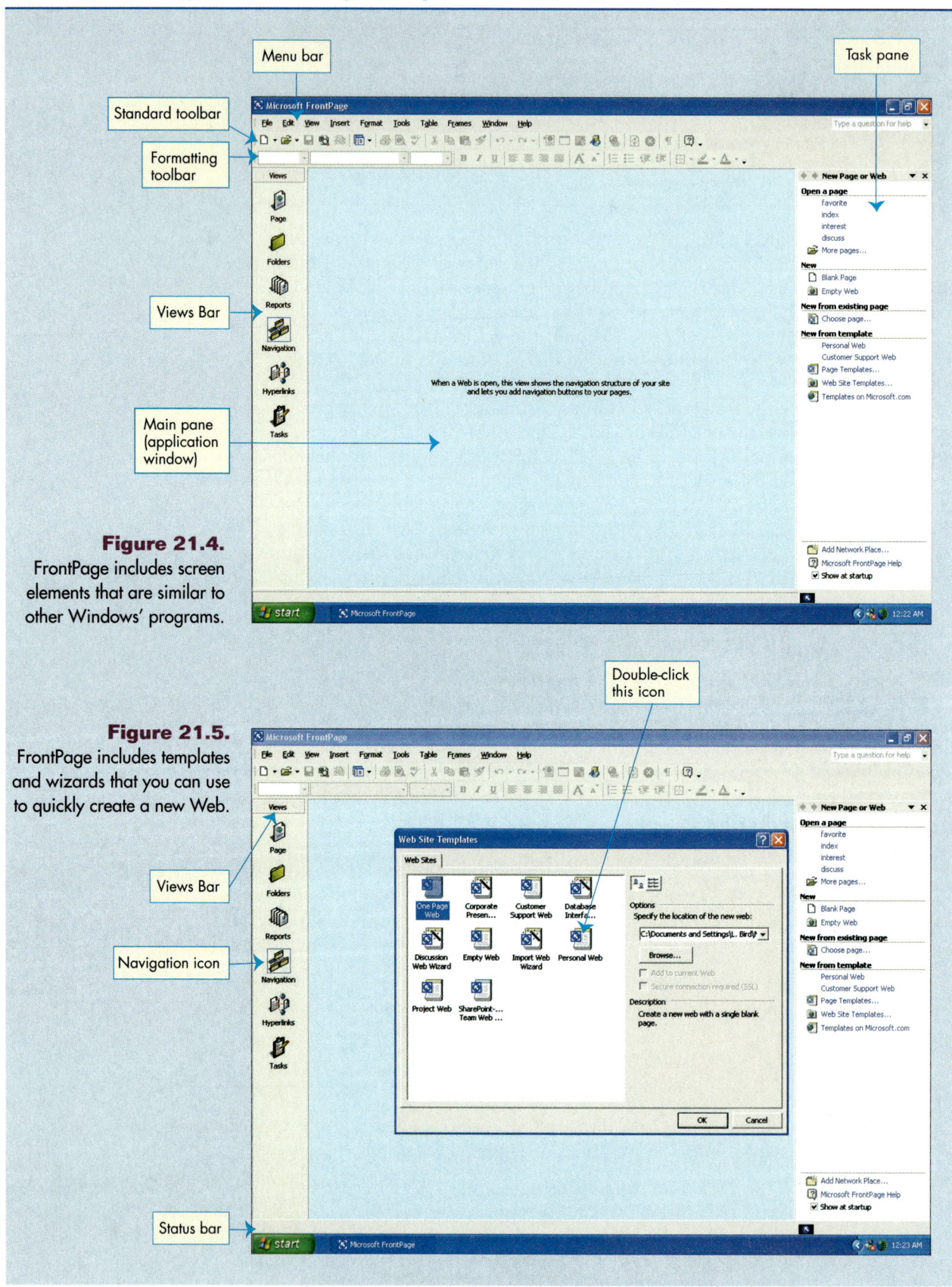

Figure 21.4. FrontPage includes screen elements that are similar to other Windows' programs.

Figure 21.5. FrontPage includes templates and wizards that you can use to quickly create a new Web.

334 Chapter 21 Using FrontPage to Develop a Web Site

ACTIVITY 21.1
Starting FrontPage and Creating a Simple Web Site

5. Double-click the Personal Web icon.
   FrontPage develops the structure for your Web. If you're observant, you might notice files being created at the bottom of the page in the status bar area. To actually *see* the structure, however, you need to switch to another view.

6. In the Views Bar, click the Navigation icon (shown in Figure 21.5).
   FrontPage switches to **Navigation view**. In this view, the structure of the Web is shown in FrontPage's main working pane. The structure is simple, but easy to follow: a home page on the first level that links to five pages on the second level (see Figure 21.6).

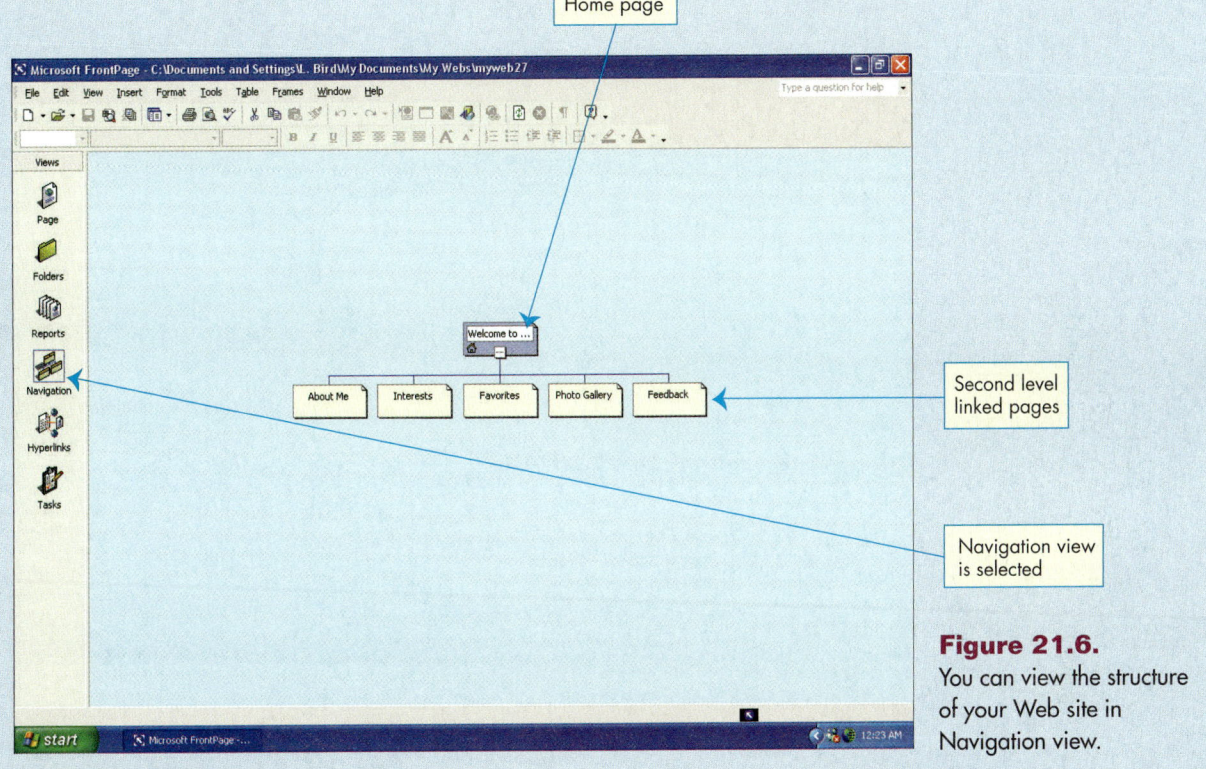

Figure 21.6.
You can view the structure of your Web site in Navigation view.

7. On the Views Bar, click the Hyperlinks icon.
   The Web is shown in **Hyperlinks view**. This view is used to illustrate the linked relationships of the pages in your Web (see Figure 21.7).

8. Click the plus (+) symbol by the aboutme.htm icon.
   The links for the page are shown (see Figure 21.8).

9. Click the minus (−) symbol for the aboutme.htm icon.
   The links for the page are no longer displayed.

10. In the Views Bar, click the Reports icon to switch to **Reports view**.
    Statistical reports for the Web are shown. These reports are useful for finding broken hyperlinks, slow-loading pages, and so on.

 INSIDE TRACK

You can also change the display to show the tasks associated with your Web. The tasks list indicates the work to be done on your Web site and is similar to a "To Do" list. Although the list is automatically generated when you use a wizard to create a Web, you can also systematically add additional tasks. To show the current listing of tasks, click the Tasks icon on the Views Bar. To add a task, display the Web in Tasks view and then choose Edit, Tasks, Add Task.

Start FrontPage and Create a Simple Web Site 335

ACTIVITY 21.1
Starting FrontPage and Creating a Simple Web Site (Continued)

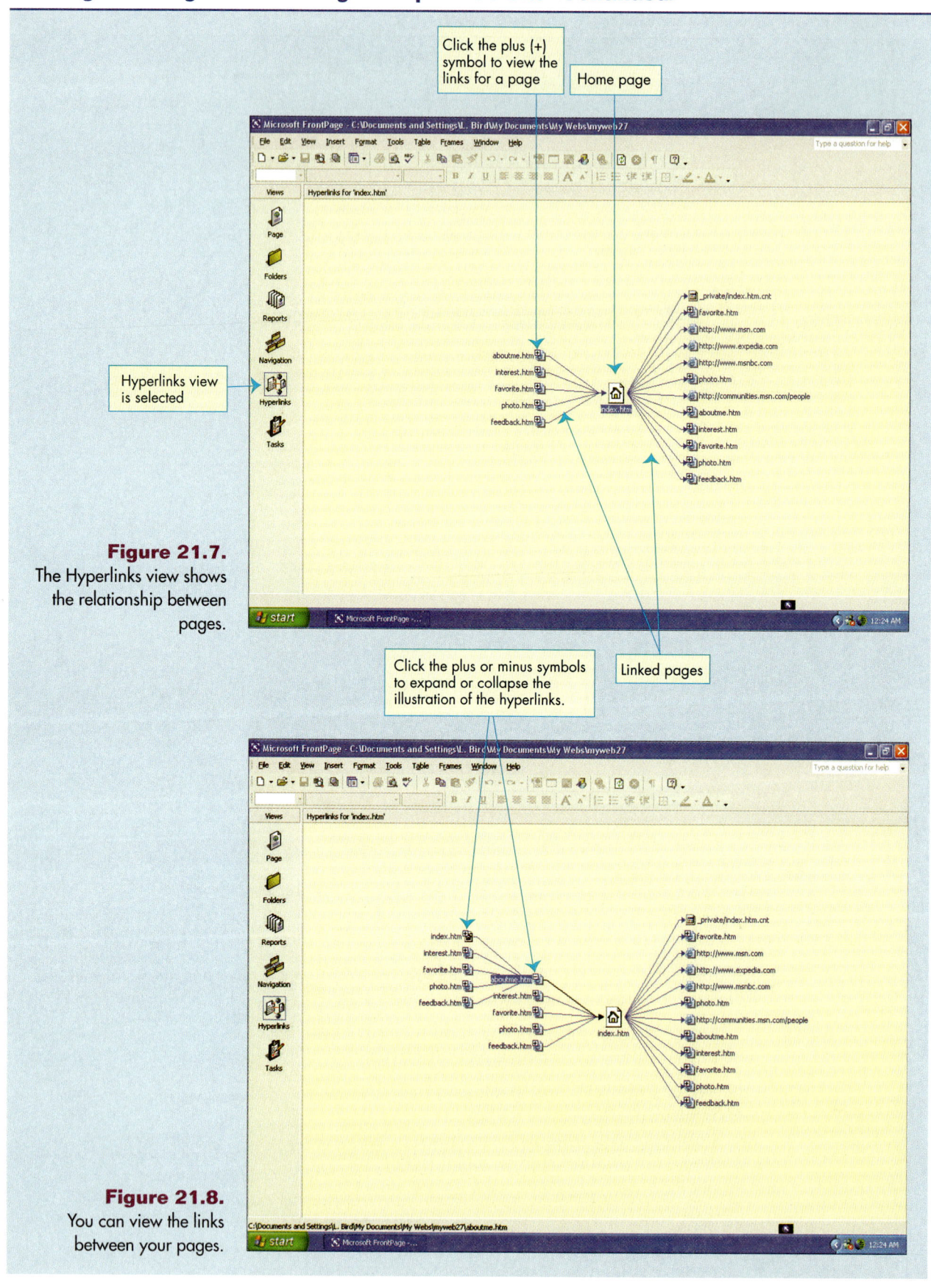

Figure 21.7. The Hyperlinks view shows the relationship between pages.

Figure 21.8. You can view the links between your pages.

ACTIVITY 21.1
Starting FrontPage and Creating a Simple Web Site

⑪ Click the Navigation icon in the Views Bar again.
   The overall structure for the Web is again shown. You can switch to Page view by double-clicking one of the page icons in Navigation view or by single-clicking a page icon in Navigation view to select it and then clicking the Page icon on the Views Bar.

⑫ In the main working pane of the FrontPage window, double-click the Home page icon (*Welcome to my Web site*).
   The Home page displays in **Page view** (see Figure 21.9). This view shows all elements on the page and is the one you work with the most to revise the page. Because you used a template to develop this page, the basic layout, elements, sample text, and formatting are already in place.
   In the next activity, you'll customize these elements for your needs, so keep FrontPage and your Web open.

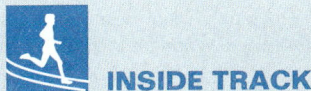
INSIDE TRACK

You can switch (toggle) the display of the files and folders associated with your Web on or off. Simply display the Web in Navigation or Page view and then choose Folder List from the View menu.

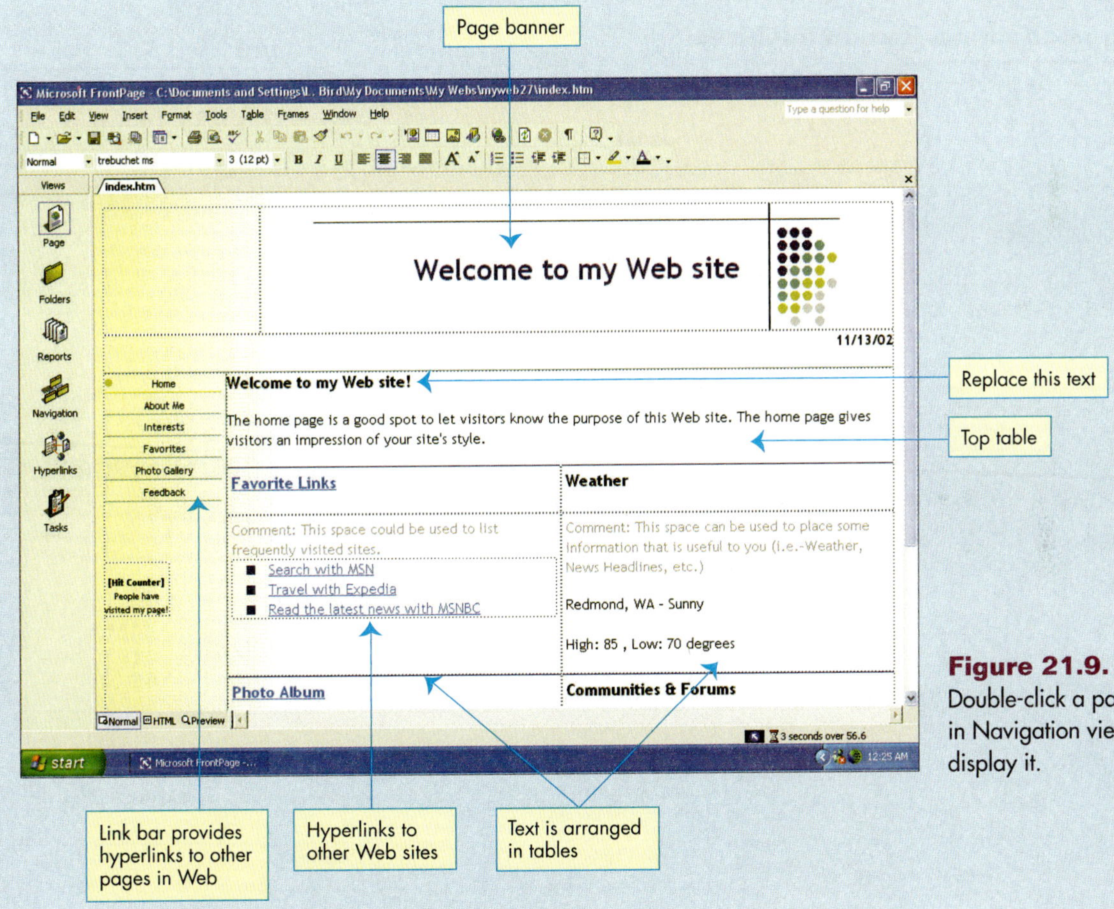

Figure 21.9.
Double-click a page icon in Navigation view to display it.

ENTER AND EDIT TEXT ON A WEB PAGE

You've already seen how easy it is to let FrontPage create the main structure of your Web, and then build on that base. A close look at the Web page shows that it's set up as a series of tables, with columns and rows—even if the table consists of one column by one row, forming a rectangle. Sectioning each Web page into tables helps to keep all the related text together (refer back to Figure 21.9).

INSIDE TRACK

A *Web* is FrontPage's term for the open group of files that make up your Web site. When the Web is open in FrontPage, all the associated files are accessible so that you can work with them.

When you initially create a Web based on a template, FrontPage creates the structure and assigns it a default name such as *Web??*. You don't need to specifically save the structure because FrontPage automatically does so. Instead, you use FrontPage's Save commands to save changes to individual pages.

The home page also includes a **link bar**, which contains the hyperlinks to other pages in the Web. Additionally, Webs created by using the wizards include sample text. In the personal Web that you've just created, you can begin to customize the Web to your needs by replacing the sample text with your own. In this activity, that's just what you'll do.

ACTIVITY 21.2
Entering and Editing Text on a Web Page

1. Make sure that the home page (*Welcome to my Web site!*) is shown in Page view.

2. Click and drag over the *Welcome to my Web site!* text in the top table cell to select it and then type `My College Connection` (refer to Figure 21.9, if necessary).

    The text you type replaces the existing text.

3. Select the text in the lower part of the same table (*The home page is a good spot...*) and then type `I'm designing this Web site so that I can keep in touch with everyone throughout college. Come and visit anytime—online or off!`

    Your page should appear similar to that shown in Figure 21.10.

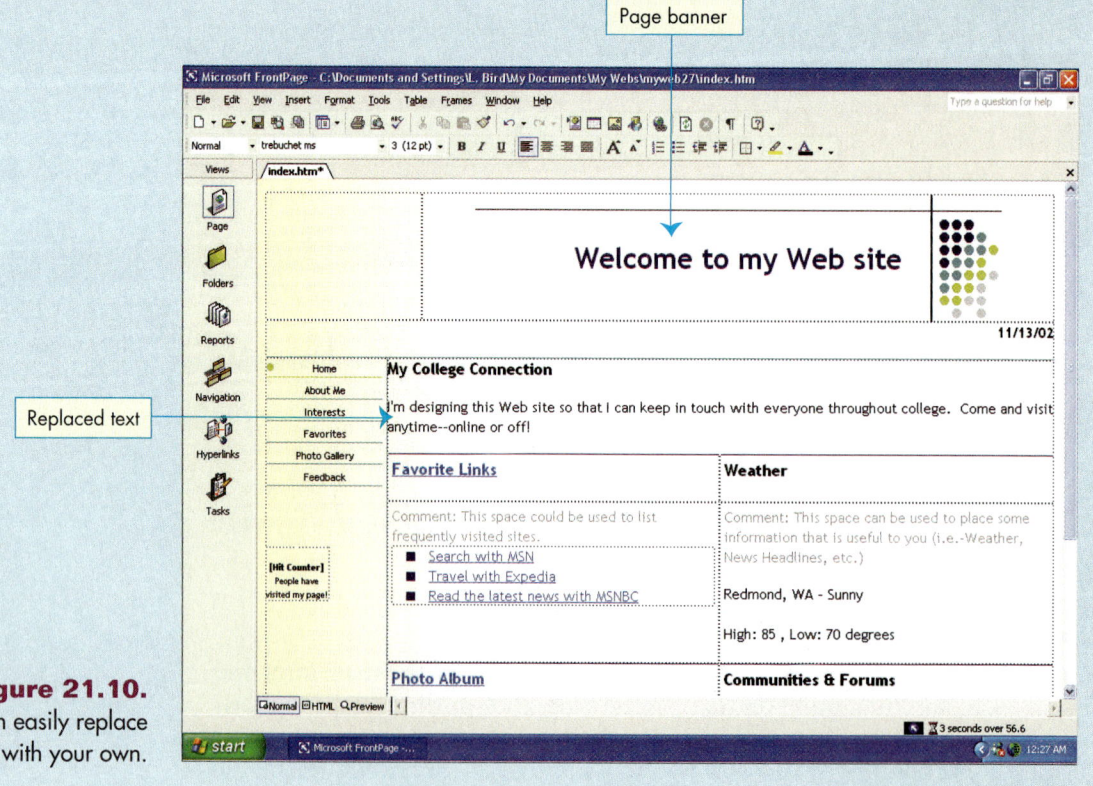

Figure 21.10.
You can easily replace sample text with your own.

ACTIVITY 21.2
Entering and Editing Text on a Web Page

 **HEADS UP!** Make sure that you're replacing the text in the first table beneath the date (as shown in Figure 21.9), not the text in the page banner area.

4 Double-click the word *designing* and then type developing.
The newly typed word replaces the selected one.

 5 Select the sentences you just typed (*I'm designing this Web site so that I can keep in touch with everyone throughout college. Come on in for a visit anytime—online or off!*) and then click the Italic button.
The text is formatted using italics.

6 Right-click the page banner text (*Welcome to my Web site*).
A shortcut menu displays (see Figure 21.11). A **shortcut menu** is a context-sensitive menu that shows commands appropriate for the object or text you're working with. (Page banner text differs from the other text you've edited; it's modified by using the associated characteristics, or properties.)

 INSIDE TRACK
The commands used to format text in FrontPage are generally found on the Formatting toolbar and are similar to those found in most other Microsoft programs. You can use FrontPage's Help to find out more about formatting your Web page text.

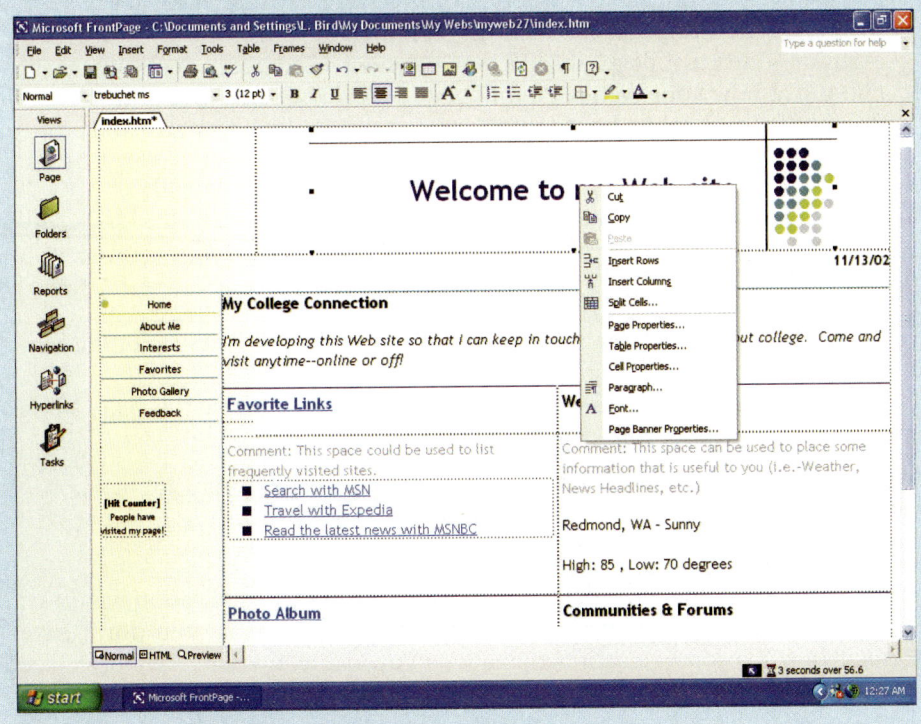

Figure 21.11.
Right-click an object to display a shortcut menu.

7 Choose Page Banner Properties on the shortcut menu.
The Page Banner Properties dialog box displays (see Figure 21.12).

8 Select the text in the *Page banner* text box; then type Yourname's Web site! Click OK.
The sample text in the page banner area is replaced by the new text.

ACTIVITY 21.2
Entering and Editing Text on a Web Page (Continued)

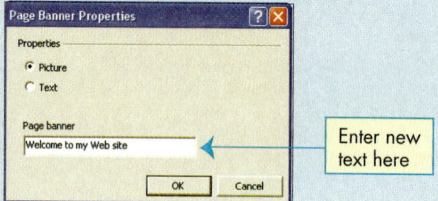

Figure 21.12.
You can modify page banner text in the Page Banner Properties dialog box.

Enter new text here

⑨ Choose File, Save All.
The Web, including all its associated files and folders, is saved using the default name assigned by FrontPage (such as *myweb1* or *myweb20*). Keep FrontPage open and your Web displayed for the next activity.

INSIDE TRACK

When you choose File, Save, the individual Web page with which you're working is saved. To save all the open pages in your Web, you choose File, Save All. Likewise, if you choose File, Close, only the individual page you're viewing is closed. To close all the open Web pages and associated files (such as graphics), choose File, Close All.

SWITCH BETWEEN THE NORMAL, HTML, AND PREVIEW PANES

So far, you've examined your Web using different views, such as the Navigation and Page views. By using different views, you can work with the Web in a variety of ways. For example, Navigation view is handy to use when you want to see the overall structure of the Web, whereas Page view is best for working with individual elements on an individual page. In this activity, you'll examine individual pages in different panes or **modes**, so that you can get a glimpse at how your Web page will look in a browser and as HTML code. You do this by switching between the three different panes available for any FrontPage Web page: Normal, HTML, and Preview.

ACTIVITY 21.3
Using the Preview and HTML Views

① Make sure that the home page of your Web is displayed in Page view and look at the buttons in the lower-left corner of the application window (see Figure 21.13).
The Web is currently shown using the Normal pane or mode. You use this pane along with Page view to edit individual Web pages.

② Click the HTML button in the lower-left corner of the FrontPage application window.
The HTML pane is shown, complete with the HTML code that controls how the Web page appears (see Figure 21.14).

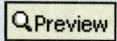

③ Click the Preview button in the lower-left corner of the FrontPage application window.
The Web appears similar to how it would in a browser, except that you don't have the usual toolbar buttons for navigating the site as you do in Internet Explorer (see Figure 21.15).

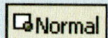

④ Click the Normal button.
The Web appears in the Normal pane again. You've already seen how you can use the Preview pane within FrontPage to get a sneak preview of how your Web page will look on the Internet. However, there's another way as well: to open the Web page in a separate browser window. This generally gives you a better idea of how the site will appear.

⑤ With the home page of your Web displayed in Page view, choose File, Preview in Browser.
The Preview in Browser dialog box appears (see Figure 21.16).

340 Chapter 21 Using FrontPage to Develop a Web Site

ACTIVITY 21.3
Using the Preview and HTML Views

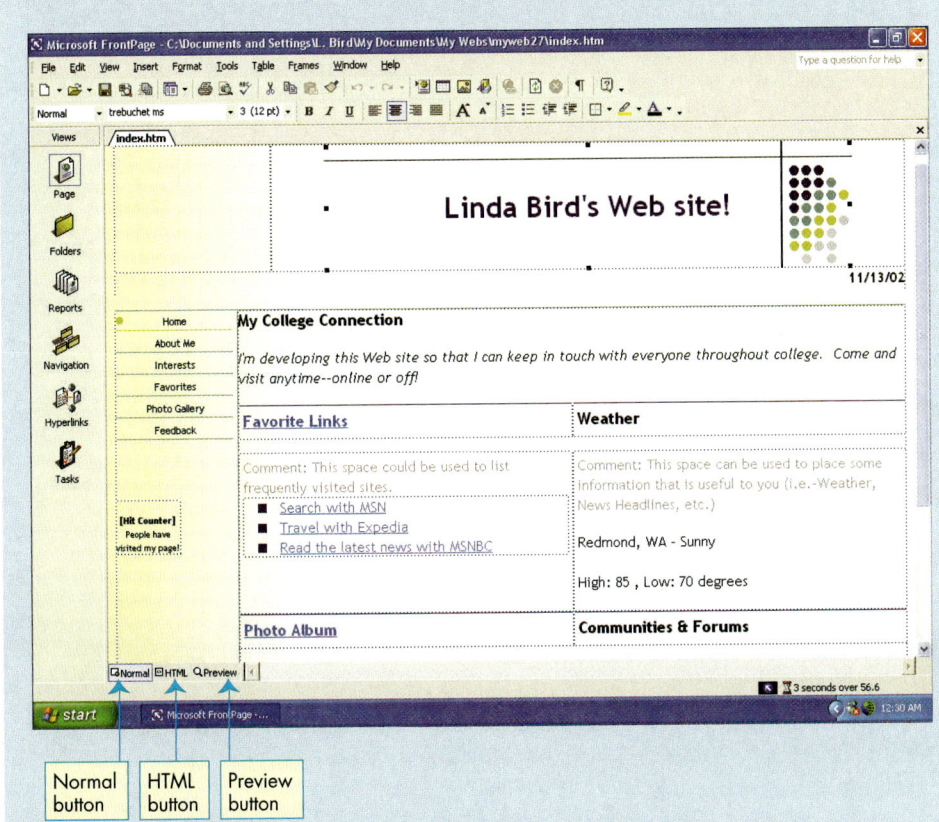

Figure 21.13.
Click a button to switch to another pane.

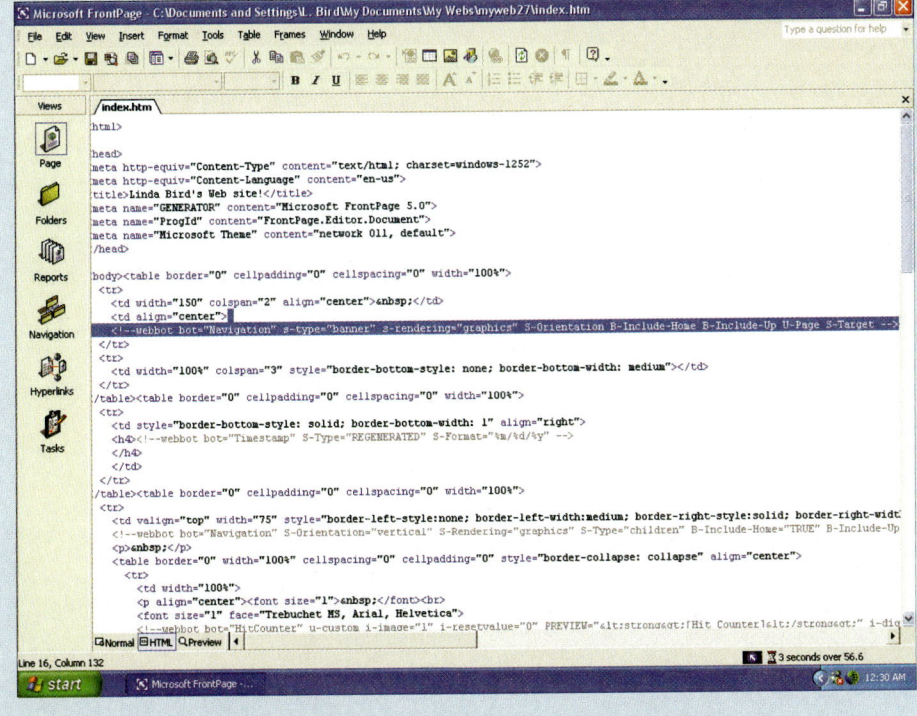

Figure 21.14.
You can display the HTML code used for your page.

ACTIVITY 21.3
Using the Preview and HTML Views (Continued)

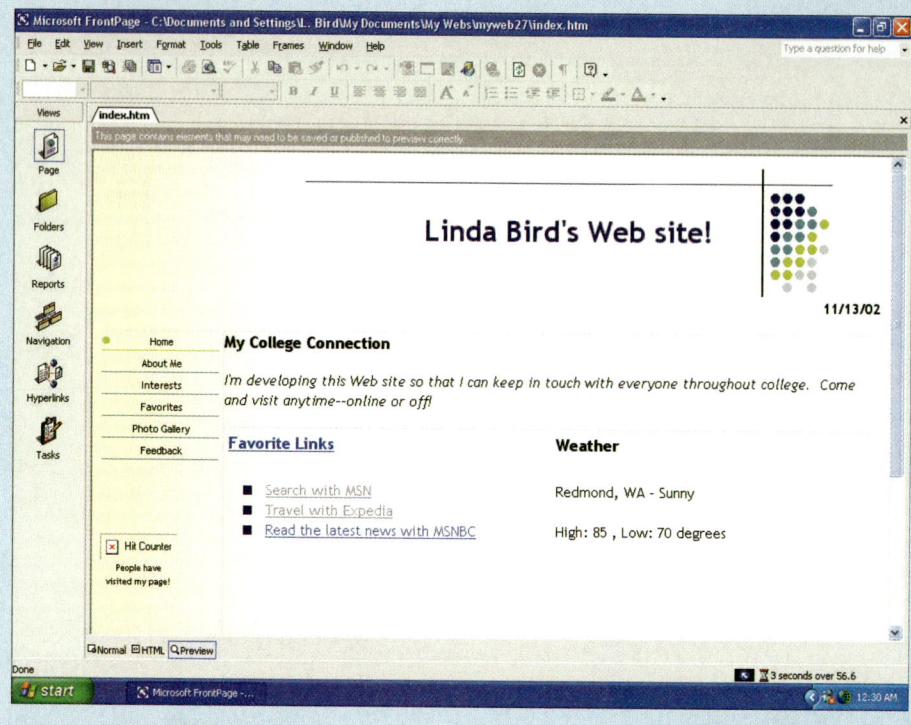

Figure 21.15.
The Preview pane gives you an idea of how the Web page will appear in a browser.

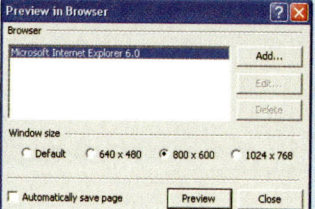

Figure 21.16.
Use this dialog box to choose a browser and screen size.

⑥ Choose the window size (such as *800 × 600*) and then click Preview.
   The Web page is displayed in a new browser window, just as it would appear in a browser on the Web. This window shows how the Web page will appear using the window size and screen resolution (800 × 600) that you indicated (see Figure 21.17).

⑦ Click the Close button in the browser window to clear it.

⑧ Press Ctrl+S to save the Web.
   Keep FrontPage open and your Web displayed for the next activity.

ACTIVITY 21.3
Using the Preview and HTML Views

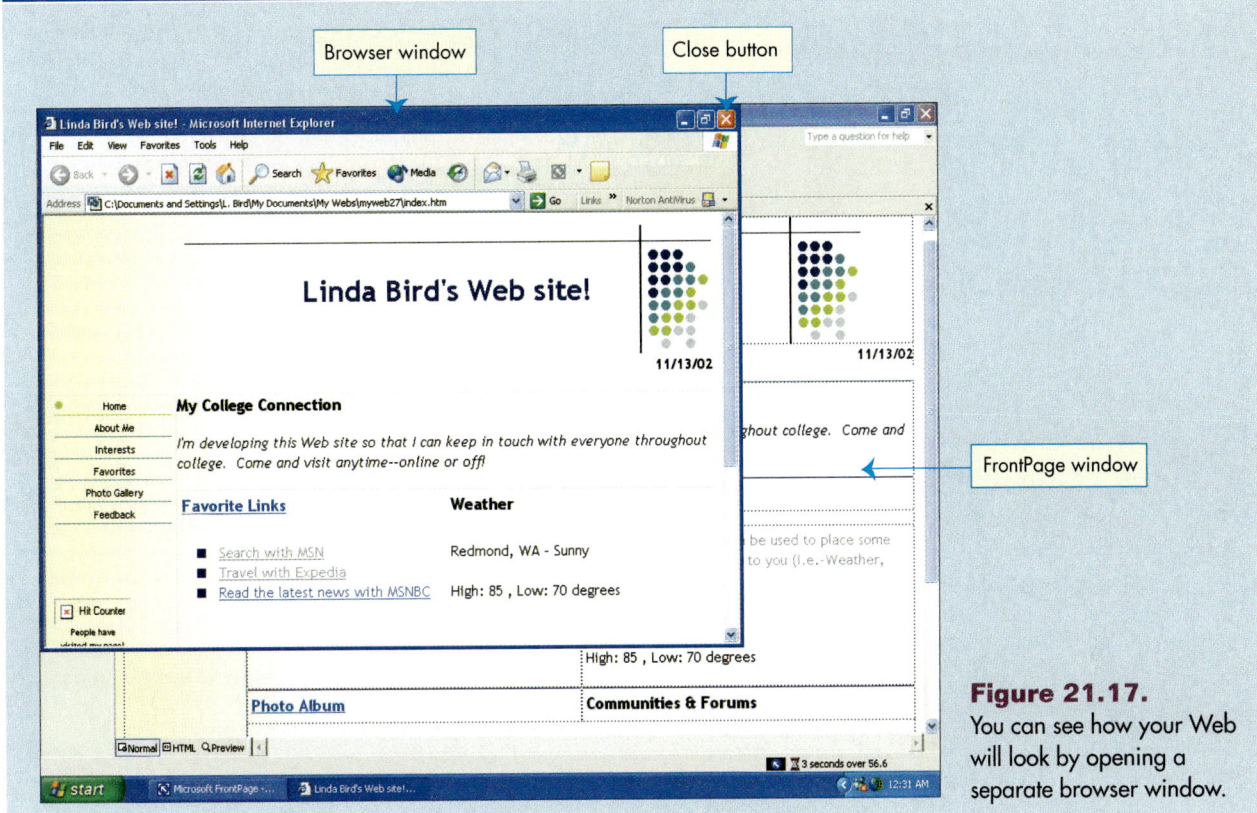

Figure 21.17.
You can see how your Web will look by opening a separate browser window.

DEVELOP A LIST AND A TABLE

The text on Web pages is easiest to follow if it's laid out in lists or as a table. A **list** is simply numbered or bulleted items that are set apart from paragraphs. A **table** is a grid with columns and rows that you can use to organize your information. The intersection of a column and row in a table is called a **cell**.

Most of the Webs you create using FrontPage's templates and wizards use lists and tables to make information easy to read. However, it's helpful to know how to modify the lists and tables that FrontPage develops. It's also useful to be able to develop these elements from scratch, if necessary. To get you up to speed on working with these features, the next activity will focus on creating and modifying lists and tables.

ACTIVITY 21.4
Developing a List and a Table

1. In the open Web, choose View, Navigation.
   The Web is displayed in Navigation view.

2. Double-click the Interests icon.
   The Interests page is shown in Page view.

3. Select the list of bulleted items and then press Del.
   Next, you'll create a new list, complete with bullets. Bullet lists are generally a good way to present information on the Web because they're easy to read.

4. Click the Bullets button and then type Skiing. Press Enter.

ACTIVITY 21.4
Developing a List and a Table (Continued)

The first item on the list (*Skiing*) is entered, and when you pressed ↵Enter the next bullet was automatically created.

5 Type `Eating pizza` and then press ↵Enter.

A second bulleted item is created on your list, and a bullet is created for your next entry.

6 Type `Walking off the pizza calories`. Press ↵Enter twice.

The insertion point moves down to a blank line. Next we'll try creating a simple table, beginning with the title.

7 Type `My Activities` and then press ↵Enter.

8 On the Table menu, point to Insert and then choose Table.

The Insert Table dialog box displays so that you can designate the number of columns and rows your table should include (see Figure 21.18).

Figure 21.18.
You can designate how many columns and rows a table should include.

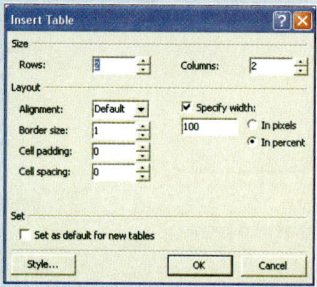

9 Click OK to accept the default settings (two rows by two columns).

A table is created on your Web page.

INSIDE TRACK
You can press ⇧Shift+Tab⇥ to move backward through cells in a table.

10 Type `Mondays`, press Tab⇥, and then type `Tennis Lesson`. Press Tab⇥.

The text is entered on the first row of your table. Notice that you needed to press Tab⇥ (not ↵Enter) to move forward through the table cells.

11 In the leftmost cell on the second row, type `Wednesdays`, press Tab⇥, and then type `Horseback Riding`. Press Tab⇥.

Your text is entered and a new row is created (see Figure 21.19).

12 In the leftmost cell on the third row, type `Fridays`, press Tab⇥, and then type `Basket Weaving`.

Although you can format your table manually, it's easier to use the Table AutoFormat feature, which applies predesigned formatting to your table.

13 Make sure that your insertion point is positioned in one of the table cells and then choose Table, Table AutoFormat.

The Table AutoFormat dialog box displays (see Figure 21.20).

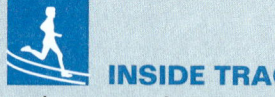

INSIDE TRACK
Just because you designate a particular structure for a table, you're not stuck with it. You can add or delete columns and rows, resize columns, and format them manually. If you want to find out more about structuring, revising, and formatting tables, see FrontPage's Help.

14 Preview several formats by single-clicking them on the Formats list.

15 Click *Simple 3* and then click OK.

The formatting is applied to your table (see Figure 21.21).

16 Choose File, Save to save the changes.

Alternatively, click the Save button on the toolbar. Keep FrontPage open and your Web displayed for the next activity.

ACTIVITY 21.4
Developing a List and a Table

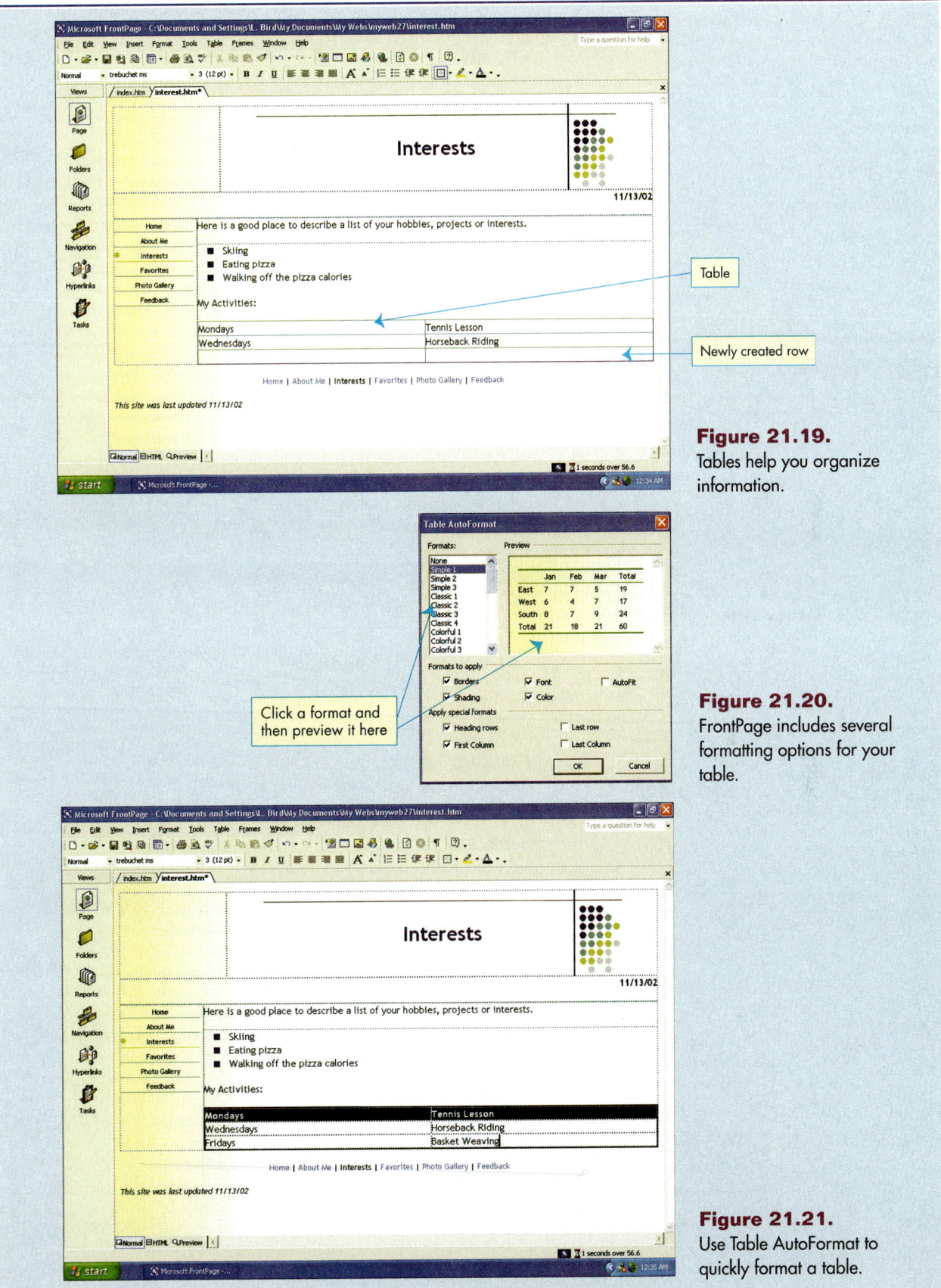

Figure 21.19.
Tables help you organize information.

Figure 21.20.
FrontPage includes several formatting options for your table.

Figure 21.21.
Use Table AutoFormat to quickly format a table.

Develop a List and a Table

APPLY A THEME

You've already seen that you can format text by using the buttons on the Formatting toolbar. However, you can also change the look of the entire Web by applying a theme. A **theme** is a group of colors, graphics, styles, and fonts that you can apply to an individual Web page or a group of pages. Using a theme is a good idea because it helps create a uniform and consistent look throughout the entire Web site. Additionally, because the themes are professionally designed, they generally include a pleasing balance of colors and designs. Finally, using themes helps you quickly produce Web pages because FrontPage already includes 23 standard themes from which you can choose.

The Web you created, like most developed using a template or wizard, already includes a theme—which is why there are already colors and graphics on it. However, you'll preview several other themes in this activity and then apply one to your Web.

ACTIVITY 21.5
Applying a Theme

① In the open Web, choose F̲ormat, T̲heme.
The Themes dialog box displays. This dialog box includes a number of professionally developed designs (see Figure 21.22).

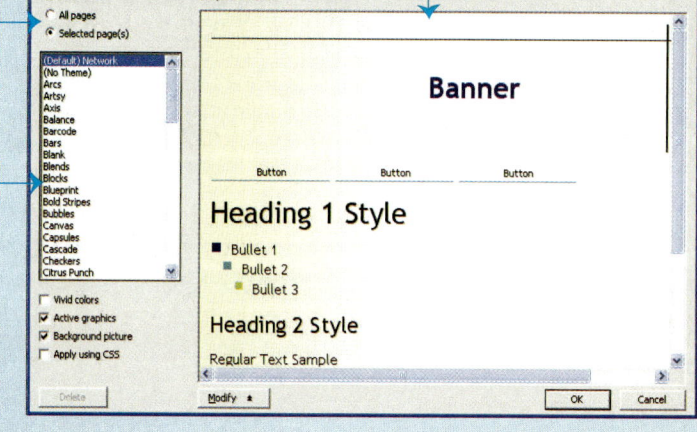

Figure 21.22.
FrontPage includes a number of professional designs—called themes—that you can use for your Web.

② In the *Apply Theme to* section, choose the *All pages* button.

③ Click the *Blends* theme.
A preview of the theme is shown in the *Sample of Theme* section of the dialog box. (If you want, preview several other themes. When you're finished, just make sure that the *Blends* theme is selected.)

 **HEADS UP!** When you complete step 4, a warning box might display. If so, choose Yes and then continue with the activity.

④ Click OK.
The theme is applied to the Web (see Figure 21.23).

ACTIVITY 21.5
Applying a Theme

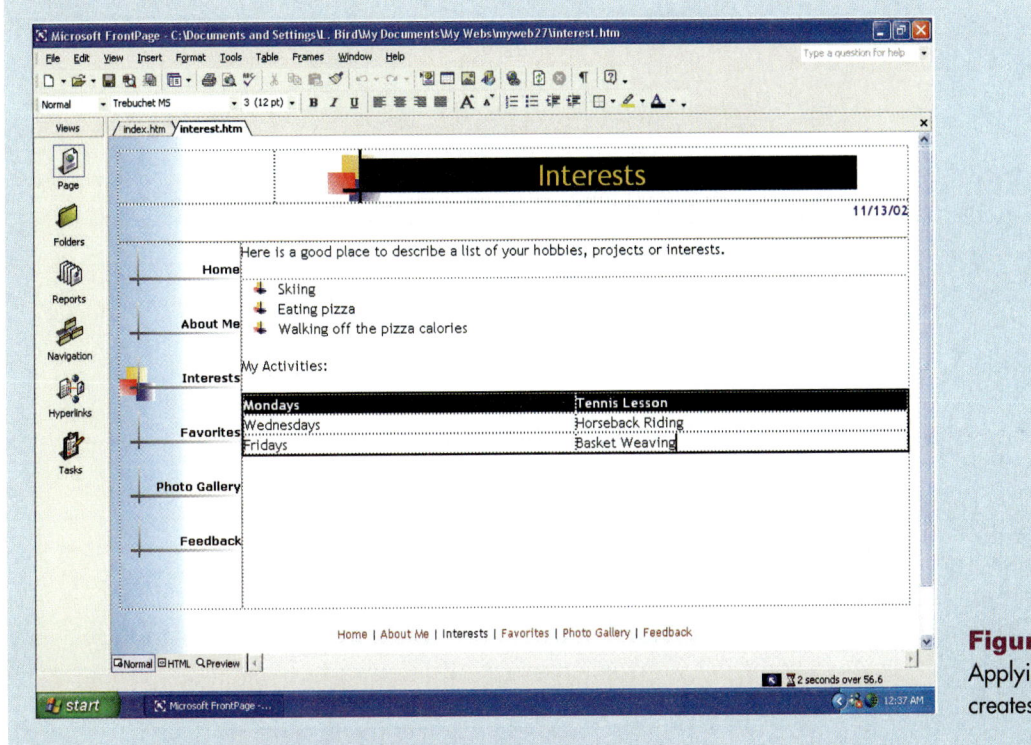

Figure 21.23.
Applying a different theme creates a distinctive look.

5. Choose File, Save to save the changes.
   Keep FrontPage open and your Web displayed for the next activity.

REVISE AND CREATE HYPERLINKS

When you use a template or wizard to create a Web within FrontPage, it usually includes several sample hyperlinks. Hyperlinks on a Web page can point to a page within the Web site, another Web site, or an e-mail address. In this exercise, you'll see how to revise the existing hyperlinks in the site and how to create a new one from scratch. You'll find out that developing hyperlinks isn't nearly as difficult as you might think. In fact, when you use FrontPage, it's downright easy!

ACTIVITY 21.6
Revising and Creating Hyperlinks

1. In the open Web, choose View, Navigation.
   The Web displays in Navigation view.

2. Double-click the Favorites icon to display the Favorites page.
   This page includes several hyperlinks. Hyperlinks are usually shown in a different color than other text.

3. Select the text for the first hyperlink (*The Microsoft Network*) and then choose Insert, Hyperlink.
   The Edit Hyperlink dialog box is shown (see Figure 21.24).

INSIDE TRACK
To edit an existing hyperlink you can also right-click it and then choose Hyperlink Properties from the shortcut menu.

ACTIVITY 21.6
Revising and Creating Hyperlinks (Continued)

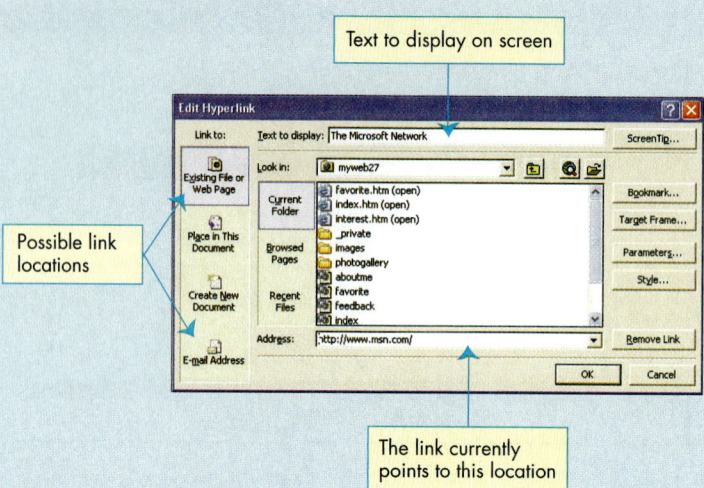

Figure 21.24.
You can edit existing hyperlinks.

- Text to display on screen
- Possible link locations
- The link currently points to this location

④ Select the existing text in the Address text box and then type `www.microsoft.com/frontpage`.
   This modifies the hyperlink so that it points to Microsoft's Web site for FrontPage.

⑤ Select the existing text in the Text to display box and then type `Microsoft's FrontPage Web site`. Click OK.

⑥ Select the text associated with the bullet below your revised hyperlink (*Microsoft FrontPage's Web site*) and then type `Help and support for working with FrontPage`.

⑦ Using steps 3–6 as a guide, revise the second hyperlink as follows:
   Text to display: `Nando Times`
   Address: `www.nandotimes.com`
   Description: `Up-to-the-minute news`

⑧ Select all the existing text associated with the third hyperlink and then delete it.

⑨ Choose File, Save to save your changes.
   Next, we'll create a new hyperlink from scratch. The procedure is similar to that for revising an existing link.

⑩ Click the index.htm tab to display the home page for your Web.

⑪ Make sure that the home page for your Web is displayed in the Normal pane and using Page view; then delete the existing text in the table cell below *Weather* (from *Comment* through *70 degrees*).

⑫ In the same cell, type `Current Weather` and then select the text.
   When you want to create a hyperlink, you must first select the text or object that you want to use for the link.

⑬ Choose Insert, Hyperlink from the menu.
   The Insert Hyperlink dialog box displays.

⑭ In the Address box, type `www.wunderground.com` and then click OK.

⑮ Click outside of the text to deselect the text; then press Ctrl+S to save your changes.
   Keep FrontPage open and your Web displayed for the next activity.

CREATE AN E-MAIL HYPERLINK

In the previous activity, you saw how to create and revise hyperlinks directed to Web sites. Hyperlinks can also point to an e-mail address. When you set up a hyperlink to an e-mail address, all the Web site visitors need to do to contact you is click the link. Doing so will automatically open a new mail message on their system with your e-mail address already filled in. Try creating an e-mail hyperlink now.

ACTIVITY 21.7
Creating an E-mail Hyperlink

1. Make sure that the home page of your Web is displayed in Page view.

2. Select *Favorite Links* in the left table area of the home page and then type `Contact Me`. The new text (*Contact Me*) replaces *Favorite Links*.

3. Select the text in the cells below *Contact Me* (from *Comment* through *MSNBC*) and then press Del.

4. Type `You can always e-mail me!`

5. Select the text you typed in the previous step (*You can always e-mail me!*) and then press Ctrl+K.
   The Insert Hyperlink dialog box displays. However, instead of linking to an existing Web page or file, you'll link to an e-mail address.

6. Click the E-mail Address button in the *Link to* section.
   The configuration of the Insert Hyperlink dialog box changes so that you can enter information related to creating an e-mail address.

ALERT!
If you plan to post this Web on the Internet, you may want to use a free, Web-based e-mail address, such as those offered through Yahoo! or Mail.com, instead of your personal e-mail address.

7. In the E-mail address box, enter your personal e-mail address and then click OK.
   Next you'll test a couple of your links using FrontPage's Preview mode.

8. With the home page of your Web displayed, click the Preview button.
   The home page is shown in the Preview pane.

9. Click the You can always e-mail me! link.
   A new mail message is created by using the mail messaging software that's installed on your system. Additionally, your e-mail address is already inserted in the *To* text box.

10. Close the mail message window and then click the *Current Weather* hyperlink.
    If your computer is connected to the Internet, the Weather Underground Web site is shown within FrontPage.

11. Click the Normal button to redisplay the home page of your Web.

12. Choose File, Save All.
    All the open Web pages are saved.
    Keep FrontPage open and your Web displayed for the next activity.

EXAMINE A LINK BAR'S PROPERTIES

In the previous two activities, you saw that you could create hyperlinks that point to either Web sites or e-mail addresses. In both cases, these were external links because they opened a window or created a link to something outside of your Web. In contrast, you can create or revise specialized hyperlinks that allow your visitors to navigate *within* your Web site. These hyperlinks can be grouped together and shown on the same location on each of your Web pages. This hyperlinked list of Web pages within a Web site is often called a **links bar** or navigation bar.

Because you relied on a template to create the Web page initially, a link bar based on the Web's structure is already included in your Web. This structure includes a parent page and several child pages. When referring to a Web's navigation structure, a **parent page** is one that has subpages at a lower level associated with it. In the same way, a **child page** is one that is connected to a higher-level parent page. However, you can easily change the items on the link bar to better fit your needs. Although extensive revision of a link bar is beyond the scope of this book, we'll point you in the right direction to do so if you're so inclined.

ACTIVITY 21.8
Examining a Link Bar's Properties

❶ Make sure that the home page of your Web is displayed in Normal view. The link bar is shown on the left side of the page (see Figure 21.25).

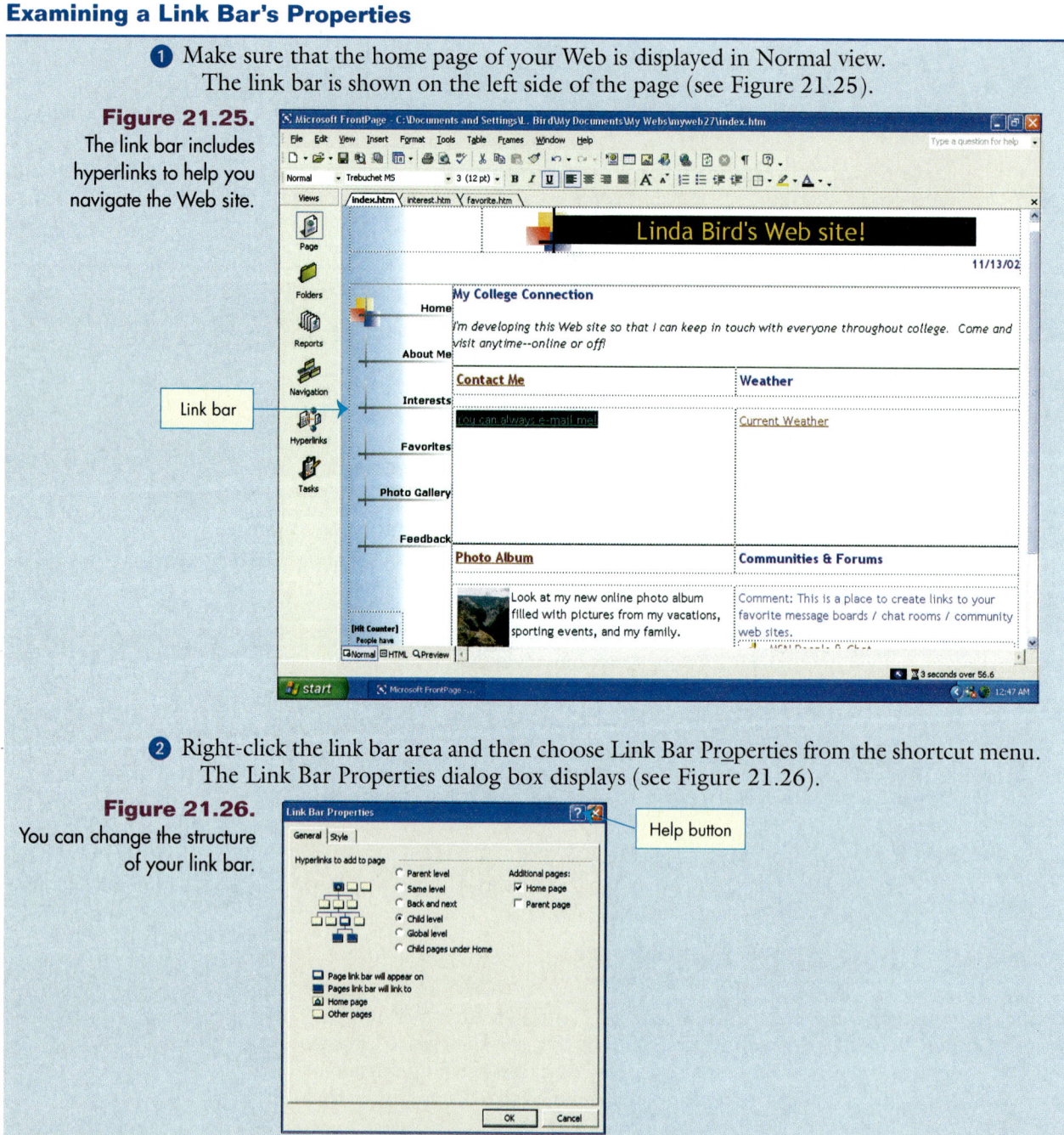

Figure 21.25.
The link bar includes hyperlinks to help you navigate the Web site.

❷ Right-click the link bar area and then choose Link Bar Properties from the shortcut menu. The Link Bar Properties dialog box displays (see Figure 21.26).

Figure 21.26.
You can change the structure of your link bar.

ACTIVITY 21.8
Examining a Link Bar's Properties

③ In the Link Bar Properties dialog box, click the Help button and then click the *Parent level* option button.
   A ScreenTip displays so that you can better understand what this option will do.

④ Click within the gray background area of the dialog box to clear the ScreenTip.

⑤ Using steps 3–4 as a guide, find out how choosing the other options in the dialog box will affect the structure of the link bar.

⑥ Choose Cancel to close the Link Bar Properties dialog box without modifying the existing options.
   Keep FrontPage open and your Web displayed for the next activity, in which you change the Web's overall structure by adding and deleting pages.

CHANGE A WEB'S STRUCTURE

The structure that was automatically created when you used the wizard to create the Web is only a starting place. You can delete pages, add additional pages, or change the navigation level on which pages appear. Of course, restructuring the Web site might also affect other elements, such as which hyperlinks appear on the links bar.

ACTIVITY 21.9
Changing a Web's Structure

① With your Web open, choose View, Navigation.
   The Web is shown in Navigation view. This is the best view to use when you want to add, delete, or otherwise modify your Web's structure.

② Single-click the *Interests* page icon; then press Del.
   The Delete Page dialog box displays.

③ Make sure the *Remove page from the navigation structure* option is selected and then choose OK.
   The page is removed from the navigation structure. Next, we'll change the order in which the pages are shown on the links bar.

④ While pointing to the About Me page icon, click and hold the mouse button.

⑤ Drag the About Me page icon to the right of the Feedback page icon.

⑥ When you see an outline of the About Me page icon's new location, release the mouse.
   The page is moved to a new location within the navigation structure. This will also change the order of the pages on the link bar.

⑦ Double-click your Web's home page icon to display it in the Normal pane.
   Notice that the order of the hyperlinks in the link bar is changed to reflect the new navigation structure. Next, we'll try adding a completely new page to your Web. Because you want to add a subpage at the level immediately below the home page, you need to first select the page.

⑧ Display the Web in Navigation view and then select the home page.

⑨ Point to New on the File menu; then choose Page or Web.
   The New Page or Web task pane displays on the right side of the application window. This task pane includes a number of options for adding a new page to an existing Web.

ACTIVITY 21.9

Changing a Web's Structure (Continued)

⑩ In the *New* section of the task pane, click *Blank Page*.

The New Page or Web task pane clears, and a new page is added as a subpage to the Web's home page (see Figure 21.27).

Figure 21.27.
It's easy to add a new page to your Web.

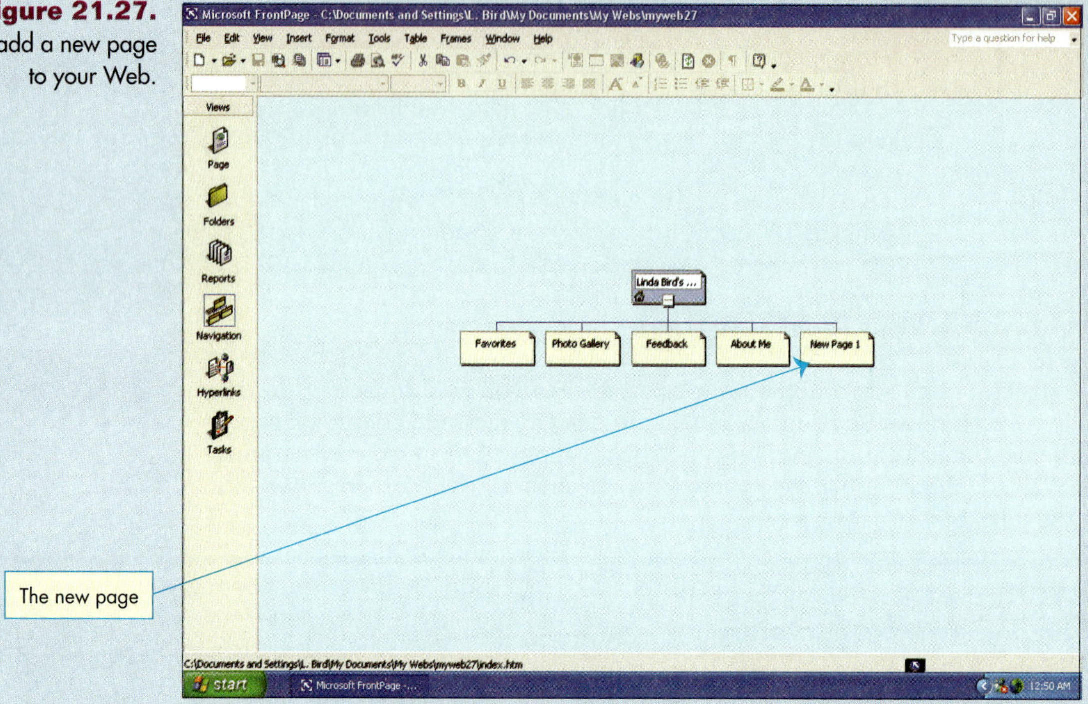

The new page

⑪ Right-click the new page and then choose Rena<u>m</u>e on the shortcut menu.

The page is shown in rename mode. You can tell that a page is in this mode when the name is selected.

⑫ Type `My Hobbies` and then click outside the page icons.

The page is renamed. Keep FrontPage open and your Web displayed for the next activity in which you test the link bar and hyperlinks.

TEST YOUR WEB

OK, you're almost ready to publish your Web to the Internet—or to add graphics and other visual elements. But before you do, you'll want to make sure everything looks as you expect and that all the hyperlinks point to the correct locations. One way to test these features is to preview the Web using FrontPage's Preview pane. Testing your Web allows you to make any revisions or corrections before publishing the Web. In this activity, you'll use this pane to take your first test run of your Web site.

ACTIVITY 21.10
Testing Your Web

1. With your Web displayed in Navigation view, double-click the home page to switch to Page view.
2. Click the Preview button to show the home page in the Preview pane.
3. Click the following hyperlinks in the link bar: *Favorites*, *Photo Gallery*, *About Me*, *Home*.
    The appropriate page displays for each link.
4. Click the *Favorites* hyperlink in the link bar of the home page.
    The Favorites page displays.
5. Click the Microsoft's FrontPage Web site hyperlink.
    If your computer is connected to the Internet, Microsoft's Web site for FrontPage is shown.
6. Click the Normal button at the bottom of the application window.
    The Web is again displayed in Normal view.
7. Choose File, Save All to save the changes to your Web.
8. On FrontPage's menu bar, choose File, Exit.
    FrontPage closes, and the Windows desktop redisplays.

INSIDE TRACK

In addition to checking the hyperlinks in your Web, it's a good idea to spell check it for errors before posting it to the Internet. To do so, choose Tools, Spelling.

In this chapter, you took a test drive of FrontPage's main features. You learned how to create a basic Web site, relying on a built-in template to create the basic structure and formatting for the site. You then revised the text, formatted, and organized the Web to better suit your needs. You also learned how to create and revise hyperlinks, work with the link bars, and test your Web within FrontPage and in a browser. In the next chapter, you'll enhance your Web site by adding graphics and other visual elements to your Web. Until then, work at getting down the basics of using FrontPage so that you'll be ready to expand on your knowledge and skills.

Don't Forget...

- You can start FrontPage and work with its interface using many of the same types of menus and commands that you have probably used in other Windows programs.
- FrontPage includes several views that you can use to work with your Web in different ways.
- You can view a page in Normal, HTML, or Preview panes.
- Lists and tables help you organize information on your Web pages.
- FrontPage includes several ready-made styles of formatting, called themes, which include text, backgrounds, colors, and other features.

- You can create or revise hyperlinks to other pages within your Web or to Web site locations on the Internet.
- You can create a hyperlink that activates a new e-mail message already set up to send to a specific recipient.
- The link bar includes links that help you navigate within a Web site.
- You can change a Web's overall structure by adding, deleting, or moving pages.
- Before publishing a Web to the Internet, it's a good idea to test your Web's links within FrontPage or in a browser.

Check This Out

MULTIPLE CHOICE

1. What is true regarding FrontPage?
   a. It helps you develop Web pages.
   b. It includes three main panes.
   c. You can develop a Web using a visual interface or by writing HTML code.
   d. All of the above

2. How can you develop a Web site in FrontPage?
   a. By using a built-in tool that already includes the site's structure and formatting
   b. By creating it from scratch, page by page
   c. By using a template; then customizing it for your needs by filling in information
   d. All of the above

3. Which of the following hyperlinks can you develop on a Web page?
   a. One that points to a Web location
   b. One that points to another page within your Web site
   c. One that opens a new mail message window
   d. All of the above

4. Which of the following is the best way to test a Web before publishing it to the Internet?
   a. Use FrontPage's Web View feature.
   b. Print out each page.
   c. Use FrontPage's Preview Pane.
   d. Examine the properties associated with the link bar.

5. What is a theme?
   a. A graphic you can insert on a Web page
   b. A professionally designed set of colors, fonts, graphics, and other elements that you can apply to your Web
   c. A way to preview your Web before publishing it to the Internet
   d. None of the above

MATCHING

a. template
b. theme
c. Navigation view
d. Web
e. Hyperlinks view
f. Page view
g. link bar
h. Reports view
i. parent page
j. table

1. A view that shows statistical reports for the Web
2. A hyperlinked list of Web pages within a site
3. In reference to FrontPage, a collection of pages that can make up a Web site
4. The view you use to work with elements on individual pages
5. A group of colors, graphics, styles, and fonts you can apply to a Web
6. A view that shows the overall structure of the Web
7. A page that has subpages at a lower level associated with it
8. A tool in FrontPage you can use to quickly develop a Web with the basic structure and formatting already in place
9. A grid with columns and rows that you can use to organize information
10. A view that shows the linked relationships of the pages in your Web

Real Life

1. Use FrontPage's wizard to develop a new Web site for a fictitious corporation that sells sports equipment online. First, open FrontPage and then point to New on the File menu. Choose Page or Web. In the New Page or Web task pane, click the link for Web Site Templates. Double-click the icon for Corporate Presence Web. When the wizard launches, work through the choices on each page, making decisions just as if you were developing the Web for a real company. When you finish, view the Web you created in each of the main views included in FrontPage.

   If time allows, replace the sample text in the Web with some of your own and apply various themes. Restructure the Web by adding another page to the Web and deleting one of the existing ones. Create or revise hyperlinks to Web sites about sports. Finally, view the Web in the Preview and HTML panes. Close the Web without saving your changes.

2. Using the steps and guidelines outlined in the previous exercise, create a Web for customer support for a store that sells music CDs online. (Hint: FrontPage includes a Customer Support template to help you specifically develop this type of Web.) Examine the Web using the various views and panes available. If time allows, replace the sample text with your own and apply various themes. When you're finished, close the Web without saving it.

3. Create a Web from scratch for a club or organization to which you belong. Assume that you're the president of the organization. Make sure to include links to related Web sites as well as an e-mail link where site visitors can contact you. If you want, apply a theme. When you're finished, close the Web without saving it.

I Spy: Privacy and Security Concerns

1. FrontPage includes a feature that allows you to import the pages from an existing Web site on the Internet to your computer. Use Help to find out how to work with this feature. Discuss with other students the implications of "borrowing" a Web site without the owner's permission, including legal, copyright, ethical, and privacy issues.
2. Think about your favorite hobby or leisure time activity; then run an Internet search to find 10 Web sites about it. View and analyze each of the Web sites, specifically looking at the contact information and the privacy policies. Are contact information and privacy policies routinely included on each site? If so, how are they similar? How are they different? What are the implications for including contact information on a site (commercial or personal)? How can you develop a Web site while still maintaining privacy?

CHAPTER 22

ADDING GRAPHICS TO YOUR WEB SITE

Key Terms

When you finish this chapter, you'll understand the following terms:

Auto Thumbnail
caption
clip art
photo gallery
Pictures toolbar
thumbnail

Chapter Objectives

After you complete this chapter, you'll be able to

- Use Clip Art
- Save Your Web Files
- Insert Picture Files
- Create and Test Thumbnails
- Create a Photo Gallery
- Modify a Photo Gallery

The Big Picture

You've probably heard that a picture is worth a thousand words. Although this isn't completely true for Web sites, you can judiciously insert graphical elements to help your audience focus on the main message, reinforce your content, or encourage them to stay longer on your site. Thoughtful inclusion of appropriate graphics can also help your site stand out from the millions of others on the Internet.

The trick is to include graphics that load quickly and reinforce your message—not distract from it. If the graphics on your site load slowly or don't have a strong relation to the site's content, visitors will quickly ditch your site in favor of others.

In this chapter, we'll show you the steps of inserting and revising clip art and pictures. You'll also learn how to use FrontPage's features to create a picture thumbnail and a photo gallery. Along the way, we'll point out design principles to keep in mind so that you don't accidentally create a hodgepodge of graphics that don't reinforce your site's content.

 INSIDE TRACK

Although we're using FrontPage as an example of Web authoring software, keep in mind that the concepts presented in this chapter can also be applied to other Web creation tools you might use, such as Dreamweaver or GoLive.

Window on the Web

FrontPage includes a number of options you can use to insert graphics on your site, including pictures and clip art. If thoughtfully used, these graphics can be used to emphasize your site's main focus. For example, Figure 22.1 shows a Web site for a woodworking school. The photograph shows some of the students and their work, which reinforces and emphasizes the site's purpose.

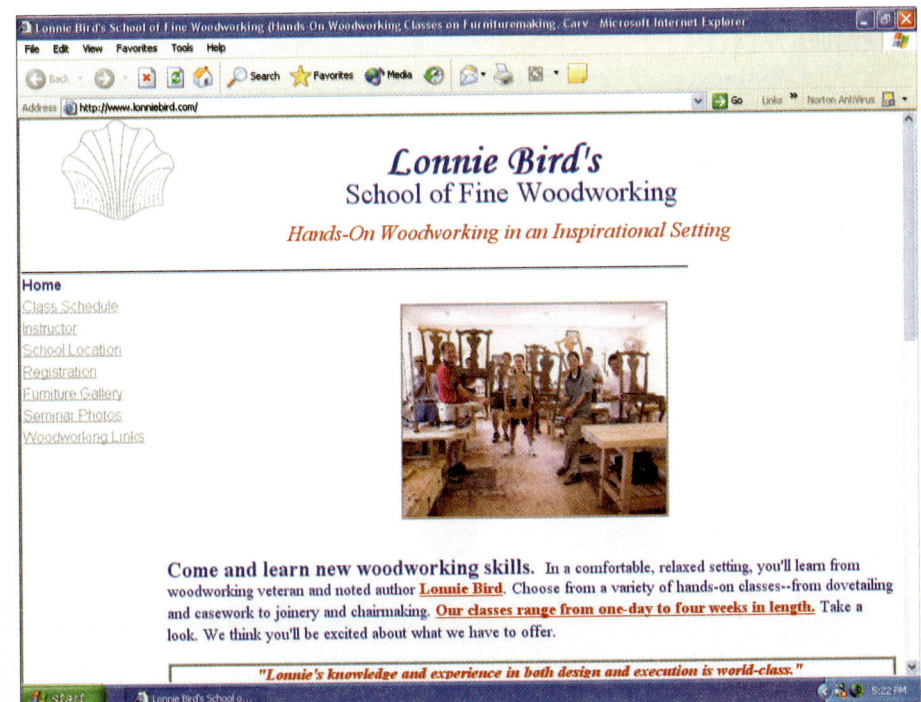

Figure 22.1.
Photographs, when carefully chosen, can reinforce a site's main purpose.

In this chapter, you'll also learn how to use FrontPage to create a photo gallery. The photo gallery consists of small images of photographs, called **thumbnails**. Site visitors can click a thumbnail to view the larger, hyperlinked image (see Figure 22.2).

However, you're not limited to photographs. You can also insert clip art images, which are line or created drawings (see Figure 22.3).

Inserting graphics on your Web page is both interesting and fun. Let's dig in and learn how to jazz up your Web site with graphics.

Figure 22.2.
FrontPage's photo galleries help you create an attractive yet quick-loading page of images.

Figure 22.3.
You can use clip art images to emphasize information.

USE CLIP ART

Clip art is non-copyrighted, electronic artwork or images that you can use in a variety of computer programs. In contrast with realistic photographic pictures, clip art images are generally line drawings created by an artist. Assuming that they have a strong relation to a Web site's content, they can be used to enhance it or draw attention to the site's purpose. Watch, however, that you don't overdo the type or number of clip art images. Doing so will create a jumbled, confusing effect that can potentially annoy your site visitors. Additionally, it might cause the page to load slowly.

FrontPage includes a number of clip art images you can use without paying a licensing fee. The best way to find these images is to use the Insert Clip Art task pane. You can think of the Insert Clip Art task pane as a library in which you can "check out" clips for your use. After you insert a clip art image you can modify, resize, or even delete it. In this activity, you'll learn the basics of finding and inserting clip art in a FrontPage Web file.

INSIDE TRACK

In addition to the clip art included in FrontPage, Microsoft includes a vast assortment of online clip art images, photographs, sounds, and animations you can use on your Web pages. These elements are available on Microsoft's Design Gallery Live Web site (*dgl.microsoft.com*). You can also create your own art from scratch using the buttons on the Drawing toolbar. To find out more about this option, see FrontPage's Help.

ACTIVITY 22.1
Using Clip Art

1. Launch FrontPage and close the *New Page or Web* task pane, if necessary.

2. Choose File, Open on the menu bar.
   The Open File dialog box displays.

3. In the Open File dialog box, navigate to the drive and folder in which the student data files for your class are stored (see your instructor for help, if necessary).

> **HEADS UP!** The icons for Web folders appear different from those for individual files within the Web. Also, if you're not sure where the student data files for this exercise are located, ask your instructor.

INSIDE TRACK

Instead of opening individual files associated with a Web, you can open the entire set of Web files at once. To do this, choose File, Open Web. Select the name of the Web in the Open Web dialog box and then click the Open button. Choose View, Navigation to display the pages in the Web.

4. Locate and then double-click the *My Personal Web* folder.
   This Web is similar to the one you developed in the last chapter. The files associated with this Web are shown in the Open File dialog box. Notice that the Web includes a file for each page in the Web as well as a number of supporting folders and files (see Figure 22.4).

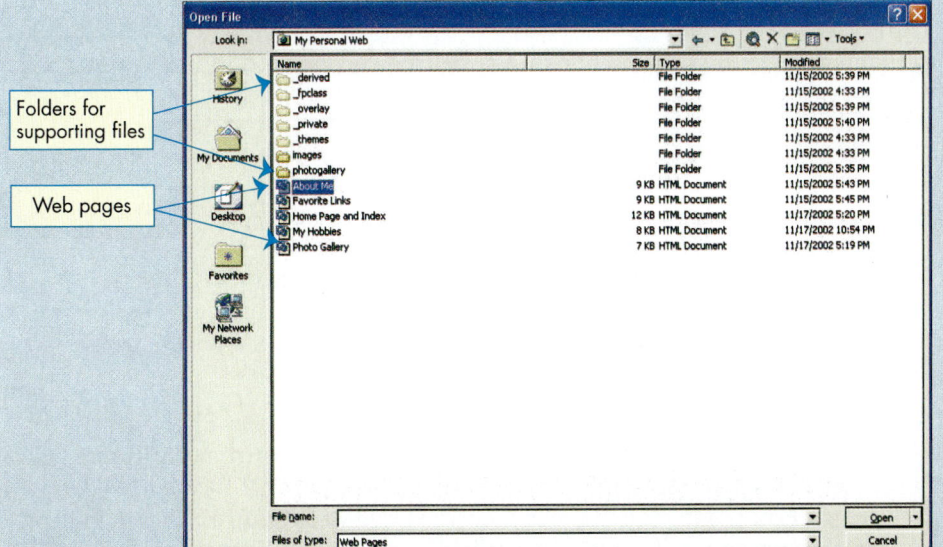

Figure 22.4.
Each Web includes a number of associated files.

ACTIVITY 22.1
Using Clip Art (Continued)

5. Single-click the *Home Page and Index* file and then click the <u>O</u>pen button.

   The home page for the Web opens in Page view (see Figure 22.5). This Web is similar to the one you developed in the previous chapter. Notice that the page is laid out in tables. This helps to group similar information together.

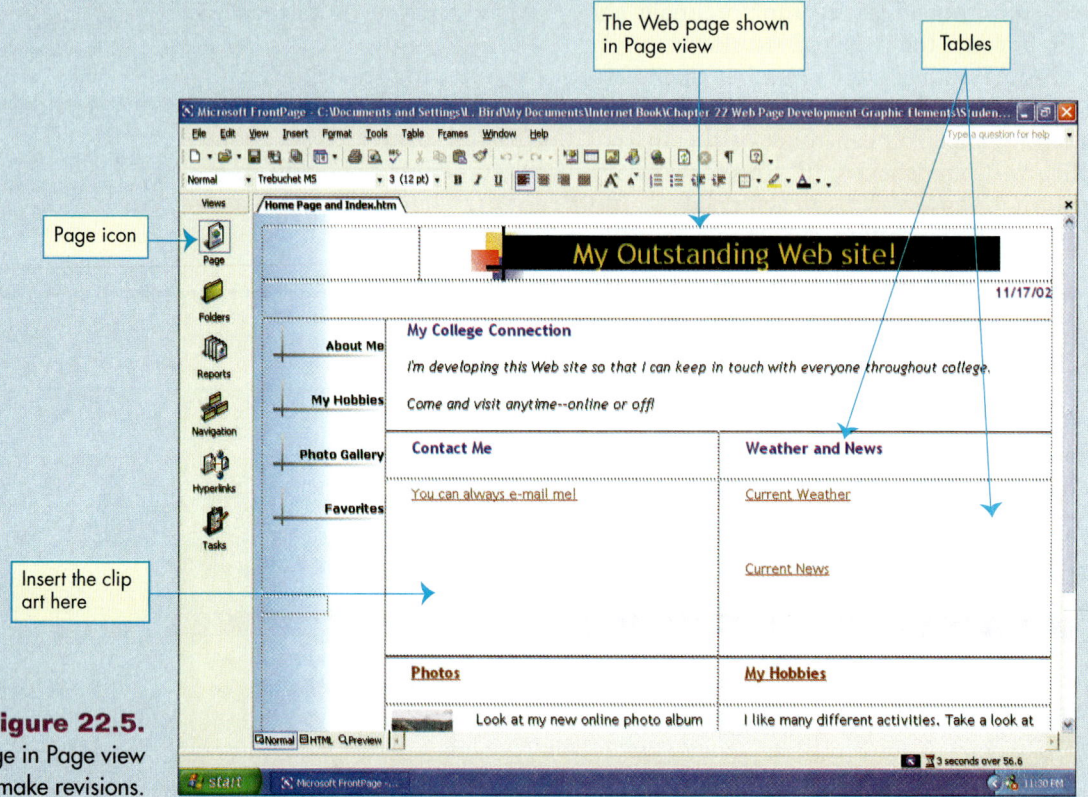

Figure 22.5.
Display a page in Page view to make revisions.

>  **HEADS UP!** If the Views Bar doesn't display in the FrontPage window, choose <u>V</u>iew, <u>V</u>iews Bar. Additionally, if the Web file on your computer doesn't match the one shown in Figure 22.5, click the Page icon on the Views Bar.

6. Click in the lower part of the *Contact Me* table, below the *You can always e-mail me!* text (refer to Figure 22.5).

   This places the insertion point (the blinking cursor) at the location in which you want to place the clip.

>  **HEADS UP!** If the Clip Organizer on your system has never been cataloged, you might see an Add Clips to Organizer message box after you complete step 7. If so, click <u>L</u>ater to close the message box and then proceed with the next step in the activity.

7. Point to <u>P</u>icture on the <u>I</u>nsert menu and then choose <u>C</u>lip Art from the submenu.

   The Insert Clip Art task pane displays on the right side of FrontPage's application window. You can search for clips by topical keyword and then display the results in the task pane (see Figure 22.6).

INSIDE TRACK
You're not limited to inserting line art clips in your Web. You can also use the Insert Clip Art task pane to insert sounds, videos, and animations on a page.

8. In the *Search text* box, type communication and then click Search.

   Clip art images that match the keyword are shown in the Insert Clip Art task pane (see Figure 22.7). Some of the clips are included as part of the FrontPage program; clips shown with a world icon are pulled in from the Internet. (These will be available only if your computer is online.)

ACTIVITY 22.1
Using Clip Art

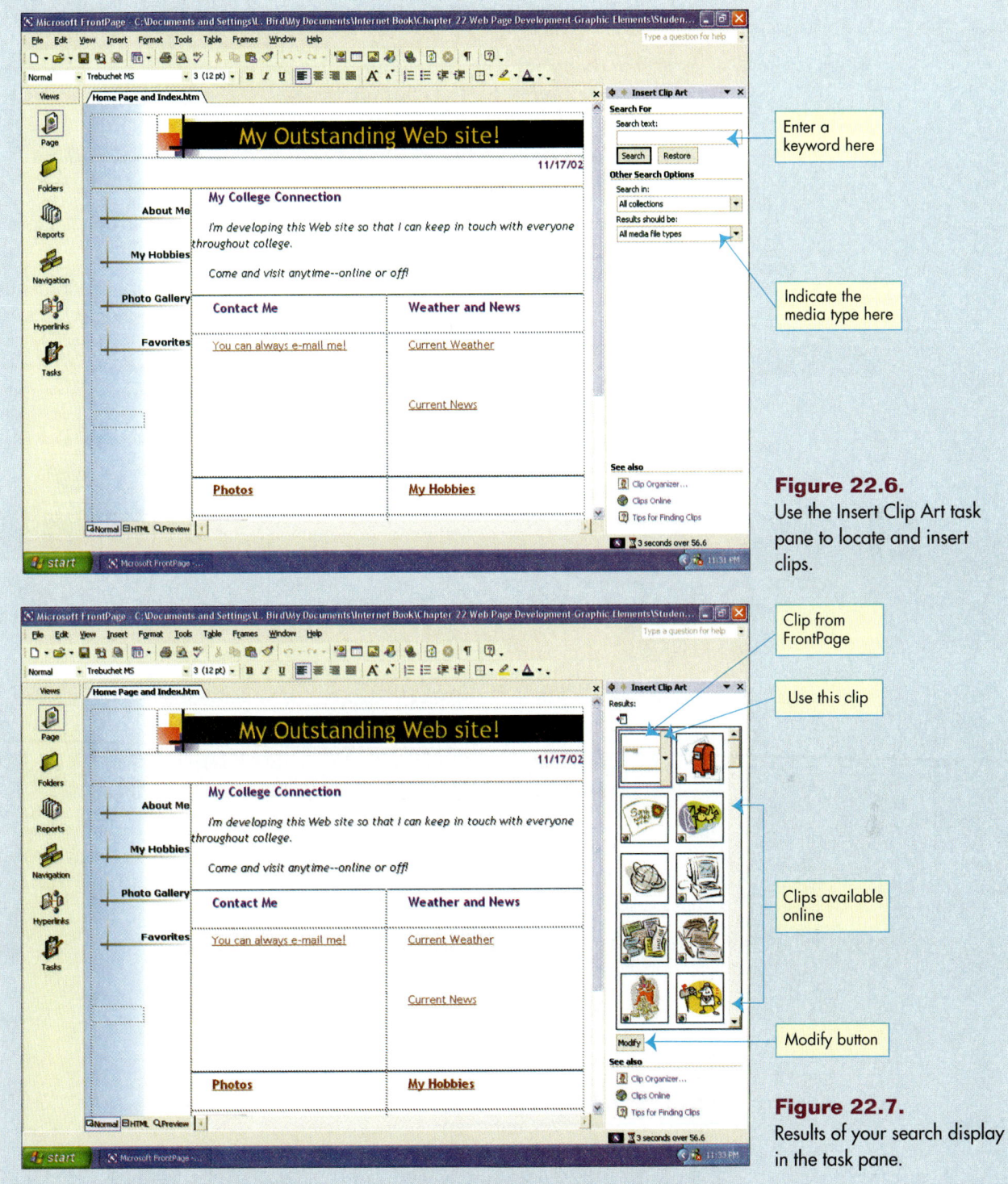

Figure 22.6.
Use the Insert Clip Art task pane to locate and insert clips.

Figure 22.7.
Results of your search display in the task pane.

⑨ Click the clip indicated in Figure 22.7. (If this clip isn't available on your system, choose a similar one.)
   The clip is inserted at the insertion point location.

⑩ Click Modify in the Insert Clip Art task pane (refer to Figure 22.7).
   The *Search text* box redisplays so that you can enter another keyword.

Use Clip Art 361

ACTIVITY 22.1
Using Clip Art (Continued)

11 Using the previous steps as a guide, insert a weather-related clip art image in the area below the *Current Weather* hyperlink.

12 Click the close button in the Insert Clip Art task pane.

The task pane closes, freeing up more room for the Web page. Your page should appear similar to the one shown in Figure 22.8.

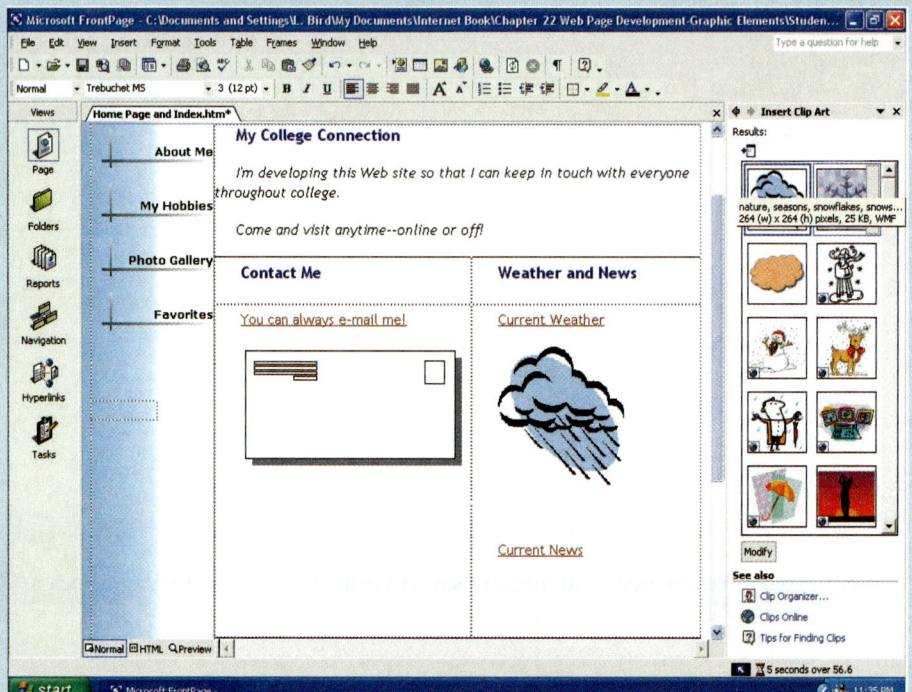

Figure 22.8.
The clip art displays on your page.

INSIDE TRACK
You can move a clip or other graphic object by selecting it and then pointing to the middle of the object and dragging it to a new location. To remove the clip from a Web page, select it and then press Del.

13 Single-click the *mail* clip.

The clip is selected, as indicated by the black selection handles that encompass its border. Next you'll try resizing one of the clips.

14 Rest the mouse pointer over the handle in the upper-right corner of the clip art object until a two-headed arrow appears; then drag down and to the left until the clip is approximately one-half of its original size. Release the mouse button.

15 Click outside of the clip art object to deselect it.

The black selection handles are no longer displayed. Keep FrontPage open and your Web displayed for the next activity in which you save the changes to your Web.

SAVE YOUR WEB FILES

INSIDE TRACK
Embedded objects are those that are created in a program (called a source program) but are placed within a different program (such as FrontPage). The objects might be text, a chart, a graphic, animation, or sound.

FrontPage includes more options related to saving your Web files than do some other software programs: You can save changes to a single page, update the existing Web by saving your modifications using the same filename and location or save the file using an entirely different name and location. Additionally, FrontPage includes a command you can use to save all the files associated with your Web.

To save changes to a single Web page, you choose File, Save. Additionally, this command prompts you to save any objects (such as graphics) that are embedded on the page. To save a single Web page using a different location or filename, you can use the File, Save As command. However, to save modifications to *all* the open files in a Web (including embedded picture and clip art files), choose File, Save All. In the next activity, you'll save the embedded graphic files as part of a single Web page. You'll also see how to close, copy, rename, and then reopen the Web.

ACTIVITY 22.2
Saving Your Web Files

❶ In the open Web, choose File, Save.
   The Save Embedded Files dialog box displays (see Figure 22.9). Because you added clip art images to a single page in the previous activity, FrontPage needs to save them as part of your Web.

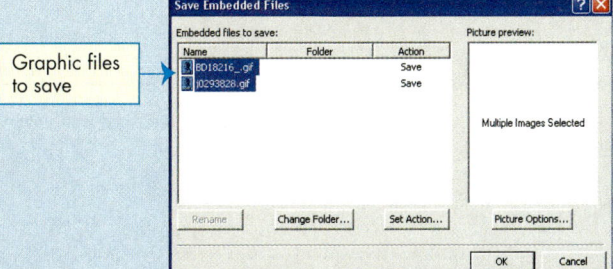

Figure 22.9.
FrontPage helps you to save graphic files as part of your Web.

INSIDE TRACK

To view the default file format used for the embedded files, click Picture Options in the Save Embedded Files dialog box. You'll notice that most clip art and line drawings use the GIF file format, which has a limit of 256 colors. In contrast, photos generally use the JPEG file format with many more colors. These files can also take up more storage space and take longer to download when used as a part of a Web site.

❷ In the Save Embedded Files dialog box, click OK.
   Now close the Web, including all the associated files.

❸ Choose File, Close Web.
   Because you already saved your changes, FrontPage doesn't prompt you to save them again. Now you'll see how to copy a Web, including all the associated files. One easy way to do this is in the Open Web dialog box.

❹ Choose File, Open Web.
   The Open Web dialog box displays.

❺ If necessary, navigate to the drive and folder where your student data files are stored; then right-click the *My Personal Web* folder.

❻ On the shortcut menu, choose Copy, then click in the white background area of the Open Web dialog box and choose Paste.
   A Copy message box displays while the files are copied. When all the files associated with the Web are copied, a folder named *Copy of My Personal Web* displays in the Open Web dialog box.

❼ Right-click the *Copy of My Personal Web* folder and then choose Rename from the shortcut menu.
   The folder's name is shown in rename mode.

❽ Type `My Outstanding Web` and then click outside of any files or folders (but within the Open Web dialog box).
   The Web is saved using the new name.

❾ In the Open Web dialog box, click the *My Outstanding Web* folder and then click the Open button.
   The Web is open in FrontPage; to see it you must use a different view, such as Navigation view.

❿ Choose View, Navigation.
   The pages for the Web are shown as page icons in Navigation view. Keep FrontPage open and your Web displayed for the next activity in which you insert pictures.

INSERT PICTURE FILES

Although drawn clip art can help to emphasize information on your Web site, you'll often find it more useful to include real photos, sometimes called *picture files*. In most cases, these picture files use the JPEG (JPG) file format.

Before locating and inserting a photograph, carefully determine whether it will enhance your site's purpose. It's also important to make sure that the file uses the lowest resolution possible, but still displays an accurate representation of the photo. Why is this so important? Because high-resolution photographic files translate into large file size—and make Web pages notoriously slow to download and view.

HEADS UP! It's important to make sure that you have the legal right to use photographs, clip art, animations, or other graphics you find on the Web. If the images are available for use at no charge, there will usually be a clear statement on the Web site to that effect. If you have any questions about the legality of using a graphic, contact the Web site's developer and ask for written permission.

After you determine the type and number of graphics to include, you can obtain Web-ready pictures in numerous ways: by scanning existing photographs to create digital files, by taking photographs with a digital camera, or by using copyright-free photographs available for download from the Internet. For example, you can download pictures from Microsoft's Design Gallery Live without paying a fee for their use. It's also possible that there are already picture files available on your personal computer system or your business or school network.

In this activity, you'll see how to insert photographic pictures into your Web. You'll also see how to estimate the time that it will take for others to view the page at different connection speeds.

ACTIVITY 22.3
Inserting Picture Files

1. With the open Web shown in Navigation view, double-click the *My Hobbies* page icon.

2. Click in the space immediately below *Sailing*.
   This indicates the location in which the picture will be inserted. In the next step, you'll insert a picture that's stored on your computer.

3. Point to Picture on the Insert menu and then click From File.
   The Picture dialog box displays.

4. Navigate to the drive and folder where the student data files for your class are stored (see your instructor for help, if necessary).

5. Double-click the *Sailing* file.
   The *Sailing* picture is inserted on your Web page (see Figure 22.10). Now use the same procedure to insert two more photos.

6. Using the previous steps as a guide, insert the *Baseball* photo below the *Baseball* text and the *Horseback Riding* photo below the *Horseback Riding* text.
   The photos on the page look great—and they reinforce the site's purpose. There's only one problem: The page will take a long time to load when used on the Internet. To help you determine how long a page will take to load, FrontPage includes an estimate in the status bar (see Figure 22.11). It's best if Web pages take no longer than 10–15 seconds to load; this page is far exceeding that limit.

7. On the status bar, click the *Estimated Time to Download* icon and then choose 14.4.
   The length of time that it will take for this page to download if a computer is connected at 14.4 K displays (approximately 146 seconds).

ACTIVITY 22.3
Inserting Picture Files

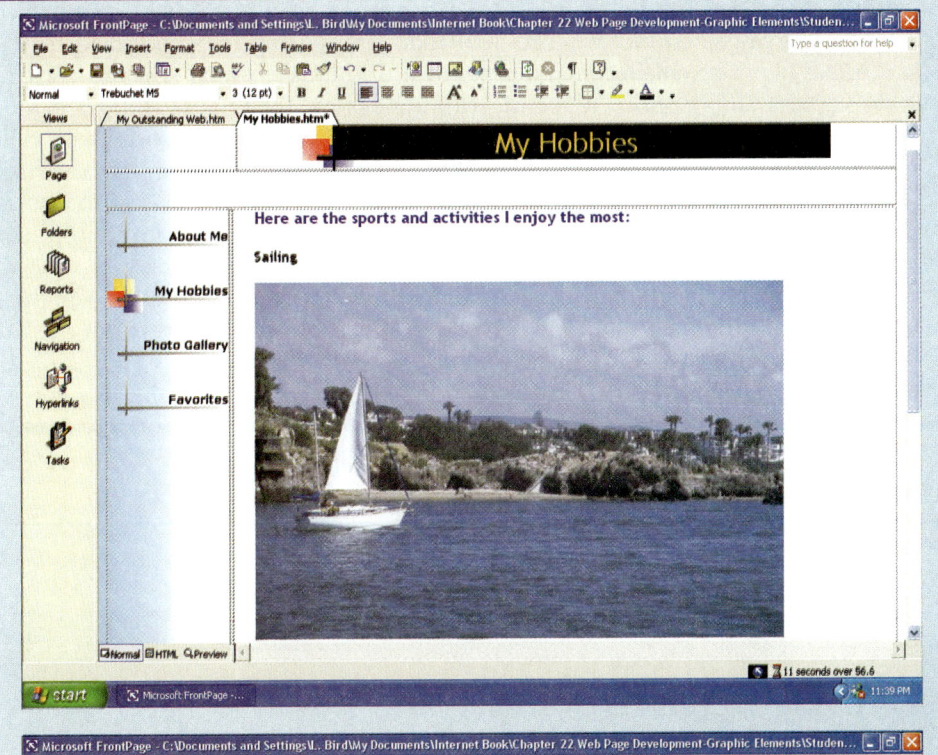

Figure 22.10.
You can insert pictures in your Web.

Figure 22.11.
FrontPage helps you estimate how long pages will take to load.

⑧ Click the *Estimated Time to Download* icon and then choose 56K.
   The download time (39 seconds) is still too long. You'll fix this problem in the next activity.

⑨ Choose File, Save.

⑩ Choose OK in the Save Embedded Files dialog box.
   Keep FrontPage open and your Web displayed for the next activity, in which you create and test thumbnails.

Insert Picture Files 365

CREATE AND TEST THUMBNAILS

So that you can use pictures in your Web but still have reasonable download times, FrontPage includes an **Auto Thumbnail** feature that you can use to convert a full-sized picture into a smaller version that is hyperlinked to the original file. The smaller image is called a thumbnail, which you can click to display the larger photo. Creating thumbnails on Web pages is a good idea because these Web pages will download more quickly than do those with full-sized photos. The visitors can then decide whether they want to take the time to download the larger images. Using thumbnails will also allow you to display more images on the page or display them in a way that the site visitors can more readily see most or all the images on the page.

In this activity, you'll convert the larger pictorial images on your Web page to smaller thumbnails and then test them. You'll also see how you can use the **Pictures toolbar** to make formatting changes to your images.

ACTIVITY 22.4
Creating and Testing Thumbnails

① Make sure that the *My Hobbies* page is shown in Page view in the open Web.

② Scroll up on the page, if necessary, until you can easily view the *Sailing* image.

 **HEADS UP!** In certain cases, the Auto Thumbnail command isn't available: If the graphic you select is already smaller than it would be as a thumbnail or if the image has a hyperlink or animation already associated with it.

③ Right-click the *Sailing* image to display the associated shortcut menu and then click the A<u>u</u>to Thumbnail command.

The full-sized image is converted to a smaller, thumbnail version (see Figure 22.12).

Now try a slightly different way of creating a thumbnail: using a button on the Pictures toolbar. First, you need to display this toolbar, which is used to modify photos.

Figure 22.12.
You can easily convert a photo to a thumbnail.

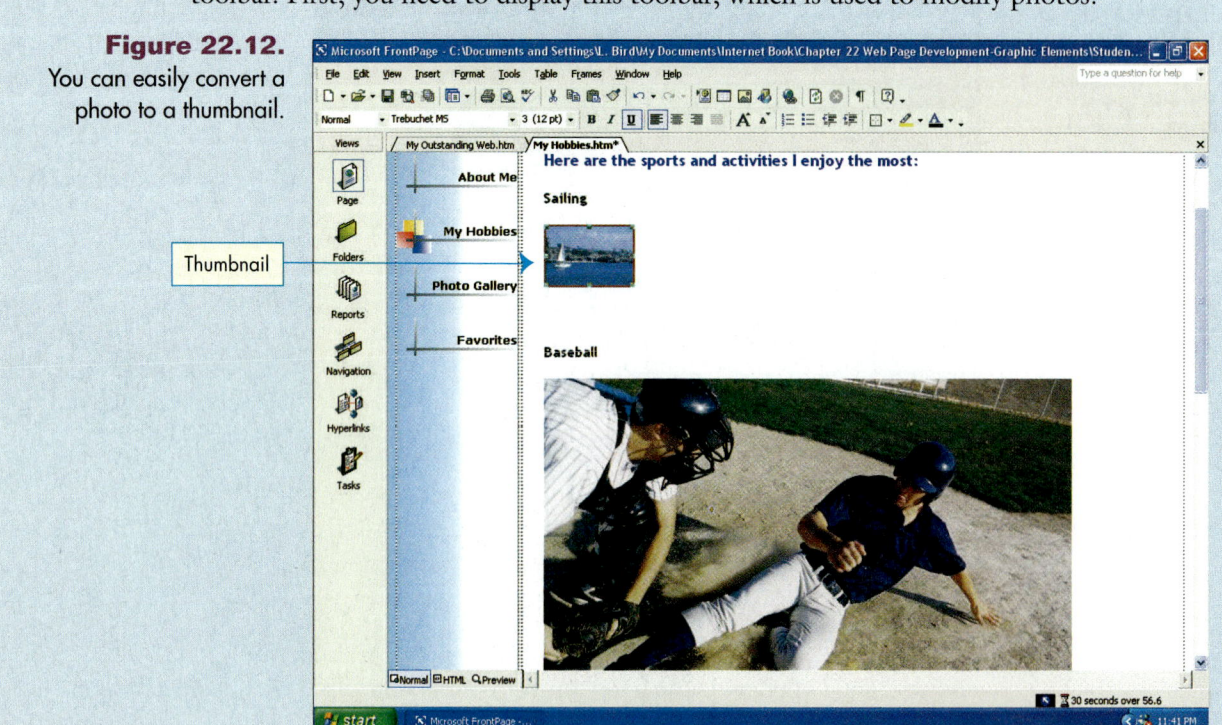

366 Chapter 22 Adding Graphics to Your Web Site

ACTIVITY 22.4
Creating and Testing Thumbnails

④ Right-click the Standard or Formatting toolbar to display a list of available toolbars and then click Pictures on the list.

The Pictures toolbar displays (see Figure 22.13). This toolbar includes buttons that you can use to create an AutoThumbnail and to format your pictures.

⑤ Single-click the *Baseball* picture to select it and then click the Auto Thumbnail button on the Pictures toolbar.

The *Baseball* picture is converted to a thumbnail.

INSIDE TRACK

If the Pictures toolbar already displays, you can skip step 4. After the Pictures toolbar is shown, you can find out what a button on the Pictures toolbar does by resting your mouse pointer over it until a ScreenTip displays.

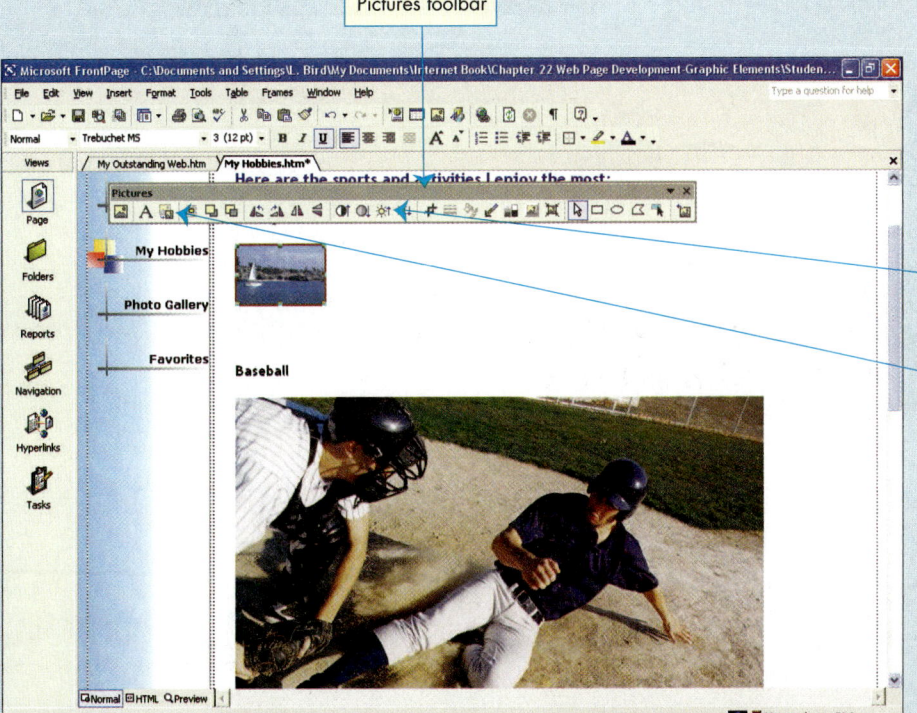

Figure 22.13.
The Pictures toolbar includes a number of tools you can use to format your pictures.

⑥ Single-click the *Horseback Riding* picture; then convert it to a thumbnail by using whichever method you prefer.

The thumbnail for this picture displays. However, this photo is a little dark. In the next step, you'll try using the More Brightness button on the Pictures toolbar to lighten it.

⑦ With the *Horseback Riding* thumbnail picture selected, click the More Brightness button on the Pictures toolbar three or four times.

The picture lightens. (If you like it as it originally displayed, click the Less Brightness button three or four times.)

INSIDE TRACK

If you want to change the default settings (such as the size or border style) for the Auto Thumbnail feature, choose Tools, Page Options. In the Page Options dialog box, click the tab for AutoThumbnail and then specify the properties, such as the default width and border thickness. Click OK and all subsequent AutoThumbnails you create will adhere to the new default settings.

⑧ Click the Preview button.

The *My Hobbies* page displays in Preview mode. This is a good mode to use when you want a quick look at how the Web will look in a browser. You can also test hyperlinks (such as AutoThumbnails) in this mode.

ACTIVITY 22.4
Creating and Testing Thumbnails (Continued)

⑨ Rest your mouse pointer over the *Sailing* thumbnail.
   A hand icon displays, indicating that this image is hyperlinked to another file or location (see Figure 22.14). In this case, it's linked to the larger photo.

Figure 22.14.
The thumbnail is hyperlinked to the larger photo.

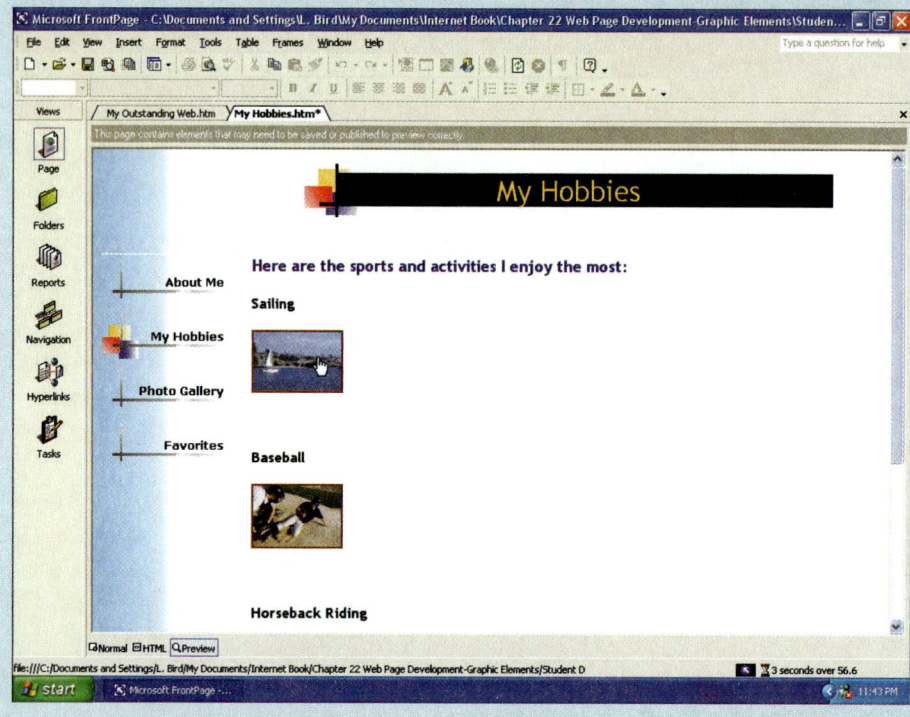

⑩ Click the *Sailing* thumbnail.
   The picture displays, using the original size of the photo.

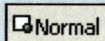

⑪ Click the Normal button.
   The Web displays using Normal mode.

⑫ Using steps 8–11 as a guide, test the thumbnails for the other two pictures on the *My Hobbies* page.

⑬ Choose File, Save.
   Because you made changes to the embedded graphics on the *My Hobbies* page, you'll need to save your modifications to them.

⑭ Choose OK in the Save Embedded Files dialog box.
   Keep FrontPage open and your Web displayed for the next activity, in which you create a photo gallery.

CREATE A PHOTO GALLERY

FrontPage includes a feature that allows you to create a photo gallery. A **photo gallery** in a FrontPage Web page consists of a group of thumbnail pictures that display using a specific arrangement. In fact, FrontPage includes four different layouts for photo galleries. Depending on the layout, you can add a label, or **caption,** to each photo. In the following activity, you'll experience how easy it is to work with this feature.

368   Chapter 22   Adding Graphics to Your Web Site

ACTIVITY 22.5
Creating a Photo Gallery

❶ In the open Web, click the Navigation icon (in the Views Bar).

❷ Double-click the icon for the *Photo Gallery* page.

❸ On the Photo Gallery page, click in the blank space below the following text: *Here are a few pictures of my family and our place near the mountains.*
This space indicates the location for the pictures in the photo gallery.

❹ Choose Insert, Picture, New Photo Gallery.
The Photo Gallery Properties dialog box displays (see Figure 22.15). You use this dialog box to indicate which pictures you want to include in the gallery.

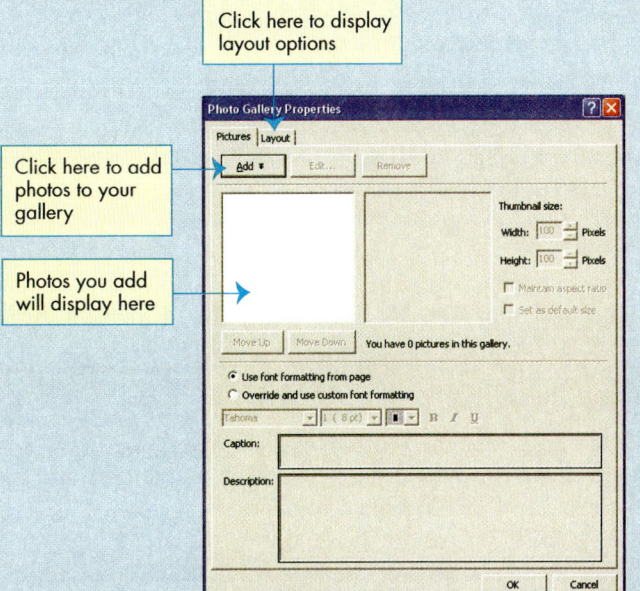

Figure 22.15.
Indicate which photos you want in the Photo Gallery Properties dialog box.

❺ In the Photo Gallery Properties dialog box, click the Add button and then choose Pictures from Files.
The File Open dialog box displays.

❻ Navigate to the drive and folder in which the student data files are stored (see your instructor for help, if necessary).
A number of picture files are available in this folder.

❼ Click the *Mountain View* file, and then click Open.
The file is added to the list in the Photo Gallery Properties dialog box (see Figure 22.16).

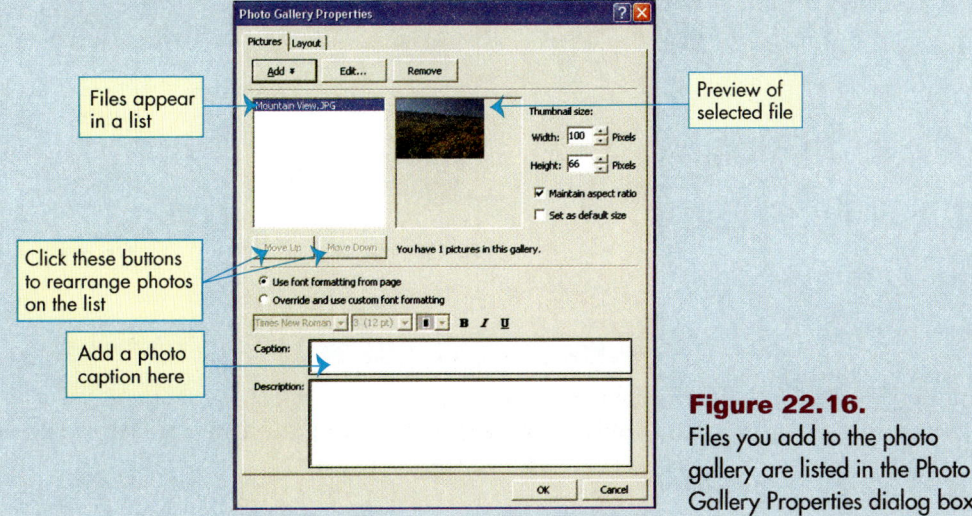

Figure 22.16.
Files you add to the photo gallery are listed in the Photo Gallery Properties dialog box.

Create a Photo Gallery 369

ACTIVITY 22.5
Creating a Photo Gallery (Continued)

⑧ With the Mountain View file selected on the list, click in the *Caption* text box and then type `We live close to the mountains!`

⑨ In the Photo Gallery Properties dialog box, click the <u>A</u>dd button and then choose Pictures from Files.

⑩ Double-click the *My Creek* file.
   The file is added to your photo gallery and appears on the list in the Photo Gallery Properties dialog box. If there are multiple files on the list, you can rearrange the order in which they appear by using the Move Up and Move Down buttons.

⑪ With the *My Creek* file still selected, click the *Move Up* button.
   The file is moved one space up on the list.

> **HEADS UP!** If you accidentally close the Photo Gallery Properties dialog box, you can reopen it by right-clicking on any photo in the gallery and then choosing Ph<u>o</u>to Gallery Properties from the shortcut menu.

⑫ Using the previous steps as a guide, add the following files to your photo gallery: *My Horse, Playing, Balancing Act, My Little Sister, Pals, Running, By My Home*.

⑬ Add a photo caption for each picture. Use the file's name for the caption (for example, use `My Horse` as the caption for the *My Horse* file).

⑭ Click OK in the Photo Gallery Properties dialog box.
   Your completed page should appear similar to that shown in Figure 22.17. Next, take a look at how each thumbnail is linked to a larger file.

Figure 22.17.
The photo gallery displays thumbnails on your page.

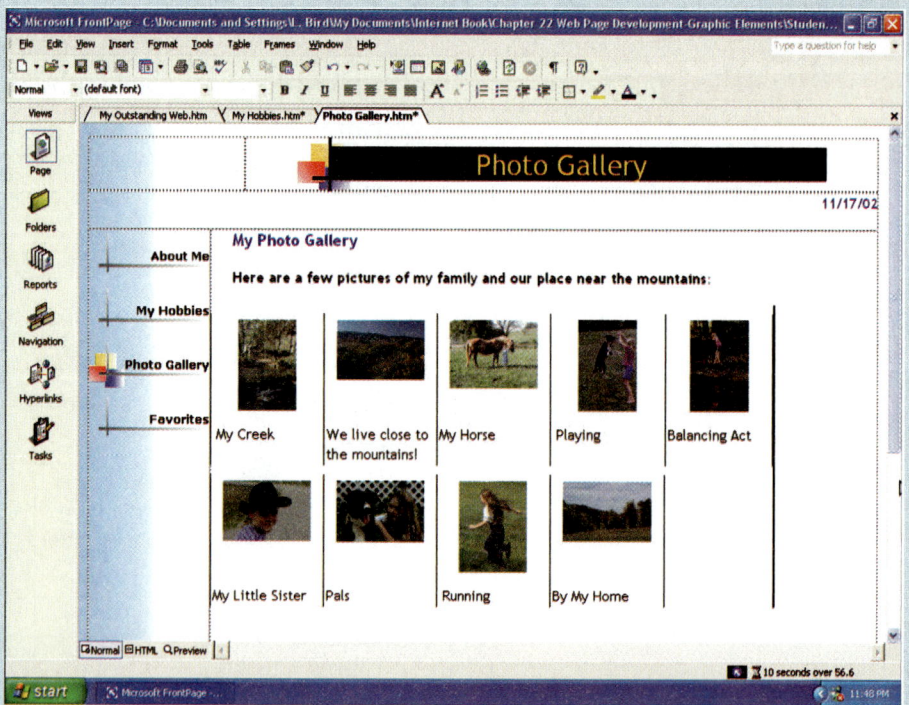

 ⑮ Click the Preview button.
   The Photo Gallery page displays in much the same way as it would appear in a browser.

ACTIVITY 22.5
Creating a Photo Gallery

⓰ Click the thumbnail for the *Mountain View* file (captioned *We live close to the mountains!*). The file displays full-screen, as you would expect. However, because this photo is too large to fit in the window, you must use the horizontal and vertical scrollbars to completely view the photo (see Figure 22.18). This reduces its Web usability. In the next activity, you'll make revisions to the photo gallery, including reducing the size of this photo which will make it much more beneficial for Web use.

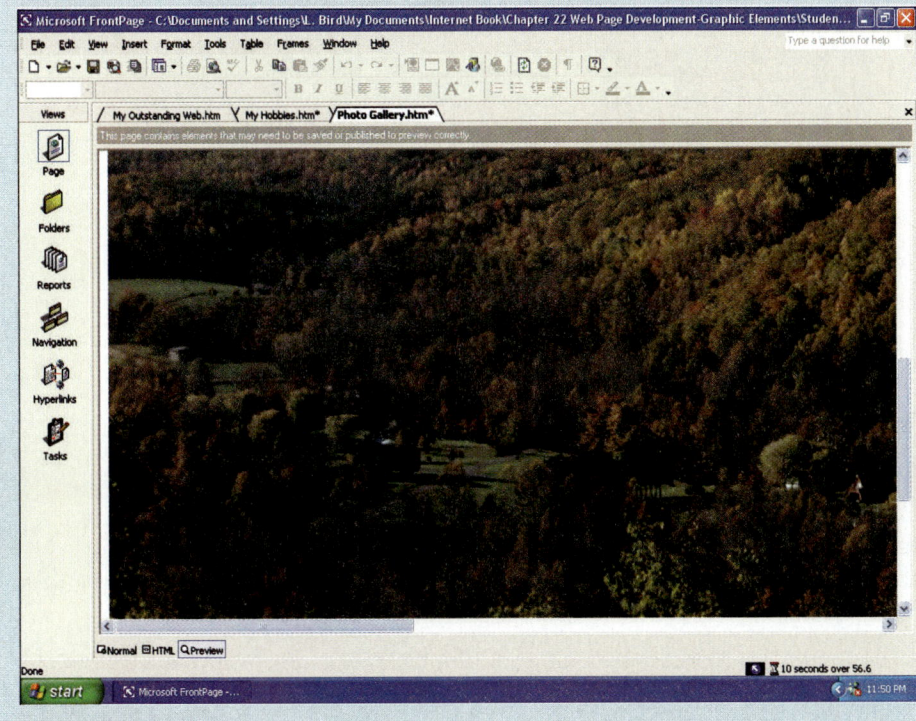

Figure 22.18.
The full-sized photo is too large to view without scrolling.

⓱ Click the Normal button to redisplay your *Photo Gallery* page.

⓲ Save the changes to your Web, including the embedded files. Keep FrontPage open and your Web displayed for the next activity.

MODIFY A PHOTO GALLERY

After you initially create a photo gallery, you have a great deal of flexibility in modifying it. For example, you can add or delete photos, rearrange the photo order, or even change the overall gallery layout. You can also make some modifications to the original pictures.

In this activity, you'll make some simple revisions to your photo gallery. To do so, you'll need to reopen the Photo Gallery Properties dialog box.

ACTIVITY 22.6
Modifying a Photo Gallery

❶ Make sure the *Photo Gallery* page of the Web is displayed in Normal mode.

❷ Right-click any of the photos on the page and then choose Ph**o**to Gallery Properties from the shortcut menu.
The Photo Gallery Properties dialog box is redisplayed.

ACTIVITY 22.6

Modifying a Photo Gallery (Continued)

❸ Click the *Playing* file on the list; then click the Remove button.

The photo is removed from the list. Next, you'll reduce the display dimensions of the *Mountain View* picture file.

❹ Click the *Mountain View* file on the list and then click the Edit button.

The Edit Picture dialog box for the picture is shown (see Figure 22.19). You can specify the picture's display dimensions in this dialog box.

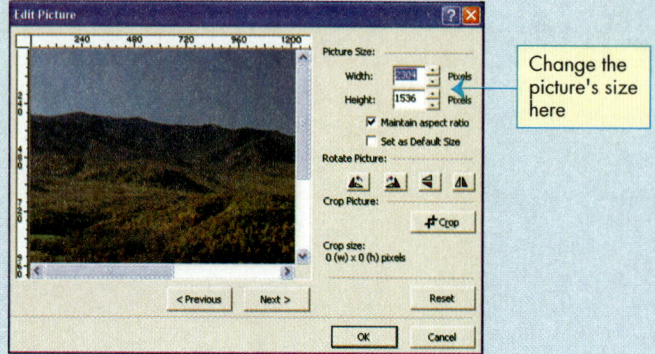

Figure 22.19.
You can use the Edit Picture dialog box to make changes to a photo's properties.

❺ Select the existing display dimensions in the Width text box and then type 500 and press Tab.

The new display dimensions (*500* by *333*) show in the Width and Height boxes.

❻ Click OK in the Edit Picture dialog box.

❼ Using steps 4–6 as a guide, change the display dimensions of the other photos in your gallery to approximately the same settings (500 wide or 500 tall, depending on the orientation of the photo).

❽ Click OK in all open dialog boxes, including the Photo Gallery Properties dialog box.

Now take a look at the size of your photos when you display them.

❾ Click the Preview button and then click the thumbnail for the *Mountain View* file (captioned *We live close to the mountains!*).

The full-sized photo now displays within the window (see Figure 22.20). Because of this, the site visitors won't have to scroll through the window to see the complete photo.

Figure 22.20.
The resized photo is completely displayed within the window.

ACTIVITY 22.6

Modifying a Photo Gallery

10 Click the Normal button, right-click a photo in the gallery, and choose Ph<u>o</u>to Gallery Properties.

11 In the Photo Gallery Properties dialog box, click the Layout tab.

The Layout page of the dialog box displays. FrontPage offers four main layout arrangements (see Figure 22.21).

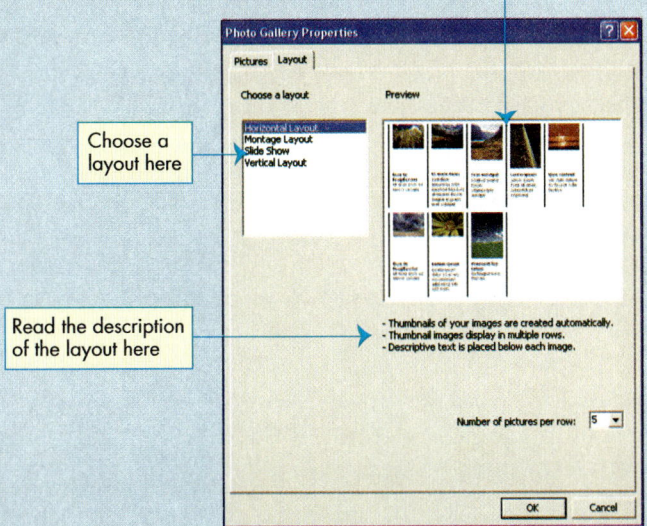

Figure 22.21.
You can change the arrangement for your photo gallery.

12 Click each of the arrangements on the *Choose a Layout* list and then preview it in the Preview area.

13 Click the Montage Layout and then click OK. (Click in the text above the photo gallery area, if necessary, to deselect the gallery.)

Your photo gallery displays using the Montage Layout. This layout differs from the default Horizontal Layout because description captions aren't displayed by the thumbnails. You can, however, rest your mouse pointer over an image to see the description. Now you're ready to save your changes.

14 Choose <u>F</u>ile, Save A<u>l</u>l and then click OK in the Save Embedded Files dialog box.

Before closing the Web, test the links and thumbnails in a browser window.

15 Choose <u>F</u>ile, Preview in <u>B</u>rowser. If necessary, choose *800 x 600* in the Preview in Browser dialog box, and then click Preview.

The Web displays in a separate browser window.

16 Click each of the hyperlinks and thumbnails in the Web. When you're finished, close the browser window.

17 Choose <u>F</u>ile, <u>C</u>lose Web. Save any changes if prompted to do so.

18 Choose <u>F</u>ile, E<u>x</u>it to clear FrontPage and redisplay the Windows desktop.

So now you know some of the ways that you can enhance a Web site and support textual content by judiciously adding clip art and photos. By sprinkling graphics throughout your site, you'll not only add interest, but spark the curiosity of your visitors and encourage them to remain at your site longer. And who knows? Perhaps you'll even be started on the path to becoming a master Web designer and a graphics guru!

Don't Forget...

- Graphics should be used on a Web site only if they will support the site's main purpose.
- Including too many graphics on a Web site can potentially annoy visitors and might cause the page to load slowly.
- Using slow-loading clips instead of thumbnails might drive visitors away from your site.
- You can insert clip art, photographs, animations, and sounds on a Web site.
- You can insert clips and photographs from a number of places, including a digital camera, the Internet, and files stored on your computer or a network.
- You can resize, move, edit, or delete a clip art image.
- Most clip art images and line drawings use the GIF file format; photos generally use the JPEG file format.
- After you insert a photograph, you can modify it, change its size, or convert it into a thumbnail.
- FrontPage photo galleries automatically use thumbnails for linked photos.

Check This Out

MULTIPLE CHOICE

1. Which of the following graphic elements can you use in a FrontPage Web?
   a. Photographs
   b. Clip art files
   c. Animations
   d. All of the above
2. Which of the following is important to consider when you insert a graphic on your Web site?
   a. Size of file
   b. Type of file
   c. Whether or not the file will reinforce the site's content
   d. All of the above
3. Which of the following file formats is usually used for digital photographs?
   a. DOC
   b. JPG
   c. GIF
   d. TXT
4. What is the major drawback of using a graphic on your Web site?
   a. It can slow down the rate at which the site loads.
   b. It won't be appealing to most site visitors.
   c. You can include only three graphics per Web site.
   d. The colors and patterns aren't displayed correctly in most browsers.
5. Which of the following can you do with a graphic after you insert it?
   a. Delete it.
   b. Format it.
   c. Resize it.
   d. All of the above

MATCHING

a. photo gallery
b. thumbnail
c. GIF
d. JPG
e. pictures
f. caption
g. layout
h. clip art
i. Photo Gallery Properties
j. Design Gallery Live

1. Online location where you can find clips
2. The type of file format used most often for clip art and line drawings, with a limit of 256 colors
3. The dialog box used to modify picture arrangements on a Web page
4. A group of thumbnail pictures you can create in FrontPage
5. The arrangement of pictures in a photo gallery
6. Type of file format usually associated with photographs
7. A small graphic that is hyperlinked to a larger version
8. A label for a picture
9. Electronic, drawn art
10. Same as photographs

Real Life

1. Create a sample Web site that you can potentially use for a club or organization. Use Microsoft's Design Gallery Live to insert several images on your site. If you want, include digital photographs from a camera or the Internet. Also, create a photo gallery with thumbnails that are linked to larger photos. Test all the links in your Web in a browser. If your instructor indicates for you to do so, save all the files associated with the Web, including embedded files.
2. Use FrontPage's Help system to find out more about creating drawings from scratch. (Hint: You'll use buttons on the Drawing toolbar to do so.) Practice creating and modifying drawings by using Help as a guide. If you want, create a Web with a blank page on which you can insert and label several drawings. If your instructor indicates for you to do so, save the Web.
3. Use FrontPage's Help system to find out how to work with WordArt. Using what you find out as a guide, create and modify WordArt objects for the titles of each page in a sample Web. If your instructor indicates for you to do so, save the Web.

I Spy: Privacy and Security Concerns

1. Use the Internet to find current sites dealing with privacy and security issues. (If you want, you can also use Web sites listed in Appendix B, Useful Web Sites.) After you locate the sites, create a Web that deals with security and privacy concerns. Make sure to design the Web with usability in mind so that it's easy for a novice Internet user to find his or her way around. Also, include appropriate graphics, including clip art or pictures that enhance the site's purpose. When you're finished, test the links by viewing the Web in a browser. If your instructor indicates to do so, save the Web, using a name of your choice.
2. Use FrontPage's Help system to find out how you can improve the security of Webs you develop using the program. (Hint: Take a look at the information in the *User Account Administration and Security* section.) Next, use the Web to find out if there are any current security holes associated with this software program. Write a report or develop an oral presentation that outlines your findings to share with others in your class.

CHAPTER 23
PUBLISHING TO THE WORLD WIDE WEB

Key Terms

When you finish this chapter, you'll understand the following terms:

- co-located server
- dedicated server
- FrontPage Server Extensions
- keyword density
- keyword frequency
- keyword prominence
- keyword proximity
- link popularity
- meta tag
- paid inclusion
- pay-per-click model
- publishing
- submitting
- Web presence
- Web Presence Provider (WPP)
- Web site positioning

Chapter Objectives

After you complete this chapter, you'll

- ▎Know How to Evaluate and Choose a Web Host
- ▎Know the Options for Getting Free Web Space
- ▎Understand the Essentials of Web Site Positioning
- ▎Understand the Basics of Publishing to the Web

The Big Picture

You've carefully considered Web site design and usability and crafted an attractive, easy-to-navigate Web. Now it's show time: You're ready to place your Web files on a Web server so that everyone in the world can view your masterpiece. After all, there's no point creating the site if no one can see it!

The process of copying your Web files to a server is called **publishing**. A site that is available on the Internet is called *live*, and having a Web site online is called having a **Web presence**. In this chapter, you'll learn important information related to publishing to the Web. You'll learn how to evaluate and choose a Web host, find free Web hosting services, and modify your Web pages so that you can ensure a better position in search engine rankings. You'll also learn how to publish your files to a Web server so that others in the Internet community can view (and admire!) your work.

 INSIDE TRACK
Instead of publishing your FrontPage Web to the Internet, you can place the files on a company or school network called an *intranet*.

 Window on the Web

As you learned in the previous chapter, your first step of publishing your Web is to verify that all the links work as you expect and that you've carefully proofread and spell checked the Web pages. Assuming that these steps are already done, you're ready to find a Web host—sometimes called a **Web Presence Provider (WPP)**—that can take care of managing (administering) your site. A Web host is a company that has servers and the means to maintain and "serve up" your files to everyone on the Internet. Web servers, as you remember, are computers that include the hardware and software necessary to host Web sites. Although you can technically set up your own computer as a Web host, the logistics of doing so are usually more than the average person wants to deal with. Instead, most people opt to hire a large, commercial Web hosting service to manage your site for you. The Web hosting services that you buy vary quite a bit, which means that you should carefully evaluate which service best meets your needs and budget. One way to do this is to use a directory such as *www.webhostdir.com* to check out the top hosting companies (see Figure 23.1).

In this chapter, you'll also learn the steps to publishing your Web to a local computer or to the Internet. You can see an example of this in Figure 23.2.

Finally, we'll give you some ideas of how you can submit your Web site to search engines (see Figure 23.3). We'll also go over the importance of positioning your Web site so that your Web site will come up high on ranking in search engines.

This chapter is the culmination of all your hard work of creating a Web in FrontPage, so come along to see how you can take your Web site to the world.

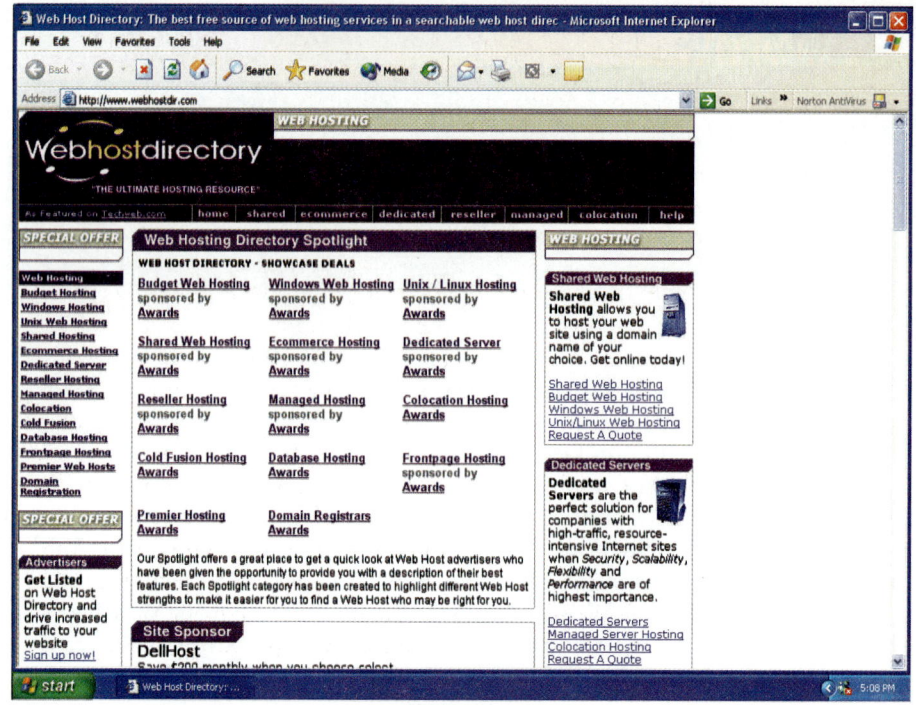

Figure 23.1.
Find the host with the most: Research which company should host your Web site.

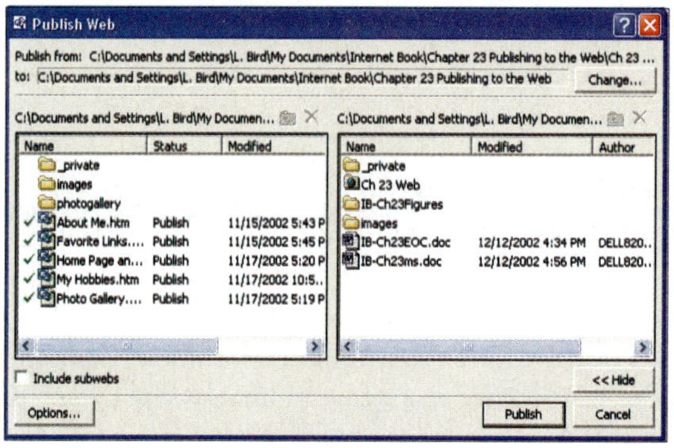

Figure 23.2.
Take your information to the world—publish it.

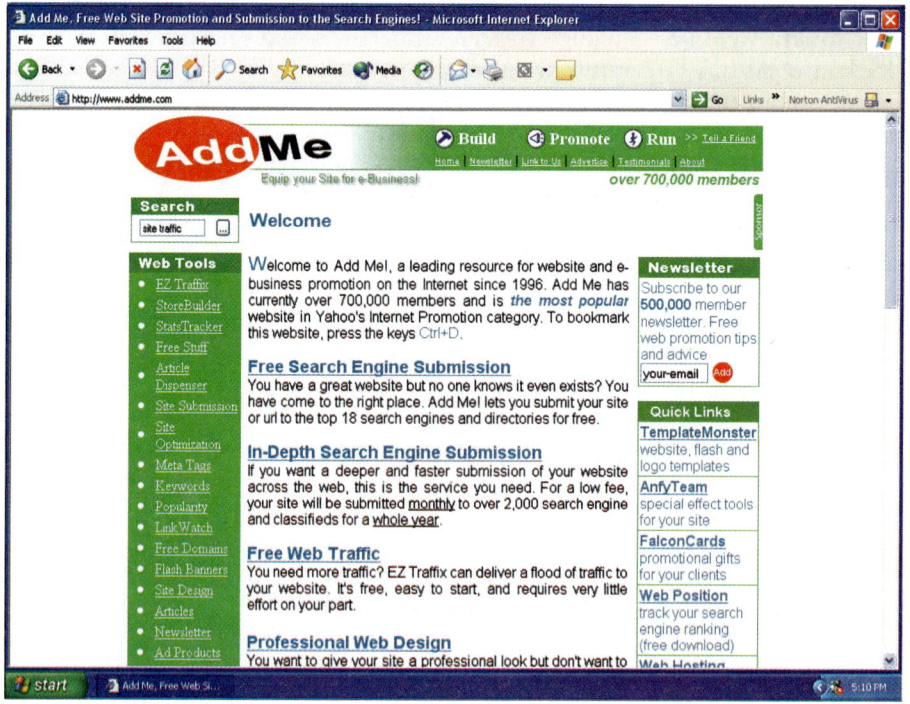

Figure 23.3.
You can better position your Web site by periodically submitting it to search engines.

KNOW HOW TO EVALUATE AND CHOOSE A WEB HOST

When you initially develop a Web site in a Web-editing program such as FrontPage, the files exist only on your computer (or a network). To share them with others via the Internet, you need to place them on a Web server. Here's a brief recap of how Web server-client architecture operates: A browser requests the files from the Web server, which then "serves" them via the browser to the local computer. In fact, you can think of the Web server for a site as a librarian who lends out the files for use by anyone who requests them.

In short, when you have a Web site, you need to determine who will be responsible for the task of serving up the files—the Web host server. Luckily, you have a couple of valid choices: You can create and maintain your own Web server or pay a monthly fee to a Web hosting service to do it.

There are advantages and disadvantages of each option. Setting up your own Web server might sound less expensive than paying a fee month after month. The exact control you can exert over the server's configuration and setup might also appeal to some people. However, running your own Web server can become more involved than you might expect. Besides efficiently serving up the files, your Web server must also be secure against attacks by crackers. Additionally, you will need to regularly back up your Web files and conscientiously maintain the server's connection to the Internet.

If this option doesn't appeal to you or sounds like too much work, you have another choice: Hire a Web hosting service to take care of the logistics of managing your Web site. The Web host will take care of the connections, security, and equipment for you; all you have to do is pay the bill.

The services provided by Web hosts vary greatly—from budget packages with limited storage space to high-end, commercial sites that include support for online shopping, databases, and interactive elements such as Java applets. The costs vary as well and can range from $8 per month for a simple budget site to several hundreds (or thousands) of dollars per month for a large, complex e-commerce site.

Not only do the costs and services vary, but the access to equipment does as well. For example, most small businesses and individuals share the host's equipment with others. This works well in most cases, especially if the businesses have simple, static HTML sites. However, if the business begins to incorporate more interactive elements, such as streaming media, they might need to switch to a dedicated server. A **dedicated server** is used by only one organization. The host owns, backs up, and maintains the server as well as providing security. Because there are no others with whom to share the host fees, the cost of this type of system is far beyond the means of the average person or small business (although it's appropriate for medium to large businesses).

The most expensive—but highest level of service—offered by a Web host is a **co-located server**. In this case, the business or organization owns the hardware, but it's located and maintained at the host's facility. This gives the business more control over the type of equipment and the connection bandwidth. However, it's typically more expensive and requires more involvement on the part of the customer.

If you're just starting out, there is another option as well: Many Internet Service Providers (ISPs) include limited space for you to post a Web site on their servers as part of your regular monthly ISP connection fee. You probably won't get your choice of a domain name (remember those easy-to-remember addresses, such as *pepsi.com*?) but you can get your feet wet in the world of Web publishing without incurring any additional expense. These services also don't offer high-end features, such as streaming media or other interactive features, but are a great option for those who want static personal sites.

If your ISP doesn't offer free Web hosting, don't despair. Geocities (*geocities.yahoo.com*) and other sites provide free Web hosting space. Again, you won't have an easy-to-remember domain name, but you will have space to place your files.

So now you're aware of some of the general Web hosting options. However, before you are ready to sign up for a Web host, you should carefully consider which features and services are most important to you. Here's a quick checklist of things you should evaluate as you're considering various Web hosting services:

>
>
> **ALERT!**
> If you plan to sign up for a free Web site, make sure that you understand the privacy policy of the site and what the host plans to do with your registration information. Most Web hosts include a privacy policy link on their Web site. You can click this link and then evaluate their policy to see if you're comfortable with the policy before signing up.

Reliability. The Web hosting service should be large enough, have up-to-date equipment, and a strong support staff to keep your Web site up and running. You should also look for a service that is up and running *at least* 90% of the time. In fact, if you're looking for a hosting service for a business or organization, see if the company provides duplicate servers and regular backups.

Connectivity. The higher the bandwidth, the faster your Web pages can potentially be delivered, especially because Web surfers are typically impatient with slow-loading sites.

Security. Find out what security features and safeguards the host uses to prevent Denial of Service attacks and other security problems. Also make sure that you understand the security procedures for the site and who is responsible for upgrading and maintaining security. Some hosts expect you to implement your own security measures, so if you don't feel comfortable doing this yourself, make sure that you find a host that will take care of it for you.

Amount of Traffic Allowed. Many Web hosting packages are set up with a limit on the amount of Web traffic allowed at your site. Depending on your plan, you could be allowed anywhere from 1–8 gigabytes of traffic each month. If you exceed the limit, you'll be charged extra fees.

Price and Billing Procedures. Everyone likes to save money, so the lower the price the better, right? True—but only if the host provides a good value on the other aspects of Web hosting. Also, make sure that you carefully read the host's billing procedures and understand the terms of the service agreement before you sign.

Availability of a Trial Period. Some hosts will let you try their service for a month or so before requiring you to make a commitment. At the very least, make sure that you don't sign up for a long-term commitment, such as a year, before giving the service a whirl.

>
>
> **INSIDE TRACK**
> Here's a little test you can conduct to determine the host's level of customer service: Call them in the middle of the night and see if they have someone available to help you. Then call them during the busiest part of the working day. If the service is good in both situations, the company is probably customer-service oriented.

Level of Customer Service. Before committing to a Web host, find out how well they service their clients. Things to consider include whether or not the company has a toll-free number and the number of hours each day they answer calls. Also find out if they have multiple methods of supporting customers, such as instant messaging, e-mail, and phone.

References. Some Web hosts will provide you with contact information for others who use their service (hopefully with the permission of those companies). If so, take a little time to make sure that the customers are satisfied with the level of service provided. Additionally, check out the Whois database (*www.whois.net*) to get additional contact information for the hosts (see Chapter 8, Getting to Know the World Wide Web, if you need a refresher on accessing this database). Another alternative? Research the Web host's background via the Internet.

Software programs supported. Web hosts vary in the operating systems (such as Windows NT or Unix) that they use to run their Web servers. Additionally, some Web hosts don't support some of FrontPage's components. For example, FrontPage includes a group of small applications that run on a Web server—called **FrontPage Server Extensions**—instead of the Web visitor's own computer. Server extensions allow Web pages created with FrontPage to use elements such as forms and hit counters. Although most Web hosts can use Web pages developed in FrontPage, they might not support the server extensions, which can limit your use of these features. Microsoft maintains a list of Web hosting services that support the server extensions at *www.microsoft.com /frontpage/wppsearch/default.htm* (see Figure 23.4).

Potential for Future Growth. Even if you're starting out small, you should think about what your Web hosting needs might be in the future. If you're publishing a personal site, you probably won't ever tap into some of the more advanced features, such as online shopping, database support, and a large bandwidth for multimedia streaming. But if you're working on a commercial site (even for a small business), keep in mind that you might want to eventually use these features. Plan for the future by making sure that the host you choose will be able to accommodate your potential needs.

Now that you have a good idea of what to look for in a paid host for your Web site, let's look at another possibility: Getting free Web space.

KNOW OPTIONS FOR GETTING FREE WEB SPACE

When the time comes for a business or organization to sign up for a Web hosting service, the careful evaluation provided by the previous section is good. However, if you're just starting to publish files to the Internet, most likely you don't want to incur a lot of expense in doing so—especially if you're primarily publishing a personal Web site. In this case, your Web hosting needs are fairly limited and a free Web hosting service will usually provide the space and services you need for your site.

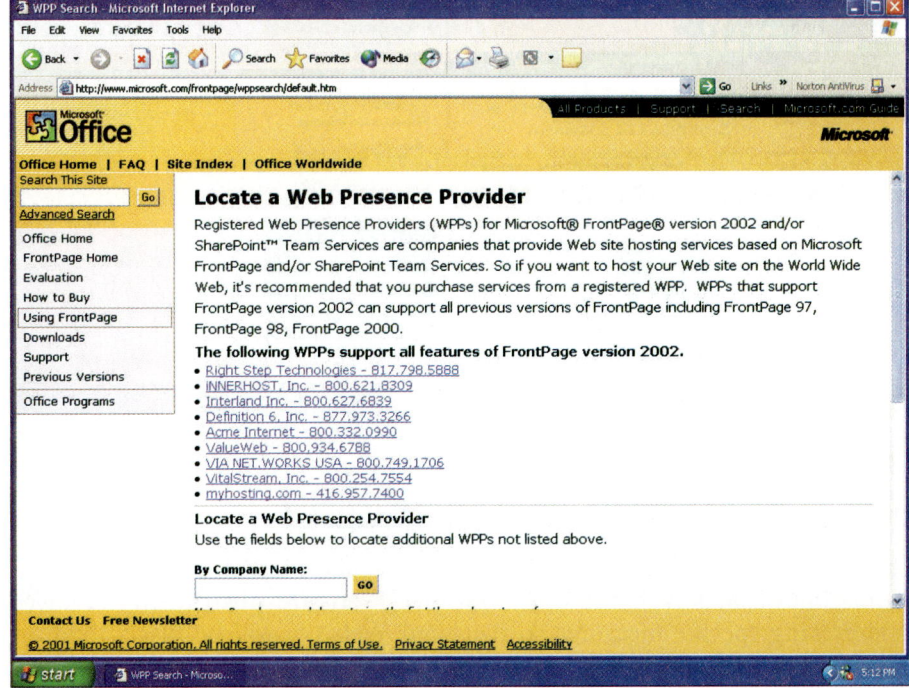

Figure 23.4.
If you plan to use all the features in FrontPage, make sure that you select a Web hosting company that supports them.

INSIDE TRACK

In Chapter 8, we explained how domain names are set up and how you can register for one. If you're interested in obtaining a domain name, look back at this chapter.

With a free service, you won't incur any upfront costs and you can often obtain free Web development tools. On the other hand, free Web hosting services generally limit the amount of storage space and Web traffic (data transfer) allowed at a freebie site. Additionally, this type of site is generally ad-supported, which means that there will probably be advertisements on it. You should also carefully consider the privacy policy of the Web hosting service because some firms use free hosting services to gather marketing information. Finally, you'll probably be "reminded" regularly about the options you have to upgrade to a paid Web hosting package. Nevertheless, if you can live with the drawbacks, you can use these services to get started in Web publishing without spending a lot of money. With these things in mind, let's look at some of the specific options available.

One place to start your search for free Web hosting is Netfirms, at *www.netfirms.com* (see Figure 23.5). Not only can you get your small business site hosted for free, but this firm also supports FrontPage Server Extensions. However, Netfirms, like most free services, comes with strings attached. Your contact information might be shared for marketing purposes, advertising will display on your page, and you'll receive many chances to sign up for Netfirms' paid service. Nevertheless, it's a good place to begin.

Yahoo! provides another free Web hosting service through its Geocities branch at *geocities.yahoo.com* (see Figure 23.6).

If you're interested in locating more free or reduced-price Web hosting companies, conduct an Internet search using keywords such as `Web hosting free`.

ALERT!

If you sign up for a free Web hosting service, be prepared to share contact information. You can be a bit "creative" with this information, but you will need an e-mail address in most cases so that the service has a place to send your password and login information. To protect your privacy, consider setting up a free e-mail account for this purpose.

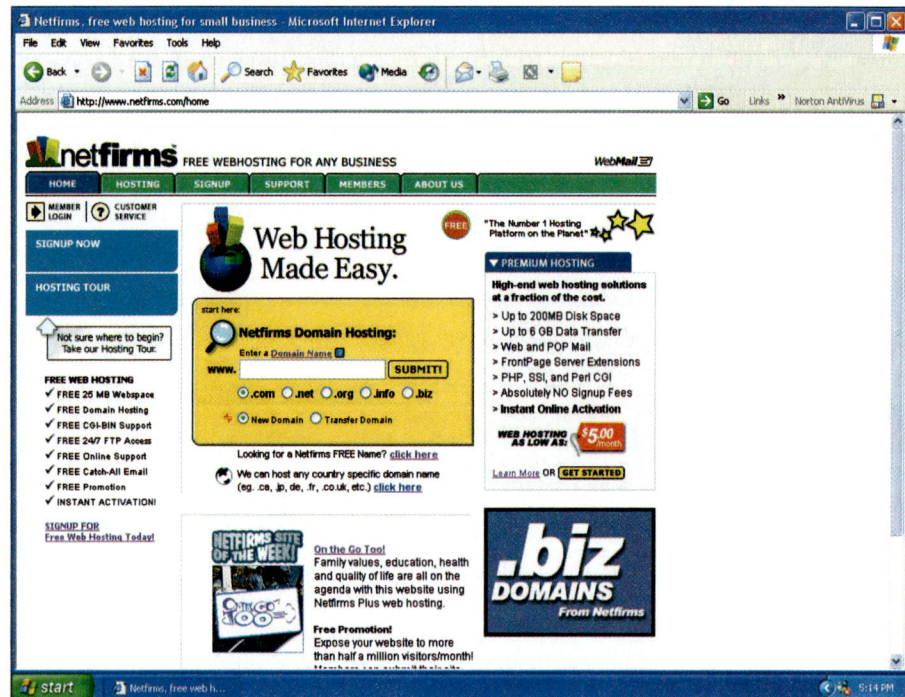

Figure 23.5.
You can sign up for free or reduced-price Web hosting at Netfirms.

UNDERSTAND THE ESSENTIALS OF WEB SITE POSITIONING

Entire books are written about the importance of Web site positioning (sometimes called Web site optimization). **Web site positioning** involves undertaking specific measures so that your Web site will be placed high in

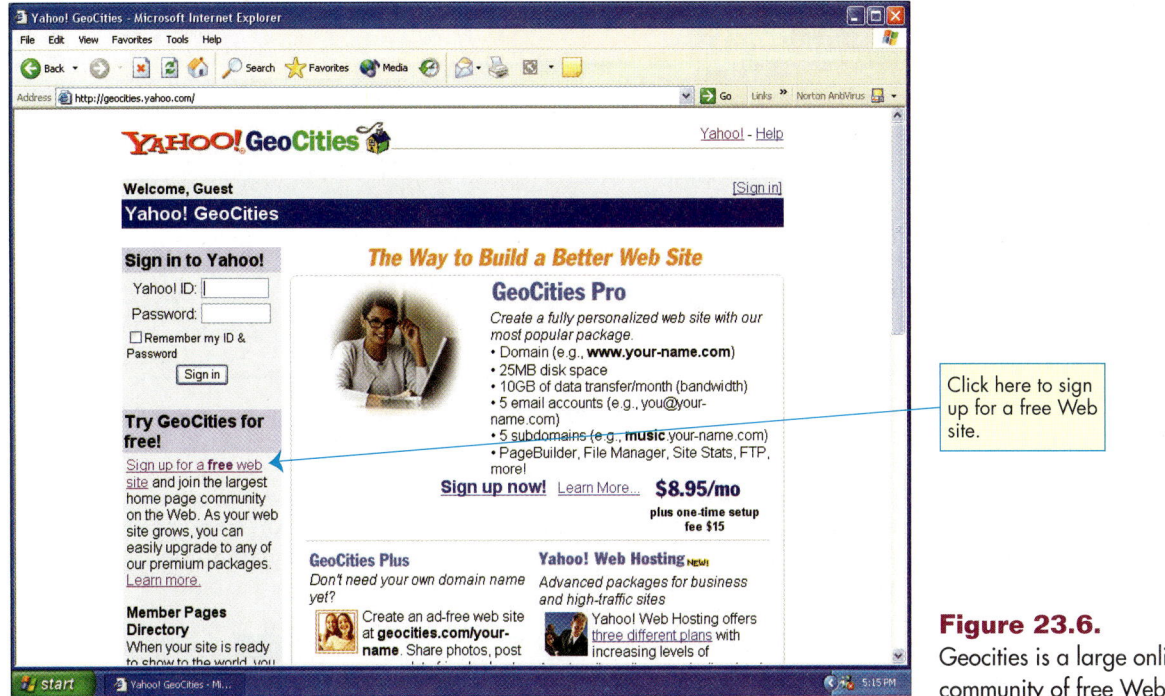

Figure 23.6.

Geocities is a large online community of free Web sites.

the rankings for the major search engines. For example, if you sell sports equipment online, having your site listed in the top 10 (or even top 20) hits whenever someone runs a search for *sports* or *sports equipment* is a great accomplishment.

Fortunately, there are a number of things that you as a Webmaster can do to ensure a better search engine placement. Although it's beyond the scope of this book to cover all the ways that you can position your site on the Web, here are a few of the tricks of the trade that savvy Webmasters use.

CAREFULLY CONSTRUCT THE HTML TITLE FOR YOUR HOME PAGE

It is important to design the HTML title for your home page correctly because search engines examine this text for relevance to the rest of your site. (For example, if your site is about an online computer class, the HTML title shouldn't have words such as *skiing* and *basketball* in it because they aren't relevant to the site.) Additionally, it's one of the first things a search engine's robot and readers see on your page. The title is also likely to be included in the search engine's results and bookmarks. Because of this, it's critical that the title describes your Web site in a succinct, catchy manner. Although it's tough to come up with a great title that appeals to both automated search engine spiders and real readers, doing so helps to better position your page in the rankings.

It's extremely helpful to position the title immediately after the *<HEAD>* tag. You can check this in your FrontPage Web by displaying the home page for the Web and then clicking the HTML button to view the associated code for the page. You can see this arrangement in Figure 23.7, which shows the underlying HTML code for eBay's site. (This code was displayed by right-clicking the site and then choosing View Source.).

Besides looking at the HTML code for the page, you can also check (or modify) the title by using the Save As command. To do so, display the home page in the Normal pane and then choose File, Save As. In the Save As dialog

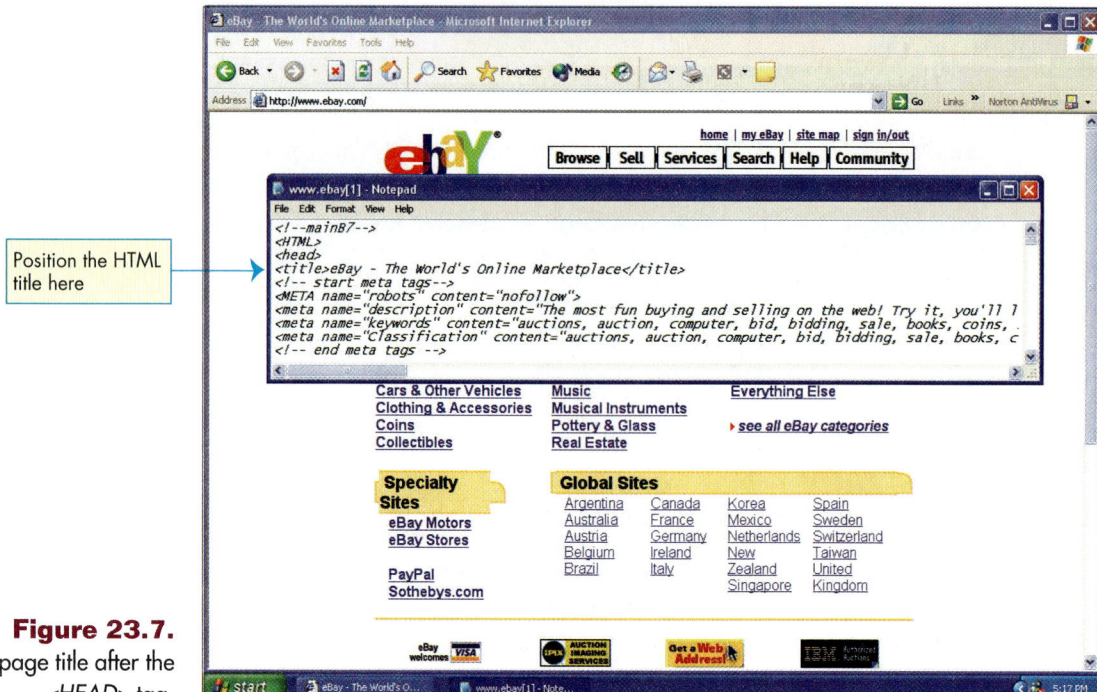

Figure 23.7.
Position the page title after the <HEAD> tag.

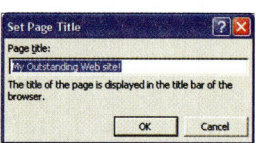

Figure 23.8.
Change your page title for better positioning.

box, click the Change title button to display the Set Page Title dialog box (see Figure 23.8). If the title isn't descriptive of your site's contents, enter a new title and click OK in the Set Page Title dialog box. Click Save in the Save As dialog box to finalize your changes.

SPRINKLE KEYWORDS APPROPRIATELY THROUGHOUT YOUR HOME PAGE

Keywords are topical words that describe your site's content to search engines. In fact, careful inclusion and placement of keywords throughout your main page is important because search engines often position Web sites based on keywords. However, each search engine considers keywords somewhat differently. For example, Google weighs the proximity of the keywords to each other more than some other search engines do.

Here are some general principles to keep in mind if you're trying to achieve a high search engine ranking:

- *Remember that home pages are critical.* Although you can certainly include keywords on pages other than your home page, some search engines look *only* at home pages. Because of this, you should concentrate your efforts on this "front door" to your site.
- *Write some text.* Make sure that your home page includes at least 100 words on it. Why? Because some search engines will ignore pages with fewer words than this.

- *Remember keyword prominence.* **Keyword prominence** refers to placing your keywords as close to the start of a page or sentence as possible. This helps with rankings because many search engines look first at the words at the top of a page.
- *Keep keyword proximity in mind.* **Keyword proximity** means placing important keywords close to each other. For example, if you were selling sports equipment, "We sell *sports equipment*" would help your rankings more than "We sell *equipment* for *sports*" because the keywords in the first sentence are closer in proximity to each other than they are in the second.
- *Use keyword density.* **Keyword density**, sometimes known as keyword weight, is the percentage of keywords to other text. The higher the percentage, the better your site's ranking. Let's take a quick look at an example: In the sentence "*We sell sports equipment,*" the percentage of keywords to other text is 50%. However, in practical terms, a keyword density of 3–7% is good. This means that keywords should comprise at least three to seven words for every 100 words on your home page. Although this might sound like a small percentage, it's sometimes difficult to include that many keywords and still have text flow and make sense.
- *Use keyword frequency.* **Keyword frequency** is a measure of the number of times that a keyword appears on a page (not the percentage). As you can imagine, keyword frequency is closely tied to keyword density. However, keyword frequency specifically looks for the number of times a keyword is repeated on a site to make sure the keyword doesn't appear in isolation.

USE META TAGS. A **meta tag** is an HTML tag that appears in the <*HEAD*> part of the page. Meta tags usually supply information about a page (such as keywords) to spiders, but don't affect the page's appearance. The tag itself is invisible to Web readers, but is examined by many search engine spiders (robots) so that they can accurately include your site in their rankings.

For example, a meta tag may list keywords for the site. If the keywords in the meta tag are similar to those typed by a Web user, your site will appear toward the beginning of the search engine rankings. Some search engines double-check these keywords against those actually used on the site. This prevents people from packing the meta tag with words that have no relevance to the site just to gain a better position. A meta tag usually appears in HTML code as follows:

```
<HTML>
    <HEAD>
    <META NAME="keywords" content="Your site's keywords here">
    </HEAD>
</HTML>
```

There are a few things to keep in mind as you develop your meta tags: Place the most important keywords first in the list, repeat the most important words, and avoid making the list too long because some search engine spiders only look at the first 1024 characters. To change the contents of your meta description tag in FrontPage, click the HTML button for your site's home page; then enter keywords between the beginning and ending tags (see Figure 23.9).

Figure 23.9.
You can affect search engine rankings by the keywords you use.

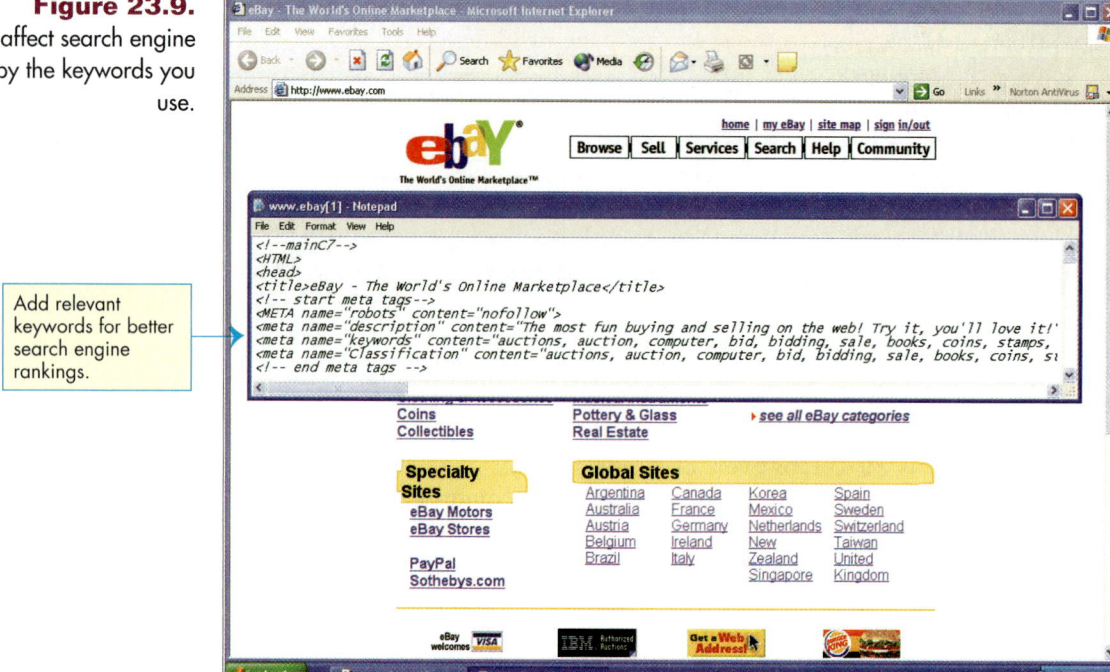

Add relevant keywords for better search engine rankings.

DEVELOP HIGH-QUALITY LINKS

Another way of helping to boost your site's ranking on the Web is to develop links from (and to) other sites. Using links to raise your Web ranking is called **link popularity**.

Here are some strategies that will help you develop links: First, it's extremely helpful to have your site listed in directories, such as Yahoo! or LookSmart. Additionally, you should ask Webmasters of major related, but non-competing sites if they'll include a link from their site to yours. For example, if you have a site that deals with medical information, you might ask the Webmaster at Medical.com or Health.com to include a link to your site. If your site is relevant, well-constructed, and doesn't compete with their site, they just might agree.

Both the quality and quantity of sites that link to your site are important. However, if you have to choose, favor having a few high-quality links from major directories to your site rather than copious links from obscure personal pages.

After you develop links to various sites, you can find out how well the search engines have located your links. Here are a couple of examples. Display the home page for Google (*www.google.com*) and then type `link:www.domainname.com` in the Search text field. (Substitute your actual domain name after the *www* in the URL, such as `link:www.lindabird.com`.) When you click the *Google Search* button, the search engine will display the sites that link to yours (see Figure 23.10).

AltaVista includes a similar feature that helps you determine the link popularity of your site. To use it, display the home page for the search engine (*www.altavista.com*), type `link:www.domainname.com` in the text box, and then click Find to list the linked sites. (You should substitute your actual domain name after *link:*—for example, `link:www.lindabird.com`.)

REALIZE THE IMPORTANCE OF SUBMITTING YOUR SITE TO SEARCH ENGINES

OK, you've carefully crafted your Web site and included all the keywords, HTML tags, and links necessary for search engines to find the site. There's

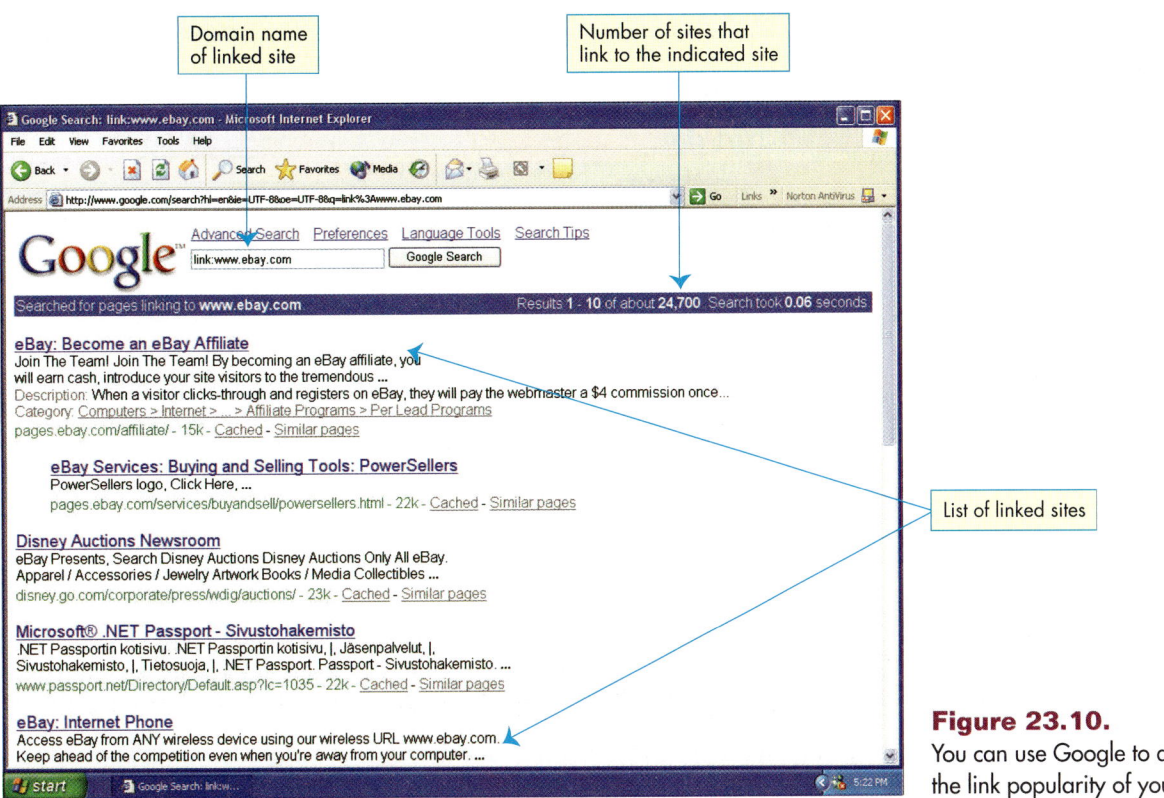

Figure 23.10.
You can use Google to analyze the link popularity of your site.

only one major step necessary to achieve a high ranking: submitting your site to the search engines and major directories, such as Yahoo!. **Submitting** your site involves making these companies aware that the site is up and running. You can do this using a variety of methods. Most involve manually telling the search engines that your site is live; some use software to automate the process.

One option for site submission is **paid inclusion**, which involves hiring a firm to present your site to the various search engines on your behalf. Some companies use automated programs to do this; others manually submit the site for you. The cost for this service varies, depending on the number of search engines to which your site is submitted (and how frequently your site will be resubmitted). Some search engines also use a **pay-per-click model**, which simply means that you pay a fee every time someone clicks your link on the ranking.

Another related option is to buy your own automated submission software program that will streamline the process of site submission for you. Although this might help you quickly submit your site to a wide variety of search engines, some services (such as AltaVista) have technology in place that specifically prevents automatic submission by software programs. Search engines do this so that the most popular sites will appear at the top of the rankings, not just those that use the best submission software. If you use an automated submission software program, be aware of this potential drawback.

A couple of no-cost options for letting search engines know that your site is up and running are AddMe at *www.addme.com* and AddPro at *www.addpro.com* (see Figure 23.11). You can use these services to systematically submit your site to approximately 20 search engines each. Although the basic submission service is free, if you want your site to be submitted to additional search engines or ensure that your site will be indexed quickly, you'll need to pay $50–100. To use AddMe or AddPro, display the respective Web site and then follow the clearly outlined directions on the site.

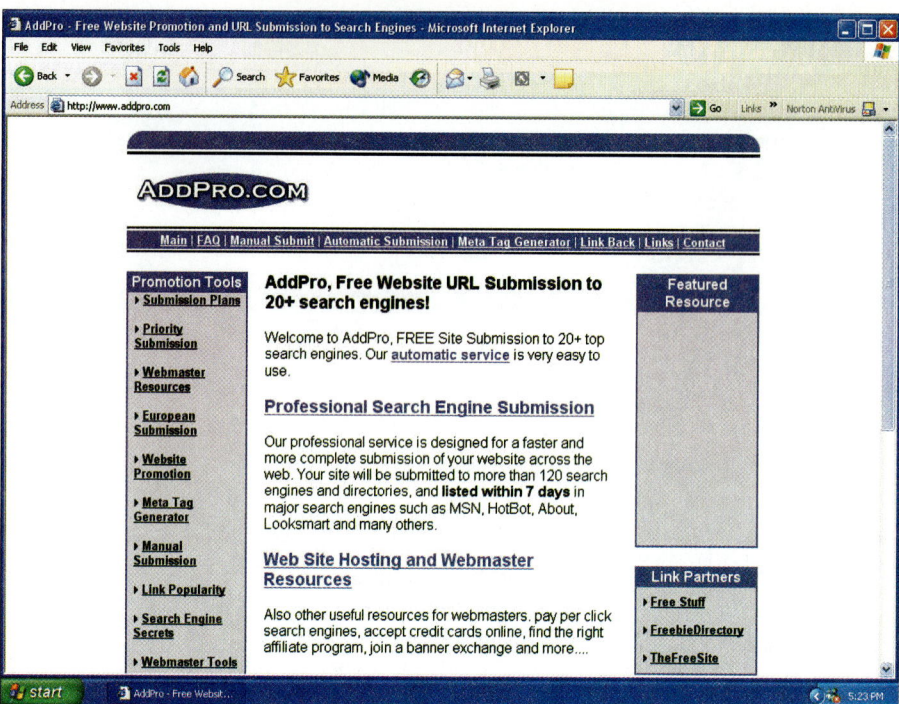

Figure 23.11.
Even free Web submission services can help you better position your site.

UNDERSTAND THE BASICS OF PUBLISHING TO THE WEB

After you've located a Web host server and understand the importance of Web site positioning, you're ready to publish your site to the Web. Publishing involves copying (uploading) your Web files to a Web server. The FrontPage program includes commands that make this process simple and seamless.

In the next activity, you'll simulate the steps necessary to publish your FrontPage Web from your computer to the Internet. Because you probably haven't actually signed up for a Web host, you can practice these steps by publishing the site to another location on your local computer. The process is essentially the same as when you publish Webs to the Internet. Because you're publishing to the local computer, you should be able to complete the steps in the activity. However, if you don't have the setup to work through the steps, just read them and then keep this book as a handy reference for when you *are* able to publish your site.

ACTIVITY 23.1
Publishing to the Web

1. In FrontPage, open the *Ch 23 Web* from the folder that contains your student data files. Display the Web in Navigation view.

2. Choose File, Publish Web.
   The Publish Destination dialog box appears, layered on top of the Publish Web dialog box. In "real life," you'll designate a location on the Web in which you want to publish your files. However, you'll instead publish the files to your local computer for this tutorial (see Figure 23.12).

3. In the *Enter publish destination* text box, type the folder location on your local computer in which your solution files are typically stored or use the Browse button to navigate to the location. (See your instructor for help, if necessary.)

Chapter 23   Publishing to the World Wide Web

ACTIVITY 23.1
Publishing to the Web

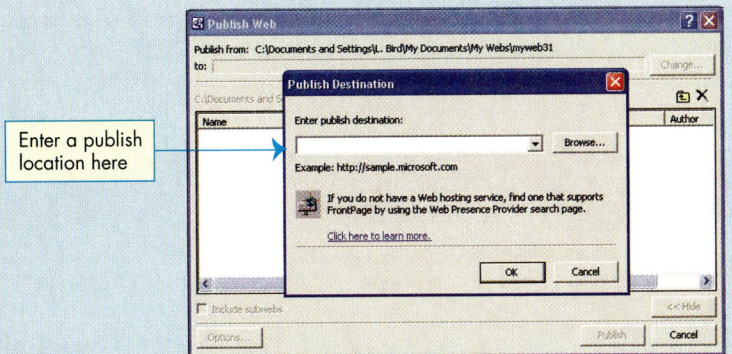

Figure 23.12.
Use the Publish Destination dialog box to designate a location in which your Web files should be published.

❹ Click OK to close the Publish Destination dialog box.

❺ Click OK in the Microsoft FrontPage message box to create a Web at the designated file location (if necessary).

The Publish Web dialog box redisplays. The left pane in this dialog box shows the source Web files you've created; the right pane displays the initial folders that appear in the destination location before you publish the pages (see Figure 23.13).

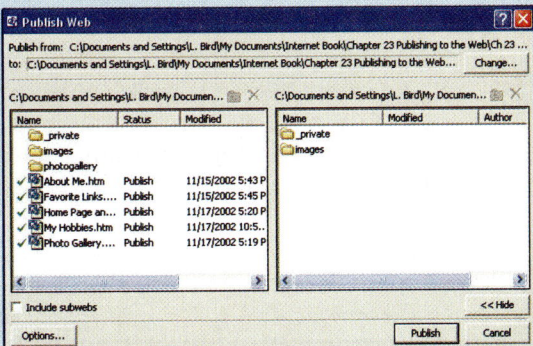

Figure 23.13.
Files are copied from the source to destination locations.

❻ In the Publish Web dialog box, click the Publish button.

The files are copied to the location you designated. When they are completely copied, a message box displays, indicating that you've published your Web site (see Figure 23.14).

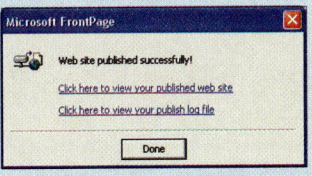

Figure 23.14.
A message box congratulates you on successfully copying your Web files.

 **HEADS UP!** If a message box displays, asking if you want to replace existing files, choose Yes to All. Also, if a Publishing FrontPage Components dialog box displays and warns you that some of the pages are dynamic and can't be published to a server without FrontPage Server Extensions installed, just click Continue.

❼ Click Done in the Microsoft FrontPage message box.

❽ Close the Web and FrontPage.

Understand the Basics of Publishing to the Web 389

So there you have it. After working through this book, you're now an accomplished Internet user. You can find virtually any information on the Internet and have a good understanding of its mechanisms. You have a heightened awareness of the security and privacy issues swirling around this cutting-edge communication tool. You also have a good idea of how to properly design and set up Web pages and then submit them so that they appear high in the rankings for various search engines. Go conquer the world.

Don't Forget...

- Copying your Web files to a server is called publishing.
- There are many Web hosting options available—each one varying in cost, service, and access to equipment.
- You can sometimes use free Web hosting if you're publishing a small personal Web with static pages.
- Web site positioning involves undertaking specific strategies so that your site will be ranked high in the major search engines.
- Changing the keywords, tags, page title, and other components on your home page can affect your site's ranking.
- You can use a variety of methods to submit your site to the major search engines.

Check This Out

MULTIPLE CHOICE

1. What is Web site positioning?
   a. The way your Web pages are arranged within FrontPage
   b. The layout of pictures on a photo gallery page
   c. Undertaking specific measures and procedures so your site will appear high in search engines' rankings
   d. None of the above

2. Which of the following do you need to consider when evaluating a Web host?
   a. Cost
   b. Amount of traffic
   c. Reliability
   d. All of the above

3. Which of the following helps to optimize your site?
   a. Including appropriate keywords in meta tags
   b. Submitting the site to various search engines
   c. Having links from a number of other related sites
   d. All of the above

4. Which of the following will probably *not* help place your site higher on search engine rankings?
   a. Including lots of graphics on the home page
   b. Increasing link popularity
   c. Increasing keyword density
   d. Writing a concise page title that describes your site's content

5. What is a way that you can submit your site to search engines?
   a. Using automated software to do so
   b. Hiring a company to submit it periodically
   c. Manually submitting it yourself using free services, such as AddMe
   d. All of the above

MATCHING

a. positioning
b. dedicated server
c. host
d. keyword prominence
e. Web presence
f. keyword proximity
g. meta tag
h. FrontPage Server Extensions
i. link popularity
j. submitting

1. FrontPage mini-applications that run from a Web server, such as hit counters
2. Same as optimizing
3. Having your Web site online
4. Placing keywords as close to the start of a page or sentence as possible
5. Placing important keywords close to each other
6. The company that administers your Web site
7. A Web server used by a single company or organization
8. An HTML tag that uses keywords to describe your site's content
9. Informing search engines that your Web site is live
10. Using links to boost your Web ranking

Real Life

1. Use the Internet to research Web hosts. Start by conducting a search on the keywords Web host. Find articles that cover how to evaluate and select a Web host and take notes on the items to consider when signing up with one. Next, use the Internet to locate 10 different Web host vendors. Develop a chart that compares the hosts' reliability (percentage of time in service), average connection speed, backup procedures, billing procedures, customer service (hours available, toll-free number), type of operating system they use, whether they support FrontPage Server Extensions, and price. Based on the information you find, which Web hosting service would you recommend for those who want to establish personal, small business, medium business, and commercial Web sites?

2. Use the Internet to run a search on the keywords Web site positioning. Read and take notes on the information on at least 10 sites, including: 1) An accurate description of Web site optimization and 2) specific methods that help Webmasters achieve a better position. Give a report on your finding to others in your class.

I Spy: Privacy and Security Concerns

1. When you submit your site to search engines, you're sometimes asked for identifying information, such as your name or e-mail address. What are the privacy implications of giving this information? What are some ways you can protect your privacy while still ensuring that your site is submitted to as many search engines as possible?

2. Discuss the possible privacy or security issues that might arise if you include an e-mail address on your Web site. For example, use the Internet to find out if Web robots collect and use e-mail information. If so, what can you do to protect your main e-mail address?

Appendix A
INTERFACING THE INTERNET WITH CELL PHONES AND PDAS

PDA OVERVIEW

If you need information wherever you go, such as your client's addresses, e-mail messages, to-do lists, and a calendar, you'll probably be interested in a class of small computers that are becoming increasingly popular. These computers are so small that most can literally fit in the palm of your hand, giving rise to the names *handheld* or *palmtop* computer. However, they're probably best known as *Personal Digital Assistants (PDAs)*. Although there are technical differences in size between the PDAs, palmtop, and handheld computers, today most people use the terms interchangeably—something we'll do as well.

PDAs lack some of the power, functionality, and features of a desktop computer; however, many people have nevertheless come to rely on them as portable communication and computing devices. Even the most basic PDAs, which include an electronic calendar and address book, make it easier to manage information when you're away from home or the office.

Although PDAs are used by students, professors, and anyone else who wants to be organized, probably the biggest group of users is mobile business professionals. For example, sales representatives, managers, and others who travel for their work often find their handheld computers almost indispensable for staying organized while on the road.

PDAs vary greatly in their features. Entry-level models, which cost around $100, provide schedulers, store phone numbers and addresses, and include features to help you develop to-do lists and notes. For $200–$500, you'll be able to get PDAs that add slimmed-down versions of popular word processing, spreadsheet, and money manager programs. Some even include features that allow you to access your e-mail and the Internet or to record voice memos. In this price range, you might also notice a number of non-business or entertainment features, such as PDAs that you can use to play music or games. The more expensive models can also include other high-end features, such as more computing memory and power, sharper display screens, and voice recognition.

Developers have also combined PDAs with digital phones to produce new, multipurpose devices. Handspring (*www.handspring.com*) recently released a device of this type that combines a PDA, wireless phone, and Web access (see Figure AA.1). Other manufacturers, such as Palm and Microsoft, followed Handspring's lead and also began to market multipurpose PDA/phone/Web-access handhelds.

As technology evolved, a number of other enhancements and accessories have been developed for handhelds. Some of them include color display, wire-

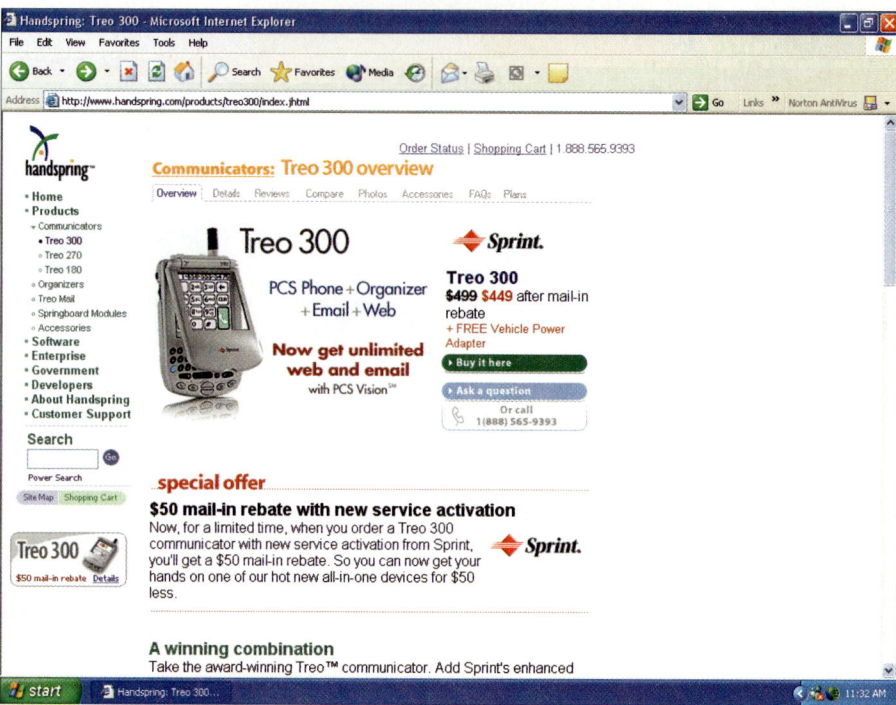

Figure AA.1.
The best of both worlds: Handspring sells a device that combines a digital phone with a Personal Digital Assistant.

less Internet access, rechargeable batteries, and mini-keyboards. Additionally, expansion slots are included in most newer PDAs so that you can connect your handheld to digital cameras, cell phones, and your desktop computer. For example, most models allow you to exchange data, such as e-mail messages, between your desktop (or laptop) computer and your handheld device. One way to do this is to attach cables between the two computers and then use software to synchronize (match) the data between them. Alternatively, PDAs might include a "cradle" that is attached to the desktop computer; when you place the PDA device in the cradle, the information is transferred. Other handheld devices use infrared ports to "beam" the information between computers using infrared light rays.

ENTERING DATA

Physically, PDAs are usually a little larger than a deck of cards in size, easily fitting into the palm of your hand; a few, however, are as large as a small notebook. A display area (sometimes called the touch screen) is used for viewing and entering information. Larger models typically include more computing power and a larger display area.

You can input data several ways. First, you can use a pen-like device, called a stylus, to write directly on the touch screen. When you do, specialized software converts your handwriting to typed text. Most of the PDAs use their own software to perform handwriting recognition. Graffiti is used by Palm for its PDAs, for example (though it also has started licensing Jot software for use in its handhelds as well). When you use Graffiti, you're required to form your letters precisely according to the program's rules or else the software won't understand how to convert them into their corresponding typed text (see Figure AA.2). In contrast, when you use Jot, you enter alphanumeric characters that appear more similar to their keyboard counterparts. In Graffiti, the letter "T" appeared similar to an upside down "L"; in Jot, a "T" looks similar to the actual letter "T." If you don't want to learn a new way of forming your letters just to use Graffiti, you can instead buy and install natural handwriting-

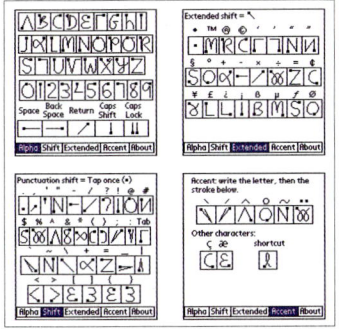

Figure AA.2.
Some handwriting recognition software requires you to enter text using very specific characters.

recognition software on any PDA. However, you'll incur the additional cost of buying the handwriting-recognition software.

Another method of entering data in a handheld involves tapping letters on an electronic keyboard in the unit's display or using the stylus to enter commands on the touch screen. Additionally, some of the units include a "thumb" (tiny) keyboard you can use to enter data. As a final keyboard option, you can attach the PDA directly to an accessory keyboard and then touch type your message as you would on any other computer keyboard (see Figure AA.3). Some of the accessory keyboards fold up to save space when not in use. Finally, if the data exists on another computer system, you can use infrared to enter the information on your PDA.

E-MAIL AND INTERNET ACCESS

Depending on the PDA model you have, you can access the Internet or send e-mail from your handheld. The technology used to access the Web or e-mail from a handheld is still in the early stages and still expensive unless you're a business professional who needs electronic information quickly. Despite the cost, however, using a PDA to access an e-mail account is essential for many mobile professionals to do their jobs efficiently.

There are a couple of ways in which you can access e-mail information and the Internet from a PDA. First, before you leave the office, you can transfer e-mail and some limited Internet content from your desktop computer to your handheld. This allows you to take your latest messages (or some saved Web pages) with you on the road. You can also do the opposite: While you're away from the office, you can write e-mail messages on your PDA and then transfer them back to your desktop computer when you return. However, if you're away from your office or home much of the time, just being able to synchronize information between your desktop and handheld computers might not fit your needs. Instead, you might find it essential to access your e-mail, including new incoming messages, no matter where you are physically located.

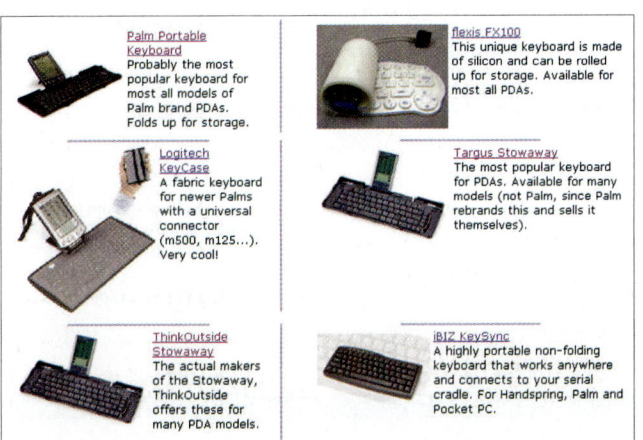

Figure AA.3.
You can attach a handheld device into an accessory keyboard and then enter your data.

Appendix A Interfacing the Internet with Cell Phones and PDAs   395

To do this, you have a couple of options. First, some handhelds include a modem (or a slot where you can add one), which you can use to dial into the Internet. For example, you can connect your PDA to the Internet using a hotel phone jack and then access your e-mail accounts or browse the Web. However, this option, although providing timely communication, does have its limitations. Handheld modems can be expensive, and you might have to pay long-distance charges if you dial into the Internet from a remote location.

The most expensive system combines your PDA's features and capabilities with a service from a wireless network that lets you send and receive data from the Internet directly, without using phone lines. Using this system, you can access the Internet from a wide variety of locations—theoretically while riding in your car, eating in a restaurant with clients, or sunning at the beach. For example, a wireless network gives sales representatives timely access to product information or inventory on the company intranet, managers can give quick feedback to their subordinates via e-mail, and information technology specialists can troubleshoot network problems remotely.

To use wireless e-mail and Internet access, you need a wireless phone in addition to the PDA. Alternatively, you can purchase a PDA with Internet and e-mail access features already built-in. Additionally, you'll need software that can access the Internet and your e-mail (although sometimes this is already preinstalled on your PDA).

Finally, you'll need to subscribe to a wireless data network service, such as those provided by Sprint or Cingular. Similar to cellular phone services, these wireless services can include a number of costs, such as those for setup, connection time, and monthly service fees. Additionally, the contracts for these services typically limit the number of e-mail messages or amount of Internet data that you can transfer; exceed the limit and you'll be charged extra. You should also realize that some PDAs use a specific wireless network, so you won't have a choice of carriers. Furthermore, most wireless networks don't have coverage in rural areas, so you will only be able to download e-mail messages or browse the Web if you're near a metropolitan area (see Figure AA.4). However, even with these limitations and costs, a wireless network service coupled with a PDA can be invaluable for many individuals and businesses.

Figure AA.4.
Wireless networks typically cover only metropolitan areas.

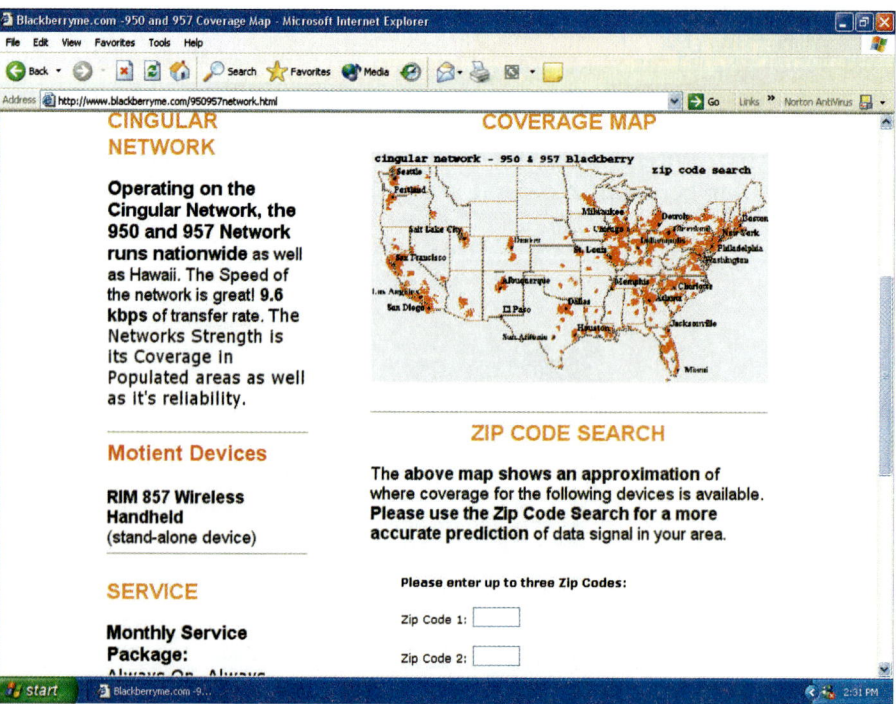

POPULAR PDA COMPANIES AND OPERATING SYSTEMS

There are several companies that produce handheld devices. Among the best known are Palm Computing, Handspring, and Microsoft. Let's take a quick look at the companies that originally pioneered handhelds and which operating systems are currently in use.

During the late 1980s and early 1990s, several companies introduced electronic organizers, such as the Sharp Wizard. However, most of these original units were too big or costly to become popular in the marketplace. Additionally, the handwriting-recognition software included in most of the devices didn't work particularly well. This changed somewhat when Palm introduced its Palm Pilot model in 1996. This device included the Graffiti handwriting software, which helped users overcome the problem of data entry, as long as you precisely followed the program's "rules" for writing letters. As a result, PDAs became more popular.

Currently, Handspring, Blackberry, Microsoft, Hewlett Packard, Compaq, and Sony are producing handhelds. You can find out more about the PDAs they sell and read reviews on the Handheld Review site at *www.handheldreviews.com* (see Figure AA.5).

In addition to the hardware, you also need software to run your PDA device, including an operating system. Just as your desktop or laptop computer uses an operating system (such as Windows XP) to run, so PDAs need a program that's responsible for running the system and any add-on applications. Most of the PDAs you'll see on the market use either a Palm or Windows-based operating system. The Palm operating system is called Palm OS. In addition to being used for Palm's own PDA devices, it's licensed by Handspring, and other companies use it in their handhelds.

Microsoft developed a version of its well-known operating system (Windows) for PDAs. The original version, Windows CE, was released in 1996. Windows CE has been replaced by the Pocket PC operating system, which is currently used by several companies in their handheld computers.

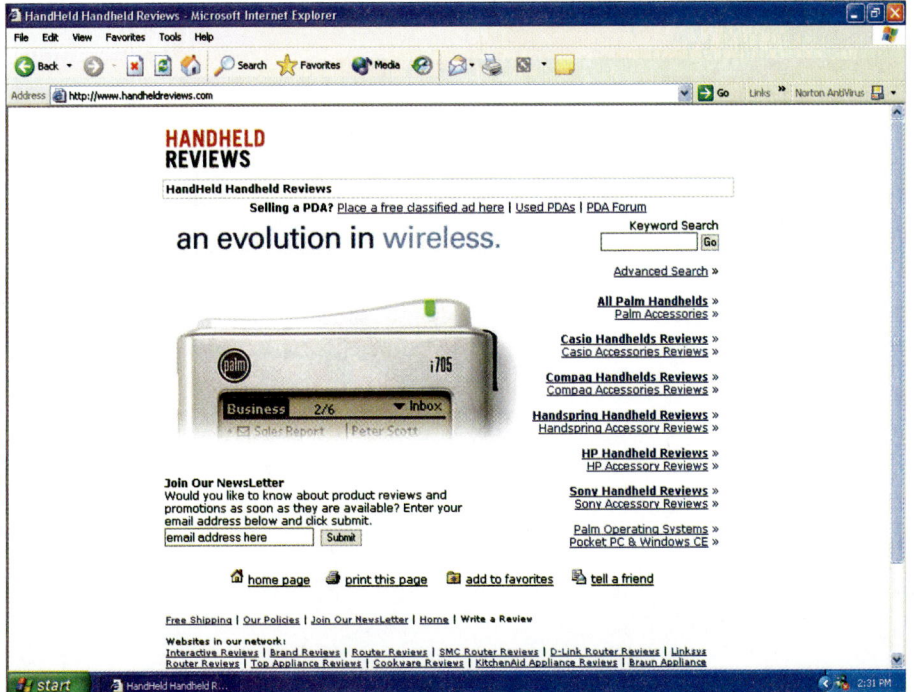

Figure AA.5.
You can evaluate handhelds on this site and find the best one for your needs.

SECURITY AND PRIVACY ISSUES

Because of the way they're used, portable devices such as laptops and handheld computers spend much of their life in public places such as airports, restaurants, stores, and subways. This fact, coupled with the size, value, and portability of these devices, makes them prime targets for thieves. It's also easy for people to lose these mobile units. For example, it's pretty easy to picture a busy professional running a PDA through an airport scanner and then is so distracted that he walks off without picking it up!

Although it can be expensive to replace the hardware and software in a PDA or other mobile unit, this cost might be minimal when compared with the loss of the data on the device. In fact, both privacy and security can be breached if a PDA is stolen or lost. For example, a thief might be able to find e-mail messages, passwords, credit card numbers, addresses, or other personal information on a handheld. Additionally, a PDA could contain important company, military, or agency information.

Besides the loss of data on the individual unit, holes in network security can open up when a PDA is stolen. For example, unless the stolen PDA includes tight security measures, it can potentially be used by a cracker or cybercriminal to gain access to a company's or agency's computer system.

To help make PDAs more secure, companies are developing software to protect the device's data. For example, one program encrypts the information inside the PDA, making it inaccessible to thieves. Another software program erases all the files in a PDA if incorrect passwords are repeatedly entered. Because most crackers use automated password cracker programs that try to bombard a computer system with a huge number of possible passwords, this method prevents thieves from accessing a PDA's data.

PDAs will continue to evolve in power and features, simultaneously providing an increase in convenience and new privacy and security issues.

Appendix B
USEFUL WEB SITES

BIOMETRICS

Identix (*www.identix.com*)   Information about this company's products, which include facial recognition, fingerprinting imaging, and other biometric technologies

DigitalPersona (*www.digitalpersona.com*)   Manufactures fingerprinting scanning security devices

Viisage (*www.viisage.com*)   Information about this company's facial recognition products

CHILDREN'S SITES

bigchalk (*www.bigchalk.com*)   Educational help and information for teachers, parents, and students

BrainMania (*www.brainmania.com*)   Includes free help with homework on a variety of subjects

DiscoverySchool.com (*school.discovery.com*)   Site with a wealth of online activities, study tools, and information

KidsPrivacy (*www.kidsprivacy.com*)   Includes information on keeping children safe online

Yahooligans! (*www.yahooligans.com*)   Combines a colorful, graphical interface with a kid-friendly directory

DOMAIN NAME REGISTRATION

Internet Corporation for Assigned Names and Numbers (ICANN) (*www.icann.org*)   Information about this organization

InterNIC (*www.internic.net*)   Site that provides information about the domain name registration services, including a number of related links

Universal Whois registry (*www.uwhois.com*)   A site that enables you to search globally for information about a domain name, such as the domain name's contact person

E-MAIL ABUSE AND SPAM

EmailAbuse.org (*www.emailabuse.org*)   Provides educational articles and tools for fighting e-mail misuse

Junkbusters (*www.junkbusters.com*)   Provides tools and information to help you limit unwanted e-mail (spam), advertisements, and cookies

Fight Spam on the Internet (*spam.abuse.net*)   Gives practical advice and steps for combating spam

Mail Abuse Prevention System (*www.mail-abuse.org*)   Information on preventing and fighting spam

Network Abuse Clearinghouse (*www.abuse.net*)   Provides a way to report e-mail abusers

Spam Laws (*www.spamlaws.com*)   Includes cases, laws, and articles about spam

Spamex (*www.spamex.com*)   Gives ideas about protecting your main e-mail address, and provides a service in which you can sign up for a disposable e-mail address

HARDWARE AND SOFTWARE VENDORS

Adobe Systems, Inc (*www.adobe.com*)   Information, news, and support for Adobe products, including Acrobat Reader

AdSubtract (*www.adsubtract.com*)   Software you can use to limit or eliminate unwanted Internet advertisements

Amaya (*www.w3.org/Amaya*)   Technical information, support, news, and downloads of W3C's editor/browser software

Apple QuickTime (*www.apple.com/quicktime*)   Learn about and download QuickTime products

Bluetooth (*www.bluetooth.com*)   Information on Bluetooth technology and developments

Cookie Central (*www.cookiecentral.com*)   Includes articles and downloadable software to control cookies

CUseeMe (*www.cuseemeworld.com*)   Information, news, and downloads about CUseeMe and videoconferencing

CyberPatrol (*www.cyberpatrol.com*)   Information on this Internet filtering software; also tips on helping to keep children safe while online

CyberSitter (*www.cybersitter.com*)   Site with information about this software, which restricts access to objectionable or harmful Internet content

Dell (*www.dell.com*)   Interactive shopping site for Dell computers and peripherals

Eudora (*www.eudora.com*)   Includes products and support for the Eudora e-mail client

Handspring (*www.handspring.com*)   Products, software, and support for Handspring's personal digital assistants and related accessories

Hotmail (*www.hotmail.com*)   Information, support, and mailboxes for free; Web-based e-mail

Kaspersky Labs (*www.kaspersky.com*)   Information, security alerts, news articles, and product information for many anti-virus and security software products

Lavasoft (*www.lavasoftusa.com*)   Distributes Ad-Aware software that detects and removes tracking components

Macromedia (*www.macromedia.com*)   Information, news, and support for Macromedia products, including Shockwave and Flash

Mail.com (*www.mail.com*)   Information and subscription information for free; Web-based e-mail

Mail2Web (*www.mail2web.com*)   Information on this Internet e-mail client and service

McAfee (*www.mcafee.com*)   Information, security alerts, news articles, and product information for many anti-virus and security software products

Microsoft (*www.microsoft.com*)   Huge, comprehensive site that provides technical information, support, and links for Microsoft products

Microsoft NetMeeting (*www.microsoft.com/windows/netmeeting*)   Information, updates, service packs, and reviews on NetMeeting

Mozilla (*www.mozilla.org*)   News and newsgroups related to Mozilla browser software as well as downloads of this program

Netscape Navigator (*www.netscape.com*)   Information on downloading Netscape products as well as links to news and other content

Opera (*www.opera.com*)   Information and downloads for the Opera browser software

Palm (*www.palm.com*)   Products, software, and support for Palm's personal digital assistants and related accessories

Pegasus Mail (*www.pmail.com*)   Includes information, technical support, and downloads for the Pegasus e-mail client

Pretty Good Privacy (*www.pgpi.org*)   Site with information and support related to this e-mail encryption software

SafeMessage (*www.safemessage.com*)   Information on SafeMessage software, which adds security and privacy to e-mail transmissions

SurfWatch (*www.surfwatch.com*)   Information on this Internet filtering software

Symantec (*www.symantec.com*)   Information, security alerts, news articles, and product information for many anti-virus and security software products, including Norton AntiVirus

Websense (*www.websense.com*)   Information on this company's workplace filtering and surveillance software

WinZip (*www.winzip.com*)   Learn and download this file compression utility

Yahoo! Mail (*mail.yahoo.com*)   Information, support, and mailboxes for free; Web-based e-mail

ZoneAlarm (*www.zonealarm.com*)   Includes security information and firewall products

INSTANT MESSAGING AND COMMUNICATION

AOL Instant Messenger (*www.aim.com*)   Information, support, and downloads for AOL Instant Messenger

Cerulean Studios (*ceruleanstudios.com/trillian*)   Information and downloads for the Trillian messaging tool

ICQ (*web.icq.com*)   Information, support, and downloads for ICQ

iVillage (*www.ivillage.com*)   Site with message boards and chat rooms

L-Soft (*www.lsoft.com*)   Information on LISTSERV

Topica (*www.topica.com*)   Information on electronic newsletters and discussions

Yahoo! Groups (*groups.yahoo.com*)   Groups and message boards on a wide variety of topics

Yahoo! Messenger (*messenger.yahoo.com*)   Information, support, and downloads for Yahoo! Messenger

INTERNET BACKGROUND INFORMATION, SURVEYS, AND STATISTICS

Jupiterresearch (*www.jupiterresearch.com*)   Detailed surveys and studies on Internet trends

MAE Services (*www.mae.net*)   Information about the Internet's switching centers (MAE, or Metropolitan Area Exchange facilities)

Nielsen//NetRatings (*www.nielsen-netratings.com*)   In-depth research on Internet demographics and usage
Nua.com (*www.nua.com*)   Information on Internet demographics and trends
Pew Internet Project (*www.pewinternet.org*)   Research on the effects of the Internet on various aspects of American life
Webopedia (*www.webopedia.com*)   Online dictionary of Internet terms and technology
World Wide Web Consortium (W3C) (*www.w3.org*)   Web site for the group that oversees the standards for the World Wide Web; provides information on the standards, software, and specifications related to the World Wide Web

INTERNET SERVICE PROVIDERS

AOL (*www.aol.com*)   Comprehensive portal for one of the largest and most popular Internet Service Providers, America Online; includes e-mail, search tools, instant messaging tools, chat, and content
AOLTV (*www.aoltv.com*)   Information about using a set-top device and AOL to access the Internet
AT&T WorldNet (*www.att.net*)   Internet Service Provider site that includes search tools, news, e-mail, shopping, and so on
EarthLink (*www.earthlink.net*)   Information on the various types of Internet access and Web hosting provided by this large ISP
ISPWorld (*www.ispworld.com*)   News and information on choosing an Internet Service Provider
Microsoft Network (*www.msn.com*)   Comprehensive portal for the MSN Internet Service Provider; also includes information on news, weather, money, and search tools
MSN TV (*www.msntv.com*)   Information about using a set-top device and Microsoft Network to access the Internet
Road Runner (*www.rr.com*)   Information on Road Runner, Time Warner Cable's broadband Internet service
SBC Yahoo! Dial (*www.prodigy.net*)   Site for this Internet Service Provider that outlines options for Internet access
The List (*www.thelist.com*)   Articles and links to help you evaluate and choose an Internet Service Provider, Web host, and Web designer
United Online (*www.unitedonline.net*)   Site for the discounted Internet Service Provider that includes Juno Online, NetZero Online, and BlueLight Internet

JOB SEARCH SITES

CareerBuilder (*www.careerbuilder.com*)   Tools and information for finding a job; includes a resume posting service and a comprehensive job search tool
EmploymentGuide.com (*www.employmentguide.com*)   Includes search tools for finding jobs, many of which are technical or computer-oriented
HotJobs (*www.hotjobs.com*)   Includes job search tools, resume layout tools, and resume posting
Monster.com (*www.monster.com*)   Provides job search tools and resume posting services

MULTIMEDIA SITES

Compression Technologies, Inc. (*www.cinepak.com*) Includes product information and support about this company's codecs

Helix Community (*www.helixcommunity.org*) Information about the Helix platform and related technologies

Internetv.com (*www.internetv.com*) Listing of online video and audio content and programs

Ligos (*www.ligos.com*) Information on this company's products, including its codecs

MPEG-4 (*mpeg4ip.sourceforge.net*) Information on the MPEG-4 technology

RealNetworks (*www.real.com*) Products, downloads, and support by RealNetworks

Sorenson Media (*www.sorenson.com*) Includes product information and support about this company's codecs

NEWS AND WEATHER SITES

AccuWeather (*www.accuweather.com*) Includes hour-by-hour predictions for weather anywhere in the world

CNN (*www.cnn.com*) News, sports, and links

MSNBC (*www.msnbc.com*) News, sports, and weather

Nando Times (*www.nandotimes.com*) Online newspaper

USAToday (*www.usatoday.com*) Online news edition of *USA Today*

Weather.com (*www.weather.com*) Popular site maintained by the Weather Channel

WildWeather (*www.wildweather.com*) Includes news stories on the most severe weather conditions in the world

Wunderground.com (*www.wunderground.com*) Weather predictions and maps

ONLINE MANNERS

List-Etiquette.com (*www.list-etiquette.com*) Guidelines and rules for proper e-mail behavior

Netiquette (*www.getnetiquette.com*) Covers rules and common courtesies for online behavior

ONLINE SHOPPING AND AUCTIONS

Amazon (*www.amazon.com*) Extremely popular online shopping site with books, electronics, toys, and so on

eBay (*www.ebay.com*) Giant, extremely popular auction site

bottomdollar.com (*www.bottomdollar.com*) Enables you to run searches for the best prices on an item

PEOPLE SEARCH SITES

Classmates (*www.classmates.com*) Includes search tools to find people from schools you've attended

Military.com (*www.military.com*) Includes general information and current events related to the military as well as a search tool you can use to find service personnel

Switchboard (*www.switchboard.com*) Includes search tools to find people, businesses, maps, and city guides

WhoWhere (*www.whowhere.lycos.com*) Has search tools you can use to find people in public records, yellow pages, or Web pages

Yahoo! PeopleSearch (*people.yahoo.com*) Includes search tools to locate people's addresses or e-mail as well as links to maps and groups

PRIVACY AND SECURITY SITES

Better Business Bureau (*www.bbb.org*) Promotes ethics in business; also includes information on privacy issues

Bugnosis (*www.bugnosis.com*) Site with information about Web bugs

CASPIAN (*www.nocards.org*) Organization that raises and discusses issues related to consumer shopping cards and online privacy

Center for Democracy & Technology (*www.cdt.org*) Includes many links and articles on data privacy and government surveillance

Child Lures Prevention (*www.childlures.com*) Lists a number of principles and safety rules that you can discuss with your children regarding interacting with strangers online

Community Emergency Response Team (CERT) (*www.cert.org*) Information on Internet security practices, alerts, and issues

Computer Security Institute (*www.gocsi.com*) Raises awareness about Internet security issues

Computer Security Resource Center (*csrc.nist.gov*) Includes information to raise awareness about security risks and vulnerabilities

CyberAngels (*www.cyberangels.com*) Information on staying safe online as well as data on viruses, cyberstalking, and hacking

Cybercrime.gov (*www.cybercrime.gov*) United States government's Web site for cybercrime, with information on cases, laws, policies, and security measures

Electronic Frontier Foundation (*www.eff.org*) Includes articles on privacy-related "hot topics" such as surveillance and censorship

Electronic Privacy Information Center (*www.epic.org*) Includes articles and information on "privacy in the information age"

Equifax (*www.equifax.com*) Credit bureau at which you can obtain your credit report and report suspected identity theft

Experian (*www.experian.com*) Credit bureau at which you can obtain your credit report or report suspected identity theft; also includes consumer alerts related to privacy and security

Federal Bureau of Investigation (*www.fbi.gov*) Includes information about cyberterrorism, misuse of social security numbers, cybercrime, and the Carnivore Diagnostic Tool

Federal Trade Commission (*www.ftc.gov*) Includes information and links to consumer protection sites; promotes fair trade practices

FirstGov for Consumers (*www.consumer.gov/idtheft*) United States government site for identity theft

Identity Theft Resource Center (*www.idtheftcenter.org*) Includes detailed information about preventing and recovering from identity theft

LinuxSecurity (*www.linuxsecurity.com*) Information and articles on Internet security

National Fraud Information Center (*www.fraud.org*) Information on preventing Internet fraud; also includes current news items about fraud

Office of Management and Budget (*www.ombwatch.org*) Promotes fiscal accountability in government

Online Privacy Alliance (*www.privacyalliance.org*)   A group of organizations and businesses that promote Internet privacy

Privacy Foundation (*www.privacyfoundation.org*)   Current news about workplace surveillance and other privacy issues

Privacy.net (*www.privacy.net*)   Information on Internet tracking; includes demonstrations of cookies and Internet tracking

Stay Safe Online (*www.staysafeonline.info*)   Information on securing home and small business computers; also includes safety and security tips for children and youth

The Privacy Rights Clearinghouse (*www.privacyrights.org*)   Information protecting personal privacy

TransUnion (*www.tuc.com*)   Credit bureau at which you can obtain your credit report or report identity theft; also includes tips for preventing identity theft

SCHOLARSHIP AND FINANCIAL AID SITES

FastWEB (*www.fastweb.com*)   Information on scholarships and colleges

FinAid! (*www.finaid.org*)   Information on college financial aid and scholarships

Peterson's (*www.petersons.com*)   Specialized search site you can use to research colleges and scholarships

SEARCH ENGINES AND DIRECTORIES

AllTheWeb (*www.alltheweb.com*)   Search engine site that also includes news

AltaVista (*www.altavista.com*)   Large search engine that also includes news and a directory, organized by topic

Anonymizer (*www.anonymizer.com*)   Information about the Anonymizer products; also includes tips on surfing safely

Ask Jeeves (*www.askjeeves.com*)   Search tool that supports natural-language searches

Dogpile (*www.dogpile.com*)   Metasearch engine site that also includes a directory and links to news and weather

Excite (*www.excite.com*)   Portal to many online activities and a search engine

Google (*www.google.com*)   Large and very popular search engine that also includes groups and news portals

HotBot (*www.hotbot.com*)   Includes four different search engines and a clutter-free look

InfoSpace (*www.infospace.com*)   Information on this online service, which includes tools to find people, businesses, government offices, and so on

LookSmart (*www.looksmart.com*)   Search engine site that also includes topical listings

Lycos (*www.lycos.com*)   Search engine site that includes news, shopping, and e-mail

Mamma (*www.mamma.com*)   Information about this metasearch engine site

MetaCrawler (*www.metacrawler.com*)   Metasearch engine site that also includes a directory and other search tools

WebCrawler (*www.webcrawler.com*)   Metasearch engine site that also includes a directory and other search tools

Yahoo! (*www.yahoo.com*)   Popular portal that includes a Web directory

SITES RELATED TO DOWNLOADING FILES

Download (*www.download.com*) Includes a topical listing of many downloadable programs and files

FTPFind (*www.ftpfind.com*) Includes search tools and a directory to help you find FTP files

FTPplanet.com (*www.ftpplanet.com*) Tutorials and information about using FTP and FTP clients

Ipswitch (*www.ipswitch.com*) The site for a company that develops software, including a well-known FTP client: WS_FTP Pro

Jumbo! (*www.jumbo.com*) Includes downloadable programs, arranged by topic

United States Copyright Office (*www.lcweb.loc.gov/copyright*) Includes information on copyright law, licensing, and records

SPECIALIZED SEARCH ENGINES AND SITES

Bright Planet (*www.brightplanet.com*) Includes information and support for searching the deep Web

CNET (*www.cnet.com*) Specialized site that includes comprehensive news and information about computers and related technologies

Consumer World (*www.consumerworld.org*) Includes alerts, news, and other consumer-related resources

FindLaw (*www.findlaw.com*) Comprehensive site with cases, legal news, and search tools

INFOMINE (*infomine.ucr.edu*) Online library and research site that includes more than 100,000 documents

Kelly Blue Book (*www.kbb.com*) Specialized search site you can use to research car values

LawGuru (*www.lawguru.com*) Large site in which you can find legal forms, get free legal advice, visit forums, and follow various links to legal resources

Library of Congress (*lcweb.loc.gov*) Huge collection of online resources

Map Quest (*www.mapquest.com*) Interactive site you can use to find driving directions and maps

Medsite (*www.medsite.com*) Specialized search site for medical and health information

Merriam-Webster (*www.m-w.com*) Online dictionary that you can use to find definitions

National Library of Medicine (*www.nlm.nih.gov*) Specialized search site for medical and health information

Northern Light (*www.northernlight.com*) Specialized search engine that includes more than 7,000 publications in its "Special Collection"

OneLook Dictionaries (*www.onelook.com*) Interactive site you can use to find a definition from more than 800 dictionaries

Online Computer Library Center (OCLC) (*www.oclc.org*) An online library and research organization

Realtor.com (*www.realtor.com*) Specialized search that helps you find properties and research various neighborhoods

Search Engine Colossus (*www.searchenginecolossus.com*) Directory of search engines from around the world

Search Engine Showdown (*www.searchengineshowdown.com*) Information on effective online searching

Search Engine Watch (*www.searchenginewatch.com*) Comprehensive site with information on creating, submitting, and positioning Web sites

SearchAbility (*www.searchability.com*)   Information on searching effectively and on using specialized search tools and technologies
yourDictionary (*www.yourdictionary.com*)   Online dictionary and thesaurus
ZDNet (*www.zdnet.com*)   Specialized search site that focuses on computer technologies, including news, downloads, trends, and reviews

TRAVEL SITES

Expedia (*www.expedia.com*)   Popular, full-service online travel site, with current information and online reservations on hotels, airfare, and car rentals
Travelocity (*www.travelocity.com*)   Full-service online travel site, with online reservations and packages

USABILITY AND WEB SITE DEVELOPMENT

FrontPage (*www.microsoft.com/frontpage*)   Microsoft's home page for FrontPage, including support, product, downloads, and technical information
Microsoft's Design Gallery Live (*dgl.microsoft.com*)   Huge collection of downloadable clips
Usable Web (*www.usableweb.com*)   Huge site with a directory listing of links about Web site usability and related design issues

WEB SITE OPTIMIZATION AND HOSTING

AddMe (*www.addme.com*)   Includes a step-by-step tutorial that helps you add your Web site to various search engines
AddPro (*www.addpro.com*)   Site you can use for free Web site submission to approximately 20 search engines
Geocities (*geocities.yahoo.com*)   Includes free hosting for personal Web sites
Search Engine Forums (*www.searchengineforums.com*)   Forums for Webmasters and developers

INDEX

A

Acceptable Use Policies (AUPs), 70–71
active content (Web pages), 160–161, 291–293
active window (multiple browser sessions), 154
ActiveX, 160, 291
   ActiveX controls, 160–161
   security, 291–293
Ad-Aware utility, 30–31
add-ins. *See* plug-ins
AddMe Web submission service, 387
AddPro Web submission service, 387
Address bars (Web browsers)
   keyword searches, 144–145
   typing URLs, 132–135
Address Book (Outlook Express), 94, 108–113
Adobe Acrobat
   Acrobat Reader, 214, 238
   Portable Document Format (PDF), 237
Adobe GoLive Web creation tool, 321
ADSL (Asymmetric Digital Subscriber Line), 54
ADSL/DSL (Asymmetric Digital Subscriber Line/Digital Subscriber Line), 48, 57–58
advertising
   banner ads, 11
   blocking ads, 156–157
   pop-up ads, 31
adware, 30–31, 263
AIM (AOL Instant Messenger), 198–200
AltaVista search engine, 140, 185–188
   analyzing link popularity of Web sites, 386
   AV Enterprise Search software, 270–271
always on connections, 57
Amaya Web browser, 127
America Online. *See* AOL
American Management Association workplace surveillance survey, 267–268, 271
AND operator (searches), 183–184
animated GIFs, 234
anonymous access
   Anonymizer browsing service, 146
   anonymous FTP, 43, 221
anti-virus software, 23, 27, 106
   anti-virus software companies, 295
      rating systems for malicious code, 295–296
   downloading updated virus definitions, 213
   Norton AntiVirus, 215
   Outlook Express anti-virus features, 112–113
   scanning downloaded files, 220, 223
AOL (America Online), 67–68
   AOL Instant Messenger (AIM), 198–200
   AOLTV, 50
   AOLTV BSP (Broadband Service Provider), 60
Apple QuickTime, 240
applets (Java), 160
archives, 219
ARPANET, 6–7
articles (newsgroups), 202
Ask Jeeves search engine, 176–177
ASP (Active Server Page) file extension, 231
asterisk (*) wildcard character, using in searches, 189
asymmetric data transfer, 54
Asymmetric Digital Subscriber Line (ADSL), 54
Asymmetric Digital Subscriber Line/Digital Subscriber Line (ADSL/DSL), 48, 57–58
AT&T WorldNet, 68
attachments (e-mail), 97
   ISP limitations, 65
   sending, 98–99
   viruses, 110–112
attack tools, 286
attackers, 285
auction fraud, 35–37
AUPs (Acceptable Use Policies), 70–71
authoring Web sites, 310. *See also* creating Web sites
Auto Thumbnail feature (FrontPage), 366
AutoComplete feature (Internet Explorer), 135
AVI (Audio Video Interleave) file extension, 231

B

back door programs, 290
Back/Forward buttons (Web browsers), 135–136, 158
backbone, 3
bandwidth, 54–55. *See also* speed of connection
   choosing ISPs, 65
banner ads, 11–12
BBS (Bulletin Board Systems), 205
best practices
   e-commerce, 300–301
   privacy checklist, 275–277
   protection from malicious code, 296–297
   security checklist, 301–303
Better Business Bureau, 11, 37
biometrics, 272–275
bitmap (bmp) file format, 234
blacklists, filtering incoming e-mail, 113–114
blended threats, 294
blocking
   advertisements, 156–157
   e-mail addresses, 114
Bluetooth, 52
BMP (bitmap) file format, 234
bookmarks (Web browsers). *See* Favorites lists
Boolean logic, 183–186
bots, 169
broadband, 54–55
Broadband Service Providers (BSPs), 55, 60
browsers. *See* Web browsers
browsing the Web. *See* surfing the Web
BSPs. *See* Broadband Service Providers
buddy lists (IM), 198
buffer overflow (IM clients), 200
buffers, 248
Bulletin Board Systems (BBS), 205

C

cable modems, 48, 57
caches (Web browsers), 152, 161–163
CareerBuilder Web site, 15, 182, 192
Carnivore Diagnostic Tool, 18, 264–266
CD burners, 251
cell phones, 51–52
Center for Democracy and Technology, 18–19
CERT (Computer Emergency Response Team), 24, 200, 283
chat rooms, 197, 201–202. *See also* IM
checklist for evaluating ISPs, 64
children
   child pages (Web sites), 350
   Family Internet Safety Pact, 39
   harmful Web sites, 37–38
   National Center for Missing and Exploited Children Web site, 40
   parental controls, 66
   privacy, 271
Children's Online Privacy Protection Act (COPPA), 271
click stream data, 30
client-server architecture, 4, 123
clients, 4
   e-mail clients, 74, 80–82. *See also* Outlook Express

FTP, 213, 221–224
Instant Messaging (IM), 198–199
mail-messaging software, 53
versus servers, 123
clip art, 359–362. *See also* graphics
    downloading, 214
CNET, 190
    Download.com site, 211
        plug-ins, 229
    Instant Messaging survey, 198
co-located servers (Web hosts), 379
Code Red, 286
codecs (streaming media), 235, 249–251
    viewing installed codecs, 251
college networks, 70–71
communication, 13–14
    Bulletin Board Systems (BBS), 205
    chat, 197, 201–202
    free speech, 18
    IM, 196–200
    LISTSERV/mailing lists, 205–206
    Netiquette, 76, 206
    newsgroups, 202–205
    video conferencing, 206–207
compressed files, 237
compression schemes (streaming media).
    See codecs
Computer Emergency Response Team. *See*
    CERT
computer monitoring software, 263,
    269–271
computer networks, 4, 7
Computer Resource Security Center, 283
Computer Security Institute financial loss
    study, 285
computers, 49–52
connecting to Internet
    college/business networks, 70–71
    connection types, 53–59
    hardware, 49–52
    Internet Service Providers. *See* ISPs
    software, 52–53. *See also* Web browsers
    speed
        comparison of connection types, 47–49,
            59
        data transfer rates, 53–55
contacts (Outlook Express Address Book),
    108–110
Content Scrambling System (CSS), 250
Cookie Central Web site, 33
cookies, 30–33, 263
    cookie management software, 277
    disabling, 32–33
COPPA (Children's Online Privacy
    Protection Act), 271
copying/pasting
    e-mail text, 97
    Web site text/graphics, 216–217
copyright infringements, 38–39
    downloading copyrighted material, 214
crackers, 39–40
crawlers, 140
creating Web sites
    design. *See* designing Web sites
    free Web creation software, 322–324
    FrontPage. *See* FrontPage
    HTML markup tags, 319, 324–327
    graphics. *See* graphics, Web pages
    publishing sites to the Web. *See* publishing
        Web sites
    Web page editors, 319–322. *See also*
        FrontPage
    Web site positioning, 382–387

critical infrastructures, 289
cross site scripting, 292
CUseeMe, 207
CyberAngels, 40–41
cybercrime, 25. *See also* Internet, misuse
    hackers/crackers, 39
    identity theft, 33–34
    Internet fraud, 35–37
    stalkers, 39–41
    United States Government Web site, 284
CyberPatrol filtering software, 40
CyberSitter filtering software, 40
cyberslacking, 267
cybersurveillance, 264
cyberterrorism, 289

D

DAT (Digital Audio Tape), 237
data snooping, 262–264. *See also* govern-
    ment surveillance
DeCSS, 250
dedicated servers (Web hosts), 379
deep Web, 190
Denial of Service (DoS) attacks, 288–289
Design Gallery Live Web site, 214
designing Web sites, 307–308
    determining goals for site, 310–311
    development of Web sites, 310
    home page design, 313–316
    reasons for creating Web pages, 309
    structure considerations, 312–313
    types of Web sites, 309
    usability considerations, 311–312
desktop shortcuts (Web site links), 139
developing Web sites, 310. *See also* creating
    Web sites
dial-up access, 48, 55–56, 65
digests (mailing lists), 205
Digital Audio Tape (DAT), 237
digital media, 234–235, 237
    stadardization, 252–253
Digital Subscriber Line (DSL), 57–58
directory services, 110
Discuss button (Internet Explorer), 158
Distributed Denial of Service (DDoS)
    attacks, 288
DivX, 250
Dogpile Web site, 142
Domain Name System (DNS), 124–125
domain names, 123–125
Download.com Web site, 211
    plug-ins, 229
downloadable media (static media), 248
downloading, 3, 54, 213–216
    audio/music files, 214
    copyrighted material, 214
    FTP, 212–213, 220–224
    graphics, 214
        copying from Web pages, 217
    Internet Explorer 6.0, 126–128
        upgrades/patches, 127
    scanning downloaded files, 220, 223
    software, 14
        FTP clients, 221–224
        Internet Explorer, 126–128
        patches/updates, 215
        registration forms, 223
        shareware/freeware, 215
        trialware, 215
    speed of connection, 49, 59
    text
        copying from Web pages, 217
        documents, 214

wallpaper, 217
Web sites
    copying from sites, 216–217
    downloading files, 219–220
    saving entire pages, 218
downstream, 54
Dreamweaver Web creation tool, 321
DSL (Digital Subscriber Line), 48, 57–58
dynamic content (Web pages), 134, 160
dynamic HTML (DHTML), 134

E

e-commerce, 10–11
    best practices, 300–301
e-mail, 2, 13, 74–75
    addressing, 78–79, 93–94
        Outlook Express. *See* Address Book
            (Outlook Express)
        distribution lists, 109
    advantages/disadvantages, 76–77
    attachments, 97
        ISP limitations, 65
        opening, 100
        scanning, 99–100
        sending, 98–99
        viruses, 26–27. *See also* viruses
    blocking e-mail addresses, 114
    clients, 53, 74, 80–82. *See also* Outlook
        Express
    copying/pasting message text, 97
    creating messages, 92–94
        assigning priority, 98–99
        spelling check, 90
    e-mailing Web pages, 147, 218
    encrypting messages, 111
    filtering incoming e-mail, 113–114
    flaming, 77
    formatting message appearance, 95–97
    forwarding messages, 100–101
    fraud, 37
    headers/header section, 92
    hyperlinks, 349
        fake Web links (viruses), 111
    mail servers, 78
    mail-messaging software. *See* e-mail clients
    mailing lists, 205–206
        LISTSERV, 41–42
    online fraud, 35–36
    privacy, best practices checklist, 276
    receiving, 78–79, 99–100
    replying, 100–101
    requesting return receipts, 107
    SafeMessage, 83
    sending, 78–79, 97
    spam, 13, 77
        avoiding, 113–114
        deleting, 114
    spoofing, 290
    standards/protocols, 79–80
    stationery, 95–96
    viruses, 110–113
    Web-based mail services, 75, 83–85
    workplace privacy, 114–115.
EarthLink, 68, 80
eBay
    auction fraud, 35–37
    usability of site, 312
Echelon, 266
Edit with button (Internet Explorer), 158
education, effects of Internet, 16–17
EIM (Employee Internet Management), 271
electronic commerce (e-commerce), 10–11
Electronic Frontier Foundation, 261

electronic mail. *See* e-mail
Electronic Privacy Information Center (EPIC), 18, 260
emerging trends/technologies, 19
Employee Internet Management (EIM), 271
encoders (streaming media), 252
encryption
   DVDs, 250
   e-mail messages, 111
entertainment, effects of Internet, 17
Equifax credit bureau, 34
error messages (Web sites), 133–134
Ethernet, 50
Eudora, 82
European Laboratory for Nuclear Research (CERN), 121
EXE file extension, 231
Experian credit bureau, 34
Extensible Hypertext Markup Language (XHTML), 233
Extensible Markup Language (XML), 6, 123, 233
eye scanning, 274

F

facial recognition technology, 274
Family Internet Safety Pact, 39
FastTrack, 271
Favorites button (Internet Explorer), 158
Favorites lists, 137–139
FBI. *See* government surveillance
Federal Trade Commission Web site, 34
fiber optics, 10
Fight Spam on the Internet Web site, 113
file attachments. *See* e-mail attachments
file extensions, 231–232
file formats, 228, 230–232
   compressed files, 237
   graphics files, 233–234
   media files, 234–237
   Portable Document Format (PDF), 237
   text files, 232
   Web pages, 233
File Transfer Protocol. *See* FTP
file-swapping programs, 30, 38–39
file downloads. *See* downloading
filtering incoming e-mail, 113–114
FinCEN (Financial Crimes Enforcement Network), 267
finding. *See* searches
FindLaw Web site, 190
fingerprint scanning, 273
firewalls, 23–25
   hacker prevention, 39–40
   personal firewalls, 297–298
   ZoneAlarm firewall program, 161
fixed wireless connections, 48, 59
flaming, 77
Flash, 239
flat rates (ISPs), 66
FOIA (Freedom of Information Act), 266
font size (Web browsers), 160
formatting e-mail messages, 95–97
Forward/Back buttons (Web browsers), 135–136, 158
forwarding e-mail messages, 100–101
frames (Web sites), 145
fraud, 35–37
free ISPs, 69–70
free speech, 18
free trials (ISPs), 67
Freedom of Information Act (FOIA), 266
freeware, 215

FrontPage, 319, 331–332
   creating simple Web sites, 333–337
   entering/editing text, 337–340
   graphics, 357–358
      captions, 368–369
      creating thumbnails, 366–368
      inserting clip art, 359–362
      inserting pictures, 364–365
      photo galleries. *See* FrontPage, photo galleries
      Pictures toolbar, 366–367
   hyperlinks
      creating/editing, 347–348
      e-mail hyperlinks, 349
      link bars, 338, 349–351
   launching, 333
   lists, 343–344
   Page Banners, 339
   photo galleries
      creating, 368–371
      editing, 371–373
   publishing Web sites, 388–389
   saving files, 338–340
   server extensions, 381
   shortcut menus, 339
   tables, 343–344
   tasks, 335
   templates/wizards, 333
   themes, 346–347
   views
      displaying Views bar, 333
      Hyperlinks view, 335
      Navigation view, 335
      Page view, 337
      Reports view, 335
      switching between Preview and HTML views, 340–342
   Webs, 333
      adding/deleting pages, 351–352
      child/parent pages, 350
      saving embedded (graphics) files, 362–363
      testing, 352–353
      uploading to the Web. *See* FrontPage, publishing Web sites
FTP (File Transfer Protocol), 42–43, 212–213, 220–224
   anonymous FTP servers, 221
   clients, 213, 221–224
   servers, 213, 220
   sites, 42–43

G

gateways. *See* proxy servers
Geocities Web hosting service, 382
GET command (Web browsers), 125
GIF (Graphics Interchange Format) files, 231, 234
gigaPoPs, 10
GoLive Web creation tool, 321
Google search engine, 131, 140
   accessing Usenet groups, 203–204
   advanced search features, 188–189
   analyzing link popularity of Web sites, 386
   keyword searches, 168–172
   newsgroups, 42
Gopher, 216
Government Computer News Web site, 279
government surveillance, 18, 264–267
   Carnivore, 264–266
   Echelon, 266
   FinCEN (Financial Crimes Enforcement Network), 267

Magic Lantern, 266
Graphical User Interfaces (GUIs), Web browsers, 120
graphics
   creating Web pages. *See* FrontPage, graphics
   disabling graphics in Web browsers, 152, 155–156
   downloading, 214, 217
   file formats, 233–234
   printing, 217
groups
   Google Groups, 203–204
   Yahoo! Groups, 205–206
GUIs (Graphical User Interfaces), Web browsers, 120

H

hackers, 39–40
hand and palm recognition systems, 273
Handspring (PDAs) Web site, 51
hardware, 49–52
   USB (Universal Serial Bus) connections, 255
   Web cams, 254–256
hash patterns (passwords), 299
headers/header section (e-mail), 92
Helix DNA platform, 252
Helix Universal Server, 252–253
hierarchy (Web sites), 313
high speed access, 55
History button (Internet Explorer), 158
History lists (Web browsers), 136–137
history of Internet, 6–8
hit counters, 381
hits (search results), 168
Hoaxbusters Web site, 112
hoaxes (viruses), 111–112
Home button (Internet Explorer), 158
home pages
   Web browsers, 159–160
   Web sites
      design considerations, 313–316
      HTML titles, 383–384
home-based business, 15
hostile work environments, 271
hosts. *See* Web hosts
HotBot, 170
HotJobs Web site, 192
Hotmail, 83–84
HTM/HTML (Hypertext Markup Language) file extension, 231
HTML (Hypertext Markup Language), 5
   code, 233, 325, 340
   dynamic HTML (DHTML), 134
   home page HTML titles, 383–384
   markup tags, 319, 324–327
   meta tags, 385
   static HTML, 134
   tags, 233
HTML editors, 319–322. *See also* FrontPage
HTML formatting (e-mail), 95–96
HTTP (Hypertext Transfer Protocol), 122
hubs, 9
hyperlinks, 5
   creating/editing, 347–349
   FrontPage
      Hyperlinks view, 335
      link bars, 338, 349–351
   navigating Web sites, 136
   thumbnail images, 367–368
   Web site positioning, 386

hypertext links. *See* hyperlinks
Hypertext Markup Language. *See* HTML
Hypertext Transfer Protocol (HTTP), 122

I
ICQ, 198–199
ID Theft Clearinghouse, 34
identity theft, 33–34
Identity Theft Resource Center Web site, 34
IM (instant messaging), 196–200. *See also* chat rooms
INFOMINE Web site, 192
information architecture, 312
information sharing, 14
InfoSpace search engine, 178
instant messaging. *See* IM
Integrated Services Digital Network (ISDN), 48, 56–57
intellectual property infringements, 38–39
Internet, 2–6
 emerging trends/technologies, 19
 history, 6–8, 121–122
 impact of Internet on the world, 10–17
 misuse, 37–41
 structure, 8–10
 versus the Web, 120–121
 workplace monitoring, 115
Internet appliances, 50
Internet Explorer, 52, 120, 126–127, 132
 AutoComplete feature, 135
 disabling cookies, 32–33
 downloading IE 6.0, 126–128
 downloading upgrades/patches, 127
 Favorites lists, 137–139
 History lists, 135–137
 Links bar, 139–140
 Outlook Express. *See* Outlook Express
 search features, 144–145
 setting
  font size, 160
  home/start page, 159–160
 Standard toolbar, 158–159
 Temporary Internet Files, 161–163
Internet fraud, 35–37
Internet Fraud Complaint Center (IFCC), 35–36
Internet Message Access Protocol (IMAP), 79–80
Internet Protocol (IP), 7
Internet Protocol (IP) address. *See* IP addresses
Internet Relay Chat (IRC), 202
Internet Service Providers (ISPs), 9
Internet worms, 294
InterNIC, 124–125
intranets, 7
intruders, 285
IP (Internet Protocol), 7
IP addresses, 124
 finding (Whois), 125
Ipswitch Web site, downloading FTP clients, 221–223
ISDN (Integrated Services Digital Network), 56–57
ISPs (Internet Service Providers), 9, 63–64
 America Online (AOL), 67–68
 AT&T WorldNet, 68
 college/business networks, 70–71
 dial-up connections, 56
 EarthLink, 68
 evaluating/choosing, 63–67
 free trials, 67
 free/discounted ISPs, 69–70

Juno, 69
market share, 67–68
Microsoft Network (MSN), 68
NetZero, 69
Prodigy, 69
propritetary software, 53
regional/local ISPs, 69
United Online, 69
Web hosting services, 379–380
ISPWorld Web site, 65
iVillage chat rooms, 201

J
Java, 160–161, 291
 applets, 160
 enabling/disabling, 160–161
 security, 291–293
JavaScript, 160, 291
 security, 291–293
jobs
 effects of Internet on jobs, 15–16
 job search Web sites, 192
JPG/JPEG (Joint Photography Experts Group) files, 231, 234
Jukebox, 235
Jumbo! download site, 212
junk e-mail, 13, 113–114
Junkbuster ad-blocking program, 157
Junkbuster's Web site, 29
Juno, 69
Jupiter Media Metrix Web site, 60

K
Kaspersky Labs (anti-virus) Web site, 27
keyboard shortcuts
 displaying recently visited Web sites, 134
 navigating Web pages, 145
keylogger programs, 263
keyword searches (Web sites), 144–145, 168–172
 using multiple keywords, 185
keywords (Web pages), 384–385
KidsPrivacy Web site, 271

L
L-Soft mailing lists, 206
languages
 HTML (Hypertext Markup Language). *See* HTML
 XML (Extensible Markup Language), 6
Lavasoft's Ad-Aware utility, 30–31
LawGuru Web site, 190
links, 5. *See also* hyperlinks
 link bars, 139–140, 338, 349–351
 popularity, 386
LinuxSecurity Web site, 279
List, The, 63
List-Etiquette.com, 206
listserv mailing lists, 41–42, 205–206
log files (Web sites), 30
logging in to e-mail services, 80
logical operators (searches), 183–186
lurking, 206

M
macro viruses, 27, 294
 disabling macros, 297
Macromedia
 Dreamweaver Web creation tool, 321
 Flash Player/Shockwave, 239
Magic Lantern, 266
Mail Abuse Prevention System Web site, 113

Mail button (Internet Explorer), 158
mail clients, 53, 74, 80–82. *See also* Outlook Express
mail servers, 78
Mail.com Web-based e-mail service, 84
Mail2Web Web-based e-mail service, 84–85
mailing lists, 41–42, 205–206
malicious code, 26. *See also* viruses
malware, 26. *See also* viruses
Mamma search engine, 178
markup tags (HTML), 324–327
mathematical operators (searches), 183
Mbps (megabits per second), 54
McAfee (anti-virus) Web site, 27. *See also* anti-virus software companies
Media button (Internet Explorer), 158
media encoders, 252
media players, 251–252. *See also* streaming media
media. *See* multimedia
Medsite Web site, 190
megabits per second (Mbps), 54
memory
 Random Access Memory (RAM), 158
 Web browser caches, 161–163
messaging clients, 196. *See also* IM
meta tags (HTML), 385
MetaCrawler search engine, 142, 144, 178
metasearch engines, 142, 178
metered rates (ISPs), 66
Metropolitan Area Exchanges (MAEs), 7
Microsoft
 Design Gallery Live Web site, 214
 Hotmail, 83–84
 NetMeeting, 207
 Outlook Express. *See* Outlook Express
Microsoft Network. *See* MSN
Military Network (MILNET), 7
MIME (Multipurpose Internet Mail Extensions), 79
MIMEsweeper, 269–270
mirror sites, 126
Microsoft FrontPage. *See* FrontPage
MLMs (mailing list managers), 205
mobile code, 291–293
modems, 48, 55–57
moderated groups, 204
Monster.com Web site, 15
Mosaic Web browser, 121
MOV file extension, 231
Mozilla Web browser, 53, 127
MP3 (MPEG-Audio Layer 3), 214, 231, 235
 MP3 players, 235–236
MP3.com Web site, 235
MPEG/MPG (Moving Picture Experts Group), 231, 235, 250
MPEG-4 Web site, 251
MSN (Microsoft Network), 68
 MSN Messenger, 198–199
 MSN TV, 50
 MSN TV BSP (Broadband Service Provider), 60
multimedia, 228, 245–247
 disabling multimedia in Web browsers, 152, 155–156
 downloading audio/music files, 214
 file formats, 234–235, 237
 QuickTime, 240
 static media, 248
 streaming media. *See* streaming media
 Web cams, 254–256
Webcasting, 254

Multipurpose Internet Mail Extensions (MIME), 79
MUSICMATCH Jukebox, 235

N

nag screens, 215
name servers, 125
NAPs (Network Access Points), 8
Napster, 38–39, 235
narrowband, 55
National Center for Missing and Exploited Children Web site, 40
National Infrastructure Protection Center (NIPC), 289
natural language search engines, 175–177
navigating
 Web pages, 145
 Web sites, 132–136
NCSA Mosaic Web browser, 121
NEAR operator (searches), 183
Net. *See* Internet; World Wide Web
Netfirms free Web hosting service, 382
Netiquette, 76, 206
NetMeeting, 207
Netscape Navigator, 52, 127
Network Access Points (NAPs), 8
Network Interface Cards (NICs), 50
networks, 4
 college/business networks, 70–71
 Ethernet, 50
 intranets, 7
NetZero, 69
newsgroups, 42–43, 114, 202–205
NICs (Network Interface Cards), 50
Norton
 AntiVirus, 215. *See also* anti-virus software
 Personal Firewall, 39
NOT operator (searches), 183–184
Notepad, 232, 325–326
NSFnet, 7

O

off-times/peak times, 157–158
offline browsing, 132, 146–147
OneLook Dictionaries Web site, 190–191
online presence, 309
Online Privacy Alliance, 261
online profiling, 29–33
online services. *See* ISPs
online shopping, 10–11
open source programs, 53
open standards (Web), 122
Opera Web browser, 127, 155
operators (searches), 183–186
Outlook, 81
Outlook Express, 75, 82–83, 89–92. *See also* e-mail
 Address Book, 108–110
 application window, 89–92
 attaching files, 98–99
 copying/pasting message text, 97
 creating e-mail, 92–94
  assigning priority, 98–99
 customizing (Options dialog box), 106–107
 encrypting e-mail messages, 111
 formatting e-mail, 95–97
 forwarding e-mail, 100–101
 launching, 90
 opening attachments, 99–100
 receiving e-mail, 99–100
 replying to e-mail, 100–101
 requesting return receipts, 107

sending e-mail, 97
Spelling tool, 90
stationery, 95–96

P

packets, 9
 packet sniffers, 263
paid inclusions (search engines), 387
Palm (PDAs) Web site, 51
parent pages (Web sites), 350
parental controls, 66
password crackers, 299
passwords, 298–300
patches (software), downloading, 127, 215
pay-per-click model (search engines), 387
payloads/payload triggers (viruses), 26
PDAs (Personal Digital Assistants), 51–52
PDF (Portable Document Format), 214, 231, 237–238
peak times/off-times, 157–158
Pegasus Mail, 82
perceptual compression, 250
Personal Digital Assistants (PDAs), 51–52
 viruses, 297
Pew Internet Project, 265
photo galleries (FrontPage)
 creating, 368–371
 editing, 371–373
pictures. *See also* graphics
 creating thumbnails, 366–368
 inserting into Web pages, 364–365
 photo galleries (FrontPage), 368–373
PKZip, 237
plain old telephone service (POTS), 55
Plain Text formatting (e-mail), 95–96
platform, 7
plug-ins, 228–229, 238–240
 Adobe Acrobat Reader, 238
 Macromedia Flash Player/Shockwave Player, 239
 media players, 251–252. *See also* streaming media
 QuickTime, 240
PNG (Portable Network Graphics) file extension, 231
PoP (Point of Presence), 79
pop-up advertisements, 31
POP3 (Post Office Protocol, version 3), 79–80
Portable Document Format (PDF), 214, 231, 237–238
portals, 141
ports (Web servers), 123
positioning. *See* publishing Web sites, Web site positioning
Post Office Protocol, version 3 (POP3), 79–80
postings (newsgroups), 202
POTS (plain old telephone service), 55
precedence (search expressions), 186
printing
 graphics, 217
 Print button (Internet Explorer), 158
 Web pages, 147
privacy, 18, 24, 29–37, 260–262
 adware, 263
 best practices checklist, 275–277
 biometrics, 272–275
 children, 271
 cookies. *See* cookies
 data snooping, 262–264
 evaluating/choosing ISPs, 65–66
 Freedom of Information Act (FOIA), 266

government surveillance, 264–267
 identity theft, 33–34
 Instant Messaging (IM), 200
 Internet fraud, 35–37
 keylogger programs, 263
 online profiling, 29–33
 sniffers, 263
 spyware, 263
 Web bugs, 263
 workplace, 115, 267–271
  computer monitoring programs, 269–271
  e-mail, 114–115
Privacy Foundation Web site, 31
 Workplace Surveillance Project, 268–271
privacy policies (Web sites), 33
Privacy Rights Clearinghouse Web site, 34
Prodigy, 69
programs. *See* software
ProtectKids.com, 38
protocols, 6–7
 e-mail, 79–80
proxy servers, 126
publishing Web sites, 377
 evaluating/choosing Web hosts, 379–381
 free Web hosting services, 381–382
 publishing from FrontPage, 388–389
 Web site positioning, 382–387
  home page HTML titles, 383–384
  keywords, 384–385
  links from/to other sites, 386
  submitting sites to search engines, 386–387
pull technology, 254
push technology, 254

Q-R

queries (search engines), 168
 keyword searches, 169–172
 natural language queries, 176
QuickTime, 240
quotation marks (" "), using in searches, 186–187
RAM (Random Access Memory), 158
rankings (search results), 169
real-time, 196
RealNetworks, 246
 Helix Producer Plus encoder, 252
 Helix Universal Server, 252–253
 RealOne Player, 235, 252
 Webcasting, 254
 Web site, 250
Realtor.com Web site, 190
receiving e-mail messages, 78–79, 99–100
refreshing Web pages, 134, 158
Remote Administration Trojans (RATs), 290
replying to e-mail messages, 100–101
results pages (search engines), 168–169
 keyword searches, 171, 185
 metasearch engines, 178
 natural language search engines, 176–177
 quotation mark (" ") searches, 186
 restricting hits using advanced search options, 189
reverse engineering, 295
revisiting Web sites, 136–140
Rich Text Format (RTF), 231–232
 e-mail, 95–96
RM (RealMedia) file extension, 231
Road Runner BSP (Broadband Service Provider), 60
robots, 169
root servers, 125
routers, 3, 9

RTF. *See* Rich Text Format

S

SafeMessage, 83
safety in chat rooms, 202
sandboxes, 291–292
satellite connections, 48, 58–59
saving. *See* downloading
SBC Internet Services, 69
scalability (Web sites), 313
scanning e-mail attachments, 99–100
Script worms, 294
scripts, 291–292
SDSL (Symmetric Digital Subscriber Line), 58
Search button (Internet Explorer), 158
search expressions, 168
SearchAbility Web site, 190
searches, 140–143
  AltaVista AV Enterprise Search software, 270–271
  Boolean logic operators, 183–186
  clip art, 360
  e-mail addresses (Outlook Express Address Book), 109–110
  finding words on Web pages, 146
  IP addresses (Whois), 125
  ISPs. *See* ISPs, evaluating/choosing
  metasearch engines, 142
  portals, 141
  quotation marks (" "), 186–187
  Search boxes (Web pages), 146
  search directories, 140–143
  search engines, 131, 140–143, 168
    advanced search features, 188–189
    AltaVista, 140, 185–188
    case-sensitivity, 189
    combination search engine/Web directories, 174–175
    Google, 131, 140, 168–172, 188–189
    HotBot, 170
    keyword searches, 168–172, 185
    link popularity, 386
    metasearch engines, 178
    natural language search engines, 175–177
    results pages, 168–169
    robots, 169
    specialized search sites, 190–192
    submitting sites to search engines, 386–387
    Web site keywords, 384–385
  search expressions, 168
  spiders, 140
  Web browser search features, 144–145
  Web directories, 172–175
  Web search sites, 141
  wildcard characters, 189
Secure Sockets Layer (SSL), 13
security, 18, 282–284. *See also* privacy
  ActiveX. *See* security, mobile code
  always on connections, 57
  back door programs, 290
  best practices
    checklist, 301–303
    e-commerce, 300–301
    viruses/malicious code protection, 296–297
  CERT (Computer Emergency Response Team), 283
  e-commerce best practices, 300–301
  e-mail (SafeMessage), 83
  evaluating/choosing ISPs, 65–66

  firewalls. *See* firewalls
  Instant Messaging (IM), 200
  Internet-based attacks
    attacks on home computers, 289–291
    critical infrastructure attacks/cyberterrorism, 289
    Denial of Service (DoS) attacks, 288–289
    financial losses due to security breaches, 285
    recent increase of security incidents, 286–287
    vulnerabilities, 285
  Java. *See* security, mobile code
  JavaScript. *See* security, mobile code
  mobile code, 291–293
    disabling in Internet Explorer, 292–293
    types of mobile code, 291–292
  passwords, 298–300
  viruses. *See* viruses
  vulnerabilities, 285
  Web browsers
    Internet Explorer 6.0 patches, 127
    Java/ActiveX controls, 160–161
self-extracting archives, 220
self-propagating malicious code, 286
Semantic Web, 143
sending e-mail, 78–79, 97
  attachments, 98–99
  encrypting messages, 111
  replies/forwarded messages, 100–101
  requesting return receipts, 107
server extensions (FrontPage), 381
servers, 4
  FTP servers, 123, 213, 220–221
  mail servers, 123
  name servers, 125
  root servers, 125
  versus clients, 123
  Web servers, 122–126
sessions (Web browsers), 153–154
set-top boxes, 50
shareware, 215
Shockwave, 239
shopping, 10–11
shortcuts
  desktop shortcuts, Web site links, 139
  keyboard shortcuts
    displaying recently visited Web sites, 134
    navigating Web pages, 145
SMTP (Simple Mail Transfer Protocol), 79–80
sniffers, 263
social engineering, 27
software
  computer monitoring software, 263, 269–271
  connecting to Internet, 52–53
  downloading. *See* downloading, software
  e-mail clients. *See* e-mail, clients
  FrontPage. *See* FrontPage
  Notepad, 232
  open source programs, 53
  Windows Media Player, 235
  WinZip, 237
spam, 13, 77
  avoiding, 113–114
  Usenet, 114
Spamex disposable e-mail address service, 114
special-purpose computers, 50
speed of connection
  choosing ISPs, 64–65

  comparison of types, 47–49, 59
  data transfer rates, 53–55
speeding up Web site access, 153–158
  blocking ads, 156–157
  customizing cache settings, 152, 161–163
  disabling graphics/multimedia, 152, 155–156
  increasing Random Access Memory (RAM), 158
  opening multiple browser windows, 153–154
  opening multiple browsers, 154–155
  peak times/versus off-times, 157–158
spelling check (e-mail messages), 90
spiders, 140
sponsored links (search results), 169
spoofing, 290
spyware, 30–31, 263
SSL (Secure Sockets Layer), 13
stalkers, 39–41
Standard toolbar, Web browsers, 158–159
standards (e-mail), 79–80
start pages, Web browsers, 159–160
static HTML, 134
static media, 248
stationery (e-mail), 95–96
Stay Safe Online Web site, 289
stock trading, 12–13
Stop button (Internet Explorer), 158
streaming media, 248–249
  buffers, 248
  codecs/compression schemes, 249–251
  media encoders, 252
  media players, 251–252
  stadardization, 252–253
  versus static (downloadable) media, 248–249
structure of Internet, 8–10
submitting Web sites to search engines, 386–387
surface Web, 190
surfing the Web, 121, 132–136
  Back/Forward buttons, 135–136
  customizing cache settings, 152, 161–163
  error messages, 133–134
  hyperlinks, 136
  multiple browser windows, 151
  navigating Web pages, 145
  refreshing Web pages, 134
  revisiting Web sites, 136–140
  searching Web sites. *See* searches
  speed. *See* speeding up Web site access
  typing into browser Address bars, 132–135
SurfWatch filtering software, 40
SWA (Shockwave) file extension, 232
switches, 9
switching, 311
Symantec/Norton (anti-virus), 27. *See also* anti-virus software companies
  security check, 284
symmetric data transfer, 54–55
Symmetric Digital Subscriber Line (SDSL), 58

T

Tagged Image File Format. *See* TIF/TIFF files
tags (HTML), 319, 324–327
  meta tags, 385
TCP (Transmission Control Protocol), 7
TCP/IP (Transmission Control Protocol/Internet Protocol), 7
technical compression, 249

technical support, ISPs, 66
telecommuting, 15
telephone access
   cell phones, 51–52
   dial-up access, 55–56
   ISDN, 56–57
   T1/T3 connections, 57
Temporary Internet Files (Internet Explorer), 161–163
text
   downloading
      copying from Web pages, 217
      documents, 214
   file formats, 232
themes (FrontPage Webs), 346–347
threads (newsgroups), 202
thumbnails, 358
   creating, 366–368
   photo galleries (FrontPage), 368–373
TIF/TIFF (Tagged Image File Format) files, 232, 234
top-level domain names, 124
Topica mailing lists, 205
Transmission Control Protocol (TCP), 7
Transmission Control Protocol/Internet Protocol (TCP/IP), 7
transport mediums, 54
TransUnion credit bureau, 34
travel, effects of Internet, 17
trialware, 215
Trillian IM client, 199
Trojan horses, 26. *See also* viruses
TV access
   cable modems, 57
   WebTV, 50
TXT file format, 232

U

U.are.U Pro fingerprint scanner, 273
Uniform Resource Locators. *See* URLs; Web site URLs
United Online, 69
Universal Serial Bus (USB), 255
universal view software, 270
university networks, 70–71
unmoderated groups, 204
updates/upgrades (software), downloading, 127, 215
uploading, 54
upstream, 54
URLs, 6, 123–125. *See also* Web site URLs
   domain names, 123–125
   FTP sites, 221
   typing into browser Address bars, 132–135
usability (Web sites), 311–312
USB (Universal Serial Bus), 255
Usenet newsgroups, 42, 197, 203–205
   spam, 114

V

VBA (Visual Basic for Applications), 232
   macro viruses, 27
VBScript (Visual Basic Scripting Edition), 291
   disabling in Internet Explorer, 293
video conferencing, 206–207
virus definitions, 295
viruses, 23–29
   anti-virus software. *See* anti-virus software
   blended threats, 294
   Computer Resource Security Center, 283
   downloaded files, 219

   downloading updated virus definitions, 213
   e-mail, 110–113
   hoaxes, 29, 111–112
   macro viruses, 27
   methods of spread, 26–27
   payloads/payload triggers, 26
   protection against, 27–28, 293–297
   scanning, 99–100, 220, 223
   social engineering, 27
   symptoms of infection, 28
Visual Basic for Applications. *See* VBA
Visual Basic Scripting Edition. *See* VBScript
voiceovers, 245
VoiceXML, 233

W

W3C (World Wide Web Consortium), 122, 233
   Amaya Web browser, 127
wallpaper, downloading, 217
WAV (waveform) file format, 232, 235
Web (World Wide Web, the Web), 5, 121. *See also* World Wide Web
Web addresses, 6
Web browsers, 6, 52–53, 126–127
   ActiveX controls, 160–161
   Amaya, 127
   Back/Forward buttons, 135–136
   caches, 152, 161–163
   disabling cookies, 32–33
   disabling graphics/multimedia, 152, 155–156
   e-mailing Web pages, 147
   Favorites lists, 137–139
   finding words on Web pages, 146
   GET command, 125
   Graphical User Interfaces (GUIs), 120
   History lists, 137
   interaction with Web servers, 125–126
   Internet Explorer. *See* Internet Explorer
   Java, 160–161
   Links bar, 139–140
   Mozilla, 127
   multiple browsers/browser windows, 151–155
   navigating Web pages, 145
   NCSA Mosaic, 121
   Netscape Navigator, 127
   Opera, 127, 155
   printing Web pages, 147
   refreshing Web pages, 134
   saving Web page data, 146
   search features, 144–145
   setting font size, 160
   setting the home/start page, 159–160
   Standard toolbar, 158–159
   Status Bar, 136
   typing URLs into Address bars, 132–135
Web bugs, 31, 263
Web cams, 246–247, 254–256
   video conferencing, 207
Web directories, 172–175
Web hosts, 319, 377
   evaluating/choosing, 379–381
   free Web creation software, 322–324
   free Web hosting services, 381–382
Web page developers, 310
Web page editors, 319–322. *See also* FrontPage
Web pages, 132. *See* creating Web sites
   downloading files from Web pages, 219–220

   e-mailing pages, 147, 218
   file formats, 233
   finding words on Web pages, 146
   graphics, 357–358
      inserting clip art, 359–362
      saving embedded files, 362–363
   HTML code, 233
   offline browsing, 132, 146–147
   printing, 147
   saving entire Web pages, 218
   saving Web page data, 146
   Search boxes, 146
   search engine optimization/positioning, 169
   viewing HTML source code, 325
Web presence, 377
Web Presence Providers (WPP), 377. *See also* Web hosts
Web servers, 122–126
   domain names, 123–125
   interaction with Web browsers, 125–126
   ports, 123
   proxy servers, 126
Web site URLs
   AddMe Web submission service, 387
   AddPro Web submission service, 387
   Adobe, 237–238
      GoLive Web creation tool, 321
   AIM (AOL Instant Messenger), 198
   AltaVista search engine, 140
   Amaya, 127
   America Online (AOL), 68
   American Management Association workplace surveillance survey, 271
   Anonymizer, 146
   AOLTV, 60
   Apple QuickTime, 240
   Ask Jeeves, 176
   AT&T WorldNet, 68
   BellSouth (ISP), 69
   Better Business Bureau, 11
   Bluetooth, 52
   BrightPlanet, 190
   CareerBuilder, 15
   Carnivore (FBI), 18
   Center for Democracy and Technology, 18
   CERT (Computer Emergency Response Team), 283
   Cinepak, 250
   CNET, 190
      Download.com, 211
   codec sites, 250
   Computer Resource Security Center, 283
   Computer Security Institute, 285
   Cookie Central, 33
   Cookie Crusher, 277
   CUseeMe, 207
   CyberAngels, 40
   cybercrime.gov, 284
   CyberPatrol filtering software, 40
   CyberSitter filtering software, 40
   digitalpersona.com, 273
   Discovery Channel, 239
   DivX, 250
   Dogpile, 142
   Earthlink, 68
   Electronic Frontier Foundation, 261
   Electronic Privacy Information Center (EPIC), 18
   Equifax credit bureau, 34
   Excite, 148
   Experian credit bureau, 34
   Family Internet Safety Pact, 39

Federal Trade Commission, 34
Fight Spam on the Internet, 113
file format sites, 231
FindLaw, 190
FreeFoto.com, 214
FTPFind, 221
ftpplanet.com, 224
Geocities Web hosting service, 382
GetNetiquette, 206
Google
  newsgroups, 42
  search engine, 140
Government Computer News, 279
Handspring (PDAs), 51
Helix Community, 252
Hoaxbusters, 112
HotBot, 148
HotJobs, 192
Hotmail, 84
HTML tag listings, 324
ICQ, 198
Identity Theft Resource Center, 34
Identix, 274
INFOMINE, 192
InfoSpace, 178
Internet Fraud Complaint Center (IFCC), 35
InterNIC, 125
Ipswitch, 221
ISPWorld, 65
iVillage, 201
Jumbo!, 212
Junkbuster ad-blocking program, 29
Jupiter Media Metrix, 60
Kaspersky Labs (anti-virus), 27
KidsPrivacy, 271
L-Soft mailing lists, 206
Lavasoft (Ad-Aware utility), 30
LawGuru, 190
Lexus Radical Contest, 239
Ligo Indeo, 251
LinuxSecurity, 279
List-Etiquette.com, 206
Macromedia, 239
Mail Abuse Prevention System, 113
Mail.com, 84
Mail2Web, 85
Mamma, 178
McAfee (anti-virus), 27
Medsite, 190
MetaCrawler, 142, 178
Metropolitan Area Exchanges, 7
Microsoft
  Design Gallery Live, 214
  hosting services that support FrontPage, 381
Microsoft Network (MSN), 68
Monster.com, 15
Mozilla, 53, 127
MP3.com, 235
MPEG-4, 251
MSN TV, 60
National Center for Missing and Exploited Children, 40
National Infrastructure Protection Center (NIPC), 289
Netfirms free Web hosting service, 382
Netscape, 127
OneLook Dictionaries, 190
Online Privacy Alliance, 261
Opera Web browser, 155

Palm (PDAs), 51
PeopleSearch, 191
Peterson's, 191
Pew Internet Project, 265
Privacy Foundation, 31
  Workplace Surveillance Project, 268
Privacy Rights Clearinghouse, 34
Prodigy, 69
ProtectKids.com, 38
QuickTime, 240
Realtor.com, 190
Road Runner, 60
SafeMessage, 83
SearchAbility, 190
Shockwave Player downloads page, 239
Sorenson Media, 250
Spamex, 114
Stay Safe Online, 289
StopCarnivore, 266
SurfWatch filtering software, 40
Sydney Opera House, 240
Symantec/Norton (anti-virus), 27
The List, 63
Topica mailing lists, 205
TransUnion credit bureau, 34
Trillian IM client, 199
United Online (ISP), 69
Usable Web, 312
Usenet, 42
Viisage, 274
W3C (World Wide Web Consortium), 122
  Amaya Web browser, 127
Web Host Directory, 377–378
WebCrawler, 178
Websense, 117, 270
WinZip, 237
World Wide Web Consortium. See W3C
Worldroom Web-based mail service, 85
Yahoo!
  Geocities Web hosting service, 382
  Groups, 42
  Mail, 84
  Messenger, 198
  PeopleSearch, 191
  Yahooligans, 271
  ZDNet, 192
  ZoneAlarm, 39
Web sites, 132. See also Web site URLs
  banner ads, 11
  cookies. See cookies
  copying Web site text/graphics, 216–217
  copyright/intellectual property infringements, 38–39
  designing. See designing Web sites
  frames, 145
  fraud, 37
  harmful sites, 37–38
  hierarchy, 313
  hit counters, 381
  log files, 30
  most popular commerce sites, 10–11
  online fraud, 35–36
  pop-up advertisements, 31
  positioning. See publishing Web sites, Web site positioning
  privacy policies, 33
  publishing to the Web. See publishing Web sites
Web-based mail services, 75, 83–85

Webcasting, 254
WebCrawler search engine, 178
Webmasters, 310
Webs (FrontPage). See FrontPage, Webs
Websense monitoring software, 117, 270
WebTV, 50
What You See Is What You Get (WYSIWYG) Web page editors, 321
whiteboards (video conferencing), 207
Whois command, 125
wildcard characters, using in searches, 189
Windows Media Audio (WMA), 232, 235
Windows Media Encoder, 252
Windows Media Player, 235, 252
WinZip, 220, 237
wireless connections, 48, 59
  wireless devices, 51–52
WMA. See Windows Media Audio
workplace privacy
  e-mail, 114–115
  workplace monitoring/surveillance, 115, 267–271
World Wide Web (Web, WWW), 5–6
  advertisements. See advertising
  deep Web, 190
  downloading, 216–220
  e-mailing Web pages, 147
  mirror sites, 126
  navigating Web pages, 145
  navigating Web sites, 132–136
  origins of the Web, 121–122
  printing Web pages, 147
  privacy. See privacy
  revisiting Web sites, 136–140
  saving Web page data, 146
  searches. See searches
  surface Web, 190
  surfing. See surfing the Web
  versus the Internet, 120–121
  Web pages versus Web sites, 132
World Wide Web Consortium (W3C), 122, 233
  Amaya Web browser, 127
Worldroom Web-based e-mail service, 85
worms, 26, 294. See also viruses
WPP (Web Presence Providers), 377. See also Web hosts
WS_FTP client program, 213, 221–224
WWW. See World Wide Web
WYSIWYG (What You See Is What You Get) Web page editors, 321

X-Y-Z

XHTML (Extensible Hypertext Markup Language), 233
XML (Extensible Markup Language), 6, 123, 233
Yahoo!
  Geocities Web hosting service, 382
  Groups, 42, 205–206
  Mail, 75, 84
  Messenger, 198–199
  PeopleSearch page, 191
  SBC Yahoo! Dial, 69
  search directory, 141
  Web directory, 173–175
  Yahooligans, 271
ZDNet Web site, 192
ZIP files, 219, 232, 237
zombies, 290
ZoneAlarm firewall program, 39, 161, 298

GLOSSARY

Acceptable Use Policy (AUP) A policy set by an organization that outlines how Internet access can be used.

active content Interactive Web sites, such as those that include animations.

active window The window for the selected program and appears on top of the rest of the open windows.

ActiveX A proprietary Microsoft technology that lets Web developers build a wide variety of applications and content into a Web page.

ActiveX controls The actual components on Web pages that run ActiveX applications.

Address bar In a browser such as Internet Explorer, this is the area directly below the Standard Buttons toolbar in which you can enter the URL for the Web site you want to view.

Address Book A list of contact information, such as names and e-mail addresses, in a mail client program such as Outlook.

Adobe Acrobat Reader A program that allows you to view a variety of documents. Adobe Acrobat Reader uses Portable Document Format (PDF) files.

adware Software that is designed to display banner or pop-up ads on Web sites. Some adware also tracks your online activities and relays this information to advertisers so that they can channel advertisements that you would be most likely to view.

always on connection An Internet connection, such as cable modem, satellite, or digital subscriber line, that you don't have to use dial-up to access. The connection to the Internet is active anytime your computer is on.

AND A search operator used to make sure that *all* the keywords joined by the AND are present on a page.

Animated GIF A series of GIF files that are shown in rapid succession to give the illusion of movement.

Anonymous FTP server An FTP server that is set up to distribute files or programs to the general public. The identification (id) used for logging on is the word "anonymous," and the password is your e-mail address.

applets (Java applets) Mini-applications written in the Java language that you can embed in an HTML document.

archive A group of files that you can extract and decompress.

ARPANET The network developed in the late 1960s and early 1970s by the Advanced Research Projects Agency (ARPA) branch of the Department of Defense.

asymmetric A technology that has a different data transfer rate for the upstream and downstream. For example, although DSL can pull data down from the Internet at a rate of 1.5Mbps; it uploads data at only approximately 128Kbps.

Asymmetric Digital Subscriber Line (ADSL) A high-speed connection to the Internet using digital subscriber lines. ADSL has different upstream and downstream data transfer rates.

attachment A file that is attached to and travels electronically with an e-mail message.

attack tools The code and techniques that cyber-criminals use to exploit security holes via the Internet.

authoring The process of developing a Web site.

Auto Thumbnail A feature in FrontPage and other Web authoring programs that you can use to convert a full-sized picture into a smaller version that is hyperlinked to the original file.

AutoComplete feature A feature in Internet Explorer that you can use to expedite entering URLs. You use the feature by typing the URL in the Address bar. Internet Explorer displays all the recently visited Web sites that match your entry on a pull-down list. From the list, click the URL that you want.

back door (Remote Administration Trojan) A security hole deliberately left on a system so that an intruder can gain control of the victim's computer.

backbone The internal infrastructure that supports the entire Internet system, including the cabling and routers.

bandwidth The transmission capacity of a communications line—the data transfer rate. Bandwidth is measured in how many bits per second (bps) can travel over the line.

banner ads Advertisements that display across the width of a displayed Web page.

best practices Optimal strategies and tactics that professionals agree work well in a particular situation.

biometrics The technology that computers can use to identify people based on unchangeable biological information. Although biometrics can be effectively used for security, it can also infringe on personal privacy when misused.

black list A list maintained by anti-spam organizations of persons who are abusing e-mail.

blended threats Hybrids, or combinations, of two types of malicious code that can include characteristics of each. Because they use multiple methods to spread and exploit Internet vulnerabilities, they can spread very rapidly and cause harm in a variety of ways.

Bluetooth A technology that uses short-range radio links between PDAs, cell phones, and other wireless devices. This technology is developed, promoted, and employed by a number of manufacturers.

Boolean logic The use of search operators such as AND, NOT, OR, and NEAR in conjunction with keywords or terms.

broadband A network that is capable of high-speed transmission of data. Alternatively, broadband can refer to the type of technology used to transfer the data, such as Digital Subscriber Line (DSL).

Broadband Service Provider (BSP) Companies that provide Internet access via a broadband service, such as DSL, satellite, or cable modem.

browser (Web browser) A client program that enables people to view hypertext documents and navigate between them on the World Wide Web. Microsoft's Internet Explorer and Netscape are two popular browsers.

browsing A process (also called *surfing*) of clicking hyperlinks to wander from page to page on the World Wide Web.

buffer An area of memory used for temporarily holding data that's in transit from one device to another. The use of a buffer keeps one device or system from slowing down another, especially if the devices operate at different speeds.

buffer overflow A security problem that results when the buffer (an area of memory used for storing messages) is flooded with more characters than it can handle.

Bulletin Board System (BBS) A computerized version of the cork bulletin boards that you might see in a public place such as a grocery store. Internet BBSs are similar to newsgroups in that they focus on a particular subject, accept postings, and use threads to keep the main messages and follow ups together.

cable modem A technology that uses a cable TV connection rather than a phone line to connect to the Internet.

cache The storage place on your hard drive and memory where your browser temporarily stores Web pages you've recently visited so that they can be reloaded quickly.

caption A label for a photo.

Carnivore Diagnostic Tool (Carnivore) A software surveillance system developed by the FBI that allows government agents to intercept and collect data transmitted over the Internet or another network.

CD burner A drive that is capable of copying ("burning") data or music to a CD capable of reading and writing (CD-RW).

cell Intersection of a column and row in a table.

CERN European Laboratory for Nuclear Research (in Switzerland) where the World Wide Web was developed so that scientists could communicate with each other more efficiently.

CERT (Computer Emergency Response Team) Carnegie Mellon University's Software Engineering Institute, which devotes itself to Internet security issues and maintains a Web site at *www.cert.org*.

chat An interactive, real-time, online discussion on a particular topic, usually with a group. Chat is similar to instant messaging in that it provides real-time communication; it differs in that chat usually involves conversing with a group of people.

chat room A specialized Web site or other virtual space that allows you to broadcast your messages to everyone who is also accessing the same location at that time.

child page In reference to a Web's navigation structure, this is a page that is connected to a higher-level parent page. For example, a customer service page might be the child page for a company's home page.

Children's Online Privacy Protection Act (COPPA) A law that specifies that Web sites targeting children under 13 years old must follow certain guidelines. For example, these sites must post a privacy policy, obtain parental consent before collecting personal information about kids, and allow parents to review the information they collect.

clickstream data The information gathered by tracking your exact movements on the Internet, such as which Web sites you access, the advertisements you click, and which newsgroups you visit.

client A user machine that connects to the server and receives information from it.

client-server architecture A network setup with a server machine and one or more client machines. One computer program (the client) requests data from another program (the server); the server responds by sending the information to the client.

clip art Non-copyrighted electronic artwork or images that you can use in a variety of computer programs. In contrast with realistic photographic pictures, clip art images are generally line drawings created by an artist.

Code Red A self-propagating worm that multiplied at such a rapid rate in 2001 that it spread globally in less than 18 hours.

codec An acronym for COder/DECoder, this is a technology that decreases the size of media data so that it can be more readily transmitted online.

co-located server A Web hosting option in which the business or organization owns the Web server hardware, but is located and maintained at the host's facility.

compression scheme Compressing data by removing non-essential data from the digital files, such as colors a human eye can't see or sounds the human ear can't hear.

computer network Computers that are linked to each other so that they can share information and resources.

computer-monitoring software Software that can track your actions, including your Web browsing history, your e-mail messages, and your keystrokes.

conceptual query A search in which the search engine returns only Web pages that are relevant to the topic, even if the words don't precisely match your keywords.

contact Identifying information for a person, such as the name, e-mail address, and phone number. E-mail client programs usually organize contacts in an electronic Address Book.

Content Scrambling System (CSS) A method of encrypting the content on a CD so that it can't be copied.

cookie A text file that a Web server places on the visitor's hard drive. This file is a unique identifier (such as a serial number) that the server can use to retrieve a user's records from their database. When the user accesses the site again, the server reads the cookie's contents to gather information about the person.

cracker A *cr*iminal h*acker* who writes malicious programs or breaks into a computer system without authorization. Usually, crackers do this with the intent of damaging a system or network or crashing an entire Web site.

critical infrastructures The underlying foundation for systems in the United States, such as banking, energy, telecommunications, transportation, or public utilities.

cross-scripting A process in which scripts (mini-programs) can be included as malicious code in a hyperlink on a Web page; when the hyperlink is clicked, the malicious code can be executed automatically by your browser.

cybercrime Criminal activity that is facilitated through use of the Internet. Cybercrime might involve terrorist activities, fraud schemes, copyright infringements, exploitation of children, spreading of malicious code, stealing of identities, or online stalking.

cyberslacking The practice by an employee of using the Internet to check personal e-mail, look at the news or weather, play games, download MP3s, or conduct other non-work related activities.

cybersurveillance Electronic monitoring by others, such as by an employer.

cyberterrorism An attack against the Internet's infrastructure.

data snoops People who try to use technology to gain access to personal information so that they can use it for their own gain. For example, an identity thief would snoop to learn your credit card and bank account numbers.

DeCSS A computer program capable of descrambling content that has been encrypted with CSS. (See also *Content Scrambling System*).

dedicated server A Web server that is used by only one organization. The host owns, backs up, and maintains the server as well as providing security.

deep Web The large portion of the Web that consists of dynamic Web pages and databases. This vast amount of content is inaccessible to conventional search engines.

demodulate To convert an analog signal to digital.

Denial of Service (DoS) An attack in which a resource on the Internet, such as a server or a Web site, experiences impaired function because the attackers launch a coordinated attack that overwhelms the target with so many bogus requests that the system can't handle them all. The most common type of DoS attack has the effect of preventing Internet users from accessing the target Web site.

dial-up Using existing telephone lines to dial into the Internet via an Internet Service Provider's network.

digest A compilation of all the daily messages for a distributed mailing list that is placed in one e-mail message.

Digital Audio Tape (DAT) A type of magnetic tape used to store digital video. The cartridge used for DAT is small—only a little larger than a credit card.

digital media Digitized audio and video.

Digital Subscriber Line (DSL) A technology that provides very fast Internet access and data transfer rates. DSL has several variations, with Asymmetric Digital Subscriber Line (ASDL) being the most well-known in the United States. Despite the fact that ADSL is only one type of DSL, the terms *ADSL* and *DSL* are used more or less interchangeably.

directory service An Internet-based search tool that helps you locate people based on various criteria.

Distributed Denial of Service (DDoS) A Denial of Service attack in which the attack originates from a variety of locations.

distribution list A group to whom you regularly send the same e-mail message.

domain name The address or Uniform Resource Locator for a Web site; the text name that corresponds to the numeric IP address.

Domain Name System (DNS) A huge database that corresponds numeric IP addresses with the text (domain) name. The DNS is maintained so that duplicate domain names aren't used on the Internet.

downloadable media files Media files that must be completely downloaded from the Internet before you can play them.

downloading The process of transferring data from the Internet to your computer.

downstream The direction of data transfers when the information is sent from the Internet (such as a Web server) to your computer.

drilling down Working your way through a directory structure by clicking the links to display a subtopic; clicking the subtopic to display *its* subtopics, and so on.

dynamic content Web information that changes frequently, such as each time a user accesses the site or in response to user input.

dynamic HTML (DHTML) Web pages that include both static HTML programming code and other types of code that can run programs (such as Java applets).

Echelon A government-maintained electronic surveillance system designed to monitor international communications.

e-commerce (electronic commerce) Conducting business, including financial transactions, over the Internet. E-commerce can include activities such as advertising goods, accepting credit cards, or trading stock online.

e-mail (electronic mail) The transmission of messages electronically over a network.

Employee Internet Management (EIM) An industry that develops software and strategies for monitoring employees.

encoder A special software tool that breaks a media file into smaller readable packets that can be streamed to a player.

encryption The process of converting a message into an encrypted (scrambled) form.

Ethernet A standard, or protocol, used for connecting computers on a network. The most common type of Ethernet is called 10BaseT.

executable file A file with an extension of EXE or VBS that performs an action or runs a program when opened.

Extensible HyperText Markup Language (XHTML) A markup language that can be used to prepare Web documents.

Extensible Markup Language (XML) The markup language promoted by W3C as a universal standard for developing Web documents.

facial recognition technology A biometric technology that uses hardware and software to scan a crowd and then converts specific characteristics of each face into digital form. It then crosschecks this information against the profiles of known terrorists and other criminals.

Favorites list A list of Web sites that you specifically intend to revisit; the Favorites list is stored in your browser.

fiber optics The transmission of data as pulses of light through fine, transparent, flexible strands that are usually comprised of glass or plastic.

file extension Represented by the last three (or four) characters of a file's name, the extension represents the data type used by the file and the program used to develop it.

file format The encoding used to store a file's information. Files created by different programs use different file formats.

File Transfer Protocol (FTP) The set of standards and rules used on the Internet to send and receive files. To transfer files using FTP, you need an FTP client and FTP server.

firewall A piece of hardware or software that protects your computer from intruders.

flaming Usenet or e-mail messages that include abusive, threatening, or inappropriate language.

flat rate The practice of charging a set rate per month for Internet access.

forum An online community in which Internet users can post and read messages on a particular topic.

frames A method of coding a Web page to organize the information into two (or more) independent sections. Technically, using frames is like loading multiple Web pages within the same browser screen.

Freedom of Information Act (FOIA) A ruling by the Federal Government that specifies what information the government must reveal to the public.

freeware Software that is available at no cost.

FrontPage Server Extensions In reference to FrontPage, this is a group of small applications that run on a Web server.

FTP client Software that resides on your local computer and can handle the FTP process. WS_FTP is a well-known FTP client.

FTP server A type of server that can transfer files via FTP.

GET command A command that uses FTP to copy files from a remote computer to your local system.

gigaPoP A high-speed interconnection point on the Internet's backbone, comprised of switching and routing intersections.

Gopher An application developed at the University of Minnesota (and named after its mascot), which helped to organize files on the Internet. Gopher is a subject-based, menu-oriented guide that helps you find and retrieve Internet files.

Graphical User Interface (GUI) An interface that allows users to interact with a program or data using graphical elements such as icons or hyperlinks. Most people find that GUIs are more intuitive to use than pure text-based systems.

graphics file A file that includes only images, such as paint program files, scanned images, photographs, clip art, or other electronic art. Graphics files are generally edited by using drawing- or photography-editing programs.

Graphics Interchange Format (GIF) A file format useful for Web applications because it supports a limited number of colors (256) and can be displayed on a variety of computer platforms. The limited number of colors reduces file size, which results in Web pages being displayed more rapidly.

hackers Programming experts who share their skills and information with others. Most hackers maintain that they don't actually cause harm to computer systems. (See also *cracker*.)

header section A text box near the top of an e-mail message window that you can use to enter the recipient's e-mail address and subject.

Helix DNA platform A set of technologies that can be used for developing, distributing, and playing digital media content. It consists of three parts: the Helix DNA client (to play digital media content), the Helix DNA encoder (to edit and encode the content), and the Helix DNA server (to distribute the content).

Helix Universal Server A server designed to distribute media content as part of the Helix DNA platform.

hierarchy A tree-like setup that begins with a single point, or root, that describes the most general characteristic of the topic. This topic is then divided into branches that contain increasingly more specific information.

high-speed access The same as broadband, this is a connection, such as DSL or satellite, that provides a fast data transfer rate between a computer and the Internet.

History list (History bar) A list that displays the most-recently-visited Web sites. You can sort the list various ways to find a site.

hit In reference to an Internet search, this is a Web page that matches the query.

hostile work environment A workplace in which the behavior of others has the effect of significantly interfering with a person's work by creating an intimidating or offensive workplace setting.

HTML tag A code that gives instructions for formatting or actions—instructions used in laying out a Web page and setting up links.

hub A common connection point for the devices on a network, such as the Internet.

Hyperlinks view A view in FrontPage that is used to illustrate the linked relationships of the pages in your Web.

hypertext links (hyperlinks) Text in an electronic document that includes special coding (usually in HTML) that links to another location, either within the document or in another document. You can click the hypertext link to follow the link and display the associated document. The World Wide Web is a hypertext system in which documents are interconnected via hyperlinks.

Hypertext Markup Language (HTML) A markup language that is used to create documents for use on the World Wide Web.

Hypertext Transfer Protocol (HTTP) The set of rules (protocol) that Web browsers and Web servers use to exchange data.

identity theft Criminals who obtain another person's personal or financial information so that the criminal can use it to impersonate the victim and/or access his or her finances.

information architecture Organizing and structuring Web data so that it's easy for users to find and Webmasters to maintain.

instant messaging (IM) A technology you can use to identify friends who are online and then exchange electronic messages with them in real time.

Integrated Services Digital Network (ISDN) A type of technology used to connect to the Internet to provide high-speed access. ISDN's technology allows one phone line to carry digital voice and data transmissions simultaneously. ISDN is faster than dial-up, but is no longer considered to be competitive with the newer technologies such as cable modem.

Internet A huge collection of computers all over the world that are connected to one another in various ways. The computers and networks use TCP/IP to communicate with each other. Through these connections, you can perform a variety of communication tasks, such as sending and receiving electronic mail, using FTP, using chat, accessing newsgroups, and viewing Web pages.

Internet fraud The practice by which criminals use Internet resources to deceive people into giving them money.

Internet Message Access Protocol (IMAP) A protocol used for storing and retrieving e-mail.

Internet Protocol (IP) address The unique number assigned to each Web site. IP addresses are set up as a series of four numbers, each separated by periods. For example, a typical IP address might appear something like 215.47.62.132. This number is converted by a Domain Name Server into the corresponding domain name.

Internet Relay Chat (IRC) A system for chatting that uses a certain set of rules and conventions as well as client/server software. IRC was one of the first ways that people could connect with other Internet users and exchange written notes in real time.

Internet Service Provider (ISP) The company that provides the computer system, software, and other support so that you can access the Internet.

Internet worm A type of worm that usually spreads via e-mail, but might also have the ability to self-activate and spread through security holes in operating systems and networks. Additionally, Internet worms can be spread via Internet Relay Chat (IRC).

intranet A computer network within an organization.

intruder (attacker) A person who breaches the security of a computer system to gain unauthorized access.

Java An object-oriented programming language used to create applications for the Web. Because Java is designed to run on any size or type of computer platform, it's heavily used to develop Web applications.

JavaScript A scripting language developed by Sun and Netscape. Although it shares many of the characteristics of Java, JavaScript was developed independently of Java. Web site authors can use JavaScript to develop interactive sites.

JPEG A graphic file format developed by the Joint Photographic Experts Group that you can use to compress graphics.

Kbps Measures the speed at which data is transferred in a communications system—1,000 bits per second equals one kilobit per second.

keyboard shortcut A combination of keystrokes that you can use to perform an action in a program.

keylogger program Specialized software that records each key pressed on a computer; then sends the information—such as credit card numbers, company reports, trade secrets, or financial data—back to the person who installed the program.

keyword Topical word that you use in a search.

keyword density The percentage of keywords to other text. The higher the percentage, the better your site's ranking.

keyword frequency A measure of the number of times that a keyword appears on a page.

keyword prominence Refers to placing your keywords as close to the start of a page or sentence as possible. This helps with site rankings because many search engines look first at the words at the top of a page.

keyword proximity Refers to placing important keywords close to each other.

link popularity Using links to raise your Web site's ranking.

Links bar In Internet Explorer, this is a bar that appears to the right of the Address bar. The Links bar is a good place to store your *most* frequently used sites because of its proximity to the Address bar.

list A series of numbered or bulleted items.

LISTSERV A distributed mailing list, in which the same e-mail message is sent to all the people who are on the list. Although LISTSERV refers to a specific, commercial product, many people use the term in a generic way to refer to any mailing list server.

log files Files kept on a Web server that track user activities or gather marketing information.

logging in The process of entering a user name and password to gain access to a network.

logical operators Operators that specify the logical relationship between elements; for example, AND, OR, NEAR, and NOT.

lurking The practice of reading messages in a distributed mailing list for a time before adding your own comments.

macro viruses Viruses that use the internal programming language of an application, such as Microsoft Word or Excel, to spread malicious code.

Macromedia Flash Player A browser plug-in that you can use to play movies and animations on Web sites.

Macromedia Shockwave Player A browser plug-in you can use to play Web multimedia games, product demonstrations, and interactive learning programs.

Magic Lantern A secretive FBI electronic surveillance project.

mail client (e-mail client) A specialized program that enables you to send, receive, and organize electronic messages on your system.

mail server A computer that initially receives your messages and stores them until they are retrieved by the mail client software on a computer.

mailing list manager (MLM) A specialized program that monitors the traffic and activity associated with a distributed mailing list.

malicious code (malware) Any computer program or code that's purposely developed to invade systems and cause problems. Viruses, worms, and Trojan horses are all common types of malware.

markup tags HTML formatting codes that control the structure and design of the text or graphical elements. The markup tags tell the browser how to format and display the text.

mathematical operators Symbols used to perform a calculation on a value.

Mbps The data transfer rate for a communications system, measured in megabits per second.

messaging client The type of software installed on a personal computer that is used to facilitate realtime communication (instant messaging) on the Internet. The most popular instant messaging clients currently on the market include AOL Instant Messenger (AIM), ICQ (for "I seek you"), MSN Messenger, and Yahoo! Messenger.

meta tag An HTML tag that appears in the <HEAD> part of the page. Meta tags usually supply information about a page (such as keywords) to spiders, but don't affect the page's appearance.

metasearch engines Large search engines that look through multiple databases simultaneously, eliminating duplicate listings as they do so. One of the best-known metasearch engines is MetaCrawler (*www.metacrawler.com*).

metered rate The practice of limiting the number of hours for Internet access and charging extra for hours that exceed the limit.

Metropolitan Area Exchange (MAE) A Network Access Point where Internet Service Providers can connect to each other; the various providers and networks transfer traffic to each other.

Military Network (MILNET) A network that was originally part of ARPANET, but split off as a military network in the mid-1980s.

mirror site An exact duplicate of an original Web site that is stored in another physical location. Mirror sites are used when Internet traffic is especially heavy to the main site.

mobile code Programming code that others write and embed in an HTML document. When your browser loads the Web page, mobile code is downloaded and executed by your browser. Mobile code gets its name from the fact that it can be passed from one system to another in this way. Java, JavaScript, and ActiveX are all examples of programming languages or technologies that can be used to create mobile code.

mode   The state of viewing the FrontPage Web in a specific pane. You can use three different panes (modes) in FrontPage: Normal, HTML, and Preview.

modem   Short for *mod*ulate and *dem*odulate, this is a device that provides an interface between the computer and communication lines, such as cable or phone lines.

moderated group   A newsgroup that has an administrator who reviews the messages before posting them.

Mosaic   The World Wide Web's first browser.

MOV   A file format used by Apple Computer's QuickTime. MOV files can be video clips or still images.

MP3   The current standard for storing and transmitting music in digital format over the Internet. Because MP3 files are smaller than WAV audio files, they are more easily shared across a network.

MPEG (Moving Picture Experts Group)   The file type associated with the Moving Picture Experts Group (MPEG) files; this is one of the current standards for storing and transmitting digital video across the Internet.

multimedia   The simultaneous use of multiple forms of media to communicate, such as combining text, audio, videos, graphics, and animations.

Multipurpose Internet Mail Extensions (MIME)   A protocol that is used to send graphic, sound, or other non-text files as e-mail attachments.

nag screens   Pop-up windows that remind you to register or buy a product, usually software.

name servers   These computers—sometimes also called *resolvers*—translate domain names into IP addresses. The name servers include the same information as the root domain servers and help to spread the workload by handling the bulk of the requests.

narrowband   A communications transmission channel, such as a dial-up line, with a data transfer less than 1.544Mbps. (See also *broadband*.)

natural language query   A search engine query that's written as a full sentence, using the same language that you might use if you were conversing with a person. Being able to use natural language queries makes the Internet more approachable for some people.

navigation bar (link bar)   A hyperlinked list of Web pages within a Web site. You should group these hyperlinks together and show them in the same location on each of your Web pages.

Navigation view   A view in FrontPage in which the structure of the Web is shown in the program's main working pane.

NEAR   A search operator used to tell the search engine to look for pages that include both terms within a specified proximity to each other (such as a certain number of words apart).

Netiquette   Using proper manners in online communications.

NetMeeting   Specialized video-conferencing software developed and marketed by Microsoft.

Network Access Point (NAP)   A major Internet connection point on the Internet where data is transferred from one Internet Service Provider to another.

network interface card (NIC)   An adapter card you install in a computer that enables you to connect the computer to a network cable.

NOT   A search operator used to eliminate pages that contain a certain word.

Notepad   The small text editor bundled with Windows.

NSFnet (National Science Foundation Network)   A high-speed network that was funded by the National Science Foundation and formed the original backbone of the academic portion of the Internet.

offline   The state when your computer is not connected to the Internet.

online presence (Web presence)   Having a Web site available on the Internet.

online profiling   Tracking a user's online actions and then compiling that information along with other data (such as e-mail addresses or information from online forms) into a demographic profile that can then be used to market goods or services to the person.

online shopping   Buying goods or services via the Internet.

open source   A program in which the programming code is shared at no cost with any software developer who wants it.

open standards   Specifications and protocols that are not proprietary and can be accessed by anyone.

OR   A search operator used to specify that *either* of the words can be present on a page.

packet A unit of data that has been prepared for sending over a network.

Page view A view in FrontPage that shows all the elements on the page and enables you to revise an individual page.

paid inclusion An option for site submission in which you hire a firm to present your site to the various search engines on your behalf.

parent page In reference to a Web's navigation structure, a parent page is one that has subpages at a lower level associated with it.

Parental controls Settings in a software program that enable administrators or parents to limit the number, type, or amount of time certain Web sites are viewed.

password A string of characters that you type so that you can access a network, online service, or Web site.

password cracker A specialized program designed to decipher passwords.

patch A minor upgrade to software that is usually created in response to a security hole or other problem in the program.

payload The damage caused by a virus or other malicious code.

payload trigger The condition or event that activates a virus, such as a date or the execution of a particular program.

pay-per-click model Paying a fee every time someone clicks your link on the search results page.

perceptual compression A compression technique that eliminates audio and visual signals that humans can't normally detect anyway.

Personal Digital Assistant (PDA) A small, handheld computer that can contain a number of programs, such as an organizer, a calendar, games, and so on.

photo gallery Small images of photographs that are laid out in a specific arrangement on the page. In some software programs, you can click a photo to enlarge the display.

Pictures toolbar A specialized toolbar in FrontPage that includes many buttons you can use to modify pictures and other graphics.

plain old telephone service (POTS) Using traditional phone lines to use dial-up connections to the Internet.

Plain Text Data that use the American Standard Code for Information Interchange (ASCII).

platform The type of operating system used for a computer system, such as Windows.

plug-in (add-in) A software program that is tightly integrated with a main program, such as a browser. Plug-ins extend the capabilities of the browser so that it can work with a wider variety of file types.

Point of Presence (PoP) The actual connection between an Internet Service Provider and the Internet's backbone. This term can also refer to the telephone number that gives people dial-up access to the Internet.

Portable Document Format (PDF) A universal format that preserves the fonts and colors of any document, no matter which platform or application was originally used to develop it. Adobe Acrobat and Adobe Acrobat Reader use the PDF format.

portal A Web site that includes content and links to other sites as well as search engine capabilities. Some portals such as Yahoo! include free e-mail, chat rooms, travel and financial information, shopping, and a directory.

Post Office Protocol, version 3 (POP3) The main protocol used for *storing* and *retrieving* messages from remote mail servers.

postings (articles) Messages submitted to a newsgroup.

precedence A component of an operator that indicates when it will be evaluated in a formula. Operators with high precedence (such as those used for multiplication and division) are completed before those with lower precedence (such as addition and subtraction). You can change the order of precedence for a search expression by placing parentheses around part of the expression; when you do, operations within the parentheses will be completed first.

privacy policy An organization's statement about its intended use of the personal information that you provide. It outlines information about what type of data it collects at the site about you and what it plans to do with that information.

protocol A set of guidelines or a standard that specifies how computers communicate with each other on a network, such as the Internet.

publishing The process of copying your Web files to a Web server.

pull technology The situation that exists when a client has to make a request before receiving data. Browsing the Web is an example of pull technology.

push technology The situation that exists when a server sends information to a client without the client requesting it. E-mail is an example of push technology; you receive messages when the sender "pushes" them to you.

query The process of typing the search expression in an engine and then "asking" the search engine to generate results.

QuickTime A technology that was originally developed by Apple Computer for Macintosh systems. This technology is used for storing sounds, graphics, and movie files.

ranking Positioning of a Web page on the results page.

real time In reference to computers, this term means that computer systems are able to process inputted information immediately; people can view and react to the data right away.

RealOne Player A technology that you can use to record, compress, transfer, decompress, and play sound (and video) files.

referrer Information sent to marketers when a user sends e-mail or browses the Web.

Reports view A view in FrontPage in which statistical reports related to the Web are shown.

results page A listing of Web pages that include the keyword(s).

retrovirus A computer virus that disarms legitimate antivirus programs. This keeps malicious code from being detected or removed.

reverse engineering A process in which a person takes something (such as malicious code) apart to figure out how it works and then reassembles it again.

Rich Text Originally designed by Microsoft, this universal way of formatting text allows for formatting, such as bold and italic.

robot See *spider*.

root servers Thirteen special computers that maintain the Domain Name System. Each of the computers includes duplicate information.

router A device that directs Internet traffic (packets). It does this by evaluating the possible paths to the destination and then finding the most efficient route based on traffic flow.

sandbox A protected area in computer memory where downloaded code can "play" without causing damage to the computer. Operating in a sandbox prevents the code from executing in the system at large because it doesn't have access to the entire computer.

satellite A type of technology you can use to access the Internet.

scalability The capability to easily adjust to changing conditions by modifying the size or configuration. For example, if you're working for a company that plans to introduce new products in the near future, it's good to structure the Web site to account for the expansion.

Script worms Worms that are created and executed using a scripting language such as VBScript.

scripts Mini-programs that can be embedded in HTML Web documents to add animations or interactivity.

search directory An organized collection of Web sites categorized by subject. These directories are usually arranged in a hierarchical structure.

search engine Software that looks for data based on some criteria. It usually does so by searching through an indexed database of Web sites. Google is a popular search engine.

search engine optimization (search engine positioning) Strategizing Web pages so that they appear near the top of a search engine's rankings.

search expression The keywords or question used to locate Web sites using a search engine.

Secure Sockets Layer (SSL) A technology used by many e-commerce Web sites that encrypts data over the Internet. SSL and related technologies are critical for conducting secure e-commerce.

security vulnerability (hole/breach) A deficiency in the hardware or software of your system that allows others to view, steal, or compromise the integrity of your data.

self-extracting archive A compressed file that includes program files. You can double-click the file to start an automated installation of the program or extract the zipped files.

self-propagating Malicious code that can relaunch itself, causing it to spread rapidly throughout the Internet.

server A machine (or software) that provides services, such as distributing e-mail or Web pages, to a client.

session Each time you open and then close a browser window.

set-top box The generic name for the special Internet appliance popularized by WebTV. Set-top boxes work with your television to help you access the Internet by using the device with a television screen.

shareware Software that is copyrighted and distributed on a free-will donation basis. To receive full support and documentation, users are typically required to pay a small fee.

shortcut menu A context-sensitive menu that shows commands appropriate for the object or text you're working with.

Simple Mail Transfer Protocol (SMTP) The protocol that is responsible for *sending* e-mail messages.

sniffer A software or hardware tool that monitors data packets on a network.

social engineering Using deception to trick a user into opening an e-mail message or revealing a password.

spam E-mail sent to a large number of people without their consent or approval; also known as *electronic junk mail*.

spiders These automated programs—also called crawlers, robots, or simply bots—collect information about Web sites around-the-clock. They search the text and coding of Web sites, evaluate the sites, and then add them to the search engine's indexed database.

sponsored links Companies that pay to have their Web sites positioned at the top of a search engine's list.

spoofing Using deception to make it appear that a message is from a different source from the one that actually sent it. Spoofing is often done so that a person is more likely to open an attachment (which could contain a Trojan horse) or reveal confidential information.

spyware A program that is deliberately planted on your computer to capture and reveal data to someone outside of your system. Spyware can track a variety of activities, such as recording keystrokes, reading e-mail, recording which Web sites a user has visited, or revealing credit card numbers.

start page (home page) The Web site that is displayed whenever you start a browser session.

static HTML Web pages that include exactly the same information each time you access them; the data returned by the source code for the page doesn't change.

static media Media that must be completely downloaded before you can play or work with it.

stationery A background pattern that you can add to your e-mail messages.

streaming media A technique used to transfer media, especially audio and video, over a network in a way that the receiving computer can process it continually. It downloads the media to your computer in a continuous flow. As soon as the first data arrives on your system, the application responsible for handling it can begin to use it without having to wait for the entire file to be downloaded.

submitting Making companies aware that your site is up and running. You can do this by using a variety of methods. Most involve manually telling the search engines that your site is live; some use software to automate the process.

surface Web Web pages that are easily accessible by conventional search engines. Many, though not all, dynamic Web pages are inaccessible on the surface Web.

switch A network device that closes a port so that data is sent in an effective or secure manner to its next destination.

switching Changing from one supplier or vendor to another.

symmetric Having the same upstream and downstream data transfer rates. (See also *asymmetric*.)

Symmetric Digital Subscriber Line (SDSL) A digital subscriber line in which upstream and downstream rates are the same.

table A grid with columns and rows that you can use to organize your information.

Tagged Image File Format (TIFF) A high-quality graphics file format. It can be used universally on different types of computers and platforms.

technical compression A compression technique that can be used to eliminate unnecessary duplicate information. For example, digitized files represent their data by binary numbers: a series of *1s* and *0s*. If a file includes a long sequence of these numbers, a technical compression scheme might be able to represent the same data with a single character.

telecommuting Working for an employer from a remote location, such as a home office. The advent of modern communication devices, such as the telephone, e-mail, and the Internet, has led to an increase in telecommuting.

Text (TXT) A file format used for documents that are text-only. Because these files don't have special characters for formatting, they can be read by most text-based programs (such as word processors) and HTML editors (such as FrontPage).

theme A group of colors, graphics, styles, and fonts that you can apply to an individual Web page or a group of pages. Using a theme is a good idea because it helps create a uniform and consistent look throughout the entire Web site.

thread A collection of follow-up messages on a newsgroup posting, sequentially ordered by date.

thumbnail Small image of a graphic or picture, such as a photograph. Users can click the image they want to see in a larger version. Creating thumbnails on Web pages is a good idea because Web pages that use thumbnails download more quickly than do those with full-sized photos.

top-level domain names Sometimes called *first-level domain names*, they include the well-known identifiers .com, .org, .net, .edu, .mil, and .gov. Within each top-level domain grouping, there can be countless second-level domains.

Transmission Control Protocol/Internet Protocol (TCP/IP) The standards (protocols) for data transmission and error correction over the Internet. TCP verifies delivery from the client to the server; IP is responsible for moving data packets between computers.

transport medium The physical connection and equipment that is used to transfer information.

trialware An evaluation copy for software. Sometimes, trialware includes limited features or is not operational after a limited time.

Trojan horse Malicious program that enters your computer hidden within legitimate software. In contrast to a virus or worm, a Trojan horse isn't able to replicate itself so it doesn't spread as quickly and the damage is typically more limited in scope.

Uniform Resource Locator (URL) Specifies the location and access method of an Internet resource. For example, *http://www.pearson.com* describes the protocol used to access the Internet (*http*), the server location, and the Web address (*www.pearson.com*).

Universal Serial Bus (USB) A place on your computer in which you can attach peripheral devices, such as Web cams.

universal view software A specialized type of software used in some organizations. This type of software acts as a search engine and allows employees to search each other's computers for the information they need.

unmoderated group A newsgroup with no administrator to review the messages that are posted.

updates New or improved features for a software program; changes to the program to make it current.

uploading The process of transferring data from your computer to the Internet.

upstream Refers to the direction of data transfer when a client (such as your computer) sends information to the Internet.

usability Refers to how easy it is for real people to interact with the Web site to perform tasks and accomplish their goals.

Usenet Worldwide distributed discussion system, in which newsgroups are organized by subject. Articles (messages) are posted to the newsgroup, and everyone who subscribes to the newsgroup can view and respond to the message.

video conferencing Holding an online meeting between multiple participants in different locations by using a network (such as the Internet or an intranet) to transmit audio and video data.

virus Self-replicating malicious code that's designed to modify the way a computer works without the permission or knowledge of the system's user.

virus definition An antivirus product that is developed to counteract malicious code.

virus hoax A false report about nonexistent viruses, usually spread via e-mail. People often use social engineering and deception to spread a virus hoax.

Visual Basic for Applications (VBA) Microsoft Office's programming language used to develop macros in Word and Excel.

Visual Basic Scripting Edition (VBScript) Similar in function to JavaScript, VBScript is used to create dynamic Web pages. VBScript was developed by Microsoft for use with Internet Explorer and can work with ActiveX.

voiceover Voice transmitted at the same time as music or video.

VoiceXML A variation of the XML format that makes it possible for people to communicate with Web servers by talking over the phone. VoiceXML combines XML with voice recognition technology.

wallpaper The background used for your Windows desktop.

Waveform (WAV) An abbreviation of *waveforms*, which is a digitized audio file format. Files that use this format are typically larger than MP3 files.

Web In FrontPage, a collection of pages, organized as a series of folders and files, which can be used to make up a Web site. Because a Web site can consist of a number of graphics, links, HTML documents, and other associated files, a FrontPage Web can easily grow to hundreds—or even thousands—of files.

Web bug A graphic on a Web page or in an e-mail message that is capable of monitoring who is viewing the Web page or message. Web bugs are typically so small that they cannot be seen on the Web page.

Web cam A small digital camera that connects to your computer system and transfers whatever image is captured on the camera to the Internet.

Web host The business that provides the equipment and services necessary to store and service your Web files and to act as the Web server.

Web page developers (designers or content managers) The people responsible for creating attractive and easy-to-use Web pages.

Web page editor (Web editor) A program that lets you create Web pages by interacting directly with the software's interface. The most well-known Web page editor is Microsoft's FrontPage.

Web pages HTML documents that can be connected via hyperlinks.

Web Presence Provider (WPP) The company responsible for hosting your Web site.

Web search site A site that includes search engine capabilities. This term is loosely used and sometimes refers to sites that are technically directories.

Web server A server that uses HTML-compatible software to distribute data. Web servers and browsers use HTTP as the protocol to communicate with each other.

Web site Web pages that are linked or grouped together for a specific purpose. For example, a commercial Web site might include pages for customer service, products, contact information, and so on.

Web site positioning Undertaking specific measures so that your Web site is placed high in the rankings for the major search engines.

Webcasting An Internet technology that some Web sites use to broadcast information, such as radio or video programming. Webcasting is similar to television broadcasting, except that it uses the Web to stream the media content to the viewers.

Webmaster The person in a company who is in charge of maintaining the content and functionality of a Web site.

What You See is What You Get (WYSIWYG) A program interface that enables you to see how your completed document will appear while you're working on it.

whiteboard Analogous to the laminated whiteboard that you might see in a corporate conference room. Electronically, the whiteboard appears in a window on the monitors of everyone in a video conference, so that they can share ideas by writing or drawing on it.

Whois A command you can use on InterNIC's site (*www.internic.net*) to find out the IP address or other information about the company or person to whom a domain name is registered.

wildcard character A special type of character that you can use in a search expression to make the search more general. The most common wildcard character is the asterisk (*), which represents any type or number of characters.

Windows Media Audio (WMA) A digital audio file format.

Windows Media Player A popular media player software program that you can use to play audio or video.

WinZip A graphical user interface program that you can use to compress files or to compress and group several files into a single archive.

wireless Devices that use a technology that doesn't employ lines or wires, working in much the same way as radio signals work.

workplace monitoring Using software or other electronic surveillance to keep track of an employee's overall Internet usage as well as e-mail communications.

workplace privacy The issue of balancing private communications at work with an employer's business interests.

workplace surveillance The practice of monitoring employees electronically, especially the practice of tracking e-mail and Internet usage.

World Wide Web (Web or WWW) A service that enables users to view and share graphic and multimedia documents that have been saved using Hypertext Markup Language (HTML) electronically and remotely over the Internet. Documents on the Web are connected by hyperlinks.

World Wide Web Consortium (W3C) A group of internationally based institutes and companies that sets universal standards for developing Web pages, such as which languages should be used and how Web documents should be linked.

worm A computer program or malicious code that is capable of making copies of itself, spreading through the Internet or other connected systems, and causing damage in a variety of ways. Because worms can self-replicate, they usually spread very quickly through a network, such as the Internet.

ZIP file A compressed archive file, usually created by PKZip (or its graphical, Windows-based cousin, WinZip); compressed files can be transferred more quickly over the Internet.

zombie A computer that is under the remote control of an intruder without the knowledge of the computer's owner. A zombie can then be used to launch DDoS attacks on other systems.